T0389699

Caliphate and Kingship in a Fifteenth-Century Literary History of Muslim Leadership and Pilgrimage

Bibliotheca Maqriziana

Edited by

Frédéric Bauden (*Université de Liège*)

OPERA MINORA

VOLUME 4

The titles published in this series are listed at *brill.com/bima*

Caliphate and Kingship in a Fifteenth-Century Literary History of Muslim Leadership and Pilgrimage

al-Ḏahab al-masbūk fī ḏikr man ḥaǧǧa min al-ḫulafāʾ wa-l-mulūk

Critical Edition, Annotated Translation, and Study by

Jo Van Steenbergen

BRILL

LEIDEN | BOSTON

Cover illustration: al-Maqrīzī, *al-Ḏahab al-Masbūk*, Cairo, 1438. Leiden, Universiteitsbibliotheek, Or. 560, fol. 115b. Copyright of the University of Leiden.

The Library of Congress Cataloging-in-Publication Data is available online at http://catalog.loc.gov
LC record available at http://lccn.loc.gov/2016040250

Typeface for the Latin, Greek, and Cyrillic scripts: "Brill". See and download: brill.com/brill-typeface.

ISSN 2211-6737
ISBN 978-90-04-32568-5 (hardback)
ISBN 978-90-04-33236-2 (e-book)

This book is printed on acid-free paper and produced in a sustainable manner.

Contents

List of Illustrations

Figure

Map

Tables

List of Plates

Abbreviations

AI	*Annales islamologiques*
AJAMES	*Annals of Japan Association for Middle East Studies*
BSOAS	*Bulletin of the School of Oriental and African Studies*
EI^2	*Encyclopædia of Islam*, Second Edition, ed. H.A.R. Gibb et al. (Leiden: E.J. Brill, 1960–2009), 13 vols.
EI^3	*Encyclopædia of Islam*, *THREE*, ed. K. Fleet, G. Krämer et al. (Leiden, Boston: Brill, 2007–).
EIr	*Encyclopædia Iranica*, ed. E. Yarshater (Winona Lake, IN: Eisenbrauns, 1982–), 15 vols. published
EQ	*Encyclopædia of the Qurʾān*, ed. J. Dammen McAuliffe (Leiden, Boston: Brill, 2001–2006), 6 vols.
GAL	Brockelmann, C., *Geschichte der arabischen Litteratur*, 2 vols. & 3 supplements (Leiden: Brill, 1943–1949 [2nd edition]).
IJMES	*International Journal of Middle Eastern Studies*
JAL	*Journal of Arabic Literature*
JAOS	*Journal of the American Oriental Society*
JESHO	*Journal of the Economic and Social History of the Orient*
JNES	*Journal of Near Eastern Studies*
JRAS	*Journal of the Royal Asiatic Society*
JSAI	*Jerusalem Studies on Arabic and Islam*
JSS	*Journal of Semitic Studies*
MSR	*Mamlūk Studies Review*
QSA	*Quaderni di Studi Arabi*
RSO	*Rivisti degli Studi Orientali*
SI	*Studia Islamica*

Acknowledgements

This analytical study, critical edition, and annotated translation of al-Maqrīzī's *al-Ḏahab al-masbūk*, a summary history of caliphs and other Muslim rulers who performed the *ḥaǧǧ*, the annual pilgrimage to Mecca, has been in the making for a long time. In the autumn of 2006 the Bibliotheca Maqriziana series editor and initiator, Frédéric Bauden, invited me to engage with this particular text and with the manuscript version that is preserved in the Leiden autograph collection of al-Maqrīzī's opuscules (Leiden, Universiteitsbibliotheek, MS Or. 560, fol. 115^{b}–135^{a}). As the relatively short text and chronographical narrative of *al-Ḏahab al-masbūk* appeared at first sight as allowing for the set-up of a manageable, pretty straightforward and clearly defined project, I happily accepted the invitation, assuming that it was an enterprise that could easily be accomplished on the side, without interfering too much with other, larger projects and commitments. As time went by, however, it transpired that this was an utterly wrong assumption and that any such liminal treatment would do grave injustice to any attempt to disclose and represent the rich complexity of this text and its meanings, and of the history and materiality of its production, reproduction and consumption. The result is that it has taken many more years and much more time than at first envisaged to accomplish the task of editing, translating, and studying this text of only 40 manuscript pages. In those years, however, this relatively brief text has compelled me to engage with a wide and highly stimulating variety of topics, debates, readings, and ideas. For this reason, this turned out to be not just a more time-consuming but also an intellectually far more rewarding enterprise than I ever could have imagined. It moreover increasingly appeared as tying in—sometimes in surprising and often also in extremely enriching ways—with my other projects, helping me to gain much better insights into how late medieval Syro-Egyptian social and cultural histories are intricately interconnected, and how the one cannot, and should not, be understood without the other. I am therefore extremely grateful to the text of *al-Ḏahab al-masbūk*, to its author Aḥmad b. ʿAlī l-Maqrīzī, and evidently also to Frédéric Bauden, for drawing me so deeply into this world of late medieval Arabic literature, Islamic historiography, Muslim political ideology, codicology, and the *ḥaǧǧ*. I genuinely hope that readers and users of *Caliphate and Kingship in a fifteenth-century literary history of Muslim leadership and pilgrimage* will be able to share at least some of these experiences. I also hope that they will not need so much time to wrestle through a book that is as much the generalising outcome of my personal explorations into various areas of Arabo-Islamic medieval specialisation as an attempt to make al-Maqrīzī's early fifteenth-century text accessible in meaningful ways to a variety of specialist and non-specialist readers in the twenty-first century.

Having been in the making for such a long time, this book owes a great deal to several institutions that hosted me while I was working on it, and to many friends and colleagues who engaged in various ways with my work on al-Maqrīzī's *al-Ḏahab al-masbūk*. First, very preliminary steps were taken when I was finishing my position as lecturer at the School of History at the University of St Andrews (UK). The main bulk of the editing, translating and annotating work for the second part of this book was done at Ghent University (Belgium), especially after I became a research professor in late 2009. A number of shorter research visits to the Netherlands-Flemish Institute in Cairo (Egypt) in 2010, 2012, and 2013 also contributed to this. The first part, presenting contextual, textual, and material analyses for *al-Ḏahab al-masbūk*, as a kind of 'cultural biography', were mainly written during my October 2014–June 2015 fellowship at the Annemarie Schimmel Kolleg 'History and Society during the Mamluk Era, 1250–1517', Bonn University (Germany). In each and every one of these institutions I had the fortunate opportunity to present my research in progress to and discuss it with a substantial host of graduate students, colleagues, and friends. I am grateful to each and every one of them. At the risk of forgetting someone, the following colleagues certainly deserve to be mentioned, for more than pleasant academic (and other) conversations and exchanges along this long road, and for the (often unconscious) contributions they made to my thinking about late medieval history and culture in general, and about al-Maqrīzī's *ḥaǧǧ* text in particular: Angus Stewart, Rob Hoyland, Hugh Kennedy, Jan Dumolyn, Kristof D'hulster, Patrick Wing, Malika Dekkiche, Urbain Vermeulen, Clément Onimus, Julien Loiseau, Konrad Hirschler, Reuven Amitai, Kate Raphael, Stephan Conermann, Mohammed Gharaibeh and Tariq Sabraa. Ideas that eventually ended up in the first part of this book were also presented at various stages of their development in different conference papers, seminar talks and lectures between 2010 and 2014 (IMC Leeds, CHESFAME Ghent, ISAP Tunis, NVIC Cairo, ASK Bonn, École française de Rome); I am grateful to organisers and audiences alike for these opportunities to receive most valuable feedback. I furthermore owe another word of gratitude to the *Bibliotheca Maqriziana* series editor, Frédéric Bauden, for identifying the extant manuscripts and the modern editions of *al-Ḏahab al-masbūk*, for providing me with electronic copies of all relevant manuscripts and of two editions, and for allowing me to work with a draft of a relevant part of his first volume of the series, on the Leiden manuscript. I finally also am most grateful to him for his valuable feedback on a full draft of this book; this has helped me a lot to fine-tune my arguments and to prevent me from making too many mistakes and infelicities. In the same vein, I would like to thank Brill's anonymous reader, whose detailed comments allowed me to produce a text that may hopefully be read more smoothly. Any remaining errors are of course my own.

A final word of gratitude I owe to my family: to my daughters Anna and Marie, to my sons Elias and Jonas, and, of course, to my wife, colleague, best friend and life partner, Maya Termonia. For all these years this book has been one among several projects that while in progress always seem to continue to grow larger, more time-consuming and more intrusive than anticipated. Even though I think that over the years I have learned to at least try and not get completely lost anymore in my late medieval worlds of texts, people and ideas, I realise that those worlds can yet remain very tough and annoying competition for them all. I am therefore extremely grateful for their endurance, and for time and again making me feel proud, happy and immensely lucky for being a member of this family. I thank Maya above all for bearing the often frustrating fact that from time to time I still get lost, for making my engagement with projects such as this one overall possible, and for her continued willingness to share this and all kinds of other worlds with me.

ألف شكر وبموت فيكي

Jo Van Steenbergen
Antwerpen, September 2015

Introduction

Number 14 in al-Maqrīzī's autograph collection of opuscules preserved in the Leiden University library (Leiden, Universiteitsbibliotheek, MS Or. 560, fols. 115[b]–135[a]) is a copy of the author's *al-Ḏahab al-masbūk*, The Moulded Gold, a summary history of the annual pilgrimage to Mecca since the days of the Prophet. This is a relatively short text of 40 handwritten pages, also known under the longer title that was later added in the header of this manuscript's fol. 115[b]: "The Book of Gold Moulded in the Format of the Report of the Caliphs and Kings Who Performed the *Ḥaǧǧ*" (*Kitāb al-Ḏahab al-masbūk fī ḏikr man ḥaǧǧa min al-ḫulafāʾ wa-l-mulūk*).

Discussing issues of caliphate, kingship and Mecca pilgrimage, this *al-Ḏahab al-masbūk* is in many ways a curious and highly intriguing little text that has so far only attracted limited scholarly attention.[1] In accordance with the long-standing status and reputation of the Egyptian scholar, administrator, and judge Aḥmad b. ʿAlī l-Maqrīzī (766–845/c. 1365–1442) as one of the most important historians of his age,[2] this attention has mainly considered the text for its historiographical value and for the convenience of its collection of diverse material concerning pilgrimages of illustrious caliphs and many other Muslim rulers. In a carefully organised chronographical manner this kind of collection allows this "report" to live up entirely to the promise of its longer title and to present all kinds of stories about a substantial list of rulers and their engagements with the *ḥaǧǧ*, the annual Muslim pilgrimage to Mecca. Starting with the Prophet's *ḥaǧǧ* of 10/632 and ending with the story of the Mecca journey in 778/1377 of the Egyptian sultan al-Malik al-Ashraf Shaʿbān (r. 764–778/1363–1377), *al-Ḏahab al-masbūk* moves from the time of the Prophet, over that of the Caliphs, to that of non-caliphal rulers' pilgrimage engagements from the eleventh century onwards. Due to the work's limited size, however, the added historiographical value of its information about pilgriming Prophet, caliphs, and kings is only very limited, and the relative neglect of the text in historical research of the Mecca pilgrimage and of the history of the caliphates and of its successor polities is therefore perfectly understandable. The booklet is rather more remarkable for other reasons, not in the least from a wider literary

1 Al-Ǧāsir (1952); al-Šayyāl (1955); al-Šayyāl (2000); Faraḥāt (2009).

2 See the biography of al-Maqrīzī by his student Ǧamāl al-Dīn Yūsuf b. Taġrī Birdī in his *al-Manhal al-ṣāfī*, 1:415–420, p. 417 ("His reputation in history and in other subjects became well-known during his life and after his death, so that he came to be referred to as a model").

DOI: 10.1163/9789004332362_002

point of view as the very first to claim to offer a more or less focused stand-alone narrative of Muslim leadership of the pilgrimage.[3]

As will be argued in this study, the disappointing historiographical nature of *al-Ḏahab al-masbūk* is actually only one residual dimension of a text that was constructed in this unique manner for far more complex purposes. It is the complexity of these particular purposes and their concomitant literary construction that makes the text so curious, intriguing, and valuable. This has to do with an author who tries to consciously communicate through his text with changing audiences. It also has to do with the larger contexts within which all three communicative partners—author, text and audiences—operated. In the early decades of the fifteenth century these contexts were defined by substantial political, socio-economic, and cultural transformations. They were also shaped by ongoing intellectual debates about the proper social order that should accommodate such transformations. At moments such as these, stories about pilgriming rulers represented very useful material for a scholar-author such as al-Maqrīzī. Many centuries of Muslim rulers' engagements with the annual pilgrimage to Mecca turned out to have produced powerful symbolic literary tools to speak about much wider issues of Muslim leadership duties and privileges. *Al-Ḏahab al-masbūk* and its particular engagement with the metaphorical options that its subject matter offered were therefore certainly also about al-Maqrīzī's personal experience of the transformations of his time, his participation in at least some of the debates that were raging, and his pursuance of some kind of impact on various people around him.

All of these issues matter for a proper understanding of the full complexity of a literary text such as al-Maqrīzī's *al-Ḏahab al-masbūk*. This book, consisting of a detailed analysis, a new critical edition, and an annotated translation of the text, wishes to present this type of comprehensive understanding. Its first part presents the first thorough study of the text, conceptualised here as the reconstruction of a kind of cultural biography of *al-Ḏahab al-masbūk*, in its changing material and immaterial manifestations from its early fifteenth-century conception onwards.[4] It will first pursue a reconstruction of those contexts that

---

3 Brockelmann's claim—following a note in the entry for *al-Ḏahab al-masbūk* in the *Kašf al-ẓunūn* by the seventeenth-century Ottoman bibliographer Ḥāǧǧī Ḫalīfa/Kātib Çelebī (1017–1067/1609–1657)—that the copy in the Leiden manuscript "only represents an excerpt from a more substantial text in five parts, completed in 841/1437 (nur ein Auszug aus einem grösseren Werk in 5 Teilen, voll. 841/1437)" was never endorsed or substantiated (*GAL*, 2:50).

4 This objective of reconstructing a cultural biography of *al-Ḏahab al-masbūk* of course refers to Kopytoff's "cultural biography of things"; this study will—even though for practical reasons mostly implicitly—take on board as key analytical tools and research questions Kopytoff's

defined the author and the production of his text as well as its reception by various audiences. The intricacies of the *ḥaǧǧ* tradition, the dynamic practices of Muslim leadership and scholarship, al-Maqrīzī's own eventful life and times, and the century-old traditions of *ḥaǧǧ* writings are like a rich canvas that serves as an indispensable background for readings and studies of this literary text to fully appreciate the depth of its forms, functions, and meanings. This first chapter therefore first discusses the Muslim pilgrimage ritual and its long and intricate history, the late medieval social and cultural worlds that connected Mecca to Cairo, and the place of al-Maqrīzī and his scholarship, his *al-Ḏahab al-masbūk* in particular, in these worlds. The second chapter moves from these defining contexts to the actual text of *al-Ḏahab al-masbūk*, set again within its wider framework of *ḥaǧǧ* writings in Arabic up to the later medieval period, but focusing above all on the detailed analysis of the textual aspects of those forms, functions, and meanings and reconstructing how in the textual interaction between author and audiences *al-Ḏahab al-masbūk* was a recipient, a transmitter, and an agent of old and new claims to historical truth. These intertextual, narratological, and semiotic readings are followed in the third and final chapter of this study by the analysis of the external, material factors of those forms, functions, and meanings that defined the life of *al-Ḏahab al-masbūk* as text and object, in al-Maqrīzī's time and beyond. This chapter consists basically of a descriptive study of the ten extant manuscript copies of *al-Ḏahab al-masbūk*. But it also moves beyond that. Tying together some of the insights gained from the other two chapters with this physical and paratextual manuscript mate-

---

explanation that "In doing the biography of a thing, one would ask questions similar to those one asks about people: What, sociologically, are the biographical possibilities inherent in its "status" and in the period and culture, and how are these possibilities realized? Where does the thing come from and who made it? What has been its career so far, and what do people consider to be an ideal career for such things? What are the recognized "ages" or periods in the thing's "life", and what are the cultural markers for them? How does the thing's use change with its age, and what happens to it when it reaches the end of its usefulness?" (Kopytoff (1986): 66–67). A parallel and similarly leading cultural biographical approach has above all been pursued in archaeology, such as proposed in a special issue of the journal *World Archaeology*, where Gosden and Marshall explain that "the central idea is that, as people and objects gather time, movement and change, they are constantly transformed, and these transformations of person and object are tied up with each", they are "social interactions involving people and objects [that] create meaning" (Gosden & Marshall [1999]: 169). Pursuing the cultural biography of *al-Ḏahab al-masbūk* as a thing, as an object, and as a literary text is then asking about its various transformations (as 'singularity' and as 'commodity'), its involvement in all kinds of social interactions, and its role in various processes of meaning-making.

rial, this final chapter actually aims to reconstruct in as much—occasionally necessarily speculative and hypothetical—detail as possible the history of the making and remaking of the text by author, copyists, readers, and all kinds of other users between the fifteenth century and today.

In this summing up of the history of *al-Ḏahab al-masbūk*'s production, reproduction, and consumption this short text's cultural biography presents itself as extremely rich and complex indeed. Rather than merely an unsatisfying fifteenth-century summary history of the pilgrimage of Muslim rulers, it appears as one literary manifestation of the many vibrant gateways that can lead modern researchers to better understandings of the social and cultural worlds that defined its life. This was a long life full of opportunities, encounters, and transformations, only a handful of which can actually be reconstructed. At every turn, however, the text appears and re-appears above all as a node in networks of people, ideas, practices, texts, and related cultural forms, which it connects and with which it is connected in ever changing configurations. Reconstructing all of these networks, connections and configurations is a much needed but also daunting task that lies far beyond the reach of this particular study of *al-Ḏahab al-masbūk*. Some of them will nevertheless make their appearances here in some relevant detail, and the contours of many others will come into sight at the horizons of this book's first part. It is hoped that in the future, this particular study's embedding within the wider scope of al-Maqrīzī's rich scholarly legacy as it is being studied in this *Bibliotheca Maqriziana* will become possible. It is only through comprehensive approaches of embeddedness, connectivity, and contextuality that these details may be further refined and that these contours may acquire more concrete shapes. It is therefore above all the combination of different cultural biographies and partially reconstructed social lives of al-Maqrīzī's many extant texts that may yield ever better and more nuanced insights into the different intellectual and practical universes that this fifteenth-century author and his regularly changing memories came to inhabit.

One important condition to achieve such enhanced understanding of arguably one of the most influential historians of pre-modern Islamic history is that we have access to his texts as he had intended them to be. As will be detailed in the third chapter of this first part, there are only a handful of modern editions of the text of *al-Ḏahab al-masbūk* and these all display in various ways important shortcomings in their relationship with the original versions of the text. The retrieval in the context of the *Bibliotheca Maqriziana* of all relevant manuscript copies and of authoritative manuscript traditions as well as the deepened understanding of the complexity of this text and of the contexts in which it operated also mean that the time certainly has come to start moving beyond current editions. Above all they all rely mainly on the same, much later copy of the text, and the only extant autograph of *al-Ḏahab al-masbūk* in the manuscript MS Or. 560 (Leiden, Universiteitsbibliotheek) has so far never been the object of any critical edition. There are therefore many good reasons to present such an edition of this text as it appears in Or. 560 in the second part of this book. In order to assure the widest possible accessibility and intelligibility of al-Maqrīzī's text, also for the non-specialist reader, this second part simultaneously presents the first English translation of al-Maqrīzī's summary history of the pilgrimage that has ever been published. A detailed reference apparatus accompanies this translation, identifying whenever possible names, places, and other phenomena that appear in the text and that continue to define in many ways its literary, historiographical and wider cultural meanings and values. A photographic reproduction of the autograph of *al-Ḏahab al-masbūk* in Or. 560 (Leiden, Universiteitsbibliotheek) follows at the end of the book, as well as a series of indexes that further supports the aim of achieving the greatest accessibility and intelligibility, both of the text and of its cultural biography.

PART 1

Study—The Cultural Biography of a Fifteenth-Century Literary Text

CHAPTER 1

Contexts: Introducing the *ḥaǧǧ*, al-Maqrīzī, and *al-Ḏahab al-masbūk* (Seventh – Fifteenth Centuries)

1 The *ḥaǧǧ* Ritual: Forms, Function, and Religious Meanings

> Q 3: 97 "Pilgrimage to the House is a duty owed to Allah by all people who can make the journey."

Ever since the dawn of Islam, the Qurʾānic injunction to perform the *ḥaǧǧ* or pilgrimage to God's House has encouraged ever more Muslims from ever more places across the globe to come to the West-Arabian region of the Hijaz. Today, more than two million male and female pilgrims every year partake in the series of prescribed acts in and near the sanctuary of Mecca that make up this pilgrimage ritual. They do so in an environment that has substantially altered since the middle of the previous century. Modernisation, particular views of Muslim orthodoxy, and various incidents with and concerns for pilgrims' health, safety and comfort, have had such a gigantic impact on pilgrimage facilities and infrastructures that conditions of travel and performance have radically changed from what they had been like for more than 1300 years. Yet the form of the *ḥaǧǧ* ritual itself, its function, and its meanings are not considered to have been affected by these or any other changes, ever since the days of the prophet Muḥammad.

For Muslims, Muḥammad performed the ritual acts of the *ḥaǧǧ* in their most pure, authentic, and correct way shortly before his death in 11/632, setting an example that ever since that time every individual pilgrim continues to have to abide by. The remembrance of this final prophetic pilgrimage, known as the Farewell Pilgrimage (*ḥiǧǧat al-wadāʿ*), was transformed into an authoritative model by the early Muslim community of the Prophet's companions, their successors, and their followers. In these early years of Arab expansion, of confrontation with other rich and powerful socio-cultural traditions, and of variegating searches for Muslim political leadership, religious authority, and social identity, the Prophet's Farewell Pilgrimage entered the community's social memory through the institutionalisation of its annual repetition in practice and through the entrenchment of its story in the community's early biographical, historical, and religio-legal textual production.

As with so many rules of good Muslim practice, this development did not prevent the survival or emergence of differences in remembrance of and in opinion on particular details of pilgrimage practice. Many of these eventually fed into the wider legal differences that marked the distinct but interconnected traditions of the Sunni schools of law, the *maḏāhib*. One of the bigger debates that continued to rage well into the later medieval period certainly concerned the distinction between the two types of pilgrimage to Mecca, the *ḥaǧǧ* and the *ʿumrah*. Whereas the *ʿumrah* is not defined by any time restrictions and only involves a series of ritual acts in and near the Mecca sanctuary, the dimensions of time and space that make for a valid *ḥaǧǧ* are very different. The correct timing of the performance of the different *ḥaǧǧ* rituals is absolutely crucial, for they can only be executed in a particular sequence on the eighth, ninth and tenth days of the twelfth month of the Muslim lunar calendar (appropriately known therefore as Ḏū l-Ḥiǧǧah, the month of the *ḥaǧǧ*). Furthermore, despite its incorporation of the *ʿumrah* rituals of circumambulation of the Kaʿbah-structure in the centre of the Mecca sanctuary (*ṭawāf*) and of running between the elevations Safa and Marwa just outside the sanctuary (*saʿy*), the *ḥaǧǧ*'s main ritual components are staged many kilometers away from Mecca, on the plain of ʿArafah at the foot of the Mountain of Mercy, and then midway between ʿArafah and Mecca, at a place called Miná, where the emblematic ritual slaughter (*aḍḥāʾ*), the laying down of the pilgrim's consecrated state (*iḥrām*), and the shaving of the head take place. The relation between these rituals of *ḥaǧǧ* and *ʿumrah*—whether they may be combined in an integrated fashion (*qirān*), have to be performed subsequently (*tamattuʿ*), or are carried out one without the other (*ifrād*)—has been the object of doctrinal debate and differing legal opinions, opposing scholars, schools, and remembrances of prophetic sayings and actions as recorded in reports of the Farewell Pilgrimage. However, these and other such discussions never really affected the general performance and sequence of the *ḥaǧǧ*'s main ritual components. Ever since the seventh century, these have always consisted of the taking on of the consecrated state upon entry of the larger Mecca region, of the circumambulation and running in Mecca, of waiting in contemplation—or 'standing' (*wuqūf*)—at ʿArafāt on the ninth of Ḏū l-Ḥiǧǧah, and of throwing pebbles (*ramy ǧamarāt*) and ritual slaughter at Miná on the tenth, followed by a few more days of celebrations, including opportunities for more pebble throwing at Miná and for further circumambulations at Mecca.

More than thirteen centuries of remembrance and re-enactment of the Farewell Pilgrimage have made it so that these main ritual forms of the *ḥaǧǧ* (and of the *ʿumrah*) have acquired an appearance of timelessness. This is also true for the basic function and meanings of the *ḥaǧǧ* and of its different ritual components. In fact, for Muslims the ritual forms, function, and meanings of the *ḥağğ* are all indeed to be understood as transcending any worldly notions of time and change. Obtaining redemption from sins and access to paradise are mentioned among the most tangible rewards that await those who successfully complete the *ḥağğ*. But performing these *ḥağğ* rituals connects pilgrims not just with the divine meaning of their individual destinies in this world and in the hereafter. Above all, it also connects them with all other pilgrims performing exactly the same sacred rituals at exactly the same sacred time at exactly the same sacred place in past, present and future. As such, these rituals remind the community of Muslims (*ummah*) of its sacred monotheist history, as progressing towards the Day of Judgement (at which all are believed to appear before God in the same simple and egalitarian capacity of the consecrated state of their *ḥağğ*, the *iḥrām*) and as following in the divinely guided footsteps of a long range of prophets and messengers, including Muḥammad's, but also above all Abraham's (Ibrāhīm). In fact, the entire *ḥağğ* ritual (as well as the wider sacred history of Mecca) is geared towards this commemoration of Abraham's engagements with the divine (and of Islam's direct descent from and reconnection with his monotheist legacy).

Considered to be the first monotheist who submitted to God's will, the first *muslim*, Abraham, his Egyptian consort Hagar, their son Ismail and their adventures in the Arabian desert are present in each and every one of the *ḥağğ*'s ritual components. The original Kaʿbah is believed to have been built more than 4,000 years ago by Abraham and Ismail, with divine guidance and assistance; the nearby source of Zamzam is thought to have been miraculously found by Hagar when she was running in despair between Safa and Marwa to look for a bit of water for her son; and at Miná the devil is claimed to have been chased away by the pebbles that Abraham threw at him when he tried to persuade him not to sacrifice his son, upon which Abraham abided by God's command to sacrifice Ismail (and not Isaac of Biblical history) and God rewarded him for his commitment by sending down a ram for slaughter instead. Eventually, Islam believes that it was Abraham himself who, upon divine instruction, set the proceedings of the *ḥağğ*. The symbolism of an individual's performance of the *ḥağğ* therefore transcends the particular case of Muḥammad by far, his paradigmatic Farewell Pilgrimage being no more than a restoration of the correct ritual, just as his wider mission is considered to be no more than a restoration of the natural, monotheist order of things, as also advocated by Abraham and many other prophets before.

It is these powerful, transcendent meanings, reminding believers of their communal place in monotheist history and of their timeless relationship with divine Will, that have always informed the Qur'ānic injunction to every individual *muslim* able to do so to perform the *ḥaǧǧ* at least once. The obligatory nature of this ritual, as already formulated in the Qur'ān, makes that together with the proclamation of faith (*šahādah*), daily prayer (*ṣalāt*), fasting during the month of Ramaḍān (*ṣawm*) and the alms tax (*zakāt*), the *ḥaǧǧ* is considered one of the five 'pillars' of Islam. It may even be argued that among these five obligatory rituals—each of which is meant to confirm a believer's relationship with the divine and each of which actively partakes in organising the monotheist rhythm of time, space, and community—the *ḥaǧǧ* stands out as special, owing to the deep commitment that speaks from a pilgrim's achievement of its demanding requirements, as well as due to the very public nature of its performance. Every year since the Prophet's Farewell Pilgrimage, the *ḥaǧǧ* has brought all kinds of people together in public spaces in Mecca, 'Arafah and Miná in a shared performance of their religious duties. Every year, too, the particular and general nature of this performance has been a matter of such wider solidarity, concern, and interest that all kinds of reports, treatises, and stories have continued to be produced about it, ranging from the textual recordings of the Farewell Pilgrimage in early Islamic history, to widespread coverage in the traditional and social media of the contemporary world.[1]

2 Pilgriming Rulers and the *ḥaǧǧ*'s Political Meanings in Islamic History

The Prophet's leadership of the Farewell Pilgrimage did not just set an example that allowed individual Muslims to reconnect with monotheist history and ritual practice. It soon also acquired more direct political meanings of legitimate Muslim rule in the Prophet's footsteps. In the decades that followed Muḥammad's death in 11/632, succession to leadership over the rapidly expanding community of believers (*ummah*) remained a vexed issue. Discussions over rules of legitimate succession were never really resolved and continued to pit supporters of different leaders and definitions of legitimate leadership against each other. In the historical reality of the regular conflicts and clashes

1 Further on these religious forms, function and meanings of the *ḥaǧǧ*, see Hawting (2001); "Ḥadjdj. iii The Islamic ḥadjdj", in *EI*² (http://referenceworks.brillonline.com/entries/encyclopaedia-of-islam-2/hadjdj-COM_0249); Armstrong (2012); Abdel Haleem (2012); Id. (2013); Peters (1994); Pearson (1994); Gaudefroy-Demombynes (1923).

through which this repeated competition for Muslim rule and sovereignty was fought out, as much as in their later explanations and remembrance by winners and losers, religious meanings of divine sanction, intervention, and guidance played important symbolic roles. As time evolved and the formulation of Muslim religious identities became more explicit, the functionality of these meanings was expanded to underscore a particular trajectory in the sacred history of a religious community and its leadership, that, in mainstream accounts, connected rulers and dynasties (the first four so-called Rightly-Guided caliphs Abū Bakr, ʿUmar, ʿUṯmān and ʿAlī in Medina [11–41/632–661], the Umayyad caliphs in Damascus [41–132/661–750], the ʿAbbāsid caliphs in Baghdad [132–656/750–1258] and in Cairo [659–922/1261–1517], and the Ottoman sultan-caliphs in Constantinople/Istanbul [c. 922–1342/1517–1924]), as though in a continuous and unbroken sequence with the leadership of Muḥammad and with his guidance along the divinely ordained path of monotheistic history.

Successful claims and performances of the leadership of the annual pilgrimage were one of the most effective, visible, and powerful ways by which this aura of legitimacy through continuity with the Prophet's example tended to be operationalised. The annual pilgrimage caravan from the Arab-Muslim empires' successive main centers (from Medina in the Hijaz, from Damascus in Syria, from Baghdad in Iraq, from Cairo in Egypt, and from Constantinople on the Bosphorus) was therefore always led by the caliph, or by one of his formally appointed representatives, and just as the Prophet had done in 10/632, the caliph or his representatives always led all pilgrims through the different stages of the pilgrimage ritual. Conflicts and competition over Muslim sovereignty therefore were often reflected in the appearance in the Mecca area of opponents' caravans and opposing claims to ritual leadership. One of the best-known and most devastating occasions of this sort occurred in 73/692, when the Meccan caliphate of ʿAbd Allāh b. al-Zubayr (r. 64–73/683–692) was violently subdued by its Umayyad rival in Damascus and the Umayyad siege of Mecca prevented rival Umayyad and Zubayrid caravans of pilgrims to complete all required rituals. Twice during this decade of Umayyad-Zubayrid competition for the caliphate the Kaʿbah itself was so severely damaged that it had to be completely rebuilt. On both occasions this happened under close political supervision. Many centuries later, in the 1040s/1630s, a third and final round of Kaʿbah reconstruction—this time occasioned by extreme flooding rather than war—was similarly pursued under close political watch, now from the Ottoman sultan of Istanbul and a specially appointed representative. All three cases illustrate how the Mecca sanctuary and the maintenance of its public buildings and services have always continued to be extremely important for those claiming some form of legitimate Muslim political leadership, often even irrespective of the distance and political realities separating them from remote Mecca.[2]

In the seventh and eighth centuries, most early caliphs still managed to personally perform their natural duty as *ḥağğ* leader, often even more than once during their tenure. After the ʿAbbāsid caliph Hārūn al-Rašīd (r. 170–193/786–809), however, the number of regional Muslim leaders who personally led the pilgrimage and performed the *ḥağğ* became surprisingly limited.[3] Over time, as safe access to Mecca became more complicated and as the religious dimension of mainstream Muslim leadership got increasingly defined in more abstract terms, priority was given to representation through symbolic acts and appointed agents and to indirect patronage through all kinds of material support, including via public construction works such as those performed on the Kaʿbah.

The contraction of caliphal power from the ninth century onwards and the concomitant realities of devolution, fragmentation, and rapid transformation of Muslim political power between the Atlantic Ocean and the Oxus and Indus valleys generated a huge increase in the need for local and regional political legitimation. This created a particular context of conflicting ideologies of power within which the *ḥağğ* often became even more than ever before one of the arenas of competition for legitimate Muslim leadership. Rulers' sovereignty continued to be represented by such symbolic forms as precedence of one's representatives in the pilgrimage's rituals, providing the annually renewed richly embroidered veil (*kiswah*) for the Kaʿbah, and mentioning one's name at the Friday *ḫuṭbah* in the Sanctuary or Ḥarām Mosque. In the competitive search for legitimate Muslim leaderships, the successful acquisition of such universally accepted symbolic forms of representation-*cum*-precedence in the *ḥağğ*'s trans-regional value system became a truly performative characteris-

---

2 For more on these political meanings of pilgrimage leadership in early Islamic history, see Sijpesteijn (2014); Munt (2013); Kennedy (2012): 76–92; McMillan (2011); Marsham (2009): 91, 124–125, 189, 268—Marsham explains most explicitly how "lists of leaders of the ḥağğ and annual campaigns [...] reveal that these poles of the religio-political calendar were kept in the control of the ruling dynasty throughout the Umayyad (and early Abbasid) period: they were assigned to the caliph himself, a relative by blood or marriage, or to the *walī al-ʿahd*; leadership of the *ḥajj* was closely associated with leadership of the *umma*, and appears to have been a prerequisite for the nomination of the *walī al-ʿahd*" (124–125); Robinson (2007): 95–100; Hawting (1993). For later Islamic history, see Faroqhi (2014) (incl. 113–120 for the Ottoman rebuilding of the Kaʿbah in the 1630s); Irwin (2012).

3 For a useful descriptive survey of Muslim leaders performing the pilgrimage up to the fifteenth century, see Möhring (1999).

tic of sovereignty, which could be effectively claimed, challenged, won, and awarded in Mecca and elsewhere along the *ḥaǧǧ* routes.[4]

Competition among local and regional Muslim rulers for these symbolic forms was furthermore exacerbated when the Ḥasanid family was established as a dynasty of local rulers (Sharifs) in Mecca in the course of the mid-tenth century. The Ḥasanid Sharifs of Mecca managed to retain their local leadership for almost a millennium, during which, at recurrent moments of political fragmentation, they took full advantage of their ability to "sell" their recognition to the highest bidder. When real and acclaimed sovereignties as well as physical control over pilgrimage routes and over the region of Mecca became extremely dispersed, localised, complicated, and often also intricately layered and diffuse, there always remained the *ḥaǧǧ*'s political dimension of treading in the Prophet's footsteps. When the Saudis conquered Mecca in 1926, for them this was also one of the many incentives to act against their Ḥasanid rivals.[5]

But the total and continued fragmentation of Muslim political communities created not just new ideological contexts that infused this trans-regional value system with adapted political meanings. It also created enormous logistical challenges for pilgrimage caravans to safely travel to Mecca, with similar political consequences. Throughout Islamic history, reports and stories of pilgrims suffering from natural disasters, famine, Bedouin attacks, or other worldly problems have always reflected badly on the reputation of their leaders. But the opposite was also always true. Whatever the time and place, assuming responsibility for the pilgrimage and for one or more of its main caravans of pilgrims has always offered huge symbolic opportunities for Muslim leaders, vis-à-vis local as well as regional audiences. It also presented them with equally huge political liabilities when things did not run smoothly. Despite the radical transformation of material circumstances, even in the contemporary globalising world this same political meaning of legitimacy in remembrance of the Farewell Pilgrimage continues to inform the connection between the local, regional, and international reputation of the Saudi patrons of the *ḥaǧǧ*'s modern logistics and the mass public event which the pilgrimage has become. From this infrastructural political perspective too, therefore, ancient as well as mod-

---

4 On the *kiswah* and other *ḥaǧǧ*-related symbols of sovereignty, see Sardi (2013); Nassar (2013); Mortel (1988); Gaudefroy-Demombynes (1954).

5 For the Ḥasanid Sharifian dynasty of Mecca, see "Makka, 2. From the ʿAbbāsid to the Modern Period", *EI*[2] (http://referenceworks.brillonline.com/entries/encyclopaedia-of-islam-2/makka-COM_0638); Meloy (2010a); Mortel (1987); Ota (2002). See also Peters (1994): 352–362.

ern reports, treatises, stories, and other representations of pilgrimage success and failure have always continued to matter.[6]

3 Cairo Sultans, Meccan Sharifs, and the Late Medieval *ḥağğ*

In 656/1258, the ephemeral remnants of the ancient ʿAbbāsid caliphate were annihilated by the Central-Asian Mongols, when they executed the 37th and last caliph of Baghdad, al-Mustaʿṣim (r. 640–656/1242–1258). By that time, for most Sunni Muslims the figure of the caliph was no longer a real political leader, but rather a divinely ordained mediator for human action, who safeguarded the connection between his community, the Prophet's example, and divine Will. The cutting of this connection by the caliph's disappearance in 656/1258 therefore generated throughout Sunni Muslim communities various challenges of legitimacy, in moral and legal as well as in political terms. These challenges, however, certainly also created a variety of opportunities, especially on the Levantine frontier of Mongol westward expansion, where that expansion forced local military leaders to close ranks behind one of theirs who had acquired the sultanate of Egypt. When in 658/1260 this partnership proved successful in pushing back the Mongol troops beyond the Euphrates and eventually also in re-integrating various Syrian and Egyptian elites and resources into the Cairo sultanate's orbit, these opportunities were intensively explored to underscore and communicate the legitimacy of the new leadership. One of the many transformative ways in which this happened was in fact by a kind of re-invention of the ʿAbbāsid caliphate in the Muslim world's new centre of gravity, Cairo. A surviving scion of the ʿAbbāsid family was proclaimed the new caliph by sultan Baybars (r. 658–676/1260–1277) and his entourage. Despite ongoing debates about the validity of the ʿAbbāsid lineage of this caliph al-Ḥākim (r. 661–701/1262–1302), his descendants maintained their position, under the sultan's continued patronage and control, until the early sixteenth century, when the Ottoman conquest of Egypt ended the sultanate as well as the Cairo caliphate.[7]

The long-standing sultanate of Cairo, thus given new military, geographical, and ideological impetus by mid-thirteenth-century military leaders such as sultan Baybars, is best known in today's academic and popular discourse as

---

6 See Faroqhi (2014); Peters (1994); Bianchi (2004).

7 Heidemann (1994); "ʿAbbāsids", in *EI*[2] (http://referenceworks.brillonline.com/entries/encyclopaedia-of-islam-2/abbasids-COM_0002).

the Mamluk Sultanate, or also as the Mamluk Empire. This Mamluk label is inspired by the continued particular social origins of the majority of its military-political elites, including of many of its sultans. Baybars was brought to Egypt a young Turkish slave (*mamlūk*) from north of the Black Sea region, and nineteen of the Cairo sultans after him shared similar *mamlūk* Central-Asian servile origins, local Arabo-Islamic and martial socialisation in the barracks of the Cairo citadel, and upward social mobility through manumission, military service, and court careerism. However, the sultanate was never the exclusive playground of any one continuous so-called Mamluk project, and this was mainly caused by the ongoing practice of slave trade and *mamlūk*s' importation, and by the recurrent pattern of the subsequent newcomer status of many of the sultans and of most of the military-political elites between the thirteenth and early sixteenth centuries. Throughout the sultanate's long history, various distinct lineages (as opposed to one Mamluk continuity) of sultans and their supporters and descendants actually tried to impose their continued control, and especially in the thirteenth and fourteenth centuries some were quite successful in this process. One of the most well-known manifestations of the latter phenomenon certainly is the century-long sultanate of Qalāwūn (r. 678–689/1279–1290) and his descendants (r. 689–784/1290–1382), including the very long reign and extremely successful rule of his son al-Nāṣir Muḥammad (r. 693–741/1293–1341, with two intervals). Such dynastic continuities, however, and their concomitant reproductive constructions of a particular dynastic political order of ideas, relationships, and things, never stopped to be challenged by rival individuals, groups, practices and ideas, resulting in continuously returning moments of elite fragmentation and transformation, when succession had to be resolved through factionalism and war, and continuities threatened to be disrupted. In this context of ongoing political complexity, of repeated competition between dynastic and non-dynastic agents, of ongoing clashes between newcomers and vested interests, and of dominance by successions of freedmen and freemen, contemporaries tended to define the various and dynamic Syro-Egyptian political environments within which they had to operate by the very generic common denominator of the *dawlat al-atrāk*, the Rule of the Turks, the latter referring in the most general terms to the inclusive and open political identity of some martial form of 'turkishness' that distinguished the urban political elites of the Cairo sultanate until, at least, the early sixteenth century.[8]

---

8 For a recent generalising impression of the sultanate's long and complex political history, carefully combining standard Mamluk narratives with more nuanced approaches, see

With power and authority in such a state of flux, sultans and their entourages were more than ever in a constant need for every kind of ideological support to explain and cement their rule. In this respect, the void left by the sudden disappearance of the ʿAbbāsids of Baghdad also created unexpected ideological space beyond the issue of caliphal authority. Soon after 658/1260, and throughout the sultanate's further existence, Cairo sultans' appropriation from the ʿAbbāsid caliphs of the symbolic forms of representation-*cum*-precedence in the *ḥaǧǧ*'s trans-regional value system remained highly appreciated as another very important and effective tool to stake out claims for legitimate leadership. This included long-standing traditions such as the annual production and dispatch of a new Kaʿbah veil (*kiswah*) and the precedence of the sultan's standard in the different pilgrimage rites. But there were also wider privileges of local sovereignty involved, such as the invocation of the sultan's name at the Friday sermon (*ḫuṭbah*) in the Sanctuary Mosque and the minting of Meccan coins in the sultan's name (*sikkah*). At the same time, sultans in Cairo continued to very proudly use the title of 'Servant of the two Sacred Places' (*Ḫādim al-ḥaramayn al-šarīfayn*), confirming their role as the main patron and protector of Mecca and Medina and of their sanctuaries (the Ḥarām Mosque with the Kaʿbah and the Prophet's Mosque with Muḥammad's grave, respectively). In 667/1269, sultan Baybars even performed the pilgrimage in person. Baybars only performed his pilgrimage in absolute secrecy though, with priority being given to an almost hagiographic remembrance rather than to public display. How this royal pilgrimage actually happened, therefore, remains unclear. The story in itself, however, already sufficed to direct the *ḥaǧǧ*'s empowering ideological effect to Baybars' royal personality. Before that, in 664/1266, similar effect had certainly already been obtained by the re-invention of a caliphal practice that was soon to develop into a highly symbolic institutional component of the annual regional *ḥaǧǧ* caravans. In that year, there was sent for the first time at the head of the Egyptian caravan the so-called *maḥmal*, a luxuriously decorated empty palanquin, raised on a camel, and symbolically representing the sultan's pilgrimage leadership along the caravan route to Mecca as well as throughout the different pilgrimage rituals. This *maḥmal* tradition was continued by Baybars' successors in Cairo, multiplied in the different caravans that departed from the sultanate's main urban centres in Syria, integrated in elaborate departure ceremonials that symbolically connected the court to the ritual performances in and around Mecca, challenged and copied by rival rulers

---

Loiseau (2014). For the contemporary use of *dawlat al-atrāk*, see Van Steenbergen (forthcoming); Yosef (2012); Ayalon (1990).

from Iraq and Yemen, maintained beyond 922/1517 under the supervision of the Ottoman sultan's representative in Cairo, and only discontinued when the Saudis acquired full control of the Mecca sanctuary in the 1920s.[9]

Whenever opportunities arose, Baybars' successors in Cairo pursued various similar and other engagements with Mecca and the *ḥağğ*. Already from the sultanate's early days onwards this particular privileged relationship between Cairo and Mecca had been institutionalised by the emergence of the official position of Commander of Mecca (*amīr Makkah*), a title conferred with befitting robes, gifts, and honours by the sultan upon the Ḥasanid Sharif. Although hardly ever representing any real control from Cairo over Mecca, the tradition of conferring this political title was continued throughout the sultanate's existence because it was mutually beneficial. For the sultan, it was a symbolic act that confirmed his sovereignty over the sacred place that Mecca was, and that time and again re-integrated the Ḥasanid rulers of remote Mecca at least theoretically into the political framework of positions and functions that were emanating from the court in Cairo. For the Sharifs, it was an official title and a formal recognition of local authority that awarded local leverage and that created distinction from other local rulers in the Hijaz and from Ḥasanid pretenders in Mecca. For both rulers, concomitant mutual oaths and arrangements furthermore provided some clarity in the rights, duties, and privileges that they owed each other. This certainly also had to do with Mecca's socio-economic subordination to Egypt. Pilgrimage brought in substantial wealth that could be easily tapped by taxation. But natural resources in the Hijaz were extremely limited so that, despite such regular income from pilgrimage, local social and political organisation depended first and foremost on the importation of staple food. For centuries, therefore, the supply of grain from Egypt had been crucial to Mecca, the Hijaz, and the annual pilgrimage, and the practice of providing for this

9 On these engagements of Cairo sultans and others after them with the *ḥağğ* and its symbolic forms, see Porter (2013); Meloy (2006); Behrens-Abouseif (1997); ʿAnkawi (1974); Jomier (1953); Dekkiche & Van Steenbergen (forthcoming). For Meloy and Jomier the *maḥmal* ritual was a tradition originating with Baybars, whereas for Behrens-Abouseif and Porter it derived from earlier symbolic practices that had originated with the later caliphs of Baghdad. On Baybars' secret pilgrimage in late 667/1269 see also Thorau (1987): 197–199; epigraphic evidence confirms that this pilgrimage, and especially its commemoration, indeed was considered a very important political event by the sultan and his entourage: a politically highly stylised (and revealing) inscription at the shrine of the Prophet Moses (*Maqām Nabī Mūsá*) in Palestine explains that it was constructed on Baybars' command in "one of the months of 668", "after the return of his noble mount from the pious *ḥağğ* and his setting out to visit holy Jerusalem" (Mayer [1933]; Amitai [2006]; Eddé [2012]).

through special arrangements with Cairo and through the set-up of religious endowments in Egypt persisted during and also after the sultanate's existence. Sultans, members from their courts, and other elite groups continued to endow yields from villages and estates that they owned in Egypt for consumption by Hijazi inhabitants and visitors, thus ensuring sufficient supplies to the Hijazi leaderships, but at the same time also furthering particular ties of patronage, reciprocity, power, and sovereignty.[10]

This privileged relationship between Cairo and Mecca and the many opportunities that it offered was of course also acknowledged by other real or would-be Muslim rulers, including by many rivals and opponents of the sultan of Cairo within and outside the sultanate's territories. A handful of rulers from the Rasūlid dynasty of Yemen (632–858/1235–1454) were notably ambitious in trying to appropriate this relationship for themselves. But most active in such respects were undoubtedly various Mongol and post-Mongol Muslim leaders in West Asia, who controlled in varying degrees populations and resources to the north and east of the sultanate. Throughout the thirteenth to early sixteenth centuries, they were regularly involved in an intense competition for regional sovereignty and for local control with, amongst others, different sultans of Cairo, and the symbolic forms of *ḥaǧǧ* representation-*cum*-precedence certainly constituted one among various arenas where such competition was fought out. This happened in particular during the first half of the fourteenth century, when this symbolism came to dominate more than anything else sultan al-Nāṣir Muḥammad's scramble for sovereignty and regional supremacy with Mongol Ilḫānid leaders. As a result of this particular competition for representation-*cum*-precedence, al-Nāṣir Muḥammad was actually pushed to personally lead the pilgrimage three times, in 712/1312, in 719/1320, and in 732/1332. These were truly unprecedented personal and very public engagements of the Cairo sultan with the *ḥaǧǧ*, every time accompanied by ever more lavish displays of his court's luxury, wealth, prosperity, and organisational capacity, by demonstrations of his generosity towards all kinds of local Hijazi elites and rulers as well as towards a diverse array of *ḥaǧǧ* participants, and by impressive manifestations of the expanding range and integrative force of his power. The elaborate representations of these royal pilgrimages in contemporary reports and texts reveal how at that time and place it almost seemed to many as though the long-forgotten glory of the classical caliphal era was finally being restored in the Islamic heartlands through the accomplished royal *per-*

10 For further details, see Meloy (2010a); Behrens-Abouseif (1999); Morisot (1998); Mortel (1997); Faroqhi (2014): 146–173; Mortel (1985); Darrag (1961): 190–194.

sona and authority of the sultan. In spite of the obvious hyperbolic nature of such literary reproductions, they were perhaps not entirely wrong either. Above all, these three pilgrimages of al-Nāṣir Muḥammad were extremely successful and effective in consolidating for many decades to follow the Cairo sultanate's supremacy in the *ḥağğ*, in the Hijaz, and in regional politics.[11]

It was only a century later, in the 830s/1430s, that this priority of the Cairo court in the *ḥağğ* rituals was once more seriously challenged, and again similar aims and strategies were employed. At that time, both the Rasūlid ruler of Yemen and the Tīmūrid ruler of Herat tried to obtain or even appropriate the right to provide a Kaʿbah veil (*kiswah*). The sultan of Cairo at that time, Barsbāy (r. 825–841/1422–1438), responded negatively, eventually managing to safeguard the rights that he had inherited from his predecessors.[12] But these were really very different times from those foregone days of al-Nāṣir Muḥammad, on the regional scene of rulers and regimes as much as locally. From a time of West-Asian crises and chaos for most of the first decade of the fifteenth century, Timurids, Ottomans, and various Turkmen dispensations had emerged as the sultanate's renewed competitors for regional supremacy and for control over political and economic resources. But simultaneously, the nature and organisation of those resources were also radically transformed, above all by the rapid growth in size, scale, and relative value of commercial interactions connecting the Indian, West-Asian, Red Sea, and Mediterranean trade systems. In the regions of the Cairo sultanate, these new commercial circuits and expanding flows of objects, commodities, and money generated all kinds of new socio-political practices and their institutionalisation, as well as unprecedented opportunities for various groups and individuals in the sultanate's centre and on its many peripheries, for new or renewed integration into the court's political orbit, for the empowering acquisition of local leverage from the court, or for a renegotiation of existing relationships with that court in Cairo. The political rise of new commercial and other economic agents of the sultan; a commercialisation of the tributary mode of surplus extraction; the installation of new types of devolved taxation via the sale of offices and similar *ad hoc* tax farming strategies; the monetisation of urban social relations; and the court's withdrawal from Egypt's and Syria's countrysides and non-urban peripheries, which was only occasionally reversed, and then mostly in a symbolic or punitive manner only: these are but some of the most currently visible interlocking

11 See Broadbridge (2008): 99–114. On Rasūlid engagements with Mecca and the *ḥağğ* see Vallet (2010): 425–469.

12 Dekkiche (2014–2015); Meloy (2010a): 138–139; Darrag (1961): 381–385.

processes of change, reform, and accommodation that made for a fifteenth-century Cairo sultanate that was very different from before, not just in political, but also in social, economic, and spatial terms.[13]

The re-imagination of political projects was certainly also part and parcel of these processes. In the 820s/1420s and 830s/1430s, sultan Barsbāy and his entourage in particular showed themselves very ambitious and active in this respect, trying to expand their political and economic reach and to renegotiate local arrangements on various frontiers, even beyond many traditional boundaries. The sultanate's conquest of Cyprus in 829/1426 was a function of this imperial policy, but so were the new engagements of Barsbāy's agents with local and regional leaderships in Syria, Southeast Anatolia, and the Hijaz. Attempts throughout the 820s/1420s at a more direct political integration of the latter West-Arabian region into Barsbāy's sultanate met with stiff and successful resistance from local elites, including most importantly from the Ḥasanids of Mecca. Instead, a policy of economic integration benefitting the court in Cairo was more successful. In their negotiations with the Ḥasanids and with other local leaders, Barsbāy's agents managed to obtain direct access to the seasonal Indo-Mediterranean commercial circulation, which in the 820s/1420s had found a new hub at Mecca's harbour of Jeddah. These mostly fiscal and tributary arrangements proved extremely effective and profitable, on local Hijazi levels as well as for Cairo's court. As a result, this economic engagement of the Cairo sultanate with the Hijaz would remain active until the sultanate's end, even under Sharif Muḥammad b. Barakāt (r. 859–903/1455–1497), when Mecca witnessed a phase of unprecedented regional empowerment, when political balances between Cairo and Mecca shifted again, and when arrangements had to be renegotiated.[14]

At such times of renegotiation, that other ongoing symbolic engagement of the sultan with Mecca through the *ḥaǧǧ* continued to prove its value. In Ḏū l-Ḥiǧǧah 884/February 1480, almost 150 years after al-Nāṣir Muḥammad, a sultan again managed to perform in person the leadership of the Egyptian *ḥaǧǧ* caravan and of the rituals in and near Mecca. Sultan Qāytbāy (r. 872–901/1468–1496)

13 For identifications and discussions of various aspects of these radical political, economic, and social transformations marking the turn of the fourteenth century, see, amongst others, Garcin (2005): 411–567: "Troisième Partie: la désurbanisation"; Garcin (1973–1974); Apellániz (2009); Rapoport (2005); Id. (2007); Loiseau (2010); Levanoni (2004); Stilt (2011); Meloy (2004); Miura (1997); Sabra (2004); Abū Ġāzī (2000); Walker (2011); Elbendary (2012); Id. (2015); Van Steenbergen, Wing & D'hulster (2016).

14 On these issues, see especially Meloy (2010a); Id. (2005); Id. (2003a); Wing (2014). For southeast Anatolia, see Wing (2015); Adriaenssens & Van Steenbergen (2016).

would actually turn out to be the last sultan in history to achieve this personal participation and leadership during his tenure. As with al-Nāṣir Muḥammad's pilgrimages before, for Qāytbāy's reign, too, this unusual royal *ḥaǧǧ* served as an impressive illustration of the accomplished nature of his long-lasting power and authority, to contemporary rivals for regional supremacy such as the Turkman leader of Tabriz, to ambitious partners such as the Sharif of Mecca, and to modern observers. This image of supreme leadership and actual control was confirmed by Qāytbāy's unprecedented patronage of endowed religious monuments in and near Mecca and in Medina, including the construction of an impressive *madrasah* adjacent to the Sanctuary Mosque and the reconstruction of the Prophet's Mosque after its complete destruction by a fire in 886/1481. Since the thirteenth century, sultans of Cairo had continued to regularly invest in Meccan and wider Hijazi real estate, public services, and religious monument construction, but never in any similar quantities or qualities as those generated by Qāytbāy's investments.[15]

A few years before Qāytbāy's pilgrimage of 884/1480, his privilege of *ḥaǧǧ* representation-*cum*-precedence had actually already been claimed through yet another tradition, when in 879/1475 his wife, the princess Fāṭimah (d. 909/1504), made the *ḥaǧǧ*, sitting in a richly decorated palanquin and accompanied by her own personal caravan, which was even claimed to have included a private orchestra. As with her husband's pilgrimage five years later, Fāṭimah was actually following in Qalāwūnid footsteps, in her case those of the princess Ṭuġāy (d. 749/1349). In 721/1321, Ṭuġāy, al-Nāṣir Muḥammad's senior wife, had performed for the first time in the sultanate's history this unusual kind of royal pilgrimage by spousal proxy, setting an example in religio-political practice as well as in the flowery literary representation and commemoration thereof, as moments of extremely luxurious display and of widespread awe for her husband, the sultan. A handful of other female royal pilgrimages followed, but this example was picked up most explicitly from 819/1416–1417 onwards. In that year, the leading royal spouse herself again made the pilgrimage, in splendid pomp and circumstance, and every successful sultan thereafter sent his wife, occasionally accompanied by sons and other members of his family, at least once on pilgrimage to Mecca. In some of these cases of spousal pilgrimage, the link with regional rivalry and competition for supremacy was obvious. In other cases, more local concerns for legitimacy and for the acceptance of the sultan's power, authority, and policies were in play. What this suggests above all is that in due course the traditional symbolic objects of representation-

15 Meloy (2010a): 184–187; Behrens-Abouseif (1999); Faroqhi (2014): 30.

cum-precedence, such as the *kiswah* and the *maḥmal*, were no longer deemed sufficient, especially when Cairo's economic interests in Red Sea commerce increased. Whereas personal participation in and leadership of the pilgrimage proved impractical for most sultans, the sending of distinguished representatives from their immediate entourage appeared as a more useful substitute to effectively continue to tap into the *ḥaǧǧ*'s networks and meanings, serving religious and political ends in Cairo, in Mecca, and everywhere in between.[16]

This pilgrimage leadership by spousal proxy happened a last time in 920/early 1515. This was a last grand occasion of royal splendour displayed from Cairo all the way to Mecca, amidst regional rivalry and competition, especially between the sultan and his very ambitious peer in Constantinople, Selim (r. 918–926/1512–1520). At the occasion of this pilgrimage, the ruler of the Hijaz, the Ḥasanid Sharif Barakāt (r. c. 903–931/1497–1525), made the unusual effort to accompany his royal guests back to Cairo. For years, this Sharif had been negotiating and fighting with local members of his family to consolidate his authority, while Mecca's (and Cairo's) profitable shares in the Red Sea commerce had been seriously affected by the arrival of the Portuguese in the Indian Ocean and in the Red Sea. In 920/1515 therefore Cairo was considered to have as much political leverage to offer to Barakāt as Mecca had to sultan Qāniṣawh al-Ġawrī (r. 906–922/1501–1516). When Selim took Cairo in January 1517, however, and sultan Qāniṣawh's successor was hanged from one of the city's gates, Barakāt had no problem switching his allegiance, including the privilege of *ḥaǧǧ* representation-*cum*-precedence, to the new supreme Muslim ruler who could offer him much needed support in his many Hijazi concerns. By this simple transfer to Ottoman sovereignty, the Sharif safeguarded his Ḥasanid family's tenure for four more centuries.[17]

4 Military Commanders and Religious Scholars between Late Medieval Mecca and Cairo

In Ḏū l-Qaʿdah 850/January 1447, a royal *ḥaǧǧ* caravan left from Cairo, led by members from the entourage of sultan Ǧaqmaq (r. 842–857/1438–1453), including two of his wives, the princess Muġul bt. al-Bārizī (d. 876/1472) and the princess Nafīsah bt. Mehmed b. Ḏūlġādir (d. 853/1449). As contemporary reports suggest this was another typical occasion of making good royal use

16 Behrens-Abouseif (1997); Johnson (2000); Dekkiche & Van Steenbergen (forthcoming).

17 Meloy (2010a): 205–232; Faroqhi (2014): 30–31.

of the empowering integrative forces inherent in the *ḥaǧǧ* value system. This royal caravan again confirmed the sultan's political sovereignty and Cairo's economic gravity through the spousal caravan's strong claim to precedence and through its lavish display and largesse in and between Cairo and Mecca.[18] An informant arriving at the court on Saturday 23 Ḏū l-Ḥiǧǧah 850/11 March 1447 allegedly reported that in this particular *ḥaǧǧ* season, however, the sultan's caravan had been confronted with challenging competition from various other regional players, an occasion remembered by the Egyptian historian al-Saḫāwī (d. 902/1497) as follows:

> The *ḥaǧǧ* had been performed by a *maḥmal* from Baghdad in a caravan of about 1,000 camels [...], by a sizeable caravan of West-Africans, by a crowd of Maghribians, and by the Ottoman vizier. [The vizier] had brought a lot of money with him for distribution among some of the needy and the poor in the two Sacred Places. He had melted 360 Egyptian sugar cones in the drinking fountain of the dome of al-ʿAbbās, to which he had added various *qinṭār*s of bee's honey. Waterskins had been filled with this, and it had been carried around during the running ceremony (*saʿy*) to quench the pilgrims' thirst.[19]

For several years throughout the 840s/1440s, *ḥaǧǧ* reports inform us of how caravans from Muslim West-Africa (Takrūr) and from the Maghrib were passing more frequently through Cairo than ever before, even culminating in 849/1446 in a pompous formal visit to Ǧaqmaq's court by a princess from the Ḥafṣid dynasty of Tunis (627–982/1229–1574).[20] One year later, in 850/1447, these two African caravans once again linked up with the Egyptian caravans, at a time when after a substantial period of interruption the Iraqi caravan was also being re-established by the Turkman ruler of Tabriz, and when also Meccan chroniclers confirm the presence of the Ottoman vizier bringing many gifts and providing both food and water for pilgrims. In this year, the sultan of Cairo therefore had very good reasons to be excessively well represented in the pilgrimage, if he wished to retain the image of his sovereignty and Muslim superiority. Various reports about sultan Ǧaqmaq's very high profile Egyptian caravan, however, reveal more than just how the 850/1447 *ḥaǧǧ* was noted by this culminating interregional dialectic of gift giving, displays of power, and competing claims to

18 Johnson (2000): 110–114.

19 Al-Saḫāwī, *al-Tibr al-masbūk*, 1:306.

20 Al-Saḫāwī, *al-Tibr al-masbūk*, 1:179, 252, 262; Ibn Fahd, *Itḥāf al-wará*, 4:223, 238, 245.

Muslim sovereignty. The spelling out in some contemporary chronicles of the distinguished identities of Egyptian and non-Egyptian participants in this particular pilgrimage is actually highly revealing. It reminds us of how, despite—or in addition to—its local and translocal political meaning, the *ḥaǧǧ* remained above all a religious event dominated by varieties of Muslims, including most notably all kinds of religious scholars (*ʿulamāʾ*) who combined the religious duty of pilgrimage to Mecca with their long-standing tradition of searching for intellectual company and acquaintance and for knowledge, beyond any political boundaries. Al-Saḫāwī again in particular provides a unique insight into the intricate networks of royals, commanders, administrators, and scholars that participated in this particular *ḥaǧǧ*.

> Those who travelled in this year are the senior princess Muġul, [who is] the daughter of the judge (*qāḍī*) Nāṣir al-Dīn al-Bārizī, the sister of the current head of the royal chancery (*kātib al-sirr*), and the wife of the sultan. The same goes for the princess who is the daughter of Ibn [Ḏūlġādir]. With the former came her daughter, and her sister, the wife of the pilgrimage's main commander. [The princess Muġul's] brother, the head of the royal chancery (*kātib al-sirr*), similarly travelled as a companion for her, together with his wife and with his daughter, the wife of al-Ǧammālī, the supervisor of the royal fisc (*nāẓir al-ḫāṣṣ*), and with a group that included [the esteemed administrators and scholars] al-Zaynī Abū Bakr b. Muẓhir [...], al-Šarafī b. al-ʿAṭṭār, al-Kamāl Abū l-Faḍl al-Nuwayrī, just mentioned [as newly appointed chief judge of Mecca], al-Šihāb b. Ṣāliḥ, Aṣīl al-Dīn al-Ḫuḍarī, the poet, our friend [the Meccan scholar and chronicler] Ibn Fahd [...], and Abū l-Waqt ʿAbd al-Awwal al-Muršidī l-Ḥanafī, who was in Cairo in this year [...]. They displayed pomp and circumstance that is beyond description, and along the roads and elsewhere they were extremely benevolent and generous [...]. When they arrived in Mecca, the lord Barakāt, its ruler, walked before the litter of the princess and of the other princesses, from the gate of al-Maʿlāh onwards. This was an arrangement considered as beautiful among those surrounded by luxury.[21]

21 Al-Saḫāwī, *al-Tibr al-masbūk*, 1:304–305. The particulars of the *ḥaǧǧ* of 850/1447 and of its diverse and competitive participation are also detailed by the Meccan contemporary chronicler Ibn Fahd, who seems to have travelled in this season's Egyptian caravan (Ibn Fahd, *Itḥāf al-wará*, 4:258–262). A summary account may be found in Ibn Taġrī Birdī, *al-Nuǧūm al-zāhirah*, 15:372.

The great variety of pilgrims who annually departed from Egypt certainly were not always accompanied by such splendour. But they did always proceed in a rather similarly organised fashion, travelling mostly in two or three Egyptian caravans (*rakb*), the first of which always included the *maḥmal* and possibly also other royal passengers, and each of which was always led, managed, and protected by a military commander (*amīr al-rakb*) and his military troops and administrative assistants, under the general supervision of the pilgrimage's main commander (*amīr al-ḥaǧǧ*). The role of these commanders was actually crucial, not only for the individual pilgrims and the success of their religious enterprise, but also for the sultan, whose credibility as a legitimate Muslim sovereign also derived from his duty vis-à-vis pilgrims' fulfilment of their religious obligation of pilgrimage. These commanders were annually appointed by the sultan, and it was their personal responsibility to safely accompany the pilgrims to and from Mecca. They were expected to provide especially the needy among them with sufficient supplies of water and food, and they had to make arrangements with Bedouin tribes along the overland caravan route that connected Cairo over the Sinai and ʿAqabat Aylah, to Medina and Mecca, so as to secure safe passage, access to sources, reliable guides, and in some cases also riding animals. Similarly organised but mostly more modest caravans departed from Damascus and from other Syrian towns, and possibly also from Baghdad and from Yemen, the latter two of course remaining beyond the sultan's authority and responsibility. Pilgrims and caravans from further away, such as from Anatolia and the North, from Iran and the East, and from Africa almost always linked up with the Syrian, Iraqi, and Egyptian caravans respectively.[22] Just as in the *ḥaǧǧ* season of 850/1447, this closely watched organisation of the main pilgrimage travel could result occasionally—in years of regional political stability and socio-economic prosperity in particular—in the arrival in Mecca of eight to ten different caravans and in the overcrowding of the town's basic facilities, as is also suggested by al-Saḫāwī for the unusually busy season of 845/1442:

> [After the arrival of the Cairo caravans], the caravan from Gaza entered [Mecca], followed by the [caravans] from Aleppo, from Damascus, from Karak, from Safad, from Baghdad, and then from with the Turkmen. As

22 Faroqhi (2014): 32–53; Irwin (2012): 142–161; see also al-Ġabbān (2011). The organisation and administration of the Egyptian *ḥaǧǧ* caravan was recorded in minute historical detail by a sixteenth-century Egyptian *ḥaǧǧ* caravan official, see al-Ǧazīrī, *Durar al-farāʾid*. In the twelfth and thirteenth centuries Crusader presence in Syria made the hazardous maritime passage through the Red Sea from the Egyptian ports of Aydhab or Quṣayr the main route for the Egyptian pilgrimage.

> a consequence, Mecca's houses, mountain paths, and mountains were filled up, and [pilgrim encampments] were stretched out all the way up to Miná.[23]

As he did for the year 850/1447, al-Saḫāwī, who displays in his chronicle *al-Tibr al-masbūk* a particular interest in reporting about pilgrimages and their participants, added to his description of the 845/1442 pilgrimage season another explicit reference to some of those who

> performed the *ḥaǧǧ*, including the judge (*qāḍī*) Bahāʾ al-Dīn b. Ḥiǧǧī, together with his young son amidst a group from his family, the master (*šayḫ*) Ṭāhir al-Mālikī, Walī l-Dīn, the son of our master (*šayḫ*) al-Sirāj al-Fahmī, and his brother; they sojourned (*yuǧāwirū*) during the following year.[24]

These and similar rudimentary lists of important pilgrims drafted by al-Saḫāwī remind us above all of how each of these caravans was first and foremost populated by several tens or sometimes even hundreds of pilgrims of diverse social, economic, cultural, and regional backgrounds, who were physically and financially capable—or at least bold enough—to temporarily leave their homes for the hazardous trip to Mecca. Obviously, these practical as well as motivational conditions made going on pilgrimage easier for some people, for successful scholars and merchants in particular, than for others. Every year various religious scholars of often towering regional reputation within and beyond their Šāfiʿī, Ḥanafī, Mālikī or Ḥanbalī schools of legal thought again travelled to Mecca for the *ḥaǧǧ*. In many cases, they combined the effort of the long and dangerous pilgrimage journey with the ambition of sojourning for some time near the Sanctuary Mosque. In that case, they acquired the particular status of *muǧāwir*, of non-resident sojourner remaining in Mecca to benefit from its many opportunities to acquire and transmit religious knowledge, and to perform the lesser pilgrimage, the *ʿumrah*.[25]

The often unparalleled size and diversity of Cairo's late medieval pilgrimage caravans, populated by many others besides royal representatives and military commanders, actually reflected not just the Cairo sultan's claim to Muslim

23 Al-Saḫāwī, *al-Tibr al-masbūk*, 1:67.

24 Ibid.

25 Irwin (2012): 163–164; "Ḥadjdj", in *EI*[2] (http://referenceworks.brillonline.com/entries/encyclopaedia-of-islam-2/hadjdj-COM_0249); "Mudjāwir", in *EI2* (http://referenceworks.brillonline.com/entries/encyclopaedia-of-islam-2/mudjawir-SIM_5307); Gellens (1990).

sovereignty. Above all, every year these caravans also epitomised the equally unparalleled metropolitan size, diversity, and efflorescence of Cairo's many urban groups and communities, and they illustrated then and now how Cairo had become a crossroads of all kinds of intersecting, competing, and overlapping cultural and economic networks that connected individuals, social groups, and cultural communities across Africa and Asia. This meant that there were many good reasons for Sunni religious scholars of all sorts of specialisation and intellectual allegiance, for Sufi masters, pupils, and practitioners, and for merchants of a variety of trades from across that wide area to continue to converge in Cairo throughout the fourteenth and fifteenth centuries, irrespective of any political or other boundaries and transformations. Cultural efflorescence, socio-economic prosperity, migration, and natural demographic growth had propelled Cairo's population to at least a quarter of a million by the first half of the fourteenth century, making it the second largest city of the Mediterranean world, and perhaps even of Eurasia, after Constantinople. From the middle of that century onwards, the Black Death pandemic and subsequent recurrent epidemics, local and regional politico-military turmoil, and economic transformation took a heavy toll on Cairo's urban constellation, but never on its regional and wider appeal and status.[26]

In Cairo, just as in any other of the deeply interconnected towns and cities of West Asia and North Africa, resident and visiting scholars and other men of religion were mostly organised along the lines of particular knowledge communities, as defined by their allegiance to one of the four dominant schools of legal thought, the Sunni *maḏhab*s, to one of the congregations of mystic learning and practice, the Sufi *ṭarīqah*s, or—as mostly was the case—to any combination of both. These scholarly communities and their diverse and dynamic urban memberships were locally and trans-locally interconnected, and often also intersected, by scholarly friendships, lineages, and teacher-student networks, by institutionalised educational, legal, and religious practices derived from scholars' monopolisation of jurisprudence and of ethico-religious authorities, and by the reproduction and transmission of particular sets of knowledge and of knowledge practice. These were therefore all extremely amorphous as well as truly imagined communities, conscious and defining components of a global community of Muslims (*ummah*), but existing in the social reality of things in the particularity of their local manifestations through relevant scholars, ideas, institutions, and practices only. That historical particularity, as it may be reconstructed today, was defined above all by the interaction between a variety

26 Berkey (1998); Raymond (2001).

of specific institutions (judgeships, teaching posts, studentships, government offices, textual traditions) and widespread social practices, of knowledge and of patronage and competition in particular. Patronage, or the intricate process of exchange of benefit for service, connected particular scholars to other scholars, as well as to varieties of other social groups, through complex webs of vertical relationships of reciprocity, confirming, establishing, or challenging social hierarchies and identities. Competition, or the equally intricate process of distinguishing the social self in the pursuance of status, authority, and legitimacy, forced the majority of horizontal relationships consciously and unconsciously into a framework of particular binary moral discourses and constructions of social order and of its continuation, protection, or rehabilitation through various sets of strategies, tools, and ideas. Above all, these vertical and horizontal practices of patronage and competition regulated access to scarce resources in the context of West-Asian and North-African late medieval redistributive political economies, where the practice of patronage generated the wider circulation of symbolic and economic assets beyond the military and political elites, and where the practice of competition organised that circulation and stimulated ongoing social transformation. For the scholarly communities, these complex practices of patronage and competition defined the particular interaction of their members with those specific ranges of institutions and with the wider circulation of resources; it regulated the local dynamics of their internal social and intellectual organisation; and it secured scholars' integration within wider West-Asian and North-African social formations, such as in the cosmopolitan urban context of late medieval Cairo.[27]

With its enormous resource flows, its rich intellectual and commercial transregional networks, and its unrivalled magnitude and diversity of social groups, including above all the sultan and his court, Cairo's social environment throughout the fourteenth and fifteenth centuries continued to display a unique cumulative intensity in these social practices of patronage and competition, affecting all, and stimulating among many other things a remarkable cultural efflorescence. Even the aforementioned radical socio-political transformation of the early fifteenth century, in many ways rooted in the accommodation of these urban practices of patronage and competition to the effects of pestilence and war, did not meaningfully interrupt that intensity nor that cultural efflorescence.[28] In the early 1990s, Carl Petry summarized the full scope,

---

27 Berkey (2003): 177–257 (Part IV: Medieval Islam, 1000–1500); Lapidus (1967); Chamberlain (1994).

28 Berkey (1998); Petry (1981); Berkey (1992); Martel-Thoumian (2001); Behrens-Abouseif (2007).

particular detail, and remarkable result of this intensity of patronage and competition in late medieval Cairo so aptly and powerfully that his impression deserves to be quoted here in a slightly updated, full version, as an extremely telling concluding generalisation of how that particular interaction between commanders and scholars was not just extremely successful, but also pivotal for the future of Islamic societies in the East and West:

> The majority of [the sultanate's] wealth was recycled back into civil society via maintenance of great households [of military commanders, including the sultan] with swarms of retainers and artisans, requisition expenditures to outfit military campaigns, and massive endowments (*awqāf*) made to found religio-academic institutions. By the fifteenth century, this latter propensity had created a network of more than two hundred mosques, colleges, and Sufi hospices in the capital alone, each supporting a core staff of clerics or faculty, instructional deputies of various specialties, and students whose needs were met out of *waqf* proceeds. The senior faculty, who held chairs (*karāsī*) in the Koranic sciences, Prophetic traditions (*ḥadīṯ*), or Shariʿ jurisprudence (*fiqh*), delivered formal lectures and certified the expertise of advanced students who presented themselves for disputation and examination. Their mentors signed authorizations (*ijāza*s) attesting to textual proficiency, which facilitated a novice's entry into the courts and/or academies. Since junior instructors handled the bulk of routine pedagogy, these senior scholars, most of whom had achieved prior renown as clerics or jurists, were left free to pen the corpus of treatises which rendered the [...] era a "Silver Age" of Islamic scholarship.[29]

5 Introducing a Scholar between Late Medieval Cairo, Damascus, and Mecca

The scholarly tradition to pursue religious duty and knowledge was certainly what drove the scholar Aḥmad b. ʿAlī l-Maqrīzī (b. 766/c. 1365; d. 26 Ramaḍān 845/7 February 1442) to join on several occasions the Egyptian caravans and to exchange from time to time the intense urban environment of his hometown of Cairo for the remote and much quieter surroundings of Sacred Mecca's Sanctuary mosque. Just as was true for any other scholar, however, whether

29 Petry (1993): 324.

in Mecca or in Cairo, metropolitan practices of competition and patronage also defined al-Maqrīzī's life, career, thinking, and scholarly production, and perhaps they even did so in even more intense and defining ways than has so far been acknowledged.

Al-Maqrīzī was born in the early 1360s in a family with a long tradition and reputation for religious status and scholarship. In the fourteenth century the different members of al-Maqrīzī's pedigree were especially highly valued in the family's hometown of Baalbek and in the nearby Syrian urban centre of Damascus. Al-Maqrīzī's father had however moved to Egypt before the 1360s to take up employment there, including as a scribe at the royal court, so that the young boy Aḥmad was born in Cairo. Aḥmad received a standard education and training in the skills and scholarship of his time, such as befitting young male members of reputed families such as his. Al-Maqrīzī's family, however, was marked by a particular regional and intellectual complexity, connecting not just the local scholarly communities of Cairo, Damascus and Baalbek, but also the intellectual *maḏhab* communities of Ḥanbalīs, of Ḥanafīs and—eventually also—of Šāfiʿīs. The latter was due to the fact that al-Maqrīzī's father and father's father were Ḥanbalīs, whereas his other grandfather was a well-known Ḥanafī scholar, and al-Maqrīzī himself switched from Ḥanafī to Šāfiʿī allegiance in the later 1380s. Although this complex family situation was certainly not entirely unusual in scholarly circles of the time, it did create a particular social and cultural context for al-Maqrīzī to grow up in. The young al-Maqrīzī would prove an eager and ambitious student of *ḥadīṯ*, *fiqh* (jurisprudence), grammar, *qirāʾāt* (Qurʾān readings), *adab* (literature) and—especially—*tārīḫ* (history). Eventually some of his biographers claimed that he personally boasted of having studied with no less than 600 teachers, in Cairo, in Damascus, and in Mecca.[30]

Al-Maqrīzī's particular family background somehow created relatively straightforward access to a range of patronage and employment opportunities for the young scholar. According to most of his biographers, he started off in the late 780s/1380s in his father's footsteps, as a scribe in the royal chancery, and from there he quickly moved on to various salaried positions of considerable standing, reputation, and impact in royal service. He served as an assistant

30 For modern biographies of al-Maqrīzī, see, amongst others, Ziyādah (1971b); Faraḥāt (2009): 5–26; Rabbat (2003); Bauden (2014). For biographies by fifteenth-century Egyptian contemporaries, see, amongst others, Ibn Taġrī Birdī, *al-Manhal al-ṣāfī*, 1:415–420; al-ʿAynī, *ʿIqd al-ǧumān*, 574; Ibn Ḥaǧar, *Inbāʾ al-ġumr*, 9:170–172; al-Saḫāwī, *al-Tibr al-masbūk*, 1:73; Id., *al-Ḍawʾ al-lāmiʿ*, 2:21–25; al-Ṣayrafī, *Nuzhat al-nufūs*, 4:242–244. See also further references in Bauden (2014): 161–162.

Šāfiʿī judge in Cairo, and he was for some time preacher in the ancient congregational mosque of ʿAmr b. al-ʿĀṣ in Fusṭāṭ and in the gigantic Sultan Ḥasan *madrasah* below the Cairo citadel. On three brief occasions between 801/1399 and 807/1405, he was appointed by the sultans Barqūq (r. 784–801/1382–1399) and his son Farağ (r. 801–815/1399–1412) to the position of *muḥtasib* of Cairo and Lower Egypt. It is generally assumed that al-Maqrīzī actually took a particular and personal interest in the latter position, sometimes translated as 'market inspector', but in fact a religio-political office of much wider local representation of the ruler in the management of urban social spaces and practices, with as a particular duty the official performance of the collective religious responsibility of 'commanding right and forbidding wrong' (*al-amr bi-l-maʿrūf wa-l-nahy ʿan al-munkar*). This interest appears above all from the unusual socio-economic detail and from the regular expression of related expert views and personal opinions on urban practice and organisation that mark some of his writings. Much to al-Maqrīzī's own frustration, however, his own known tenures of this important position of *muḥtasib* never were very successful. They lasted between one and seven months only, and none left any clear traces of policy, practice, or impact—not even in al-Maqrīzī's own writings—except for brief references to his appointments and replacements by rival candidates. In fact, al-Maqrīzī's last referenced appointment to the position of *muḥtasib*, in Šawwāl 807/April 1405, is his last known appointment to any position of similar—or any other—standing and responsibility in Cairo.[31]

Some two years later, there was yet a new episode of appointment, as teacher of *ḥadīṯ* in the Ašrafiyyah and Iqbāliyyah *madrasah*s in Damascus. It seems, however, that this concerned at best an ephemeral episode of tenure only, which unlike the Cairo *muḥtasib*ship was even left entirely unreferenced in al-Maqrīzī's own writings. Al-Saḫāwī, in his biography of al-Maqrīzī, explains that from these years onwards, "he relinquished all that (i.e. his salaried positions) and abided in his home city, obsessed by the occupation of history, so that he acquired a well-known reputation for it, his fame in it spread wide, and he got a series of writings in it." The reality of al-Maqrīzī's life in the 1410s, '20s and '30s may have been more complex than al-Saḫāwī's summary suggests here, if only because al-Maqrīzī is known to have spent considerable time away from his home in Cairo's Barğuwān area, in Damascus and in Mecca. Throughout these many years, he actually performed three more pilgrimages to Mecca (in

---

31 On these specific points, see the afore-mentioned biographies and also: Broadbridge, (1999): 88–91; Stilt (2011): 65; Allouche (1994): 3–7, 120. The three appointments to the position of *muḥtasib* are also referred to by al-Maqrīzī himself in his *al-Sulūk*, 3:930, 970, 1155.

825/1422, in 834/1431, and in 838/1435), and also sojourned there regularly, twice between 834/1431 and 840/1436 in particular. But there is little reason not to accept the bottom-line of al-Saḫāwī's assessment of this second phase in al-Maqrīzī's life, as very different from before, and as prolific and successful in scholarly terms. Nor is there much reason to doubt the general feeling that emerges from contemporary biographies as well as from modern studies that the data, theories, and opinions that fed the more than two hundred works of history, which he eventually claimed to have authored, created a particular reputation and profile for this professional historian that deeply divided his widening audiences of students, readers, and colleagues into either admirers or opponents. When al-Maqrīzī eventually died an old man nearing his eighties in Ramaḍān 845/February 1442, he was buried in the so-called Cemetery of the Sufis immediately outside Cairo's Northern wall, but only few people seem to have taken much notice. By that time and age, the construction of the ivory tower of his scholarship had been successfully completed; his books and essays rather than his person aroused, and would continue to arouse, attention and debate.[32]

The puzzling issue of this remarkable transformation that Aḥmad b. ʿAlī l-Maqrīzī went through, from a very active and relatively successful career in the political, socio-economic and cultural limelight of city and sultanate, to a life of critical observation, detached contemplation, even unrelenting frustration, and widening yet mixed public reception, has continued to intrigue scholars since al-Saḫāwī. In current scholarship, there is a general consensus that this was indeed a rather slow process, of gradual withdrawal to the background of elite social life, beginning in the eventful years of sultan al-Nāṣir Faraǧ's reigns (r. 801–815/1399–1412), and taking a decisive turn in the days of his successor, sultan al-Muʾayyad Šayḫ (r. 815–824/1412–1421). Whether it really was a voluntary process and whether al-Saḫāwī's suggestion of an obsession with history sufficiently explains it are questions that continue to arouse debate. Some modern scholars, such as Bauden, Ziyādah and Faraḥāt, follow al-Saḫāwī's explanation of consciously giving in to the appeal of a life of intellectual scholarship. They present this transformation moreover as enabled by a liberation from material concerns, when, by 813/1410, al-Maqrīzī would have inherited sufficient property and income from his parents and grandparents to become

32 These issues are detailed in the afore-mentioned biographies; for the quote by al-Saḫāwī, see al-Saḫāwī, *al-Tibr al-masbūk*, 1:73; Id., *al-Ḍawʾ al-lāmiʿ*, 2:22. For al-Maqrīzī's sojourning in Mecca, see especially Bauden (2014): 165, fn. 12, and also al-Maqrīzī, *Ḍawʾ al-sārī*, 12, 47.

financially independent.[33] Anne Broadbridge, however, made a very different analysis, from the perspective of a socio-economic reality within which patronage and competition were the main social practices defining relationships of power, flows of resources, and individuals' lives. Broadbridge demonstrates how during the reign of al-Nāṣir Farağ al-Maqrīzī gradually lost contacts and patrons among the political elites, and how he, after 815/1412, proved incapable of attracting new patronage and of obtaining new access to income, whereas the very opposite happened to some of his peers. "In terms of the competitive arena and Mamluk patronage practices", Broadbridge concluded, "al-Maqrīzī seems to have died a failure."[34] Nasser Rabbat, finally, agrees with this latter view of socio-economic isolation, but also qualifies it further by adding an emotional perspective of despair and reclusion. In doing so, he suggests an even more gloomy picture, of a middle aged man's intentional resignation that was inspired on the one hand by al-Maqrīzī's gradual "leaning toward *zuhd*, the 'mild ascetism' professed by a number of ulama in the medieval period", but on the other hand also by "a feeling of despondency", caused by the endless political intriguing, by the ongoing military confrontations, and by the unusually bloody violence that had plagued Egypt and Syria in the first dozen years of the fifteenth century and that had cost him his patrons and friends.[35]

6 Contextualising al-Maqrīzī's Authorship

A further contextualisation of this transformatory process in al-Maqrīzī's life actually enables an even better understanding of how these three interpretations of scholarly pursuit, of social failure, and of asceticism and despair connect to each other and to this particular epoch of the early fifteenth century, with important repercussions for current assessments of al-Maqrīzī's writings, not in the least of his *ḥağğ* treatise *al-Ḏahab al-masbūk*.

As explained above, the early years of the fifteenth century in Egypt and Syria were marked by processes of radical change, reform, and accommodation that, even despite the long-term continuation of social practices and cultural efflorescence, made for the emergence of an entirely different Cairo sultanate, in political as much as in any other terms of organisation, discourse,

33 Bauden (2014): 166; Ziyādah (1971b); Faraḥāt (2009).

34 Broadbridge (1999) (quote p. 105).

35 Rabbat (2003) (quotes p. 16). Bauden equally refers to "the loss of most of his relatives" as an additional reason for al-Maqrīzī to decide "to retire from public life and to devote himself full-time to his passion for writing history" (Bauden [2014]: 166).

and memberships. Al-Maqrīzī's career was very much confronted with those radical changes, which really started to set in just after his first appointment to the position of *muḥtasib* in 801/1399, when sultan Barqūq died. At that time dynastic arrangements around Barqūq's royal household proved strong enough to enable his succession by his young son al-Nāṣir Farağ. Simultaneously, however, a whole range of phenomena and events and their direct and indirect effects turned into an explosive cocktail that proved destructive for all kinds of social formations in the Asian hemisphere. These ranged from the post-Mongol Central-Asian military leader Tīmūr's (r. 771–807/1370–1405) ruthless and unstoppable campaigns of Asian conquest and booty, hitting Syria and Anatolia shortly after Farağ's accession; over the gradual but total reconfiguration of West-Asian leaderships in Timūr's wake, including the fragmentation of Cairo's political elites into an unstable and uncontrollable range of military factions from 807/1405 onwards, spreading over Egypt and Syria in increasingly lethal cycles of confrontation and violence; to the deep and systemic crises of traditional socio-economic systems, when political-military upheaval coincided with the cyclical effects of epidemics (the plague) and of natural disasters and when as a consequence century-old urban-rural balances were gravely disturbed.[36] This is not the place to expand on any of these transformative local and trans-local phenomena that pushed West-Asian social groups and formations onto a road of no-return towards adaptation. It is however clear that the impact on traditional social and economic resources in Egypt and Syria and on the different urban elites that had for at least two centuries relied and thrived on such resources was substantial.[37]

As with anyone around him, al-Maqrīzī was also therefore forced to deal with these socio-economic changes on a daily and very personal basis. This did not just involve direct confrontations with disease and death through the loss of almost all of his relatives and children, including in 826/1423 his last surviving daughter Fāṭimah.[38] In al-Maqrīzī's unfortunate case, these radical changes moreover occurred just when, by the turn of the century, after careful preparation and with the help of family, friends, and patrons, he was about to firmly establish his person, his reputation, and his access to resources among the Cairo sultanate's ruling circles. Changes in patronage structures regularly

---

36 On these issues, see especially Onimus (2013); Manz (1999); Borsch (2005): 40–54.

37 For various appreciations of these impacts and accommodations, see Walker (2011): 233–271; Loiseau (2010); Apellániz (2009); Meloy (2005); Bacharach (1973); Garcin, (1973–1974); Elbendary (2015).

38 Bauden (2014): 166; Rabbat (2003): 17; Ziyādah (1971b): 16.

accompanying the accession of a new sultan and the natural dynamics of competition with peers may well help to explain initial adverse turns in this career, after sultan Barqūq's death in 801/1399. But when al-Maqrīzī himself added a rare personal note that he had only accepted his short-lived re-appointment to the position of *muḥtasib* in Šawwāl 807/April 1405 "reluctantly, and after the sultan's threefold repeated insistence", it becomes clear that by 807/1405 this wariness may have had most to do with growing political tension that was about to culminate in two military confrontations in and near Cairo in Ḏū l-Ḥiğğah 807/June 1405 and in sultan Farağ's temporary abdication between Rabīʿ I and Ğumādá II of the next year (September–November 1405).[39] The same contextuality needs to be taken into account when considering al-Maqrīzī's surprising refusal in 810/1407 of sultan Farağ's offer of the leadership over Šāfiʿī court justice in Syria, which according to most observers was his last known engagement with salaried positions.[40] This actually occurred when he had travelled in the royal entourage to Syria, during the sultan's fourth Syrian expedition against rival amirs (Muḥarram-Rabīʿ II 810/July–September 1407). This expedition ended with sultan Farağ's victory at the battle of Baalbek and with the death of one of his opponents, his former tutor Yašbak al-Šaʿbānī. But this outcome did nothing at all to end a competition for power that was gradually spiralling out of anyone's control and that was causing chaos and havoc in Syria, uncertainty in Egypt, and a radical reconfiguration of the sultanate's political landscapes, all of which was to culminate in 815/1412 in the public execution of sultan Farağ in Damascus.[41] Although this unprecedented outcome

39 On the events of 1405, see Onimus (2013): 463–481 ("la fragmentation du milieu émiral"), 747. For the quote, see al-Maqrīzī, *al-Sulūk*, 3:1155. On this moment in the life of al-Maqrīzī and in the history of the position of the *muḥtasib* of Cairo, see also Meloy (2003b): 190; Allouche (1994): 3–4, 120; ʿAbd al-Rāziq (1977): 153. Al-Maqrīzī's deep political involvement is suggested by Meloy's speculative claim that one of his earliest treatises, the *Iġāṯat al-ummah*, may well have been written as a piece of economic advice for Farağ's young brother ʿAbd al-ʿAzīz, who briefly sat on the throne as al-Malik al-Manṣūr (r. September–November 1405) (Meloy (2003b): 190).

40 See Broadbridge (1999): 91 (where confusion over the reasons for this refusal is expressed), 92 (where al-Saḫāwī's claim that al-Maqrīzī was appointed to a teaching post in the Muʾayyadī mosque complex in the 1410s is shown to have been unlikely); Rabbat (2003): 15–16 (who assigns the refusal to "weariness" and "the traditional pious alim's fear of inadvertently committing injustice while holding the position of judge").

41 On these events and their consequences, see the detailed analyses in Onimus (2013): 481–512 ("Entre concentration et fragmentation: le second règne de Farağ"), 649–657 ("La radicalisation des pratiques guerrières"). See also Bauden (2014): 166 (where al-Maqrīzī's direct exposure to these events is suggested by the explanation that after being "part of

was anything but evident to al-Maqrīzī and his colleagues in 810/1407, by then the ongoing violent political tension and lack of local control surely already offered very good reasons for his not wanting to accept the position of Šāfiʿī chief judge of Syria, and for not showing much obvious ambition for any other function of import in these and in subsequent years.

Personal loss, anxieties, and fears in times of political violence and socio-economic upheaval had a substantial impact on al-Maqrīzī's career. But as both Anne Broadbridge and Nasser Rabbat demonstrate, this withdrawal of course also had to do with the gradual disappearance of a range of patrons and powerful close friends, just as al-Maqrīzī was reaching middle age, leading to social bereavement, stimulating an attitude of asceticism, and possibly even causing despondency. This emergence of a new, adverse social reality around al-Maqrīzī however also deserves further contextualisation, especially since his known patrons and friends in high places all belonged to a particular group of political, administrative, and cultural elites who were all greatly affected by the crises of the early fifteenth century. So far, four political patrons have been clearly identified in contemporary biographies and in modern studies. These included of course first and foremost the royals Barqūq and his son Faraǧ. In the former's case, al-Maqrīzī is even claimed to having been one of the sultan's boon companions (*nadīm*), whereas his membership in Faraǧ's entourage on the latter's various expeditions to Syria between 810/1407 and 815/1412 also suggests a certain, yet much more qualified, closeness. Al-Saḫāwī's biographies of al-Maqrīzī furthermore suggest a very close and beneficial friendship with the above-mentioned military commander Yašbak al-Šaʿbānī, a former *mamlūk* of sultan Barqūq and sultan Faraǧ's tutor, who had however a very complex relationship with the latter sultan, ranging from moments of support and Yašbak's *de facto* rule in Faraǧ's name, to equally regular moments of competition for power and of military confrontation, culminating in Yašbak's death at the battle of Baalbek on 13 Rabīʿ II 810/17 September 1407.[42] Caught between the often opposing interests of these two high-profile patrons, al-Maqrīzī finally also seems to have nurtured more stable good relations with the head of the chancery at

a group which accompanied the sultan on a trip to Damascus in 810/1407 [...] it seems likely that he did not remain in the town continuously and returned to Cairo each time the sultan did."), 168 (where the same suggestion follows from the statement that "[al-Maqrīzī's] ties with the sultan al-Nāṣir Faraǧ were to increase two years later, when he accompanied the latter in his various sojourns in Damascus").

42 See Broadbridge (1999): 88 (Yašbak & Barqūq, including reference to Ibn Taġrī Birdī's boon-companionship claim), 89 (Barqūq), 91 (Yašbak). See also al-Saḫāwī, *al-Tibr al-masbūk*, 1:73; Id., *al-Ḍawʾ al-lāmiʿ*, 2:22.

the royal court in Cairo, the royal secretary (*kātib al-sirr*) Fatḥ Allāh al-Tabrīzī (d. 816/1413), who, according to Rabbat, "was both a dependable and resourceful patron and a faithful friend for more than twenty years". This converted Jew from Tabriz, who was actually a doctor and who had been the official chief of doctors in Cairo (*ra'īs al-aṭibbā'*) when sultan Barqūq transferred him, despite his lack of qualifications, to the position of royal secretary, had remained in office for many years under Barqūq and Farağ, until his dismissal and murder in 815–816/1413 by order of Farağ's executioner and successor, sultan al-Mu'ayyad Šayḫ.[43] What each of these latter two patrons Yašbak and Fatḥ Allāḥ have in common is their close connections to Barqūq, and to the royal household that was constructed around this sultan from the 1380s onwards, and that continued to be dominant—albeit eventually in an extremely fragmented and destructive way—until the execution of its leader Farağ in 815/1412.[44] Al-Maqrīzī's loss of his patrons between Barqūq's death in 801/1399 and Fatḥ Allāh's murder in 816/1413 were therefore not isolated events or unfortunate co-incidences. This rather was symptomatic of the gradual implosion and total disappearance of a particular power constellation and of a particular socio-political order during the first decade of the century, and of how this anything but premeditated outcome also deeply affected scholars such as al-Maqrīzī.

Al-Maqrīzī's personal history of social transformation and withdrawal is then not merely a story of mild asceticism, frustration, and failure. It is also the story of much wider changes that affected the political, economic, and social worlds in which he lived, and that had a huge impact on traditional social structures and elites in Cairo and beyond. It is above all the story of how he—willingly or not—chose to deal with these changes. With traditional socio-economic conditions in an unprecedented state of flux, and with the social field of politics undergoing rapid and violent transformation, old routes and trodden paths for social advancement were dwindling for people such as

---

43 See Rabbat (2003): 16 (also describing al-Maqrīzī as "suddenly jolted by the dismissal and then brutal killing of his last confirmed patron, Fatḥ Allāh the *kātib al-sirr*, which took place after a painful six-month imprisonment (Šawwāl 815–Rabīʿ al-Awwal 816/January–June 1413)"). See also the biography of Fatḥ Allāh by Ibn Taġrī Birdī (*al-Manhal al-ṣāfī*, 8:375–377), where it is explained that "he was an eager collectioner of precious books", a particularity that might be somehow related to the wide range of al-Maqrīzī's scholarship.

44 See Onimus (2013): 316–514 ("Quatrième partie: *al-bayt wa l-ḥizb*, l'ascension de la maison sultanienne face au factionnalisme émiral"); and Loiseau (2010): 179–214 ("4. Refondation de l'état, redistribution du pouvoir: vers un nouvel ordre mamelouk"), 287–330 ("6. Le sultan et les siens. Usages politiques et stratégies sociales dans la fondation de la maison du sultan [al-Ẓāhir Barqūq, al-Nāṣir Farağ]").

al-Maqrīzī. Simultaneously, however, new opportunities certainly also continued to arise, but they required new skills and assets, new friends and roads to patronage, and new dealings with old and new competitors. These were new circumstances that turned out to be more favourable for some than for others, including for some of al-Maqrīzī's peers, such as the great Šāfiʿī judge and specialist of *ḥadīṯ* Ibn Ḥaǧar al-ʿAsqalānī (773–852/1372–1449) or the *muḥtasib* and historian Maḥmūd al-ʿAynī (762–855/1361–1451). The former's membership in an ancient wealthy family of spice merchants may have proven an incredible asset when traditional income from land came under immense pressures, whereas the latter's southeast-Anatolian origins, professed Ḥanafism, and cultural proficiency in Turkish secured his direct access to the new rulers and their patronage.[45] In al-Maqrīzī's case nothing much is known indeed of further advancements in terms of salaried positions, nor of any explicit ambitions in that respect; on the contrary, his attitude, as expressed through his writings, rather has been reconstructed so far as one of regular criticism of the ruling sultans and their representatives (eventually even including his former patron Barqūq),[46] of total abandonment of his former activism (though not of his political and socio-economic interest and concern), and of occasional frustration and despair with his personal circumstances, often even expressed as a longing for a better past, when things would have been—in the eyes of a historian such as him at least—much clearer and much better organised.[47]

7 Contextualising al-Maqrīzī's *al-Ḏahab al-masbūk*

The preceding micro-historical contextualisation undoubtedly enables a more nuanced understanding of Anne Broadbridge's assertion that "in terms of the competitive arena and [...] patronage practices al-Maqrīzī seems to have died a failure."[48] She however also added to this assessment that "in terms of academic endeavour, [he died] a resounding although not unqualified success with at least his followers, although not his detractors."[49] Considering that this second phase in al-Maqrīzī's life coincided with what Bauden, Ziyādah, and Faraḥāt, after al-Saḫāwī, have also identified as a consciously constructed high-point in his scholarly production, it was clearly not just all melancholy, depression,

45 Broadbridge (1999): 86–87, 89–91, 94–97.
46 Ibid., 93–94. See also Levanoni (2001); Massoud (2003).
47 Rabbat (2003): 16–18; Id. (2000); Id. (2012).
48 Broadbridge (1999): 105.
49 Ibid.

isolation, and frustration that made him—in the words of one of his students and successors as a historian, Ǧamāl al-Dīn Yūsuf Ibn Taġrī Birdī (813–874/1411–1470)—into "the historian of his time whom no one could come near";[50] neither can it have been simply a story of mild asceticism and aloofness that made al-Maqrīzī himself explicitly write down that in 833/1429 an ambassador from the Tīmūrid court in Herat came to Cairo requesting the sultan for a copy of his *Kitāb al-Sulūk*, his ongoing project of chronicling the late medieval Cairo sultanate.[51] Obviously, the reality of al-Maqrīzī's professional life in the 810s/1410s, '20s and '30s was more complex than any one explanation can account for. Whereas changing times and contexts, past experiences, personal intellectual developments, and ongoing encounters with loss and despair continued to inform and define al-Maqrīzī's personality and mindset, it should also be made clear that in those decades his personal ambition had definitely moved away from direct participation in the newly composed post-815/1412 ruling establishments and its institutions, towards a life of observation and teaching, of describing that new organisation of the Cairo sultanate of his days from various *longue durée* perspectives, and even of connecting with its practices of patronage and competition in equally new ways.

As is well known, al-Maqrīzī mainly engaged in the production of historiographical scholarship in two different ways. On the one hand, he produced a number of carefully constructed and deeply interconnected grand works of Egyptian topography, biography, and history, in which he collected, surveyed, and preserved the history of Egypt, its Muslim capitals, and its changing elites from the seventh-century Arab conquest until his own days; apart from the above mentioned *Kitāb al-Sulūk*, which was itself a continuation of two other works by al-Maqrīzī dealing with Egypt's history up to the emergence of the Cairo sultanate in the later twelfth century, these works include the famous *Ḫiṭaṭ* on the history of the city of Cairo, and the *Kitāb al-Tārīḫ al-Kabīr al-Muqaffá li-Miṣr* with biographies of people who lived in Egypt or visited the region.[52] On the other hand, al-Maqrīzī also produced simultaneously with these multi-volume works a high number of short books, topical essays, and

---

50 Ibid., 92–93, referring to Ibn Taġrī Birdī, *History of Egypt*, 8:143.

51 Ibid., 103, referring to al-Maqrīzī, *al-Sulūk*, 4:818, and adding that Ibn Ḥaǧar's and al-ʿAynī's references to this embassy make no mention of a request for al-Maqrīzī's *al-Sulūk*. The ongoing nature of this chronographical project is explained in Ziyādah, "ʾAḥmad b. ʿAlī l-Maqrīzī", and it is further qualified in Bauden (2014): 181.

52 Bauden (2014): 167–196; Ziyādah (1971a): 18–19; al-Šayyāl (1971): 23–24. To these grand works should certainly also be added a biography of the prophet Muḥammad (*Imtāʿ al-asmāʿ li-mā li-l-rasūl min al-anbāʾ wa-l-aḥwāl wal-ḥafadah wa-l-matāʿ*) and a more

little treatises, on various socio-economic, cultural, or political subjects, and almost always including a perspective of identifying precedents, continuities, and changes for precisely defined historical phenomena from past or present; these undoubtedly made up the majority of the alleged number of more than 200 works by al-Maqrīzī, even though today only about twenty-five opuscules of this undoubtedly optimistically counted set have survived.[53]

The production of most of al-Maqrīzī's grand works of history was a long-term project that was only more or less completed in the years immediately before his death.[54] Yet, the conception, set-up, and writing of most of them clearly fitted in some sort of coherent plan of scholarly action that he must have started to think of seriously in the course of the 810s/1410s, if not earlier.[55] These works were therefore never directly connected to any obvious form of commissioning or cultural patronage, even though through their size, subject matter, and detailed scholarship they obviously attracted a substantial level of high-profile attention. This is certainly suggested for the *Kitāb al-Sulūk*, when in 833/1429 this Arabic chronicle's fame already turned out to have travelled all the way to the Persianate Tīmūrid court in Herat, many years before it was actually completed.[56] Similar stories of renown and possibly also reward may

traditional universal history of mankind since Creation (*al-Ḫabar ʿan al-Bašar*), both of which were written during the final decade of al-Maqrīzī's life (see Bauden [2014]: 171, 196–199).

53 Bauden (2014): 168; al-Šayyāl (1971): 25–37; Faraḥāt (2009): 19–25 (listing an overall number of 34 extant or known books by al-Maqrīzī—some of the titles listed by Faraḥāt may however only refer to parts from other works, such as number 8, the unpublished *Tārīḫ al-Ǧarākisah* [Oxford, Bodleian Library, MS Or. 458], which upon inspection turns out to be a copy from a part of the *Kitāb al-Sulūk* covering the years 807–830 AH). Al-Saḫāwī claimed to have read "in [al-Maqrīzī's] own handwriting that his compositions consisted of more than two hundred large volumes" (al-Saḫāwī, *al-Ḍawʾ al-lāmiʿ*, 2: 23).

54 See, in general, Bauden (2014): 173 (*Ḫiṭaṭ*), 181 (*al-Sulūk*), 191–192 (*al-Muqaffá*). For the *Ḫiṭaṭ*, see also Sayyid (1979): 240; Broadbridge (1999): 100; Bauden (2008): 99. Al-Maqrīzī's major annalistic chronicle *Kitāb al-Sulūk* runs up to the end of the year 844 AH (May 1441), which means that he continued adding material to it until shortly before his death (Ziyādah [1971a]: 11; Bauden [2014]: 181). In the bibliographical section that Ibn Taġrī Birdī added to al-Maqrīzī's biography, he stated that the latter had confided to him that "if this history [i.e. *Kitāb al-Tārīḫ al-kabīr al-muqaffá*] had been completed the way I prefer, it would have consisted of more than eighty volumes", suggesting that it was indeed never completed (Ibn Taġrī Birdī, *al-Manhal al-ṣāfī*, 1: 419; also referred to in al-Šayyāl (1971) 24); al-Saḫāwī, who repeated the same statement, claims that eventually only sixteen volumes were completed (al-Saḫāwī, *al-Ḍawʾ al-lāmiʿ*, 2: 22).

55 Bauden (2008): 71–72; Id. (2010); Id. (2014): 168–169, 176; Ziyādah (1971b): 18–19.

56 Broadbridge (1999): 103, referring to al-Maqrīzī, *al-Sulūk*, 4: 818; Ibn Taġrī Birdī, *al-Nuǧūm*

surely be true for the reception of al-Maqrīzī's other, equally highly admired works, such as his multi-volume *al-Muqaffá* and his *al-Ḫiṭaṭ*.[57]

This matter of the production, reproduction, and consumption of al-Maqrīzī's written word is obviously more diverse and complex for those many smaller texts. There are a few patterns that may be reconstructed here too, though, and that above all have some relevance for the historical contextualisation of one of these texts, which is this study's main subject, the *Kitāb al-Ḏahab al-masbūk*. In the case of a number of these texts, at least the perception of a genuine personal scholarly interest is created as the main reason for writing them. Thus, a short treatise on the history of Arab tribes in Egypt, the *Kitāb al-Bayān wa-l-iʿrāb ʿammā bi-arḍ Miṣr min al-Aʿrāb*, begins with the clear statement that "I noted down [this treatise] for myself (*li-nafsī*) and for whom God wants from my brethren (*abnāʾ ǧinsī*)."[58] Other treatises, such as the monetary history *Šuḏūr al-ʿuqūd* and the legal inquiry of a Hebron endowment, the *Ḍawʾ al-sārī li-maʿrifat ḫabar Tamīm al-Dārī*, make explicit claims to having been commissioned for particular purposes, in these two cases respectively by sultan al-Muʾayyad Šayḫ (r. 815–824/1412–1421), soliciting monetary advice from al-Maqrīzī, and by the heirs of a Companion of the Prophet, Tamīm al-Dārī, seeking some form of support for their appeal to justice.[59] A third and final category of treatises seems to have been conceptualised by al-Maqrīzī for similar particular occasions and purposes, but with the explicit aim of soliciting or confirming relations of cultural patronage and impact. This is suggested to have been the case with one of the first known historical texts produced by al-Maqrīzī, the economic treatise *Iġāṯat al-ummah*, which seems to have been written as an advice text for the sultan ʿAbd al-ʿAzīz b. Barqūq when he briefly replaced his brother Faraǧ on the throne in the autumn of 1405.[60] This motive of socio-cultural promotion and of soliciting royal patronage also seems to have

---

al-zāhirah, 14:336. The seminal contemporary status of the *Kitāb al-Sulūk* is certainly also illustrated by the fact that it was explicitly continued by at least two mid-fifteenth-century chronicles, one by Ibn Taġrī Birdī (*Ḥawādiṯ al-duhūr fī madá l-ayyām wa-l-šuhūr*; see also Ibn Taġrī Birdī, *al-Manhal al-ṣāfī*, 1:418) and the other by al-Saḫāwī (*al-Tibr al-masbūk fī ḏayl al-Sulūk*). Bauden similarly concludes that "the work was hugely successful, as demonstrated by the large number of manuscripts preserved in libraries across the world" (Bauden [2014]: 182).

57 For Ibn Taġrī Birdī, the *Ḫiṭaṭ* managed to attain "extreme beauty (*fī ġāyat al-ḥusn*)" (Ibn Taġrī Birdī, *al-Manhal al-ṣāfī*, 1: 419).

58 Al-Maqrīzī, *Bayān*, 6. See also Al-Šayyāl (1971): 25–26.

59 Meloy (2003b): 197; al-Maqrīzī, *Ḍawʾ al-sārī*, 47–49.

60 Meloy (2003b): 190 ("… al-Maqrīzī may have taken advantage of the interregnum of al-Malik al-Manṣūr ʿAbd al-ʿAzīz ibn Barqūq … to submit his recommendations to be put into practice").

caused, almost thirty years later, the production of al-Maqrīzī's treatise on the legal rulings and historical practice of circumcision, the *al-Iḫbār ʿan al-iʿḏār*; this is at least suggested by the author himself in an autobiographical note in his *Kitāb al-Sulūk*, added to a brief report of festivities organised for the circumcision of sultan Barsbāy's son, Ǧamāl al-Dīn Yūsuf (827–868/1424–1463, r. 841–842/1438), in mid-Šaʿbān 837/late March 1434:

> At that occasion, I wrote a book (*kitāb*^{an}) which I entitled 'The Report on the Feast of Circumcision' (*al-Iḫbār ʿan al-iʿḏār*). As far as I am aware nothing similar has ever been produced before, [considering] what it contains of stories and traditions, of rulings by the authoritative pioneers of Islam, of deeds of caliphs and rulers, and of memorable events and impressive cases.[61]

This combination of occasion, of promotion, and of seeking, confirming, or abiding by the rules of cultural patronage is even more explicitly suggested by al-Maqrīzī as the main ground for his writing of the short history of the pilgrimage to Mecca, which is the focus of this study. In the opening lines of this 'Book of Moulded Gold' (*Kitāb al-Ḏahab al-masbūk*) al-Maqrīzī actually makes a number of extremely informative and useful statements, enabling an unusually precise historical contextualisation of this text and its production. In this very personal literary reflection, the author dedicates his booklet directly to an individual whom he identifies clearly as a person of high standing and as his patron; he then explains at length that he wrote it as a present befitting the occasion of the latter's preparation for the *ḥaǧǧ*; and he finishes his introduction with some good wishes for his patron's safe journey.

> I demand God—supplicating Him and stretching out my hand to Him—to cause the days of the noble lord to be followed by similarly good and additionally abundant ones ever after, such that every fortune that he anticipates and [every] expectation that he nurtures will come true, outdoing anyone who preceded him and unmatched by anyone who follows him. [...] The word has spread that the high-born intention was set on undertaking the *ḥaǧǧ* and to be endowed with the noise and blood of rituals. It has become common practice for servants to present a gift to their masters, for which reason I considered the situation of clients that owe presents on the occasion of an event like this, and I decided to

61 Al-Maqrīzī, *al-Sulūk*, 4:913.

> follow their example. [...] Since knowledge is the most precious and most valuable of treasures, the most glorious and the longest remembered of deeds, I collected for the benefit of the esteemed library of our lord—may God support it with long life for its owner—a volume that comprises the report of those caliphs and kings who performed the *ḥaǧǧ*. [...] May God protect our lord whenever he does not expect it and may He guard him whenever he does not think of it; may He be with him as a guardian when traveling, and as a supporter and helper when he is staying somewhere.[62]

As the long version of the title of the booklet already announces—"The Book of Gold Moulded in the Format of the Report of Those Caliphs and Kings Who Performed the *Ḥaǧǧ*"—, the text that follows this dedicatory introduction is organised around the *ḥaǧǧ*. Instead of approaching this subject from a traditional didactic or religio-legal perspective of the pilgrimage's religious forms, function, and meanings, al-Maqrīzī decided to focus first and foremost on "those caliphs and kings who performed the *ḥaǧǧ*", on pilgriming rulers. This focus, however, was not meant to offer its dedicatee any sort of guidance on or historical examples of the *ḥaǧǧ* journey, of good pilgrimage practice, or on ritual rules and regulations. As will be explained in detail in the next chapter, the combination of the subject of the *ḥaǧǧ* with that of rulers of caliphal or royal standing allowed al-Maqrīzī first and foremost to inform his audience about the *ḥaǧǧ*'s political meanings, and about how those meanings had been, and could or should be, operationalised throughout Islamic history. *Al-Ḏahab al-masbūk* is therefore not a religious or merely historiographical text, but rather above all a political didactic text, which would certainly have been entertaining and instructive for a larger readership, but which was meaningful first and foremost to a political audience, and which was therefore perhaps even as programmatic as some of al-Maqrīzī's socio-economic texts, such as the *Iġāṯat al-ummah* and the *Šuḏūr al-ʿuqūd*, had been.

This brings up the issue of the nature of that political audience, of the identity of the booklet's dedicatee and of al-Maqrīzī's patron, of the occasion and time of its composition, and finally also again of al-Maqrīzī's radically changed but clearly yet ongoing engagement with the social practice of patronage beyond the 1410s. Some scholars, such as the booklet's first editor Ǧamāl al-Dīn al-Šayyāl and then also Karam Ḥilmī Faraḥāt more recently, claimed that *al-Ḏahab al-masbūk* was written in May 1438.[63] This is however the result

62 See below, §§1, 2, 4, 5.

63 Al-Šayyāl (1955): 24–26; Id. (2000): 25–27; Faraḥāt (2009): 27–29. See also al-Šayyāl, (1971): 27; *GAL*, 2:50.

of a misinterpretation of the reference to this date (Ḏū l-Qaʿdah 841) in some manuscript colophons, as a reference to the work's composition, whereas in fact it only refers to the moment when al-Maqrīzī collated, corrected, and finalised a copyist's copy of the text.[64] Ḏū l-Qaʿdah 841/May 1438 can therefore only serve as a *terminus ante quem*. Furthermore, there is one clear internal reference in the text to the author's own time, which is explicitly situated after Šaʿbān 815/November 1412, a date that therefore can serve as a *terminus post quem*.[65] This leaves a substantial level of doubt regarding the actual time of production of *al-Ḏahab al-masbūk*, at some undefined moment between 815/1412 and 841/1438. Contextualising the text's production from the perspective of patronage may actually help to offer some more clues to resolve this issue.

Most scholars who have looked at the question of dedication and patronage for this text have felt extremely frustrated by the combination of, on the one hand, al-Maqrīzī's explicitness in dedicating the text and explaining the occasion for its production and, on the other hand, his silence on the actual identity of the patron whom he was writing it for, only referred to in the introduction by generic titles and epithets such as "the noble lord" (*al-maqarr al-maḫdūm*), "the high-born intention" (*al-ʿazm al-šarīf*), "for the benefit of the esteemed library of our lord" (*bi-rasm al-ḫizānah al-šarīfah al-maḫdūmiyyah*), "the high-born mind" (*al-ḫāṭir al-šarīf*), and "the lord" (*al-maḫdūm*).[66] On the basis of the prominent appearance of the first title in particular, al-Šayyāl, and Faraḥāt after him, concluded that this patron had to be a high-ranking amir, who performed the pilgrimage in 841/1438, but whose identity could not be further established.[67] There are however good reasons, both internal and external to

64 These issues are discussed in more detail in Chapter 3 of this study.

65 See p. 61 ("Until today, the situation has remained like that, the Friday sermon in Mecca never being spoken in the name of any of the ʿAbbāsid caliphs of Egypt, except for [the name of] the caliph al-Mustaʿīn bi-llāh Abū l-Faḍl al-ʿAbbās b. Muḥammad, [which was mentioned] for a few days in the year 815.") Al-Mustaʿīn reigned as sultan between March and November 1412 ("al-Mustaʿīn", in *EI*[2] (http://referenceworks.brillonline.com/entries/encyclopaedia-of-islam-2/al-mustain-SIM_5620)).

66 The first reference, *al-maqarr al-maḫdūm*, appears three times, the others only once (see below, §§1–5).

67 See al-Šayyāl (1955): 24–26; id. (2000): 25–27; referring to the formal classification of titles such as *al-maqarr*, including *al-maqarr al-šarīf* and *al-maqarr al-maḫdūmī*, in the sultanate's chancery practice, as recorded in al-Qalqašandī, *Ṣubḥ al-aʿšá*, 5:494; 6:130–133, 146–148, 154–155, 161. This argument is repeated word-for-word by Faraḥāt (2009): 27–29. The other editor of *al-Ḏahab al-masbūk*, Ḥamad al-Ǧāsir, suggests that this amir was al-Maqrīzī's former patron Yašbak al-Šaʿbānī, referring to a similar statement in the entry for *al-Ḏahab al-masbūk* in the seventeenth-century bibliography *Kašf al-ẓunūn* (al-

the text, to develop some more precise ideas about the identity of this patron, moving beyond the formal question of titulature and introducing two rather different potential dedicatees of an engaged political booklet such as this *ḥaǧǧ* history. One option is that it was dedicated in about 834/1431 to Ǧamāl al-Dīn Yūsuf, the aforementioned son of al-Ašraf Barsbāy. Another option is that a first version of *al-Ḏahab al-masbūk* was already written at a much earlier date, in 821/1418, for sultan al-Mu'ayyad Šayḫ. An argument can actually be made in favour of each of these two options.

Both potential dedicatees concern persons of royal status, and this tallies well with the text's obvious royal set-up, with its focus on caliphs and other Muslim rulers and their political patronage of the *ḥaǧǧ*. These are subjects befitting a sultan or a sultan's heir, but they are highly unsuitable or at least hazardous to dedicate in a similarly programmatic way to a senior amir from a sultan's entourage.[68] The first suggested option of the dedication of *al-Ḏahab al-masbūk* to Yūsuf would also be in line with al-Maqrīzī's aforementioned composition in 837/1434 of another treatise on the occasion of the same Ǧamāl al-Dīn Yūsuf's circumcision. A similar occasion for the production of another dedicated text, but then on the politics of the *ḥaǧǧ*, certainly would have presented itself to al-Maqrīzī three years earlier, in the summer of 834/1431, when the author himself had been sojourning in Mecca, and when sultan

Ǧāsir [1952]: 5–6); as suggested above, however, Yašbak died at the battle of Baalbek on 17 September 1407, making it highly unlikely—given the explicit reference to the 1412 sultanate of caliph al-Mustaʿīn—that al-Maqrīzī would have dedicated it to him posthumously; the dedication rather suggests the text's mediation of a patron-client relationship that is still active. The entire argument in favour of a high-ranking amir, however, is rather weak and follows from the conclusion that *al-maqarr* cannot formally be used in this combination with *al-maḫdūm* for the sultan, nor for a non-military member of the court, so that it can only have been meant for an amir (even though the combination does not entirely match chancery usage for high-ranking amirs either, and the other titles and epithets that were mentioned do not match such known usage at all); for an alternative potential explanation for the generic nature of these titles and epithets, and for their non-representative character for that patron, from the perspective of wider socio-literary tradition rather than from chancery practices, see chapter three of this first part.

68 Another potential dedicatee that at least should be suggested here—even though a strong case cannot really be made for him—is the amir Qurqmās al-Šaʿbānī (d. 842/1438), deeply engaged in the affairs of the Hijaz as sultan Barsbāy's main local agent and eventually, in 842/1438 (shortly after the production of the Leiden manuscript), Ǧaqmaq's main rival for Barsbāy's succession, in which context he was considered a valuable "candidate for the sultanate" (*taraššaḥa li-l-salṭanah*) in al-Maqrīzī's *al-Sulūk* (4:1105) (see Van Nieuwenhuyse & Van Steenbergen [forthcoming]).

Barsbāy's senior wife, the princess Ǧulbān al-Hindī (d. 839/1436), had been sent on the first of the two spousal pilgrimages that were organised during Barsbāy's reign. Confirming or re-establishing her royal husband's privilege of representation-*cum*-precedence and his sovereignty along the road and in Mecca at a time of growing regional competition, Ǧulbān travelled in full royal splendour, bringing her entourage and family with her. Her only male son with sultan Barsbāy, Ǧamāl al-Dīn Yūsuf—at that time a boy of about seven years old, living with his mother in the royal harem—was most certainly among those family members who participated in this 834/1431 *ḥaǧǧ* with her.[69] This particular context of the first royal pilgrimage from Cairo since 819/1417 obviously would have befitted the production of a text constructed around the history and political symbolism of this kind of meaningful royal engagement with the Hijaz,[70] and its dedication by the author to the only living son of sultan Barsbāy, who was at that occasion following in the royal footsteps of many an illustrious predecessor of his father, would then evidently have imposed itself.

But there are also good reasons to follow a second option, of the booklet's dedication to an actual sultan of Cairo: al-Malik al-Mu'ayyad Šayḫ. As with Yūsuf, this would certainly also be in line with another known textual enterprise that similarly connected al-Maqrīzī to Šayḫ: the case of the *Šuḏūr al-ʿuqūd*, which was, as explained, a text of advice commissioned by this sultan.[71] As with Yūsuf, an occasion for the production of this particular type of text certainly also presented itself, when in Šaʿbān 821/September 1418 al-Mu'ayyad Šayḫ's plans to go on pilgrimage to Mecca were made public.[72] By

69 For al-Maqrīzī's 'sojourning' in Mecca at this time, see Ibn Fahd, *Itḥāf al-wará*, 4:55–56 (I am grateful to M. Dekkiche for providing me with this reference); al-Maqrīzī, *Ḍaw' al-sārī*, 12; Bauden (2014): 165. On the *ḫawand al-kubrā* Ǧulbān al-Hindī and her pilgrimage, "accompied by her family and relatives (*wa-maʿahā ahluhā wa-aqāribuhā*)", see Ibn Taġrī Birdī, *al-Manhal al-ṣāfī*, 5:15; also al-Maqrīzī, *al-Sulūk*, 4:858; Dekkiche & Van Steenbergen (forthcoming). On growing regional competition and the symbolical role of the *ḥaǧǧ* and of Mecca, see Dekkiche (2014–2015).

70 For the ḥaǧǧ of sultan al-Mu'ayyad Šayḫ's *ḫawand al-kubrā* Ḫadīǧah (d. 833/1430) in 819/1417 (coinciding with the wife [*ḫātūn*] of the ruler of the Mongol Golden Horde joining the Damascus caravan for the *ḥaǧǧ* and with a sizeable caravan from Takrūr joining the Egyptian caravan), see al-Maqrīzī, *al-Sulūk*, 4:368, 371; Ibn Ḥaǧar, *Inbā' al-ġumr*, 7:223.

71 Meloy (2003b): 197–203; Broadbridge (1999): 92; Id. (2003): 239–240.

72 See al-Maqrīzī, *al-Sulūk*, 4:458–459 (parading in Cairo of the sultan's camels selected for the trip to the Hijaz [*li-l-safar maʿahu ilá l-Ḥiǧāz*] and Syrian troubles urging for the abortion of the plans [*inṯaná ʿazm al-sulṭān ʿan al-safar ilá l-Ḥiǧāz*]); similarly reported in Ibn Ḥaǧar, *Inbā' al-ġumr*, 7:315 (but reformulated as "he gave up his intention to perform the *ḥaǧǧ* [*inṯaná ʿazmuhu ʿan al-ḥaǧǧ*]"); Ibn Taġrī Birdī, *al-Nuǧūm al-zāhirah*,

this, Šayḫ would actually follow in the footsteps of only three other sultans who are claimed to have undertaken this journey from Cairo—al-Ẓāhir Baybars, al-Nāṣir Muḥammad, and al-Ašraf Šaʿbān. Each of them was given an entry in *al-Ḏahab al-masbūk* and al-Ašraf Šaʿbān's pilgrimage story even closed the booklet, creating then the impression of Šayḫ—if indeed he was the dedicatee—pursuing or stepping into a historical sequence that was reconstructed for him by al-Maqrīzī. There are also two more internal reasons that make this a very valid option. One has to do with an explicit reference in the text to the fact that the inner *kiswah* of sultan al-Nāṣir Ḥasan "is still present today"; this inner *kiswah* of sultan Ḥasan was actually replaced by sultan Barsbāy's in the course of 826/1423, which would then move back the text's *terminus ante quem* substantially (provided at least that al-Maqrīzī would have known about this new inner *kiswah* arrangement), making a 821/1418 date of composition more likely.[73] This relatively early date would certainly also help to explain one puzzling auto-referential feature in the text, which is then the second internal reason for linking the text to al-Muʾayyad Šayḫ's patronage. As will be detailed in the next chapter, there are a handful of explicit references throughout the text to other writings by al-Maqrīzī, explaining how more information on this or that ruler may be found in one or more of his other texts. However, the chronologically last ruler to receive this kind of references is sultan al-Ẓāhir Baybars, for whom al-Maqrīzī adds that more may be found in "his biography in the *Kitāb al-Tārīḫ al-Kabīr al-Muqaffá* and the *Kitāb Aḫbār Mulūk Miṣr*."[74] The abrupt ending of this pattern of auto-referencing in the narrative of Baybars may then be explained by the simple fact that by 821/1418 the production of works such as that *Kitāb Aḫbār Mulūk Miṣr*—better known to later generations as the annalistic chronicle *Kitāb al-Sulūk li-maʿrifat duwal al-mulūk*—had not yet advanced nor perhaps even been conceptualised beyond Egypt's history in the thirteenth century, making similar auto-references in the narratives of the next four fourteenth-century rulers simply impossible.[75]

14:68 (adding to a detailed parading report that by that act "it was confirmed to everyone that the sultan was going to travel for the *ḥağğ*"). In a personal communication Nasser Rabbat informed me that he has also developed in his forthcoming biography of al-Maqrīzī a similar argument for *al-Ḏahab al-masbūk*'s dedication to al-Muʾayyad Šayḫ on the occasion of this 821/1418 pilgrimage project.

73 See p. 81; the particular history of the decoration with Barsbāy's new inner *kiswah* in 826/1423 was certainly known to al-Maqrīzī's Meccan student, colleague, and friend Ibn Fahd (see Ibn Fahd, *Itḥāf al-wará*, 3:596); Dekkiche (2014–2015).

74 See p. 82.

75 This suggestion of *al-Ḏahab al-masbūk*'s predating the composition of most of the *Kitāb al-*

This factor of royal dedication then finally brings up again the issue of al-Maqrīzī's asceticism, despair, and alleged failure to engage with new patronage in the second phase of his live, or at least his withdrawal from active participation in the sultanate's new, post-1412 ruling establishments. This attitude certainly may have been the case as far as salaried positions, court privileges, and government duties were concerned. The above presentation and historical contextualisation of his writings suggests, however, that things may have been rather different with his involvement in socio-cultural patronage. As is generally accepted, al-Maqrīzī certainly persevered with actively pursuing royal attention and patronage during the reign of al-Muʾayyad Šayḫ, and it may well be that *al-Ḏahab al-masbūk* was part and parcel of that social strategy (even though the text soon lost its direct value when Šayḫ's pilgrimage was aborted due to Syrian troubles).[76] Whether effective and successful or not, the same practice of a particular cultural production aimed at the sultanate's political elites may have been continued by al-Maqrīzī during the reign of Šayḫ's successor Barsbāy, and in the 1430s it may even have engaged with the entourage of the sultan's wife Ǧulbān al-Hindī (d. 839/1436) and of their only son Yūsuf.[77] Past

Sulūk would certainly also help to explain three obvious dating mistakes in two narratives from the post-Baybars era (the dating of al-Ḥākim's pilgrimage to the year 699 AH rather than to 697 AH, of al-Mujāhid ʿAlī's second pilgrimage to 752 AH rather than to 751 AH, and of the same ruler's death to 769 AH rather than to 767 AH); in *al-Sulūk* the correct dates are mentioned in all three cases, which makes for a remarkable inconsistency between both texts that can only be explained by the fact that for the production of these narratives in *al-Ḏahab al-masbūk* the *al-Sulūk* and the material used for it were not yet available to the author for easy reference. It has to be admitted, however, that this argument on the basis of internal suggestions in the text of *al-Ḏahab al-masbūk* does not agree well with Bauden's conclusion that "by 820/1417 [al-Maqrīzī] had already written the whole part [of *al-Sulūk*] covering the years 567/1171–791/1389, the equivalent of three volumes, as there is a comment that a practice which he described is still current at the time he wrote the passage, that is to say the year 820/1417" (Bauden (2014): 181); in the latter case the absence of further references to and the dating discrepancies with the *al-Sulūk* remain rather enigmatic. From the reference to the *al-Sulūk* as *Kitāb Aḫbār Mulūk Miṣr* it is anyway clear that *al-Ḏahab al-masbūk* was written before the *al-Sulūk* was awarded the more poetic title by which it has become known to later generations.

76 See al-Maqrīzī, *al-Sulūk*, 4:459; Ibn Ḥaǧar, *Inbāʾ al-ġumr*, 7:315 Ibn Taġrī Birdī, *al-Nuǧūm al-zāhirah*, 14:68.

77 An illustration of that entourage's status and position in the 1430s is the fact that Ibn Taġrī Birdī was quite impressed by the charisma of Ǧulbān and by her empowerment in her son's slipstream, as suggested by his claim that "if she had lived until her son al-ʿAzīz became sultan, she would have managed his reign most efficiently" (Ibn Taġrī Birdī, *al-Manhal al-ṣāfī*, 5:16).

experiences with radical socio-political transformation and with personal loss, and stark or even controversial personal opinions about social order, justice, and socio-economic policy surely continued to inform his writings in various direct, indirect, and above all dynamic ways, which certainly require further exploration.[78] But neither this particular mindset nor the choice for a life of scholarship from the 810s/1410s onwards meant that al-Maqrīzī—as he himself also explains in the introduction of *al-Ḏahab al-masbūk*—ever really wished, tried, or would have been able to escape from the context of patronage and competition that defined the field of socio-cultural practice for any fifteenth-century Egyptian scholar and his audiences. In this social reality of things, and despite his own death in solitude, al-Maqrīzī may even be claimed to have been quite successful, given the long survival of his post-815/1412 scholarship's fame, remembrance, and textual production among patrons, peers, and pupils, and among admirers as well as among opponents.

The suggestion of the existence of an aspired or even actual bond of scholarship and cultural patronage between al-Maqrīzī and Ǧamāl al-Dīn Yūsuf in the 1430s of course remains tenuous and speculative, standing on one explicit textual leg only (the reference in *al-Sulūk* to the reason for writing *al-Iḫbār ʿan al-iʿḏār*). The full picture nevertheless begs the final question whether it was really merely a coincidence that—as will be explained below—the careful preparation for publication of a selection of al-Maqrīzī's shorter texts, including *al-Ḏahab al-masbūk*, happened at about the same time as the illness that confined sultan Barsbāy to his deathbed and that caused his son Yūsuf's official nomination as heir apparent soon thereafter, in late 841/mid-1438.[79] This particular publication project had of course everything to do with an old man's general concern to preserve his scholarly legacy and to organise the orderly

78 One issue demanding further exploration certainly is the afore-mentioned fact that quite a few of these sultans, from Barqūq over Šayḫ to Barsbāy, receive a very negative press from al-Maqrīzi, albeit apparently always posthumously (Bauden [2014]: 182; Broadbridge [1999]: 93–94; but also Id. [2003], offering a didactic purpose as an explanation).

79 The Leiden autograph, including *al-Ḏahab al-masbūk*, was produced by a copyist at some time between early 1437 and early 1438, and it was corrected by al-Maqrīzī between February–March and June–July 1438 (see chapter 3). Sultan Barsbāy's fatal illness apparently started to manifest itself from Rajab 841/January 1438 onwards (al-Maqrīzī, *al-Sulūk*, 4:1027); he officially installed his son Yūsuf as heir apparent in early Ḏū l-Qaʿdah 841/late April 1438, when it became clear that an epidemic was decimating the membership of the sultan's household (al-Maqrīzī, *al-Sulūk*, 4:1040, 1041–1042, 1042–1045); Barsbāy died 12 Ḏū l-Ḥiǧǧah 841/6 June 1438, and was succeeded by his son the next day (al-Maqrīzī, *al-Sulūk*, 4:1051, 1053–1054, 1065–1066).

and authentic transmission of the various kinds of knowledge that over time he had been engaging with. But even in the ivory tower of al-Maqrīzī's scholarly pursuit such concerns betray an ongoing interest in the impact of his writings and in issues of readership and of his own status and identity as an authoritative member of the scholarly community. Al-Maqrīzī may then actually also have seen a good occasion in the events, changes, and re-alignments affecting the sultanate's elites in 841/1438 and coinciding with his publication project to draw (renewed) attention to the many merits of his scholarly production.

From this perspective of ongoing scholarly communication and performance in a socio-cultural context that is rooted in practices of patronage and competition the two dedicatory options suggested above for *al-Ḏahab al-masbūk* may not even be mutually exclusive.[80] It seems sound to claim that the case for dedication to al-Mu'ayyad Šayḫ is quite strong, but also that at the same time the aborted plan of this sultan's *ḥaǧǧ* in 821/1418 must have made the text somewhat meaningless. It may then well be that it was never published in this original form, and that it was recycled many years later by its author, when new contexts arose that re-aligned with at least some of the text's meanings and that justified renewed investments in its preparation for publication. The 834/1431 pilgrimage of Ǧulbān al-Hindī and her family as well as the accession of al-ʿAzīz Yūsuf on 13 Dhū l-Ḥiǧǧah 841/7 June 1438 certainly provided for occasions that tallied well with the political text that *al-Ḏahab al-masbūk* was meant to be.

At the same time, however, Yūsuf's extremely short-lived tenure of the sultanate, between 13 Ḏū l-Ḥiǧǧah 841 and 18 Rabīʿ I 842/7 June and 8 September 1438 only, as well as Šayḫ's aborted pilgrimage twenty years earlier may have added yet other moments of disappointment and despair to al-Maqrīzī's long life, moments of despondency for more lost channels of access to his audiences indeed, perhaps even inviting for unhappy musings similar to the ones that Nasser Rabbat identified to have been added in al-Maqrīzī's hand at the bottom of the cover page of the autograph manuscript of the first volume of the *al-Sulūk*:

> I have been afflicted by such bad fortune, that whenever it goes up, it immediately comes down, and whenever it stands up, it inevitably falls down, and whenever it goes straight, it surely bows down again, and

80 A similar suggestion was made for the textual history of al-Maqrīzī's *Šuḏūr al-ʿuqūd* and its changing dedication from al-Mu'ayyad Šayḫ in the 1410s to "Barsbāy's successor" in 1438, see Meloy (2003b): 197, fn. 54.

whenever it runs smoothly, it at once encounters obstacles, and whenever it becomes alert, it soon sleeps again. [...]

By your life, I do not lack a banner of glory
Nor did the horse tire of competing
Instead, I am afflicted with bad fortune
Just like a beautiful woman is inflicted with divorce.[81]

81 Rabbat (2003): 17.

CHAPTER 2

Texts: *al-Ḏahab al-masbūk* between Narratives, Stories, and Meanings

1 The *ḥaǧǧ* in Arabic Writing and Literature: Between *fiqh* and *tārīḫ*

Just as the Prophet's Farewell Pilgrimage of 10/632 (*ḥiǧǧat al-wadāʿ*) had established itself as a normative paradigm in the social and cultural realities of the performance and leadership of the annual pilgrimage, so did its remembrance and reproduction in Arabic writings on the *ḥaǧǧ* from the seventh century onwards. Already at an early date in the Islamic community's complex socio-cultural history the Farewell Pilgrimage was singled out as a separate and important subject of more or less coherence among the many stories (*aḫbār*) of the Prophet's life and of the early Muslim community's history. These stories of Muḥammad's actions and sayings during the Farewell Pilgrimage, transmitted in various and often also conflicting versions, soon acquired with many others of these reports much larger moral, political, and religious meanings. Moulded in this particular context, the Farewell Pilgrimage account started a life in Arabic writing and literature as one of those bundles of codified prophetic narratives that continued to provide guidance, food for debate and conflict, and a powerful model for emulation, into the contemporary period.

Between the seventh and ninth centuries, all these prophetic reports of varying size, detail, origins, value, and reliability underwent a substantial transformation towards becoming an integral component of the emerging community's social memory. The variety of Farewell Pilgrimage reports fully shared in this transformatory process of transmission, from stories' collection through oral and written practices, over their reproduction in comprehensive books, to their selective incorporation and organisation as authoritative traditions (*ḥadīṯ*) in specialist genres, emerging simultaneously with the rise of particular branches of Islamic learning. In that process, the Farewell Pilgrimage made its way as a valid subject to write on—as did so many aspects of the Prophet's biography—into two increasingly distinct but never fully disconnected branches: jurisprudence (*fiqh*) and history (*tārīḫ*). These interlocking traditions in the field of Arabo-Islamic culture and literature—the one looking to the past in order to retrieve normative precedents for individual guidance towards a predetermined future, the other searching the past for points of reference to imagine and explain a community and its varied memberships in a temporal continuum that gave meaning to the present—have continued to write about the *ḥaǧǧ* for many centuries, arguably even until today.[1]

The reports about the Prophet's pilgrimage experience, as well as about similar experiences of those in his early community who followed in his footsteps, were successfully and in a formative manner integrated into more or less coherent narratives in the first chronographies of Muḥammad's life and of the exploits of the first generations of Muslims that were produced in the eighth and early ninth centuries. The biography of Muḥammad by Ibn Isḥāq (d. 150/767), as preserved in its edition by Ibn Hišām (d. 218/833), and the accounts of the events and of the generations of people involved in the Muslim community's first two centuries or so by al-Wāqidī (d. 207/823) and by Ibn Saʿd (d. 230/845), all produced deeply interrelated versions of the Prophet's Farewell Pilgrimage that were to be preserved and reproduced in legal as well as in historical texts from the ninth century onwards.[2]

Islamic legal thought and writing, which acquired their first distinct intellectual and cultural identities simultaneously with these chronographies and in competitive and often even conflicting socio-cultural and political contexts, incorporated these and related reports about the Prophet's Farewell Pilgrimage in legal texts that were meant to produce, preserve, and communicate authoritative rules, regulations, and guidelines for good Muslim behaviour. A 'book of the *ḥaǧǧ*' (*Kitāb al-ḥaǧǧ*), informed by reports of the Prophet's Farewell Pilgrimage and related texts, became a standard component of all seminal works of *ḥadīṯ* and of legal rules, regulations, and categorisations that were composed since the ninth century. The great and widespread diversity in legal views in these early centuries of Islamic jurisprudence, however, also reflected in the varieties of opinions on the particularities of various pilgrimage rules, as expressed in different 'books of *ḥaǧǧ*' and as supported by differing interpretations of reports of the Prophet's Farewell Pilgrimage. From the eleventh century, at latest, onwards, some of these legal works, their 'books of *ḥaǧǧ*', and their particular opinions about pilgrimage rules acquired seminal status, within the much larger context of the crystallisation of religio-legal differences and debates into a mainstream consensus around particular knowledge practices—with priority being given to the normative example of the Prophet, or *Sunnah*, as embodied in the *ḥadīṯ*—and around the valid (although not

1 See especially Khalidi (1994): 1–82 ("1. The birth of a tradition"; "2. History and *Hadith*"); Robinson (2003); McMillan (2011): 167–179.

2 See Ibn Hišām, *al-Sīrah*, 1091–1095; al-Wāqidī, *al-Maġāzī*, 3:1088–1116; Ibn Saʿd, *al-Ṭabaqāt*, 2/1:124–136.

always uncontested) co-existence of only a handful of distinct knowledge communities of Sunni legal thought and practice—the *maḏāhib* or schools of law. Differences of opinions, including about *ḥaǧǧ* rules and regulations, were thus accepted, codified, and furthered in thought, debate, and writing within the increasingly impermeable intellectual boundaries of the different Sunni legal traditions.[3]

On an individual rather than on a communal level, simply accepting the validity of these differences continued to prove difficult for many members of these scholarly communities. Even though over time inter-*maḏhab* competition and polemics gradually shifted from sometimes violent confrontations to much more peaceful and mostly intellectual interactions and disagreements, this generalising diachronic picture needs to be qualified by the particular cases of quite a few individual legal scholars who continued to try and transcend or challenge in varieties of ways emerging institutional boundaries. The conscious shift early in his life to the Šāfiʿī *maḏhab* of the author of *al-Ḏahab al-masbūk*, Aḥmad b. ʿAlī al-Maqrīzī, has been mentioned before. In the late-fourteenth-century case of the young al-Maqrīzī there were surely sound pragmatic reasons for making this intellectual and socio-cultural switch in the Šāfiʿī-dominated Egyptian context. Nasser Rabbat, as well as some of al-Maqrīzī's

3 On the formation and crystallisation of differing socio-legal views and practice in general, see Berkey (2003): 141–151, and Melchert (1997); for books of the *ḥaǧǧ* and the related codification of differences of scholarly opinion in particular, see Adang (2005): 114–115. A 'book of *ḥaǧǧ*' may be found in each of the six canonical *ḥadīṯ* collections: in the *Ṣaḥīḥ*s of al-Buḫārī (d. 256/870), of Muslim (d. 261/875) and of al-Tirmiḏī (d. 279/892), and in the *Sunan*s of Abū Dāwūd (d. 275/888), al-Nasāʾī (d. 303/915) and of Ibn Māǧah (d. 273/887). It may also be found in each of the *maḏhab*s' seminal texts: in Saḥnūn b. Saʿīd's (d. 240/854) *al-Mudawwanah* and in al-Qayrawānī's (d. 386/996) *al-Risālah* for the Mālikīs, in al-Marġīnānī's (d. 593/1197) *al-Hidāyah* for the Ḥanafīs, in al-Šāfiʿī's (d. 204/820) *Kitāb al-Umm*, and in Ibn Qudāmah's (d. 620/1223) *al-Muġnī* for the Ḥanbalīs. Many specialist legal *ḥaǧǧ* manuals, or *manāsik* books, have furthermore been produced and preserved, such as by al-ʿAdawī (d. c. 156/773) (*Kitāb al-Manāsik*), by al-ʿUtbī (d. 255/869) (*Kitāb al-Ḥaǧǧ*), and by al-Nawawī (d. 677/1277) (*Kitāb al-Īǧāz fī l-Manāsik*); by Ibn Taymiyyah (d. 728/1328) (*Ahamm al-aḥkām fī manāsik al-ḥaǧǧ wa-l-ʿumrah ʿalá hady ḫayr al-anām*; *Šarḥ al-ʿUmdah fī bayān manāsik al-ḥaǧǧ wa-l-ʿumrah*), by al-Tabrīzī (fl. 737/1337) (*Kitāb al-Ḥaǧǧ min Miškat al-maṣābīḥ*), by Ibn Ǧamāʿah (d. c. 767/1366) (*Hidāyat al-sālik ilá l-maḏāhib al-arbaʿah fī l-manāsik*), by al-Ǧundī (d. c. 766/1365) (*Manāsik ʿalá maḏhab al-imām Mālik*), by Ibn Farḥūn (d. 799/1397) (*Iršād al-sālik ilá afʿāl al-manāsik*); by Ibn al-Ḍiyāʾ (d. c. 855/1451) (*al-Baḥr al-ʿamīq fī manāsik al-muʿtamir wa-l-ḥāǧǧ ilá bayt Allāh al-ʿatīq*), by Ibn Ẓuhayrah (d. 889/1484) (*Kifāyat al-muḥtāǧ ilá l-dimāʾ al-wāǧibah ʿalá l-muʿtamir wa-l-ḥāǧǧ*; *Ġunyat al-faqīr fī ḥukm al-ḥaǧǧ al-aǧīr*), by al-Kirmānī (d. c. 883/1478) (*al-Masālik fī l-manāsik*), by al-Suyūṭī (d. 911/1505) (*Kitāb al-Ḥaǧǧ*), and by many others.

contemporaries and biographers suggest that this however may also have been part of a much longer intellectual process, related to those emerging institutional boundaries, and in which this scholar developed an increasingly critical attitude vis-à-vis some dominant interpretative and accommodating applications of legal sources and ideas of justice. "Al-Maqrīzī was known later in his life", so Rabbat explains, "for his bias against, even his antipathy toward, the Hanafis, ostensibly because of his unconfirmed leaning toward the by-then uncommon Ẓāhirī *maḏhab*."[4]

The latter *maḏhab* actually was one of those religio-legal traditions of Islamic thought that would prove intellectually too strict and socio-culturally too narrow to survive the above-mentioned process of Sunni crystallisation, even though it seems to have retained some limited popularity and acquaintance with individual scholars into the early fifteenth century.[5] One of the main reasons for this temporary survival certainly was the fact that the main written formulations of this uncompromising literalist approach to understanding Qur'ān and *ḥadīṯ* had been produced by a formidable and highly influential intellectual personality from eleventh-century al-Andalus: the man of letters, philosopher, religious scholar, and polemicist Abū Muḥammad ʿAlī b. Aḥmad b. Saʿīd Ibn Ḥazm (d. 456/1064). Among the different works by Ibn Ḥazm that codified Ẓāhirī religio-legal thought, there actually also figures a unique and remarkable piece of writing, entitled "The Farewell Pilgrimage" (*ḥiǧǧat al-wadāʿ*), in which the author isolated the topic of the Prophet's Farewell Pilgrimage from traditionally much wider legal or historical discussions. Ibn Ḥazm's aim with this treatise was indeed to transcend boundaries, and to resolve once and for all the disagreement on the rules for the proper performance of the *ḥaǧǧ*, by imposing a clean, clear, and easily accessible version of the Farewell Pilgrimage, explained by an explicit literalist Ẓāhirī reading of relevant *ḥadīṯ* and by an equally explicit refutation of diverging interpretations. Despite the work's highly polemic approach and its subsequent failure to actually resolve *maḏhab* disagreements, its particular and easily accessible nature proved very influential for later religio-legal writings about the Prophet's Farewell Pilgrimage. At least, in the fourteenth century prominent Syrian scholars such as Ibn Taymiyyah (d. 728/1328) and Ibn Kaṯīr (d. 774/1372) praised the quality of the work, even though they did not entirely agree with its arguments.[6]

---

4 Rabbat (2003): 12; referring to, among others, Ibn Taġrī Birdī, *al-Manhal al-ṣāfī*, 2: 417. Also Bauden (2014): 164–165.

5 On the Ẓāhirīs in fourteenth- and fifteenth-century Egypt and Syria, see especially Wiederhold (1999): 204–206.

6 Adang (2005): 113–116.

In the early fifteenth century, al-Maqrīzī equally considered Ibn Ḥazm's contribution to the scholarship of the Prophet's Farewell Pilgrimage a moment of the utmost importance in that Pilgrimage's intellectual trajectory. This emerges from the fact that in his own pilgrimage book, the *al-Ḏahab al-masbūk*, he decided to open his summary discussion of it by referring his readers to Ibn Ḥazm's work and to his own discussion, in another (now lost) book, of some of the debates that had arisen around Ibn Ḥazm's *ḥiǧǧat al-wadāʿ*:

> The books of *ḥadīṯ* are full of reports of the pilgrimage of the Prophet—may God bless him and grant him salvation. Out of all of these the jurist and *ḥāfiẓ* Abū Muḥammad ʿAlī b. Aḥmad b. Saʿīd Ibn Ḥazm al-Andalusī created an important single volume (*muṣannaf^an ǧalīl^an*). I responded in the book *Šāriʿ al-naǧāt* (The Road to Deliverance) to certain passages in it to which objections were raised.[7]

As mentioned above, the formative collections and chronographies of Ibn Isḥāq, al-Wāqidī, and Ibn Saʿd also had a defining impact on the Farewell Pilgrimage's representations in Arabo-Islamic historiography. The multifarious textual production of what today tends to be considered under that label gradually developed into a more or less separate branch of learning simultaneously with the emergence of other specialisms. A clear distinction in aims, scope, and material between *ḥadīṯ* scholarship, *fiqh*, and other cultural modes such as *adab*, however, only emerged very slowly, not in the least because many of its practitioners continued to pursue many if not all branches of traditional scholarship. Among the different genres and categories that emerged within this only loosely definable historiographical tradition, chronography in particular attached some importance in its writings to the annually returning event of the pilgrimage to Mecca. The fixed and genuinely Islamic time-space dimensions of the *ḥaǧǧ* provided a useful and very meaningful point of reference for writing about and imagining a newly emerging transregional political and socio-cultural community. Especially the genre of annalistic chronography, which emerged in the course of the ninth century and which remained a dominant form of Arabic historiography until modern times, incorporated *ḥaǧǧ* reports as a useful pattern for closing its annual cycles of variously recorded events. In doing so, these particular types of memory texts obviously also looked beyond the increasingly codified stories about the particular engagements of the Prophet and his early community with the annual *ḥaǧǧ*. The latter

---

7 See below, § 6.

stories continued to be incorporated in manners that closely mirrored their representations in *ḥadīṯ* and *fiqh* texts. However, historiography's growing presentist concerns in the increasingly consolidated spatial and social contexts of Islamic caliphate and cultural order also stimulated the incorporation of a variety of reports about subsequent generations' regular and occasionally equally eventful engagements with the same rituals. Recording reports about caliphs' literally stepping in the Prophet's footsteps, about their or their representatives' engagements with *ḥaǧǧ* caravans and infrastructures, and eventually even about the experiences of growing varieties of pilgrims *en route* and in Mecca, contributed in important ways to the pre-dominant purpose of a long range of such historiographical works to explain their present as meaningfully connected to an expanding community's glorious past. In this process of the historiographical production and reproduction of *ḥaǧǧ* and *ḥaǧǧ*-related reports in annalistic and other types of Arabic chronography, and eventually also in biographies and in related prosopographical and hagiographical genres, many of these reports became fixed in form to particular plots and related stories, in ways reminding us of the codified reproductions of the Farewell Pilgrimage. From the eleventh century onwards, therefore, if not earlier already, historians seeking to incorporate *ḥaǧǧ* reports in their works of communal or individual history were always bound by the particular choices, framings, and models imposed on this as on any other similarly valuable material by earlier generations of textual producers and consumers, if at least these post-1000 historians truly wished to participate in and meaningfully contribute to the textual discourses of the Arabo-Islamic historiographical genre and its audiences.[8]

A key moment in this standardisation of, amongst other things, annual *ḥaǧǧ* reports was undoubtedly represented by the *magnum opus* of pre-1000 CE Arabo-Islamic historiography: the voluminous *History of Messengers and Kings* (*Tārīḫ al-rusul wa-l-mulūk*) by the Iraqi scholar Muḥammad b. Ǧarīr al-Ṭabarī (d. 310/923). This expansive composition of Muslim world history from the moment of creation until the Muslim year 302 (/915) was so comprehensive in the reports that it managed to integrate and so tuned in to the meticulous transmission methods of *ḥadīṯ* scholarship that it became a crucial point of reference for the remembrance of almost any historical phenomenon from the formative period of Islam. In the annalistic representation of the first 300 years of the Muslim era in the final part of this chronicle, focus is really on the whereabouts of the leading characters of the community, which obviously includes

8 For comprehensive accounts of the formation of the Arabo-Islamic historiographical genre, see, amongst others, Khalidi (1994); Robinson (2003).

their annual engagements with the *ḥaǧǧ*. A few other works of history, such as the entirely different but equally impressive *Meadows of Gold* (*Murūǧ al-ḏahab*) by al-Ṭabarī's near-contemporary al-Masʿūdī (d. 345/955), also include detailed lists of *ḥaǧǧ*-leaders. But none set the standards for future representations as al-Ṭabarī did.[9]

Beyond the eleventh century, the achievement of al-Ṭabarī was above all transformed into a normative standard representation of the formation of Islam by the work of a scholar from Mosul, in the historical region of the Jazira (Northern Iraq), ʿIzz al-Dīn Ibn al-Aṯīr (d. 630/1233). His *Complete History* (*al-Kāmil fī l-tārīḫ*) is an equally impressive multi-volume annalistic chronicle of Muslim world history, incorporating the work of al-Ṭabarī and also of others, accommodating this material to the requirements of his time, and complementing it with annalistic reports up to the Muslim year 628 (/1231). By Ibn al-Aṯīr's time, the production of historiography had actually moved much closer to the circles of rulers and their courts than ever before, in the urban socio-cultural realities of patronage and competition as much as in its authors' overwhelming interest in politics, in lineages of Muslim leaderships, and in the relationships that connected individuals across time and space. The growing pre-dominance of a so-called *siyāsah*-oriented trend in an Arabic historiography that no longer needed to justify the religious past, but that rather was meant to try to understand, connect, and legitimate the complex socio-political present, manifested itself in particular in a booming production. From the time of Ibn al-Aṯīr onwards, annalistic chronicles, but also individual biographies, impressive prosopographical collections of biographical dictionaries, multi-volume encyclopaedic works of history and geography, and combinations of these and of similar works of historiographical interest started to be written, published, consumed, and reproduced in unprecedented numbers, first mostly in Syria and in the Jazira, but from the fourteenth century onwards increasingly predominantly by cultural elites who convened in Cairo or who had at least strong connections with this trans-regional metropolis.[10]

---

9 Khalidi (1994): 73–81; McMillan (2011): 168–173; Marsham (2009): 91, 124–125. Marsham in particular explains how "lists of leaders of the hajj and annual campaigns [...] form two of the earliest strands in Islamic historiography".

10 See especially Khalidi (1994): 182–231 ("Chapter 5: History and *Siyasa*"); Robinson (2003): 97–102 ("Chapter 5: Historiography and traditionalism—1000 to 1500: New directions"). For Ibn al-Aṯīr's *al-Kāmil*, see also Ibn al-Aṯīr, *Chronicle*; Richards (1982).

This—as Konrad Hirschler phrased it—"veritable explosion that history writing experienced in Syria and Egypt from the thirteenth century onwards" went hand in hand with other, deeply related cultural processes of transformation. Thomas Bauer has argued convincingly that there occurred a general literarisation of communication among educated (and increasingly also non-educated) individuals and groups, with poetry and ornate prose becoming widespread accepted forms and norms of socio-cultural interaction, resulting in a huge production of anthologies as well as of new literary material of all sorts (most of which remains to be discovered and fully appreciated). According to Hirschler, this happened simultaneously with a process of textualisation of cultural life, when the consumption of texts gradually became possible for more and more people as general reading skills and availability of texts improved. Expanding from what Carl Petry—as quoted in the previous chapter—described as the emergence of a huge "corpus of treatises which rendered the era a 'Silver Age' of Islamic scholarship", Hirschler even identified this efflorescence as part and parcel of a much wider socio-cultural trend: the popularisation of textual production, a growing active participation in bustling literary life from the course of the fourteenth century onwards by increasing numbers of people who are not regularly considered among the cultural elites. When al-Maqrīzī therefore re-oriented his life in the 810s/1410s to that of an active historian, he did so in a context that was not only remarkable for its many historiographical engagements with a complex present and with set precedents—including a continued interest in the Farewell Pilgrimage and in many other leadership engagements with the *ḥaǧǧ*—, but that was also particular because of the widespread literarisation of the forms and channels of communication that made up its culture in general.[11]

11 See Bauer (2005); Id. (2013a); Hirschler (2013) (quote p. 161); Id. (2012); Petry (1993): 324. Apart from *fiqh* and historiography, other genres of Arabo-Islamic culture and literature also obviously engaged with the memories and representations of the *ḥaǧǧ*, including Arabic poetry and travel writings (most famously the texts associated with the pilgrimages and travels of Ibn Ǧubayr [d. 614/1217] and Ibn Baṭṭūṭah [d. c. 779/1377]), but they will not be considered here because they are not directly relevant for contextualising al-Maqrīzī's *al-Ḏahab al-masbūk* (see e.g. Van Gelder [1998]: "Large portions of the famous travel accounts by Ibn Jubayr and Ibn Battuta describe the holy sites of Islam. The pilgrimage, a major theme already in the poetry of ʿUmar b. Abi Rabiʾa, remained the source of literary inspiration, for frivolous poets like Abu Nuwas as well as pious ones. In the poems and prose writings of the great mystics such as the Egyptian Ibn al-Farid and Ibn al-ʿArabi from Spain, the Hijaz is very much present"; Netton [2008]; Waines [2010]).

2 Introducing *al-Ḏahab al-masbūk*: Prophet, Caliphs, and Kings between Narratives and Stories

When Aḥmad b. ʿAlī l-Maqrīzī composed and recomposed *al-Ḏahab al-masbūk fī ḏikr man ḥağğa min al-ḫulafāʾ wa-l-mulūk* between 821/1418 and 841/1438, he straightforwardly engaged with the different traditions of Arabic writing that had emerged over time around the memory of the Prophet and that continued to define the historiography-of-pilgrimage discourse of his time. Legal texts' representations of the Farewell Pilgrimage, early historiography's interest in the precedents of pilgriming caliphs, and the booming business of *siyāsah*-historiography and its presentist concerns for questions of non-caliphal pilgrimage leadership all received their due attention in this booklet. Starting with the Prophet's *ḥağğ* of 10/632 and ending with the story of the *ḥağğ* in 778/1377 of the Cairo sultan al-Ašraf Šaʿbān (r. 764–778/1363–1377), *al-Ḏahab al-masbūk* moved from the time of the Prophet, over that of the Caliphs, to that of non-caliphal rulers' pilgrimage engagements from the eleventh century onwards. Due to the work's limited size, however, the added legal or historiographical value of the diverse material about pilgriming Prophet, caliphs, and kings is only very limited. The booklet is rather more remarkable for other reasons, not in the least, from a wider literary point of view, as the very first—at least, by the present state of acquaintance with the field of Arabic literary production up to al-Maqrīzī's time—to claim to offer a more or less focused narrative of Muslim leadership of the pilgrimage. In order to try and come to some level of understanding of what this means, it is this chronographical material, the language, styles, and narrative forms in which it was cast, and the precise literary context of historiographical precedents and antecedents with which it interacted that first require a more detailed explanation.

Following the minimalist literary conventions of *siyāsah*-historiography, the adoption in most parts of the text of a language and style that seem to aim at straightforwardness, accessibility, and clarity rather than at any sort of complexity is entirely in line with al-Maqrīzī's writing practice in his other known works of history. It is a practice that prioritises chronography over literary aesthetics as a guiding principle, and that is therefore deeply embedded in the historiographical genre's process of formation and crystallisation out of the many individual reports of varying size, length, value and authenticity, the *ḫabar*s, that informed and defined the early Muslim community's social memory. Ornate prose is largely absent from the text of *al-Ḏahab al-masbūk*, and only at four particular occasions a handful of lines of poetry are included, when quotes from others' poetic repertoires were considered relevant for the plotting of a story.[12] As with many texts of this type, however, this booklet opens with a general introduction that stands as an exception to this general rule of literary sobriety. Unbound by restrictions of genre and tradition, al-Maqrīzī used this introduction to explain his motives for writing this particular kind of history in a far more belletrist and personalised prose, also embellished by four lines of poetry. Dedicating—as discussed in the previous chapter—the work in the best of Arabic literature's panegyric tradition to an unnamed patron, the author describes in flowery language how his personal quest for finding a gift that befitted the occasion of this patron's *ḥaǧǧ* eventually resulted in his "collecting for the benefit of the esteemed library of our lord [...] a volume that comprises the report of those caliphs and kings who performed the *ḥaǧǧ*", a history of pilgriming Muslim rulers which he then decided to entitle "The Moulded Gold" (*al-Ḏahab al-masbūk*).[13]

The main storyline of *al-Ḏahab al-masbūk* is indeed just this "report of those caliphs and kings who performed the *ḥaǧǧ*": a simple identification of all the Muslim rulers who, according to al-Maqrīzī, had meaningfully and actively engaged with the *ḥaǧǧ* during eight centuries of Muslim history. Starting from the Prophet's Farewell Pilgrimage, a comprehensive chronological list

12 See below, §§ 27, 31, 66, 129.

13 See below, § 4. In the Leiden autograph, the actual title page of this text is missing (as explained in chapter 3 of this study) and in the text itself only *al-Ḏahab al-masbūk* was explicitly mentioned by al-Maqrīzī and his copyist as the booklet's title. The second part of the longer title by which it is now generally known (*al-Ḏahab al-masbūk fī ḏikr man ḥaǧǧa min al-ḫulafāʾ wa-l-mulūk*) only appears in the lines preceding this short title, as an explanation of its contents rather than as any part of its intended title (*"ǧuzʾan yaḥtawī ʿalá ḏikr man ḥaǧǧa min al-ḫulafāʾ wa-l-mulūk sammaytuhu l-Ḏahab al-masbūk"*). That longer title is present in the header of the text's first page in the Leiden autograph, but this is an addition by a different, later hand (see Leiden, Universiteitsbibliotheek, MS Or. 560, fol. 115[b]). By the early seventeenth century, however, the longer, two-tiered title had become the standard way to refer to the text, including in the manuscript copies that were then and later produced (see chapter 3). In al-Maqrīzī's biographies by Ibn Taġrī Birdī and al-Saḫāwī, however, it is only this explanatory addition to the title that is used to identify this text (Ibn Taġrī Birdī, *al-Manhal al-ṣāfī*, 1:419: *kitāb fī ḏikr man ḥaǧǧa min al-ḫulafāʾ wa-l-mulūk*; al-Saḫāwī, *al-Tibr al-masbūk*, 1:73; Id., *al-Ḍawʾ al-lāmiʿ*, 2:23: *ḏikr man ḥaǧǧa min al-mulūk wa-l-ḫulafāʾ*). Yet another version of the title may be found in al-Ǧazīrī's sixteenth-century manual and history of the *ḥaǧǧ*, *Durar al-farāʾid*, where it is claimed that al-Maqrīzī "called [his text] (*sammāhu*) *l-Ḏahab al-masbūk fī tārīḫ man ḥaǧǧa min al-mulūk*" (al-Ǧazīrī, *Durar al-farāʾid*, 2:325); this 'non-caliphal version' of the title is also the one by which the text was listed in the *Kašf al-ẓunūn* by the seventeenth-century Ottoman bibliographer Ḥaǧǧī Ḫalīfah/Kātib Çelebī (1017–1067/1609–1657) (Kātib Çelebī, *Kašf al-ẓunūn*, 1:828).

of twenty-seven leaders is presented and combined with twenty-seven equally diverse leadership narratives, consisting of simple or complex strings of variegated stories about some of their leadership experiences that were mostly somehow related to the Mecca sanctuary. Before looking at the complex issue of how al-Maqrīzī squeezed all this material into his *al-Ḏahab al-masbūk*, however, it is the complexity of this particular list that deserves a few comments. At first sight, this list of twenty-seven appears not just as constructed along a chronographical plan, but also as conveying a sequential vision of Muslim rule since the Prophet's time. Upon further inspection, this apparent sequence is quite remarkable for certain choices that were made by the author, mostly to include certain rulers, but also to exclude some others. Among the latter there were at least one ʿAbbāsid caliph and a handful of mostly African rulers who did not make it to al-Maqrīzī's final selection.[14] Among the former al-Maqrīzī's unquestioning inclusion of the caliphate of ʿAbd Allāh b. al-Zubayr (r. 64–73/683–692) stands out as a remarkable counter-narrative to certain assumptions about the end of the Hijazi caliphate in the late 30s/650s and

14 From the late medieval ʿAbbāsid caliphs of Cairo, only the pilgrimage in 1298 of al-Ḥākim was recorded; according to al-Maqrīzī's own historiographical texts, however, another of these caliphs, al-Muʿtaḍid bi-llāh (d. 763/1362), also performed the *ḥaǧǧ* twice, in 1354 (754 AH) and in 1359 (760 AH) (*al-Sulūk*, 2:903; 3, 77; *al-Ḫiṭaṭ*, 3:785; *Durar al-ʿuqūd al-farīdah*, 2:210—I am grateful to Dr Mustafa Banister (Univ. Toronto) for providing me with these references). According to al-Ǧazīrī, the ʿAbbāsid caliph al-Maʾmūn (r. 197–218/813–833) performed the *ḥaǧǧ* in 212/828, but he adds his doubts since this was a story acquired from the early-fourteenth-century Syrian scholar al-Ḏahabī only (al-Ǧazīrī, *Durar al-farāʾid*, 2:345–346); al-Maqrīzī himself anyway makes the explicit claim that after al-Maʾmūn's father, Hārūn al-Rašīd, no ʿAbbāsid ever performed the *ḥaǧǧ* again from Baghdad (§ 82). Apart from the West-African ruler Mansā Mūsá (r. 712–738/1312–1337), *al-Ḏahab al-masbūk* also makes explicit reference to three of his predecessors—Sarbandānah, the legendary first Muslim ruler of Mali; Mansá Ulī (r. 653–668/1255–1270, son of the legendary Māri Ǧātā [also known as Sundjata Keïta, r. 627–653/1230–1255]), and the usurper Sākūrah (r. 684–699/1285–1300)—who would have already performed the pilgrimage before Mansā Mūsá; they were not however awarded any separate narratives in the text, but fully integrated into that of Mansā Mūsá (see § 203) (see also al-Ǧazīrī, *Durar al-farāʾid*, 2:359–364 [*ḏikr man ḥaǧǧa min mulūk al-Takrūr*]; Möhring [1999]: 326). Al-Ǧazīrī mentions a handful of other pilgriming rulers that did not make it into al-Maqrīzī's list, even though they were not really dissimilar from those that were included: "Mawlāy al-Sulṭān Ḥillī ʿAbd al-ʿAẓīm, the sulṭān al-Maġrib", performing the *ḥaǧǧ* in 766/1365, the Marīnid "Ṣāḥib Fās" sultan ʿAbd al-ʿAzīz shortly before 774/1372, the Ayyūbid "Ṣāḥib Ḥiṣn Kayfā" al-Malik al-Ṣāliḥ in 776/1375 and the East-African "Ṣāḥib Kilwa" Ḥasan b. al-Muʾayyad Sulaymān b. al-Ḥusayn in 813/1411 (al-Ǧazīrī, *Durar al-farāʾid*, 2:367; see also Möhring [1999]: 327, listing even a few more cases).

about the continuity of the Syrian Umayyad caliphate between 41/661 and 132/750.[15] Another remarkable moment occurs in the text when it suddenly leaps forward by almost 500 years, from the glorious days of the ʿAbbāsid Hārūn al-Rašīd (r. 170–193/786–809)—after whom "there was no other caliph who performed the pilgrimage from Baghdad"—to the thirteenth and last caliph in the list, al-Ḥākim (r. 661–701/1262–1302), the second ʿAbbāsid caliph of Cairo whose lineage would continue to represent the caliphate throughout the fourteenth and fifteenth centuries. In al-Ḥākim's case, it is above all al-Maqrīzī's plotting of the story of this caliph's 697/1298 pilgrimage against a background of powerlessness and defunct authority that reads as an anticlimactic moment in the text, after the great deeds and exemplary exploits of al-Ḥākim's twelve caliphal predecessors.[16]

In many ways, this moment then announces and explains the transition of the author's focus from the caliphs to the kings of the booklet's title. Actually, al-Maqrīzī's concluding sentence of this caliphal part of the text is auspiciously programmatic in this particular respect. Connecting the sequence of caliphs to his own time, he subtly explains this transition by zooming in on the long-standing tradition of mentioning the ruler's name in the Friday sermon (*ḫuṭbah*) in the Mecca sanctuary:

> Until today, the situation has remained like that, the Friday sermon in Mecca never being delivered in the name of any of the ʿAbbāsid caliphs of Egypt, except for the caliph al-Mustaʿīn bi-llāh Abū l-Faḍl al-ʿAbbās b. Muḥammad, [in whose name the Friday sermon was delivered] for a few days in the year 815 [1412].[17]

---

15 On these assumptions of Umayyad continuity, constructed in modern scholarship rather than by premodern Muslim historians, see esp. Robinson (2007): 31–35. On this discussion among historiographers of how to record in Arabic chronography the complex turmoil of the second *fitnah* (c. 60–72/680–692), see also Robinson (2003): 76 (from which al-Maqrīzī's pragmatic approach in *al-Ḏahab al-masbūk* appears indeed as historiographically less unusual than might be expected from modern scholarship). This particular portrayal of the caliphate of Ibn al-Zubayr as a legitimate and integral part of Muslim sacred history does not just transpire from what al-Maqrīzī mentions in the narrative that goes by this Meccan leader's name. It is also made explicit in the next narrative, where al-Maqrīzī explains that the Umayyad ʿAbd al-Malik (r. 65–86/685–705) "remained in the office of caliph after Ibn al-Zubayr for 13 years and 4 months less 7 nights", thus presenting Ibn al-Zubayr's death as the real starting point for the caliphate of ʿAbd al-Malik. See below, 25–27, 28.

16 For Hārūn, see below, §§ 82–107; for al-Ḥākim, see below, §§ 108–110.

17 See below, § 110.

Al-Ḥākim's scion al-Mustaʿīn (r. 808–816/1406–1414) was indeed briefly awarded this supreme Muslim rulership privilege. This, however, derived from al-Mustaʿīn's accession to Muslim kingship rather than from his caliphal authority, when during a short span of time in 815/1412 al-Mustaʿīn was made sultan, uniquely combining the by now empty shell of the ʿAbbāsid caliphate with the sovereignty of the Cairo sultanate.[18] Non-caliphal Muslim kingship, including the sultanate of Cairo, is therefore what al-Maqrīzī focused on in the next part of the booklet. In general, this part confronts the reader with far less coherent narratives than the previous caliphal part, mainly due to the fact that at first sight this chronological list of 'kings' seems to be made up merely by those non-caliphal local or regional Muslim leaders who shared the privilege of having *al-malik*, 'the king', in their titles. What was already true for the sequence of caliphs is therefore even more so relevant for al-Maqrīzī's chronological listing of these 'kings': any first appearance of historical sequence is qualified by remarkable, even disruptive textual moments.

The first ruler on the list, ʿAlī b. Muḥammad al-Ṣulayḥī (d. 473/1081), is almost as surprising a character as his immediate caliphal precededecessor on the list. ʿAlī is immediately identified as "one of the world's revolutionaries (*aḥad ṯuwwār al-ʿālam*)" and as an agent of the anti-ʿAbbāsid Shiite Fāṭimid caliphate of Cairo (358–567/969–1171), who briefly gained control over Yemen and over Mecca in the Fāṭimids' name. In the staunchly Sunni and anti-Shiite environment of fifteenth-century Cairo this is a surprising—if not indeed revolutionary—way for any author to start a list such as this one.[19] The second and third rulers are then also surprising, but this is for the simple reason that their actual engagements with the *ḥaǧǧ* is tenuous rather than for the fact that these two unmistakable champions of Sunni Islam, Nūr al-Dīn Maḥmūd (r. 541–569/1146–1174) and Saladin's brother Tūrān Šāh (d. 576/1178), represent a strong and explicit symbolic counterbalance to the Shiite case of ʿAlī l-Ṣulayḥī.[20] Then there is the fifth ruler, Tūrān Šāh's nephew al-Masʿūd Yūsuf (d. 626/1229), whose case

18 On this caliph, see "al-Mustaʿīn", in *EI*[2] (http://referenceworks.brillonline.com/entries/encyclopaedia-of-islam-2/al-mustain-SIM_5620).

19 On al-Maqrīzī's own link with the Fāṭimids, his stance towards Shiism in general, and the discussions and debates that arose around these issues in fifteenth-century Cairo, see Rabbat (2003): 6–10; Walker (2003). On the anti-Shiite climate in late medieval Egypt and Syria in general, see Winter (1999).

20 The alleged pilgrimage of Nūr al-Dīn in 556/1161 does not feature at all in the narrative, but is rather tucked away and pushed to the very end, where it suddenly appears in the format of the shortest possible reference only (see below, § 122); substantial doubts

stands out as one of wrongful violence and of violation of the sacred character of the *ḥağğ* rituals and of the Mecca sanctuary.[21] Finally, after the prodigious cases of the Rasūlid ruler of Yemen al-Muẓaffar Yūsuf (r. 647–694/1249–1295), of the Egyptian sultans al-Ẓāhir Baybars (r. 658–676/1260–1277) and al-Nāṣir Muḥammad (r. 693–694/1293–1294; 698–708/1299–1309; 709–741/1310–1341), and of the West-African Mansā Mūsá (r. 712–738/1312–1337), unlawful violence and violation of sacred rules return as defining the twelfth and the thirteenth cases of this list of non-caliphal rulers, of the Rasūlid al-Muğāhid ʿAlī (r. 721–764/1322–1363) in the pilgrimage season of 1352, and of the Qalāwūnid sultan al-Ašraf Šaʿbān in 778/1377. The story of Šaʿbān is actually told here in as anticlimactic a manner as that of the caliph al-Ḥākim was presented before. This last ruler of the entire list left his seat of government in Cairo for the pilgrimage, but he never made it to Mecca due to a series of rebellions in his own royal entourage. This then appears as a final moment of political failure and chaos that contrasts in dark ways with the redemptive theme of pilgrimage and that provided the booklet with a rather fatalistic end. In this rather negative line of thought, al-Maqrīzī aptly concluded both Šaʿbān's case and *al-Ḏahab al-masbūk*'s text with the claim that "the last that is known about [sultan Šaʿbān] is that he was killed by strangulation—God knows best".[22]

What can be made out of this complex general whole of particular arrangements that define the organisation of *al-Ḏahab al-masbūk*? The meanings that are conveyed through this text, the authorial decisions and choices by which it was created, and the morality that it bespeaks will be discussed in some detail below. Suffice it to claim here already that for all the winding roads that the text seems to be taking along a very mixed variety of stories about Muslim leaders

have indeed been raised about the veracity of Nūr al-Dīn's pilgrimage, which was left unnoticed by his own chroniclers and which seems to have been recorded in the early fifteenth century only, in *al-Ḏahab al-masbūk* and—in an equally very brief reference—in the writings of al-Maqrīzī's Meccan contemporary al-Fāsī (d. 832/1429) (see Möhring [1999]: 318). For Saladin's brother Tūrān Šāh reference is only made to his performance of the lesser pilgrimage, the *ʿumrah*, which means that technically speaking he did not deserve to be included in this list of non-caliphal rulers performing the *ḥağğ* (see below, §125). These rulers' Sunni championship speaks from the explicit references to Nūr al-Dīn's active restoration of Sunni Islam in Shiite dominated Aleppo, and to Tūrān Šāh's leading role in Saladin's victories over the Fatimid black troops in Cairo and over a *Ḫāriğī* ruler in Yemen (see below, §§117, 123, 125).

21 As al-Maqrīzī explains, he spilled the blood of pigeons in the sacred mosque and he got drunk from drinking wine during his stay in Mecca (see below, §142).

22 See below, §221.

great and small, there is more that connects those stories than just the issue of pilgrimage. Formally, it transpires at least that clear and conscious choices were made about the general lay-out of the text, when it is realised that it has a structural unity that transcends any issues of chronographical organisation.[23] *Al-Ḏahab al-masbūk* actually is made up of three parts that were each demarcated by explanatory titles that define these parts as three separate chapters, one on the Prophet, one on caliphs, and one on kings.[24] By sheer size, the second and third chapter clearly function as the text's main structural blocks, and this is not in the least also suggested by the fact that these two chapters are symmetrically aligned in two units of exactly thirteen Muslim leaders. Thirteen pilgriming caliphs (Abū Bakr, ʿUmar, ʿUṯmān, Muʿāwiya, ʿAbd Allāh b. al-Zubayr, ʿAbd al-Malik, al-Walīd, Sulaymān, Hišām, al-Manṣūr, al-Mahdī, Hārūn al-Rašīd, and al-Ḥākim) are thus succeeded by thirteen pilgriming 'kings' (ʿAlī al-Ṣulayḥī, al-ʿĀdil Nūr al-Dīn Maḥmūd, al-Muʿaẓẓam Tūrān Šāh, al-Muʿaẓẓam ʿĪsá, al-Masʿūd Yūsuf, al-Manṣūr ʿUmar b. ʿAlī b. Rasūl, al-Nāṣir Dāwūd, al-Muẓaffar Yūsuf, al-Ẓāhir Baybars, al-Nāṣir Muḥammad, Mansā Mūsá, al-Muǧāhid ʿAlī, al-Ašraf Šaʿbān). The first, much shorter chapter on the Farewell Pilgrimage then

23 At three occasions in the text al-Maqrīzī also clarifies how he himself considered the overall structural nature of the entire booklet, identifying it as representing a '*ǧuz*'', a comprehensive volume (a term that is mostly used in *ḥadīṯ* studies to identify a selection of *ḥadīṯ* by one transmitter—I am grateful to F. Bauden for this clarification). In the introduction, the author thus clarifies the nature of his textual endeavour by explaining that he "collected for the benefit of the esteemed library of our lord [...] a volume (*ǧuz'an*) that comprises the report of those caliphs and kings who performed the *ḥaǧǧ*"; in the first chapter on the Prophet, he similarly opens the text with the personal statement that "I began this volume (*hāḏā l-ǧuz'*) with [the Prophet's pilgrimage]"; and in the narrative of the ʿAbbāsid caliph Hārūn al-Rašīd he hints at certain rules regulating the composition of such a *ǧuz'* when he explains the summary nature of a story by suggesting that "its report does not fit within the parameters of this volume (*min šarṭ hāḏā l-ǧuz'*)" (see below, §§ 4, 6, 91). The confusion and wrong expectations that a term such as *ǧuz'* may cause (as does 'volume' in English) appears from the statement in the entry for *al-Ḏahab al-masbūk* in the *Kašf al-ẓunūn* by Ḥāǧǧī Ḫalīfah/Kātib Çelebī that the text had been produced by al-Maqrīzī "*in five volumes* (*fī ḫamsat aǧzā'*)" (Kātib Çelebī, *Kašf al-ẓunūn*, 1:828; see also GAL, 2:50) (see also chapter 3 for further explanations of the latter confusion).

24 "Chapter on the pilgrimage of the Messenger of God", "Chapter with the report of the caliphs who went on pilgrimage during their caliphate", and "The report of the kings who went on pilgrimage when they were king". Just as the Farewell Pilgrimage, also the caliphal part was explicitly identified as a full-fledged "chapter" (*faṣl*), suggesting that—although the term was not explicitly used there—the third part was also considered as such. See below, pp. 185, 201, 303.

clearly was constructed by al-Maqrīzī as a sort of textual axis and as a touchstone for each of the other two chapters of thirteen rulers, reminding of the way in which the example of the Prophet was referential for Muslim rulers in general.

This clearcut structure of three chapters and two sets of thirteen Muslim rulers emanating from the Prophet surely goes a long way toward explaining al-Maqrīzī's sometimes surprising choices for or against the inclusion of particular rulers. But there may be much more than meets the eye, even structurally. If some of the most remarkable moments in the text—the powerless caliph al-Ḥākim, the revolutionary ʿAlī l-Ṣulayḥī, and the doomed al-Ašraf Šaʿbān—are mapped on to this larger structural perspective of two times thirteen Muslim rulers, it transpires that these moments coincide with particular structural junctures in the text. These representations of Muslim rule at its nadir really come across as repeating each other in their parallel anticlimactic tones at beginning or end, and as thus confirming and explaining the structural boundaries of the booklet's two main narrative blocks. On both occasions, they immediately follow reconstructions of particularly glorious moments of Muslim rule, such as under the ʿAbbāsid caliphs al-Manṣur, al-Mahdī, and al-Rašīd, and under the Egyptian sultans al-Ẓāhir Baybars and al-Nāṣir Muḥammad. In this structural combination, then, al-Ḥākim's, ʿAlī's and Šaʿbān's stories all bespeak the idea of a cycle of rise, decline, and fall, as manifested in the caliphal line, and then again in the non-caliphal line of Muslim rulers and their multiple engagements with pilgrimage.

In this literary construction of Muslim caliphal and non-caliphal rulership as bound, even doomed, by the internal logic of successive historical cycles of rise, decline, and fall, the separate prophetic chapter again stands out as entirely different, in many ways reminding of the notion that the Prophet's example escapes from the particular historical logic of mankind and of its rulers. This brief first chapter follows its own literary construction, thus indeed remaining far removed from the numerical and cyclical symmetries of the following chapters two and three. In fact, it displays its own particular internal logic of two distinct narratives, the one primarily historical and the other mainly jurisprudential. On the one hand, there is a summary chronography of the prophet's performance of the farewell pilgrimage in 10/632, presented in the spirit of Sunni traditionalism as setting the historical norm for a Muslim future. On the other hand, there are embedded into this narrative four separate moments when in the best of Sunni *fiqh* traditions certain points of legal debate (the relationship between *ḥaǧǧ* and *ʿumrah*, the bringing of oblational animals, the noon prayer of 10 Ḏū l-Ḥiǧǧah, the timing of the call to pilgrimage) are discussed. Deeply intertwined in the chapter's text, these two narratives are clearly separated in various micro-structural ways. The frame narrative of the farewell pilgrimage is told in a quick and summarising chronological manner from a bird's eye outsider perspective. The embedded legal debate narrative—especially concerning the first two issues of *ʿumrah* and of oblational animals—develops in much slower and much more detailed ways and is told from constantly moving perspectives and points-of-view that include those of various contemporary or later participants in those debates. This particular plotting enabled above all the introduction of particular views, opinions, and some Shāfiʿī partisanship into the set text of the Farewell Pilgrimage. It also made it possible for al-Maqrīzī to even construct another remarkable end note to this legal narrative, and to the first chapter as a whole, surprisingly connecting this prophetic example to one of the eponymous non-caliphal rulers of his own days, sultan al-Ẓāhir Baybars (r. 658–676/1260–1277). Just as the Prophet—according to an explanatory note at the opening of the chapter—"showed to the people the milestones of their religion" by preceding them in their pilgrimage rituals, so was Baybars alleged to have shown the way by installing another great and longstanding *ḥaǧǧ* tradition: the parading of the *maḥmal*. In its structural relationship with that opening reference this final note at least seems to suggest in all but subtle ways that al-Maqrīzī thought of this parallel when he ended this prophetic chapter by stating summarily and quite unexpectedly that "the first one to organise the parading of the *maḥmal* was al-Malik al-Ẓāhir Baybars al-Bunduqdārī—may God's mercy be upon him."[25] By this kind of ritual closure as much as by its particular internal structure, the first chapter indeed remains firmly separate from the two very differently organised chapters that follow. The presence of Prophet and Baybars as pioneers of *ḥaǧǧ* rituals at the beginning and end of the chapter, however, make it so that, for the reader, this structural separation happens without the chapter being entirely out of touch with the caliphal successors of the Prophet and the royal peers of Baybars who populate the narratives that follow.

Beyond their larger structural definition along numerical and cyclical symmetries these narratives of chapters two and three also deserve further brief consideration from more particular, micro-structural perspectives. This is not in the least so because the latter perspectives demonstrate how internally these chapters are both much more different as well as alike than so far might appear. Each of these two chapters' twenty six individual ruler narratives are more or less similar in their general framing within opening contexts that share an inter-

25 See below, §§ 6, 15.

est in naming and lineage, and in most cases also in oaths of allegiance or other accession-to-power particulars, often expanded with term-of-office highlights or with references to when or how these terms came to an end.[26] The focus of the individual narratives themselves is then in most cases not directly derived from these general introductory frames of legitimate rulership, but rather from subsequent summary chronologies of pilgrimage participation that identify how many and what pilgrimages the narrative's ruler actually participated in. Thus, for Hārūn al-Rašīd, the narrative is structured along the nine pilgrimages that he performed. The same happened for al-Nāṣir Muḥammad and his three pilgrimages, for Baybars and his secret pilgrimage of 667/1269, for ʿAlī l-Ṣulayḥī and his two pilgrimages, for the caliph ʿUmar and three of the nine or ten pilgrimages that he performed, and in parallel ways for most of the other listed rulers and their singular or multiple pilgrimage engagements. This actually created a generally shared internal narrative hierarchy of introductory rulership frame, pilgrimage chronography, and stories that were mostly occasioned by the latter, but that often also continued to refer to the former. In some cases, however, the disturbance of this hierarchy by the oscillating of different stories between rulership and pilgrimage—both acting in those cases as two extremes in a structural continuum rather than as hierarchical partners—leave disparate and confusing overall impressions on a reader.[27] For the author, this kind of flexible structuring, wavering between hierarchy and continuum, clearly enabled the inclusion of a great variety of material, and hence the creation of a complex, multilayered text. It even enabled the inclusion of absolute outsiders to

26 This general rule can be observed for all caliphal narratives, but not for all non-caliphal ones, where the accession-to-power factor is missing from the Mansā Mūsá (ruler n° 11) and the al-Muǧāhid ʿAlī (12) narratives. The non-caliphal narratives for al-Muẓaffar ʿĪsá (4) and to some extent also al-Nāṣir Dāwūd (7) are also different due to the inclusion of educational data (references to the study of particular texts and with particular teachers) that remind of a religious scholar's biography (*tarǧamah*); in the non-caliphal cases of al-Masʿūd Yūsuf (5), al-Muǧāhid ʿAlī (12) and al-Ašraf Šaʿbān (13) this type of rulership framing has been expanded beyond an introductionary functionality, structuring the entire narrative instead.

27 This is especially the case for the caliphs Ibn al-Zubayr (caliph n° 5) (whose regular pilgrimage leadership is mentioned, but not as a cause for the two rulership stories that are recorded here) and al-Walīd (7) (whose narrative also includes stories about public works in and around Medina that are entirely devoid of any pilgrimage connection), and for the non-caliphal rulers Nūr al-Dīn Maḥmūd (ruler n° 2) and Tūrān Šāh (3) (see next footnote), and al-Masʿūd Yūsuf (5) and al-Nāṣir Dāwūd (7) (whose pilgrimages are merely included among the strings of stories that are occasioned by a structurally dominant rulership chronography).

the general theme of pilgriming rulers, such as the non-caliphal rulers Nūr al-Dīn Maḥmūd and Tūrān Šāh, whose pilgrimage engagements were, as mentioned before, rather tenuous. For both of them, al-Maqrīzī could legitimately reduce any necessary pilgrimage references to a bare and marginalised minimum, without really jeopardising the structural unity and coherence of his booklet on pilgriming rulers.[28]

This complex and flexible micro-structure of the twenty-six individual ruler narratives enabled al-Maqrīzī to include accounts of or references to more than 120 different stories that he considered relevant for *al-Ḏahab al-masbūk*'s topic and purpose.[29] They are all spread in a rather amorphous way over the different ruler narratives, some reproducing one story only, and others really consisting of strings of stories, connected through the frames of rulership or pilgrimage. Two narratives—of the caliphs Abū Bakr and Muʿāwiyah—actually have no stories attached to them at all, consisting of rulership and pilgrimage frames only.[30] At the other end of this quantitative scale, there are a handful of narratives that are the complete opposite in having not just complex frames, but also large numbers of intricate stories attached to them. For the sake of clarifying the above argument and its relation with these stories, the diverse yet parallel structures of these narratives of the caliphs al-Manṣūr, al-Mahdī and Hārūn, and of the non-caliphal rulers Baybars and al-Nāṣir Muḥammad deserve to be schematically reconstructed here.

The al-Manṣūr narrative (n° 10)

- rulership frame
- pilgrimage frame (6 pilgrimages)
  - pilgrimage 1: story 1
  - pilgrimage 2: story 2
  - pilgrimage 6: story 3

28 These references were limited to the following statements: "[Nūr al-Dīn] died on 11 Šawwāl of the year 569 in Damascus, after he had performed the pilgrimage in the year 556" (see below, § 122); "[Tūrān Šāh] came to Mecca and performed the lesser pilgrimage, and he moved on to Zabīd" (see below, § 125).

29 I counted 126, but this can only be an approximate number, due to the fragmented nature of some stories, and the blurred boundaries between others, making this counting impossible to claim any authority of exactness. Rather than any mathematical exactness, it is of course their numerous presence and participation in this textual construction that is the point here.

30 See below, §§ 16–20, 35–36.

  - pilgrimage 6: story 4
  - story 5
  - story 6
  - story 7
  - story 8

The al-Mahdī narrative (n° 11)

- rulership frame
- pilgrimage frame (1 pilgrimage)
  - story 1
  - story 2
  - story 3
  - story 4
  - story 5
- rulership + pilgrimage frame
  - story 6
  - story 7
  - story 8

The Hārūn al-Rašīd narrative (n° 12)

- rulership frame
- pilgrimage frame (9 pilgrimages)
  - pilgrimage 1: story 1
  - pilgrimage 2: story 2
  - pilgrimage 3: story 3
  - pilgrimage 4: story 4
  - pilgrimage 5
    - story 5
    - story 6
    - story 7
    - story 8
    - story 9
  - pilgrimage 7
    - story 10
    - story 11
  - pilgrimage 9: story 12
- pilgrimage frame (bis)
  - story 13

- rulership + pilgrimage frame
  - story 14/version a
  - story 14/version b

The Baybars narrative (n° 9)

- rulership frame
- pilgrimage frame (1 pilgrimage)
  - story 1
  - story 2
  - story 3
  - story 4
  - story 5
  - story 6
  - story 7
  - story 8
  - story 9

The al-Nāṣir Muḥammad narrative (n° 10)

- rulership frame
  - pilgrimage story 1
- pilgrimage frame (3 pilgrimages)
  - pilgrimage 1
    - story 2
    - story 3
  - pilgrimage 2
    - story 4
    - story 5
    - story 6
    - story 7
    - story 8
    - story 9
    - story 10
    - story 11
  - pilgrimage 3
    - story 12
    - story 13
    - story 14
    - story 15

- story 16
- story 17
- story 18

The actual workings of factors of micro-structural variation and flexibility within and between narratives clearly transpire from this very schematic reconstruction of the booklet's five most sizeable and most complex narratives. Elicited by issues of rulership, pilgrimage, or both, all the stories themselves moreover also vary enormously in contents and size, some merely referring to well-known stories in one or two sentences only, others explaining in much and often dramatised detail what the story was all about. Whereas many stories are thus retold in summarised or more panoramic ways and from bird's-eye perspectives, some thirty-five stories are rather differently plotted, sometimes taking up much more space within the narratives as a result. These stories—or at least certain parts of them—are staged for the reader to slowly and sometimes quite dramatically unfold in front of his or her reading eyes. To this effect they often also include vivid dialogues that contain direct speech that is explicitly put in the mouth of named speakers. The story of the caliph ʿUmar assigning shares in Egyptian supplies thus develops through his dialogue with an entrepreneurial merchant, whereas the story of ʿUmar's humble origins is told through his monologue about the memories that his passage through a valley of his youth evokes.[31] The narrative of the Umayyad caliph Sulaymān develops through one story only, a relatively detailed account of the construction, inauguration, and eventual gradual deconstruction of a watering system that he commissioned for the Mecca sanctuary.[32] For the ʿAbbāsid caliph al-Mahdī, a prophecy story for his accession is included that is constructed around an opponent retelling in scenic fashion a dream that he had about an epigraphic inscription in the mosque of Medina.[33] Another such story is told in similarly appealing ways about the non-caliphal ruler Tūrān Šāh, for whom one Ibn al-Ḫaymī is brought up saying that in a dream he had seen him giving away his burial shroud from the grave.[34] Then there also is the narrative of the Cairo sultan al-Nāṣir Muḥammad, which actually really stands out as full of this kind

31 See below, §§ 24, 30. ʿUmar's narrative contains seven different stories in all; two more stories of this dramatised type both have to do with prophecies of his murder.

32 See below, §§ 51–52.

33 See below, § 80. Al-Mahdī's narrative consists of eight stories; these include one other of this dramatised type, about his overhearing a bedouin woman bewailing the fate of her kin (see below, § 81).

34 See below, §§ 128, 129. This is the only story told about Tūrān Šāh.

of slowly developing and highly dramatised stories, such as how his very good relationship with the bedouin causes confusion among his courtiers, how he refuses special treatment in the sanctuary mosque, how his pilgrimage is prepared with minute care by his agents, how a storm causes havoc and fear in his camp, or how his return to Cairo is an occasion for festivities and splendour.[35]

There is thus substantial internal variation between these thirty-five slowly plotted and therefore relatively longer stories[36] and the many others that are presented in much more rapid modes throughout the different narratives. Even among the former, however, there is substantial variation between dialogues that run on for pages—such as between Hārūn al-Rašīd and the ascetic al-Fuḍayl b. ʿĪyāḍ (d. 187/803)[37]—and other scenic stories that only take up a paragraph at most. From this feature another complex and potentially confusing structural dimension emerges for the text of *al-Ḏahab al-masbūk*, as developing along speeds that continuously varied between the different narratives, and also on many occasions within them. Again, therefore, the overall impression that remains is that of stories being pitched by the author on a continuum, but this time one of modes of speed, oscillating between very rapidly and very slowly developing plots.

---

35 See below, §§ 191, 193, 195, 200, 202. Al-Nāṣir Muḥammad's narrative of 18 stories has, apart from the five mentioned here, three more stories that include this kind of dramatised material, about the sultan's entry in Damascus in 1313, about his arrival in Cairo in 1320, and about his conflict with an amir in 1332 (see below, §§ 189, 197, 199–201).

36 The 19 other not yet mentioned stories concern the following events and occasions: ʿUṯmān's ritual prayer at Miná (see below, § 33), ʿAbd al-Malik's Friday sermon in Medina (see below, § 44), al-Walīd's meeting with Saʿīd b. al-Musayyab in the mosque of Medina (see below, § 48), the prophecy of al-Manṣūr's death and his encounters with the Medinan judge Muḥammad b. ʿImrān (see below, §§ 65–67, 68–70), Hārūn's encounters with Fuḍayl b. ʿIyāḍ (see below, §§ 97–105, 106–107), al-Nāṣir Dāwūd's conflict with the caliph of Baghdad (see below, § 158), different events, encounters and adventures happing during al-Ẓāhir Baybars' secret pilgrimage (see below, §§ 165–182), Mansā Mūsá's reception by al-Nāṣir Muḥammad (see below, § 204), and al-Muǧāhid ʿAlī's confrontations with Hijazi and Egyptian amirs in Mecca and his reception by al-Nāṣir Muḥammad in Cairo (see below, §§ 212–213, 214).

37 See below, §§ 97–105. There also is a second version of this al-Fuḍayl story, much shorter but equally scenic and including a dialogue with the caliph (§§ 106–107). The al-Fuḍayl story is moreover among the few, in the caliphal narratives only, in which there is a narrator identified who even actively participates in the story (also in the three last stories about ʿUmar involving amongst others ʿĀʾišah and ʿAlī, and in the stories about Hišām and Abū l-Zinād and about al-Mahdī and his dreaming competitor for the caliphate) (see below, §§ 26–28, 29; 54; 80).

Between the structural continuum that connects frames and stories and the modal continuum that connects stories and the way they are being presented, chronology continues to figure as an organising principle to hold on to for the author and his audiences. Years, dates, and chronography continued to be important tools on the micro-structural level of *al-Ḏahab al-masbūk* too, and al-Maqrīzī pursued a chronological arrangement of his stories wherever the available material allowed for such a set-up. As on the macro-structural level also micro-structurally the order of time is taken seriously for the order of telling stories. There are the more general rulership and pilgrimage participation statements, providing not just for a narrative macro-structure but also for a temporal frame of terms-of-office, years of pilgrimage participation, and times of death for situating, arranging, and connecting stories. Although again never applied rigidly or similarly, this frame is obstructed only very rarely by references that suddenly move time forward or backward between or within stories.[38]

It is rather a very different kind of disruption that occasionally interferes in this congruence of time and telling and that actually tends to transcend plots, stories, and narratives and connect them with metatextual and other realities. On a number of occasions, short references appear in the narratives that subtly introduce al-Maqrīzī's own early fifteenth-century experiences into the text. In the list of caliphs, this happened when he explains that al-Ḥağğāğ made the Kaʿbah "as it still is today", that in the time of al-Mahdī the *kiswa* was not annually removed "as it is the practice now", that after al-Ḥākim "the caliphate has remained with his offspring to this day", and finally that since

38 In two cases, stories within other stories occur that seem to disrupt the orderly flow of time: a story about the death of the caliph al-Manṣūr is followed by a story of the miraculous announcement to al-Manṣūr of his approaching death and then by three more stories about his encounters with Muḥammad b. ʿImrān (see below, §§ 63, 65–67, 68–70); the story of how one of Hārūn al-Rašīd's pilgrimages was performed on foot is followed by references to how the Byzantine emperor Heraclius once similarly performed the pilgrimage, and to how the caliph's earlier marriage with his brother's widow had been the reason for this particular behaviour (see below, §§ 88, 89). A rare example of time disruptions in the arrangement of stories may be found in the caliph Ibn al-Zubayr's narrative, where the story of his execution by al-Ḥağğāğ is followed by that of the different reconstructions of the Kaʿbah, first by the caliph and then by his executor (see below, §§ 39–41). Time disruptions within stories may be found in the *kiswah*story of the caliph al-Mahdī, where his removal of the *kiswah* introduces a story about *kiswah* practices going back to the time of the Umayyad Hišām and before (see below, § 73); and in the story about ʿAlī l-Ṣulayḥī's conquest of Mecca, generating safety for its population and visitors "such as they had not experienced before him" (see below, § 114).

the days of al-Ḥākim "until today […] the Friday sermon [is] never being delivered in the name of any the ʿAbbāsid caliphs of Egypt, except for the caliph al-Mustaʿīn bi-llāh Abū l-Faḍl al-ʿAbbās b. Muḥammad, [in whose name the Friday sermon was delivered] for a few days in the year 815 [1412]."[39] In the list of non-caliphal rulers, this includes such brief and isolated references as "the Darb Šams al-Dawlah in Cairo was named after" Tūrān Šāh and "the Masʿūdī *dirhams* in Mecca are named after" al-Masʿūd Yūsuf, but also the more elaborate explanations that "the Friday sermon […] continued to be delivered from the *minbar* of Mecca in the name of the rulers of Yemen until our own days, [but then nowadays only] after the sermon [is delivered] in the name of the sultan of Egypt", and—in the same narrative of al-Muẓaffar Yūsuf of Yemen—that "the *kiswah* of al-Muẓaffar, which he had the inside of the Kaʿbah covered with, continued to be present until in the year 761 [1360] al-Malik al-Nāṣir Ḥasan b. Muḥammad b. Qalāwūn covered it with this *kiswah* which is still present today."[40] These sudden intrusions of these carefully and consciously constructed narratives and stories by chronologically atypical and highly disconnected symbolic and ritual practices are one more remarkable characteristic of this text, obviously operating as points of direct contact for readers who shared the same frameworks of cultural reference with al-Maqrīzī and for whom *kiswah* practices, Cairo's Darb Šams al-Dawlah, Meccan Masʿūdī *dirhams*, and political dedications of sermons were equally meaningful.

A similar, but even more complex, process seems at work with another type of such metatextual material that also disturbs the strict chronological flow of narratives and stories in notable ways. In the above cases, as well as in quite a few others, references are often also included to other works of literature and history, not just to occasionally indicate sources for particular stories, but also to situate narratives or stories explicitly within their wider historiographic, jurisprudential, and literary contexts as these had developed up to the early fifteenth century. Just as the first prophetic chapter was explicitly linked up with discussions arising around Ibn Ḥazm's Farewell Pilgrimage text,[41] so did al-Maqrīzī also add a reference to one of his own books, the *Kitāb Šāriʿ al-naǧāt*, apparently a work of religious history and jurisprudence that has furthermore

---

39 See below, §§41, 73, 109, 110; similar, but less explicit, occasions concern the discussion of differences in naming (eg. Ibn al-Zubayr's *kunyah*: "ʾAbū Bakr—and it was said Abū Bukayr", see below, p. 229) or the explanation of the spelling and genealogy of the Banū Lihb in one story in the ʿUmar narrative ("Lihb—with the vowel i after the *lām*—is one of the clans of al-Azd, known for harbouring feelings of aversion and reprimand"), see below, §25.

40 See below, §§130, 146, 160, 161.

41 See below, §6.

remained unknown.[42] The wording of this reference actually suggests that this opening chapter is really only a summary of the relevant passages in that text. This particular inter-textual arrangement is made even more explicit for a number of other references to texts of al-Maqrīzī elsewhere in the narratives. For the Kaʿbah story of Ibn al-Zubayr's narrative, al-Maqrīzī thus adds that he has "reported that in great detail in the book *al-Išārah wa-l-iʿlām bi-bināʾ al-kaʿbah al-bayt al-ḥarām* [Advice and Information Regarding the Construction of the Kaʿbah, the Sacred House]"; for ʿAbd al-Malik, he explains in the context of a summarily reported story about rebels that "the stories about them were recorded in their proper place", whereas he also added in the general narrative frame that this caliph's term-of-office was also "reported in his biography and in the biography of his father in *al-Tārīḫ al-kabīr li-Miṣr* [the Great History (in Continuation) of Egypt]".[43] Similar references occur elsewhere, as in the narrative of Tūrān Šāh, which was concluded by the author's personal statement that "I [= al-Maqrīzī] reported his biography in detail in the book *al-Mawāʿiẓ wa-l-iʿtibār bi-ḏikr al-ḫiṭaṭ wa-l-āṯār* [Admonitions and Reflections on the Quarters and Monuments (in Fusṭāṭ and Cairo)] and in the book *al-Tārīḫ al-kabīr al-muqaffá li-Miṣr* [The Great History of Egypt in Continuation]",[44] and in the narrative of Baybars, where it was written by al-Maqrīzī that "there is a long story (*ḫabar ṭawīl*) of that which I have reported in his biography (*fī tarǧamatihi*) in the book *al-Tārīḫ al-kabīr al-muqaffá* [The Great History in Continuation] and the book *Aḫbār Mulūk Miṣr* [The Stories of the Kings of Egypt]".[45] The primary literary, jurisprudential, and historiographical contexts that readers are referred to by this meta- and—at the same time—intertextual material was therefore first and foremost the fruit of al-Maqrīzī's own productive pen, in the format of both his grand works of Egyptian history and of any other books that he had already began to write at the time of *al-Ḏahab al-masbūk*'s initial composition.

42 According to al-Maqrīzī's biographer al-Saḫāwī (who is the only one to refer to this text) this *Kitāb Šāriʿ al-naǧāt* "consisted of all the differences in the principles and substance of mankind's religions, including an exposition on their proofs and on their guidance towards the truth" (al-Saḫāwī, *al-Ḍawʾ al-lāmiʿ*, 2: 23; see also Faraḥāt [2009]: 23).

43 See below, §§ 41, 42, 43.

44 See below, § 131.

45 See below, § 163. Other similar references are found in the narratives of Hārūn (see below, § 93), of al-Muʿaẓẓam ʿĪsá (see below, § 139), of al-Masʿūd Yūsuf (see below, § 145), and of al-Nāṣir Dāwūd (see below, § 157), in each of these four cases referring to the "*Kitāb al-Tārīḫ al-kabīr al-muqaffá*"; the ʿUmar narrative, finally, includes another reference to al-Maqrīzī's *Ḫiṭaṭ* (see below, § 23); in all, there are twelve auto-references, seven of which refer to the *Kitāb al-Tārīḫ al-kabīr al-muqaffá*, in the narratives of a total of nine rulers (four caliphs and five non-caliphal rulers).

However, a few other historiographical contexts and literary texts were also included explicitly in particular narratives or stories in this chronologically disturbing, metatextual manner. For the caliphs ʿUmar, ʿUṯmān, Muʿāwiyah, Ibn al-Zubayr and Sulaymān, al-Maqrīzī included references to discussions that had arisen in later scholarly circles around their pilgrimage and rulership stories.[46] The identity of only one of those scholars involved in these discussions is revealed, when al-Maqrīzī explains for the caliphate of ʿUṯmān that unlike others the historian "Ibn al-Aṯīr reported that ʿUṯmān led the people on the pilgrimage in the first year [of his term of office]".[47] This type of naming external textual origins also happens in one of the stories about the caliph ʿUmar, which is explicitly linked to the writings of al-Wāqidī and of the Andalusian scholar Ibn ʿAbd al-Barr al-Namarī l-Qurṭubī (d. 463/1070).[48] A reference to Ibn Ḥazm returned in the narrative of Hārūn al-Rašīd, where the story of the caliph's marriage to his brother's widow is explained as stemming from Ibn Ḥazm's work of Arabic genealogy, the *Ǧamharat al-ansāb*.[49] In the same narrative, the two final stories about the caliph's encounter with the ascetic al-Fuḍayl b. ʿIyāḍ are moreover referenced as being taken from the *Kitāb al-Ḥilyah*, a biographical dictionary of ascetics and mystics by Abū Nuʿaym al-Iṣfahānī (d. 430/1038).[50] But these are all the references there are, and they are really only minor exceptions

---

46 For ʿUmar, al-Maqrīzī explains that "he performed the pilgrimage in all of [these years], except for one year only, […] It was [also] said that ʿUmar rather performed the pilgrimage every year of [his caliphate]." (see below, § 21); for ʿUṯmān, he details to some extent the discussions on what pilgrimages the caliph had actually participated in (see below, § 33); for Muʿāwiyah, al-Maqrīzī refers to discussions on the year of the main oath of allegiance to him (see below, § 35) and on the exact number of pilgrimages which he actually participated in (see below, § 36); for Ibn al-Zubayr mention is made of discussions on his *kunyah* (Abū Bakr or Abū Bukayr) (see below, p. 229); and for Sulaymān, al-Maqrīzī explains that it was unclear whether he reigned for two years and eight months "and 5 days" or "less 5 days" (see below, § 50).

47 See below, § 33. For Ibn al-Aṯīr and the importance of his *al-Kāmil fī l-tārīḫ*, see above (Chapter 2, 1).

48 See below, § 28. For al-Wāqidī, see above (Chapter 2, 1); Ibn ʿAbd al-Barr was an Andalusian scholar whose scholarly portfolio included *al-Istīʿāb fī maʿrifat al-aṣḥāb*, a compendium of biographies of Companions (see "Ibn ʿAbd al-Barr", in *EI*² [http://referenceworks.brillonline.com/entries/encyclopaedia-of-islam-2/ibn-abd-al-barr-SIM_3027]).

49 See below, § 89.

50 See below, § 97. The religious scholar Abū Nuʿaym Aḥmad al-Iṣfahānī (336–430/948–1038) is best known as the author of this *Kitāb Ḥilyat al-awliyāʾ wa-ṭabaqāt al-aṣfiyāʾ*, a biographical encyclopaedia of individuals from the earliest days of Islam onwards, who, at least according to the author, were to be regarded as ascetics and mystics ("Abū Nuʿaym

of external interferences in a text that is clearly first and foremost constructed around a conscious authorial persona and his very intricate and particular narrative methodologies.

3 The Sources of *al-Ḏahab al-masbūk*: Between *ḫabar* and *tarǧamah*

Explicit references such as to the writings of Ibn al-Aṯīr, Ibn ʿAbd al-Barr, Ibn Ḥazm or Abū Nuʿaym illustrate how al-Maqrīzī constructed the narratives of *al-Ḏahab al-masbūk* employing a fully conscious acquaintance with the Arabic literary heritage of his age. As detailed above, the environment of textual and literary forms within which he and his peers operated was one of longstanding as well as more recent historiographical antecedents and precedents, many of which had been set to paradigmatic basic forms and meanings that by the standards of early fifteenth-century social norms and cultural aesthetics could not be simply discarded. Al-Maqrīzī's literary environment constituted, as it were, a historically socialised as well as socialising matrix of meanings embodied in literary forms, defined by and defining authors and scholars as well as their production, reproduction, and consumption of knowledge. This is not at all particular to early fifteenth-century Cairo, of course. But for its booming business of historiography it meant that it was above all through reproductive strategies of selection, re-organisation, or reformulation of this extant literarised material that textual communication, authorial identities, and innovative ideas had to be constructed.[51] This was certainly the case for the different traditions of Arabic writing that had emerged over time around the memory of the Prophet and that continued to define the historiography-of-pilgrimage imagination into al-Maqrīzī's own time. At least, that is what is

---

al-Iṣfahānī", in *EI*³ [http://referenceworks.brillonline.com/entries/encyclopaedia-of-islam-3/abu-nuaym-al-isfahani-COM_23648]).

51 For this particular nature of al-Maqrīzī's literary environment and related issues of understanding intertextuality, communication and literary aesthetics of 'medieval' Arabic literary texts, see especially Bauer (2005); Id. (2007); Id. (2013a); Id. (2013b). On the idea of a matrix of cultural forms and meanings, and of how also issues of social identity and social performance are related to this literary matrix, see Van Steenbergen (2012). The substantial textual interdependence of Arabic historiographical texts from late medieval Egypt and Syria has been demonstrated in some of its technical detail in the following: Haarmann (1969); Little (1970); Massoud (2007). On al-Maqrīzī's engagement with his literary environment—in particular the technicalities of his "working method"—and with intertextuality, see the detailed analyses by Frédéric Bauden in his Maqriziana series of articles, in particular Bauden (2008); Id. (2009); Id. (2010).

suggested when *al-Ḏahab al-masbūk* is approached from this perspective of its inevitable embeddedness in a longstanding and socio-culturally disciplined Arabic historiographical tradition, and in this tradition's discourse on rulership and pilgrimage in particular. As will be reconstructed in some detail here, explicit and implicit intertextual relationships with this discursive tradition provided al-Maqrīzī with the necessary material for the creative process of constructing particular narratives, awarding the text at the same time the aura of historiographical authority and authenticity that it aspired.

A first level of intertextuality is perhaps the most obvious and conspicuous one, at least to the text's learned contemporary readership. This level derives from the booklet's title that was clearly specifically chosen to position the text—or at least educated readers' expectations about it—in one very particular and rather surprising web of texts and authors, usually considered under the literary rubric of the Mirrors-for-Princes genre (*naṣīḥat al-mulūk*). The booklet's title, as identified by the author himself in the opening chapter—"I entitled it: 'The Moulded Gold' (*al-Ḏahab al-masbūk*)"—,[52] clearly entered into direct communication with similar titles of seminal status by well-known authors from eleventh- and twelfth-century Iraq. This was the case in particular with a work by the Baghdadi Ḥanbalī scholar Ibn al-Ǧawzī (d. 597/1201), similarly entitled *al-Ḏahab al-masbūk fī siyar al-mulūk* (The Gold Moulded around the Conduct of Kings), and above all with the epitome of this genre, a work of princely advice in Persian attributed to the towering scholarly authority of Abū Ḥāmid Muḥammad al-Ġazālī (d. 505/1111) and known in Arabic in a late twelfth-century translation as *al-Tibr al-masbūk fī naṣīḥat al-mulūk* (The Gold Moulded around the Advice to Kings). The latter text in particular was widely known and read in late medieval Egypt and Syria, making the relationship between *al-Tibr al-masbūk* and al-Maqrīzī's choice of title real, conspicuous, and discursively meaningful. The interaction with titles such as these may at least have raised particular textual expectations with *al-Ḏahab al-masbūk*'s readership. Beyond this very particular level of a repeated literary wordplay in the title, however, there appears no further direct relationship whatsoever between the booklet's contents and these popular works of political advice, at least not as far as any other textual similarities and intertextualities are concerned.[53]

52 See below, §4, and see also above fn. 13, for a discussion of the different formats and versions of this title.

53 On these Mirrors-for-Princes texts, the *al-Tibr al-masbūk* in particular, see Marlowe; Crone (1987); Hillenbrand (1988). For Ibn al-Ǧawzī's *al-Ḏahab al-masbūk*, see *GAL*, 1:661; *GAL S* 1:915; this text currently only seems to be available in the format of a summary repro-

The actual nature of the material with which al-Maqrīzī constructed *al-Ḏahab al-masbūk*, of the building blocks of the micro-structural components of his text, are quite different. They are identified most explicitly in one passage that refers unusually explicitly to the origins of the lines of text that tell the story of a jinn's elegy for ʿUmar. "This story (*hāḏā l-ḫabar*)", al-Maqrīzī explains, "was thus transmitted by the *ḥāfiẓ* Abū ʿUmar Yūsuf b. ʿAbd Allāh b. ʿAbd al-Barr al-Namarī."[54] The passage that preceded is indeed a literal reproduction of how this story was plotted in *al-Istīʿāb fī maʿrifat al-aṣḥāb*, a compendium of biographies of Companions of the Prophet by the Andalusian scholar Ibn ʿAbd al-Barr al-Namarī (d. 463/1070).[55] As mentioned above, there are a few other explicit references to such intertextual connections, especially to Ibn Ḥazm's work of Arabic genealogy, the *Ǧamharat ansāb al-ʿArab*, for the story of Hārūn's marriage to his brother's widow,[56] and to the *Ḥilyat al-awliyāʾ*, a biographical compendium of ascetics and mystics by the Isfahani traditionist Abū Nuʿaym (d. 430/1038), for two versions of the story of Hārūn's encounter with the ascetic al-Fuḍayl b. ʿIyāḍ.[57] In both cases, again the relevant passages concern identical textual reproductions from the *Ǧamharat ansāb al-ʿArab* and *Ḥilyat al-awliyāʾ* respectively. In the latter case, al-Maqrīzī actually stated very frankly that he was merely copying Abū Nuʿaym's selected versions of the story, when he opened the passage with the announcement that "among the qualities of [Hārūn] al-Rašīd, there was what the great transmitter Abū Nuʿaym selected (*aḫraǧa*) in the *Kitāb al-Ḥilyah*." What it was that had been selected first by Abū Nuʿaym in *Ḥilyat al-awliyāʾ*, and that had been faithfully reproduced by al-Maqrīzī in *al-Ḏahab al-masbūk*, obviously was a *ḫabar*, a story, as made clear in the fragment from Ibn ʿAbd al-Barr al-Namarī. In all three cases, *ḫabar*-like versions of stories, transmitted in classics such as *al-Istīʿāb*, *Ǧamharat ansāb al-ʿArab* and *Ḥilyat al-awliyāʾ*, were infused into the particular narrative structures of *al-Ḏahab al-masbūk*, without any authorial interference, but with due acknowledgement.

---

duction that presents a short biographical history of the caliphate from al-Walīd b. ʿAbd al-Malik (r. 86–96/705–715) to al-Mustaʿṣim (r. 640–656/1242–1258) (see Ibn al-Ǧawzī/al-Irbīlī, *Ḫulāṣat al-ḏahab al-masbūk*). *Al-Tibr al-masbūk fī tawārīḫ al-mulūk* by the scholar and Ayyubid prince/sultan from Hama Abū l-Fidāʾ (672–732/1273–1331) may represent another possible point of this type of intertextual reference (see Abū l-Fidāʾ, *al-Tibr al-masbūk*).

54 See below, § 28.

55 See "Ibn ʿAbd al-Barr", *EI*²; Wasserstein (1998).

56 See below, § 89. For Ibn Ḥazm, see "Ibn Ḥazm", *EI*²; and also Adang et al. (2012).

57 See below, § 97. For Abū Nuʿaym, see "Abū Nuʿaym al-Iṣfahānī", *EI*².

As is well known to scholars of Islamic history, these handful of *ḫabar*s belong to an enormous repertoire of such reports of varying size, value, and authenticity, in which stories and anecdotes about individuals, places, or events from Muslim history were set to particularly constructed and often juxtaposed, overlapping, or dispersed forms. *Ḫabar*s formed, informed, and defined the Muslim community's social memory since the early days of the Arabic historical tradition, and they continued to represent the basic building blocks of that memory through the centuries. When from the tenth century onwards annalistic chronography and *siyāsah*-oriented historiography became dominant macro-structural formats of historiographical communication, *ḫabar*s retained, within those larger formats, normative status for the transmission of knowledge about early Islamic history. As a literary form, the self-contained textual unit of the *ḫabar* arguably even seems to have retained some level of micro-structural appeal for the recording of contemporary history in certain literary historiographies such as *al-Ḏahab al-masbūk*.[58] This genealogical process, which physically connects the different generations of Arabic historiographical and related texts through the growing body of *ḫabar*s that informed their stories, is in fact central for any understanding of *al-Ḏahab al-masbūk*. It is present in direct and explicit ways in the handful of *ḫabar*s that connect *al-Ḏahab al-masbūk* with *al-Istīʿāb*, *Ǧamharat ansāb al-ʿArab*, and *Ḥilyat al-awliyāʾ*. It is equally present in direct but implicit ways in dozens of similar types of *ḫabar*s that were reproduced in many of the more than 120 stories of *al-Ḏahab al-masbūk*, positioning the text in a web of very meaningful (and discursively inevitable) textual ties with a handful of other classics of Arabic historiography. This was a textual reality especially for the first and second chapters, with its stories about Prophet and caliphs really mainly being made up of *ḫabar* material that throughout the centuries had been thoroughly codified in form and meaning by the increasingly shared social memory of mainstream Muslim communities from east and west (a process of transregional community-building that is also exemplified by the explicit presence in this Egyptian text

58 See Khalidi (1994): 137–151; Robinson (2003): 92–97. Al-Maqrīzī occasionally is very explicit about his qualification of the textual units with which he constructed *al-Ḏahab al-masbūk*, as well as some of his other texts, as *ḫabar/aḫbār*, as in the following cases: *kamā qad ḏakartu ḫabarahu* (see below § 23); *fa-kāna min aḫbārihim mā qad ḏukira fī mawḍiʿihi* (see below, § 43); *wa-qad ḏakartu ḫabar ḏālika mabsūṭ*^{an} *fī tarǧamat al-Maʾmūn* (see below, § 93); *wa-qad istawfaytu aḫbārahu* (see below, § 145); *wa li-ḏālika ḫabar ṭawīl qad ḏakartuhu fī tarǧamatihi* (see below, § 163). Other similar terms were sometimes also used (*ḏikr, qiṣaṣ, anbāʾ*), but they occur far less frequently than terms related to *ḫabar* do (throughout the text, *ḫabar* and derived verbal forms occurr no less than fifteen times).

of material from Ibn Ḥazm's and Ibn ʿAbd al-Barr's al-Andalus and from Abū Nuʿaym's Persia). But also for the third chapter on non-caliphal rulers, intertextuality of its stories along *ḫabar*-lines may be reconstructed, even though that material was far less burdened by transcendent and translocal communal meanings.

As suggested above, two key moments in the genealogical process of *ḫabar* transmission and codification were the *History of Messengers and Kings* (*Tārīḫ al-rusul wa-l-mulūk*) by the Iraqi scholar al-Ṭabarī (d. 310/923) and the *Complete History* (*al-Kāmil fī l-tārīḫ*) by Ibn al-Aṯīr (d. 630/1233). For the majority of the second chapter's stories for which so far a genealogy could be reconstructed, the normative historiographical status of these works of history is reflected in al-Maqrīzī's heavy reliance on *ḫabar*s that can be traced back to these texts.[59] In fact, it is always Ibn al-Aṯīr's version of a *ḫabar* that al-Maqrīzī is reproducing, with occasionally only slight adaptations in wording, phrasing, or detail, but without ever identifying this textual relationship.[60] For six caliphal narratives this canonical *ḫabar* tradition even is the sole source for all related stories.[61] In four narratives, however, this *ḫabar* tradition is entirely absent, either because there are no stories, as with the caliph Muʿāwiyah, or because the narrative post-dates Ibn al-Aṯīr's time, as with al-Ḥākim, or because other *ḫabar* traditions were prioritised. In the narrative of Ibn al-Zubayr it thus seems to have been al-Maqrīzī's own history of the Kaʿbah, *al-Išārah wa-l-iʿlām*, that was followed (and explicitly named as such), whereas

59 For the second chapter of the text of *al-Ḏahab al-masbūk*, we counted 34 moments of direct textual interdependence between *ḫabar*s in the text and other texts; 24 of these moments have been identified as connecting directly with the Ibn al-Aṯīr/al-Ṭabarī tradition (further details are provided in the footnotes that follow). Each of these moments has been duly referenced in the critical apparatus of the edition of the Arabic text.

60 On three occasions, a *ḫabar* could be traced back to Ibn al-Aṯīr's *al-Kāmil* only, and not to al-Ṭabarī's *Tārīḫ* (Abū Bakr's pilgrimage leadership in 12 AH [not a story as such, but only a brief reference to the conflicting reports about the leadership of that year's *ḥaǧǧ*], ʿAbd al-Malik's public Friday sermon in Medina, and Hārūn's confronting the *ḫāriǧī* rebellion of al-Walīd b. Ṭarīf in 177 AH; see below, §§ 19, 44, 86–87). Slight variations in the wording, phrasing or detail of the *ḫabar* texts may have to do with al-Maqrīzī's working method of first taking notes from other texts in a personal notebook, sometimes slightly adapting or summarising them for his personal use, and then quoting from the notebook rather than from the actual texts when drafting his own texts (see the detailed analysis in Bauden [2008]; Id. [2009]).

61 All *ḫabar*s (or pilgrimage/rulership references) making up the narratives of Abū Bakr (no. 1), ʿUṯmān (3), ʿAbd al-Malik (6), al-Walīd (7), Hišām (9) and al-Mahdī (11) stem directly from the Ibn al-Aṯīr/al-Ṭabarī tradition.

the narrative of Sulaymān is entirely constructed (again, however, without any explicit reference) around a single *ḫabar* from the *Reports of Mecca* (*Aḫbār Makkah*), attributed to the ninth-century Meccan historian al-Azraqī.[62] The caliphal narratives of ʿUmar, al-Manṣūr, and al-Rašīd, finally, were also made up of substantial material from the Ibn al-Aṯīr *ḫabar* tradition, but added to that there are *ḫabar*s from other traditions, either explicitly identified, such as with the aforementioned five stories from *al-Istīʿāb*, *Ǧamharat ansāb al-ʿArab*, and *Ḥilyat al-awliyāʾ*, or on two other implicit occasions in the ʿUmar narrative from Ibn ʿAbd al-Ḥakam's ninth-century *Conquest and Other Reports Concerning Egypt* (*Futūḥ Miṣr wa-aḫbāruhā*).[63] The latter actually was as authoritative a *ḫabar* tradition for Egyptian local history as the Ibn al-Aṯīr/al-Ṭabarī tradition was for the history of the caliphate, and al-Azraqī's for that of Mecca and its sanctuary, which is then possibly one of the reasons why there was no need for al-Maqrīzī to make these particular genealogies explicit. Unlike in the case of *al-Istīʿāb*, *Ǧamharat ansāb al-ʿArab*, and *Ḥilyat al-awliyāʾ*, *ḫabar*s from the latter three codified traditions simply identified themselves, plugging *al-Ḏahab al-masbūk* almost automatically into a web of textual ties and authorities that were well-known, widely acknowledged, and historiographically normative.

This issue of intertextuality is far more difficult to establish for the third chapter. Its narratives of non-caliphal rulers are even richer in story material than the second chapter, and many of these stories continue to present themselves *ḫabar*-wise as self-contained textual units of varying size and detail. Identifying this chapter's *ḫabar* genealogy, however, turns out to be less evident. The non-caliphal rulers around whom the narratives and their stories were constructed simply were far less transcendent politico-cultural characters than many of their caliphal predecessors continued to be. By the early

62 See below, §§40–41, 51–52. On the Meccan historian Abū l-Walīd Muḥammad b. ʿAbd Allāh b. Aḥmad al-Azraqī and his unique history of Mecca and its sanctuary, see "al-Azraḳī", in *EI*[2] (http://referenceworks.brillonline.com/entries/encyclopaedia-of-islam-2/al-azraki-SIM_0958).

63 See below, §§23–24 (related, without acknowledgment, with Ibn ʿAbd al-Ḥakam's *Futūḥ*), §§25–28 (with Ibn ʿAbd al-Barr's *al-Istīʿāb*), §89 (with Ibn Ḥazm's *Ǧamharah*), §§97–105, 106–107 (with Abū Nuʿaym's *Ḥilyah*) and §§68, 70 (demonstrating some indirect textual relationship with the Baghdadi scholar Wakīʿ's [d. 306/918] *The Reports of the Judges* (*Aḫbār al-quḍāt*) [see "Wakīʿ", in *EI*[2] (http://referenceworks.brillonline.com/entries/encyclopaedia-of-islam-2/waki-SIM_7834)]). On ʿAbd al-Raḥmān b. ʿAbd Allāh Ibn ʿAbd al-Ḥakam (d. 257/871) and his *Futūḥ Miṣr*, see Khalidi (1994): 65–67; "Ibn ʿAbd al-Ḥakam", *EI*[2] (http://referenceworks.brillonline.com/entries/encyclopaedia-of-islam-2/ibn-abd-al-hakam-SIM_3028).

fifteenth century time had moreover not yet allowed specific memories to crystallise into equally authoritative *ḫabar* traditions. But memories and traditions there undoubtedly were, and even if they had not yet been—nor ever would be—crystallising into anything resembling the globally meaningful al-Ṭabarī/Ibn al-Aṯīr tradition, they were yet already forming into something that was at least as meaningful for Egyptian elites' localising social memory as the Ibn ʿAbd al-Ḥakam tradition was.[64] Obviously, al-Maqrīzī's own prolific historiographical production represented an important moment in this particular (but not necessarily intentional) genealogical process, which was then continued or challenged by colleagues and students alike (and extremely successful up to this day).[65] Chapter three of *al-Ḏahab al-masbūk* was very much part and parcel of this, which explains why it is set within al-Maqrīzī's own growing production of works of Egyptian history even more explicitly than was done in the second chapter.[66] This may also be one of the reasons why, unlike in

---

64 Conermann interestingly explains this 'natural' process of crystallisation in pre-modern history writing as "a willingness to reduce the complexity of human experience into stereotypes according to 'literary canons' which could be utilized easily to make a moral point" (Conermann [2008]: 3). On the question of whether or not there were in late medieval *siyāsah*-oriented Arabic historiography distinct local/regional traditions of historiographical production, including thirteenth-to-fifteenth-century Syrian and Egyptian 'schools', referring for the latter even to some form of "court culture" that may have had a substantial formative impact, see Guo (1997): 29–33, 37–41; see also Id. (2010): 450–451. For a general appreciation of late medieval Syro-Egyptian Arabic historiographical writing, see Little (1998). For detailed micro-historical analyses of particular sets of intertextual historiographical traditions, see especially Little (1970); Massoud, (2007).

65 Little, however, approached this characteristic rather more from a negative perspective: "... until such time as the annals of *al-Sulūk* have been compared with those of other historians, [...] al-Maqrīzī's significance as a historian will remain as a compiler and preserver of the work of others" (Little [1998]: 436–437, esp. 437).

66 The second chapter has four references to al-Maqrīzī's own production: one to the aforementioned Kaʿbah history, one to the *Ḫiṭaṭ* (referring any reader interested in how a canal between the Nile and the Red Sea was famously redug to this topographical work of history of his), and two to the biographical collection *al-Tārīḫ al-kabīr al-muqaffá* (referring to his biographies of ʿAbd al-Malik and of his father Marwān, and to his account of the story of Hārūn's problematic succession in the biography of the caliph al-Maʾmūn) (see below, §§41, 23, 42, 93). The third chapter has seven similar references: five to the biographical collection *al-Tārīḫ al-kabīr al-muqaffá* (for each of the Ayyubid and Mamluk rulers Tūrān Šāh, al-Muʿaẓẓam ʿĪsá, al-Masʿūd Yūsuf, al-Nāṣir Dāwūd and al-Ẓāhir Baybars, but not for the fourteenth-century sultans al-Nāṣir Muḥammad and al-Ašraf Šaʿban), one to the *Ḫiṭaṭ* (for Tūrān Šāh) and one to the chronicle *Kitāb al-Sulūk* (for Baybars) (see below, §§131, 139, 145, 157, 163). Whereas for chapter two these references have to do with particular

the second chapter, the author did not feel any need to identify explicitly any other textual ties beyond those rather more forward looking ones with his own scholarly production in full progress. Either there simply were no ties considered valuable enough by him for the establishment of the text's authority, or there were such ties, but then rooted in local *ḫabar* traditions that had already become so dominant and well-known by the early fifteenth century that they too could do without any explicit reference. The latter must certainly have been the case with the 667/1269 secret pilgrimage *ḫabar*s that were used to construct al-Ẓāhir Baybars' narrative, and that all referred directly—with the occasional omission of some details only—and without any acknowledgement back to the panegyric biography that Baybars' personal secretary, Muḥyī al-Dīn Ibn ʿAbd al-Ẓāhir (d. 692/1292), wrote for his sultan, *al-Rawḍ al-zāhir fī sīrat al-Malik al-Ẓāhir*.[67] For three Yemeni rulers—ʿAlī l-Ṣulayḥī and the Rasūlids Nūr al-Dīn ʿUmar and his son al-Muẓaffar Yūsuf—some *ḫabar*s can similarly be traced back to one of the Meccan histories by a contemporary of al-Maqrīzī, Taqī l-Dīn Muḥammad al-Fāsī (775–832/1373–1429), the *Šifāʾ al-ġarām bi-aḫbār al-Balad al-Ḥarām*.[68] No further similarly clear textual ties have so far come to light, but if these two cases suggest anything already, it certainly is that in the third chapter al-Maqrīzī also continued to root his stories within a web of *ḫabar* intertextualities, that these ties represented distinct recent and localised *ḫabar* genealogies that were gradually being codified in their own locally meaningful ways, and that further publication and exploration of thirteenth- and fourteenth-century historiographical texts may reveal much more about the genealogies and impact of these emerging later historiographical traditions for situating *al-Ḏahab al-masbūk* as well as for understanding the wider cultural field of the era's exploding historiographical production.

With a second chapter that is directly plugged into heavily codified globalising *ḫabar* traditions, and a third chapter that does the same with localising

---

stories within the narratives only, for chapter three they often concern the entire narrative and the clarification that much more comprehensive accounts about these five particular rulers may be found in one of al-Maqrīzī's other works.

67 See below, §§ 164–181. For Ibn ʿAbd al-Ẓāhir and his panegyric of al-Ẓāhir Baybars, see Holt (1982): 20–24; Id. (1985): 129–133; "Ibn ʿAbd al-Ẓāhir", in *EI*[2] (http://referenceworks.brillonline.com/entries/encyclopaedia-of-islam-2/ibn-abd-al-zahir-SIM_3034).

68 See below, §§ 114, 152–153, 160. For the Meccan scholar al-Fāsī and his history of the city of Mecca, see "al-Fāsī", *EI*[2] (http://referenceworks.brillonline.com/entries/encyclopaedia-of-islam-2/al-fasi-SIM_2311); "al-Fāsī, Taqī al-Dīn Muḥammad", *EI3* (http://referenceworks.brillonline.com/entries/encyclopaedia-of-islam-3/al-fasi-taqi-l-din-muhammad-COM_27018).

ḫabar traditions in formation, the first chapter stands out as as distinct in intertextual ways, as it also was structurally. As mentioned before, the chapter opens explicitly with references to Ibn Ḥazm's Farewell Pilgrimage text, and to al-Maqrīzī's own work of comparative theology, the Road to Deliverance (*Šāriʿ al-naǧāt*). In terms of intertextuality, however, its text does not seem to be related to either one but rather to the relevant passage in a separate text of prophetic biography by the Damascene *ḥadīṯ* specialist and historian Ibn Kaṯīr (700–774/1300–1373).[69] The entire chapter turns out to be reproduced without hardly any variation from Ibn Kaṯīr's *al-Fuṣūl fī sīrat al-rasūl*, and most of it eventually figured in very similar but more elaborate fashion in another, later work by al-Maqrīzī on prophetic biography, the multi-volumous *Imtāʿ al-asmāʿ bi-mā li-l-nabī min al-aḥwāl wa-l-amwāl wa-ḥafaḍah wa-l-matāʿ*.[70] This ties *al-Ḏahab al-masbūk* up with yet another web of textual production, this time of a particular *ḫabar* tradition of longstanding Syro-Iraqi *ḥadīṯ* scholarship, widely known and respected for its contribution to the articulation of Sunni Islamic socio-cultural identities and memories.[71]

These very deeply rooted multiple intertextualities surely endowed *al-Ḏahab al-masbūk* with particular types of textual authority and socio-cultural meaning. But first and foremost they clearly had a very strong impact on the contents of the three chapters of *al-Ḏahab al-masbūk*, nuancing the intentionality of their structural organisation. At least aforementioned micro-structural elements such as the plotting of stories along a modal continuum, their continued chronological organisation, and even the first chapter's embedded legal debate narrative, were then imposed rather by the particularities of different extant *ḫabar* traditions than merely by the author's intentions. Authorial decisions mainly played on the macro-structural level of selecting particular stories and related *ḫabar*s, of devising particular rulership-pilgrimage frames for each

---

69 Ibn Kaṯīr, *al-Fuṣūl*, 214–217. For Ibn Kaṯīr, see "Ibn Kaṯīr", *EI*[2] (http://referenceworks.brillonline.com/entries/encyclopaedia-of-islam-2/ibn-kathir-SIM_3237).

70 Al-Maqrīzī, *Imtāʿ al-asmāʿ*, 2:102–120. This extensive work on the Prophet's biography was produced between 832/1429 and 836/1433 (Bauden [2014]: 196–197). The idea that the Farewell Pilgrimage text in the *Šāriʿ al-naǧāt* (the production date of this now lost text remains unclear) was somehow different and predated that in *al-Ḏahab al-masbūk* is suggested by explicit references in the latter's chapter one, such as "I responded in the book *Šāriʿ al-naǧāt* to certain passages in [Ibn Ḥazm's text] …" and, especially, that an argument for the combination of *ḥaǧǧ* and *ʿumrah* "has also been transmitted … by sixteen successors, whom I have mentioned in the book *Šāriʿ al-naǧāt*" (see below, §§ 6, 9).

71 On this particular genealogical tradition of *ḥadīṯ* scholarship, see Lucas (2004): 109–112. For this tradition's central role in the articulation of a particular historiographical genre in Mamluk Syria and Egypt, see Guo (1998): 82–87.

and every narrative—formally directly related to the *tarǧamah* or individual biography of the biographical genre[72]—, and of wrapping those narratives in an equally particular three-tiered structure of communicating chapters. Micro-structurally reproduction is the key word to understand *al-Ḏahab al-masbūk*, situating the text within rich and discursively even inevitable intertextual contexts of global and local *ḫabar* traditions. Macro-structurally, however, production rather is the key word, al-Maqrīzī creating something entirely new within the textual webs that connect those traditions. It was this authorial creative process of the production of particular, innovative kinds of *tarǧamah*s and chapters that endowed the text with its most obvious meanings.

4 The Meanings of *al-Ḏahab al-masbūk*: Between Author and Ruler

The construction of a historical text such as *al-Ḏahab al-masbūk* along particular structural dynamics and its positioning within particular genealogical webs of Arabic literary canons are obviously part of a set of authorial decisions, some consciously taken and others rather more imposed by the conventions of genre, of discourse, and of the author's wider contexts of time and space. These decisions actually define the text's intersubjectivity, connecting particular social memories and claims to veracity to discursive imaginations of the author's present and generating the communication of particular cultural and social meanings. As this kind of authorial construct *al-Ḏahab al-masbūk* is actually one among many remnants of the growing body of textual 'makers' in the cultural and social realities of late medieval Egypt that were all participating in this socio-cultural agency in remarkable and widely penetrating ways. Indeed, the historiographical partners in the aforementioned double process of expanding textual consumption and production were not merely representing, reconstructing, transmitting, or preserving some externalised and objective real world. On the contrary, they all actively contributed to making that world, in all the subjectivity of its many social and cultural manifestations.[73] In

72 On the set formalities of the *tarǧamah* (with its textual references organised in subcategories of name, of dates, of social and textual relations, and of *aḫbār* and similar anecdotes), see al-Qāḍī (1998): 151–152. In *al-Ḏahab al-masbūk* the technical term *tarǧamah* occurs several times (see below, §§42, 93, 131, 139, 163), but always to refer the reader to the full-blown biographical entries for caliphs and kings that al-Maqrīzī had produced elsewhere, explaining that the material in *al-Ḏahab al-masbūk* were topical derivatives of such full *tarǧamah*s only.

73 For more on these issues of the historical agency of late medieval Arabic historiographical

many ways they were even that world, constituting some of the hard facts that not just reproduced but also produced late medieval Egyptian realities, along the diverse, changing, and segmented pathways by which their growing bodies of authors and readers experienced, imagined, and tried to make sense of these realities.

Al-Ḏahab al-masbūk is part and parcel of these formative and performative socio-cultural processes, operating in the general context of late medieval Egyptian social practices and value systems as well as in the specific contexts of al-Maqrīzī's authorship and life. It reproduced and produced meaningful relations for both contexts, and to some extent, a glimpse of these can still be grasped, even though the passage of time has obviously radically transformed or even annihilated contexts and relations alike. As suggested above, it is the authorial creative process of the production of particular innovative kinds of chapters and narratives for selected sets of reproductive historical material that endowed the text with its most relevant meanings. Considering *al-Ḏahab al-masbūk*'s core business of pilgriming Prophet, caliphs, and non-caliphal rulers, these meanings obviously operated first and foremost on the level of making the past of Muslim kingship meaningful for the present of al-Maqrīzī's early fifteenth-century readership. Before considering those relational meanings of Muslim kingship, however, another level also needs to be briefly contemplated, directly related to the latter present of al-Maqrīzī's readership, and made explicit by the author himself on various occasions, above all in his ornate introduction of the text.

As mentioned before, in this introduction al-Maqrīzī dedicates the text to an anonymous patron, describing how his personal quest for finding a gift that befitted the occasion of this princely patron's *ḥaǧǧ* eventually resulted in his production of *al-Ḏahab al-masbūk*.[74] Although this is nothing unusual for this type of literary dedication, the explicit presentation of the text as a gift and—above all—of the author's skills and knowledge as special and relevant for such an exchange certainly reveals some of his intentions and therefore deserves to be reproduced here:

---

and other texts, see Hirschler (2006); Id. (2013): 167–180; Conermann (2008): 1–4 ("With the aid of such 'literary canons', the chroniclers could use past figures and events as explanations and modes of legitimizing present political life", p. 4), 21–24. See also Bauer (2013a): 53 ("Literature, especially poetry and ornate prose, was central, it permeated every field of life and was an important medium of educated communication [...]. It was always also a means of distinction as well as a means of creating group identity."); Van Steenbergen (2012).

74 See below, §§1–5.

> The word has spread that the high-born intention was set on undertaking the *ḥaǧǧ* and to be endowed with the noise and blood of rituals. It has become common practice for servants to present a gift to their masters, for which reason I considered the situation of clients that owe presents on the occasion of an event like this, and I decided to follow their example. But then I thought: I could offer my soul as a present, but it already belongs to the noble lord; I could offer my property, but that is his already; I could offer my love and gratitude, but they already are his full and undivided due. I abhored [the idea of] draining this intention [of my lord] from its habitual practice and of becoming as a result one of those that are considered negligent, or [the idea of] claiming to possess what can meet the noble lord's due and becoming as a result one of those that are considered liars.
>
> I cannot present my soul, because he already owns it, so I am only guarding it as the most precious sort of noblesse;
> Nor can I present any wealth, because he has donated it, so I am the one who owes him thankfulness.
> Nor can I present my gratitude, because it is a pawn until the end of time for your comeliness.
> When the sun rises, she does not need to be lit by the full moon's highness.
>
> Since knowledge is the most precious and most valuable of treasures, the most glorious and the longest remembered of deeds, I collected for the benefit of the esteemed library of our lord—may God support it with long life for its owner—a volume that comprises the report of those caliphs and kings who performed the *ḥaǧǧ*. I entitled it: 'The Moulded Gold', as a reminder to the high-born mind that what comes from me is better informed, more entitled to be considered useful, and more appropriate. In what I do and compose, I am like someone who presents drops of water to the sea, or who sends light to the moon, and fragrance to flowers, or even better, like someone who sends the rays of light to the sun, and the breath of life to the soul: apart from the fact that there is sinlessness in such a man's noble manners and that there is a satisfying aspect in the purity of his sweat, what is given is little but also surpasses things that are a fault and a shortcoming.

A remarkable concern to display the individuality, speciality, and authenticity of al-Maqrīzī's authorship appears from these opening statements. This concern finds confirmation throughout the text in various aforementioned meta- and intertextual references by which *al-Ḏahab al-masbūk* and al-Maqrīzī's authorial person and wider authorship became explicitly and tightly interwoven. Already the very first word of this introduction—"I demand" (*fa-as'al*)—leaves no doubt about this authorial presence, as it immediately introduces al-Maqrīzī into the text through a first person reference.[75] This is also repeated at the very start of the actual text, where the first prophetic chapter begins with a similar auto-reference—"I began" (*iftataḥtu*)—that leaves no doubt about the author's personal textual agency.[76] This decisive authorial authority is also emphasised in the many first-person references in the above passage from the introduction, making clear how the text is intended by its author "as a reminder to the high-born mind that what comes from me is better informed, more entitled to be considered useful, and more appropriate" (*li-yakūna taḏkiratan li-l-ḫāṭir al-šarīf bi-mā huwa minnī adrá wa-aḥaqq bi-ifādatihi wa-aḥrá*). The relation between author and patron is then not just simply hierarchical[77] but also reciprocal, and the text is meant to mediate this dyadic relationship as a confirmation of its validity, or at least as an agent of the author's related claims to distinction, identity, and socio-cultural entitlement.

This mediation of the relation between the author and his wider socio-cultural environment also appears from various other meta- and intertextual occasions. In the opening chapter, al-Maqrīzī makes very clear not just that the text's macro-structural organisation was his own conscious decision ("I began this volume with [the Prophet's pilgrimage] because ..."), but also that he had much more to say about this in another work of his.[78] Similar auto-references appear in chapters two and three. For two particular stories in the second chapter—al-Manṣūr's will and the pilgrimage of Hārūn al-Rašīd's wife Zubaydah—al-Maqrīzī intrudes into the text to explain explicitly how he limits himself to summary references for practical reasons only, suggesting at the same time that space and time allowing he indeed would have had much more

75 See below, § 1.

76 See below, § 6.

77 A hierarchy that is also quantitatively represented in the introduction, with 31 direct references to this patron ('he', 'him', 'his', and once in a more direct manner 'your' ["for your beautiful acts"]), compared to only 18 references to al-Maqrīzī himself ('I', and once 'me').

78 See below, §§ 6, 9. ("I responded in the book *The Road to Deliverance*"—"It has also been transmitted ... by sixteen successors, whom I have mentioned in the book *The Road to Deliverance*").

to say.[79] A similar connotation emerges from ten further auto-references,[80] equally spread over both chapters and each allowing the author to intrude in parallel authoritative ways and to explain that more has been said about many of these particular narratives and stories in his other literary works.[81] To this meta- rather than intertextual kind of material should certainly also be added the aforementioned short references to *kiswah* practices, Cairo's Darb Šams al-Dawlah, Meccan Masʿūdī *dirham*s, and political dedications of sermons.[82] In subtle ways these similarly introduce al-Maqrīzī's own early fifteenth-century experiences into the text, operating not just as recognizable points of direct contact for his readers, but also as points of reference for displaying his own knowledgeability about these and similar cultural practices. The primary literary, jurisprudential, historiographical, and heuristic contexts that readers are referred to by this metatextual material were therefore first and foremost the fruits of al-Maqrīzī's own mind and productive pen. Wrapped in carefully constructed narratives, stories, and *ḫabar*s, these fruits are displayed here as legitimate, authoritative, and comprehensive containers of knowledge about Muslim history, from the days of the Prophet until al-Maqrīzī's own time and

79 See below, § 63 ("… if it were not for its length, I would mention it [here]"); § 91 ("… its report does not fit within the parameters of this volume [*min šarṭ hāḏā l-ǧuzʾ*], and therefore, I will leave out this report").

80 "As I have reported" (*kamā qad ḏakartu ḫabarahu*) (see below, § 23); "as I have reported that in great detail" (*kamā qad ḏakartu ḏālika ḏikr^an^ šāfiy^an^*) (see below, § 41); "as I reported in his biography" (*kamā qad ḏakartu tarǧamatahu*) (see below, § 42); "stories about them were recorded in their proper place" (*fa-kāna min aḫbārihim mā qad ḏukira fī mawḍiʿihi*) (see below, § 43); "I have extensively reported the story of that in the biography of al-Maʾmūn" (*wa-qad ḏakartu ḫabar ḏālika mabsūṭ^an^ fī tarǧamat al-Maʾmūn*) (see below, § 93); "I reported his biography in detail" (*wa-qad ḏakartu tarǧamatahu mabsūṭat^an^, wa-qad ḏakartu tarǧamatahu mustawfāt^an^*) (see below, §§ 131, 139); "I have recorded his stories in much more detail" (*wa-qad istawfaytu aḫbārahu*) (see below, § 145); "there are tales and tidings about him which I have reported" (*wa kānat lahu qiṣaṣ wa-anbāʾ ḏakartuhā*) (see below, § 157); "there is a long story of that which I have reported in his biography" (*wa li-ḏālika ḫabar ṭawīl qad ḏakartuhu fī tarǧamatihi*) (see below, § 163).

81 As explained in the previous chapter these auto-references end with al-Ẓāhir Baybars, fourteenth-century rulers such as al-Nāṣir Muḥammad, Mansā Mūsá, al-Muǧāhid ʿAlī and al-Ašraf Šaʿbān surprisingly not receiving any similar notes (even though al-Maqrīzī does deal with them extensively in other works of his); as suggested, this may hint at the early date of composition of the work's first draft, as predating al-Maqrīzī's treatment of any of these later rulers in any of his texts.

82 See below, §§ 110, 130, 146, 161, 160.

from Rasūlid Yemen to Muslim West-Africa. This highly functional translation of communal past to authorial present then generates nothing less than a textual performance of al-Maqrīzī's mastery of historical knowledge, announced in the introduction as "the most precious and most valuable of treasures, the most glorious and the longest remembered of deeds" and presented throughout the text as though monopolised by its author. *Al-Ḏahab al-masbūk* thus pursues a very particular and highly personalised social and cultural mediation, exchanging the hierarchy of material patronage for a reversed immaterial one of knowledge and making strong and effective claims to wider socio-cultural entitlement.

Against this background of the assumption of an authorial and then socio-cultural authority that transcends *al-Ḏahab al-masbūk* as a text but not as an agent, other relations become apparent that are similarly hierarchical in reversed order, that derive their full meaning from that reversal, and that communicate in didactic ways particular moral values from the author via the agency of the text to his royal audiences. It is at this level above all that the particular past of Muslim kingship could be made meaningful for the author's early fifteenth-century present and that the creative process of the production of particular, innovative kinds of chapters and narratives for selected sets of codified and authoritative historical material acquired its true meanings. Not surprisingly the author's selection of particular stories about caliphal and non-caliphal rulers and their framing in narratives of rulership and pilgrimage participate above all in the communication of the grand old theme of legitimate Muslim kingship. Throughout the chapters, the narratives, and the stories that make up the text, its audience learns from a kaleidoscope of examples what it means to be a good ruler, from ʿUmar securing Egyptian supplies for the Hijaz, over ʿAbd al-Malik fighting rebels, al-Manṣūr submitting to the law, and al-Mahdī making *kiswah* arrangements and organising the Arabian postal system, to Hārūn heroically performing the pilgrimage on foot and seeking moral advice from pious men of learning; from ʿAlī l-Ṣulayḥī spreading justice in the Hijaz, over al-Muʿaẓẓam ʿĪsá distributing alms in Mecca and Medina, Nūr al-Dīn ʿUmar abolishing unlawful taxes, Baybars performing a secret pilgrimage, and al-Nāṣir Muḥammad being welcomed with pomp and circumstance, to Mansā Mūsá exchanging royal gifts. Ritual precedence and distinction, public works and patronage, generosity and largesse, order and justice, victory and sovereignty, piety and knowledge, modesty, lineage and charisma: they all are there one way or another, emerging as the main qualities of good rule from this incongruous wealth of material.

The kaleidoscope, however, occasionally also takes strange or surprising turns that make connections with legitimate Muslim kingship less obvious and rather suggest the opposite. The non-Umayyad ʿAbd Allāh b. al-Zubayr is portrayed as a legitimate caliph, because he received the oath of allegiance (*bayʿah*); at the same time it is his public execution that restores political order, after "the earth had been covered in warfare" and when "fortune was on the side of (*sāʿadat al-aqdār*) ʿAbd al-Malik b. Marwān, and all those who opposed him were killed".[83] The lineage of the Cairo caliph al-Ḥākim is the object of "disagreement" (*ʿalā ḫilāf fī nasabihi*), and his claims to legitimacy are simply not accepted in Mecca.[84] ʿAlī b. Muḥammad is "one of this world's revolutionaries" (*aḥad ṯuwwār al-ʿālam*) and an agent of the Shiite Fāṭimid dynasty (*aḥad duʿāʾ al-dawlah al-fāṭimiyyah*), who dies at the hand of an opponent.[85] Tūrān Šāh dies leaving an enormous debt, due to "the wealth of his generosity and the wide extent of his benevolence" (*wa-sabab hāḏā l-dīn kaṯrat ǧawdihi wa-saʿat ʿaṭāʾihi*).[86] Al-Masʿūd Yūsuf "committed gravely sinful deeds of insolence towards God" (*wa-aẓhara min al-ǧarʾa ʿalá llāh qabāʾiḥ*), including shooting pigeons and drinking wine in Mecca's sacrosanct area.[87] Al-Nāṣir Dāwūd, ruler of Damascus, "began to oppress the populace, seizing their property and abandoning himself to amusements" (*wa-aḫaḏa l-Nāṣir fī ẓulm al-raʿiyyah wa-aḫḏ amwālihim wa-l-inhimāk fī l-laʿib*), and he experienced the loss of Damascus, of family and supporters, and eventually even of any principality to rule.[88] Due to misfortune and bad weather *en route*, Mansā Mūsá lost two-thirds of his enormous West-African royal entourage and was forced to borrow money (*iḥtāǧa ilá qirḍ māl kaṯīr*), after first having brought "impressive gifts and lots of gold" (*hadāyā ǧalīlah wa-ḏahab kaṯīr*).[89] Al-Muǧāhid ʿAlī overplayed his hand when he tried to gain control over Mecca, "contriving a despicable innovation" (*tabtadiʿu bidʿah fāḥišah*) by bringing weapons into the sanctuary, and only managing to return to Yemen after much trouble, including even a period of captivity in Cairo.[90] Al-Ašraf Šaʿbān, finally, failed to deliver his entourage's travel allowance (*nafaqah*) and to command sufficient loyalty, resulting in rebellion, defeat, and violent death.[91]

83 See below, § 42.
84 See below, p. 297, § 110.
85 See below, §§ 111–112, 115.
86 See below, § 127.
87 See below, § 142.
88 See below, §§ 156–157.
89 See below, §§ 204, 207.
90 See below, §§ 212–217.
91 See below, § 221.

These are all but examples of good, legitimate Muslim rule. At the same time, however, their selection and inclusion in the text clearly also served related didactic purposes, illustrating in often graphic ways the opposites of good rule, as well as the consequences of such unwelcome behaviour. Therefore the negative counterparts of those qualities of good rule found almost metaphorical expression in these stories: defunct authority (vs. charisma), faulty lineage (vs. lineage), excesses (vs. modesty), sinfulness and ignorance (vs. piety and knowledge), defeat and loss (vs. victory and sovereignty), disorder and injustice (vs. order and justice), indulgence and shortage (vs. generosity and largesse), and negligence (vs. public works and patronage). Even the royal need for ritual precedence and distinction is similarly highlighted through opposition, such as in the story of the Rasūlid al-Manṣūr ʿUmar, who wanted to provide a new *kiswah* for the Kaʿbah in 643/1246, but was allowed only a rudimentary restoration of the old *kiswah* when the *šayḫ al-ḥaram* insisted on this being an exclusively caliphal prerogative; in the story of ʿUmar's descendant al-Muǧāhid ʿAlī in 742/1342 being denied outright the right to provide any *kiswah*, making him "leave in anger"; or in the story of al-Ḥākim, requesting in vain for the privilege of having his name mentioned in the Friday prayer in Mecca.[92] These very different cases thus present some of the many pitfalls and temptations that Muslim rulers may also find on their way, illustrating by doing so in again incongruous metaphorical ways a well-known wisdom about the many moral dangers involved in being a Muslim ruler in this world. This wisdom was actually expressed most explicitly in one of Hārūn's stories, about the mystic al-Fuḍayl b. ʿIyāḍ's advice to the caliph, such as in the following greeting: "Never have I seen anyone with a face more beautiful than yours; if you are able not to blacken this face with the heat from the fire [of Hell], then do so."[93]

Most selected stories thus contributed along a winding, kaleidoscopic road of didactic examples to making the very same moral point of what a good ruler should and should not do, with pilgrimage representing in this a secondary thematic tool only for selecting stories and for providing the kaleidoscope with some coherence. What that winding kaleidoscope moreover suggests—

---

92 See below, §§153, 211, 110.

93 See below, §107. See also Crone (1987): 172–173. For al-Maqrīzī's stance on such issues of rulership and social order, see also more in general Anne Broadbridge's extremely pertinent assessment that "indeed, al-Maqrīzī does demonstrate a marked interest in [...] the connections among royal authority, justice, and the maintenance of order in society. In al-Maqrīzī's hands, however, the concept is most frequently shown in reverse as the weakening of royal authority, the proliferation of injustice and the resultant spread of societal disorder." (Broadbridge [2003]: 236).

or at least what impression it produces—is that al-Maqrīzī presents history in *al-Ḏahab al-masbūk* not as a simple Whiggish and black-and-white process, but rather as developing along similarly winding roads, where being a ruler is serious business and hard work with limited hope for future reward and positive recompense. Rulers are then portrayed in stories and narratives alike not just as a human kind apart, but also as always qualified by the transcendent reality of divine sovereignty. Even they cannot escape their larger destiny, as suggested in several prophecy stories announcing the deaths of the caliphs ʿUmar and al-Manṣūr,[94] in the ways ʿAlī l-Ṣulayḥī and al-Masʿūd Yūsuf are presented as dying *en route* to or in Mecca, in the ways Nūr al-Dīn Maḥmūd and Tūrān Šāh are presented as passing away in peaceful circumstances after rich lives of conquest and warfare, and in the booklet's final line, where al-Ašraf Šaʿbān is made to leave the scene "killed by strangulation", a passage tellingly ending in the fatalist mode of divine providence with the well-known saying "God knows best".[95] This separate secondary theme of the absolute sovereignty of divine will finally certainly also explains the inclusion in the al-Manṣūr narrative of three stories about the caliph's encounters with the Medinese judge Muḥammad b. ʿImrān (fl. 2nd/8th c.), each illustrating rulers' absolute subordination to God's Law and its human agents, the *qāḍīs*.[96]

These universal themes of good Muslim rule and divine sovereignty are paired by at least three related but more particular moral themes, similarly communicated from the author via the agency of the text to his royal audiences. For a number of non-caliphal rulers, the author constructs his narrative so as to also make room for a conspicuous set of recurrent statements about the proper political relationship between Cairo and Yemen. This set of Cairo-Yemen statements begins in the narrative of ʿUmar al-Ṣulayḥī, who upon his conquest of Yemen is presented as "publicly proclaiming allegiance to the Imam al-Mustanṣir bi-llāh Abū Tamīm Maʿadd b. al-Ẓāhir b. al-Ḥākim, one of the Fāṭimid caliphs in Cairo".[97] It is continued in the narrative of Saladin's brother Tūrān Šāh, who "took control of the territories of Yemen, assumed

94 See below, §§ 25, 65–67.

95 See below, 116, 145, 123, 128, 222.

96 See below, §§ 68–70. This emphasis on "the ephemeral character of power and the [preeminence of] divine will which makes and destroys rulers, seemingly on a whim" appears also elsewhere in al-Maqrīzī's writings as a recurrent and powerful subtext (see Bauden [2014]: 184).

97 See below, § 113.

the honorific al-Malik al-Muʿaẓẓam and had the Friday sermon delivered in his own name, after [that of] the ʿAbbāsid caliph."[98] Then it moves to the narrative of Tūrān Šāh's nephew, al-Masʿūd Yūsuf, which explains that he was appointed by his father, the ruler of Egypt, over Yemen in 611/1214–1215, that "he occupied it and he acquired control over Tihāmah, Taʿizz, Sanaa and all the territories of Yemen", and that in 622/1225 he "left Nūr al-Dīn ʿUmar b. ʿAlī b. Rasūl al-Kurdī as his agent to govern it" when he travelled to Egypt.[99] This ʿUmar (d. 647/1249), the eponymous founder of the ruling dynasty of Yemen up to al-Maqrīzī's time, the Rasūlids (632–858/1235–1454), and two of his successors, his son al-Muẓaffar Yūsuf and a later descendant al-Muǧāhid ʿAlī, are then all accorded separate narratives. In each one, however, the same theme of Yemen's particular relationship with the sultan of Egypt returns. ʿUmar is presented as having "sent a precious gift to al-Malik al-Kāmil [in Egypt], saying 'I am the representative of the sultan over the lands'." Yūsuf "had the inside of the Kaʿbah covered with [a *kiswah*, which] continued to be present until in the year 761 [1360]", when it was replaced by that of the sultan of Cairo. And the Cairo-Yemen statements really culminated in the narrative of al-Muǧāhid ʿAlī, which explains that he was defeated by the sultan's agents in Mecca and that he was eventually brought to Cairo as the sultan's captive twice, each time to be scorned for his insubordination and to be reminded of his proper place in the sultan's shadow; this included that he was made "to kiss the ground before the sultan al-Malik al-Nāṣir Ḥasan b. Muḥammad b. Qalāwūn", that "he was chided and seriously reprimanded by the amirs", and that "he was obliged to annually transfer money [to the sultan], as was the habit".[100] Meanwhile, the same theme of Cairo's sovereignty over Yemen appeared in the narrative following that of al-Muẓaffar Yūsuf and dedicated to his Egyptian contemporary, sultan al-Ẓāhir Baybars, in the format of the story of a letter sent by Baybars reproaching Yūsuf for falling short of his leadership duties and urging him to follow in Baybars' pilgriming and warring footsteps:

> I have composed [this letter] from glorious Mecca, which I have travelled to in seventeen steps' […] 'the ruler is he who performs for God the duty of his *ǧihād*, and who exerts himself in defending the territory of Islam. If I were a ruler, I would go out and confront the Mongols![101]

98 See below, §125.

99 See below, §§141, 143.

100 See below, §§147, 161, 212–216.

101 See below, §175.

Egypt's sovereignty over Yemen (and thus also over other similar polities) emerges from all these story lines and recurrent statements not just as historically qualified since at least the early eleventh century, but also as morally defined, and therefore as the only proper way of cultivating the relationship between Cairo sultan and Rasūlid ruler into the early fifteenth century. In the al-Muẓaffar Yūsuf narrative this idea of Egypt's regional sovereignty is indeed brought up to al-Maqrīzī's own time, by the explanation that "the sermon [...] continued to be delivered from the *minbar* of Mecca in the name of the rulers of Yemen until our own days, [but then nowadays only] after the sermon [is delivered] in the name of the sultan of Egypt".[102]

It is al-Maqrīzī's construction of chapters rather than that of the *tarǧamah*-like narratives within them, however, that endowed the text with what may be considered its most particular, imminent, and programmatic meanings. It was already explained before that some of the most remarkable moments at the extremes of the text's two main chapters—the powerless caliph al-Ḥākim, the revolutionary ʿAlī l-Ṣulayḥī, and the doomed al-Ašraf Šaʿbān—bespeak the idea of a rise, decline, and fall, as manifested in the caliphal line, and then again in the non-caliphal line of Muslim rulers and their multiple engagements with pilgrimage. As suggested, the separate and very differently constructed prophetic chapter then reminds in many ways of the prevalent idea in Sunni Islam that the Prophet's example escapes from the particular historical logic of mankind and its rulers. Together with the other two chapters' internal logic of successive historical cycles of rise, decline, and fall a particular historical appeal is made by the author, not just to support a particular communal understanding of sacred history, but above all to promote a much more localised, political vision of past, present, and future. Against the background of the interlocking moralising themes of divine sovereignty, of the challenges of good Muslim rule, and of the realities of Egyptian sovereignty, the text was actually communicating in subtle and discursively grounded ways two powerful political ideas to its royal audiences that emerge in particular from situating their reproduction within the larger socio-cultural and ideological contexts that made them meaningful.

These ideas appear above all in the remarkable, anticlimactic, and therefore surprising ways by which chapters two and three end, with the defunct authority of the ʿAbbāsid caliph of Cairo, al-Ḥākim, and with the violent murder of sultan Šaʿbān in Ḏū l-Qaʿdah 778/March 1377 respectively. As mentioned before, the former issue of defunct caliphal authority was extended to al-

102 See below, §160.

Maqrīzī's own time at the very end of the al-Ḥākim narrative, and thus of the entire caliphal chapter, when the text explains not just that "until today" the authority of the ʿAbbāsid caliph of Cairo was never accepted in Mecca, but also that one exception to this general picture had to be made "for the caliph al-Mustaʿīn bi-llāh Abū l-Faḍl al-ʿAbbās b. Muḥammad, [in whose name the Meccan Friday sermon was delivered] for a few days in the year 815 [1412–1413]."[103] As was undoubtedly still fresh in the memories of al-Maqrīzī's readers it had not been al-Mustaʿīn's caliphal authority that had thus been acknowledged in 1412, but rather the authority of the sultanate of Cairo, which the caliph had briefly been made to occupy at that time, smoothening the disruptive and violent transition between the public execution of sultan al-Nāṣir Farağ (r. 801–815/1399–1412) and the accession of the emerging new strong man Šayḫ al-Maḥmūdī (r. 815–824/1412–1421). In this peculiar reference's closing combination with the cyclical nature of the caliphal chapter—including also al-Maqrīzī's explicit statement that the soundness of the lineage of al-Mustaʿīn's ancestor al-Ḥākim remained debated—the transition from the caliphate to non-caliphal rule is legitimated, not just in the author's construction of the text, but also in his consideration of Muslim history's moral order in general.[104] In fact, what al-Maqrīzī seems to suggest through the balanced double chapter structure of 13 caliphs and then 13 non-caliphal rulers is that as far as good Muslim rule is concerned the rulers of his days inhabit the same universe as the caliphs of old did. By taking this stance the author was actually tapping into a local ideological discourse on the relationship between caliphate and sultanate that remained much debated, that was highly accommodating to Syro-Egyptian political circumstances, and that had been promulgated most explicitly by towering scholars such as the early fourteenth-century Šāfiʿī chief judge Ibn Ğamāʿah (d. 733/1333) and al-Maqrīzī's own teacher Ibn Ḫaldūn (d. 808/1406).[105] Participants to this powerful discourse claimed that over time the divinely ordained political role of the caliphs to lead Muslims in accordance with God's will had indeed been taken over by other local rulers, or, as Ibn Ḫaldūn formulated it when discussing the conditions of the caliphate,

---

103 See below, § 110.

104 If Šayḫ was the text's original dedicatee, as was put forward as a hypothesis in the preceding chapter, it may even be read as also directly underscoring, via this set-up of its chapters, the particular transition from al-Mustaʿīn the caliph to Šayḫ the non-caliphal ruler in 815/1412.

105 For more details and relevant references, see especially Hirschler (2006): 109–113; "Khalīfa. (ii) in political theory", in *EI*[2] (http://referenceworks.brillonline.com/entries/encyclopaedia-of-islam-2/khalifa-COM_0486).

> we consider it a [necessary] condition for the person in charge of the affairs of the Muslims that he belong to the people who possess a strong group feeling, superior to that of their contemporaries, so that they can force the others to follow them and the whole thing can be united for effective protection. [...] Qurashite [= including ʿAbbāsid] [group feeling] was all-comprehensive, since the mission of Islam, which the Quraysh represented, was all-comprehensive, and the group feeling of the Arabs was adequate to that mission. Therefore, [the Arabs] overpowered all the other nations. At the present time, however, each nation has people of its own who represent the superior group feeling [there].[106]

This pragmatic idea of the demise of the caliphate and its replacement or absorption by more localised rulers such as the sultans of Cairo and, related to that, of the appropriation of local power itself as sufficient to provide legitimacy,[107] is then also clearly propagated through the general authorial construction of *al-Ḏahab al-masbūk* in three chapters that consider Prophet and caliphal and non-caliphal rulers on an equal footing of legitimate Muslim leadership.[108] It appears as an overarching organisational mechanism rather than as an explicitly formulated ideological stance, first and foremost, but it never-

106 Ibn Ḫaldūn, *al-Muqaddimah*, 1: 401 (Chapter III/24: 'The differences of Muslim opinion concerning the laws and conditions governing the caliphate').

107 For this particular phrasing, referring to Ibn Ǧamāʿah's ideas as formulated in his advice text *Taḥrīr al-aḥkām fī tadbīr ahl al-islām*, see Hirschler (2006): 111: "The sultan took the caliph's position, or, more precisely the sultanate absorbed the caliphate. The sultanate was now directly subordinate to God without the intermediary position of the caliph. Most importantly, Ibn Jamāʿa argued that the seizure of power itself was sufficient to detain legitimate authority."

108 The idea, dominant in Sunni circles of relevant scholarship, that any ruler, even an unjust one, is better than rebellion, discord, and *fitnah* in the community, may then also explain al-Maqrīzī's rather unproblematic inclusion in his list of legitimate Muslim rulers of some characters that were apparently lacking in proper Muslim conduct, such as al-Masʿūd Yūsuf (n° 5) (see Crone [2004]: 255–256). It needs to be noted here, however, that this sub-text of the legitimacy of post-caliphal rule in *al-Ḏahab al-masbūk* squarely contradicts Bauden's suggestion, derived from his preliminary study of the *al-Sulūk*, the *Imtāʿ al-asmāʿ* and *al-Ḫabar ʿan al-bašar*, that "it is also possible to infer here an expression of the wish that the Arabs should be the holders of power and that the caliph, who should come from the family of the Prophet (the Banū Hāshim), should regain his rightful power" (Bauden [2014]: 184); given the fact that the production of *al-Ḏahab al-masbūk* seems to predate these three works, this difference may well suggest that throughout the 1420s and '30s there occurred a radical shift in al-Maqrīzī's thinking about political legitimacy.

theless clearly positions the text within this particular political discourse that explained and underscored the Cairo sultanate and its political order from the perspective of its main religious communities.

Finally, this propagation of the end of the caliphate closing chapter two and, more generally again, the balanced cyclical chronological construction of both chapters suggest that the end of chapter three, with its rebellion against and murder of a Muslim ruler, is similarly pitched as the end of an era, and thus that the post-778/1377 time of writing *al-Ḏahab al-masbūk* belonged to another era at which a new cycle was unfolding. Of course, nowhere in the actual text is this idea really explicitly formulated, and it may even have been an unintentional consequence of the author's infusion of the text's many complex narratives with codified historical material. But this textual construction's coinciding with a turn of the century that was a time of personal, political, and socio-economic crises for the author and his audiences alike—as also reminded by the reference to al-Mustaʿīn's unorthodox tenure of the sultanate in 815/1412—at least suggests that the readership of *al-Ḏahab al-masbūk* may have been highly susceptible to ideas of causality through moral decay (that is, rebellion and murder in 778/1377), of restoration of good and legitimate Muslim rule, and of revival of Egyptian sovereignty that may also be read between the booklet's many lines.[109] In the specific context of the royal patronage relationship that the text mediated, generating that reversed hierarchy of the knowledgeable author and his susceptible audiences, it makes a lot of sense then to consider *al-Ḏahab al-masbūk* as participating not just in a more passive tradition of

109 These ideas of moral decay, its causality, and its resolution by the restoration of a traditional order certainly also emerge as important themes in some of al-Maqrīzī's other texts, such as in the *Iġāṯat al-ummah* (See Meloy [2003b]: 188–197), and in the ongoing project of his grand history of Egypt, the *Kitāb al-Sulūk*, where the account of the event that ended *al-Ḏahab al-masbūk*, the murder of al-Ašraf Šaʿbān, was actually concluded with a remarkable personal comment that reveals how al-Maqrīzī indeed considered this a matrix moment in recent social and political history, a beginning of the end, related to the collapse of proper social order and political hierarchy that followed from the sudden collapse of al-Ašraf Šaʿbān's rule: "There occurred a rise of the lowest (*irtifāʿ al-asāfil*) which was such that there is a lesson to be learned from it for those who care to contemplate such matters (*mā fīhi ʿibrah li-man iʿtabara*). The junior *mamlūk*s (*al-mamālīk al-aǧlāb*), who only yesterday had been too trivial to be noticed (*aqall al-maḏkūr*), but [who] then pursued a path of murder, eviction, and all kinds of torture, became rulers (*mulūk*) for whom the fruits from everything were collected and who reigned over the realms of the land as they saw fit. From then onwards, the region's situation changed because of its people's transformation (*wa-min ḥīna'iḏ taġayyarat aḥwāl al-bilād bi-taġayyur ahlihā*)" (al-Maqrīzī, *al-Sulūk*, 3:289).

history-writing to explain a political present, but also in another ancient literary tradition of pursuing an impact in that political present by offering advice to the ruler.[110]

The themes of legitimate and good Muslim rule in general and of the Egyptian sultanate's supremacy in particular, set within a wider theme of acknowledging divine sovereignty, certainly obtain a coherence, relevance, and deeper meaning when viewed from this contextualised 'advice-to-rulers' perspective. The cure that al-Maqrīzī then suggests to his readership to overcome their present predicaments is that of a moral political programme of connecting again with the line that had begun with the Prophet, that had been furthered by the caliphs first and then, for better or worse, by a series of non-caliphal rulers, and that had materialised in—among many other things—their continued physical and symbolic leadership of the pilgrimage to Mecca.[111] In the text, this historical line actually culminated in the reign and political morality of the sultans of Cairo, a process that, as mentioned above, was already announced in the first prophetic chapter's sudden ending with an explicit reference to sultan Baybars stepping in the Prophet's foundational footsteps. There is then a complexity of meanings that are reproduced and communicated by *al-Ḏahab al-masbūk*, some undoubtedly more intentionally constructed by its author than others, and some more readily acceptable to its audiences than others. But they all seem to converge in these prophetic footsteps, or perhaps even more in the vexed political road of legitimate, sovereign, and good Muslim leadership along which these prophetic footsteps were meant to be leading.

110 For a parallel interpretation of al-Maqrīzī's *Iġāṯat al-ummah* and his *Šuḏūr al-ʿuqūd* as advice-for-rulers texts, see Meloy (2003b): 186–187, and Broadbridge (2003): 238–239. This would also help to explain the afore-mentioned textual relationship that is suggested by *al-Ḏahab al-masbūk's* title with advice texts attributed to Ibn al-Ǧawzī and to al-Ġazālī.

111 *Al-Ḏahab al-masbūk* actually communicates, seen from this advisory perspective, a politico-religious programme that nicely pairs with and complements the economic agenda of similarly constructed texts such as the *Iġāṯat al-ummah* and, especially, the potentially more contemporary *Shuḏūr al-ʿuqūd*, summarised by John Meloy as follows: "For al-Maqrīzī, sound economics then was based on the excellences of predecessors, which required a review of previous monetary exempla. By using the notion of such *faḍāʾil* to present his case, al-Maqrīzī in effect composed in the *Shudhūr* a monetary mirror for princes. As with the other branches of Islamic statecraft, such knowledge required a grounding in the excellent examples of predecessors. History in the *Shudhūr* comes across clearly as a didactic subject and its role here was to provide advice for sound economic policy." (Meloy [2003b]: 197–198).

CHAPTER 3

Production, Reproduction, and Consumption: *al-Ḏahab al-masbūk*'s Life and Times (Fifteenth – Twentieth Centuries)

Al-Ḏahab al-masbūk is an extremely complex text, made up of many layers that were not just defined by its internal construction and meanings but also by its social history as a cultural product that went through many different hands, from its author's and copyists' to its readers' and users'. It is in this materiality of production, reproduction, and consumption that the intricate textual structures and semiotics of *al-Ḏahab al-masbūk* and the rich socio-cultural contexts within which it existed connected, interacted, and engaged with each other. It is there that a text such as *al-Ḏahab al-masbūk* acquired, and re-acquired time and again, its value and that it lived its complex social life, from its inception in the fifteenth century until its study, re-edition, and translation some six centuries later.

1 Producing *al-Ḏahab al-masbūk* (821–841/1418–1438)

Some scholars, such as the booklet's first modern editor Ǧamāl al-Dīn al-Šayyāl and then also its more recent editor Karam Ḥilmī Faraḥāt, claimed that *al-Ḏahab al-masbūk* was written in Ḏū l-Qaʿdah 841/May 1438.[1] As explained before, this assumption is actually the result of a misinterpretation of the reference to this date in the colophons of the two oldest extant manuscript versions of the text. In MS Escorial árabe 1771 (E)—a codex dated to the sixteenth century and containing a copy of two of al-Maqrīzī's shorter treatises (see below)—the colophon on fol. 75[b] explains that this copy

> "was written down from an original [that was] handwritten by its composer; its author—may God have mercy upon him—said:

1 Al-Šayyāl (1955): 24–26; Id. (2000): 25–27; Faraḥāt (2009): 27–29. See also al-Šayyāl (1971): 27; *GAL*, 2:50.

> It was corrected by me—its author Aḥmad b. ʿAlī al-Maqrīzī—to the best of [my] abilities, so that it is correct, in Ḏū l-Qaʿdah of the year 841"
>
> *Kutiba min aṣl bi-ḫaṭṭ muṣannifihi qāla muʾallifuhu raḥimahu llāh ḥarrartuhu ǧuhd al-qudrah fa-ṣaḥḥa muʾallifuhu Aḥmad b. ʿAlī l-Maqrīzī fī Ḏī l-Qaʿdah sanat 841.*[2]

In MS Leiden Universiteitsbibliotheek Or. 560 (L)—a fifteenth-century codex mainly containing twenty shorter texts and notes on a variety of subjects by al-Maqrīzī (see below)—the colophon on fol. 135^r similarly states that

> "It was corrected to the best of [his] abilities by its author Aḥmad b. ʿAlī l-Maqrīzī, so that it is correct, in Ḏū l-Qaʿdah of the year 841"
>
> *Ḥarrarahu ǧuhd al-qudrah fa-ṣaḥḥa muʾallifuhu Aḥmad b. ʿAlī l-Maqrīzī fī Ḏī l-Qaʿdah sanat 841.*[3]

These colophons—added in the latter case by al-Maqrīzī himself—clearly suggest that L was actually the "original [that was] handwritten by its composer" in 841/1438 from which E was then copied about a century or more later. Just as several colophons of other texts in L (and various other features) equally explain (see below), these colophons confirm above all the key status of L as an autograph manuscript for the text of *al-Ḏahab al-masbūk*, created by a professional copyist who had probably been hired for the task by al-Maqrīzī, and copy-edited in Ḏū l-Qaʿdah 841/May 1438 by the author himself. What these colophons finally also clarify, however, is that there must have been an earlier holograph draft of the text of *al-Ḏahab al-masbūk* for the copyist to produce his copy from and for al-Maqrīzī to collate that copy with. As the author complained in another colophon elsewhere in the manuscript, the copying of this and of all other texts in this codex turned out to have been poorly done, requiring a lot of editorial work, which in different colophons and revision notes al-Maqrīzī explicitly claimed to have carried out between Ramaḍān 841/February–March 1438 and Muḥarram 842/June–July 1438. As suggested before, the date of Ḏū l-Qaʿdah 841/May 1438 can therefore have been no more than a *terminus ante quem* for the actual production of the text of *al-Ḏahab*

---

2 Ms. Escorial árabe 1771, fol. 75^b.

3 Ms. Leiden Universiteitsbibliotheek Or. 560, fol. 135^a.

al-masbūk and for its draft from which the copy in L was produced in particular. It has furthermore been suggested that the copyist of L did his work some time earlier, between al-Maqrīzī's known completion in the course of the second half of the year 840/the first half of 1437 of another text that was copied into L, and the start of his editorial activities in Ramaḍān 841/February–March 1438. The *terminus ante quem* for the production of this now lost holograph draft of *al-Ḏahab al-masbūk* should therefore be slightly moved further back in time, to the beginning of 841/mid-1437, when the copying of L seems to have started, at the very latest.[4]

In the preceding chapters of this study I developed the argument that al-Maqrīzī actually may have produced a first version of the text of *al-Ḏahab al-masbūk* already in 821/1418, when the sultan al-Mu'ayyad Šayḫ intended to perform the pilgrimage and when the complex construction of the text around the theme of legitimate, sovereign, and good Muslim leadership made a lot of sense. The premature abortion of the sultan's pilgrimage plans may have resulted in the parallel abortion of al-Maqrīzī's plans, leaving the text at the draft stage of its production. This may then have been the same holograph draft that was eventually brought to some proper use when al-Maqrīzī in the early 840s/the second half of the 1430s decided that there were good reasons to collect and publish in one single codex most of the shorter literary works that he had written in the course of the 810s/1410s, '20s and '30s.

It can however also be suggested that before this reproduction in L the history of *al-Ḏahab al-masbūk* may have been a bit more complex than that. Dedicated to a ruler such as, perhaps, sultan al-Mu'ayyad Šayḫ, with powerful didactic and moral as well as very personal socio-cultural objectives in mind, the titles and epithets that were explicitly used in the introduction to identify

4 A similar suggestion for the staged production process of another one of the different texts in L has recently been formulated by Fabian Käs (al-Maqrīzī, *al-Maqāṣid al-saniyyah*, 4, 7; referring also to Dozy [1847–1851]: 17–27, esp. 18); the suggestion of the author's production of a pre-publication draft copy conforms also with al-Maqrīzī's general working method as that has been reconstructed by Frédéric Bauden (Bauden [2008]). L is described and analysed in the fullest detail in Bauden [2017] (I am grateful to F. Bauden for providing me with a draft copy of relevant parts of this forthcoming publication); the codicological presentation and analysis in the current volume of the *Bibliotheca maqriziana* will therefore remain limited to a minimum that is relevant for the present study, as informed by Bauden's study. For the suggested dating of the copying and correction of L, see Bauden (who demonstrates that the copyist had a draft of all of al-Maqrīzī's texts available when he started his copying work) and al-Maqrīzī, *Ḍaw' al-sārī*, 38–39, 47–49 (where it is demonstrated by Frenkel that the work on *Ḍaw' al-sārī li-maʿrifat ḫabar Tamīm al-Dārī* must have started in Raǧab 840/January 1437).

the dedicatee as a patron and the text as a mediator in a particular author-patron relationship stand out as remarkably generic. "The noble lord" (*al-maqarr al-maḫdūm*), "the high-born intention" (*al-ʿazm al-šarīf*), and their like appear as surprisingly neutral signifiers of intended audience for a text that is otherwise extremely explicit in very subtle ways about any other aspect of the communicative relationship that it was meant to mediate. In line with a wider literary practice to functionally adjust dedications in the reproduction of texts, it may therefore well be that the draft that was used to copy L from was only a neutralised later version of the original 821/1418 draft. In the latter, original draft the dedicatee would have been explicitly identified in a full and flowery style that was the only correct way to represent a sultan's high social status as well as the hierarchical relationship between such a patron and the text's author. At some point between 821/1418 and the late 840s/mid-1430s—perhaps even, as suggested above, at the occasion of the pilgrimage in 834/1431 of sultan al-Ašraf Barsbāy's wife Ǧulbān al-Hindī and her family—a new, more generic version of the text must then have been produced by al-Maqrīzī. In this hypothetical textual scenario, the revision of at least parts of the introduction actually redirected the text and its meanings from the very particular context and relationships of 821/1418 to a more general—or certainly more flexible and accommodating to ever changing circumstances—level of communication, performance, and author-audience interaction. This transformation also made the text of *al-Ḏahab al-masbūk* more fit for wider publication, as seems to have been the intention when this allegedly second version of the text became the draft from which the copy in L was made.[5]

Manuscript L, produced between early 841/mid-1437 and early 842/mid-1438 by an anonymous copyist and then by Aḥmad b. ʿAlī l-Maqrīzī himself, consists of a codex with 205 leaves of oriental laid paper. It entered the library of Leiden University already in 1668, as part of a uniquely rich collection

5 This practice of producing two versions of a text, one explicitly dedicated and the other rewritten in more generic and publishable terms, has been identified as a common socio-literary tradition by Thomas Bauer (Bauer [2013a]: 26–29.) For the particular case of al-Maqrīzī's texts and their reproduction in 841/1438, John Meloy also notes similar corrections to the introduction of the text of the *Šuḏūr al-ʿuqūd* (Meloy [2003b]: 197, fn. 54: "Note that some of the manuscripts of the *Šuḏūr* include the name of al-Mu'ayyad Shaykh: 'Inspire our master the sultan [al-Mu'ayyad Šayḫ] with the …,' while others simply state 'the sultan'. But there is ambiguity to the imperative appeals to 'Our master the sultan,' which suggests that perhaps al-Maqrīzī's corrections to the text in Ramaḍān 841 [February–March 1438] eliminated these so that the text could be used as an appeal to Barsbāy's successor. Barsbāy fell ill in Šaʿbān 841 and died by the end of the year.").

of Oriental manuscripts bequeathed to his *alma mater* by a Dutch scholar, merchant, and diplomat to the sultan of Istanbul, Levinus Warner (1619–1665). Nothing much seems to be known of the manuscript's whereabouts between the mid-fifteenth and the mid-seventeenth centuries. Most of the different texts in L, including *al-Ḏahab al-masbūk*, were copied in the same clear and legible *nasḫ* handwriting, using the same creamy paper, text frame, *misṭarah* or ruling board of 25 lines per page, black carbon ink, and red ink for specific text markers. The current binding of the text is a European one, done after the arrival of the manuscript in Leiden. It has been demonstrated that in the course of this (or an earlier) binding a rearrangement of the different texts of the manuscript occurred, for unknown reasons. The copied text of *al-Ḏahab al-masbūk*, occupying 34 pages (fol. 115[b]–135[a], minus fols. 122, 123, 126 [see below]), therefore is currently number fourteen of the collection, whereas originally it had been copied by the copyist as one of the last texts of the codex. In both bindings it immediately follows al-Maqrīzī's treatise on the family of the Prophet, *Maʿrifat mā yağib li-āl al-bayt min al-ḥaqq*, and in the original set up it was followed by al-Maqrīzī's history of the Kaʿbah, *al-Išārah wa-l-iʿlām bi-bināʾ al-kaʿbah al-bayt al-ḥarām*. In the current binding the first page of *al-Ḏahab al-masbūk* is on the verso of the last leaf of the preceding text, the *Maʿrifat* (fol. 115). The verso of the final leaf of *al-Ḏahab al-masbūk* itself was left blank. The latter physically separating arrangement of beginning a new text's copy on a new separate leaf actually seems to have been the copyist's standard practice, and *al-Ḏahab al-masbūk*'s copy starting on another text's verso really stands out as unusual in the manuscript. The reason for this is that when correcting the preceding text of the *Maʿrifat* al-Maqrīzī decided to make substantial final additions, for which he eventually also had to use a slip of paper that was inserted after fol. 114 in the manuscript, and that was eventually pasted on the recto of fol. 115. Originally, however, this fol. 115 had indeed been reserved for copying *al-Ḏahab al-masbūk* only.[6]

These general features of the copyist's writing practices, as applied between mid-840/early 1437 and mid-841/early 1438, created a physically coherent, uniform, and polished outlook for these copies of al-Maqrīzī's different texts throughout this single codex. All that was left for the author himself to do was to complete the titles of some texts, to emend any inevitable copying errors, and to add colophons and correction notes confirming and closing this process of careful and authoritative preparation for publication. This was all

6 For this codicological information and for further detailed analyses and discussions, see Bauden (2017).

done by al-Maqrīzī between Ramaḍān 841/February–March 1438 and Muḥarram 842/June–July 1438, the chronological order of his authorial proofreading as documented in the different colophons diligently following the original arrangement of text copies in L. The copy of *al-Ḏahab al-masbūk* was thus identified as one of the five text copies in L that were collated and re-appropriated by their author in Ḏū l-Qaʿdah 841/April–May 1438. However, as just explained, the recto of this particular copy's first leaf, which in the case of other texts in L was consistently used for the addition of title and authorship details, is no longer visible. Another later user or owner (perhaps Muḥammad al-Muẓaffarī, one of L's first owners after al-Maqrīzī, according to a note on L's title page) therefore briefly added details of title and author on the text's actual first page, currently fol. 115ᵇ, above the first line of the *misṭarah*.[7] As in many other copies, on this first line, left blank on purpose by the copyist, a typical opening *basmalah* invocation was added in a carefully executed, ornate, and vowelled version of al-Maqrīzī's own peculiar handwriting ("In the name of God, the Merciful, the Compassionate. My Lord, ease [my task], o Noble One"). Just as in the other copies of texts in L al-Maqrīzī then also collated the copyist's version of the text of *al-Ḏahab al-masbūk*, making more than 200 textual corrections and providing more than 100 additions of words or phrases, in both cases apparently making up for at least part of the copy's large number of scribal errors, omissions, or inaccuracies. As detailed above an appropriate authorial colophon was eventually also added at the end of the text, on the last line of the *misṭarah* of fol. 135ʳ—again left blank on purpose by the copyist—, explaining to anyone consulting L the particular status of this copy, as corrected and authenticated by its author.

As a collection of at least sixteen of al-Maqrīzī's texts, all made uniform, polished, and upgraded, L was thus fully prepared and finalised by the author for disclosure to a wider readership in early 842/the summer of 1438. This entire

7 In the introduction of the text of *al-Ḏahab al-masbūk* al-Maqrīzī only identifies this text with the short title of *al-Ḏahab al-masbūk* ("I entitled it 'The Moulded Gold' […]", see below, § 4, L fol. 115ᵇ), rather than with the longer twofold title that was added to the top of fol. 115ᵇ of L ('The Gold Moulded in the Format of the Report of Those Caliphs and Kings Who Performed the *Ḥağğ*'), that made its appearance in this same passage in the introduction in later manuscript copies of the text ("I entitled it 'The Gold Moulded in the Format of the Report of Those Caliphs and Kings Who Performed the *Ḥağğ*", see e.g. Y fol. 27ᵃ), and by which the text is generally known today. It remains therefore unclear to what extent *al-Ḏahab al-masbūk fī ḏikr man ḥağğa min al-ḫulafāʾ wa-l-mulūk* was indeed the title that al-Maqrīzī had intended for this text (see also chapter 2, fn. 13, for different references to this text's title from the fifteenth century onwards).

complex process of many months of copying and editing therefore indeed cannot have been anything less than the carefully planned publication by the author of a consciously constructed, unified collection of a range of different shorter texts of his. In this publication project, however, the forms, functions, and meanings of these individual texts—including those of *al-Ḏahab al-masbūk*—were radically re-imagined and re-directed from the varied particular contexts, which had defined the production of each, to a very different setting, in which it was their combination and relative arrangement rather than their particularity that was considered most meaningful by al-Maqrīzī. Those transformed forms, functions, and meanings that made for L transcend the particularity of any of these individual texts, including that of *al-Ḏahab al-masbūk*, and can therefore only be accounted for in their joint study as full and complementary partners in the particular communicative act that, in early 842/the summer of 1438, gave shape to L.[8]

L, however, does not just consist of 205 leaves with clearly produced and critically annotated text. Fifteen slips of paper of different sizes, types, and qualities were also inserted at various locations throughout the manuscript. They all bear varying numbers of irregular lines of text, and they were all written—or rather scribbled—in black ink in al-Maqrīzī's own cursive and difficult to read handwriting. These inserts all contain additions by al-Maqrīzī that were apparently too large or too extensive to be put in the margins of the copyist's text. In the case of the copy of *al-Ḏahab al-masbūk* three inserts were added by al-Maqrīzī (fols. 122, 123, and 126), leaving reference marks (*signes-de-renvoi*) in the text at the exact places where these inserted texts should be added. At some point in the history of L—most probably at the moment of rebinding—these three inserts were actually misplaced so that the connection between them and the original copy was lost.[9] Most importantly, it remains unclear whether these inserts were produced during al-Maqrīzī's revision work between Ramaḍān 841/February–March 1438 and Muḥarram 842/June–July 1438 or whether they were later additions.[10] Whatever may have been the case, the three inserts (fols. 122, 123, 126) that he added in L to this copy of the text

---

8 For further detailed analyses and discussions, see Bauden (2017). For the original list and arrangement of al-Maqrīzī's opuscula, and for the chronology of his work on L, see also al-Maqrīzī, *al-Maqāṣid al-saniyyah*, 8–9.

9 The text of 19 and 13 lines on fol. 126 is an addition that was marked for insertion in the copy on fol. 121[b]; the proper order of fols. 122 and 123 was even reversed and their text, starting on fol. 123[b] and ending on fol. 122[a] and written in 16, 15, 16, and 10 lines respectively, was marked for insertion on fol. 125[b].

10 For further detailed analyses and discussion of these inserts, see Bauden (2017).

of *al-Ḏahab al-masbūk* were definitely more than mere authorial emendations in the proofreading process. To a certain extent these notes actually produced a new version of that same text that al-Maqrīzī may have first written in very different circumstances twenty years earlier, that in the same scenario must have been revised a first time before early 841/mid-1437, and that had been meant to be finally published as part of this larger collection in early 842/mid-1438. These inserted notes now added a handful of new stories to the original text, suggesting indeed that they were most probably only inserted some time after al-Maqrīzī's collation of the copy with his draft of *al-Ḏahab al-masbūk* in Ḏū l-Qaʿdah 841/May 1438. They seem to confirm also that by that later time L indeed continued in its entirety to be revised by him, as though a work-in-progress consisting of this unique selection, combination, and collection of his texts, to which notes from various sources could still be added.

In the case of *al-Ḏahab al-masbūk*, such notes were added at the end of two caliphal narratives, the one of al-Manṣūr and the other of al-Rašīd. Both narratives had been brought to a perfect structural close in the earlier draft, ending with the story of the death and burial of al-Manṣūr *en route* to Mecca and with the story of the mythical riches and benevolence of al-Rašīd after that of his last pilgrimage, respectively. In the latter case, apart from inserting a reference mark al-Maqrīzī made no real attempt at creating any explicit structural connection between this old text and the new addition. He simply began the added text on the insert with the statement that "among the qualities (*faḍāʾil*) of al-Rašīd, there was what the great transmitter Abū Nuʿaym selected in the *Kitāb al-Ḥilyah*." This introduction of the nature and source of this piece of text was then followed by a word-by-word reproduction of two versions of the same story from Abū Nuʿaym al-Iṣfahānī's work. In the former case of the al-Manṣūr narrative, a more explicit connection was made, at least physically, when the last line of the original version of the narrative was erased and replaced by a new line of text in al-Maqrīzī's own handwriting, making an introductory statement similar to the one for al-Rašīd that "among the unusual things (*badīʿ*) that were told about him, [there was the following:] When he had performed the pilgrimage and was about to reach the Prophet's Medina". This introduction and first line of the newly inserted text was then again followed by a mark referring to the inserted slip, where the text simply continues with three stories about the caliph's encounters with the Medinan judge Muḥammad b. ʿImrān.[11]

---

11 See below §§ 68–70, 97–107 for these passages in the text, and fols. 121^{b} + 126 (al-Manṣūr) and fols. 125^{a} + 123–122 (al-Rašīd) of L.

To sum up, the argument about the production history of *al-Ḏahab al-masbūk* that has been developed here on the basis of material remains, textual and paratextual characteristics, and historical contexts suggests that al-Maqrīzī produced at least three different versions of his text: one in 821/1418, a second one before early 841/mid-1437, and the third one after early 842/mid-1438. It also suggests that at least on two occasions, in 821/1418 and in 841–842/1438, al-Maqrīzī saw good reason to try and publish a final, polished version of the text. It is finally also argued that the 841–842/1438 publication project substantially changed *al-Ḏahab al-masbūk*'s function and meaning due to that project's ambitious nature of collecting and combining more than a dozen different texts in one coherent whole, perhaps meant above all to transmit as well as to speak of al-Maqrīzī's achievements after a lifelong career of scholarship.

L undoubtedly represents an important if not crucial material node in this complex web of versions, drafts, and publication projects. It began its life as the object of al-Maqrīzī's ambitious publication project in the final months of sultan Barsbāy's reign, and it contains as a consequence an emended and authenticated copy of the second version of *al-Ḏahab al-masbūk*. But it soon transformed again when the author continued to make revisions, so that it also contains yet another version of the text of *al-Ḏahab al-masbūk*, and perhaps even of some of the other texts too. The latter fact of al-Maqrīzī's continued work on different texts in L (with a potentially negative impact on the legibility of the text, as appears from the eventually wrong arrangements of the three inserts in this copy of *al-Ḏahab al-masbūk*) suggests that between mid-842/late 1438 and his death about three years later, in Ramaḍān 845/February 1442, the possibility should not be ruled out that the publication of another fine version of this collection of texts was at least considered. It may of course well be that the changed arrangement of texts in later manuscript versions of this collection no longer had anything to do with al-Maqrīzī's editorial work. It may also well be that the faithful and correct reproduction of the very latest version of the text of *al-Ḏahab al-masbūk*—including, without any notice and in their proper place, the texts from the three inserts—in each one of these later manuscripts was entirely due to later scribes' diligent and careful copying from L. But it is certainly also possible that that changed arrangement and correct and full reproduction sprang from a final published and now lost version of the collection that was made from the revised L shortly before al-Maqrīzī's death.[12]

12 A similar possibility of the author's drafting of a final post-L version is briefly referred to as an equally hypothetical option for al-Maqrīzī's *al-Maqāṣid al-saniyyah* by Käs ("unklar ob weitere Korrektur je durchgeführt—keine Belege") (al-Maqrīzī, *al-Maqāṣid al-saniyyah*, 6).

2 Reproducing *al-Ḏahab al-masbūk* (Sixteenth – Twentieth Centuries)

Al-Maqrīzī's conscious production of L in the course of 841/1437–1438 and beyond created a different, new work of literature in his scholarly portfolio, which would prove much larger than the sum of its individual constituents. At least as far as the text of *al-Ḏahab al-masbūk* is concerned, the importance of this transformation is suggested by the fact that no separate copies of it have been preserved. In the manuscript reproduction of al-Maqrīzī's work texts such as this one were mainly considered relevant, interesting, or meaningful in their combination with other shorter texts by the same author, in the tradition that was established by al-Maqrīzī himself with his production of L. It is therefore only in the comprehensive study of these different extant collections of al-Maqrīzī's shorter texts that that history of textual reproduction, stretching between the sixteenth and nineteenth centuries, can be fully accounted for. This study's necessary focus on the manuscript reproduction of one of these texts only, *al-Ḏahab al-masbūk*, is by default distorted, can only purport to contribute to lifting a small tip of a much larger and far more complex veil, and will as a result be of a restricted nature only.[13]

Today there are—apart from L—nine more extant and known manuscripts that have preserved a copy of the text of *al-Ḏahab al-masbūk* in their collection of al-Maqrīzī's shorter texts.[14] Three of these are fragmentary remnants of such collections, having preserved in their current status two or three of such texts only. The others all tend to follow more or less, with recurrent exceptions, the selection of texts that was already made in L, even though none adopted these texts' original arrangement from L. A collation of the different copies of *al-Ḏahab al-masbūk* in these manuscripts enables the preliminary reconstruction of a rudimentary *stemma codicum* that—with the caveat of distorting partiality—will be presented below. But first, the material and paratextual features of these different manuscripts and of *al-Ḏahab al-masbūk*'s copies in them will be briefly introduced in a chronological description.[15]

---

13 For this history of manuscript reproduction from the only correct and full perspective of L, see Bauden (2017).

14 This full set of manuscripts containing a copy of *al-Ḏahab al-masbūk* has been identified by the editor of the series *Bibliotheca maqriziana*, Frédéric Bauden; I am grateful to him for sharing this information with me and for providing me with a high-resolution digital copy for each of these manuscripts.

15 For further details and references, see Bauden (2017); unless otherwise stated the information in this entire section has been taken from Bauden.

a *Madrid/San Lorenzo de el Escorial, Real Biblioteca del Monasterio, MS Árabe 1771, fols. 22ᵇ–75ᵇ [E] (Sixteenth Century?) Plates 1–2*

E is a codex of 76 paper leaves, containing a copy of two of al-Maqrīzī's shorter texts: *Šuḏūr al-ʿuqūd fī ḏikr al-nuqūd* and *al-Ḏahab al-masbūk*. The texts are written in a careful *nasḫ* by the same hand throughout the manuscript, applying a *misṭarah* of 15 lines on each page. The copy of *al-Ḏahab al-masbūk* begins on the verso of fol. 22 and is reproduced on 53 leaves. These have no marginal notes, corrections, or any other addenda, apart from three cases only where words were added or completed that fell outside of the text frame (fols. 24ᵃ, 36ᵃ). The entire copy successfully and faithfully integrates into the text all the marginal, interlinear, and inserted corrections and additions that al-Maqrīzī had made in L. A full title page on fol. 2ʳ introduces the first text, but this is not the case for the text of *al-Ḏahab al-masbūk*, which is only introduced by its title and by a brief reference to its author (*li-l-Maqrīzī*) on the first four lines of the *misṭarah* of its first page (fol. 22ᵇ, plate 1). As explained above, a scribal colophon (fol. 75ᵇ) explicitly identifies this manuscript as a direct copy from the text of *al-Ḏahab al-masbūk* in L, the authorial colophon of which was copied into this scribal colophon; it does not however provide any details about E's own origins (plate 2).

As a result of these characteristics the fragmentary manuscript E turns out to contain a very fair copy of *al-Ḏahab al-masbūk*, which very closely resembles what that copy should have looked like in a final re-published version of L's collection of texts. Unfortunately, however, very little is known about E's own history. Fol. 1ʳ contains several different Arabic and Persian notes, but they appear as aphorisms rather than as any more revealing statements. Another note added to the left top corner of fol. 2ʳ is more useful as it makes the following statement in clear Maghribi script:

> Glory to God.
>
> It was in the possession of the servant of God the Exalted, Zaydān, the Commander of the Faithful,
>
> son of Aḥmad al-Manṣūr, the Commander of the Faithful, al-Ḥasanī, may God grant him long life.
>
> *al-ḥamd li-llāh*
>
> *tamallakahu ʿabd Allāh taʿālá Zaydān amīr al-muʾminīn*
>
> *Ibn Aḥmad al-Manṣūr amīr al-muʾminīn al-Ḥasanī ḫallada llāh lahu*

Mawlāy Zaydān al-Ḥasanī (r. 1016–1036/1608–1627) was a member of the Saʿdians, a Sharifian dynasty that ruled as sultans of Morocco from 961/1554 to c. 1070/1659. His ownership mark places E in early-seventeenth century Morocco, while the Arabic and Persian notes in Oriental scripts suggest that the manuscript had had a life in the East before arriving in Morocco. E was therefore most probably produced in the course of the sixteenth century, if not before. It undoubtedly ended up in Spain in the course of 1021/1612 already, as part of the 73 boxes of Arabic books that Zaydān is said to have sent ahead when he tried to leave Morocco in the face of rebellion and that were declared war-booty when intercepted by the Spanish.[16]

b *New Haven, Yale University, Beinecke Rare Book and Manuscript Library, MS Landberg 111, fols. 26ᵃ–62ᵇ [Y] (1018/1609) (Plates 3–5)*

Y is a codex of 108 paper leaves, containing a copy of three of al-Maqrīzī's shorter texts: *Ḍaw' al-sārī li-maʿrifat ḫabar Tamīm al-Dārī*, *al-Ḏahab al-masbūk* and *al-Nizāʿ wa-l-taḫāṣum fīmā bayna Banī Umayyah wa-Banī Hāšim*. The text is written by the same hand throughout the manuscript, in what has been defined as a scholar's *nasḫ*, making consistent use of a *misṭarah* of 19 lines. The copy of *al-Ḏahab al-masbūk* begins on the recto of fol. 26 and it was reproduced on 39 paper leaves, 37 of which are still extant and in fairly good condition (there are two lacunae of one leaf between fols. 41–42 and 61–62). Again there are no marginal notes, corrections, or any other addenda in this copy of the text, apart from the different subtitles that were repeated by the copyist in the margins for easy reference, and apart from different notes and scribbles that were added by the manuscript's late-nineteenth-century owner. Apart from the introduction of a number of scribal errors (see below) the entire copy again stands for a rather faithful representation of al-Maqrīzī's last known version of the text. Y has furthermore preserved the first extant copy of a proper title page introducing the text of *al-Ḏahab al-masbūk* (fol. 26ᵃ) (but unusually omitting the author's *ism* and *nasab*, only naming him as "Taqī l-Dīn al-Maqrīzī l-Šāfiʿī") (plate 3). A scribal colophon (fol. 62ᵇ) clarifies that this was actually one of five copies that had so far been made of this text by one and the same scribe, ʿAlī b. Muḥammad al-Mallāḥ, and that this one was done on 5 Ǧumādá II 1018/5 September 1609 (plate 5).[17]

---

16 "Saʿdids", in *EI*² (http://referenceworks.brillonline.com/entries/encyclopaedia-of-islam-2/sadids-SIM_6417).

17 Perhaps there is a direct link between this early-seventeenth-century reference to five copies being made of the text, and the afore-mentioned puzzling note in the entry for *al-*

This reproduction of *al-Ḏahab al-masbūk* again very closely resembles what the text should have looked like in a final re-published version of L's collection. It has indeed been established that the fragmentary Y with its three texts originally had been part of such a larger codex containing al-Maqrīzī's texts, all produced by al-Mallāḥ in 1018/1609. Parallel scribal references in the colophons of the other extant text copies as well as one other remaining fragmentary manuscript (Leiden, Universiteitsbibliotheek, MS Or. 3019, dated 20 Shawwāl 1017/27 January 1609 and explicitly identified in its colophon as "the fourth copy" prepared by ʿAlī b. Muḥammad al-Mallāḥ) confirm that Y was part of the fifth copy in a series of at least five full copies that had all been prepared by the same copyist. The colophon of the *Ḍawʾ al-sārī* on Y's fol. 25[b] even claims that the copying of this and the other texts had happened from "a copy that has been emended in the author's handwriting (*nusḫah muṣaḥḥaḥah bi-ḫaṭṭ muʾallifihā*)". Al-Mallāḥ's early-seventeenth-century reproductions of al-Maqrīzī's collection of shorter works, including *al-Ḏahab al-masbūk*, thus claimed an authoritative status that paralleled that of the copy to which E had once belonged. The son of this scribal entrepreneur, Yūsuf b. ʿAlī b. Muḥammad al-Mallāḥ, is furthermore identified by Bauden as the scribe of another fragment of al-Maqrīzī's work (Riyadh, Maktabat Ǧāmiʿat al-Malik Saʿūd, MS 2170). This manuscript's colophon states that it was produced at about the same time as his father's fifth copy (15 Ǧumādá I 1018/16 August 1609). This fragment then was presumably also part of yet another copy of al-Maqrīzī's collection that was produced by Yūsuf in circumstances very similar to those defining his father's copies, suggesting that there may even have been more copies that were made at that time. The first decade of the seventeenth century and father and son al-Mallāḥ thus represent an important moment in the history of the reproduction of al-Maqrīzī's collection, from which obviously also the reproduction of *al-Ḏahab al-masbūk* benefited.

c *Istanbul, Atıf Efendi Kütüphanesi, MS 2814, fols. 84[a]–107[a] [Ia] (1041/1632) (Plates 6–8)*

Ia is a codex of 216 paper leaves, containing a copy of fifteen of al-Maqrīzī's shorter texts, most of which are also to be found in L (but in a different order). The text is written by the same hand throughout the manuscript, in a *nasḫ* script making consistent use of a *misṭarah* of 25 lines. The copy of *al-Ḏahab*

Ḏahab al-masbūk in the *Kašf al-ẓunūn* by the Ottoman bibliographer Ḥāǧǧī Ḫalīfah/Kātib Çelebī (1017–1067/1609–1657) that it was "a report involving 26 people ... *in five volumes* (*fī ḫamsat aǧzāʾ*), which [al-Maqrīzī] completed in Ḏū l-Qaʿdah of the year 841" (Kātib Çelebī, *Kašf al-ẓunūn*, 1:828; see also GAL, 2:50).

al-masbūk is the sixth text in this collection, preceded by *Ḍawʾ al-sārī* and followed by *al-Nizāʿ wa-l-taḫāṣum*, an arrangement that parallels that of the fragmentary Y. The text of *al-Ḏahab al-masbūk* begins on the recto of fol. 84 and it was reproduced on 24 leaves. Again there are no marginal notes, corrections, or any other addenda in this copy of the text, apart from the different titles that were—as in Y—repeated by the copyist in the margins for easy reference, and apart from one marginal note in another hand (fol. 87^{a}) that emends a scribal omission that was also present in Y (Y fol. $31^{a}1$, Ia fol. $87^{a}17$: *Lihb maksūr qabīlah min qabāʾil al-Azd*; emended Ia fol. 87^{a} left margin: *ḥ Lihb bi-lām maksūrah fa-hāʾ sākinah qabīlah min qabāʾil al-Azd*; the original in L fol. $117^{b}15$–16, E fol. $29^{a}14$: *Lihb maksūr al-lām qabīlah min qabāʾil al-Azd*). Apart from such scribal errors (see below) the entire copy of *al-Ḏahab al-masbūk* in Ia again represents a rather faithful representation of al-Maqrīzī's last known version of the text. Just as in Y, Ia also begins with a proper title page introducing the text of *al-Ḏahab al-masbūk* (fol. 84^{r}) and naming its author as "Taqī l-Dīn al-Maqrīzī l-Šāfiʿī" (plate 6). A scribal colophon (fol. 107^{r}) explains that the unnamed copyist finished his work "on Thursday 20th of the noble [Ḏū] l-Ḥiǧǧah", without however mentioning the year (plate 8). Following the colophon of the third text in this collection (*Kitāb Naḥl ʿibar al-naḥl*)—completed on "Tuesday 11th of the noble [Ḏū] l-Ḥiǧǧah of the months of the year 1041 of the prophetic *hiǧrah*" (fol. 62^{b})—this should refer to 20/12/1041, corresponding to Thursday 8 July 1632. For five texts (8 to 12) in this collection's copy in Ia an exact reproduction of authorial colophons from L preceded these scribal colophons, suggesting some link with the latter autograph. This explicit authorial reference was however not copied at the end of this copy of *al-Ḏahab al-masbūk*.

d *Istanbul, Nuruosmaniye Kütüphanesi,* MS *4937, fols. 145^{a}–186^{a}* [*In*] (*1085/1674*) (*Plates 9–11*)

In is a codex of 363 paper leaves, also containing a copy of fifteen of al-Maqrīzī's shorter texts in exactly the same order as they appear in the preceding Ia (and—presumably—in the original of Y). The text is written by the same hand throughout the manuscript, in a careful and conspicuous *nastaʿlīq* script making consistent use of a *misṭarah* of 17 lines. The copy of *al-Ḏahab al-masbūk* is again the sixth text in this collection, preceded by *Ḍawʾ al-sārī* and followed by *al-Nizāʿ wa-l-taḫāṣum*. It begins on the recto of fol. 145 and it was reproduced on 42 leaves. There are no marginal notes, corrections, or any other addenda in this copy of the text (not even marginal titles), apart from one marginal note in another hand (fol. 158^{a}: *fī ǧamāʿah ṣaḥḥa*) that corrects a scribal omission. Interestingly, the scribal omission that was also present in Ia and Y (*Lihb maksūr qabīlah min qabāʾil al-Azd*) has also been reproduced in In (fol. 150a2–3). Apart from some more scribal errors (see below) the entire copy of *al-Ḏahab al-masbūk* in In once again makes up a rather faithful representation of al-Maqrīzī's last known version of the text. Just as in Y and Ia, In also begins with a proper title page introducing the text of *al-Ḏahab al-masbūk* (fol. 145a) and naming its author as "Taqī l-Dīn al-Maqrīzī l-Šāfiʿī" (plate 9). The scribal colophon (fol. 186a) only consists of a brief religious final formula, devoid of any paratextual data (plate 11). The more detailed scribal colophons of four other texts in this collection situate the production of In between 24 Šaʿbān 1085/23 November 1674 and 4 Shawwāl 1085/1 January 1675. The scribal colophon of In's last text (*Ḥall luġz al-māʾ*) moreover identifies its copyist as one Abū l-Ṣalāḥ Muḥammad al-Ḥanafī, "known as al-Qaṭarī (*al-šahīr bi-l-Qaṭarī*)" (fol. 363a). Similar to what was found in Ia, finally, in In, seven texts (8 to 14)—but not the copy of *al-Ḏahab al-masbūk*—have an exact reproduction of authorial colophons from L preceding their scribal colophons.

e *Istanbul, Beyazıt Devlet Kütüphanesi, MS Veliyüddin 3195, fols. 64a–85a [Iv] (1101/1690) (Plates 12–14)*

Iv is a codex of 201 paper leaves, again containing a copy of the same fifteen shorter texts of al-Maqrīzī, but this time differently arranged from how these same texts appeared in Ia, In, and—presumably—Y. The text is written by the same hand throughout the manuscript, again in a careful and conspicuous *nastaʿlīq* script making consistent use of a *misṭarah* of 25 lines. The copy of *al-Ḏahab al-masbūk* is now the fifth text in this collection and it is preceded by the *Kitāb Naḥl ʿibar al-naḥl* and followed by the *Kitāb al-Bayān wa-l-iʿrāb ʿammā fī arḍ Miṣr min al-Aʿrāb*. It begins on the recto of fol. 64 and it was reproduced on 22 leaves. There are only four marginal notes and corrections in this fair and carefully made copy of the text, and all four are in the copyist's own hand (fol. 79a: *maṭlab šarāfat Makkah al-musharrafah*, fol. 80a: *maṭlab*; and fol. 65b: *muḥaqqiqī ṣaḥḥa*, fol. 85b: *yawm al-aḥad ṣaḥḥa*, in the latter two cases correcting a scribal omission). Again the scribal omission that has been identified above for In, Ia, and Y (*Lihb maksūr qabīlah min qabāʾil al-Azd*) was also reproduced in Iv (fol. 67a5–6). Apart from this and quite a few other scribal errors (see below) the entire copy of *al-Ḏahab al-masbūk* in Iv once again represents rather faithfully al-Maqrīzī's last known version of the text. Just as Y, Ia, and In did, Iv also begins with a proper title page introducing the text of *al-Ḏahab al-masbūk* (fol. 64a), but now referring to its author as "Taqī l-Dīn al-Maqrīzī" only (plate 12). As in In, the scribal colophon of this copy of *al-Ḏahab al-masbūk* in Iv (fol. 85a) only consists of a brief religious final formula, devoid of any paratextual data (plate 14). Similar to what was found in Ia and In also in Iv seven texts (the same as in In, here numbered 6, 8–10, 12–14)—but not the copy of *al-Ḏahab al-masbūk*—have an exact reproduction of authorial colophons from L preceding their scribal colophons.

A number of more detailed scribal colophons of other texts in this collection situate the production of Iv between 19 Šaʿbān and 17 Ḏū l-Qaʿdah 1101/28 May and 22 August 1690 (fols. 27[a], 201[a]). They furthermore repeatedly name its copyist as Muḥammad al-Qaṭarī, who is identified explicitly on various occasions as *imām* and *ḫaṭīb* of a mosque in Jedda and as producing this copy in the town of Jedda. This confirms that In and Iv were produced by the same religious scholar/copyist, who clearly was able to make money out of copying al-Maqrīzī's collection in the 1080s/1670s as he still did in 1101/1690. In due course, however, it also seems that Muḥammad al-Qaṭarī had learned to do so in creative ways, changing the order of the texts from how they had been arranged in most of the extant seventeenth-century manuscripts.

f *Cambridge, University Library, MS Add. 746, fols. 78ᵃ–105ᵇ [Ca] (1112/1701) (Plates 15–17)*

Ca is a codex of 260 leaves of different qualities and paper types (some dyed in red, yellow, and green), containing a combination of copies of only ten texts from al-Maqrīzī's collection of opuscules (fols. 1–164) and of five other unrelated texts that were added to the textblock at some later date. The copies of al-Maqrīzī's ten texts were all done in the same hand, in a clear *nasḫ* script making consistent use of a *misṭarah* of 25 lines. The copy of *al-Ḏahab al-masbūk* is now the fourth text in this collection of ten (which in its current arrangement does not seem to follow that of any other manuscript), and it is preceded by the *Kitāb Naḥl ʿibar al-naḥl* and followed by the *Kitāb al-Nizāʿ wa-l-taḫāṣum*. It begins on the recto of fol. 78 and it was reproduced on 28 leaves. There are more than 35 marginal notes in this copy of the text, mostly addenda of scribal omissions written in the scribe's own hand. Five technical marks (*balaġa*) in the outer margins of fols. 82[a], 86[a], 92[b], 101[b], and 104[a] suggest that most of those marginal notes were the result of the copyist's careful collation of his copy with one or more other copies; three of these marginal notes actually explicitly identify alternative readings from such a copy (referred to as *nusḫah*) (fols. 82[a], 94[b], 103[a]). Apart from such scribal errors (see also below) the entire copy in Ca once again is a rather faithful representation of al-Maqrīzī's last known version of the text. Just as in Y, Ia, In and Iv, Ca also begins with a proper title page introducing the text of *al-Ḏahab al-masbūk* (fol. 78[a]), but in the case of Ca its author is fully named as "Taqī l-Dīn Aḥmad b. ʿAbd al-Qādir al-Maqrīzī". These title and author references are inserted in an inverted triangle in red ink. On the lower half of the same title page a royal pilgrimage *ḫabar* that is absent from any other manuscript has been inserted. It starts with the explanatory phrase that "al-Ṯaʿālabī in his book *Laṭāʾif al-maʿārif* reported about Ǧamīlah bt. Nāṣir al-Dawlah b. Ḥamdān that she performed the pilgrimage in the year 366 [977], which then became an exemplary and remembered act (*fa-ṣāra ḥağğuhā maṯal*[an] *wa-tārīḫ*[an])."[18] (fol. 78ᵃ, plate 15)

The scribal colophon (fol. 105ᵃ) only consists of the briefest possible note ("The book is done; glory to God alone") (plate 17). Two more detailed scribal colophons of two other texts in this collection (fols. 18ᵃ, 77ᵃ) identify its copyist as one Yūsuf b. Muḥammad "known as Ibn al-Wakīl al-Mallawī" and they situate the production of al-Maqrīzī's ten texts in Ca around January and February 1701 (Šaʿbān and Ramaḍān 1112). The last of these two colophons actually refers to the earliest of these two dates, suggesting that the original arrangement of these texts was changed at some point in this manuscript's history.

g *Paris, Bibliothèque nationale de France, MS arabe 4657, fols. 101ᵇ–131ᵃ [P] (Mid-Eighteenth C.) (Plates 18–19)*

P is a codex of 266 leaves of two types of paper. It again contains a copy of the full set of fifteen shorter texts of al-Maqrīzī, arranged in the same order as in Ia, In, and—presumably—Y. The text is written by the same hand throughout the manuscript, in a clear *nasḫ* making consistent use of a *misṭarah* of 25 lines. The copy of *al-Ḏahab al-masbūk* is the sixth text in this collection and it is preceded—as in Ia, In, and Y—by the *Ḍawʾ al-sārī* and followed by *al-Nizāʿ wa-l-taḫāṣum*. It begins on the verso of fol. 101 and it was reproduced on 31 leaves. There are no marginal notes, corrections, or any other addenda in this copy of the text, apart from a number of titles that were repeated by the copyist in the margins for easy reference, without however pursuing this as a systematic and consistent practice. On more than twenty pages, moreover, the copyist had to make up his repeated failures to fully fit a line's final word within the page's text frame by adding remaining letters or word parts in the relevant line's direct margin. Interestingly, the scribal omission that was also present in Iv, In, Ia and Y (*Lihb maksūr qabīlah min qabāʾil al-Azd*) has been reproduced once again in P (fol. 105ᵃ11–12). A paragraph was furthermore lost when in the turning of leave 120 the copyist mistakenly substituted two references to the year 600 (*wa-sittimiʾah*) and the text in between was not copied. Apart from some more of these old and new scribal errors (see also below) the entire copy of *al-Ḏahab al-masbūk* in P consists of another rather faithful representation of al-Maqrīzī's last known version of it. The text is not identified by any title or authorial reference (nor is any of P's other texts),

18 For this paradigmatic story of royal female patronage, see also Behrens-Abouseif (1997): 93; Meloy (2006): 407.

even though fol. 101^{r} was probably left blank by the copyist for the purpose of their later addition. As in Iv and In, the scribal colophon of this copy of *al-Ḏahab al-masbūk* in P (fol. 131^{a}) only consists of a brief religious formula, devoid of any paratextual data (plate 19). Actually, none of the scribal colophons in P provide any information about the identity of P's copyist or about its date of production. However, a datable paper filigree and owner's stamp make clear that the latter must have happened some time between 1749 and 1781. Finally, also in P five texts (the same as in Ia, 8 to 12)—but not the copy of *al-Ḏahab al-masbūk*—have a reproduction of authorial colophons from L preceding their scribal colophons.

h *Cambridge, University Library, MS Qq. 141, fols. 1^{a}–37^{a} [Cq] (1232/1817) (Plates 20–22)*

Cq is a codex of 86 paper leaves, containing a copy of three of al-Maqrīzī's shorter texts only: *al-Ḏahab al-masbūk*, *Naḥl ʿibar al-naḥl*, and *al-Ṭurfah al-ġarībah min aḫbār Wādī Ḥaḍramawt al-ʿağībah*. The text is written by the same hand throughout the manuscript, in what may be defined as a scholar's *nasḫ*, making consistent use of a *misṭarah* of 19 lines. The copy of *al-Ḏahab al-masbūk* begins on the recto of fol. 1 and it was carefully reproduced on 37 leaves. There are no marginal notes, corrections, or any other addenda in this copy of the text. Interestingly, the scribal omission that has been identified above for Iv, In, Ia, and Y (*Lihb maksūr qabīlah min qabāʾil al-Azd*) was also reproduced in Cq (fol. 5^{b}17–18). Apart from a number of such scribal mistakes (see also below) the entire copy again makes for a rather faithful representation of al-Maqrīzī's last known version of the text. Just as in Y, Ia, In, Iv, and Ca, Cq also begins with a proper title page introducing the text of *al-Ḏahab al-masbūk* (fol. 1^{a}), but in the case of Cq its author is now only referred to as "Aḥmad b. ʿAlī l-Maqrīzī" (plate 20). A scribal colophon (fol. 37^{a}) clarifies that this copy was finished by an unnamed scribe on 15 Ṣafar 1232/4 January 1817 (plate 22). This manuscript entered Cambridge University Library two years later already, in 1819, as part of the bequest of the Swiss traveller J.L. Burckhardt. Burckhardt must have acquired this manuscript shortly before his death in Cairo in October 1817. This tight timing between Cq's production and Burckhardt's death make it likely that it was especially copied in Cairo for Burckhardt and for the newly emerging Orientalist markets that he represented.[19]

---

19 Browne (1900): 82, no. 442.

i *Ḥuraydah, Maktabat al-ʿAṭṭās* [Ḥ]

This codex, preserved in a Yemeni private collection, has so far remained inaccessible. It has been identified as containing a copy of a set of thirteen of al-Maqrīzī's shorter texts. These include that of *al-Ḏahab al-masbūk*, as well as most other texts featuring in the complete sets of Ia, In, Iv, P and L. Unfortunately, no further material, textual, or paratextual information about this copy is currently available.

To sum up, these nine manuscripts with fragmentary or complete sets of copies of the shorter texts that al-Maqrīzī had chosen to publish as one collected volume in L span a substantial timeframe, ranging between the sixteenth and the early nineteenth centuries. Despite the substantial temporal, material, and also geographical distances that separated these specimens of an ongoing reproduction, and despite the fact that some copies (E, L, Cq, and also P) were all removed from local flows of circulation and reproduction at rather early dates in their material lives (ending up in European libraries in the early seventeenth [E, L] and early nineteenth centuries [Cq, P] respectively), many of these manuscripts, and of the copies of *al-Ḏahab al-masbūk* in them, share certain features that deserve to be repeated here.

- Four manuscripts (Ia, In, Iv, P) have a full set of fifteen texts, and three of them (Ia, In, P) share the same arrangement of these texts. There are good reasons to suggest that Y represents a fragmentary remnant of a similar manuscript, and that also Ca and Ḥ originally had followed this tradition, or at least somehow derived from it.
- Six manuscripts (E, Y, Ia, In, Iv, P) include authorial colophons or related paratextual claims to authenticity in at least a number of their texts, referring to or repeating word-for-word al-Maqrīzī's authorial colophons in L. Two manuscripts (In, Iv) include such colophons for seven texts and two (Ia, P) do so for five texts. E uniquely has such reference for *al-Ḏahab al-masbūk*, whereas the equally fragmentary Y only hints at this claim indirectly in another text.
- Five manuscripts (Y, Ia, In, Iv, Ca) may be roughly dated to the same seventeenth century. Y in particular represents a specimen of an important moment in this history of reproduction, being one of at least six copies that were produced in the early seventeenth century by father and son al-Mallāḥ. The reproduction of In and Iv by the same copyist al-Qaṭarī in Jedda in the last quarter of this century represents a similar cluster of scribal entrepreneurship organised around al-Maqrīzī's collection of texts.
- Six copies of *al-Ḏahab al-masbūk* (in Y, Ia, In, Iv, Ca, Cq) begin with a genuine title page (which is missing in E and also in P), with some slight variations in

the references to the author's name: Taqī l-Dīn al-Maqrīzī l-Šāfiʿī (Y, Ia, In); Taqī l-Dīn al-Maqrīzī (Iv); Taqī l-Dīn Aḥmad b. ʿAbd al-Qādir al-Maqrīzī (Ca); Aḥmad b. ʿAlī l-Maqrīzī (Cq).
- Three copies of *al-Ḏahab al-masbūk* (in Y, Ia, P) have subtitles that are repeated in the margins of the text, for easy reference. In P, however, this practice was not pursued consistently.
- All copies of *al-Ḏahab al-masbūk* in all manuscripts faithfully represent the very last version of al-Maqrīzī's text as copied, collated, and revised in L, but they do so in remarkably uncritical ways. None display any clear signs of systematic collation with L or with any other copy, because none of these copies bear any relevant number of scribal marks or other notations to that effect (even though scribal errors did occur; see below). The only exception to this general rule is the copy in Ca, but the absence of reproductions of authorial colophons in this manuscript (as in E, Y, Ia, In, Iv, P) and its incomplete nature and complex material history (consisting of ten texts by al-Maqrīzī only, which were combined with later copies of an unrelated set of texts) make it impossible to say much more about its relationship with other copies.
- The copies of *al-Ḏahab al-masbūk* in six manuscripts (Y, Ia, In, Iv, P, Cq) all display a remarkable reproduction of the same scribal omission (*Lihb maksūr*). This attests to this shared practice of uncritical copying and lack of collation (in Ia, there is a marginal note to correct this, but this correction seems not to have happened after collation because this scribal suggestion [*Lihb bi-lām maksūrah fa-hāʾ sākinah*] differs from what L says [*Lihb maksūr al-lām*]). This also suggests that these manuscripts were somehow all connected to the eldest among them, Y, rather than to L directly. Further collation actually confirms this and allows in combination with the above for a more precise preliminary reconstruction of those connections.

This collation of all the currently known manuscript copies of *al-Ḏahab al-masbūk* from L, as corrected and revised by al-Maqrīzī in and beyond early 842/mid-1438, and from the eight codices that are currently available for study, has resulted in the identification of many dozens of scribal errors across the entire field of reproduction. As may be expected for a field spread out between substantial temporal, material, and geographical ranges, these errors represent all of the traditional types that are well-known in Arabic manuscript studies: omissions, additions, substitutions, transpositions, corrections, variations, and cacography.[20] None had any relevant impact on the meanings of the text of *al-*

20 Gacek (2009): 234–235.

Ḏahab al-masbūk, but they do provide further suggestions about relationships between these different manuscript copies and about the relative distances separating these copies from L and from each other. In order to get a better sense of these relationships and distances a selection has been made of the 58 most relevant scribal errors across the reproductive field. These were listed in a table in which every column details how these 58 textual moments appear in one of these nine manuscript copies and in which every row identifies continuities and changes across the different copies in the reproduction of one of these 58 moments. Changes in these rows, representing the appearance of a scribal error in a copy, were highlighted with different colours, every colour identifying a particular copy of the text and, if relevant, the reproduction of its error across the other manuscripts (table 1).

Even though this collation table is biased towards the identification of errors and limited by its working with a relevant sample only, this visualisation does provide further strong suggestions about how at least the texts within these different manuscript copies were related. Thus, the 1018/1609 copy of *al-Ḏahab al-masbūk* by ʿAlī b. Muḥammad al-Mallāḥ, Y, introduces into the table a total of 19 of these 58 scribal errors. Ten of these errors were fully reproduced in all of the six later copies and five more errors were fully reproduced in three, four or five copies. As was already suggested by the reproduction of the *Lihb maksūr* error mentioned above, Y therefore clearly stands as a representative of a particular and powerful tradition in the reproduction history of the text of *al-Ḏahab al-masbūk*. This tradition, coinciding with the scribal entrepreneurship of the al-Mallāḥ family in the early seventeenth century, acquired archetypal status for most of the manuscripts that followed at a time when al-Maqrīzī's autograph, L, was acquired by the Dutch diplomat Warner and disappeared from local circulation.

The opposite appears to be the case for manuscript E. It remains unclear whether its two texts originally did or did not belong to a codex with the full set of al-Maqrīzī's shorter texts, as in L. The close relationship between E's copy of *al-Ḏahab al-masbūk* and that in L is nevertheless obvious, also from this collation. But so is the fact that in the text's circulation E was first sidelined in Morocco and then isolated in Spain, therefore leaving no relevant traces in a reproduction history of this text that seems to have focused on eastern Arabic regions first and foremost.

Manuscripts In and Iv, both produced by the scholar and scribe Abū l-Ṣalāḥ Muḥammad al-Ḥanafī l-Qaṭarī in the last quarter of the seventeenth century, fully engaged with the archetypal tradition represented by Y. But they also represent their own tradition of reproducing the text of *al-Ḏahab al-masbūk*, which not only reproduced most of Y's errors but also introduced 17 new ones.

The latter can be found in In and Iv only, establishing—in this table at least—al-Qaṭarī's scribal activities in Jedda as a particular and separate enterprise. In the 1101/1690 manuscript Iv al-Qaṭarī introduced even more new errors (11 in the table) that were not reproduced in any other extant copy.

One of the more puzzling manuscripts in the list certainly is Ca, mainly consisting of substantial remnants of copies made in 1112/1701 by Yūsuf b. Muḥammad Ibn al-Wakīl al-Mallawī. On the one hand, Ca clearly participated in the reproduction of *al-Ḏahab al-masbūk* from the archetypal tradition represented by Y. On the other hand, it also followed its own very particular dynamics of reproduction, adding its own scribal errors to the list and—as mentioned above—being far more critical in its reproduction than any of the other manuscripts (avoiding thus even the *Lihb maksūr* error). As the product of collation with more than one model (which cannot have been L or E, since these had disappeared to Europe in the course of the seventeenth century) Ca probably derives from two different archetypal traditions, only one of which has actually been preserved in Y.

These particular relationships, clustering, and grouping of the extant manuscript copies of *al-Ḏahab al-masbūk* are finally also suggested in very illustrative ways when these same continuities and changes for L and the nine other copies, for Y and the seven later copies, and for In and Iv are calculated and expressed in percentages of reproduction (Table 2).

The close relationship, or short textual distance, between L and E speaks very strongly from this table, as does the short distance between Y and Ia-Cq-P-Ca and between In and Iv. At the same time, this table reveals that as far as these scribal errors are concerned Iv is farthest removed from L, and it gives an indication of the substantial relative distance separating L from Y, as well as Y from In. With due acknowledgement of the very particular and partial nature of these data and of the chosen parameters from which they emerge, L, Y, and In again appear as representatives of particular moments in the history of the reproduction of the text of *al-Ḏahab al-masbūk*.

Above all, many parallel appearances of relationships and distances and of clustering, and grouping emerge from these different sets of qualitative and quantitative descriptions. A genuine *stemma codicum* defining precise connections between individual copies cannot be constructed from what remain above all appearances of similarity and dissimilarity that may be explained in multiple ways.[21] Nevertheless, particular relationships and distances between scribal versions of the text and particular clusters and families of manuscript copies there most certainly were (see also figure 1):

21 See also Gacek (2009): 268.

- The autograph L was part of an authorial cluster of mostly non-published versions, and with E this cluster represents an important early family of copies of the text of *al-Ḏahab al-masbūk*. Specimens of this family of copies seem to have survived by chance only when they were variously removed from local flows of consumption, reproduction, and circulation in the course of the seventeenth century.
- Y represents an early seventeenth-century cluster of at least half a dozen manuscripts, produced within a particular context of entrepreneurship, as though participating in a process of commodification of al-Maqrīzī's collection of 15 texts.[22] This cluster soon transformed into an archetypal tradition of substantial reproductive impact of its own, to which all other known manuscripts are related. The Y-cluster itself was somehow closely related to the L-E family, if only because explicit references to the latter awarded textual authority and value to the former. The exact nature of this relationship remains unclear, however, and given the distance between L and Y it is not unlikely that one or more other copies interfered as models for the production of this cluster.
- In and Iv represent a third deeply related cluster of copies, produced within another particular context of entrepreneurship and commodification. It stands out above all as a highly independent and distant cluster within the larger family of manuscripts that emerged around the Y-cluster.
- The 1112/1701 manuscript Ca finally is part of this larger family too, but it reveals at the same time that parallel archetypal traditions may have also been reproduced, at least into the early eighteenth century, either directly from lost remnants of the L-E-cluster, or indirectly from a now lost archetypal tradition that existed side by side with that of the Y-cluster.

In the post-World-War-II period the survival of the text of al-Maqrīzī's *al-Ḏahab al-masbūk* in this complex multitude of copies resulted in its renewed reproduction in four printed editions.[23] Most important among these are the two editions that were done independently from each other in the early 1950s, by Ǧamāl al-Dīn al-Šayyāl in Cairo and by Ḥamad al-Ǧāsir in Riyadh. The

22 On the process of commodification (or also 'commoditization'), that is, of the transformation of 'singularities' into commodities, or of the acquisition by things and relations of market values instead of or in addition to their social values, see Kopytoff (1986); Van Binsbergen (2005).

23 I am again grateful to the series editor, Frédéric Bauden, for sharing his information about these four editions with me, and for providing me with a copy of the al-Šayyāl 2000 and the al-Ǧāsir 1952 editions.

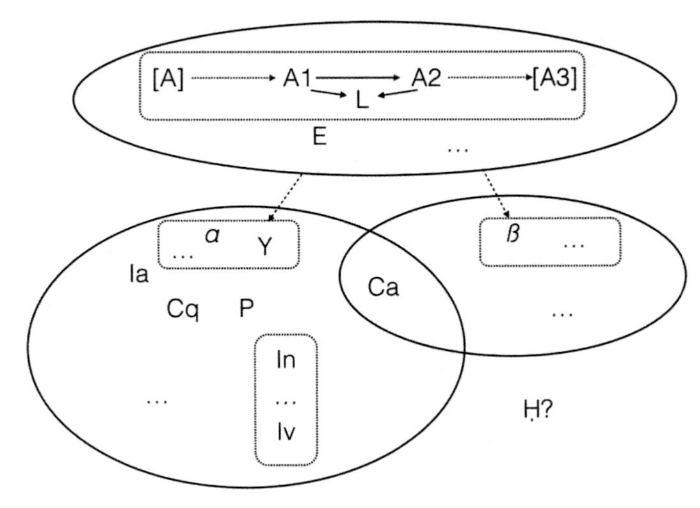

FIGURE 1 *Visual representation of apparent mss. relationships and distances.*

symbols: *A = 821/1418 version [hypothetical] / A1 = pre-841/1437 version in autograph L / A2 = post-842/1438 version in autograph L / A3 = revised published version [hypothetical] / α = archetype 1 / ß = archetype 2 / L, E, Y, Ia, In, Iv, Ca, P, Cq, Ḥ: mss. (see above) / ... = other unknown and lost mss.*

arrows: *red = production / black = reproduction / full line = direct attested relationship / broken line = indirect attested relationship (via lost intermediaries) / dotted line = hypothetical relationship*

Venn diagrams: *full line = family (related group of mss.) / dotted line = cluster (related mss. of a particular shared quality appearing closely together at a particular time and place)*
Distances between mss. are represented by their relative positioning in the diagram.

other two editions, published in 2000 and in 2009, are actually no more than reproductions of al-Šayyāl's 1955 edition, in the format of a complete and unchanged reprint in one case and of an update in quantitative rather than in qualitative terms in the second case.[24] Al-Šayyāl's edition, which was first published in 1955, was part of a larger publication project—the *Maktabat al-Maqrīzī al-Ṣaġīrah* series—in which it was the third (and apparently also the last) to be published. As is explained by the al-Maqrīzī specialist al-Šayyāl in a brief study preceding and introducing the text and his work on it, his edition was first done from P and Iv, and he had considered Iv as the *aṣl* to work from because it was the oldest of the two. Al-Šayyāl then details how, after finishing

24 Al-Maqrīzī, *al-Ḏahab al-masbūk*[3]; al-Maqrīzī, *al-Ḏahab al-masbūk*[4].

the edition, he discovered a third ms., which was E and which proved much more authoritative because it was a stated copy from an autograph; his edition was therefore collated with E, and variations were noted in footnote or added in the text. Nevertheless, the heavy reliance on Iv for this edition of *al-Ḏahab al-masbūk* left many traces and certainly not all of them were effaced in this process of collation.[25]

Three years earlier, in 1952, Ḥamad al-Ǧāsir, "member of the Academy for the Arabic Language in Damascus", had published his own work on the same text of al-Maqrīzī, in a serial edition in seven monthly instalments as an annex to volume six of the *Maǧallat al-Ḥaǧǧ* ('The Pilgrimage Journal'), appearing between Raǧab 1371 AH and Muḥarram 1372/April–September 1952. In his brief introduction, this editor al-Ǧāsir explains that he had relied for his work on microfilmed copies in Cairo and in Mecca from Iv and Ca, and that he had chosen Iv as his *aṣl* to work from as he considered it to be of better quality than Ca.[26] Unlike al-Šayyāl's work, which was reprinted and re-edited in the early twenty-first century, al-Ǧāsir's edition does not seem to have had much of a long-lasting impact.

More generally, considering—as detailed above—the distance separating Iv, and the cluster to which it pertains, from L, it appears as highly problematic that this handful of modern textual reproductions of al-Maqrīzī's *al-Ḏahab al-masbūk* continue until today to rely first and foremost on this Iv. In their critical readings, reproductions, and explanations of the text, these two editions have had substantial merit; the identification of other relevant copies and authoritative manuscript traditions as well as the deepened understanding of the complexity of this text and of the contexts in which it was produced and reproduced simultaneously also demonstrate their limitations.

3 Consuming *al-Ḏahab al-masbūk*: From Memory to History

The conscious communicative act that al-Maqrīzī's *al-Ḏahab al-masbūk* was did not just involve the participation of its author and of scribal reproducers, but obviously also of the audiences and recipients of its message. Producing and reproducing any text is only meaningful if it is also provoking interest,

---

25 Al-Maqrīzī, *al-Ḏahab al-masbūk*². We so far identified more than 60 variant readings of words or phrases between this al-Šayyāl edition and the L-E Mss. family. The collation with E seems to have resulted above all in referring to it in footnote rather than in making any textual amendments.

26 Al-Maqrīzī, *al-Ḏahab al-masbūk*¹.

read, studied, thought about, debated, and preserved. It is from this variegated consumption above all that webs of people, of things, and of ideas continued to be woven around texts and that all kinds of intended, unintended, and changing meanings became effective nodes in those webs. Given its long social life in various forms, shapes, and contexts this must certainly also have been the case for *al-Ḏahab al-masbūk*. However, available textual, paratextual, and material data for this other side of this text's life prove rather limited, allowing for making no more than a few general assumptions only. The transfer of *al-Ḏahab al-masbūk* in the early 840s/later 1430s from being a separate text of moral-didactic purpose to becoming only one particle in the large and complex whole of al-Maqrīzī's collection as it appeared in L has a lot to do with that silence. This story of consumption again appears first and foremost as one that can and should only be told for the full complexity of that collection. At the same time, however, the early 840s/later 1430s represent a moment of such radical transformation in the consumption as much as in the production of *al-Ḏahab al-masbūk*, that this change in communication certainly offers some powerful clues for this particular text too.

It has been argued above that *al-Ḏahab al-masbūk* was first and foremost produced as a programmatic text of moral-didactic purpose, which used the formats of pilgriming ruler narratives and leadership stories to communicate ideas of good Muslim rule, Egyptian supremacy, and divine sovereignty. Its first intended audience was therefore the ruler and his court, most likely the sultan al-Muʾayyad Šayḫ and his advisors. However, when the plans for the sultan's 821/1418 pilgrimage had to be cancelled, the casting of this message in the format of an innovative pilgrimage text proved futile and the text was therefore probably never published for nor received by its originally intended audience.

As a consequence, when the text of *al-Ḏahab al-masbūk* entered the collection of L some twenty years later, it may have done so in a slightly altered, more generic and less specific form, taking into account the new audiences whose interests it still might serve. These audiences were certainly still members of the political and other elites, and they possibly even included Barsbāy's son and short-lived successor al-ʿAzīz Yūsuf and his entourage.[27] At that same time, however, political circumstances had substantially changed and the imminent relevance of the text's original meaning of political restoration after the deep crisis that had ended the Barqūqid era (784–815/1382–1412) was for ever lost.

27 See—as mentioned before—also John Meloy's parallel suggestion for the *Šuḏūr al-ʿuqūd*, another treatise in the same collection, that "al-Maqrīzī's corrections to the text in Ramaḍān 841 (February–March 1438)" perhaps made possible "that the text could be used as an appeal to Barsbāy's successor" (Meloy [2003b]: 197, fn. 54).

Due to the lack of any reading notes or external references it remains unclear how the text was actually read by its new readership in the 830s and 40s/1430s, if not for its political message. The inclusion of *al-Ḏahab al-masbūk* in al-Maqrīzī's collection of texts covering a wide range of subjects is nevertheless quite suggestive, as is this text's constant featuring along many others in long lists of al-Maqrīzī's scholarly production that were drafted by contemporary biographers such as Ibn Taġrī Birdī and al-Saḫāwī.[28] A particular expectation is at least created about one of the meanings that may have been intended by the author and perhaps even understood by most of his fifteenth-century audiences. The latter lists, as well as the former collection, certainly speak of al-Maqrīzī's authoritative achievements in a wide range of related fields of scholarship. It was demonstrated above how the text of *al-Ḏahab al-masbūk* certainly was also meant to mediate such more personal socio-cultural meanings of the author's claims to distinction, identity, and entitlement. It could be argued then that despite the loss of the acuteness of its political meanings the text continued to be relevant (and continued to be redrafted) for the more personal socio-cultural meanings that it communicated. What remained was its textual performance of al-Maqrīzī's mastery of historical knowledge, announced in the introduction as "the most precious and most valuable of treasures, the most glorious and the longest remembered of deeds" and presented throughout the text by inter- and metatextual means as though monopolised by its author. In the particular combination with the other texts in the collection, *al-Ḏahab al-masbūk* thus continues to attest above all to the accomplished scholarship of its author.

However, as time went by and al-Maqrīzī as well as those scholars who derived some level of socio-cultural authority from his status gradually disappeared from the scenes of textual consumption, this level of personalised socio-cultural meanings evidently retreated to the background too. Al-Maqrīzī and his texts obviously retained an authority that is exemplified by the temporal, geographical, and material dimensions of the field of reproduction of the collection that includes *al-Ḏahab al-masbūk*. But in the ongoing consumption of this collection and of different other products of al-Maqrīzī's pen, texts such as *al-Ḏahab al-masbūk* increasingly derived their meanings from that authority rather than that they were merely meant to perform it. Their consumption thus transformed from accepting them (or not) as presenting particular social

28 Ibn Taġrī Birdī, *al-Manhal al-ṣāfī*, 1:418–419; al-Saḫāwī, *al-Ḍaw' al-lāmi'*, 2:22–23. One reference in a recently published bibliography suggesting that al-Saḫāwī even would have produced a text with the same title as al-Maqrīzī's turns out to be an unfortunate bibliographic conflation of *al-Ḏahab al-masbūk*'s title with that of al-Saḫāwī's continuation of the *al-Sulūk*, *al-Tibr al-masbūk fī ḏayl al-Sulūk* (see al-Musawi [2015]: 418).

claims about historical knowledge to understanding them as privileged carriers and transmitters of that knowledge. As far as *al-Ḏahab al-masbūk* is concerned, this process made that eventually its historical character was prioritised over the different other meanings that it communicated, and that an understanding of the particular ways in which it had been constructed to pursue the latter communication was side-lined for retrieving names, data, and *ḫabar*s of pilgriming Muslim rulers.

Already in the sixteenth century, this changed pattern of consumption had become the norm for the text of *al-Ḏahab al-masbūk*. In those early modern Ottoman times, as Suraiya Faroqhi explained, the historical example of predecessors of the Ottoman rulers in affairs of the pilgrimage had become a matter of political exigency.

> Sixteenth- and seventeenth-century authors dealing with the Ottoman sultans in their role of protectors to the pilgrimage, have often measured Ottoman performance against the yardstick of what had been done, really or presumably, by their Mamluk predecessors. This explains why Ottoman sultans adhered as closely as they could to the practices connected with the names of Qāytbāy (r. 878–901/1468–1496) and Qāniṣawh al-Ġawrī (r. 906–922/1501–1516).[29]

This context certainly explains why reproductions of texts such as that of *al-Ḏahab al-masbūk* and its accounts of Ottoman predecessors found fertile ground in sixteenth- and seventeenth-century Ottoman times. Substantial reference is actually even made to al-Maqrīzī's text in a unique account of the pilgrimage that was written by a mid-sixteenth-century Egyptian scholar who had been employed in the Ottoman administration of pilgrimage caravans from Egypt. This ʿAbd al-Qādir al-Ǧazīrī (d. c. 977/1570) wrote an extensive text on that administration of the *ḥaǧǧ* and its history, including an account of "notable men and women" performing the pilgrimage to Mecca in the seventh and last part (*bāb*) of this book.[30] At the start of that chapter, al-Ǧazīrī explains metaphorically that

> some of the later [historians] such as al-Maqrīzī have spoken about similar things as there are in this part; he entitled it The Gold Moulded in the Format of the History of Those Kings Who Performed the Pilgrimage [*al-Ḏahab al-masbūk fī tārīḫ man ḥaǧǧa min al-mulūk* (sic)]. I consulted

29 Faroqhi (2014): 33.

30 Al-Ǧazīrī, *Durar al-farāʾid*, 2:325. On al-Ǧazīrī (also known as al-Ǧazarī) and his text, see also Faroqhi (2014): 33–35.

> it, stripped off that product of smelting, and added it as a purifier to this silver [= this seventh part]. Whoever reads my book, may he say: there is no further trail [to follow] after [being quenched by] a source [such as this one].[31]

Throughout the text of this last part of his book then, al-Ğazīrī appeals to the authority and information of al-Maqrīzī's booklet to produce his own chronography of rulers performing the pilgrimage. Unlike al-Maqrīzī, however, al-Ğazīrī wants this to be a comprehensive historical account, and he therefore also has to come to some terms with how *al-Ḏahab al-masbūk* is lacking in that respect. He thus explicitly notes textual lacunae and interdependencies, such as between al-Maqrīzī's *ḫabar* about Hārūn's barefoot pilgrimage and that of Ṣibṭ Ibn al-Ğawzī (d. c. 654/1256) in the *Mir'āt al-zamān*.[32] Al-Ğazīrī provides more material from other sources, and eventually also adds many more names of caliphs and, especially, of non-caliphal rulers to al-Maqrīzī's limited list of 26.[33] In all, one may claim that for al-Ğazīrī al-Maqrīzī's text on the matter clearly stands as the main authority and point of reference, but that his purely historiographical approach to it proved all but straightforward when it came to the details.

It remains nevertheless this historiographical approach of al-Ğazīrī that seems to have continued to dominate the textual consumption of *al-Ḏahab al-masbūk*.[34] In the twentieth century, at least, similar readings from the perspective of useful "summary biographies of selections of rulers" still provided the main types of meanings and values that were prioritised in any specific study of the text, such as by al-Šayyāl in the 1950s, and by Faraḥāt in his adapted introduction to the re-edition of the text in 2009.[35] Parallel to what was concluded about the current state of the reproduction of *al-Ḏahab al-masbūk*, therefore, it should be acknowledged that also as far as its consumption is concerned current appreciations certainly have their merits, but that the deepened understandings of the complexity of this text and of the contexts in which it was produced, reproduced, and consumed simultaneously also demonstrate that much more can and should be read in al-Maqrīzī's *al-Ḏahab al-masbūk*.

---

31 Al-Ğazīrī, *Durar al-farā'id*, 2:325.

32 Ibid., 2:345.

33 Ibid., 2:345–374.

34 *Al-Ḏahab al-masbūk* was also referred to and used in this historicising manner by the Ottoman Egyptian historian al-Ğabartī (1167–1241/1753–1825) (as suggested by Ayalon [1960]: 221).

35 See al-Šayyāl (1971): 25 (*al-tarğamah al-muḫtaṣarah li-mağmū'ah min al-mulūk*); see also al-Šayyāl (1955): 10–24; Faraḥāt (2009): 29–34.

Map, Plates and Tables

Map

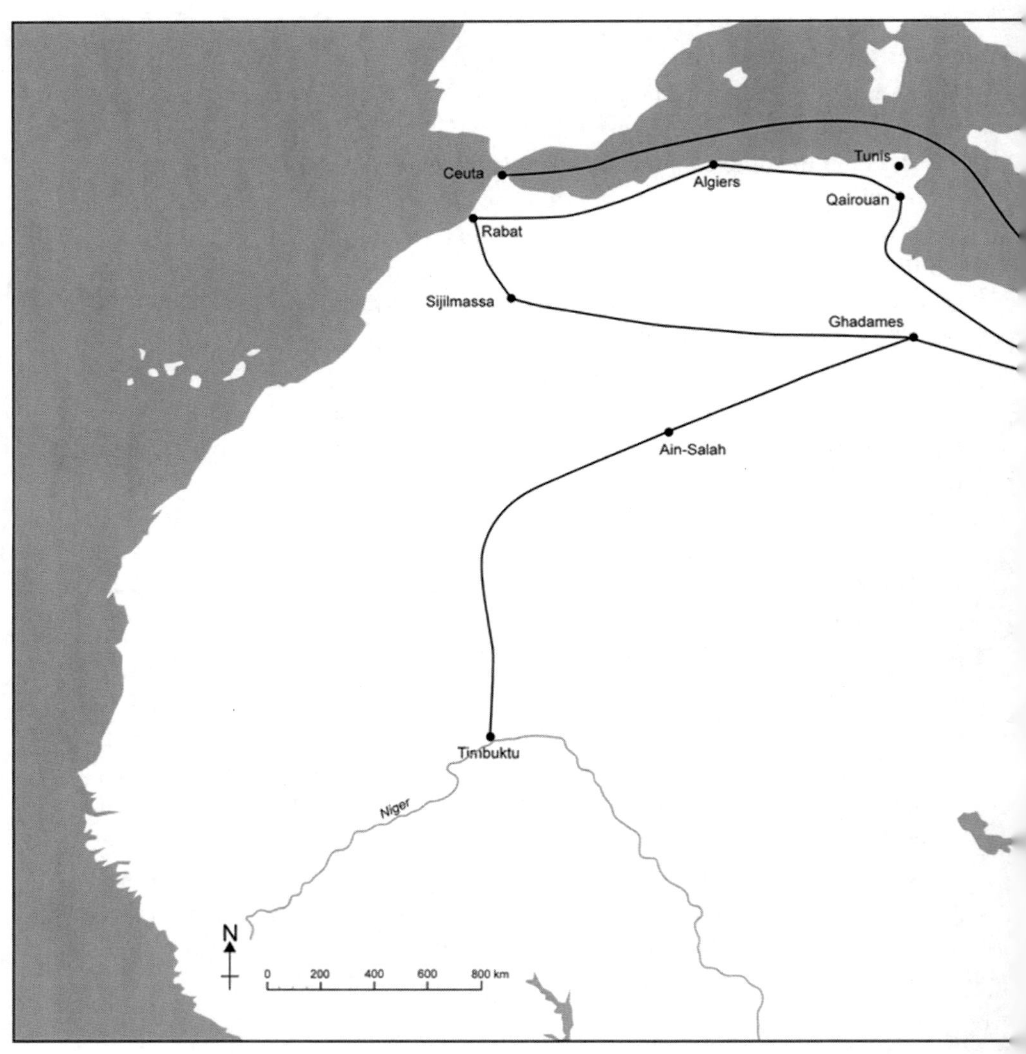

Map of the Middle East and North Africa, with the main medieval ḥaǧǧ routes and the most important cities, towns, and places mentioned in this book (map drawing courtesy of Erik Smekens, 2016)

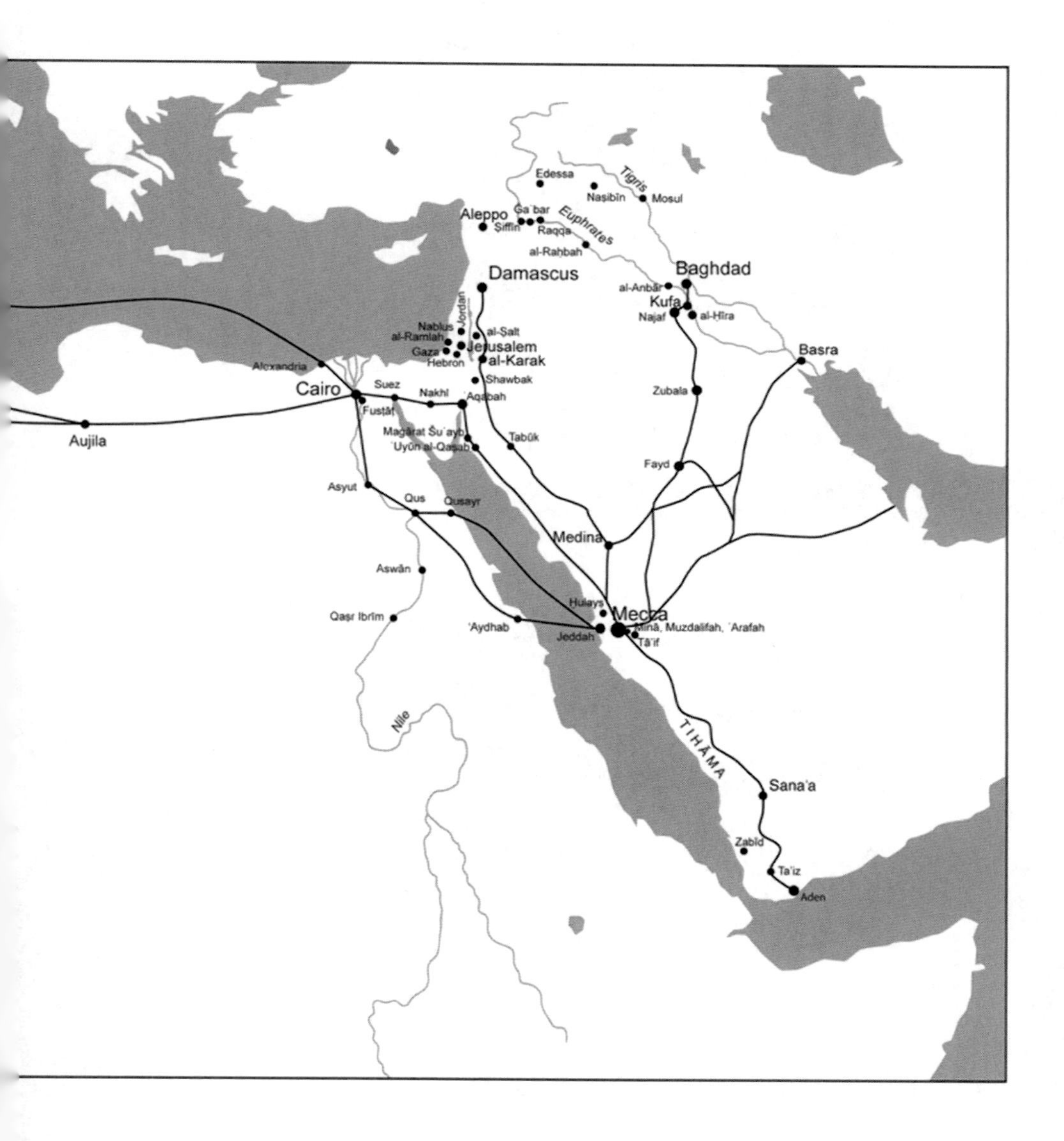
Edessa
Tigris
Naṣibīn
Mosul
Aleppo
Ǧa`bar
Ṣiffīn
Raqqa
Euphrates
al-Raḥbah
Damascus
Baghdad
al-Anbār
Kufa
Najaf
al-Ḥīra
Jordan
Nablus
al-Ramlah
al-Ṣalt
Jerusalem
Gaza
Hebron
al-Karak
Alexandria
Shawbak
Basra
Cairo
Suez
Nakhl
ʿAqabah
Zubala
Fusṭāṭ
Aujila
Maġārat Šuʿayb
ʿUyūn al-Qaṣab
Tabūk
Fayd
Asyut
Qus
Qusayr
Medina
Aswān
Hulays
Mecca
Qaṣr Ibrīm
ʿAydhab
Jeddah
Minā, Muzdalifah, ʿArafah
Tāʾif
Nile
TIHĀMA
Sanaʿa
Zabīd
Taʿiz
Aden

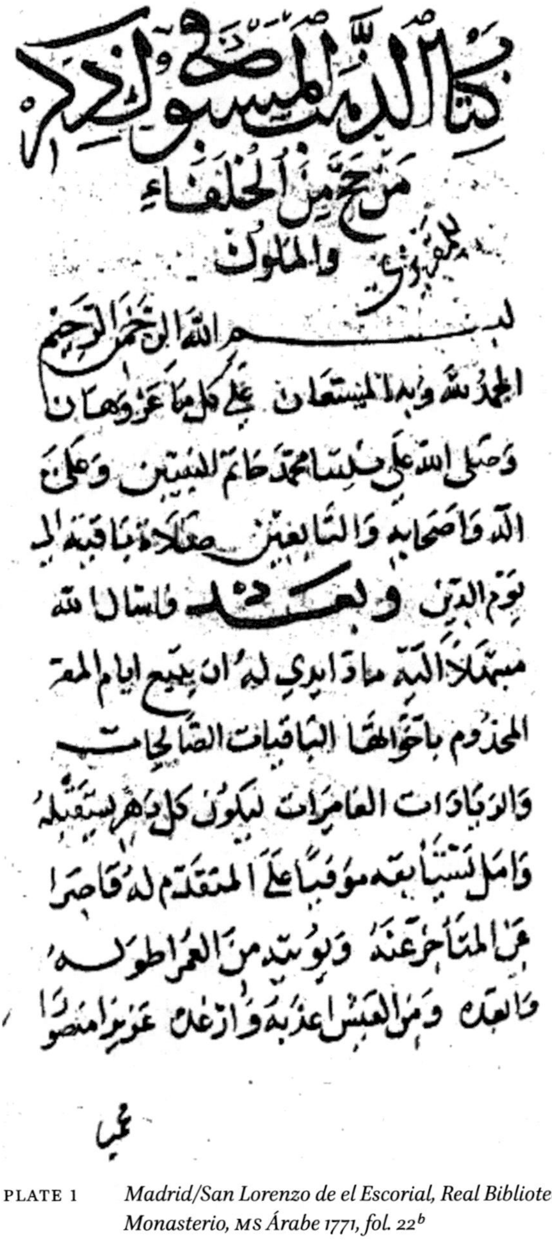

كتاب الذهب المسبوك في ذكر من حج من الخلفاء والملوك

بسم الله الرحمن الرحيم

الحمد لله وبه المستعان على كل ما عز وهان
وصلى الله على سيدنا محمد خاتم النبيين وعلى
آله وأصحابه والتابعين صلاة باقية إلى
يوم الدين وبعد فأسأل الله
مبتهلا إليه مادا يدي له أن يجعل أيام المقر
المخدوم بأخواتها الباقيات الصالحات
والزيادات العامرات ليكون كل دهر يستقبله
وأمد يستأنفه موفيا على المتقدم له قاصرا
عن المتأخر عنه ويزيد من العمر طوله
والعز ومن العيش أعذبه وأرغده عزيزا منصورا

PLATE 1 *Madrid/San Lorenzo de el Escorial, Real Biblioteca del Monasterio,* MS *Árabe 1771, fol. 22*^{b}

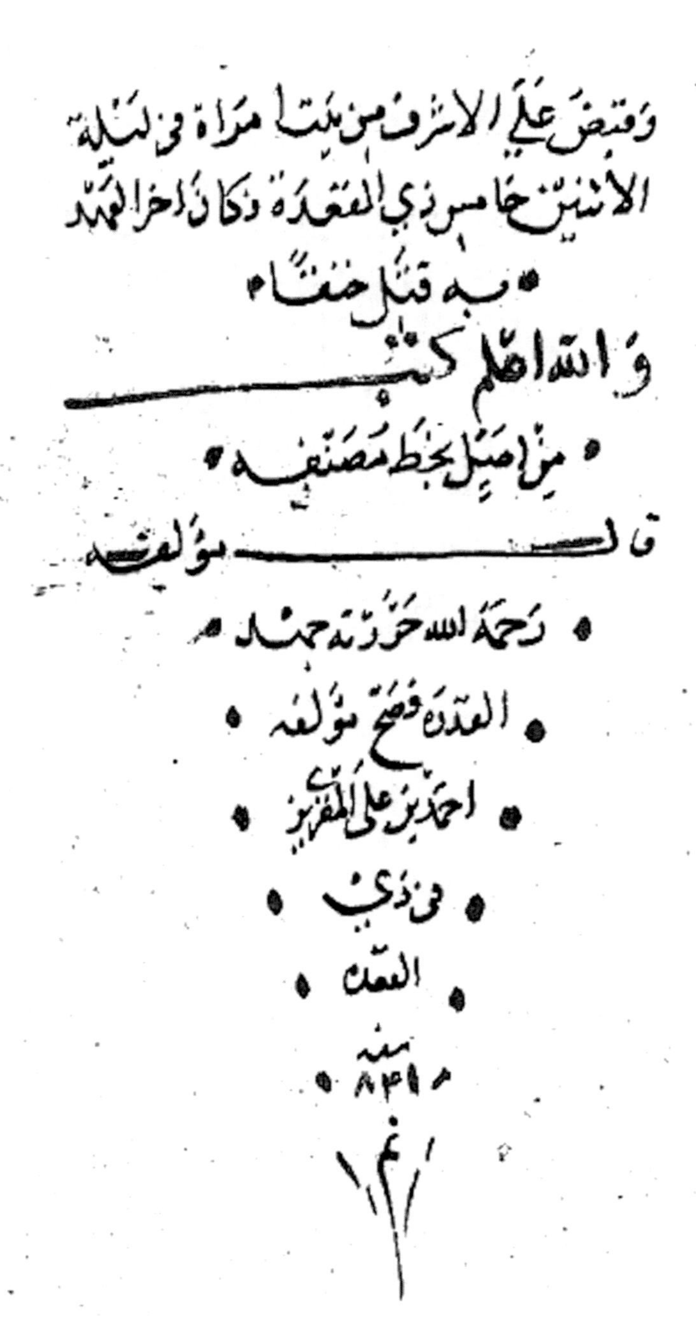

وقبض على الاشرف من بيتنا مرة في ليلة
الاثنين خامس ذي القعدة وكان اخر العهد
به قبل [illegible]
والله اعلم كتب
من اصل بخط مصنفه
قال مؤلفه
رحمه الله [illegible]
العبد فضح مؤلفه
احمد بن علي المقريزي
في ذي
القعدة
سنة
٨٤١

PLATE 2 *Madrid/San Lorenzo de el Escorial, Real Biblioteca del Monasterio, MS Árabe 1771, fol. 75*[b]

كتاب الذهب المسبوك في ذكر
من حج من الخلفا والملوك تاليف
الشيخ الامام والعلامة الهمام
المحدث المورخ تقي الدين
المقريزي الشافعي
تغمده الله برحمته
ولكاتبه والمسلمين
امين

PLATE 3 *New Haven, Yale University, Beinecke Rare Book and Manuscript Library,* MS *Landberg 111, fol. 26*[a]

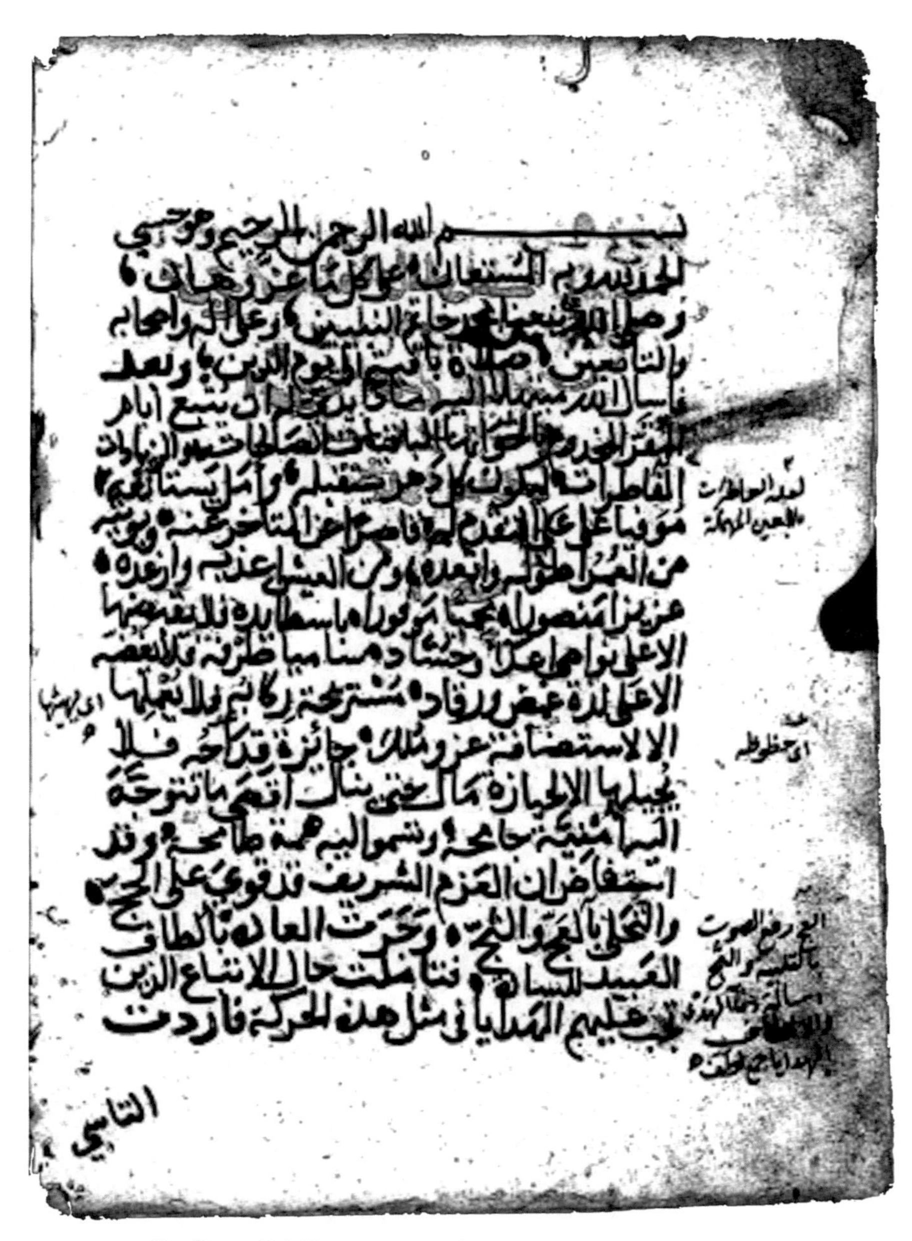

PLATE 4 *New Haven, Yale University, Beinecke Rare Book and Manuscript Library, MS Landberg 111, fol. 26b*

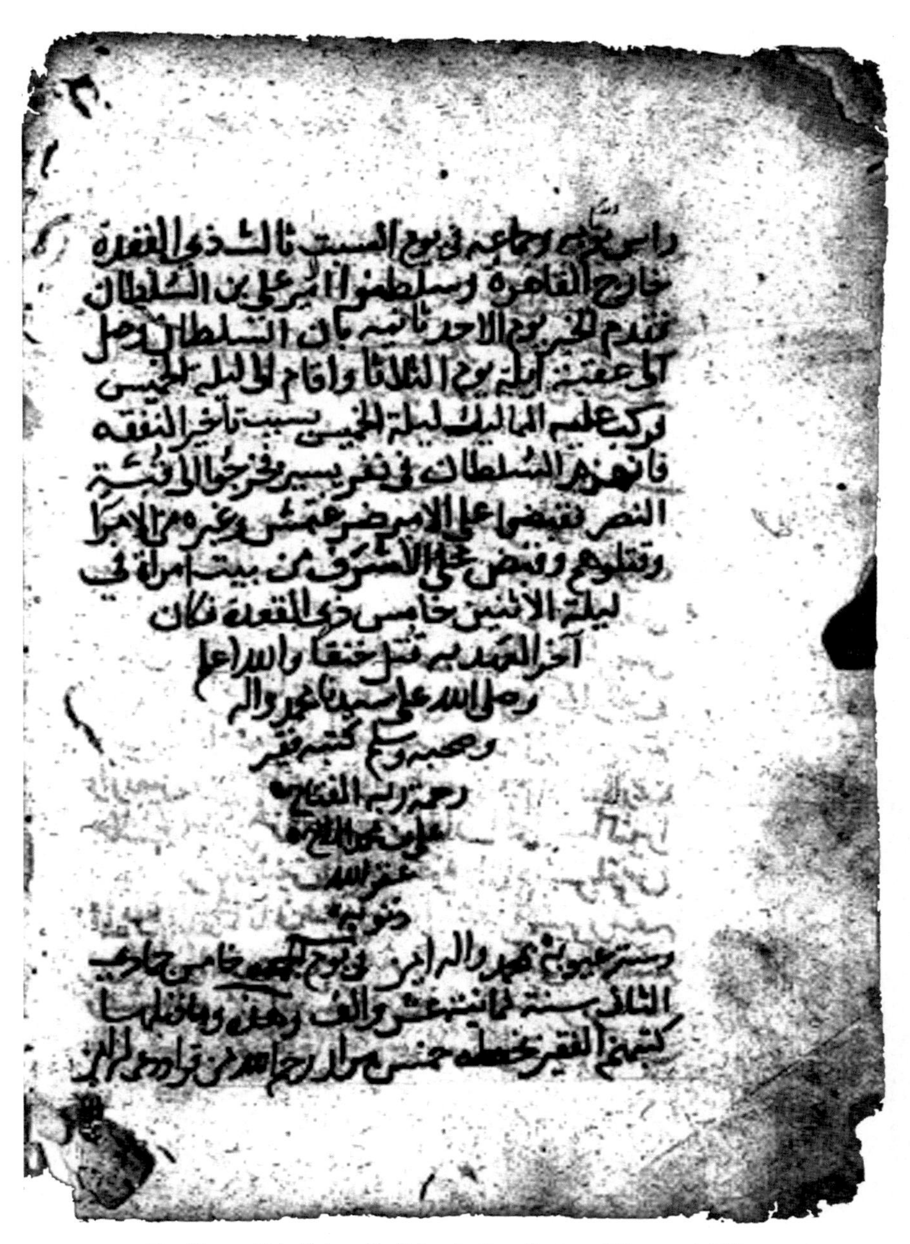

راس ... وجماعته في يوم السبت ثالث ذي القعدة
خارج القاهرة وسلطنوا الامير علي بن السلطان
تقدم الخبر يوم الاحد ثانيه بان السلطان وصل
الى عقبة ايلة يوم الثلاثا واقام الى ليلة الخميس
تركب عليه المماليك ليلة الخميس بسبب تاخير النفقة
فانهزم السلطان في نفر يسير فخرجوا الى قبة
النصر فقبضوا على الامير ضرغتمش وغيره من الامرا
وقتلوهم وقبض على الاشرف من بيت امراة في
ليلة الاثنين خامس ذي القعدة فكان
اخر العهد به قتل خنقا والله اعلم
وصلى الله على سيدنا محمد واله
وصحبه وسلم كتبه فقير
رحمة ربه الفتاح
علي بن محمد [illegible]
غفر الله
ذنوبه
وستر عيوبه [illegible] في يوم الخميس خامس [illegible]
الثاني سنة [illegible] والف [illegible]
كتبه الفقير [illegible]

PLATE 5 *New Haven, Yale University, Beinecke Rare Book and Manuscript Library, MS Landberg 111, fol. 62ᵇ*

PLATE 6 *Istanbul, Atıf Efendi Kütüphanesi,* MS 2814, *fol.* 84^a

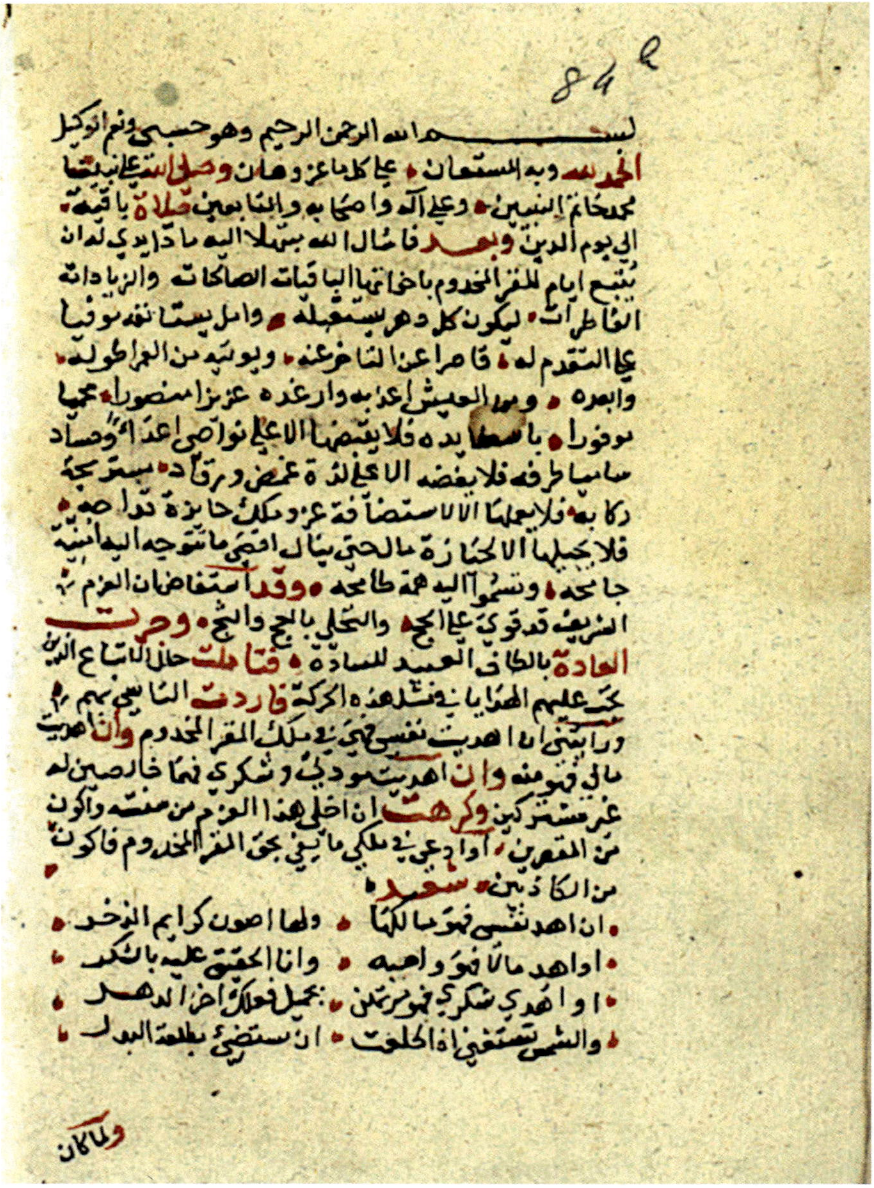

84b

بسم الله الرحمن الرحيم وهو حسبي ونعم الوكيل
الحمد لله وبه المستعان على كل ما عز وهان وصلى الله على نبينا
محمد خاتم النبيين وعلى آله واصحابه والتابعين صلاة باقية
الى يوم الدين وبعد فاسال الله ان يسهل اليه ما ادّاريك له ان
يُتبع ايام المقر المخدوم باخواتها الباقيات الصالحات والزيادات
المتطاولات ليكون كل دهر يستقبله واملًا يستانفه موفيا
على المتقدم له قاصرا عن المتأخر عنه ويوتيه من العمر اطوله
وابعده ومن العيش اعذبه وارغده عزيزا منصورا محميا
موفورا باسطا يده فلا يقبضها الا على نواصي اعدائه وحساده
ساميا طرفه فلا يغضه الا على لذة غمض ورقاده ميسرة حجة
ركابه فلا يعملها الا استضافة عز وملك حايزة ثوابا جم
فلا يحملها الا الحيازة مال حتى ينال اقصى ما توجه اليه امنيه
جامحه وتسمو اليه همة طامحه وقد استفاض ان العزم
الشريف قد قوي على الحج والتحلي بالحج والنجح وجرت
العادة بالطاف العبيد للسادة فتاملت حال الاتباع الذين
يجب عليهم الهدايا في مثل هذه الحركة فرددت التاسي بهم
ورايتني ان اهديت نفسي فهي في ملك المقر المخدوم وان اهديت
مالي فهو منه وان اهديت مودتي وشكري فهما خالصين له
غير مشتركين وكرهت ان اخلي هذا العزم من منتسه واكون
من المقصرين او ادعي في ملكي ما يفي بحق المقر المخدوم فاكون
من الكاذبين شعر

ان اهد نفسي فهو مالكها ... ولها اصون كرايم الذخر
او اهد مالا فهو واهبه ... وانا الحقيق عليه بالشكر
او اهد شكري فهو مرتهن ... بجميل فعلك آخر الدهر
والشمس تستغني اذا طلعت ... ان تستضيء بطلعة البدر

ولما كان

PLATE 7 *Istanbul, Atıf Efendi Kütüphanesi, MS 2814, fol. 84*[b]

١٠٧

107a

الاجلاب وشرع بالاهتمام بالحج في سنة ثمان وسبعين
وخرج الجلاب الاتي للسفر يوم السبت ثاني عشر شوال وخرج
طلب السلطان يوم الاحد ثالث عشره فجر عشرين قطار هجن
بقماش ذهب وخمسة عشر قطارا بعبي حرير وقطارا ملبس
خليفتي وقطارا بقماش ابيض برسم الاحرام ومائة راس خيل
مشهرة وكجاوتين وستة محفات كلها باغشية حرير مزركش
وستة واربعين زوج محاير وخزانة عشرين جمل وقطارين
جمال تحمل خضر مزدرعة ومن الجمال المحملة شيا كثيرا وركب
يوم الاثنين رابع عشره فاقام بسرياقوس الى يوم الثلاثا ثاني
عشرينه واستقل بالمسير وتقدم من الامرا المقدمين تسعة ومن
الطبلخاناه خمسة وعشرون ومن العشرات خمسة عشر فركب
طاش تمر المحمدي اللفاف احد العشرات وقرطاي راس نوبة وجماعة
في يوم السبت ثالث ذي القعدة خارج القاهرة وسلطنوا
امير علي ابن السلطان فقدم الخبر يوم الاحد ثانيه بان السلطان
وصل الى العقبة ايله يوم الثلاثا واقام الى ليلة الخميس فركب
عليه المماليك ليلة الخميس بسبب تاخير النفقة فانهزم السلطان
في نفر يسير فخرجوا الى قبة النصر فقبضوا على الامير صرغتمش وغيره
من الامرا وقتلوهم وقبض على الاشرف من بيت امراة في ليلة
الاثنين خامس ذي القعدة فكان اخر العهد به قتل خنقا والله
تعالى اعلم وصلى الله على سيدنا محمد وعلى اله وصحبه وسلم تسليما
كثيرا الى يوم الدين امين اللهم اغفر لمولفه ولكاتبه ولصاحبه ولمن
قرا فيه ونظر بوضعا واصلحه ولوالديهم ولمن دعا لهم
بالمغفرة وللمسلمين اجمعين امين وكان الفراغ من هذه
النسخة يوم الخميس عشرين الحجة الحرام من الهجرة
النبوية على صاحبها افضل الصلاة
والسلام

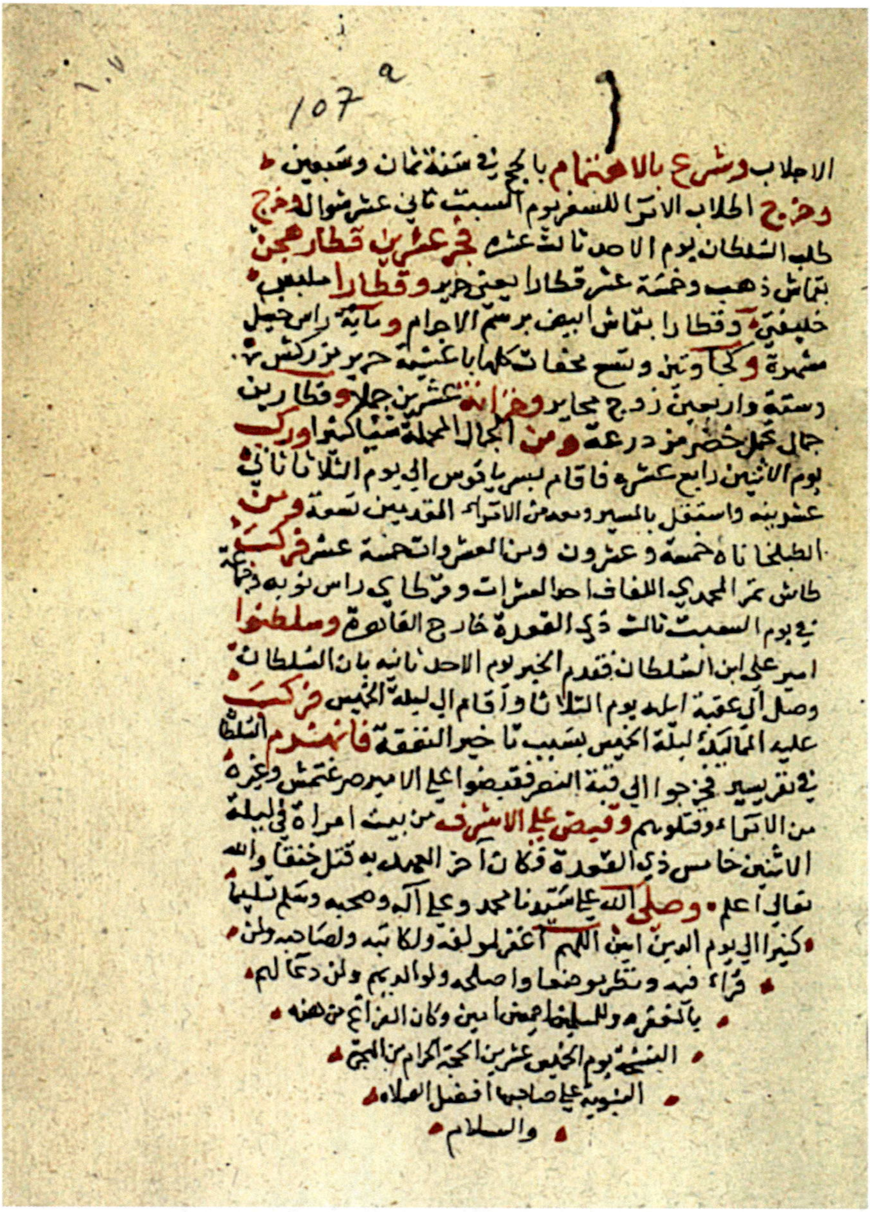

PLATE 8 *Istanbul, Atıf Efendi Kütüphanesi,* MS *2814, fol. 107*[a]

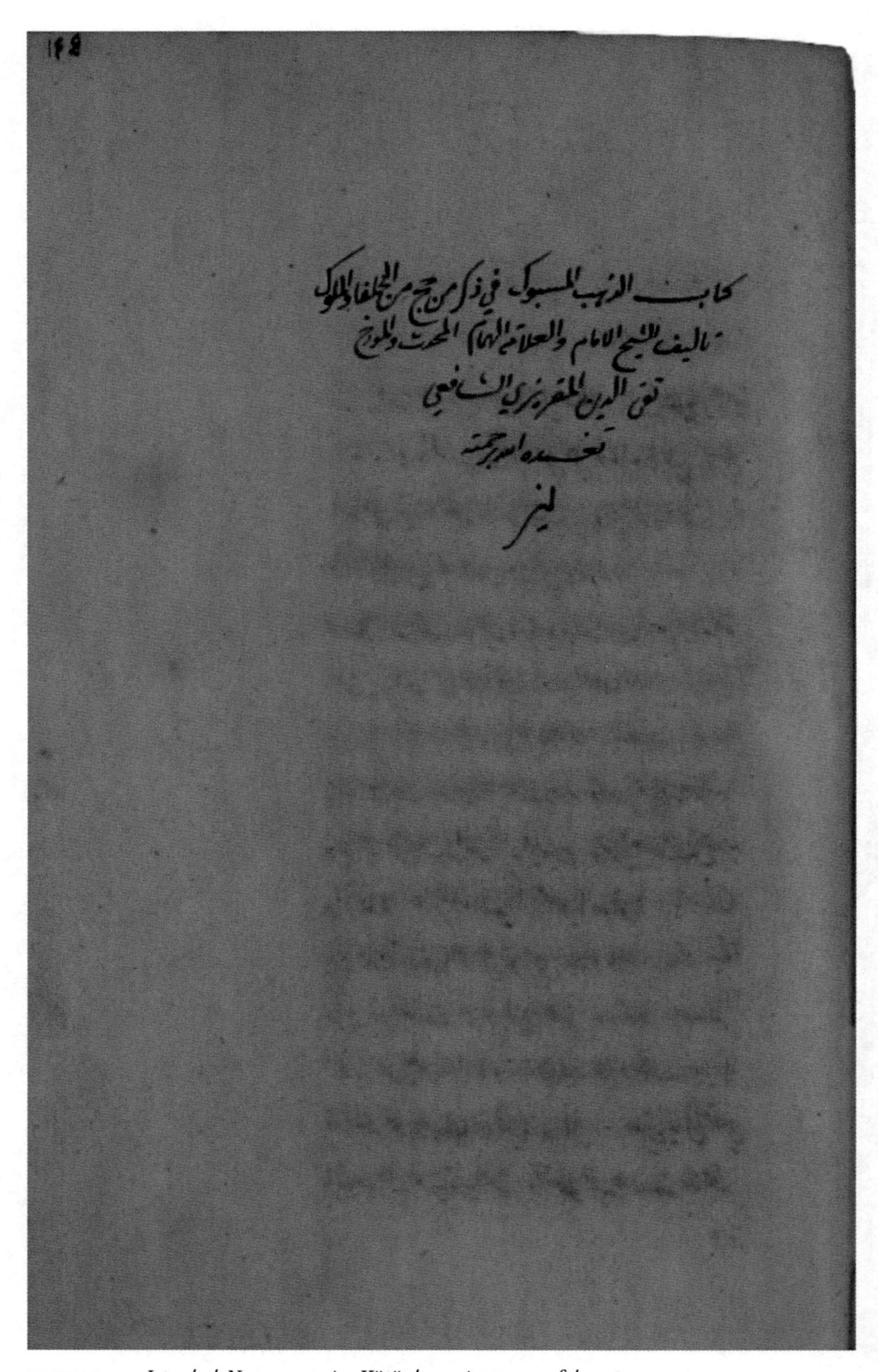

كتاب الذهب المسبوك في ذكر من حج من الخلفاء والملوك
تاليف الشيخ الامام والعلامة الهمام المحدث والمورخ
تقي الدين المقريزي الشافعي
تغمده الله برحمته

PLATE 9 *Istanbul, Nuruosmaniye Kütüphanesi,* MS *4937, fol. 145*[a]

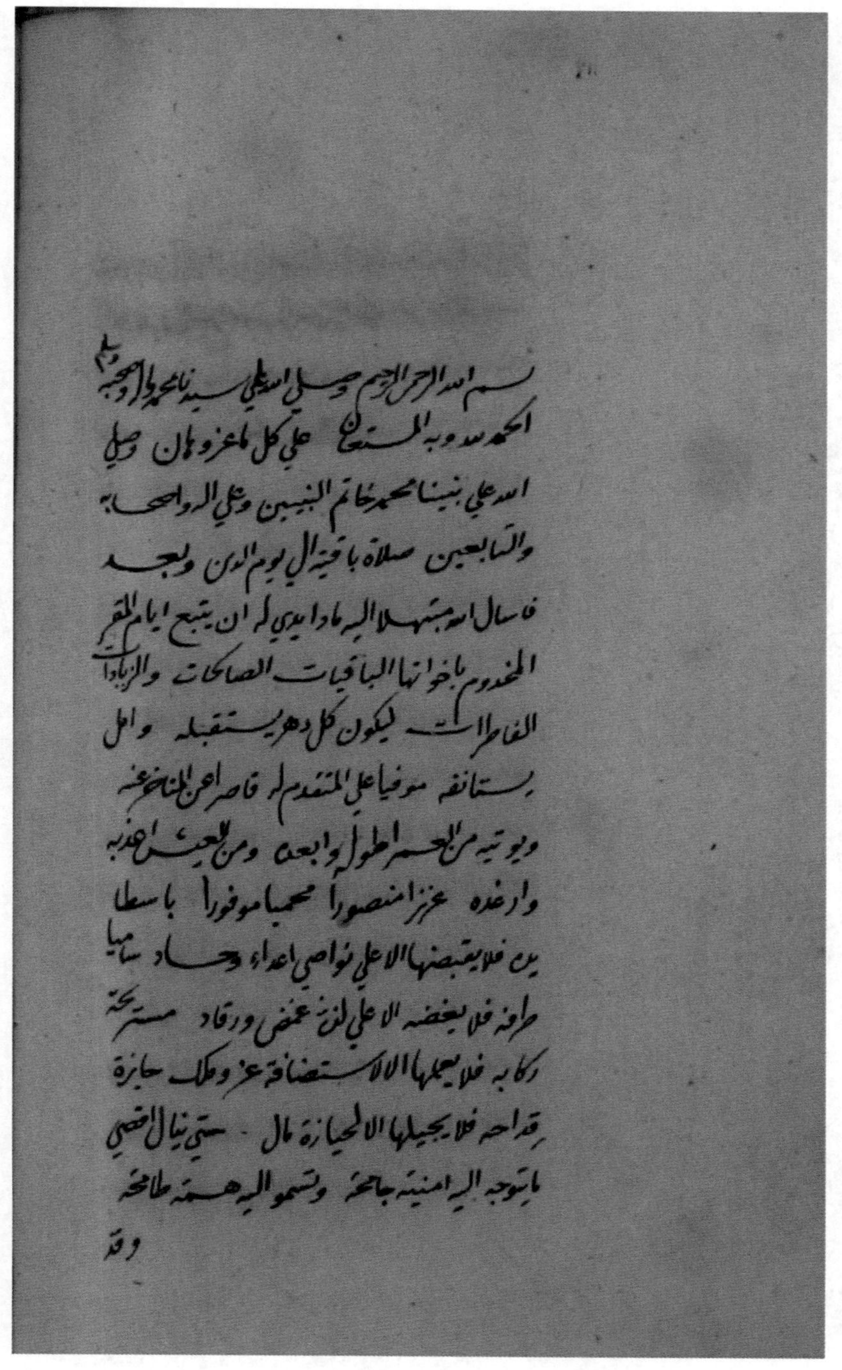

بسم الله الرحمن الرحيم وصلى الله على سيدنا محمد واله وصحبه وسلم
الحمد لله وبه المستعان على كل ما عز وهان وصلى
الله على نبينا محمد خاتم النبيين وعلى اله واصحابه
والتابعين صلاة باقية الى يوم الدين وبعد
فاسال الله مبتهلا اليه مادا يدي له ان يتبع ايام المقر
المخدوم باخواتها الباقيات الصالحات والزيادات
الفاطرات ليكون كل دهر يستقبله وامل
يستانفه موفيا على المتقدم له قاصرا عن المتاخر عنه
ويوتيه من العمر اطوله وابعده ومن العيش اعذبه
وارغده عزيزا منصورا محببا موفورا باسطا
يدا فلا يقبضها الا على نواصي اعداء وحساد ساميا
طرفه فلا يغضه الا على لذة غمض ورقاد مستريحة
ركابه فلا يعملها الا لاستضافة عز وملك حائزة
قداحه فلا يجيلها الا لحيازة مال حتى ينال اقصى
ما يتوجه اليه امنية جامحة وتسمو اليه همة طامحة
وقد

PLATE 10 *Istanbul, Nuruosmaniye Kütüphanesi,* MS *4937, fol. 145*[b]

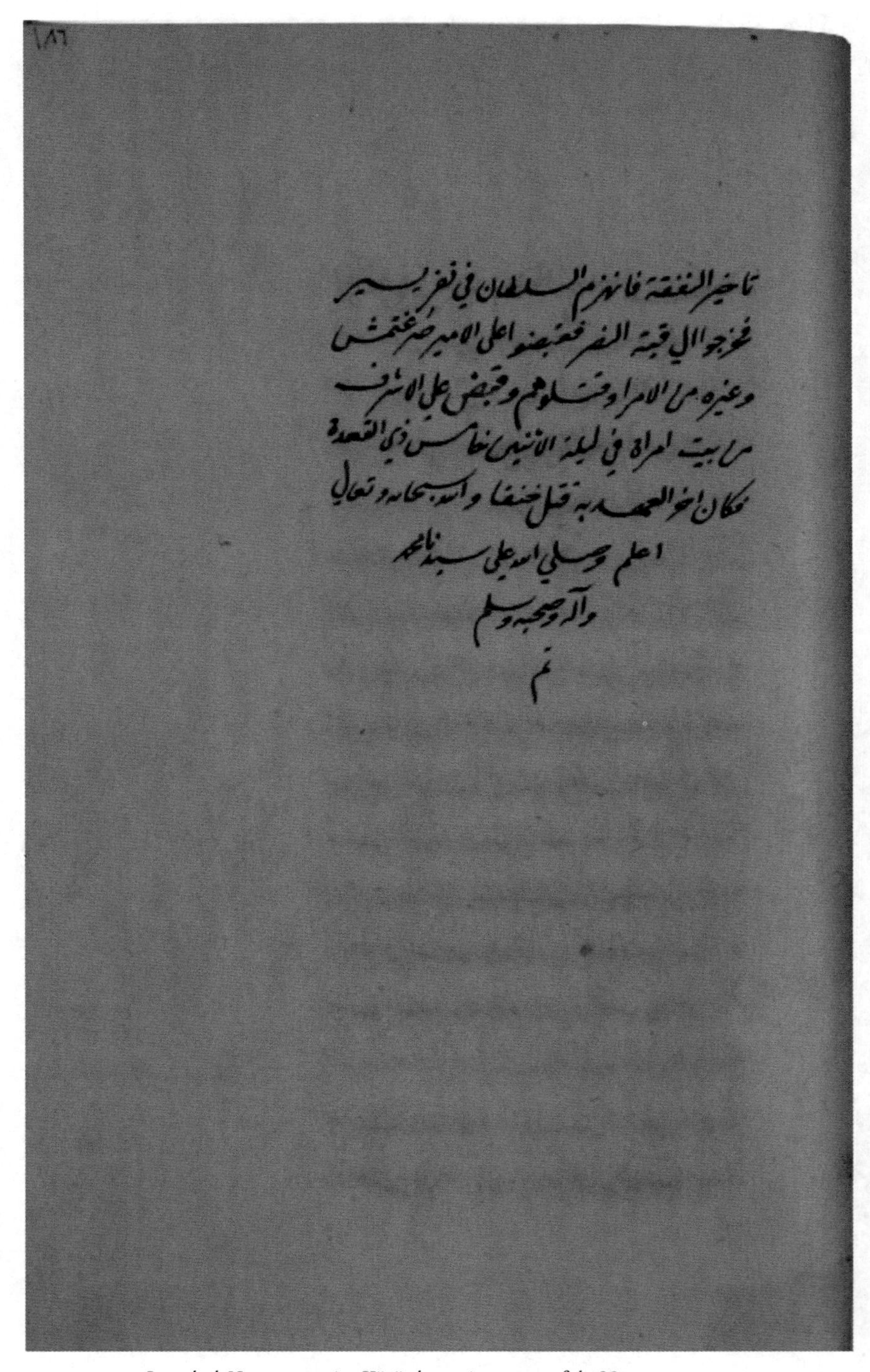

١٨٦

تاخير النفقة فانهزم السلطان في نفر يسير
فخرجوا الى قبة النصر فقبضوا على الامير صرغتمش
وغيره من الامرا وقتلوهم وقبض على الاشرف
من بيت امراة في ليلة الاثنين خامس ذي القعدة
فكان اخر العهد به قتل خنقا والله سبحانه وتعالى
اعلم وصلى الله على سيدنا محمد
وآله وصحبه وسلم
تم

PLATE 11 *Istanbul, Nuruosmaniye Kütüphanesi, MS 4937, fol. 186[a]*

٦٤

كتاب الذهب المسبوك في ذكر من حج من الخلفاء والملوك
تاليف الشيخ الامام العلامة الهمام المحدث
والمورخ تقي الدين المقريزي
الشافعي رحمه الله
تعالى

PLATE 12 *Istanbul, Beyazıt Devlet Kütüphanesi, MS Veliyüddin 3195, fol. 64[a]*

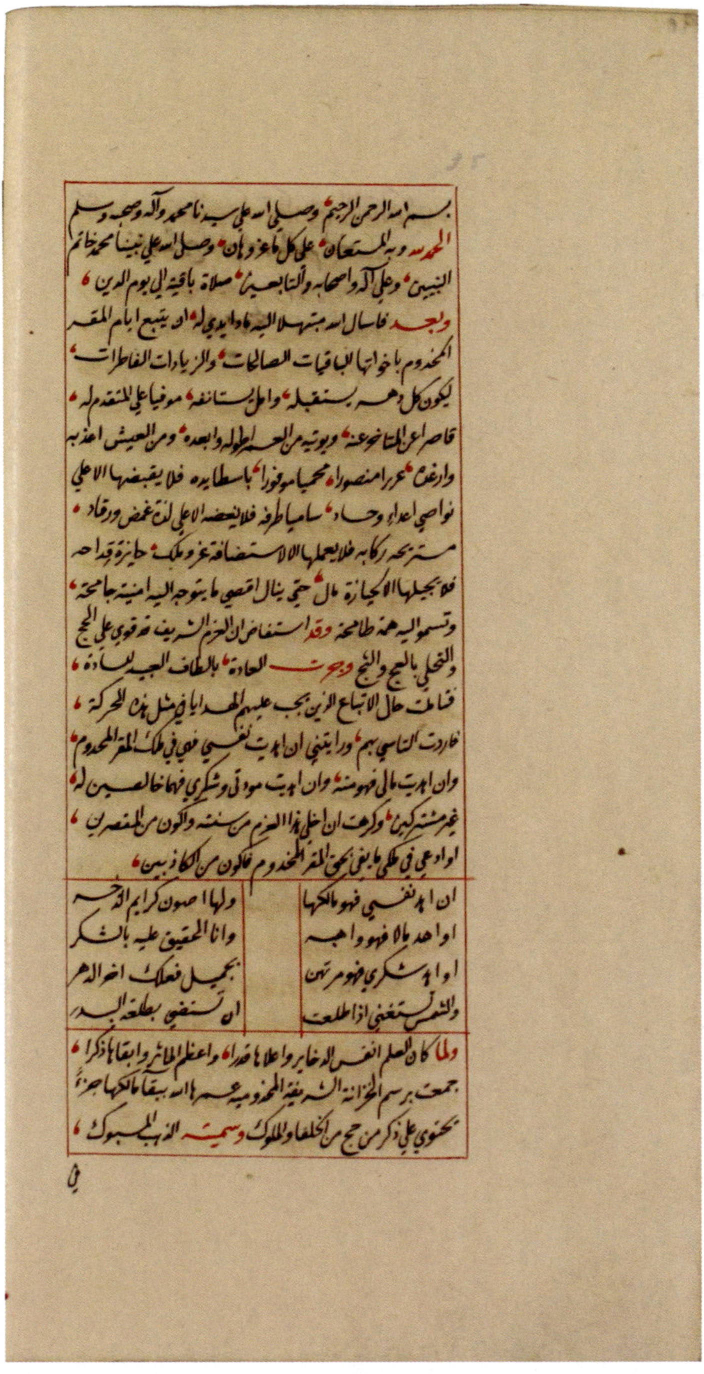

بسم الله الرحمن الرحيم وصلى الله على سيدنا محمد وآله وصحبه وسلم
الحمد لله وبه المستعان على كل ما عز وهان وصلى الله على نبينا محمد خاتم
النبيين وعلى آله واصحابه والتابعين صلاة باقية إلى يوم الدين
وبعد فاسال الله مبتهلا اليه مادا يدي له ان يتبع ايام المقر
المخدوم باخواتها الباقيات الصالحات والزيادات الفاطرات
ليكون كل دهر يستقبله واول يستانفه موفيا على المتقدم له
قاصرا عن المتاخر عنه ويوتيه من العمر اطوله وابعده ومن العيش اعذبه
وارغده عمرا منصورا محيا موفورا باسطا يده فلا يقبضها الا على
نواصي اعداء وحساد ساميا طرفه فلا يغضه الا على لين غمض ورقاد
مستريحة ركابه فلا يعملها الا لاستضافة عز وملك حائزة قداحه
فلا يجيلها الا لحيازة مال حتى ينال اقصى ما يتوجه اليه امنية جامحة
وتسمو اليه همة طامحة وقد استعفاه ان الحرم الشريف فقوي على الحج
والتخلي بالعج والثج وجرت العادة بالطاف العبيد لسادة
فسامت حال الاتباع الذين يجب عليهم الهدايا في مثل هذه الحركة
فاردت التاسي بهم ورايتني ان اهديت نفسي فهي في ملك المقر المخدوم
وان اهديت مالي فهو منه وان اهديت مودتي وشكري فهما خالصين له
غير مشتركين وكرهت ان اخلي هذا العزم من سنته واكون من المقصرين
او ادعي في ملكي ما يبقى بحق المقر المخدوم فاكون من الكاذبين

ان اهد نفسي فهو مالكها ولها اصون كرايم الذخر
او اهد مالا فهو واهبه وانا الحقيق عليه بالشكر
او اهد شكري فهو مرتهن بجميل فعلك آخر الدهر
والشمس تستغني اذا طلعت ان تستضي بطلعة البدر

ولما كان العلم انفس الذخاير واعلاها قدرا واعظم الماثر وابقاها ذكرا
جمعت برسم الخزانة الشريفة المخدومية عمرها الله ببقاء مالكها جزءا
يحتوي على ذكر من حج من الخلفاء والملوك وسميته الذهب المسبوك

PLATE 13 *Istanbul, Beyazıt Devlet Kütüphanesi,* MS *Veliyüddin 3195, fol. 64*[b]

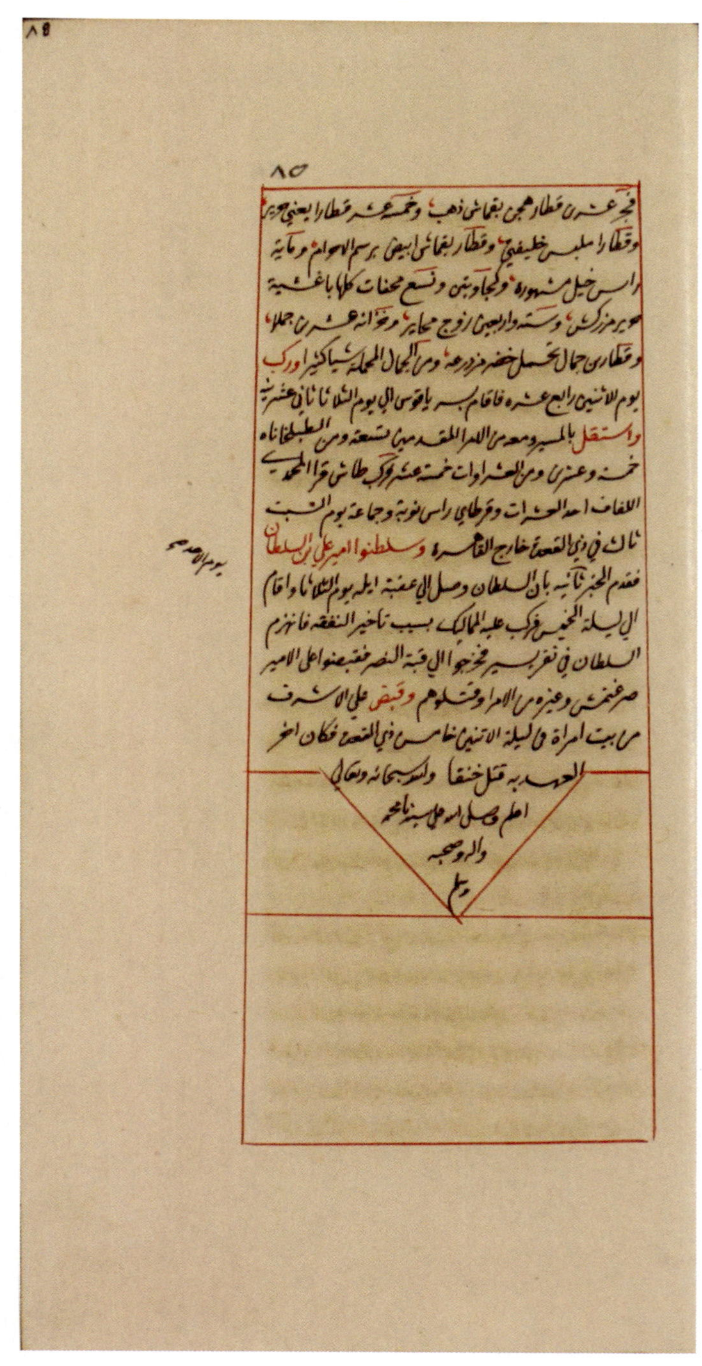

٨٥

٨٥

فيه عشرين قطار هجن بقماش ذهب وخمسة عشر قطارا بعبي حرير
وقطارا ملبس خليفتي وقطار بقماش ابيض برسم العوام ومائة
راس خيل مشهورة وكجاوتين وتسع محفات كلها باغشية
حرير مزركش وستة واربعين زوج محاير ومن خزانة عشرين جملا
وقطارين جمال تحمل خضر مزروعة ومن الجمال المحملة شيا كثيرا وركب
يوم الاثنين رابع عشره فاقام ببر ياقوس الى يوم الثلاثا ثاني عشرينه
واستقل بالمسير ومعه من الامرا المقدمين تسعة ومن الطبلخاناه
خمسة وعشرين ومن العشراوات خمسة عشر وركب طاش تمر المحمدي
اللفاف احد العشرات وقرطاي راس نوبة وجماعة يوم السبت
ثالث في ذي القعدة خارج القاهرة وسلطنوا الامير علي ابن السلطان
فقدم الخبر ثانيه بان السلطان وصل الى عقبة ايلة يوم الثلاثا واقام
الى ليلة الخميس فركب عليه المماليك بسبب تاخير النفقة فانهزم
السلطان في نفر يسير فخرجوا الى قبة النصر فقبضوا على الامير
صرغتمش وغيره من الامرا وقتلوهم وقبض على الاشرف
من بيت امراة في ليلة الاثنين خامس ذي القعدة فكان اخر
العهد به قتل خنقا والله سبحانه وتعالى
اعلم وصلى الله على سيدنا محمد
واله وصحبه
وسلم

يوم الاحد

PLATE 14 *Istanbul, Beyazıt Devlet Kütüphanesi,* MS *Veliyüddin 3195, fol. 85*[a]

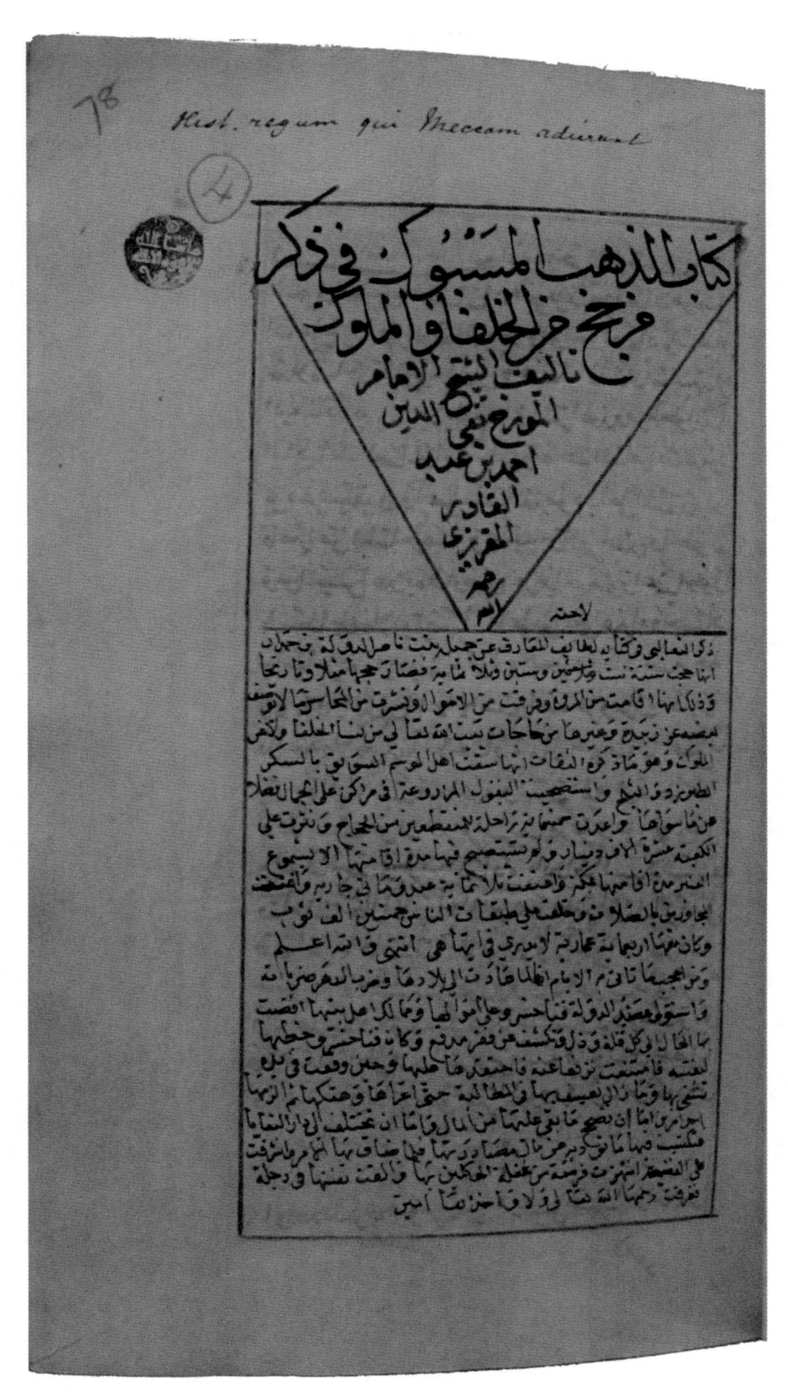

78

Hist. regum qui Meccam adierunt

كتاب الذهب المسبوك في ذكر
من حج من الخلفا والملوك
تأليف الشيخ الإمام
المؤرخ تقي الدين
أحمد بن عبد
القادر
المقريزي
رحمه
الله

PLATE 15 *Cambridge, University Library, MS Add. 746, fol. 78[a]*

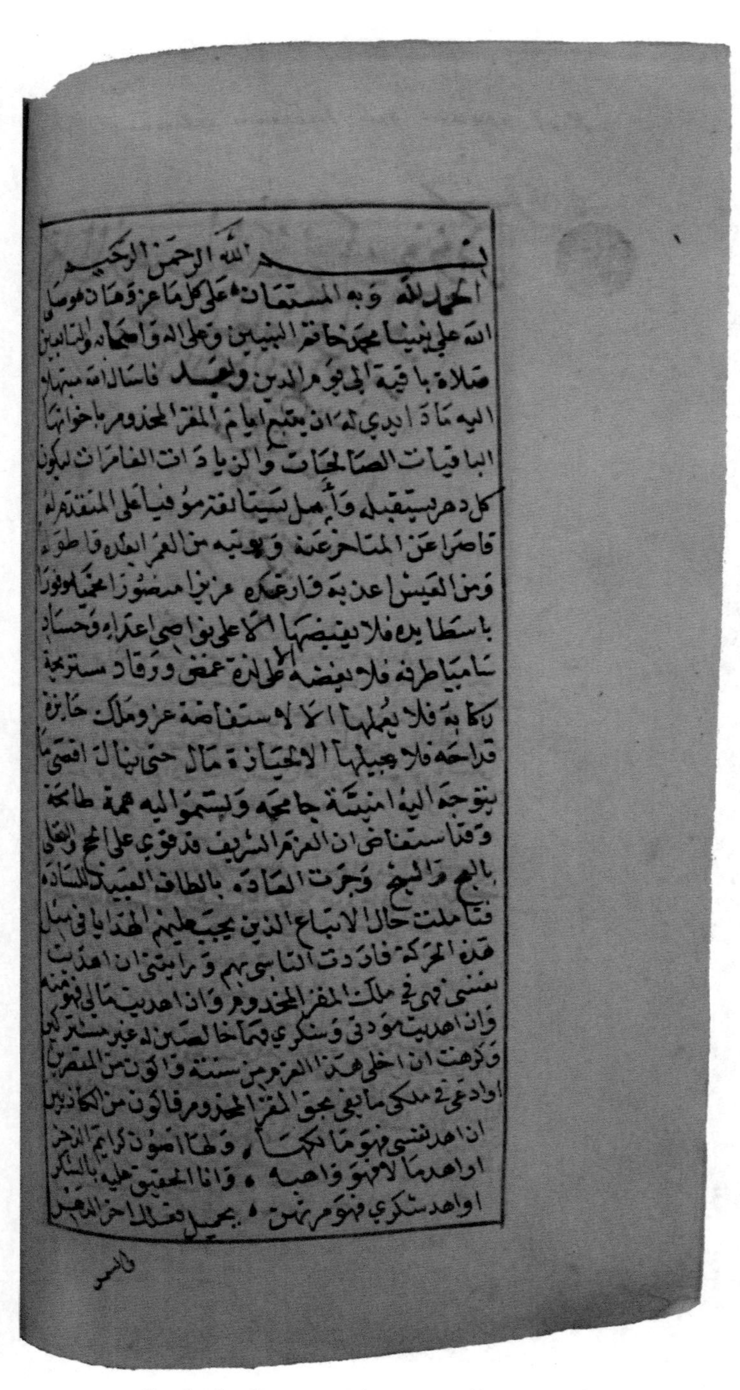

بسم الله الرحمن الرحيم
الحمد لله وبه المستعان على كل ما عز وهان وصلى
الله على نبينا محمد خاتم النبيين وعلى آله وأصحابه والتابعين
صلاة باقية إلى يوم الدين وبعد فأسأل الله سبحانه
إليه مادة أيديه أن يمتع أيام المقر المخدوم بأخواتها
الباقيات الصالحات والزيادات العامرات ليكون
كل دهر يستقبله وأمل يستأنفه موفيا على المتقدم له
قاصرا عن المتأخر عنه ويهب له من العمر أبلغه وأطوله
ومن العيش أعذبه وأرغده عزيزا منصورا محميا موفورا
باسطا يده فلا يقبضها إلا على نواصي أعدائه وحساده
ساميا طرفه فلا يغضه إلا على لذة غمض ورقاد مستريحة
ركابه فلا يعملها إلا لاستفاضة عز وملك حائزة
قداحه فلا يجيلها إلا لحيازة مال حتى ينال أقصى ما
يتوجه إليه أمنية جامحة ويسمو إليه همة طامحة
وقد استفاض أن العزم الشريف قد قوي على الحج [illegible]
بالبر والنجح وجرت العادة بالطاف العبيد للسادة
فتأملت حال الأتباع الذين يجب عليهم الهدايا في مثل
هذه الحركة فأردت التأسي بهم ورأيتني إن أهديت
نفسي فهي في ملك المقر المخدوم وإن أهديت مالي فهو منه
وإن أهديت مودتي وشكري فهما خالصين له غير مشتركين
وكرهت أن أخلي هذا العزم من سنة وأكون من المقصرين
أو أدعي في ملكي ما يبقى بحق للمقر المخدوم فأكون من الكاذبين
إن أهديت نفسي فهو مالكها ، وهذا أصون لرائم الذخر
أو أهديت مالي فهو واهبه ، وأنا الحقيق عليه بالشكر
أو أهديت شكري فهو مرتهن ، بجميل فعله آخر الدهر

PLATE 16 *Cambridge, University Library,* MS *Add. 746, fol. 78*[b]

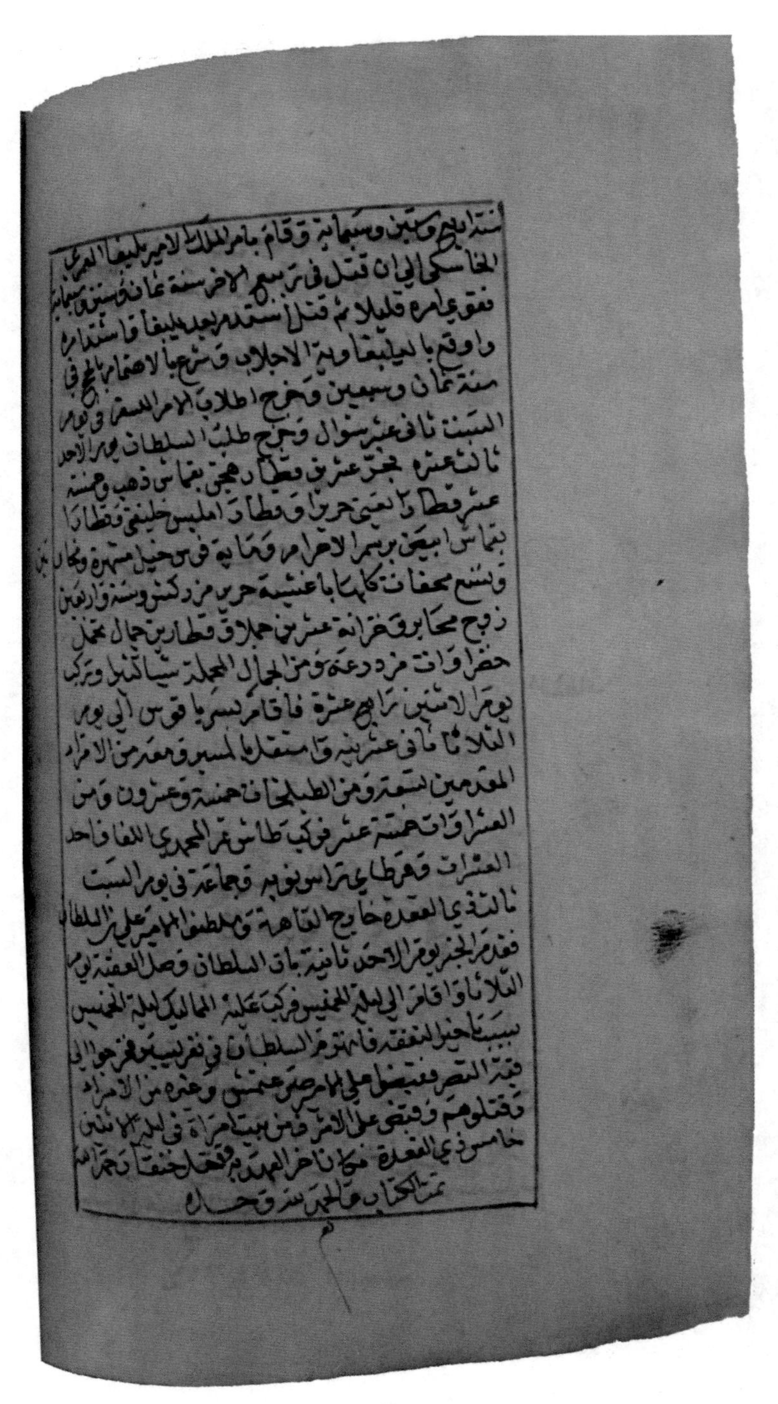

PLATE 17 *Cambridge, University Library, MS Add. 746, fol. 105*[b]

بسم الله الرحمن الرحيم
الحمد لله وبه المستعان على كل ما عز وهان
وصلى الله على نبينا محمد خاتم النبيين وعلى آله وأصحابه
والتابعين صلاة باقية إلى يوم الدين وبعد
فأسأل الله مبتهلا إليه مادا يدي له أن ينسئ أيام
المقر المخدوم بأخواتها الباقيات الصالحات
والزيادات الغامرات ليكون كل دهر يستقبله وأمل
يستأنفه موفيا على المتقدم له قاصرا على المتأخر
عنه ويؤتيه من العمر أطوله وأبعده ومن العيش أعذبه
وأرغده عزيزا منصورا محجبا موفورا باسطا يده
فلا يقبضها إلا على نواصي أعداء وحساد حاميا
طرفه فلا يغضه على لذة تمحيص ورقاد مستغنية
ركابه فلا يعملها إلا لاستفاضة عز وملك حائزة
قد أحد فلا يجيلها إلا لحيازة مال حتى ينال أقصى
ما يتوجه إليه أمنية جامحة وتسمو إليه همة طامحة
وقد استفاض عندي أن العزم الشريف قد قوي على الحج
والتحلي بالعود والحج وجرت العادة لألطاف
العبيد للسادة فتأملت حال الأتباع الذي يجب
عليهم الهدايا في مثل هذه الحركة فأردت التأسي بهم
ورأيتني إن أهديت نفسي فهي في ملك المقر
المخدوم وإن أهديت مالي فهو منه وإن أهديت
مودتي وشكري فهما خالصان له غير مشترك فيهما
وكرهت أن أخلي هذا العزم من سنة وأكون من العصري
أو أدعي في ملكي ما هو حق المقر المخدوم فأكون من
الكاذبين شعر

ان

PLATE 18 *Paris, Bibliothèque nationale de France,* MS *arabe 4657, fol. 101*[b]

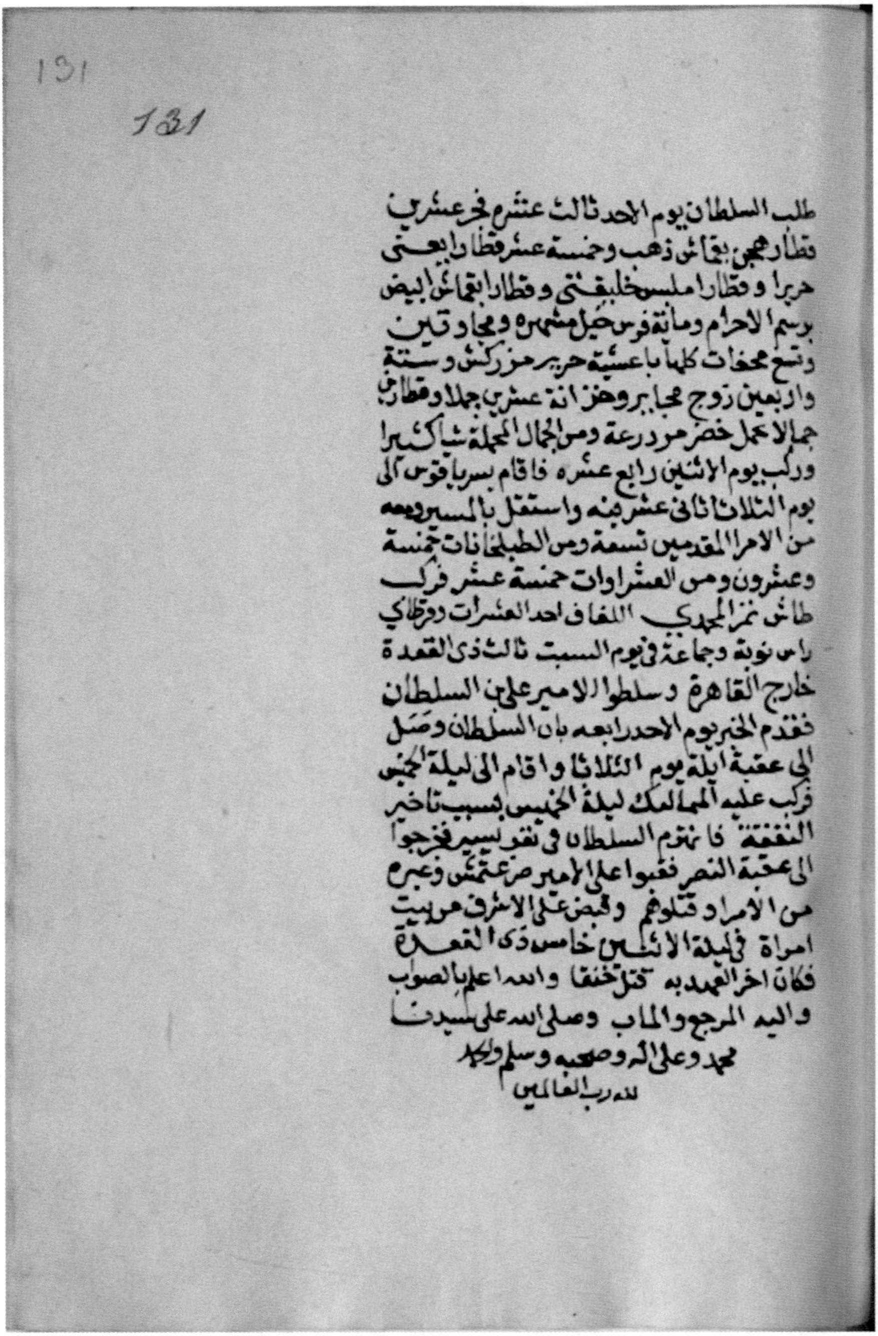

131

131

طلب السلطان يوم الاحد ثالث عشره فخرج عشرين
قطار هجن بقماش ذهب وخمسة عشر قطارا بعني
حريرا وقطارا ملبس خليفتي وقطارا بقماش ابيض
برسم الاحرام ومائة فرس خيل مشهورة ومحادتين
وتسع محفات كلها باغشية حرير مزركش وستة
واربعين زوج محاير وخزانة عشرين جملا وقطارين
جمال لحمل خضر مزدرعة ومن الجمال المحملة شيا كثيرا
وركب يوم الاثنين رابع عشره فاقام بسرياقوس الى
يوم الثلاثا ثاني عشرينه واستقل بالمسير ومعه
من الامرا المقدمين تسعة ومن الطبلخاناة خمسة
وعشرون ومن العشراوات خمسة عشر فركب
طاش تمر الجهركسي اللفاف احد العشرات دوقطاي
راس نوبة وجماعة في يوم السبت ثالث ذي القعدة
خارج القاهرة وسلطنوا الامير علي بن السلطان
فقدم الخبر يوم الاحد رابعه بان السلطان وصل
الى عقبة ايلة يوم الثلاثا واقام الى ليلة الخميس
فركب عليه المماليك ليلة الخميس بسبب تاخير
النفقة فانهزم السلطان في نفر يسير فخرجوا
الى عقبة النصر فقبضوا على الامير صرغتمش وغيره
من الامرا وقتلوهم وقبض على الاشرف من بيت
امراة في ليلة الاثنين خامس ذي القعدة
فكان اخر العهد به قتل خنقا والله اعلم بالصواب
واليه المرجع والماب وصلى الله على سيدنا
محمد وعلى اله وصحبه وسلم والحمد
لله رب العالمين

PLATE 19 *Paris, Bibliothèque nationale de France, MS arabe 4657, fol. 131a*

الذهب المسبوك في ذكر من حج من الخلفاء والملوك
تاليف الشيخ الامام الرحلة الحافظ
المحدث احمد بن علي
المقريزي تغمده
الله برحمة

PLATE 20 *Cambridge, University Library, MS Qq. 141, fol. 1*[a]

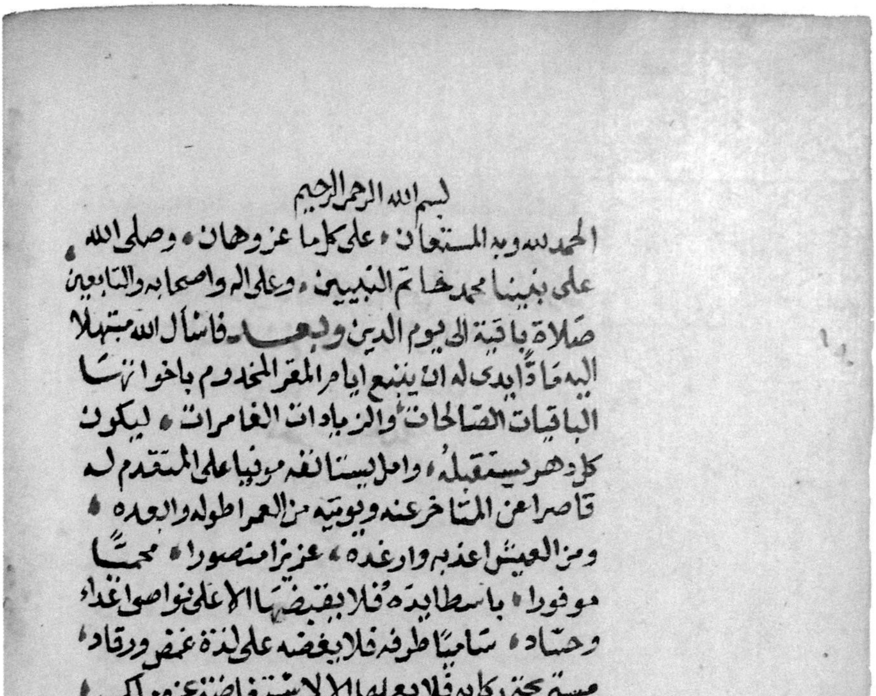

بسم الله الرحمن الرحيم

الحمد لله وبه المستعان ، على كل ما عز وهان ، وصلى الله
على نبينا محمد خاتم النبيين ، وعلى آله واصحابه والتابعين
صلاة باقية الى يوم الدين وبعد فاسال الله متبهلا
اليه مادًّا يدي له ان يتبع ايام المقر المخدوم باخواتها
الباقيات الصالحات والزيادات الغامرات ، ليكون
كل دهر يستقبله ، وامل يستانفه موفيا على المتقدم له
قاصرا عن المتاخر عنه ويومه من العمر اطوله والعده
ومن العيش اعذبه وارغده ، عزيزا منصورا ، محميا
موفورا ، باسطا يده فلا يقبضها الا على نواصي اعداء
وحساد ، ساميا طرفه فلا يغضه على لذة غمض ورقاد
مسترجية ركابه فلا يعملها الا لاستفاضة عز وملك
حايزة قداحه فلا يجيلها الا لحيازة مال حتى ينال اقصى
ما يتوجه اليه امنية جامحه ، وتسموا اليه همة طامحه
وقد استفاض ان العزم الشريف قد قوى على الحج ، والتحلي
بالعج والثج ، وجرت العادة بالطاف العبيد للسادة
فتاملت حال الاتباع الذي يجب عليهم الهدايا في
مثل هذه الحركة فاردت التاسي بهم ورايتني ان
اهديت نفسي وهي في ملك المقر المخدوم وان اهديت

مالي

PLATE 21 *Cambridge, University Library, MS Qq. 141, fol. 1[b]*

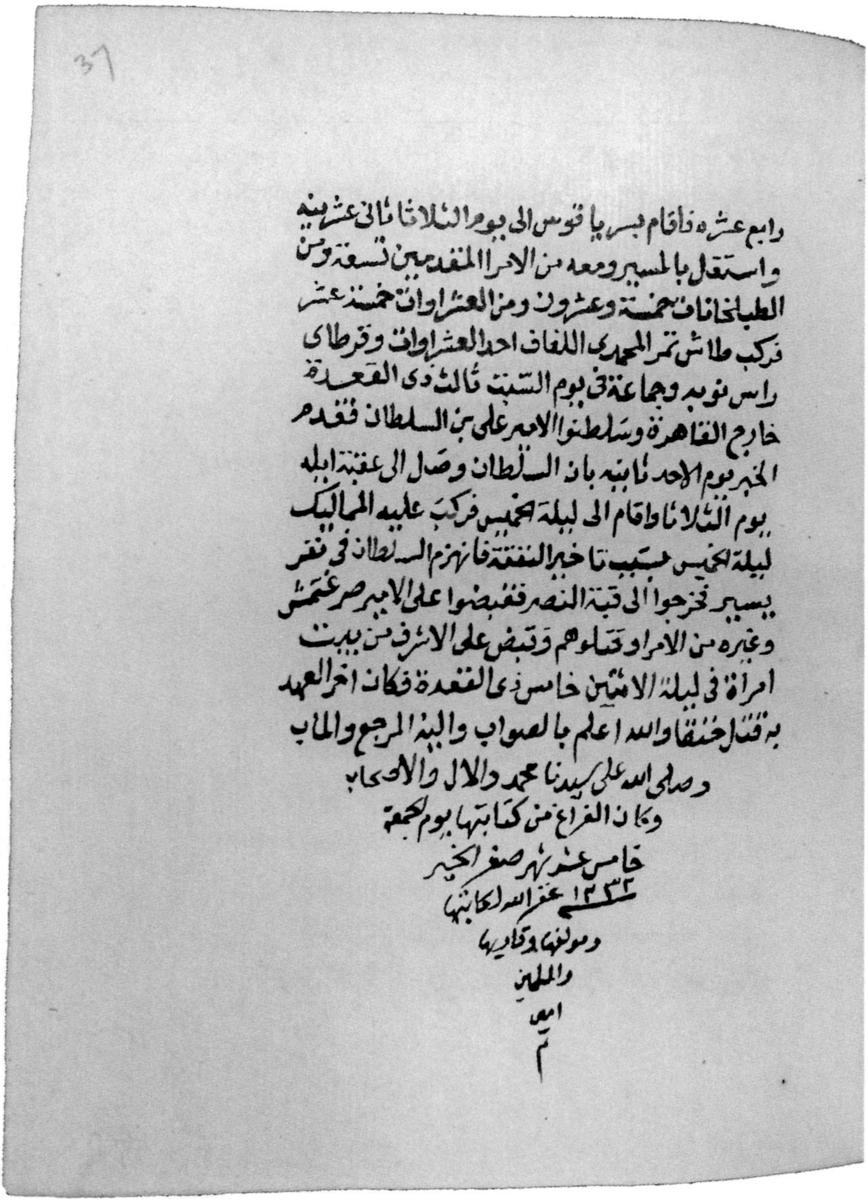

37

رابع عشره فاقام بسرياقوس الى يوم الثلاثا ثاني عشريه
واستقل بالمسير ومعه من الامرا المقدمين تسعة ومن
الطبلخاناة خمسة وعشرون ومن العشراوات خمسة عشر
فركب طاش تمر المحمدي اللفاف احد العشراوات وقرطاي
راس نوبة وجماعة في يوم السبت ثالث ذي القعدة
خارج القاهرة وسلطنوا الامير علي بن السلطان فقدم
الخبر يوم الاحد ثانيه بان السلطان وصل الى عقبة ايلة
يوم الثلاثا واقام الى ليلة الخميس فركب عليه المماليك
ليلة الخميس بسبب تاخير النفقة فانهزم السلطان في نفر
يسير فخرجوا الى قبة النصر فقبضوا على الامير صرغتمش
وغيره من الامرا وقتلوهم وقبض على الاشرف من بيت
امراة في ليلة الاثنين خامس ذي القعدة فكان اخر العهد
به قتل خنقا والله اعلم بالصواب واليه المرجع والماب
وصلى الله على سيدنا محمد والال والاصحاب
وكان الفراغ من كتابتها يوم الجمعة
خامس عشر شهر صفر الخير
سنة ١٢٣٢ غفر الله لكاتبها
ومولفها وقاريها
والمسلمين
امين
تم

PLATE 22 *Cambridge, University Library,* MS *Qq. 141, fol. 37*[a]

TABLE 1 *Collation table of 58 scribal errors in mss. L (white [= scribe]/orange [= author]), E (yellow), Y (light blue), Ia (purple), In (grey), Iv (dark blue), Ca (red), P (dark green), Cq (light green)*

Leiden UB MS Or 560, ff. 115^b^–135^a^ (*aṣl*) → L [A1 + A2] / 1438	**Escorial, MS Ar. 1771, ff. 22^b^–75^b^ → E / 16th c.**	**New Haven, Yale UL, MS Landberg 111, ff. 26–62 → Y / 1609**	**Ist. SK, MS Atıf Efendi 2814, ff. 84^b^–107^b^ → Ia / 1632**
سميته الذهب المسبوك (١١٥ب)		سميته الذهب المسبوك في ذكر من حج من الخلفاء والملوك (١٢٧)	
يامره عن ربه تعالى (١١٦)			
وامر من كان معه هدي (١١٦ب)			
فقال له صلى الله عليه وسلم بما اهللت قال باهْلال كاهْلالِ النبي صلى الله عليه وسلم (١١٦ب)	(١٢٦) /		
ثم حل من كل شي حَرُم منه صلى الله عليه وسلم وخطب ثاني يوم النحر (١١٦ب)		ثم حل من كل شي حرم منه صلى الله عليه وسلم ثاني يوم النحر ثم خطب (١٢٩)	
في تلك الحجة (١١٩)			
المنصف (١١٩ب)		النصف (٣٤ب)	

Ist., SK, MS Nuruosmaniye 4937, ff. 145ª–186ª →In / 1674–1675	Ist. SK, MS Veliüddin 3195, ff. 64–85 → Iv / 1690	Cambridge UL, MS Add. 746, ff. 78–105 → Ca / 1701	Paris, BnF, MS arabe 4657, ff. 101ᵇ–131ª → P / mid-18th c.	Cambridge UL, MS Qq. 141, ff. 1–37 → Cq / 1817
		وسميته بالذهب المسبوك في ذكر من حج من الخلفاء والملوك (١٧٩)		
	يامره عن ربه عز وجل (١٦٥)			
وامر من كان معه (١٤٧ب)				
		ثم حل من كل شيء احرم منه صلى الله عليه وسلم ثاني يوم النحر ثم خطب (١٨٠-ب)		
في تلك السنة (١١٥٣)				

Leiden UB MS Or 560, ff. 115b–135a (*aṣl*) → L [A1 + A2] / 1438	Escorial, MS Ar. 1771, ff. 22b–75b → E / 16th c.	New Haven, Yale UL, MS Landberg 111, ff. 26–62 → Y / 1609	Ist. SK, MS Atıf Efendi 2814, ff. 84b–107b → Ia / 1632
وبعث الوليد الى ملك الروم بما عزم عليه (١١٩ب)			
بجزُرٍ (١٢٠)		بجزور (٣٥ب)	
الذي سقاكم المآ العذب الزلال النُقَاخَ العَذْب (١٢٠)			
(١٢٠ب) /			
من بغداد الى مكة (١٢١)			
ومن بديع ما يحكي عنه (١٢١ب-١٢٦ب)	ومن بديع ما حكى عنه ... (٣٩ب)		
وعن حسبك (١٢٦ب)	وعن حَيْبك (٤١ب)		
ولما دخل الرشيد مكة (١٢٤ب)			
والكسوة الظاهرة (١٢٥)		/	

Ist., SK, MS Nuruosmaniye 4937, ff. 145ª–186ª →In / 1674–1675	**Ist. SK, MS Veliüddin 3195, ff. 64–85 → Iv / 1690**	**Cambridge UL, MS Add. 746, ff. 78–105 → Ca / 1701**	**Paris, BnF, MS arabe 4657, ff. 101ᵇ–131ª → P / mid-18th c.**	**Cambridge UL, MS Qq. 141, ff. 1–37 → Cq / 1817**
وبعث الوليد بما عزم عليه الى ملك الروم (١٥٤ا)				
	الذي سقاكم المآ العذب الزلال النقاخ (٦٩ب)			
		والله المعين (١٨٦)	والله المعين الهادي الى طريق الارشاد (١١٠ا)	والله المعين الهادي الى طريق الرشاد (١١ب)
	من بغداد الى الكوفة (١٧٠ا)			
ولما دخل الرشيد مكة وهو خليفة (١٦٢ا)				
الكسوة الطاهرة (١٦٢ب)	والكسوة الظاهرة الفاخرة (١٧٢ا)			

Leiden UB MS Or 560, ff. 115b–135a (*aṣl*) → L [A1 + A2] / 1438	Escorial, MS Ar. 1771, ff. 22b–75b → E / 16th c.	New Haven, Yale UL, MS Landberg 111, ff. 26–62 → Y / 1609	Ist. SK, MS Atıf Efendi 2814, ff. 84b–107b → Ia / 1632
ومن فضايل الرشيد (١٢٣ب)		/	
ثم قال له (١٢٣ا)			
(١٢٥ب) /			
قسيم الدولة بن اقسنقر (١٢٥ب)			
والمارستان (١٢٥ب)			
وستماية (١٢٧ا)		وخمسماية (٤٦ب)	
بالحرمين (١٢٧ا)			
وبالغ في الاحسان (١٢٧ا)			
كفني (١٢٧ب)			
جزيلة (١٢٧ب)		جليلة (١٤٨)	
والجنايات (١٢٨ب)		الجبايات (٤٩ب)	

Ist., SK, MS Nuruosmaniye 4937, ff. 145^{a}–186^{a} → In / 1674–1675	Ist. SK, MS Veliüddin 3195, ff. 64–85 → Iv / 1690	Cambridge UL, MS Add. 746, ff. 78–105 → Ca / 1701	Paris, BnF, MS arabe 4657, ff. 101^{b}–131^{a} → P / mid-18th c.	Cambridge UL, MS Qq. 141, ff. 1–37 → Cq / 1817
		وقال (٩١ب)		
	والله سبحانه وتعالى اعلم (١٧٥)			
			قسيم الدولة بن آق (١١٧ب)	
والبيمارستان (١٦٧ب)		والبيمارستانات (٩٣ب)		
بالحرمين الشريفين (١٦٨ا)				
وبالغ في الاحسان رحمه الله تعالى (١٦٨ا)				
الكفن (١٦٨ب)				
			(١٢٠ب) /	

Leiden UB MS Or 560, ff. 115^{b}–135^{a} (*aṣl*) → L [A1 + A2] / 1438	Escorial, MS Ar. 1771, ff. 22^{b}–75^{b} → E / 16th c.	New Haven, Yale UL, MS Landberg 111, ff. 26–62 → Y / 1609	Ist. SK, MS Atıf Efendi 2814, ff. 84^{b}–107^{b} → Ia / 1632
والجنايات (١٢٨ب)		الجبايات (٤٩ب)	
(١٢٨ب) /			
سلطنة مصر (١٢٨ب)			
ان الشتته (١٢٨ب)	ان التشتت (١٥٧)	ان تشتت (٥٠ب)	
ولم تزل كسوة المظفر التي كساها للكعبة (١٢٩ا)			
الفوار (١٣٠ا)	النوار (٦٠ب)	الفور (١٥٣)	
يوم الخميس خامس شهر شوال (١٣٠ا)			
وبلاد الشام (١٣١ا)			
مهابة السلطان (١٣١ا)			
قتل اخيه الملك الأشرف صلاح الدين خليل بن قلاوون (١٣١ب)			

Ist., SK, MS Nuruosmaniye 4937, ff. 145ª–186ª →In / 1674–1675	Ist. SK, MS Veliüddin 3195, ff. 64–85 → Iv / 1690	Cambridge UL, MS Add. 746, ff. 78–105 → Ca / 1701	Paris, BnF, MS arabe 4657, ff. 101ᵇ–131ª → P / mid-18th c.	Cambridge UL, MS Qq. 141, ff. 1–37 → Cq / 1817
	والله سبحانه وتعالى اعلم (٧٧ب)			
سلطنته (١٧١ب)				
ولم تزل كسوة الكعبة التي كساها المظفر (١٧٣ا)			ولم تزل كسوة المظفر التي كساها الكعبة (١٢١ب)	
	يوم الخميس خامس شوال (١٧٩)			
	والشام (١٨٠)			
	مهابته (١٨٠)			
		اخيه الملك الاشرف صلاح الدين خليل بن قلاوون (١٠٠ا)		

Leiden UB MS Or 560, ff. 115b–135a (*aṣl*) → L [A1 + A2] / 1438	Escorial, MS Ar. 1771, ff. 22b–75b → E / 16th c.	New Haven, Yale UL, MS Landberg 111, ff. 26–62 → Y / 1609	Ist. SK, MS Atıf Efendi 2814, ff. 84b–107b → Ia / 1632
اشلون بنت شكاي (١٣١ب)	اسَلُون بنت شكراي (١٦٤)		
فقدم (١٣١ب)			
وتقطاي الساقي (١٣١ب)		ونقطاي الساقي (١٥٦)	
وسلمهم (١٣١ب)			
ومنهم من له خمسون عليقة (١٣٢ب)			ومنهم من له خمسين عليقة (١٠٣ب)
بعد ما كان سلوكها مشقا (١٣٢ب)			
وتقدم اليه قاضي القضاة بدر الدين ابن جماعة (١٣٢ب)	وتقدم اليه ابن جماعة (١٦٨)		
مدة سنين (١٣٣ا)			
وصاروا يَدِلون عليه ادلالا زائدا (١٣٣ا)			
والاحمدي مستمر عليه زرديه وسيفه (١٣٣ب)		وكل احد مشتمل عليه زرديه وسيفه (٥٩ب)	
ومعه ماية حجارا (١٣٣ب)		ومعه ماية حجار (١٦٠)	

Ist., SK, MS Nuruosmaniye 4937, ff. 145[a]–186[a] →In / 1674–1675	Ist. SK, MS Veliüddin 3195, ff. 64–85 → Iv / 1690	Cambridge UL, MS Add. 746, ff. 78–105 → Ca / 1701	Paris, BnF, MS arabe 4657, ff. 101[b]–131[a] → P / mid-18th c.	Cambridge UL, MS Qq. 141, ff. 1–37 → Cq / 1817
		اسلون بنت سكاي (١٠٠ا)		
	فتقدم (٨٠ب)			
	واسلمهم (٨١)			
بعدما كان سلوكه صعب (١٨٠ا)				
		والاحمدي مشتمل عليه زرديه وسيفه (١٠٣ا)	والاحمدي مستمر زرديه وسيفه (١٢٨ا)	

Leiden UB MS Or 560, ff. 115b–135a (*aṣl*) → L [A1 + A2] / 1438	Escorial, MS Ar. 1771, ff. 22b–75b → E / 16th c.	New Haven, Yale UL, MS Landberg 111, ff. 26–62 → Y / 1609	Ist. SK, MS Atıf Efendi 2814, ff. 84b–107b → Ia / 1632
مَسًّا (١٣٣ب)		منسا (٦٠ب)	
انا رجل مالكي المذهب (١٣٤ا)			
وقربه اليه (١٣٤ا)			
فلم يمكنه امير مكة من ذلك (١٣٤ا)		فلم يمكنه من ذلك امير مكة (٦١ا)	
وعنف تعنيفا كثيرا (١٣٥ا)		؟	
وقام بامر المملكة (١٣٥ا)		وقام بامر الملك (٦٢ا)	
وهو محفات كلها باغشية حرير مزركش (١٣٥ا)		كلها باغشية حرير مزركش (٦٢ا)	
طاش تمر المحمدي اللفاف (١٣٥ا)			
ليلة الخميس (١٣٥ا)			
والله اعلم (١٣٥ا)		والله اعلم وصلى الله على سيدنا محمد واله وصحبه وسلم (٦٢ب)	والله تعالى اعلم وصلى الله على سيدنا محمد والى آله وصحبه وسلم تسليما كثيرا الى يوم الدين امين اللهم (١٠٧ا)

Ist., SK, MS Nuruosmaniye 4937, ff. 145[a]–186[a] →In / 1674–1675	**Ist. SK, MS Veliüddin 3195, ff. 64–85 → Iv / 1690**	**Cambridge UL, MS Add. 746, ff. 78–105 → Ca / 1701**	**Paris, BnF, MS arabe 4657, ff. 101[b]–131[a] → P / mid-18th c.**	**Cambridge UL, MS Qq. 141, ff. 1–37 → Cq / 1817**
انا مالكي المذهب (١٨٣ا)				
وقربه (١٨٣ا)				
وعنف تعنيفا كبيرا (١٨٤ا) ؟				وعنف تعنيفا (١٣٦)
طاش قرا المحمدي اللفاف (١٨٥ب)				
(١٨٥ب) /				
والله سبحانه وتعالى اعلم وصلى الله على سيدنا محمد وآله وصحبه وسلم (١٨٦ا)		رحمه الله تمت الكتاب والحمد لله وحده (١٠٥ب)	والله اعلم بالصواب واليه المرجع والمآب وصلى الله على سيدنا محمد وعلى اله وصحبه وسلم والحمد لله رب العالمين (١٣١ا)	والله اعلم بالصواب واليه المرجع والمآب وصلى الله على سيدنا محمد والال والاصحاب (١٣٧ا)

TABLE 2 *Calculation of the reproduction from L, Y, or In in other relevant manuscripts (Y only has data for 55 errors due to missing pages in the manuscript) (number of cases of exact reproduction in one of the manuscripts/58 cases selected as comparative model in L, Y [only 55] or In)*

	L [A1 + A2] 1438	E 16th c.	Y 1609	Ia 1632	In 1674–1675	Iv 1690	Ca 1701	P mid-18th c.	Cq 1817
L	58/58	51/58	36/55	40/58	24/58	9/58	34/58	37/58	39/58
% reprod.	100	87,95	64,45	68,97	41,38	15,52	58,62	63,8	67,24
Y			55/55	52/55	38/55	28/55	43/55	46/55	47/55
% reprod.			100	94,55	69,09	50,91	78,18	83,63	85,45
In					58/58	44/58			
% reprod.					100	75,86			

PART 2

Critical Edition and Annotated Translation of al-Maqrīzī's al-Ḏahab al-masbūk fī ḏikr man ḥaǧǧa min al-ḫulafāʾ wa-l-mulūk

∵

Introduction

As explained in the third chapter of this monograph's first part, the four modern editions of the text of *al-Ḏahab al-masbūk* that have so far been published are all rooted one way or another in the early 1950s, when almost simultaneously but independently from each other two editions were produced, by Ǧamāl al-Dīn al-Šayyāl in Cairo and by Ḥamad al-Ǧāsir in Riyadh. The retrieval in the context of the *Bibliotheca Maqriziana* of all relevant manuscript copies and of authoritative manuscript traditions as well as the deepened understanding of the complexity of this text and of the contexts in which it operated also mean that the time certainly has come to revisit these editions. Above all this has made clear that this handful of modern textual reproductions relies on one of the more distant manuscript clusters in the material history of the text, and that the only extant autograph of *al-Ḏahab al-masbūk* in the manuscript L (Leiden, Universiteitsbibliotheek, MS Or. 560, fol. 115^{b}–135^{a}) has so far never been the object of any critical edition. There are therefore many good reasons to present such a new edition of this text as it appears in L in this second part of this book. This new critical edition tries to faithfully reflect the text as al-Maqrīzī continued to add some material to it during and after late 841/mid-1438 (A2), and as it eventually also would be reproduced in the course of the sixteenth century in E, and thereafter in all known other manuscripts. The nature and extent of these collations, emendations, and additions by al-Maqrīzī are indicated and clarified in the critical apparatus (in Arabic), so that al-Maqrīzī's substantial corrections of the copyist's work as well as his additions to the pre-841/-1437 version of the text (A1) continue to stand out, as they do in L. Wherever relevant this Arabic critical apparatus also clarifies where the orthography of L (especially regarding the writing and/or support of the *hamza*) was aligned with modern standards, and where for reasons of legibility L's many orthographic idiosyncrasies and particularities (especially regarding the presence/absence of consonantal diacritics) had to be adjusted. The critical apparatus finally also identifies references to al-Maqrīzī's and others' texts, parallels with other texts, and the text's handful of Qurʾānic verses.

Side by side with this new critical edition, this second part also presents the first ever English translation of al-Maqrīzī's summary history of the pilgrimage and of his identification of all the Muslim rulers who, according to the author, had meaningfully and actively engaged with the *ḥaǧǧ* during eight centuries of Muslim history. This also enables non-specialist readers to engage directly with *al-Ḏahab al-masbūk*'s twenty-seven diverse leadership narratives and with their simple or complex strings of variegated stories about some of these rulers' leadership experiences that were mostly somehow related to the Mecca sanctuary. In order to enhance the accessibility and intelligibility of this convoluted literary construct a detailed reference apparatus accompanies this translation, identifying whenever possible names, places, and other phenomena that appear in the text and that continue to define in many ways its literary, historiographical, and wider cultural meanings and values. Published English translations of parallel passages in other texts (especially from *The History* of al-Ṭabarī) are also identified in this reference apparatus.

Abbreviations and Symbols

﴾…﴿	Qur'ānic Verses
[...]	Interpolation
{...}	Correction
|	Used in the Arabic text to indicate the passage to the next folio (number indicated in the left margin)
L/الأصل	Leiden, Universiteitsbibliotheek, MS Or. 560, fols. 115[b]–135[a]
E/أ	Madrid/San Lorenzo de el Escorial, Real Biblioteca del Monasterio, MS Árabe 1771, fols. 22[b]–75[b]

Edition and Translation of al-Maqrīzī's

al-Ḏahab al-masbūk [fī ḏikr man ḥaǧǧa min al-ḫulafāʾ wa-l-mulūk]

كتاب الذهب المسبوك [في ذكر من حج من الخلفاء والملوك]

The Book of Gold Moulded [in the Format of the Report of Those Caliphs and Kings Who Performed the Ḥaǧǧ]

∵

115b

كِتَابُ الذَّهَبِ المَسْبُوك
في ذِكرِ مَنْ حَجَّ من الخُلَفاءِ وَالمُلُوك

تأليف المقريزي

١–٣ كِتَابُ ... المقريزي : في الهامش الأعلى بخط مختلف عن خط الناسخ.

The Book of Gold Moulded in the Format of the Report of Those Caliphs and Kings Who Performed the *Ḥağğ*

by al-Maqrīzī

بِسمِ اللّٰهِ الرَّحمن الرَّحِيم

رب يسِّر يا كريم

الحمد لله، وبه المستعان، على كل ما عز وهان، وصلى الله على نبينا محمد خاتم النبيين، وعلى آله وأصحابه والتابعين، صلاة باقية إلى يوم الدين.

٥ وبعد فأسأل الله مبتهلا إليه مادا يدي له أن يتبع أيام المقر المخدوم بأخواتها الباقيات الصالحات والزيادات الغامرات، ليكون كل دهر يستقبله وأمل يستأنفه، موفيا على المتقدم له قاصرا عن المتأخر عنه، ويؤتيه من العمر أطوله وأبعده ومن العيش أعذبه وأرغده، عزيزا منصورا محميا موفورا، باسطًا يده فلا يقبضها إلا على نواصي أعداء وحساد، ساميا طرفه فلا يغضه إلا على لذة غمض ورقاد، مستريحة ركابه فلا يَعمِلها إلا لإستضافة عز وملك، حائزة قِدَاحُه فَلا يَجيلها
١٠ إلا لحيازة مال حتى ينال أقصى ما تتوجه إليه أمنية جامحة، وتسمو إليه همة طامحة.

وقد استفاض أن العزم الشريف قد قوي على الحج والتحلي بالعج والثج. وجرت العادة بإلطاف العبيد السادة، فتأملت حال الأتباع الذين يجب عليهم الهدايا في مثل هذه الحركة، فأردت التأسي بهم، ورأيتني أن أهديت نفسي فهي في ملك المقر المخدوم، وأن أهديت مالي فهو منه، وأن أهديت مودتي وشكري فهما خالصين له غير مشتركين. وكرهت أن أخلي هذا العزم من سُنته وأكون من
١٥ المقصرين، أو أدعى في ملكي ما يفي بحق المقر المخدوم فأكون من الكاذبين: [الكامل]

٣ كل : ناقصة في الأصل، مضافة بخط المقريزي في الهامش الأيسر من الأسفل إلى الأعلى + صح، يشير إليها الرمز ˥ بعد كلمة "على". ٥ مبتهلا : تصحيح في الأصل بخط المقريزي. ٦ قاصرا : تصحيح في الأصل بخط المقريزي. ٧ ومن : تصحيح في الأصل بخط المقريزي. ٨ يده : تصحيح في الأصل بخط المقريزي. || أعداء : "اعدآ" في الأصل. ٩ حائزة : تصحيح في الأصل بخط المقريزي ("حايرة"). ١٠ وتسمو : "تسموا" في الأصل. || همة : ناقصة في الأصل، مضافة بخط المقريزي في الهامش الأيسر من الأسفل إلى الأعلى + صح، يشير إليها الرمز ˥ بعد كلمة "إليه". || طامحة : تصحيح في الأصل بخط المقريزي. ١٣ أن : تصحيح في الأصل بخط المقريزي.

In the name of God, the merciful, the compassionate

O Lord, make it easy, o Noble One!

Praise be to God, who is being sought for help against all that overpowers and humiliates. May God bless our Prophet Muḥammad—the seal of prophets—, his folk, his companions, and the generation that followed them, and may He continue to do so until the Day of Judgment.

§ 1 I demand God—supplicating Him and stretching out my hands to Him—to cause the days of the noble lord to be followed by similarly good and additionally abundant ones ever after, such that every fortune that he anticipates and [every] expectation that he nurtures will come true, outdoing anyone who preceded him and unmatched by anyone who follows him. [I demand God that] He gives him the longest and most extensive lifetime, a life of the utmost sweetness and pleasance, in circumstances of high standing, victory, protection, and opulence; [a life during which he] spreads out his hand, only to close it for grasping enemies and enviers by the forelock; [a life during which he] raises high his look, only to bring it down for the pleasure of sleeping and lying down; [a life during which] his riding camels find rest, only to be used by him for welcoming majesty and kingship; [a life during which] his divining arrows are well-arranged, only to be moved about by him for collecting wealth. [I demand God all of this] so that he achieves the highest that untamable aspiration can pursue and that high-aiming ambition can reach for.

§ 2 The word has spread that the high-born intention was set on undertaking the *ḥaǧǧ* and to be endowed with the noise and blood of rituals. It has become common practice for servants to present a gift to their masters, for which reason I considered the situation of clients that owe presents on the occasion of an event like this, and I decided to follow their example. But then I thought: I could offer my soul as a present, but it already belongs to the noble lord; I could offer my property, but that is his already; I could offer my love and gratitude, but they already are his full and undivided due. I abhorred [the idea of] draining this intention [of my lord] from its habitual practice and of becoming as a result one of those that are considered negligent, or [the idea of] claiming to possess what can meet the noble lord's due and becoming as a result one of those that are considered liars. [*Kāmil* meter]

إن أهـد نفسي فهو مالـكها ولها أصون كرائم الذخر

أو أهـد مـالاً فهو واهـبه وأنا الحقيـق عليه بالشكر

أو أهد شكري فهو مرتهـن بجميـل فعلك آخر الدهـر

والشمس تستغني إذا طلعت أنْ تستضيئ بطلعة البدر[1]

٥ ولما كان العلم أنفس الذخائر وأعلاها قدرا وأعظم المآثر وأبقاها ذكرا، جمعت برسم الخزانة الشريفة المخدومية—عمرها الله ببقاء مالكها—{جُزءا} يحتوي على ذكر من حج من الخلفاء والملوك سميته **الذهب المسبوك**، ليكون تذكرة للخاطر الشريف بما هو مني أدرى وأحق بإفادته وأَحْرى. وإني—فيما فعلت وصنعت—كمن أهدى القطر إلى البحر، أو بعث النُور إلى القمَر والأَرَج إلى الزهر، بل كالذي أرسل الضياء إلى | الشمس وروح الحيٰوة إلى النفس، غير أن في كريم أخلاقه الزكية، 116a
١٠ وزا كي أعراقه المرضيّة ما يقبل اليسير ويتجاوز عن الخطأ والتقصير.

رعى الله المخدوم من حيث لا يرتقب، وحرسه من حيث لا يَحْتَسِب. وكان له في سفره خفيرا، أو في حضره عونا وظهيرا بمنه.

١ ولها ... الذخر: ناقصة في الأصل بسبب ثقب في المخطوطة، مضافة هنا من أ، ص. ٢٣ب ("لها اَصُون كرايم الذخر"). ٦ ببقاء: "ببقا" في الأصل. || جُزءا: "جُزا" في الأصل. || الخلفاء: "الخلفآ" في الأصل. ٧ وإني: "وانى" في الأصل. ٩ الضياء: "الضيآ" في الأصل. ١١ رعى: "رعا" في الأصل. || من[2]: ناقصة في الأصل، مضافة بخط المقريزي في الهامش الأيمن من الأعلى إلى الأسفل + صح؛ يشير إليها الرمز ⌝ بعد كلمة "حرسه". || يَحْتَسِب: تصحيح في الأصل بخط المقريزي. || خفيرا: "حفير" في الأصل. ١٢ عونا: ناقصة في الأصل، مضافة بخط المقريزي في مكانها الصحيح في الجملة عند آخر السطر بعد كلمة "حضره". || وظهيرا: "ظهيرَ" في الأصل، الواو والألف لتنوين الفتح من إضافة المقريزي.

[1] راجع خبرا مساويا عن الشاعر العباسي أبي عثمان سعيد بن حميد بن سعيد (ت. ٨٧٣/٢٥٩)، على شكل مختلف ولكن بمفردات وجمل ومعان متشابهة، في الخالديان، التحف والهدايا، ص. ٢٨، ٣٣. هذه البيوت الأربعة كلها لسعيد بن حميد الا الكلمتان الأخيرتان اللتان في شعر سعيد "بسنّة البدر".

§ 3 I cannot present my soul, because he already owns it,
so I am only guarding it as the most precious sort of noblesse;

Nor can I present any wealth, because he has donated it,
so I am the one who owes him thankfulness.

5 Nor can I present my gratitude, because it is a pawn
until the end of time for your comeliness.

When the sun rises, she does not need
to be lit by the full moon's highness.[1]

§ 4 Since knowledge is the most precious and most valuable of treasures, the
10 most glorious and the longest remembered of deeds, I collected for the benefit of the esteemed library of our lord—may God support it with long life for its owner—a volume that comprises the report of those caliphs and kings who performed the *ḥağğ*. I entitled it: 'The Moulded Gold', as a reminder to the high-born mind that what comes from me is better informed, more
15 entitled to be considered useful, and more appropriate. In what I do and compose, I am like someone who presents drops of water to the sea, or who sends light to the moon, and fragrance to flowers, or even better, like someone who sends the rays of light to the sun, and the breath of life to the soul: apart from the fact that there is sinlessness in such a man's noble manners
20 and that there is a satisfying aspect in the purity of his sweat, what is given is little but also surpasses things that are a fault and a shortcoming.

§ 5 May God protect our lord whenever he does not expect it and may He guard him whenever he does not think of it; may He be with him as a guardian when traveling, and as a supporter and helper when he is staying
25 somewhere.

1 This poem, as well as the preceding discussion of the reciprocal obligations between patrons and clients, demonstrates an obvious (for the poem even almost word for word) intertextual relationship with reports about the poet Saʿīd b. Ḥumayd (d. 259/873) writing a letter to his patron at the ʿAbbāsid court, as these may be found, amongst others, in the section on gifts (*al-hadāyā*) in al-Ḫālidiyyān, *al-Tuḥaf wa-l-hadāyā*, 28, 33. The latter tenth-century belletrist text on gift-giving has been identified as a source for al-Maqrīzī's *Ḫiṭaṭ*, which makes it highly likely that it also informed the current passage (I am grateful to Frédéric Bauden for this suggestion).

فصل في حجة رَسُول الله ﷺ

افتتحت بها هذا {الجزء} إذ كان ﷺ هو الذي بين للناس معالم دينهم وقال: "خُذُوا عني مناسككم". وقد امتلأت كتب الحديث بذكر حجة رسول الله ﷺ، وأفردَ فيها الفقيهُ الحافظ أبو محمد علي بن أحمد بن سعيد بن حزم الأندلسي مُصنفًا جليلا[٢]، قد اعترُض عليه في مواضع منه، أجبتُ عنها في ٥ كتاب شارع النجاة.[٣]

وملخص حجة الوداع[٤] أن رسول الله ﷺ لما دخل ذو القعدة تجهز للحج، وأمر الناس بالجهاز له، وأذن فيهم، فاجتمعوا. ثم صلى الظهر يوم الخميس لستٍ بقين من ذي القعدة سنة عشر من الهجرة بالمدينة أربعاً، وخرج منها بمن معه من المسلمين من أهل المدينة ومن تجمع من الأعراب—

---

٢ الجزء: "الجزو" في الأصل. || هو: تصحيح في الأصل بخط المقريزي. ٤ اعترُض: تصحيح في الأصل بخط المقريزي. ٧ وأذن: تصحيح في الأصل بخط المقريزي. || عشر: كشط المقريزي تاء مربوطة. ٨ أربعاً: تصحيح في الأصل بخط المقريزي.

---

[٢] راجع ابن حزم، حجّة الوداع، ص. ١٣٩-١٦٥ (ذكر حجة الوداع وترتيبها وصفتها) خصوصا. [٣] كتاب "شارع النجاة" للمقريزي مذكور في ترجمة المقريزي للسخاوي (الضوء اللامع، ج. ٢، ص. ٢٣: "يشتمل على جميع ما اختلف فيه البشر من أصول دياناتهم وفروعها مع بيان أدلتها وتوجيه الحق منها")، ولكنه حسبما عرف مفقود. [٤] هذا الملخص كله موجود على نفس الشكل تقريبا في ابن كثير، الفصول، ص. ٢١٤-٧ (فصل حجة الوداع). وأكثر أخبار حجة الوداع المذكورة هنا موجودة أيضا على شكل مساو في كتاب آخر للمقريزي: راجع المقريزي، إمتاع الأسماع، ج. ٢، ص. ١٠٢-١٢٠.

---

2 Abū Muḥammad ʿAlī b. Aḥmad b. Saʿīd Ibn Ḥazm (384–456/994–1064) was an Andalusian poet, historian, jurist, philosopher, and theologian; he is especially renowned for his codification of the literalist Ẓāhirī doctrine and the application of its method to all the religious sciences (see R. Arnaldez, "Ibn Ḥazm", in *EI*[2] http://referenceworks.brillonline.com/entries/encyclopaedia-of-islam-2/ibn-hazm-COM_0325). For Ibn Ḥazm's discussion of the Prophet's farewell pilgrimage, see in particular Adang (2005).

Chapter on the Pilgrimage of the Messenger of God—may God bless him and grant him salvation

§ 6 I began this volume with [the Prophet's pilgrimage] since he—may God bless him and grant him salvation—is the one who has shown to the people
5 the milestones of their religion, saying: "learn your pilgrimage rituals from me". The books of *ḥadīṯ* are full of reports of the pilgrimage of the Prophet—may God bless him and grant him salvation. Out of all of these the jurist and *ḥāfiẓ* Abū Muḥammad ʿAlī b. Aḥmad b. Saʿīd Ibn Ḥazm al-Andalusī[2] created an important single volume. I responded in the book *Šāriʿ al-naǧāh*
10 [The Road to Deliverance] to certain passages in it to which objections were raised.[3]

§ 7 The farewell pilgrimage[4] can be summarised [as follows]: The Messenger of God—may God bless him and grant him salvation—prepared for the pilgrimage when [the month of] Ḏū l-Qaʿdah began, and he ordered the
15 people to prepare for it as well. He called [to prayer] among them, so they gathered. Then, on Thursday 24 Ḏū l-Qaʿdah of the tenth year since the *hiǧrah* [20 February 632], while still in Medina, he prayed the midday prayer in four [*rakʿahs*],[5] and he left from there, together with the Muslims from among the people of Medina and with those Bedouins that had assembled—

3 Al-Maqrīzī's "Road to Deliverance" is mentioned by his biographers, such as by al-Saḫāwī (d. 902/1497) (*al-Ḍaw' al-lāmiʿ*, 2:23), but no copy of the work is so far known to have been preserved.

4 This name is derived from the fact that this pilgrimage occurred only a few months before Muḥammad's death, bidding his community 'farewell' by taking the lead in the rituals of the pilgrimage to Mecca; these rituals are believed to have obtained their definite form at this particular occasion, and the farewell pilgrimage has therefore acquired a referential status for any discussion of the rituals and meanings of the *ḥaǧǧ*, one of the five 'pillars' of Islam (see D.J. Stewart, "Farewell Pilgrimage", *EQ* http://referenceworks.brillonline.com/entries/encyclopaedia-of-the-quran/farewell-pilgrimage-SIM_00151).

5 The word *rakʿah* refers to a fixed sequence of specific positions and movements of the body, always in combination with set phrases and words in Arabic, that make up the substance of the Islamic ritual prayer (*ṣalāt*); every ritual prayer consists of at least two successive *rakʿahs* (see G. Monnot, "Ṣalāt", in *EI*2 http://referenceworks.brillonline.com/entries/encyclopaedia-of-islam-2/salat-COM_0983).

وهم عشرة آلاف—، بعدما استَعْملَ على المدينة أبا دُجَانة الساعدي—ويقال سِبَاع بن عُرْفُطَة الغِفَاري. فصلى العصر بذي الحُلَيفة ركعتين وبات بها.

وأتاه آت من ربه عز وجل في ذلكَ الموضع—وهو وادي العقيق—يأمره عن ربه تعالى أن يقول في حجته: "هذه حجة في عمرةٍ."[٥] ومعنى هذا أن الله سبحانه أمره بأن يقرن الحج مع العمرة.

---

٥ راجع ابن حنبل، المسند، ج. ١، ص. ٢٩٩-٣٠٠ (مسند عمر بن الخطاب، ١٦١: سمعتُ رسول الله ﷺ وهو بالعقيق يقول: "أتاني الليلة آتٍ من ربّي فقال: صَلِّ في هذا الوادي المبارك وقُلْ: عمرةٌ في حَجَّةٍ")، وراجع أيضا البخاري، الجامع الصحيح، ج. ٢، ص. ١٣٥-١٣٦ (كتاب الحج، باب قول النبي ﷺ العقيق وادٍ مباركٌ، ١٥٣٤: سمعتُ النّبيّ ﷺ بوادي العقيق يقول: "أتاني اللّيلة آتٍ من ربّي فقال: صَلِّ في هذا الوادي المبارك وقُلْ عمرةٌ في حَجَّةٍ")، وج. ٣، ص. ١٠٧ (كتاب الحرث والمزارعة، ٢٣٣٧: قال: "اللّيلة أتاني آتٍ من ربّي وهو بالعقيق أنْ صَلِّ في هذا الوادي المبارك وقُلْ عمرةٌ في حَجَّةٍ")، وراجع أيضا أبو داود، السنن، ص. ٢٩٤ (كتاب المناسك، باب في الإقران، ١٨٠٠: سمع رسول الله ﷺ يقول: "أتاني اللّيلة آتٍ من عند ربّي عز وجل، وقال: وهو بالعقيق، فقال: "صَلِّ في هذا الوادي المبارك وقال: عمرةٌ في حَجَّةٍ")، وراجع أيضا ابن ماجة، السنن، ج. ٣، ص. ٣٣ (كتاب المناسك، باب التّمتّع بالعمرة إلى الحجّ، ٢٤٢٨/ ٣٠٣١: سمعتُ رسول الله ﷺ يقول وهو بالعقيق: "أتاني اللّيلة آتٍ من ربّي فقال: صَلِّ في هذا الوادي المبارك وقُلْ: عمرةٌ في حَجَّةٍ").

---

6 Abū Duğānah Simāk b. Ḫarašah was a respected companion from one of the Arab tribes of Medina who had welcomed and supported the Prophet after his departure from Mecca; Abū Duğānah was especially known for his courage and horsemanship (see his short biographical note in al-Ṭabarī, *History XXXIX*, 286, fn. 1297).

7 Sibāʿ b. ʿUrfuṭah al-Ġifārī was a member of the Ḥiğāzī tribe of Ġifār that are remembered for their alliance with the Prophet in the course of the 620s, and most of whom converted to Islam before 8/630. Sibāʿ is believed to have been left as a representative in Medina during a number of the Prophet's expeditions (J.W. Fück, "Banū Ghifār." in *EI*² http://referenceworks.brillonline.com/entries/encyclopaedia-of-islam-2/banu-ghifar-SIM_2501).

8 Dū l-Ḥulayfah: until today, this site—today's Abar ʿAlī, about ten kilometers from Medina—marks one of the *mīqāt*, the place where people performing the pilgrimage from Medina assume the *iḥrām*, a pilgrim's state of temporary consecration (J. Jomier, A.J. Wensinck, "Iḥrām", in *EI*² http://referenceworks.brillonline.com/entries/encyclopaedia-of-islam-2/ihram-SIM_3506).

they numbered 10,000. Before that, he had appointed over Medina Abū Duǧānah al-Sāʿidī,[6] and it was said [that the appointee rather was] Sibāʿ b. ʿUrfuṭah al-Ġifārī.[7] He prayed the afternoon prayer in two *rakʿah*s at Ḏū l-Ḥulayfah,[8] and he stayed there for the night.

5 § 8 At that place—Wādī l-ʿAqīq[9]—there came to him from his Lord—may He be strong and lofty—the instruction, on authority of his Lord, the exalted, to say regarding this pilgrimage of his: 'this is a pilgrimage within a lesser pilgrimage.'[10] The meaning of this is that God—may He be praised—ordered him to integrate[11] the pilgrimage with the lesser pilgrimage. The next morn-

---

9 Wādī l-ʿAqīq: a valley passing just West of Medina, along which in the Prophet's time the first stage of the route from Medina to Mecca ran (up to Ḏū l-Ḥulayfah) (G. Rentz, "al-ʿAḳīḳ", in *EI*[2] http://referenceworks.brillonline.com/entries/encyclopaedia-of-islam-2/al-akik-SIM_0477). See also Eskoubi (2006).

10 The lesser pilgrimage or visitation (*ʿumrah*) refers to a set of rituals in and around Mecca that are very similar or even identical to those of the pilgrimage (*ḥaǧǧ*), but that are fewer in number and that are therefore considered to make up a separate, lesser type of ritual visitation to Mecca; unlike the pilgrimage—which is one of the five 'pillars' of Islam, and therefore obligatory—, the lesser pilgrimage is an act of devotion and piety that is not obligatory; it may be performed simultaneously with the pilgrimage (the timing of which is fixed in the Muslim calendar) or at any other moment. As transpires from this issue of timing as well as from the current passage, the relationship between pilgrimage and lesser pilgrimage has been a point of vehement discussions ever since the time of the Prophet; in due course, however, scholarly consensus has accepted the idea of a threefold relationship: *qirān* (integration, without breaking the *iḥrām* between their performance), *tamattuʿ* (combination, with a break in the *iḥrām* between them) and *ifrād* (completely separate performance) (R. Paret, E. Chaumont, "ʿUmra", in *EI*[2] http://referenceworks.brillonline.com/entries/encyclopaedia-of-islam-2/umra-COM_1292). As the *ḥadīṯ* referred to here occupies an important position in these discussions, it is remarkable to note that al-Maqrīzī, following Ibn Kaṯīr (and probably also Ibn Ḥazm [see below]), reversed the original word order of this passage authorising integration (*qirān*), for in the main hadith collections this phrase—attributed to God, and therefore part of a *ḥadīṯ qudsī*, an instance of extra-scriptural divine revelation—is preserved as stating: "say: [there is] a lesser pilgrimage in a pilgrimage (*wa-qul: ʿumratun fī ḥiǧǧatin*)" (see Ibn Ḥanbal, *al-Musnad*, 1:299–300; al-Buḫārī, *al-Ǧāmiʿ al-ṣaḥīḥ*, 2:135–136, 3:107; Abū Dāwūd, *al-Sunan*, 294; Ibn Māǧah, *al-Ṣaḥīḥ*, 3:33). For a detailed discussion of this point of contention in Ibn Ḥazm's text (with reference to the actual context of this short passage: the discussion whether women on pilgrimage who get their periods should put off *iḥrām* or not, thus going for combination or integration of *ʿumra* and *ḥaǧǧ*), see Adang (2005): 114, 120, 135–144.

11 *Qirān* or integration of *ḥaǧǧ* with *ʿumrah* (see previous footnote).

فأصبح ﷺ فأخبر الناس بذلك. وطاف على نسائه يومئذ بغسل واحدٍ—وهُنَّ تسعٌ وقيل إحدى عشرة. ثم اغتسل وصلى عند المسجد ركعتين، وأَهَلّ بحجة وعمرة معاً.

هذا الذي رواه بلفظه ومعناه عنه ﷺ ستة عشر صحابيا، منهم خادمه أنس بن مالك رضي الله عنه. وقد رواه عنه ﷺ ستة عشر تابعياً قد ذكرتهم في **كتاب شارع النجاة**. وهذا صريح لا يحتمل التأويل ٥ إلا أن يكون بعيدًا، وما عدا ذلك مما جاء من الأحاديث الموهمة التمتع أو ما يدل على الإفرَاد، فليس هَذا محل ذكرها. والقِرَان في الحج هو مذهب إمامنا أبي عبد الله محمد بن إدريس الشافعي رحمة الله عليه، وقد نصره جماعة من محققي أصحابه، وهو الذي يحصل به الجمع بين الأحاديث

١ نسائه : "نسآيه" في الأصل. || يومئذ : "يوميذ" في الأصل. || إحدى : "احدي" في الأصل، والياء مضافة بخط المقريزي في مكانه في السطر. ٢ عشرة : "عشر" في الأصل، والتاء المربوطة مضافة بخط المقريزي في مكانه في آخر الكلمة. ٤ تابعياً : "تابعا" في الأصل، وحرف الياء مضافة في مكانها في الكلمة بخط المقريزي.
٥ مما : ناقصة في الأصل، مضافة بخط المقريزي في الهامش الأيمن من الأعلى إلى الأسفل + صح؛ يشير إليها الرمز ⌐ بعد كلمة "ذلك". || جاء : "جآ" في الأصل.

ing, he—may God bless him and grant him salvation—informed the people of that. On that same day, he went around among his wives—they were nine, or some say eleven—, performing one single ritual ablution. Thereafter he performed [another] ritual ablution, prayed two *rakʿah*s at the mosque, and entered into *iḥrām* for the pilgrimage and the lesser pilgrimage together.

§ 9 This is what has been transmitted in letter and spirit about him—may God bless him and grant him salvation—by sixteen companions, including his servant Anas b. Mālik[12]—may God be pleased with him. It has also been transmitted about him—may God bless him and grant him salvation—by sixteen successors, whom I have mentioned in the book *Šāriʿ al-naǧāh* [The Road to Deliverance]. This is therefore unambiguous and does not allow for interpretation, for that could only be far-fetched. This is not the place either to mention those *ḥadīṯ*s that have come down and instill the delusion of the principle of combination[13] [of the pilgrimage and the lesser pilgrimage] or those that point at the principle of complete separation.[14] The principle of integration during the pilgrimage is the doctrine of our *imām* Abū ʿAbd Allāh Muḥammad b. Idrīs al-Šāfiʿī[15]—may God's mercy be upon him—, supported by a group of authoritative adherents of his, for he is the one who managed in this matter to collate all the *ḥadīṯ*s. Some scholars say that it is obligatory.

12 Anas b. Mālik was a young servant of the Prophet in Medina, who became an important transmitter of *ḥadīṯ* and an authoritative figure in later collections; he died in Basra in the early years of the second/eighth century (A.J. Wensinck, J. Robson, "Anas b. Mālik", in *EI*² http://referenceworks.brillonline.com/entries/encyclopaedia-of-islam-2/anas-b-malik-SIM_0654).

13 *Tamattuʿ* or combination of *ḥaǧǧ* and *ʿumrah* (see footnote 10).

14 *Ifrād* or complete separation of *ḥaǧǧ* from *ʿumrah* (see footnote 10).

15 Muḥammad b. Idrīs al-Šāfiʿī is the well-known eponymous pioneer of a method of jurisprudence (*fiqh*) that was to crystallise over time in a coherent intellectual community of legal thinkers and practicioners, the Šāfiʿī *maḏhab*, one of the four 'schools of law' that acquired authoritative status in matters of Islamic law; al-Šāfiʿī was born in 150/767 and he died in Egypt in 204/820; his main contributions to the field of Islamic jurisprudence concern his narrowing down of the definition of authoritative custom to the *Sunna* of the Prophet, and his systematisation of analogical reasoning (see E. Chaumont, "al-Shāfiʿī", in *EI*² http://referenceworks.brillonline.com/entries/encyclopaedia-of-islam-2/al-shafii-COM_1020; Kecia [2011]).

كلها. ومن العلماء | من أوجبه، وممن قال بأفضليته الإمام أبو حنيفة النُعمٰن بن ثابت رحمه الله، 116b
وهو رواية عن الإمام أبي عبد الله أحمد بن حنبل الشيباني رحمه الله.

وساق ﷺ الهدي من ذي الحليفة، وأمر من كان معه هدي أن يُهل كما أهل ﷺ. وسار ﷺ
والناس بين يديه وخلفه وعن يمينه وشماله أمما لا يُحصَون كثرةً، كلهم قدم ليأتم به ﷺ. فلما قدم
٥ ﷺ مكة لأربع ليال خلون من ذي الحجة طاف للقدوم. ثم سعى بين الصفا والمروة، وأمر الذين لم

١ العلماء: "العلمآ" في الأصل. ‖ النُعمٰن بن: تصحيح في الأصل بخط المقريزي ("النعمن ن").

16 Abū Ḥanīfah al-Nuʿmān is another eponymous pioneer of a method of jurisprudence (*fiqh*) that crystallised over time into the Ḥanafī *madhab*; he lived in Iraq, where he died in 150/767; his legal thought, only transmitted via the writings of his pupils, is especially known for its high degree of reasoning using personal judgment and analogy (see J. Schacht, "Abū Ḥanīfa al-Nuʿmān", in *EI*² http://referenceworks.brillonline.com/entries/encyclopaedia-of-islam-2/abu-hanifa-al-numan-SIM_0194).

Among those that say that it is preferable there is the *imām* Abū Ḥanīfah al-Nuʿmān b. Ṯābit[16]—may God have mercy upon him—, as transmitted on the authority of the *imām* Abū ʿAbd Allāh Aḥmad b. Ḥanbal al-Šaybānī[17]—may God have mercy upon him.

5 § 10 He—may God bless him and grant him salvation—drove the oblational animals[18] on from Ḏū l-Ḥulayfah, and he ordered who had brought an oblation animal with him to enter into *iḥrām* just as he—may God bless him and grant him salvation—had. When he—may God bless him and grant him salvation—moved on, an innumerable amount of people from 10 all nations were before and after him, and to his right and left. All of them came to follow his—may God bless him and grant him salvation—example. When he—may God bless him and grant him salvation—reached Mecca on 4 Ḏū l-Ḥiǧǧah [1 March], he performed the circumambulation [of the Kaʿbah] for the occasion of the arrival.[19] Thereafter he performed the ritual 15 of running between al-Ṣafā and al-Marwah.[20] He commanded to those who

17 Aḥmad b. Ḥanbal is yet another eponymous pioneer of a method of jurisprudence (*fiqh*), which crystallised over time into the Ḥanbalite *maḏhab*; he lived in Baghdad, where he died in 241/855; Ibn Ḥanbal is especially associated with the triumph of traditionalism in the formation of Sunni Islamic thought and practice (see H. Laoust, "Aḥmad b. Ḥanbal", in EI² http://referenceworks.brillonline.com/entries/encyclopaedia-of-islam-2/ahmad-b-hanbal-COM_0027; Melchert [2006]).

18 *Hady* is an ancient Arabic term meaning 'oblation'; in the context of Islamic pilgrimage it refers to the animals that are to be offered to God as part of the pilgrimage rituals (J. Chelhod, "Hady", in EI² http://referenceworks.brillonline.com/entries/encyclopaedia-of-islam-2/hady-SIM_2611).

19 *Ṭawāf* refers to the ritual of walking or running seven times counterclockwise around the Kaʿbah at Mecca; it is one of the rituals that must be performed for the pilgrimage to be valid; there are three sets of *ṭawāf*: that of 'the arrival' (*al-qudūm*), that of 'the overflowing' (*al-ifāḍah*) or of the visitation on 10 Ḏū l-Ḥiǧǧah—marking the end of *iḥrām* restrictions—, and the non-obligatory one of the departure (*wadāʿ*) (U. Rubin, "Circumambulation", in EI³ http://referenceworks.brillonline.com/entries/encyclopaedia-of-islam-3/circumambulation-COM_25135).

20 *Saʿy* is the ritual of running between al-Ṣafā and al-Marwah, two hills to the south and north-west of the Kaʿbah, connected by a 300-meter-course which pilgrims have to travers seven times in all; this ritual is obligatory at the arrival and recommended at the departure of all pilgrims; it symbolises the prophetic story of Hagar's running in search for water for her son Ismāʿīl (T. Fahd, "Saʿy", in EI² http://referenceworks.brillonline.com/entries/encyclopaedia-of-islam-2/say-SIM_6675).

يسوقوا هَدْيا أن يفسخوا حجهم إلى عمرة ويتحللوا حِلًّا تاما، ثم يُهلوا بالحج وقت خروجهم إلى منى.[21] وقال ثمَّ: "لو استقبلت من أمري ما استدبرت ما سقت الهدي، ولجعلتها عمرة."[٦] وهذا دليل ظاهر أنه ﷺ لم يكن متمتعا كما ذهب إليه بعض أصحاب الإمام أحمد وغيرهم.

وقَدِم علي بن أبي طالب رضي الله عنه من اليمن، فقال له ﷺ: "بما أهللت؟" قال: "بإهْلالٍ كإهْلالِ النبي ﷺ." فقال له النبي ﷺ: "إني سقت الهدي وقَرَنْتُ." روى هذا اللفظ أبو داود وغيره من الأئمة ٥

٥ الأئمة: "الايمة" في الأصل.

٦ راجع أبو داود، السنن، ص. ٣٠٧ (كتاب المناسك، باب صفة حجّة النّبيّ، ١٩٠٥: "إنّي لو استقبلتُ من أمري ما استدبرتُ لم أَسُقِ الهَدْيَ ولجعلتُها عمرةً")؛ وراجع أيضا أبو داود، السنن، ص. ٢٩٠ (كتاب المناسك، باب في إفراد الحجّ، ١٧٨٤: "لو استقبلتُ من أمري ما استدبرتُ لما سُقْتُ الهَدْيَ")، والنسائي، السنن، ج. ٥، ص. ١٤٣ (كتاب مناسك الحجّ، الكراهية في الثّياب المصبّغة للمحرم، ٢٧١٢: "لو استقبلتُ من أمري ما استدبرتُ لم أَسُقِ الهَدْيَ وجعلتُها عمرةً")، وابن حنبل، المسند، ج. ٢١، ص. ٣٢٠ (مسند أنس بن مالك، ١٣٨١٣: "لو استقبلتُ من أمري ما استبدتُ لجعلتُها عمرةً ولكن سُقْتُ الهدْيَ وقَرنتُ الحجّ والعمرة").

21 Miná is a town in the hills east of Mecca on the road to ʿArafah, where on 10 Ḏū l-Ḥiǧǧah part of the pilgrimage rituals are performed, such as the throwing of pebbles, the sacrifice, and the shaving or cutting of the pilgrims' hair; it is also the site for the three-day-celebration after the conclusion of the pilgrimage, on 11, 12 and 13 Ḏū l-Ḥiǧǧah (Fr. Buhl, "Minā", in *EI*[2] http://referenceworks.brillonline.com/entries/encyclopaedia-of-islam-2/mina-SIM_5201).

had not brought along an oblational animal to rescind their pilgrimage [and to transform it] into a lesser pilgrimage, to completely end their state of *iḥrām*, and to enter into *iḥrām* [again] at their departure for Miná.[21] He said: "Had I known at the beginning of my case what I knew at the end
5 thereof, I would not have driven on the oblation animal and thus would have made it a lesser pilgrimage."[22] This is a clear proof that he—may God bless him and grant him salvation—was not combining [pilgrimage and lesser pilgrimage], as was believed by some companions of the *imām* Aḥmad[23] and by others.

10 § 11 ʿAlī b. Abī Ṭālib[24]—may God be pleased with him—arrived from Yemen, and he—may God bless him and grant him salvation—said to him: "How did you enter into *iḥrām*?" He said: "In the way the Prophet—may God bless him and grant him salvation—entered into *iḥrām*." The Prophet—may God bless him and grant him salvation—said to him: "Verily, I led on the
15 oblation animal and integrated [the pilgrimage with the lesser pilgrimage]." This wording was transmitted by Abū Dāwūd[25] and by other *imāms*, via

---

22 For the translation of the more detailed parallel passage in Ibn Ḥazm's text, regarding this discussion of the requirements following from bringing along sacrificial animals, see Adang (2005): 121–122.

23 For Aḥmad b. Ḥanbal, see above, note 17.

24 ʿAlī b. Abī Ṭālib is the nephew and son-in-law of the Prophet; he was married to the Prophet's daughter Fāṭimah, with whom he had two sons: al-Ḥasan and al-Ḥusayn; he was one of the first believers in Muḥammad's mission, and succeeded in 36/656 to the leadership of the Muslim community as the fourth successor to Muḥammad, or caliph, in a context of general upheaval, discord, and competition (the first *fitnah*) that prevented his authority from ever being generally accepted; he was murdered in the mosque of Kufa, Iraq, in 40/661; his lineage, the ʿAlids, and their various supporters eventually crystallised into a separate religious community, the *šīʿat ʿAlī* (ʿAlī's party) or the Shiites, who believe in the transhuman nature and mission of ʿAlī and his designated descendants, the imāms (L. Veccia Vaglieri, "ʿAlī b. Abī Ṭālib", in *EI*[2] http://referenceworks.brillonline.com/entries/encyclopaedia-of-islam-2/ali-b-abi-talib-COM_0046).

25 Abū Dāwūd al-Siǧistānī (d. 275/889) is the compiler of one of the six collections of *ḥadīṯ* that are considered canonical in Sunni Islam (Christopher Melchert, "Abū Dāwūd al-Sijistānī", in *EI*[3] http://referenceworks.brillonline.com/entries/encyclopaedia-of-islam-3/abu-dawud-al-sijistani-SIM_0024; Melchert [2008]).

بإسناد صحيح، وهو صريح في القِرَان.[7] وقدم مع علي رضي الله عنه من اليمن هَدَايا. فأشركه ﷺ في هَدْيه أيضا، فكان حاصلهما مائة بدَنَة.

ثم خرج ﷺ إلى منى، فبات بها، وكانت ليلة الجمعة التاسع من ذي الحجة. ثم أصبح، فسار إلى عرفة، وخطب بنَمِرَة خطبة عظيمة شهدها من أصحابه نحو من أربعين ألفا رضي الله عنهم أجمعين. وجمع ٥ بين الظهر والعصر. ثم وقف بعرفة، فحج على رَحْل، وكانت زاملته. ثم بات بالمزدلفة وجمع بين المغرب والعشاء ليلتئذ. ثم أصبح، فصلى الفجر في أول وقتها. ثم سار قبل طلوع الشمس إلى مِنَى، فرمى جمرة العقبة، ونحَر وحلق. ثم أفاض، فطاف بالبيت طواف الفرض، وهو طواف الزيارة.

١ صريح : تصحيح في الأصل بخط المقريزي. ٢ مائة : "ماية" في الأصل. ٦ والعشاء ليلتئذ : "والعشآ ليلتيذ" في الأصل. || الشمس : تصحيح في الأصل بخط المقريزي.

[7] راجع أبو داود، السنن، ص. ٢٩٢ (كتاب المناسك، باب في الإقران، ١٧٩٧: فلما قدم عليّ من اليمن على رسول الله ﷺ قال: ... فأتيتُ النّبيّ ﷺ فقال لي رسول الله ﷺ: "كيف صَنَعْتَ؟" فقال: قُلْتُ: "أهللتُ بإهلال النّبيّ ﷺ." قال: "فإنّي قد سُقْتُ الهَدْيَ وَقَرَنتُ")، راجع أيضا النسائي، السنن، ج. ٥، ص. ١٤٩ (كتاب مناسك الحج، القران، ٢٧٢٥: فلمّا قدم على النّبيّ ﷺ قال عليّ: "فأتيتُ رسول الله ﷺ فقال لي رسول الله ﷺ: "كيف صَنَعْتَ؟" قلتُ: "أهللتُ بإهلالِكَ." قال: "فانّي سُقْتُ الهَدْيَ وَقَرَنْتُ")، وص. ١٥٨ (كتاب مناسك الحجّ، الحجّ بغير نيّة يقصده المحرم، ٢٧٤٥: فلمّا قدم عليّ على النّبيّ ﷺ قال عليّ: "... فأتيتُ النّبيّ ﷺ فقال لي: "كيف صَنَعْتَ؟" قُلْتُ: "أهللتُ بما أهللتَ." قال: "فإنّي قد سُقْتُ الهَدْيَ وَقَرَنتُ").

an authentic chain of transmission, being very clear about the principle of integration. ʿAlī—may God be pleased with him—brought oblational animals from Yemen, and he also gave him—may God bless him and grant him salvation—a share of his oblational animals. They jointly received 100 head of cattle.

§ 12 Then he—may God bless him and grant him salvation—left for Miná, where he spent the night. This was the night of Friday 9 Ḏū l-Ḥiǧǧah [6 March]. The next morning he went to ʿArafah.[26] He delivered a sublime sermon at Namirah,[27] witnessed by about 40,000 of his companions—may God be pleased with all of them—, and he combined the noon and afternoon prayer. Then he performed the standing [before God] at ʿArafah. He performed the pilgrimage on a mount which was his pack camel. Then he spent the night at Muzdalifah,[28] combining there and then the sunset and evening prayer. At early dawn of the next morning, he performed the morning prayer [at Muzdalifah], and before sunrise he went to Miná, where he performed the throwing at Ǧamrat al-ʿAqabah, the sacrifice, and the shaving of his hair. Then he ran back in an enthusiastic manner, and performed around the house [of God] the obligatory circumambulation, which is the circumambulation of the visitation.[29] There is disagreement on where exactly he

26 ʿArafah or Mount ʿArafāt refers to a wide plain with an isolated hill on it, situated about 21 kilometers east of Mecca, where pilgrims perform the "standing before God" (*wuqūf*) from noon to sunset of 9 Ḏū l-Ḥiǧǧah, after a public sermon (*ḫuṭbah*) and a combination of the noon and afternoon prayer; it is one of the rituals that must be performed for the pilgrimage to be valid, and it is generally believed that the sins of pilgrims performing it are forgiven (Uri Rubin, "ʿArafāt", in EI[3] http://referenceworks.brillonline.com/entries/encyclopaedia-of-islam-3/arafat-COM_22903).

27 Namirah is claimed to be the name of a site near ʿArafah, with a cave in which the Prophet is believed to have stayed before beginning the ritual at ʿArafah (Rubin, "ʿArafāt").

28 Muzdalifah is—next to ʿArafah—the second place outside Mecca's *ḥaram*-area which pilgrims are to visit during the pilgrimage; it is on the route between Mecca and ʿArafah; pilgrims combine the sunset and evening prayer and then spend the night between 9 and 10 Ḏū l-Ḥiǧǧah at this site, finishing with another but much shorter standing before God (*wuqūf*) and the morning prayer (A.J. Wensinck, J. Jomier, "Ḥadjdj", in EI[2] http://referenceworks.brillonline.com/entries/encyclopaedia-of-islam-2/hadjdj-COM_0249).

29 *Ṭawāf al-ifāḍah* or *ṭawāf al-ziyārah*, see above note 19.

واختلف أين صلى الظهر يومئذ، وقد أشكل ذلك على كثير من الحفاظ. ثم حل من كل شيء حَرُم منه ﷺ. وخطب ثاني يوم النحر خطبة عظيمة أيضا، ووصى وحذر وأنذر، وأشهدهم على أنفسهم بأنه بلغهم الرسالة. فنحن نشهد أنه بلغ الرسالة، وأدى الأمانة، ونصح الأمة ﷺ تسليما كثيرا إلى يوم الدين. ثم أقبل ﷺ منصرفا إلى المدينة، وقد أكمل الله | له دينه. 117a

١ يومئذ : "يوميذ" في الأصل. ‖ شيء : "شي" في الأصل. ٢ ثاني … وحذر : ناقصة في الأصل، مضافة بخط المقريزي في الهامش الأيسر، من الأسفل إلى الأعلى + صح؛ يشير إليها الرمز ⌐ بعد كلمة "خطب". ‖ وأشهدهم : تصحيح في الأصل بخط المقريزي.

performed the noon prayer on that day—this has been a source of confusion for many experts. Then everything that had been forbidden for him—may God bless him and grant him salvation—became lawful again. On the day after the Day of Immolation, he delivered another sublime sermon, and he gave counsel, cautioned, and admonished. He called upon them as a witness for themselves that he had told them about [God's] message. We similarly testify that he—may God bless him and grant him total salvation until Judgement Day—told about [God's] message, led to [God's] faithfulness, and gave good counsel to the community. Thereafter he—may God bless him and grant him salvation—began to return to Medina. Thus God had made his religion complete for him.

لطيفة

النداء بالحج سُنّةٌ للمسلمين. ويُنادى بديار مصر في رجب، وهو قياس ندائه عليه السلام أول ذي القعدة لأن مسافة الحج مِن المدينة عشرة أيام فقدم النداء بثلاثة أمثالها، ومسافة الحج في البر من مصر أربعُونَ يومًا، فقدم النداء بثلاثة أمثالها، فكانت الجملة من أول رجب إلى انقضاء عشر ذي ٥ الحجة خمسة أشهر وعشرة أيام.

وكذلك بدمشق.

وأول من أدار المحمل الملك الظاهر بيبرس البندقداري رحمه الله.

٢ النداء : "الندآ" في الأصل. ‖ ندائه : "ندآيه" في الأصل. ٣ النداء[1] : "الندآ" في الأصل. ٤ النداء[2] : "الندآ" في الأصل. ‖ انقضاء : "انقضآ" في الأصل. ٧ البندقداري : مضافة بخط المقريزي في مكانها الصحيح في الجملة بعد كلمة "بيبرس". ‖ رحمه الله : ناقصة في الأصل، مضافة بخط المقريزي في الهامش الأيمن، من الأعلى إلى الأسفل + صح، يشير إليها الرمز ⌐ بعد كلمة "البندقداري".

Brief note

§ 13 The public call for the pilgrimage is a binding tradition for Muslims. In the regions of Egypt, the call is done in Rağab. This is by analogy with the call by him—peace be upon him—on 1 Ḏū l-Qaʿdah: the distance for
5 the pilgrimage from Medina is 10 days, whereas the call is done 3 times the same amount [of days] before; the distance for the pilgrimage over land from Egypt is 40 days, whereas the call is done 3 times the same amount [of days] before, there being in all 5 months and 10 days between 1 Rajab and the end of 10 Ḏū l-Ḥiğğah.

10 § 14 The same is true [for the public call for the pilgrimage] in Damascus.

§ 15 The first one to organise the parading of the *maḥmal*[30] was al-Malik al-Ẓāhir Baybars al-Bunduqdārī[31]—may God's mercy be upon him.

30 Since the mid-thirteenth century the *maḥmal* was a central component of rulers' pilgrimage paraphernalia, consisting of an empty palanquin covered with an elaborately decorated cloth that accompanied the main pilgrimage caravans (from Egypt, from Syria, from Iraq …) to Mecca; it symbolised the presence and (aspired) reality of a ruler's authority along the route and in Mecca, as well as his patronage of the caravan and pilgrimage rituals; *maḥmal*s were in use into the twentieth century (see Jomier [1953]); on the legendary origins of the *maḥmal* parade, see Behrens-Abouseif (1997).

31 Al-Ẓāhir Baybars was sultan of Egypt and Syria between 658/1260 and 676/1277 (P. Thorau, "Baybars I, al-Malik al-Ẓāhir Rukn al-Dīn", in *EI*³ http://referenceworks.brillonline.com/entries/encyclopaedia-of-islam-3/baybars-i-al-malik-al-zahir-rukn-al-din-COM_23709; Thorau [1987]).

فصل في ذكر من حج من الخلفاء في مدة خلافته

أبو بكر الصديق رضي الله عنه.

اسمُهُ عبد الله بن أبي قحافة عثمان بن عامر بن عمرو بن كعب بن سَعْد بن تَيْم بن مُرة بن كعب بن لُؤَي بن غالب بن فهر بن مالك القرشي التيمي، خليفة رسول الله ﷺ.

٥ بويع له بعد وفاة رسول الله ﷺ بيعة العامة يوم الثلٰثاء ثالث عشر شهر ربيع الأول سنة إحدى عشرة من الهجرة.

فحج بالناس في هذه السنة عَتَّابُ بن أَسِيْد، وقيل: عبد الرحمن بن عوف رضيَ الله عنهما.

١ الخلفاء: "الخلفآ" في الأصل. ٥ له: ناقصة في الأصل، مضافة بخط المقريزي في مكانها الصحيح في الجملة فوق السطر. ‖ العامة: "العآمة" في الأصل. ‖ الثلٰثاء: "الثلثا" في الأصل. ٦ عشرة: التاء المربوطة ناقصة في الأصل، مضافة بخط المقريزي في مكانها في السطر.

Chapter with the Report of the Caliphs Who Went on Pilgrimage During Their Caliphate

1. Abū Bakr al-Ṣiddīq[32]—May God be pleased with him.

§16 His name is ʿAbd Allāh b. Abī Quḥāfah ʿUṯmān b. ʿĀmir b. ʿAmr b. Kaʿb b. Saʿd b. Taym b. Murrah b. Kaʿb b. Luʾayy b. Ġālib b. Fihr b. Mālik al-Qurašī l-Taymī, Successor of the Messenger of God—may God bless him and grant him salvation.

§17 The public oath of allegiance was sworn to him after the passing of the Messenger of God—may God bless him and grant him salvation—on Tuesday, the 13th of the month Rabīʿ al-Awwal, of the year 11 since the *hiǧrah* [9 June 632].

§18 In this year ʿAttāb b. Asīd[33]—it was said ʿAbd al-Raḥmān b. ʿAwf,[34] may God be pleased with both of them—led the people on the pilgrimage.

---

32 Abū Bakr al-Ṣiddīq was the first to succeed the Prophet as leader of Muḥammad's community, as 'Commander of the Faithful' and 'Caliph'; he is remembered as a longstanding close companion of Muḥammad and as the father of his favourite wife, whose main achievement during his brief caliphate was the continuation and consolidation of Muḥammad's achievement in the Hijaz and on the Arabian peninsula; he died in 13/634 (W.M. Watt, "Abū Bakr", in *EI*[2] http://referenceworks.brillonline.com/entries/encyclopaedia-of-islam-2/abu-bakr-SIM_0165; Madelung [1997]: 28–56).

33 ʿAṭṭāb b. Asīd b. Abī l-ʿĪṣ b. Umayyah was a member of the Umayyad clan, the leading clan of pre-Islamic Mecca, who changed sides upon Muḥammad's capture of Mecca in 8/630 and who was made governor of Mecca shortly afterwards; he continued to hold this post during the caliphate of Abū Bakr, and died between 12/634 and 23/644 ("ʿAttāb", in *EI*[2] http://referenceworks.brillonline.com/entries/encyclopaedia-of-islam-2/attab-SIM_0856).

34 ʿAbd al-Raḥmān b. ʿAwf was an early convert and companion of Muḥammad, with considerable standing in Muḥammad's community; he was a close advisor of Abū Bakr and eventually he also was a member of the council (*šūrá*) that arranged the succession to the caliph ʿUmar in 23/644; he died in about 31/652 (M. Houtsma; W.M. Watt; "ʿAbd al-Raḥmān b. ʿAwf", in *EI*[2] http://referenceworks.brillonline.com/entries/encyclopaedia-of-islam-2/abd-al-rahman-b-awf-SIM_0113).

وحج أبو بكر رضي الله عنه بالناس سنة اثنَتي عشرة، واستخلف على المدينة عثمان بن عفان رضي الله عنه، وقيل: حج بالناس عمر بن الخطاب أو عبد الرحمن بن عَوْف رضي الله عنهما، والأول أصح.[٨]

وتوفي أبو بكر رضي الله عنه على رأس سنتين وثلٰثة أشهر واثني عشر يومًا، وقيل غير ذلك.

[٨] راجع هذا الخبر على نفس الشكل تقريبا في ابن الأثير، الكامل، ج. ٢، ص. ٢٥١.

§ 19 Abū Bakr—may God be pleased with him—led the people on the pilgrimage in the year 12 [634]. He left as his deputy over Medina ʿUṯmān b. ʿAffān[35]—may God be pleased with him. There was said that ʿUmar b. al-Ḫaṭṭāb[36] or ʿAbd al-Raḥmān b. ʿAwf—may God be pleased with both of 5 them—led the people on the pilgrimage. But the first statement is the most authentic.

§ 20 Abū Bakr—may God be pleased with him—passed away after exactly two years, three months, and twelve days [in office]—it was said otherwise.

35 ʿUṯmān b. ʿAffān was a member of the Umayyad clan of pre-Islamic Mecca, but also an early convert and a close companion and son-in-law of Muḥammad, and therefore a highly respected member of his community; in 23/644 he was chosen to succeed ʿUmar in the caliphate, which he held—with mixed success—until 35/656; he was murdered in Medina by tribal groups dissatisfied with his centralising policy vis-à-vis recently acquired rich provinces such as Egypt and Iraq (G. Levi Della Vida, R.G. Khoury, "ʿUṯmān b. ʿAffān", in *EI*[2] http://referenceworks.brillonline.com/entries/encyclopaedia-of-islam-2/uthman-b-affan-COM_1315; Madelung [1997]: 78–140).

36 ʿUmar b. al-Ḫaṭṭāb was one of the closest companions to Muḥammad, who was married to his daughter; upon Muḥammad's death, he undoubtedly was one of the community's most charismatic leading members, which resulted in his succession to Abū Bakr in 13/634; his leadership until his death in 23/644 was a pivotal moment in the community's early history, taking a defining course that included its successful expansion beyond the Arabian peninsula and the set-up of embryonic organisational structures that were soon to transform into the basic features of the early Islamic empire (G. Levi Della Vida; M. Bonner, "ʿUmar (I) b. al-Khaṭṭāb", in *EI*[2] http://referenceworks.brillonline.com/entries/encyclopaedia-of-islam-2/umar-i-b-al-khattab-SIM_7707; Madelung [1997]: 57–77).

عُمر بن الخطاب

ابن نُفَيل بن عبد العُزّى بن {رياح} بن عبد الله بن {قُرط} بن رَزاح بن عَدي بن كعب القرشي العدوي، أبو حفص، أمير المؤمنين رضي الله عنه.

ولي الخلافة بعد أبي بكرٍ الصديق رضي الله عنه. بويع له بها باستخلافه له في جمادى الآخرة سنة ثلث عشرة، واختلف في اليوم كما اختلف في يوم وفاة أبي بكر رضي الله عنه. وقتل مطعُونًا بيدِ ٥
أبي لُؤلؤة—غلام المغيرة بن شعبة—لثلاث بقين من ذي الحجة سنة ثلث وعشرين. فكانت خلافته عشر سنينَ ونصف، حج في جميعها إلا السَّنَة الأُولى فقط، فإنه حج بالناس فيها عتاب بن أَسيد، وقيل: بل حج عمر بالناس سِنيه كلها.

وفي سنة سبع عشرة اعتمر رضي الله عنه وبنى المسجد الحرام ووسع فيه، وأقام بمكة عشرين ليلة.
وهدم على قوم أبوا أن يبيعوا دورهم وعوضهم أثمانها من بيت المال. وجدد أنْصَابَ الحَرَم على يد ١٠

٢ العُزّى: "العُزَّي" في الأصل. ‖ {رياح}: "رَباح" في الأصل وهو خطأ. ‖ {قُرط}: "قُرَظ" في الأصل وهو خطأ ومن الظاهر أن المقريزي صحح الظاء. ‖ بن°: تصحيح في الأصل بخط المقريزي. ٤ باستخلافه: الفاء والهاء في الهامش الأيسر على نفس السطر بخط الناسخ. ٨ بل: تصحيح في الأصل بخط المقريزي. ‖ سِنيه: تصحيح في الأصل بخط المقريزي. ٩ رضي ... عنه: ناقصة في الأصل، مضافة بخط المقريزي في مكانها الصحيح في الجملة على آخر السطر في الهامش الأيسر.

2. ʿUmar b. al-Ḫaṭṭāb

b. Nufayl b. ʿAbd al-ʿUzzá b. Riyāḥ b. ʿAbd Allāh b. Qurṭ b. Razāḥ b. ʿAdī b. Kaʿb al-Qurašī l-ʿAdawī, Abū Ḥafṣ, Commander of the Faithful—may God be pleased with him.

5 § 21 He occupied the position of caliph after Abū Bakr al-Ṣiddīq—may God be pleased with him. The oath of allegiance was sworn to him for [this position], following his appointment as successor by [Abū Bakr] in Ǧumādá II of the year 13 [August 634]. There are different opinions on the exact date, just as there are different opinions on the day of the demise of Abū 10 Bakr—may God be pleased with him. [ʿUmar] was stabbed to death by Abū Luʾluʾah, the slave of al-Muġīrah b. Šuʿbah,[37] on 27 Ḏū l-Ḥiǧǧah of the year 23 [4 November 644]. His caliphate lasted for ten years and a half. He performed the pilgrimage in all of [these years], except for one year only, because in [that year] ʿAttāb b. Asīd led the people on the pilgrimage. It was 15 [also] said that ʿUmar rather performed the pilgrimage every year of [his caliphate].

§ 22 In the year 17 [638] he—may God be pleased with him—performed the lesser pilgrimage. He carried out building works on the sacred mosque,[38] creating more space inside. He stayed in Mecca for twenty nights. He had 20 [the properties] demolished of people who refused to sell their [neighbouring] houses and he compensated them with their market values from the public treasury. He had the stones that stake out the sacrosanct area (*ḥaram*)

37 On the murder of ʿUmar by Abū Luʾluʾah, a Christian slave of the then governor of Basra and companion al-Muġīrah b. Šuʿbah (d. c. 51/671), and a refused appeal against a tax as its main motive, see Levi Della Vida; Bonner, "ʿUmar (I) b. al-Khaṭṭāb", *EI*²; Madelung (1997): 68–70.

38 The Meccan sanctuary of *al-masǧid al-ḥarām*, the sacred mosque, was originally constructed as a place of Muslim worship in 8/630 by Muḥammad, on the small open space around the Kaʿbah and incorporating the related sacred sites of the Maqām Ibrāhīm and the well of Zamzam; soon proving too small for its purpose, this mosque has continuously been enlarged, embellished, and added to by a long list of political rulers, from the days of the caliph ʿUmar until contemporary engagements by the Saʿūdī kings (A.J. Wensinck, "al-Masdjid al-Ḥarām", in *EI*² http://referenceworks.brillonline.com/entries/encyclopaedia-of-islam-2/al-masdjid-al-haram-SIM_4999; see also Grabar [1985]: 4–7; al-Harigi [1994]).

مَخْرَمة | بن نوفل في آخرِين. واستأذنه أهل المياة في أن يبنوا منازل بين مكة والمدينة، فأذن لهم 117b
وشرط عليهم أن ابن السبيل أحق بالظل والماء.[9]

ثم خرج من المدينة عام الرمادة[10] حاجا أو معتمرا، فأتى الجار ليرى السفن التي قدمت من مصر في الخليج الذي احتفره عَمرو بن العاص، كما قد ذكرت خبره في **كتاب المواعظ والاعتبار بذكر**

٢ أحق : ناقصة في الأصل، مضافة بخط المقريزي في الهامش الأيسر، من الأسفل الى الأعلى + صح؛ يشير إليها الرمز ⌐ بعد كلمة "السبيل". ‖ والماء : "والمآ" في الأصل. ٣ معتمرا : ناقصة في الأصل، مضافة بخط المقريزي في مكانها الصحيح في الجملة على آخر السطر في الهامش الأيسر. ‖ فأتى : تصحيح في الأصل بخط المقريزي. ‖ ليرى : تصحيح في الأصل بخط المقريزي. ٤ الذي : تصحيح في الأصل بخط المقريزي. ‖ ذكرت : تصحيح في الأصل بخط المقريزي.

[9] راجع هذا الخبر على نفس الشكل تقريبا في ابن الأثير، الكامل، ج. ٢، ص. ٣٨٢؛ وفي الطبري، تاريخ الرسل والملوك، ج. ١/٥، ص. ٢٥٢٨-٢٥٢٩. [10] عام الرمادة هو سنة ١٨ (ابن الأثير، الكامل، ج. ٢، ص. ٣٩٦؛ الطبري، تاريخ الرسل والملوك، ج. ١/٥، ص. ٢٥٧٠).

renewed by Maḫramah b. Nawfal,[39] amongst others. The overseers of the wells asked for his permission to build way stations [on the route] between Mecca and Medina. He gave them permission, but made it conditional upon them that the wayfarer[40] would always be entitled to shelter and water.[41]

5 § 23 Then he left Medina in the Year of the Drought,[42] either performing the pilgrimage or the lesser pilgrimage. He came to al-Ǧār[43] to view the ships that came from Egypt via the canal which ʿAmr b. al-ʿĀṣ[44] had dug out—as I have reported in the book *al-Mawāʿiẓ wa-l-iʿtibār bi-ḏikr al-ḫiṭaṭ wa-l-āṯār*

---

39 Maḫramah b. Nawfal b. Uhayb b. ʿAbd Manāf (d. 54/673–674) was a member of the Quraysh of Mecca who converted to Islam in 8/630; he is remembered in particular by later authorities for his knowledge of Quraysh traditions, of their geneaology, and of these stones that demarcated the sacrosanct area of Mecca and that are believed to have been put there by the prophet Ibrāhīm under the supervision of the angel Ǧibrīl (see his biography in al-Ṭabarī, *History* XXXIX, 42–43).

40 In pre-Islamic and early Islamic society, the term 'wayfarer' (*Ibn al-sabīl*) referred to a specific social group that enjoyed a particular protected social status among settled people (see al-Ṭabarī, *History* XIII, 109, fn. 375).

41 For the translation of the parallel text in al-Ṭabarī's History, see al-Ṭabarī, *History* XIII, 109.

42 In his history, al-Ṭabarī explains that "in this year, I mean 18 (639), the people were afflicted by a severe famine and a drought of catastrophic proportions. This is the year that is called the Year of the Drought (*ramādah*)" (al-Ṭabarī, *History* XIII, 151); he furthermore explains the use of the specific Arabic noun *ramādah* (derived from *ramād*, meaning ashes) as follows: "In the reign of ʿUmar the people in Medina and its surrounding territory were afflicted by a drought in which the world was awhirl with dust when the wind blew, as if it rained ashes. That is why this year was called the Year of Drought" (al-Ṭabarī, *History* XIII, 154).

43 Al-Ǧār was Medina's supply port on the Red Sea until the eighteenth century; from the days of the caliph ʿUmar until the middle of the second/eighth century, this supply consisted predominantly of grain brought from Egypt (A. Dietrich, "al-Djār", in *EI*[2] http://referenceworks.brillonline.com/entries/encyclopaedia-of-islam-2/al-djar-SIM_1999).

44 ʿAmr b. al-ʿĀṣ was a Meccan leader and companion of the Prophet, who acquired his fame especially in his leading involvement in the Arabic conquests of Palestine and of Egypt; he consolidated Arab authority over Egypt and became Egypt's first Muslim governor; he was dismissed by the third caliph, ʿUṯmān, but returned to the governorship of Egypt after successfully siding with the Umayyad Muʿāwiyah against the caliph ʿAlī in 36–38/656–658; he died in office at an allegedly very advanced age in 42/663 (A.J. Wensinck, "ʿAmr b. al-ʿĀṣ", in *EI*[2] http://referenceworks.brillonline.com/entries/encyclopaedia-of-islam-2/amr-b-al-as-SIM_0633).

الخطط والآثار.[11] وقال للناس: "سيروا بنا ننظر إلى السفن التي سيرها الله إلينا من أرض فرعون." وأكل في سفره هذا وهو محرم لحم ظبي أصابه قوم حلال. فلما نزل على البحر قال: "إغتسلوا من ماء البحر فإنه مبارك."

ثم صك للناس بذلك الطعام صكوكا، فتبايع التجار الصكوك بينهم قبل أن يقبضوها. فلقي عمر العلاء بن الأسود، فقال: "كم ربح حكيم بن حِزَام؟" فقال: "إبتاع من صكوك الجار بمائة ألف ٥ درهم، وربح عليها مائة ألف." فلقيه عمر، فقال: "يا حكيم، كم ربحت؟" فأخبره بمثل خبر العلاء. قال: "فبعته قبل أن تقبضه؟" قال: "نعم." قال: "فإن هذا بيع لا يصلح، فاردده." قال: "ما علمت أن هذا لا يصلح وما أقدر على رده." قال: "ما بد." قال: "والله، ما أقدر على ذلك، وقد تفرق وذهب، ولكن رأس مالي ورِبْحي صدقة."[12]

٣ ماء : "مآ" في الأصل. ٤ صك : تصحيح في الأصل بخط المقريزي. ٥ العلاء : "العلآ" في الأصل. ‖ بن[1] : تصحيح في الأصل بخط المقريزي. ‖ فقال : ناقصة في الأصل، مضافة بخط المقريزي في الهامش الأيسر، من الأسفل الى الأعلى + صح؛ يشير إليها الرمز ˥ بعد كلمة "الاسود". ‖ بمائة : "بماية" في الأصل. ٦ مائة : "ماية" في الأصل. ‖ العلاء : "العلآ" في الأصل. ٩ ورِبْحي : تصحيح في الأصل بخط المقريزي.

[11] راجع المقريزي، الخطط، ج. ١، ص. ١٩١؛ ج. ٣، ص. ٣٧٦. [12] راجع خبر عام الرمادة على نفس الشكل تقريبا في ابن عبد الحكم، فتوح مصر، ص. ١٦٦.

[Admonitions and Reflections on the Quarters and Monuments (in Fusṭāṭ and Cairo)].[45] He said to the people: "Come along with us to watch the ships that God has sent to us from the land of Pharao." During this trip of his, he ate the meat of a gazelle shot by respectable people, while he was in the state of *iḥrām*. When he came down to the sea, he said: "Perform the ritual ablution with water from the sea, for it is blessed."

§ 24 Then he assigned to the people fixed shares in that food [that was brought from Egypt to Arabia via al-Ǧār].[46] But the merchants sold the shares among each other before they had actually acquired [the food]. So when ʿUmar met with al-ʿAlāʾ b. al-Aswad,[47] he said: "How much profit did Ḥakīm b. Ḥizām[48] make?" He said: "He purchased the shares of al-Ǧār for 100,000 *dirhams* and made a profit on them of 100,000 [*dirhams*]." ʿUmar met with him and said: "Ḥakīm, how much profit have you made?" He reported to him just as al-ʿAlāʾ had reported. [ʿUmar] said: "Did you sell it before you had acquired it?" He said: "Yes." [ʿUmar] said: "This is a sale that is not permitted, so return [the money]." He said: "I did not know that this is not permitted, and I cannot return it." [ʿUmar] said: "There is no other way." He said: "By God, I cannot do that, because [the money] has been distributed and spent. But my capital and my profit are charitable gifts [that should make up for this]."

45 See al-Maqrīzī, *al-Ḫiṭaṭ*, 1:191; 3:376.

46 Vehement discussions on the permissibility of trade in fixed shares, or assignments (*ṣukūk*), for grain from the storehouses in al-Ǧār are well-attested from the earliest extant writings of Islamic legal discourse (Dietrich, "Al-Djār", *EI*²); today, the term *ṣukūk* continues to be used in Islamic banking for a specific type of bonds that complies with Islamic requirements, with the prohibition of interest in particular (see eg. Suhaib [2009]).

47 Al-ʿAlāʾ b. al-Aswad: His name appears in the chain of transmitters of a *ḥadīṯ* reported by al-Buḫārī as al-ʿAlāʾ b. al-Aswad or al-Aswad b. al-ʿAlāʾ b. Ǧāriyah who transmitted the tradition from ʿĀʾišah (al-Buḫārī, *al-Taʾrīḫ al-kabīr*, 7:209). Apart from that, I have so far not been able to retrieve any further information on this person.

48 Ḥakīm b. Ḥizām b. Ḫuwaylid b. Asad b. ʿAbd al-ʿUzzá b. Quṣayy was an old member of the Meccan clan of Quraysh and a nephew of the Prophet's first wife Ḫadīǧah; he is believed to have converted to Islam with his four sons in the year 8/630, and they were therefore all considered to belong to the Prophet's Companions; Ḥakīm is said to have died in Medina in the year 54/674, at the highly advanced age of 120 (see his biographies in al-Ṭabarī, *History* XXXIX, 40–42).

واتفق في آخر حجة حجها عمر رضي الله عنه أنه لما رمى الجمرة أتاه حجر فوقع على صلعته، فأدماه. وثَم رجل من بني لِهْب، فقال: "أُشْعِر أميرَ المؤمنين لا يحج بعدها." ثم جاء إلى الجمرة الثانية، فصاح رجل: "يا خليفة رسول الله." فقال: "لا يحج أمير المؤمنين بعد عامه هذا." فقتل عمر رضي الله عنه بعد رجوعه من الحج. لِهْب—مكسور اللام—قبيلة من قبائل الأزْد تُعرَف فيها العِيافة والزَّجْر.[١٣]

٥ وعن عائشة رضي الله عنها أن عمر أذن لأزواج النبي ﷺ أن يحججن في آخر حجة حجها. قالت: "فلما ارتحل من الحَصْبة، أقبل رجل متلثم، فقال وأنا أسمع: "أين كان منزل أمير المؤمنين؟" فقال قائل وأنا أسمع: "هذا كان منزله،" فأناخ في منزل عمر، ثم رفع عَقِيْرتَه يتغنى: [الطويل]

---

١ عمر ... عنه: ناقصة في الأصل، مضافة بخط المقريزي في الهامش الأيسر، من الأسفل الى الأعلى + صح، يشيرإليها الرمز ⌐ بعد كلمة "حجها". ٢ جاء: "جآ" في الأصل. ٥ عائشة: "عايشة" في الأصل. ٦ قائل: "قايل" في الأصل.

---

[١٣] راجع هذا الخبر على نفس الشكل تماما في ابن عبد البر، الاستيعاب، ج. ٣، ص. ٢٤٠.

§ 25 During the last pilgrimage which ʿUmar—may God be pleased with him—performed, it so happened that while he was throwing at the [first] Ǧamrah,[49] a stone flew at him and fell on a wen he had, making him bleed. There was a man from the Banū Lihb who said: "I sense that the Commander of the Faithful will not make another pilgrimage." Then ʿUmar came to the second Ǧamrah, where a man shouted: "O Successor of the Messenger of God", and he said: "The Commander of the Faithful will not perform the pilgrimage beyond this year." ʿUmar—may God be pleased with him—was indeed killed after his return from the pilgrimage. Lihb—with the vowel i after the *lām*—is one of the clans of al-Azd, known for harbouring feelings of aversion and reprimand.[50]

§ 26 [It is transmitted] on the authority of ʿĀʾišah[51]—may God be pleased with her—that during the last pilgrimage that ʿUmar performed he allowed the wives of the Prophet—may God bless him and grant him salvation—to perform the pilgrimage. She said: "When I departed from the pebble throwing, I ran into a veiled man. He said, while I heard him: "Where is the dwelling of the Commander of the Faithful?" Someone else said, while I heard him: "This was his dwelling." He dismounted at the dwelling of ʿUmar, and then he raised his voice and started singing: [*Ṭawīl* meter]

---

49 The three sites at Miná where pebbles are to be thrown as part of the pilgrimage rituals, are each referred to as al-Ǧamrah ("the pebble"), the first one to be encountered on the way back from ʿArafah being known as al-Ǧamrah al-Ūlà ("The First Ǧamra"), the second one some 150 metres further as al-Ǧamrah al-Wuṣṭà ("The Middle Ǧamra"), and the third one 115 metres on as Ǧamrat al-ʿAqabah (the Ǧamrah of the mountain pass) (F. Buhl, J. Jomier, "al-D̲jamra", in *EI*² http://referenceworks.brillonline.com/entries/encyclopaedia-of-islam-2/al-Djamra-SIM_1977).

50 The name for two ancient Arab tribal groupings, the Lihb belonging to the largely settled Azd Sarāt of the highlands of ʿAṣir (see G. Strenziok, "Azd", in *EI*² http://referenceworks.brillonline.com/entries/encyclopaedia-of-islam-2/azd-SIM_0946).

51 ʿĀʾišah was the daughter of the caliph Abū Bakr and one of the Prophet's wives; it is generally believed that she was the Prophet's favourite wife; in the field of the transmission of stories and traditions about the Prophet and the first caliphs, ʿĀʾišah is considered an important and authoritative source of information due to her highly respected status that continued up to her death in 58/678 (W.M. Watt, "ʿĀʾis̲h̲a Bint Abī Bakr", in *EI*² http://referenceworks.brillonline.com/entries/encyclopaedia-of-islam-2/aisha-bint-abi-bakr-SIM_0440).

عليك سلام من أمير وباركت يــــد الله في ذاك الأديم الممزّق

فمن يَجْرِ أَوْ يركَبْ جناحَيْ نعامة ليدرك ما قدمت بالأمس يُسْبَق

قضيتَ أُمورًا ثم غادرت بعدها بــــوائج في أكمامــــها لم تُفَتَّــــق"

قالت عائشة: "فقلت لبعض أهلي: "أعلموا لي من هذا الرجل؟" فذهبوا، فلم يجدوا في مناخه أحدًا."

٥ قالت عائشة: "فوالله، إني لأحسبه من الجن." فلما قُتل عمر نحل الناس هذه الأبيات للشماخ بن ضِرار أو لأخيه مُزَرِّد. هكذا روى هذا | الخبر الحافظ أبو عُمر يوسف بن عبد الله بن عبد البر 118a النَمَرِي.[١٤] وذكر محمد بن عمر الواقدي في كتاب **الفتوح** هذه الأبيات بزيادة في عدتها.[١٥]

١ وباركت: تصحيح في الأصل بخط المقريزي. ٤ عائشة: "عايشة" في الأصل. ٥ عائشة: "عايشة" في الأصل. || بن: "ابن" في الأصل والالف مضافة بخط المقريزي في مكانها الصحيح في الكلمة فوق السطر وبيمينها خط قلم يشير إلى شطبها. ٦ الخبر: تصحيح في الأصل بخط المقريزي.

[١٤] راجع ابن عبد البر، الاستيعاب، ج. ٣، ص. ٢٤٤. [١٥] كتاب الفتوح للواقدي مفقود.

52 In Islam, the *ǧinn* are conceived of as intelligent beings just as mankind and angels, with bodies composed of vapour or flame; Muḥammad was sent to them just as he was sent to mankind; they cannot be perceived as such by human senses, but they can appear under different forms; their relationship with the devil remains somewhat ambiguous, and in particular in popular thought and folklore there has always existed a rich tradition of how *ǧinn* interfere in man's life and vice versa (see Lebling [2010]).

§ 27 May there be upon you a peace that is a commander's due
May this torn skin by God's hand be blessed

One who runs ahead or rides the wings of an ostrich
surely realises that what you forwarded yesterday will be passed

5 You accomplished things whereafter you departed
[leaving behind] calamities the sleeves of which could not be unstitched."

§ 28 'Ā'išah said: "So I said to some of my folk: 'Let me know who this man is', so they left, but they did not find anyone where he had dismounted."
10 'Ā'išah said: "By God, I truly think he is one of the *ǧinn*."[52] When 'Umar was killed, the people attributed these verses to al-Šammāḫ b. Ḍirār or to his brother Muzarrid.[53] This story was thus transmitted by the *ḥāfiẓ* Abū 'Umar Yūsuf b. 'Abd Allāh b. 'Abd al-Barr al-Namarī.[54] Muḥammad b. 'Umar al-Wāqidī mentioned these verses in the *Kitāb al-Futūḥ* [Book of Conquests],[55]
15 augmenting their number.

53 Al-Šammāḫ b. Ḍirār is the name of a poet of the northern Ḏubyān tribe, who converted to Islam, actively participated in the Arab conquests and died in the course of them, allegedly in 30/650; he belonged to a family of well-reputed pre-islamic and early islamic poets, that also included his brother al-Muzarrid, and he is known for the superb quality of his poetry (hence his nickname al-Šammāḫ—the proud one) (see A. Arazi, "al-Shammākh b. Ḍirār", in *EI*[2] http://referenceworks.brillonline.com/entries/encyclopaedia-of-islam-2/al-shammakh-b-dirar-SIM_6806).

54 See Ibn 'Abd al-Barr, *al-Istī'āb*, 3:240. Abū 'Umar Yūsuf Ibn 'Abd al-Barr (368–463/978–1070) was a highly reputed Andalusian scholar of *ḥadīṯ*, law, and genealogy, and a *qāḍī*, who left a considerable number of scholarly works, including *al-Istī'āb*, a compendium of biographies of Companions (see Ch. Pellat, "Ibn 'Abd al-Barr", in *EI*[2] http://referenceworks.brillonline.com/entries/encyclopaedia-of-islam-2/ibn-abd-al-barr-SIM_3027).

55 Muḥammad b. 'Umar al-Wāqidī (130–207/747–822) was an Islamic scholar and historian from Medina, whose writings are considered of paramount importance for the construction and transmission of knowledge about the first decades of Islamic history; his work only survived in part in the *Kitāb al-Maġāzī*, and through all kinds of references in later historical writings (M. Leder, "al-Wāḳidī", in *EI*[2] http://referenceworks.brillonline.com/entries/encyclopaedia-of-islam-2/al-wakidi-SIM_7836). The passage in the *Kitāb al-Futūḥ* referred to here does not seem to have survived.

وقال أبو عثمان النهدي: "رأيت عمر يرمي الجمرة وعليه إزار مرقوع بقطعة جراب." وقال علي بن أبي طالب: "رأيت عمر يطوف بالكعبة وعليه إزار فيه إحدى وعشرون رقعة فيها من أدم."

وعن سعيد بن المسيب، قال: "حج عمر، فلما كان بضَجْنَان قال: "لا اله الا الله العلي العظيم المعطي من شاء ما شاء، كنت أرعى إبل الخطاب بهذا الوادي في مدرعة صوف، وكان فظا يتعبني إذا عملت، ويضربني إذا قصرت، وقد أمسيت وليس بيني وبين الله أحد." ثم تمثل: [الكامل] ٥

لا شيء مما تَرى تَبْقى بشاشَتُه يبـقى الإلهُ ويُودَى المَالُ والولَـدُ

لم تغن عن هرمُزٍ يومًا خزائنه والخلدَ قد حاولت عَادٌ فما خلَدُوا

٢ إحدى : تصحيح في الأصل بخط المقريزي. || وعشرون : تصحيح في الأصل بخط المقريزي. ٤ من : تصحيح في الأصل بخط المقريزي. || شاء[1] : "شآ" في الأصل. || ما : تصحيح في الأصل بخط المقريزي. || شاء[2] : "شا" في الأصل. ٦ شيء : "شي" في الأصل. || والولَدُ : تصحيح في الأصل بخط المقريزي. ٧ لم ... خلَدُوا : هذا البيت كله مضاف في السطر الصحيح في الأصل بخط المقريزي تصحيحا. || خزائنه : "خزاينه" في الأصل.

56 Abū ʿUṯmān al-Nahdī, from the clan Nahd b. Zayd, only converted to Islam during the reign of ʿUmar; he came to live in Kufa and Basra, and he died in 83/702–703 (al-Ṭabarī, *History* XXXIX, 214–215).

§ 29 Abū ʿUṯmān al-Nahdī[56] said: "I saw ʿUmar throwing at the Ǧamrah, wearing a cloak patched with a piece of leather bag." ʿAlī b. Abī Ṭālib said: "I saw ʿUmar circumambulating the Kaʿbah, wearing a cloak made up of twenty-one pieces of cloth, some of which were of leather."

5 § 30 [It was transmitted] on the authority of Saʿīd b. al-Musayyab,[57] who said: "ʿUmar went on pilgrimage. When he was at Ḍaǧnān[58] he said: 'There is no god but God, the Great, the Sublime, the Giver to whomever He wishes of whatever He wishes. I used to graze the camels of al-Ḫaṭṭāb in this valley, wearing a woollen cloak; [my father] was a rude [man] who wearied me
10 when I was working and who beat me when I fell short [of doing my work properly]. Now, however, my situation has become thus that there is no one between me and God.' Then he recited: [*Kāmil* meter]

§ 31 There is nothing of what you see whose joy lingers on
[only] the divine lingers on, whereas wealth and offspring will be
15 destroyed.

The treasures of Hurmuz[59] have been of no avail to him, [not even] for a day;
[The people of] ʿĀd[60] have tried to achieve eternity, but they did not abide;

---

57 Saʿīd b. al-Musayyab was a highly respected early Muslim scholar and genealogist from Medina, who died in 94/712–713 (al-Ṭabarī, *History* XXXIX, 316, fn. 1462).

58 Ḍaǧnān: a small mountain close to Mecca, on the route to Medina (see al-Ṭabarī, *History* XIV, 131, fn. 648).

59 Hurmuz is a name that was borne by five rulers of the Sassanid dynasty of late antique Persia; the most well-known in history and in Arabic literature was Hurmuz IV (r. 579–590), who was executed following a successful rebellion against his rule (Cl. Huart, H. Massé, "Hurmuz", in *EI*² http://referenceworks.brillonline.com/entries/encyclopaedia-of-islam-2/hurmuz-SIM_2963; A. Shapur Shahbazi, "Hormozd IV", in *EIr*, 12:466–467).

60 ʿĀd is the name of an ancient Arab tribe, known from pre-Islamic poetry and Arabic mythology; they are referred to in the Qurʾān as the people to whom the Arabian prophet Hūd was sent, but who rejected him and who were then destroyed by a violent wind, which is referred to in the next verse of this poem (A. Rippin, "ʿĀd.", in *EI*³ http://referenceworks.brillonline.com/entries/encyclopaedia-of-islam-3/ad-COM_26300; R. Tottoli, "ʿĀd", in *EQ* http://referenceworks.brillonline.com/entries/encyclopaedia-of-the-quran/ad-SIM_00008).

ولا سليمان إذْ تجري الرياح له والإنس والجن فيما بينها بَــرد

أين الملوك التي كانت نوافلها من كل أوب إليها راكب يَفِـدُ

حوض هناك مورود بلا كدر لا بُدَّ مِنْ ورده يومًا كما ورَدُوا[١٦]

[١٦] راجع هذا الخبر عن ابن المسيب على نفس الشكل إلا لبعض التفاصيل في ابن الأثير، الكامل، ج. ٢، ص. ٤٥٦-٤٥٧؛ وفي الطبري، تاريخ الرسل والملوك، ج ٥/١، ص. ٢٧٦٤-٢٧٦٥؛ وراجع هذا الخبر على شكل مختصر في ابن عبد البر، الاستيعاب، ج. ٣، ص. ٢٤٣.

And neither did Sulaymān,[61] despite the fact that the winds blew for him and that man and *ǧinn* were made weak among themselves.

Where are the kings to whose gifts
from every direction a rider used to come?

5 [At the end of life] there is a pool which is like a watering place that can be reached without having to wade through mud:
It is unavoidable that one day [we] will reach it, just as [others already] have reached [it]."[62]

---

61 The Muslim Sulaymān is identical with the biblical king Solomon, known in Islam as one of the most powerful rulers on earth, with deep knowledge, unparalleled wisdom, and great powers of magic and divination; he is frequently mentioned in the Qur'ān, where he is presented as a messenger of God and as a prototype for Muḥammad, and where it is also claimed that a strong wind was subjected to him (J. Walker, P. Fenton, "Sulaymān b. Dāwūd", in *EI*² http://referenceworks.brillonline.com/entries/encyclopaedia-of-islam-2/sulayman-b-dawud-SIM_7158; P. Soucek, "Solomon", in *EQ* http://referenceworks.brillonline.com/entries/encyclopaedia-of-the-quran/solomon-COM_00188).

62 For the translation of the parallel text of this story transmitted on account of Saʿīd b. al-Musayyab in al-Ṭabarī's *History*, see al-Ṭabarī, *History* XIV, 131.

عثمان بن عفان

ابن أبي العاصي بن أُمَيَّة بن عبد شمس بن عبد مناف بن قُصَي القرشي الأُمَوي، أبو عبد الله وأبو عمرو، ذُو النورَيْن، أمير المؤمنين رضي الله عنه.

بويع له بالخلافة يوم السبت غرّة المحرم سنة أربع وعشرين، بعد دفن عمر بن الخطاب رضي الله عنه بثلاثة أيام، بإجتماع الناس عليه. وقتل بالمدينة يوم الجمعة لثمان عشرة أو سبع عشرة خلت من ذي الحجة سنة خمسٍ وثلثين، وذلك على رأس إحدى عشرة سنة وأحد عشر شهرا واثنين وعشرين يوما من مقتل عمر رضي الله عنه.

حج فيها كلها إلا السنة الأُولى والاخيرة. وذكر ابن الأثير أنه حج بالناس في السنة الأولى وقيل: بل حج بالناس عبد الرحمن بن عوف بأمر عثمان.[١٧] ولما حج في سنة تسع وعشرين ضرب فسطاطه بمنًى، فكان أول فسطاط ضربه عثمٰن بمنى. وأتم الصلاة بها وبعرفة. فكان أول ما تكلم به الناس في عثمان ظاهرا حين أتم الصلاة بمنى، فعاب ذلك غير واحد من الصحابة، وقال له علي رضي

---

٢ عبد٢: ناقصة في الأصل، مضافة بخط المقريزي في الهامش الأيمن من الأعلى إلى الأسفل + صح؛ يشير إليها الرمز ⌐ بعد كلمة "بن". || القرشي: تصحيح في الأصل بخط المقريزي. ٤ الخطاب: تصحيح في الأصل بخط المقريزي. ٤–٥ رضي ... عنه: ناقصة في الأصل، مضافة بخط المقريزي في مكانها الصحيح في الجملة على آخر السطر في الهامش الأيسر. ٨ الأُولى: "الأُولي" في الأصل. || الأولى: "الاولي" في الأصل. ١١–1.220 رضي ... عنه: ناقصة في الأصل، مضافة بخط المقريزي في الهامش الأيمن من الأعلى إلى الأسفل + صح؛ يشير إليها الرمز ⌐ بعد كلمة "علي".

---

[١٧] ابن الأثير، الكامل، ج. ٢، ص. ٤٧٥؛ وراجع أيضا خبرا مساويا في الطبري، تاريخ الرسل والملوك، ج. ٥/١، ص. ٢٨٠٩.

3. ʿUṯmān b. ʿAffān

b. Abī l-ʿĀṣī b. Umayyah b. ʿAbd Šams b. ʿAbd Manāf b. Quṣayy al-Qurašī l-Umawī, Abū ʿAbd Allāh and Abū ʿAmr, Ḏū l-Nūrayn [Possessor of the two lights[63]], Commander of the Faithful—may God be pleased with him.

§ 32 The oath of allegiance was sworn to him for the office of caliph on Saturday, the first day of Muḥarram of the year 24 [6 November 644], three days after the burial of ʿUmar b. al-Ḫaṭṭāb—may God be pleased with him—, as a result of the people's consensus on [the succession by] him. He was killed in Medina on Friday, the 18th or 17th of Ḏū l-Ḥiǧǧah of the year 35 [17 June 656], exactly 11 years, 11 months, and 22 days after the murder of ʿUmar—may God be pleased with him.

§ 33 He went on pilgrimage in each of those years, apart from the first and the last. Ibn al-Aṯīr[64] reported that he led the people on the pilgrimage in the first year, whereas it was said that rather ʿAbd al-Raḥmān b. ʿAwf led the people on the pilgrimage by order of ʿUṯmān. When he performed the pilgrimage in the year 29 [650], he set up his tent at Miná—it was the first tent ʿUṯmān set up at Miná—and he fulfilled the ritual prayer there and at ʿArafah [with two additional *rakʿah*s]. It was the first thing about ʿUṯmān that the people openly spoke about, when he fulfilled the ritual prayer at Miná. More than one of the Companions[65] found fault with that. So ʿAlī—may God

63 ʿUṯmān's epithet *Ḏū l-nūrayn* ("possessor of the two lights") is traditionally explained as referring to his consecutive marriages with two of the Prophet's daughters, Ruqayyah and Umm Kulṯūm.

64 See Ibn al-Aṯīr, *al-Kāmil*, 2:475. ʿIzz al-Dīn Abū l-Ḥasan ʿAlī Ibn al-Aṯīr (d. 630/1233) was a scholar from Mosul who gained a towering socio-cultural reputation, above all as a historian recording the history of the local Syro-Mesopotamian dynasty of the Zangids as well as that of the wider Muslim community of his time, in Arabic works of mainly annalistic history that soon acquired authoritative historiographical status; his grand work is the multi-volume *al-Kāmil fī l-tārīḫ* [The Complete History] (see F. Rosenthal, "Ibn al-Athīr", in EI[2] http://referenceworks.brillonline.com/entries/encyclopaedia-of-islam-2/ibn-al-athir-SIM_3094).

65 The Companions (*ṣaḥābah*) refers to the first generation of Muslims who are distinguished from other generations by their direct contact with the Prophet; they are as a result key authoritative figures in early Islamic history as well as for the development of Muslim thought and practice (M. Muranyi, "Ṣaḥāba", in EI[2] http://referenceworks.brillonline.com/entries/encyclopaedia-of-islam-2/sahaba-SIM_6459).

الله عنه: "ما حدث أمر، ولا قدم عهد، ولقد عهدت النبي ﷺ وأبا بكر وعمر يصلون | ركعتين، 118b
وأنت صليت ركعتين صدرا من خلافتك." فما درى ما يرجع إليه، وقال: "رأي رأيته." وبلغ الخبر
عبد الرحمن بن عوف رضي الله عنه وكان معه، فجاءه وقال له: "ألم تصل في هذا المكان مع رسول
الله ﷺ وأبي بكر وعمر ركعتين {وصليتها} أنت ركعتين؟" قال: "بلى ولكني أُخْبرت أن بعض من
٥ حج من اليمن وجُفاة الناس قالوا إن الصلاة للمقيم ركعتين، واحتجوا بصلاتي، وقد اتخذت بمكة
أهلا ولي بالطائف مال." فقال عبد الرحمن بن عوف: "ما في هذا عُذر. أما قولك "اتخذت بها
أهلا،" فإن زوجك بالمدينة تخرج لها إذا شئت وإنما تسكن بسكاك. وأما مالك بالطائف فبينك
وبينه مسيرة ثلث ليال. وأما قولك عن حاج اليمن وغيرهم، فقد كان رسول الله ﷺ ينزل عليه
الوحي والإسلام قليل، ثم أبو بكر وعمر فصلوا ركعتين وقد ضرب الإسلام بجرانه." فقال عثمن:
١٠ "هذا رأي رأيته." فخرج عبد الرحمن، فلقي عبد الله بن مسعود، فقال: "أبا محمد، قد غير ما تعلم."

١ حدث: تصحيح في الأصل بخط المقريزي. ‖ عهد: تصحيح في الأصل بخط المقريزي. ٢ الخبر: تصحيح في الأصل بخط المقريزي. ٣ رضي ... عنه: ناقصة في الأصل، مضافة بخط المقريزي في الهامش الأيسر، من الأسفل الى الأعلى + صح؛ يشير إليها الرمز ⌐ بعد كلمة "عوف". ‖ فجاءه: "فجاه" في الأصل. ٤ وصليتها: في الأصل "صليتهما"، والتصحيح من السياق ومن ابن الأثير، الكامل في التاريخ، ج. ٢، ص. ٤٩٤. ‖ أُخْبرت: تصحيح في الأصل بخط المقريزي. ٦ بالطائف: "بالطايف" في الأصل. ٧ شئت: "شيت" في الأصل. ‖ بالطائف: "بالطايف" في الأصل. ٩ والإسلام: تصحيح في الأصل بخط المقريزي.

be pleased with him—said to him: "Whenever something new happens that is without any precedent, I adhere to [the example of] the Prophet—may God bless him and grant him salvation—, of Abū Bakr and of ʿUmar, [just as in this case, where they used to] perform the prayer in two *rakʿah*s, just as you performed it in two *rakʿah*s at the beginning of your term as caliph." [ʿUṯmān] did not know what he could base [his changes] upon, so he said: "[This is] a personal opinion that I have." The story reached ʿAbd al-Raḥmān b. ʿAwf—may God be pleased with him—, while he was in [the caliph's] entourage. So he came to him and said to him: "Did you not perform the prayer at this spot together with the Messenger of God—may God bless him and grant him salvation—, with Abū Bakr, and with ʿUmar in two *rakʿah*s? [I'm sure that] you did perform it in two *rakʿah*s!" [ʿUṯmān] said: "Surely, but I learned that some from Yemen who went on pilgrimage and [other] uncouth people said that for someone permanently residing [at Mecca] the ritual prayer is to be performed in two *rakʿah*s, and they advanced as an argument my ritual prayer, because I have become connected [by marriage] to a family in Mecca and I have property in Ṭāʾif."[66] But ʿAbd al-Raḥmān b. ʿAwf said: "This is no excuse, not your saying 'I have become connected to a family there', because your wife in Medina [only] leaves it when you want her to, and she merely lives where you do; nor is your property in Ṭāʾif [an excuse], because there are three nights of travel between you and [Ṭāʾif]; nor is your saying about the pilgrims of Yemen and others. Revelation descended upon the Messenger of God—may God bless him and grant him salvation—while Islam was small, whereas Abū Bakr and ʿUmar performed the prayer in two *rakʿah*s when Islam had become firmly established." ʿUṯmān said: "[This is] a personal opinion that I have." So ʿAbd al-Raḥmān b. ʿAwf left, and he met ʿAbd Allāh b. Masʿūd[67], saying: "O Abū Muḥammad, whatever

66 The town of Ṭāʾif in the Arabian Hijaz was dominated in the early days of Islamic history by the tribe of Ṯaqīf; it is situated to the southeast of Mecca, and it was known for its pleasant climate and for the fertility and prosperity of its mountainous environment, for which reason various members of the Meccan elite are recorded to have developed, already before Muḥammad's prophetic mission, estates in the valleys around Ṭāʾif and to have had close connections with the town and its inhabitants (M. Lecker, "al-Ṭāʾif", in *EI*², http://brillonline.com/entries/encyclopaedia-of-islam-2/alTaif-SIM_7324).

67 ʿAbd Allāh b. Masʿūd was a widely respected Companion, Qurʾān transmitter and early scholar; he is believed to have died in 32/652–653, either in Medina or in Kufa (J.-C. Vadet, "Ibn Masʿūd", *in EI*² http://referenceworks.brillonline.com/entries/encyclopaedia-of-islam-2/Ibn-masud-COM_0338).

قال: "فما أصنع." قال: "إعمل بما ترى وتعلم." فقال ابن مسعود: "الخلاف شر، وقد صليت بأصحابي أربعا." فقال عبد الرحمن: "قد صليت بأصحابي ركعتين، وأما الآن فسوف أصلي أربعًا." وقيل: كان ذلك سنة ثلثين.[18]

وَلم يحج أمير المؤمنين علي بن أبي طالب في خلافته لاشتغاله بحرب الجمل وصِفّين.

١ الخلاف: تصحيح في الأصل بخط المقريزي.

[18] راجع هذا الخبر كله على نفس الشكل تقريبا في ابن الأثير، الكامل، ج. ٢، ص. ٤٩٤؛ وراجع هذا الخبر على شكل مساو أيضا في الطبري، تاريخ الرسل والملوك، ج. ١/٥، ص. ٢٨٣٣-٢٨٣٥.

you know has been changed." He said: "How should I then proceed?" He said: "Do as you see fit and [as] you know [to be right]." Ibn Masʿūd said: "Disagreement is an evil thing, so I have performed prayer in four [*rakʿahs*] with my companions [following ʿUṯmān's example]." ʿAbd al-Raḥmān said: 5 "I have been performing prayer in two *rakʿahs* with my companions, but from now on I shall perform prayer in four [*rakʿahs*]." It was said that this happened in the year 30 [651].[68]

§ 34 The Commander of the Faithful ʿAlī b. Abī Ṭālib did not perform the pilgrimage during his caliphate, due to his preoccupation with the Battle of 10 the Camel[69] and with [the Battle of] Ṣiffīn.[70]

---

68 For the translation of the parallel text of this story, transmitted by al-Wāqidī on account of Ibn ʿAbbās and of ʿAbd al-Malik b. ʿAmr b. Abī Sufyān al-Ṯaqafī, in al-Ṭabarī's *History*, see al-Ṭabarī, *History* XV, 38–40; 39, fn. 65, explains the reasoning behind ʿUṯmān's changes to the ritual prayer as follows: "ʿUthmān's point is twofold: (1) Many ordinary Muslims were ignorant of the different numbers of ritual prostrations (*rakʿas*) connected with the act of prayer at different times. Hence, they would assume that all prayers were to be performed with two *rakʿas*, although in fact only those who were travelling or on pilgrimage were permitted to abbreviate the usual four *rakʿas* in that manner. (2) ʿUthmān's property holdings and family ties made him a permanent resident in Mecca and al-Ṭāʾif as well as Medina; hence, he felt obligated to observe the complete rite of four *rakʿas* even during the Pilgrimage season."

69 The Battle of the Camel is the name given to the 36/656 military confrontation near Basra in Iraq between ʿAlī and his supporters on the one hand, and the Companions Ṭalḥah and al-Zubayr with their associates—including the Prophet's widow ʿĀʾišah—on the other, in which the latter were defeated; this was the culmination of a conflict over the succession of the caliph ʿUṯmān, that had begun in the aftermath of his murder, when ʿAlī had assumed the caliphate without consultation of Companions such as Ṭalḥah and al-Zubayr; the name 'Battle of the Camel' is derived from the fact that tradition claims that the worst fighting occurred around the camel that carried ʿĀʾišah in a litter on its back (A. Afsaruddin, "ʿĀʾisha bt. Abī Bakr", in *EI*³ http://referenceworks.brillonline.com/entries/encyclopaedia-of-islam-3/aisha-bt-abi-bakr-COM_23459).

70 The Battle of Ṣiffīn refers to the 37/657 confrontation in Syria between the Iraqi forces of the caliph ʿAlī and the Syrian forces of the Syrian governor Muʿāwiyah b. Abī Sufyān, generated by the fact that Muʿāwiyah—an Umayyad kinsman of the murdered caliph ʿUṯmān—was denied the right to avenge the murder of his kinsman; the outcome of the battle of Ṣiffīn, near Raqqa by the Euphrates, was inconclusive, but it did set several historical processes in motion that generated, by 40/661, the murder of ʿAlī and the general acceptance of Muʿāwiyah's caliphate from Damascus (M. Lecker, "Ṣiffīn", in *EI*² http://referenceworks.brillonline.com/entries/encyclopaedia-of-islam-2/siffin-SIM_7018); see also Hinds (1972); Humphreys (2006).

مُعَٰوية بن أبي سُفيَٰن

واسمه صَخْر بن حَرْب بن أُمية بن عبد شمس بن عبد مناف القرشي الأموي، أبو عبد الرحمن، أمير المؤمنين.

كان أميرًا بالشام نحو عشرين سنة. وبايع له أهل الشام خاصة بالخلافة سنة ثمان أو تسع وثلٰثين،
٥ واجتمع الناسُ عليه حين بايع له الحَسَنُ بن علي وجماعَةُ مَنْ معَهُ في ربيع [الآخر] أو جمادى [الأولى] سنة إحدى وأربعين، وقيل سنة أربعين. وأقام في الخلافة تسع عشرة سنة وتسعة أشهر وثمانية وعشرين يومًا، وقيل غير ذلك.

وحج بالناس عدة سنين أولها سنة أربع وأربعين. ولم يحج سنة خمس وأربعين، فحج بالناس مروان

٢ صَخْر: تصحيح في الأصل بخط المقريزي. ‖ عبد١: تصحيح في الأصل بخط المقريزي. ٤ خاصة: "خآصة" في الأصل. ٥ الآخر: ناقصة في الأصل، مضافة من السياق. ٦ الأولى: ناقصة في الأصل، مضافة من السياق. ٨ خمس: تصحيح في الأصل بخط المقريزي.

71 Muʿāwiyah was the son of one of pre-Islamic Mecca's leaders; upon his conversion to Islam in about 8/630, he was allowed to retain his privileged position, but now in the Prophet's entourage at Medina. Muʿāwiyah participated in the Arab conquest of Syria, and eventually, in 18/639, he became this former Byzantine province's first Muslim governor, who managed to transform Syria into a powerful Arab-Muslim powerbase; after the inconclusive confrontation with ʿAlī at Ṣiffīn, Muʿāwiyah obtained supreme leadership over the caliphate, which he retained from 41/661 until his demise in 60/680; in doing so he shifted the Arab empire's headquarters to Syria and initiated what is considered to be the first dynasty of Islam: the Umayyad caliphate (41–132/661–750) (see M. Hinds, "Muʿāwiya", in *EI*² http://referenceworks.brillonline.com/entries/encyclopaedia-of-islam-2/muawiya-i-SIM_5279; Humphreys [2006]).

4. Muʿāwiyah b. Abī Sufyān[71]

His name is Ṣaḫr b. Ḥarb b. Umayyah b. ʿAbd Šams b. ʿAbd Manāf al-Qurašī l-Umawī, Abū ʿAbd al-Raḥmān, Commander of the Faithful.

§ 35 He was a governor in Syria for about 20 years. [Then,] in the year 38 or 9 [659], mainly the people of Syria swore the oath of allegiance to him for the office of caliph. [Most of the other] people only agreed on him [as their caliph] once al-Ḥasan b. ʿAlī[72] and a group of his associates swore the oath of allegiance to him in Rabīʿ [II] or Ǧumādá [I] of the year 41 [August–September 661], and it was said: of the year 40 [660]. He remained in the office of caliph for 19 years, 9 months and 28 days; and it was said otherwise.

§ 36 He led the people on the pilgrimage during several years, the first of which was the year 44 [665]. He did not perform the pilgrimage in the year 45 [666], when Marwān b. al-Ḥakam[73] led the people on the pilgrimage.

---

72 Al-Ḥasan b. ʿAlī was born in 3/624–625; he was the grandson of the Prophet, through his mother, the Prophet's daughter Fāṭimah; his father was the caliph ʿAlī. Upon his father's murder in Kufa in 41/661, al-Ḥasan was proclaimed caliph by the Iraqis; eventually, however, in the face of renewed hostilities with the Syrians, he renounced his office in favour of Muʿāwiyah and returned to a quietist life in Medina, where he died in the year 49/669–670. Al-Ḥasan is considered by all Shiite groups alike as the second divinely inspired *imām*, designated by his father to succeed him as the only legitimate leader of the faithful (see L. Veccia Vaglieri, "(al-)Ḥasan b. ʿAlī b. Abī Ṭālib", in *EI*[2] http://referenceworks.brillonline.com/entries/encyclopaedia-of-islam-2/al-hasan-b-ali-b-abi-talib-COM_0272).

73 Marwān b. al-Ḥakam (c. 2–65/ 623–685) was a well-respected Companion and a cousin of caliph ʿUṯmān, who acted as a governor on several occasions during the reign of caliph Muʿāwiyah. By the time of Muʿāwiyah's death in 60/680, Marwān was considered the most senior of the Umayyad clan in the Hijaz; when by 63/683 the Umayyads were on the defense on several fronts, Marwān and his family were forced to flee to Syria. In 64/684 he emerged victoriously from a major confrontation among Syrian Arab tribes, and was proclaimed the Umayyad caliph in Damascus. Marwān died in 65/685, and was succeeded in the Umayyad caliphate by his son ʿAbd al-Malik. All Umayyad caliphs after Marwān were from his lineage, and they are therefore known as the Marwānids (C.E. Bosworth, "Marwān I b. al-Ḥakam", in *EI*[2] http://referenceworks.brillonline.com/entries/encyclopaedia-of-islam-2/marwan-i-b-al-hakam-SIM_4979).

ابن الحكم. ثم حج معٰوية سنة خمسين، وقيل: بل حج بالناس ابنه يزيد بن معٰوية. وقيل: حج معٰوية عدة سنين أكثر من هذه.

Thereafter Muʿāwiyah again went on pilgrimage in the year 50 [670–671], and it was said [that in that year] rather his son Yazīd b. Muʿāwiyah[74] led the people on the pilgrimage. There was said [that] Muʿāwiyah went on pilgrimage for several more years than these.

74 Yazīd b. Muʿāwiyah succeeded his father to the Umayyad caliphate in 60/680; although as capable a leader as his father, he is remembered especially for the fact that his agents slaughtered the Prophet's grandson al-Ḥusayn and his family at Karbalāʾ in Muḥarram 61/October 680. Yazīd died in 64/683, while his armies were confronting opposition against his rule in the Hijaz (G.R. Hawting, "Yazīd (I) b. Muʿāwiya", in *EI*[2] http://referenceworks.brillonline.com/entries/encyclopaedia-of-islam-2/yazid-i-b-muawiya-SIM_8000).

عبد الله بن الزبير

ابن العوام بن خويلد بن أسد بن عبد العُزى بن قصي القرشي الأسدي، أبو بكر—وقيل: أبو بكير—وأبو حبيب، أمير المؤمنين رضي | الله عنه. 119a

بويع له بالخلافة سنة أربع—وقيل: خمس—وستين، بعد موت معاوية بن يزيد بن معٰوية بن أبي سفيٰن. وكان قبل ذلك لا يدعي بالخلافة. واجتمع على طاعته أهل الحجاز واليمن والعراق وخراسان. ٥

وحج بالناس ثماني حجج.

وقُتل رحمه الله على يد الحجاج بن يوسف الثقفي في أيام عبد الملك بن مروان بن الحكم، يوم الثلٰثاء

٧ الثلٰثاء: "الثلثا" في الأصل.

75 ʿAbd Allāh b. al-Zubayr was a renowned Companion, who became leader of the Hijaz group that contested the legitimacy of the succession of the caliph Muʿāwiyah in 60/680 by his son Yazīd. This opposition was locally successful, giving rise to the so-called second civil war (*fitnah*); when the Umayyads of Syria got into disarray after Yazīd's early death in 64/683, Ibn al-Zubayr successfully claimed the caliphate and his leadership was established over most of the Arab empire; eventually, however, the Syrian Umayyads, led by Marwān b. al-Ḥakam and his son ʿAbd al-Malik, fought back, generating the siege of Mecca and the murder of the caliph Ibn al-Zubayr in 73/692, and the recreation of the Umayyad caliphate (H.A.R. Gibb, "ʿAbd Allāh b. al-Zubayr", in *EI*[2] http://referenceworks.brillonline.com/entries/encyclopaedia-of-islam-2/abd-allah-b-al-zubayr-SIM_0069).

5. ʿAbd Allāh b. al-Zubayr[75]

b. al-ʿAwwām b. Ḫuwaylid b. Asad b. ʿAbd al-ʿUzzá b. Quṣayy al-Qurašī l-Asadī, Abū Bakr—and it was said Abū Bukayr—and Abū Ḥabīb, Commander of the Faithful, may God be pleased with him.

5 § 37 The oath of allegiance for the office of caliph was sworn to him in the year 64 [684]—and it was said: [in the year 6]5 [685]—, after the death of Muʿāwiyah b. Yazīd b. Muʿāwiyah b. Abī Sufyān.[76] He did not use to make any claims for the office of caliph before. The people of the Hijaz, of Yemen, of Iraq, and of Ḫurāsān agreed to submit to him.

10 § 38 He led the people on the pilgrimage eight times.

§ 39 He—may God's mercy be upon him—was killed by the hand of al-Ḥaǧǧāǧ b. Yūsuf al-Ṯaqafī[77] in the days of ʿAbd al-Malik b. Marwān b. al-

76 Muʿāwiyah b. Yazīd b. Muʿāwiyah b. Abī Sufyān, or Muʿāwiyah II, was the son and successor of the Umayyad caliph Yazīd; he reigned very briefly in 64/683–684 amidst great turmoil in Syria and beyond; Muʿāwiyah II moreover died, probably from a disease, before he had been able to nominate a successor. His shortlived reign, which was never widely accepted anyway, and thus presaged the temporary collapse of Umayyad power (C.E. Bosworth, "Muʿāwiya II", in *EI*[2] http://referenceworks.brillonline.com/entries/encyclopaedia-of-islam-2/muawiya-ii-SIM_5280).

77 Al-Ḥaǧǧāǧ b. Yūsuf al-Ṯaqafī was one of the main military agents and commanders for the Umayyad caliph ʿAbd al-Malik b. Marwān. After bringing a violent end to the caliphate of Ibn al-Zubayr in Mecca and after a brief governorship over the Hijaz, al-Ḥaǧǧāǧ was appointed governor of Iraq in 75/694, from where he successfully consolidated Umayyad Syrian authority over Iraq and further East; he remained in charge of the whole of the Islamic East in name of the Umayyad caliph of Syria until his death in 95/714 (A. Dietrich, "al-Ḥadjdjādj b. Yūsuf", in *EI*[2] http://referenceworks.brillonline.com/entries/encyclopaedia-of-islam-2/al-hadjdjadj-b-yusuf-SIM_2600).

لسبع عشرة خلت من جمادى الأولى—وقيل: جمادى الآخرة—سنة ثلٰث وسبعين، وصلب بعد قتله بمكة.

وبدأ الحجاج بحصاره من أول ليلة من ذي الحجة سنة اثنتين وسبعين. وحج بالناس الحجاج في ذلك العام، ووقف بعرفة وعليه ذرع ومغفر. ولم يطوفوا بالبيت في تلك الحجة. فحاصره الحجاج ستة أشهر ٥ وسبعة عشر يوما إلى أن قتل.

ولما غزاه أهل الشام في أيام يزيد بن معٰوية احترقت الكعبة—في سنة أربع وستين—فتركها ابن الزبير ليشنع بذلك على أهل الشام. فلما مات يزيد واستقر الأمر له، هدمها إلى الأرض وبناها على قواعد إبراهيم عليه السلام، وأدخل فيها الحِجْرَ وجعل لها بابين. فلما قتل الحجاجُ عبدَ الله بن الزبير هدم بناء ابن الزبير من الكعبة في سنة أربع وسبعين وجعلها على ما هي عليه الآن، كما قد ذكرت ١٠ ذلك في **كتاب الإشارة والإعلام ببناء الكعبة البيت الحرام** ذكرا شافيا.[١٩]

١ الأولى: "الاولي" في الأصل. ٥ يوما: تصحيح في الأصل بخط المقريزي. ٧ ليشنع: تصحيح في الأصل بخط المقريزي. ٨ عليه السلام: ناقصة في الأصل، مضافة بخط المقريزي في الهامش الأيمن من الأعلى إلى الأسفل + صح؛ يشير إليها الرمز ⌝ بعد كلمة "إبراهيم". ٩ هدم: تصحيح في الأصل بخط المقريزي. ‖ بناء: "بنآ" في الأصل. ‖ ابن: تصحيح في الأصل بخط المقريزي. ‖ عليه الآن: ناقصة في الأصل، مضافة بخط المقريزي في الهامش الأيسر، على نفس السطر + صح؛ يشير إليها الرمز ⌐ بعد كلمة "هي". ١٠ ببناء: "ببنآ" في الأصل.

[١٩] راجع المقريزي، بناء الكعبة، ص. ١٥٦-١٥٨.

Ḥakam,[78] on Tuesday 17 Ǧumādá I—and it was said Ǧumādá II—of the year 73 [4 October/3 November 692]. After his murder in Mecca [his body] was exposed on a cross.

§ 40 Al-Ḥaǧǧāǧ began besieging him from the first night of Ḏū l-Ḥiǧǧah of 5 the year 72 [24 April 692]. In that year, al-Ḥaǧǧāǧ led the people on the pilgrimage. At ʿArafah, he performed the ritual of standing while he was wearing a coat of mail and a helmet. During that pilgrimage, they did not circumambulate the house [of God]. Al-Ḥaǧǧāǧ besieged him for 6 months and 17 days, until [Ibn al-Zubayr] was killed.

10 § 41 When the Syrians attacked [Ibn al-Zubayr] in the days of Yazīd b. Muʿāwiyah, the Kaʿbah was burnt down. [This happened] in the year 64 [683]. Ibn al-Zubayr left it [untouched] so as to defame the Syrians by that. But when Yazīd died and leadership was vested in him, he destroyed it to the ground and built it on the foundations of Abraham[79]—may there be peace 15 upon him. He included the *ḥijr*[80] into it and he made two doors for it. When al-Ḥaǧǧāǧ killed ʿAbd Allāh b. al-Zubayr, he demolished Ibn al-Zubayr's construction of the Kaʿbah—[this happened] in the year 74 [693]—and he made it as it still is today, as I have reported that in great detail in the book *al-Išārah wa-l-iʿlām bi-bināʾ al-kaʿbah al-bayt al-ḥarām* [Advice and Informa- 20 tion Regarding the Construction of the Kaʿbah, the Sacred House].[81]

78 ʿAbd al-Malik b. Marwān b. al-Ḥakam was Umayyad caliph between 65/685 and 86/705; he managed to restore Umayyad power throughout the Arab empire and to consolidate his authority East and West in unprecedented Arabo-Islamic imperial fashion (H.A.R. Gibb, "ʿAbd al-Malik b. Marwān", *in* EI[2] http://referenceworks.brillonline.com/entries/encyclopaedia-of-islam-2/abd-al-malik-b-marwan-SIM_0107; Robinson [2007]).

79 In Islam, the prophet Ibrāhīm—Abraham of the Judeo-Christian tradition—is accredited with building, together with his son Ismāʿīl, the Kaʿbah in Mecca by direct order from God, as the cosmic centre of the original monotheistic cult of mankind; upon completing the Kaʿbah's construction, Ibrāhīm and Ismāʿīl are furthermore believed to have established the rites of pilgrimage to it, which were then only revived by Muḥammad (R. Paret, "Ibrāhīm", in EI[2] http://referenceworks.brillonline.com/entries/encyclopaedia-of-islam-2/ibrahim-SIM_3430; see also Cook [1983]: 36–37).

80 The *ḥiǧr* or *ḥiǧr Ismāʿīl* refers to a small open area between the Kaʿbah's north-west wall and a semi-circular low wall of white marble, which is believed to contain the graves of Ibrāhīm's son Ismāʿīl and of Ismāʿīl's mother Hagar (Wensinck, Jomier, "Kaʿbah", EI[2]).

81 Al-Maqrīzī, *Bināʾ al-Kaʿbah*, 156–158 (*Ḏikr bināʾ al-Ḥaǧǧāǧ b. Yūsuf al-Kaʿbah* ['Report of al-Ḥaǧǧāǧ b. Yūsuf's construction of the Kaʿbah']).

عبد الملك بن مروان

ابن الحكم بن أبي العاص بن أمية بن عبد شمس بن عبد مناف بن قُصَي.

قام بدمشق بعد موت أبيه في شهر رمضان سنة خمس وستين، وبمكة عبد الله بن الزبير يدعى له بالخلافة، وعلى العراق المختار بن أبي عُبَيد الثقفي يدعو لمحمد بن الحنفية. والأرض تستعر حربا منذ ٥ قتل الحسين بن علي بن أبي طالب رضي الله عنهما. فساعدت الأقدار عبد الملك بن مروان، وقتل جميع من خالفه. وأقام في الخلافة بعد ابن الزبير ثلٰث عشرة سنة وأربعة أشهر إلا سبع ليال، كما قد ذكرت ترجمته وترجمة أبيه في **التاريخ الكبير لمصر**، فإنهما دخلاها.[٢٠]

٤ يدعو: "يدعوا" في الأصل. ٥ رضي ... عنهما: ناقصة في الأصل، مضافة بخط المقريزي في الهامش الأيمن، من الأعلى إلى الأسفل + صح؛ يشير إليها الرمز ⌐ بعد كلمة "طالب". ٦ عشرة: تصحيح في الأصل بخط المقريزي.

[٢٠] هتان الترجمتان ناقصتان من المخطوطات المعروف وجودها لهذا الكتاب. راجع المقريزي، المقفى، ج. ٨، الفهارس العامّة.

82 Al-Muḫtār b. Abī ʿUbayd al-Ṯaqafī was the leader of a movement that controlled Kufa in 66–67/685–687 in the name of Muḥammad b. al-Ḥanafiyyah, a son of ʿAlī b. Abī Ṭālib whom they claimed to be the only legitimate heir to the caliphate; eventually al-Muḫtār and his supporters were defeated by the agents of Ibn al-Zubayr, al-Muḫtār being killed in battle on 14 Ramaḍān 67/3 April 687 (G.R. Hawting, "al-Mukhtār b. Abī ʿUbayd", in *EI*^{2} http://referenceworks.brillonline.com/entries/encyclopaedia-of-islam-2/al-mukhtar-b-abi-ubayd-SIM_5473).

6. ʿAbd al-Malik b. Marwān

b. al-Ḥakam b. Abī l-ʿĀṣ b. Umayyah b. ʿAbd Šams b. ʿAbd Manāf b. Quṣayy.

§ 42 He came to power in Damascus after the demise of his father in the month Ramaḍān of the year 65 [April 685]. [At that time] there was in Mecca ʿAbd Allāh b. al-Zubayr for whom the office of caliph was claimed, and over Iraq there was al-Muḫtār b. Abī ʿUbayd al-Ṯaqafī,[82] who claimed [the office of caliph] for Muḥammad b. al-Ḥanafiyyah.[83] [At that time also] the earth had been covered in warfare, ever since the killing of al-Ḥusayn b. ʿAlī b. Abī Ṭālib[84]—may God be pleased with them both. But fortune was on the side of ʿAbd al-Malik b. Marwān, and all those who opposed him were killed. He remained in the office of caliph after Ibn al-Zubayr for 13 years and 4 months less 7 nights, as I reported in his biography and in the biography of his father in *al-Tārīḫ al-kabīr li-Miṣr* [The Great History (in Continuation) of Egypt][85] (because both of them entered [Egypt and were therefore recorded in that history]).

83 Muḥammad b. al-Ḥanafiyyah was the son of ʿAlī b. Abī Ṭālib by a woman of the Banū Ḥanīfah; he lived a politically quietist life in the turbulent days of the early Muslim community; but when the leadership of his half-brothers, the Prophet's grandsons al-Ḥasan and al-Ḥusayn, had become impossible by the early 60s/680s, some supporters of the leadership of ʿAlī's lineage—al-Muḫtār in Kufa in particular—briefly turned to him to lead their cause; after the failure of al-Muḫtār's movement, Muḥammad continued to try and live his quietist life in the Hijaz until his death in 81/700–701 (Fr. Buhl, "Muḥammad b. al-Ḥanafiyya", in *EI*² http://referenceworks.brillonline.com/entries/encyclopaedia-of-islam-2/muhammad-ibn-al-hanafiyya-SIM_5351).

84 Al-Ḥusayn b. ʿAlī b. Abī Ṭālib was the youngest son of ʿAlī and Fāṭimah, the Prophet's daughter; he is especially remembered for the unfortunate fate he encountered near Karbalāʾ, in Iraq, in 60/680, when after accepting an invitation from an anti-Umayyad movement to come to Kufa and assume leadership over the community, he was stopped on the road by Umayyad troops and killed (L. Veccia Vaglieri, "(al-)Ḥusayn b. Abī Ṭālib", in *EI*² http://referenceworks.brillonline.com/entries/encyclopaedia-of-islam-2/al-husayn-b-ali-b-abi-talib-COM_0304).

85 Both biographies seem to have been lost, as they are not mentioned in any of the extant fragments of this voluminous biographical history of Egypt by al-Maqrīzī (see al-Maqrīzī, *al-Muqaffá*). For a detailed discussion of this compilation's title and its translation (*al-Tārīḫ al-kabīr al-muqaffá*—The Great History in Continuation), see Witkam (2014): 96–101. I am grateful to professor Witkam for drawing my attention to this publication.

وحج عبد الملك في خلافته سنتين، {إحداهما} سنة خمس وسبعين. فهم شبيب بن يزيد—أحد الخوارج—أنْ يفتك به، فبلغه ذلك، فاحترس وكتب إلى الحجاج بن يوسف بعد انصرافه يأمره بطلب صالح بن مسرح وغيره من الخوارج. فكان من أخبارهم ما قد ذكر في موضعه.[٢١]

وخطب عبد الملك الناس بالمدينة النبوية، فقال—بعد حمد الله | والثناء عليه: "أما بعد فإني 119b
٥ لست بالخليفة المستضعف—يعني عثمٰن رضي الله عنه، ولا بالخليفة المداهن—يعني معٰوية، ولا بالخليفة المأبون—يعني يزيد بن معٰوية، ألا وإني لا أداري هذه الأمة إلّا بالسيف، حتى تستقيم لي قناتكم وإنكم تكلفونا أعمال المهاجرين الأولين ولا تعملوا مثل أعمالهم، وإنكم تأمرونا بتقوى الله

١ إحداهما: "إحديهما" في الأصل. ٤ والثناء: "الثنآ" في الأصل. ٥ رضي ... عنه: ناقصة في الأصل، مضافة بخط المقريزي فوق كلمة "عثمن" رأسا على عقب.

[٢١] راجع هذا الخبر على شكل مساو في ابن الأثير، الكامل، ج. ٤، ص. ١٥٠؛ وأيضا في الطبري، تاريخ الرسل والملوك، ج. ٢/٢، ص. ٨٨١.

§ 43 During his caliphate, ʿAbd al-Malik went on pilgrimage in two years. One of them was in the year 75 [695], when Šabīb b. Yazīd,[86] one of the *Ḫāriǧīs*,[87] intended to murder him. But he was informed of that, so he took his precautions. He wrote to al-Ḥaǧǧāǧ b. Yūsuf—after his departure [from the Hijaz for the governorship of Iraq]—ordering him to summon Ṣāliḥ b. Musarriḥ[88] and other *Ḫāriǧīs*. The stories about them were recorded in their proper place.

§ 44 ʿAbd al-Malik delivered a public Friday sermon to the people in the Prophet's Medina. After praising and lauding God, he said: "Now then, I am not like the weakling caliph, that is ʿUṯmān—may God be pleased with him—, nor [am I] like the sycophant caliph, that is Muʿāwiyah, nor [am I] like the catamite caliph, that is Yazīd b. Muʿāwiyah; on the contrary, I will only treat this community with the sword, so that your lances will be correctly lined up for us again. You charge us with following the actions of the first emigrants,[89] but you do not act according to their actions; and you

86 Šabīb b. Yazīd b. Nuʿaym al-Šaybānī (c. 25–78/c. 646–697) was an Arab leader from the region of Mosul who participated in some of the many Iraqi uprisings against the Syrian Umayyads, traditionally referred to as *Ḫāriǧī* rebellions; between 76/695 and 77/696 Šabīb lead one such rebellion himself in Northern and Central Iraq (K.V. Zettersteen, C.F. Robinson, "Shabīb b. Yazīd", in *EI*² http://referenceworks.brillonline.com/entries/encyclopaedia-of-islam-2/shabib-b-yazid-SIM_6728).

87 The term *Ḫāriǧī* is used to denote a member of the earliest of the religious sects of Islam, which emerged in the mid-seventh century as a result of ongoing competition and conflicts for legitimate leadership over the young Muslim community; *Ḫāriǧīs* appeared especially in the sources for the early Islamic period in the context of continunous rebellions against central Muslim authorities (G. Levi Della Vida, "Khāridjites", in *EI*² http://referenceworks.brillonline.com/entries/encyclopaedia-of-islam-2/kharidjites-COM_0497).

88 Ṣāliḥ b. Musarriḥ was another rebel against Umayyad authority; he was killed in battle in Northern Iraq shortly after this caliphal pilgrimage, in 76/695, whereupon the abovementioned Šabīb b. Yazīd continued his rebellion, or at least recuperated Ṣāliḥ's forces for his own rebellion (Robinson, "Shabīb b. Yazīd", in *EI*²).

89 The term 'First Emigrants' refers to the group of people from Mecca who accepted Muḥammad's call to prophetic leadership and who converted before his migration (*hiǧrah*) to Medina in 0/622; they all migrated with him—hence their name; their early conversion in the adverse circumstances of polytheist Mecca and their closeness to the Prophet have awarded them a special status in the remembrence of the early days of the Muslim community.

وتنسون ذلك من أنفسكم. والله، لا يأمرني أحد بتقوى الله بعد مقامي هذا إلا ضربت عنقه!" ثم نزل.[٢٢]

[٢٢] راجع هذه الخطبة على نفس الشكل في ابن الأثير، الكامل، ج. ٤، ص. ١٥٠.

order us to fear God, but you forget that for yourself. By God, no one will order me anymore to fear God after this rise in rank of me, or I will have his head cut off." Then he came down [from the *minbar*].

الوليد [بن] عبد الملك بن مروان

بويع بعد موت أبيه بعهده إليه المنصف من شوال سنة ست وثمانين، وكانت خلافته تسع سنين وسبعة أشهر.

وعمر مسجد رسول الله ﷺ في سنة ثمان، وكان على يد عمر بن عبد العزيز وهو على المدينة. فكتب
٥ إليه في ربيع الأول يأمره بإدخال حجر أزواج النبي في مسجد رسول الله ﷺ، وأن يشتري ما في نواحيه حتى يكون مائتي ذراع في مثلها، وأن يقدم القبلة. فقوم عمر الأملاك قيمة عدل، وأعطى الناس أثمانها، وهدم بيوت أزواج النبي ﷺ، وبنى المسجد، وأتته الفعلة من الشام. وبعث الوليد إلى ملك الروم بما عزم عليه، فبعث له مائة ألف مثقال ذهبا ومائة عامل وأربعين حملا من الفسيفساء، فحمل الوليد ذلك إلى عمر بن عبد العزيز. فحضر عمر ومعه الناس فوضعوا أساس
١٠ المسجد وابتدؤوا بعمارته.[٢٣]

---

١ الوليد ... مروان : بالرغم من العناوين الأخرى في الأصل، عنوان باب الخليفة الوليد هذا بالمداد الأسود. ‖ بن[١] : ناقصة في الأصل، مضافة من السياق. ٢ المنصف : تصحيح في الأصل بخط المقريزي. ٥ وأن : تصحيح في الأصل بخط المقريزي. ‖ يشتري : ناقصة في الأصل، مضافة بخط المقريزي في الهامش الأيسر، من الأسفل إلى الأعلى + صح؛ يشير إليها الرمز ⌐ بعد كلمة "ان". ٦ مائتي : "مايتى" في الأصل. ‖ قيمة : تصحيح في الأصل بخط المقريزي. ٧ وأعطى : "واعطا" في الأصل. ‖ ﷺ : ناقصة في الأصل، مضافة بخط المقريزي في الهامش الأيسر، من الأعلى إلى الأسفل + صح؛ يشير إليها الرمز ⌐ بعد كلمة "النبي". ‖ وبنى : "وبنا" في الأصل. ٨ مائة : "ماية" في الأصل. ‖ ومائة : "ماية" في الأصل. ١٠ وابتدؤوا : "وابتدوا" في الأصل.

---

[٢٣] راجع هذا الخبر على شكل مساو في ابن الأثير، الكامل، ج. ٤، ص. ٢٤٦-٢٤٧؛ وراجع هذا الخبر بتفاصيله في الطبري، تاريخ الرسل والملوك، ج. ٢/٢، ص. ١١٩٢-١١٩٤.

7. Al-Walīd b. ʿAbd al-Malik b. Marwān[90]

§ 45 The oath of allegiance was sworn to him after his father's death, by designation from him, on 15 Šawwāl of the year 86 [9 October 705]. His term of caliph lasted for 9 years and 7 months.

5 § 46 He had the mosque of the Messenger of God—may God bless him and grant him salvation—built in the year 88 [707]. That happened by the hand of ʿUmar b. ʿAbd al-ʿAzīz,[91] while he was [governor] over Medina. [Al-Walīd] wrote to him in Rabīʿ I [February] ordering him to incorporate the apartments of the Prophet's wives into the mosque of the Messenger of 10 God—may God bless him and grant him salvation—, to acquire what was surrounding it so that it would measure 200 cubits on each side, and to move the *qiblah* forward. So ʿUmar assessed the value of the properties in a fair manner and he gave the people their prices. He pulled down the rooms of the wives of the Prophet—may God bless him and grant him salvation—and 15 he built the mosque. [Soon afterwards] workmen came to him from Syria. Al-Walīd sent [word] to the ruler of the Byzantines [informing him] of what he intended. [The Byzantine emperor] sent to him 100,000 *miṯqāls*[92] of gold, 100 workers, and 40 loads of mosaic. Al-Walīd had [all] that transported to ʿUmar b. ʿAbd al-ʿAzīz. Then ʿUmar came [to the site] while the leading people [of 20 Medina] were with him. They laid the foundations of the mosque and started its construction.[93]

---

90 Al-Walīd succeeded his father ʿAbd al-Malik b. Marwān b. al-Ḥakam in the Umayyad caliphate in 86/705 without opposition; he remained in office until his death in 96/715, continuing his father's policies and generating a period of internal peace and external expansion (R. Jacobi, "al-Walīd", in *EI*² http://referenceworks.brillonline.com/entries/encyclopaedia-of-islam-2/al-walid-SIM_7846).

91 ʿUmar b. ʿAbd al-ʿAzīz b. Marwān b. al-Ḥakam was the son of caliph ʿAbd al-Malik's brother; he was governor of Medina on behalf of al-Walīd between 87/706 and 93/712. In 99/717 he succeeded al-Walīd's brother Sulaymān b. ʿAbd al-Malik in the Umayyad caliphate, and he remained in office until his death in 101/720 (P.M. Cobb, "ʿUmar (II) b. ʿAbd al-ʿAzīz", in *EI*² http://referenceworks.brillonline.com/entries/encyclopaedia-of-islam-2/umar-ii-b-abd-al-aziz-COM_1282).

92 A measurement of weight, equalling about 5 grams, one silver coin and a half, or one gold coin.

93 For the translation of the parallel text of this story, transmitted by Muḥammad b. ʿUmar, in al-Ṭabarī's *History*, see al-Ṭabarī, *History* XXIII, 141–142.

وكتب أيضا إلى عمر أن يُسَهِل الثنايا ويحفر الآبار ويعمل الفوارة بالمدينة. فعملها وأجرى ماءها. فلما حج الوليد ورآها أعجبته، فأمر لها بقوام يقومون عليها، وأمر أهل المسجد أن يستقوا منها. وكتب إلى جميع البلاد بإصلاح الطرق وعمل الآبار بطريق الحجاز ومنع المجذمين من الخروج على الناس وأجرى لهم الأرزاق.[٢٤]

٥ وكان حجه في سنة إحدى وتسعين. فلما دخل المدينة، غدا إلى المسجد ينظر إلى بنائه، وأخرج الناس منه، ولم يبق غير سعيد بن المسيب، فلم يجسر أحد من الحرس يخرجه. فقيل له: "لو قمت." فقال: "لا أقوم حتى يأتي الوقت الذي كتب أقوم فيه." فقيل: "فلو سلمت على أمير المؤمنين." قال: "والله، لا أقوم إليه." قال عمر بن عبد العزيز: "فجعلت أعدل بالوليد في ناحية المسجد لئلا يراه." فالتفت الوليد إلى القبلة، فقال: "من ذلك الشيخ؟ أهو سعيد؟" قال | عمر: "نعم، ومن حاله كذا وكذا، ولو 120a

١٠ علم بمكانك لقام فسلم عليك، وهو ضعيف البصر." قال الوليد: "قد علمت حاله، ونحن نأتيه." فدار في المسجد، ثم أتاه، فقال: "كيف أنت، أيها الشيخ؟" فوالله، ما تحرك سعيد، فقال: "بخير، والحمد لله. فكيف أمير المؤمنين وكيف حاله؟" فانصرف الوليد وهو يقول لعمر: "هذا بقية الناس."[٢٥]

---

١ يُسَهِل: تصحيح في الأصل بخط المقريزي. ‖ ماءها: "ماها" في الأصل. ٢ يستقوا: تصحيح في الأصل بخط المقريزي. ٣ من: تصحيح في الأصل بخط المقريزي. ٤ وأجرى: "اجري" في الأصل. ٥ بنائه: "بنايه" في الأصل. ٨ لئلا: "ليلا" في الأصل. ٩ ولو: تصحيح في الأصل بخط المقريزي. ١٠ علمت: ناقصة في الأصل، مضافة بخط المقريزي في الهامش الأيمن، من الأعلى إلى الأسفل + صح؛ يشير إليها الرمز ⌐ بعد كلمة "قد".

---

[٢٤] راجع هذا الخبر على نفس الشكل تقريبا في ابن الأثير، الكامل، ج. ٤، ص. ٢٤٧؛ وراجع هذا الخبر بتفاصيله في الطبري، تاريخ الرسل والملوك، ج. ٢/٢، ص. ١١٩٥-١١٩٦. [٢٥] راجع هذا الخبر على نفس الشكل تقريبا في ابن الأثير، الكامل، ج. ٤، ص. ٢٦٢-٢٦٣؛ وأيضا في الطبري، تاريخ الرسل والملوك، ج. ٢/٢، ص. ١٢٣٢-١٢٣٣.

§ 47 [Al-Walīd] also wrote to ʿUmar [instructing him] to facilitate [passage through] the narrow mountain passes [around Medina], to dig out wells and to construct a drinking fountain in Medina. [ʿUmar] constructed it and caused its water to flow. When al-Walīd performed the pilgrimage and saw 5 [the fountain], he was impressed by it. He assigned caretakers for it who had to look after it, and he ordered that the people of the mosque should be given to drink from it. He wrote to all the regions [instructing them] to repair the roads and to dig wells along the road of the Hijaz, and he prevented lepers from going out among the people, arranging for allowances to be allocated 10 to them.[94]

§ 48 His pilgrimage happened in the year 91 [710]. When he entered Medina, he immediately went to the mosque to inspect its construction. The people were cleared out of it, no one remaining behind except for Saʿīd b. al-Musayyab.[95] None of the guards dared to make him leave, so it was said 15 to him: "if only you stood up." But he said: "I will not stand up until the time has come that was written for me to stand up." Then it was said: "and if only you greeted the Commander of the Faithful." He said: "By God, I shall not stand up for him." ʿUmar b. ʿAbd al-ʿAzīz said: "I began making al-Walīd turn towards the [other] side of the mosque so as not to see him." But 20 al-Walīd turned his face towards the *qiblah* and said: "who is that elderly man? Is he not Saʿīd?" ʿUmar said: "Yes, but his condition is so-and-so, and if he had known that you are standing here, he certainly would have stood up and greeted you; but [he did not because] his sight is weak." Al-Walīd said: "I already know about him; let us go towards him." So he went around 25 the mosque and then came to him. He said: "How are you, *šayḫ*?" But, by God, Saʿīd did not move. He said: "I'm well, praise to God; and how is the Commander of the Faithful and how is his condition?" Al-Walīd left, saying to ʿUmar: "This is the last remaining one from the [first generation of the community's] leading people."[96]

---

94 For the translation of the parallel text of this story, transmitted by Muḥammad b. ʿUmar and by Ibn Abī Sabrah, in al-Ṭabarī's *History*, see al-Ṭabarī, *History* XXIII, 144.

95 The Medinan scholar Saʿīd b. al-Musayyab (d. 94/712–713) was remembered for refusing to swear allegiance to al-Walīd, for which he ended up in prison (al-Ṭabarī, *History* XXXIX, 316, fn. 1462 [see also fn. 57]).

96 For the translation of the parallel text of this story, transmitted by Muḥammad b. ʿUmar, in al-Ṭabarī's *History*, see al-Ṭabarī, *History* XXIII, pp. 179–180.

وقسم بالمدينة أموالا كثيرة، وصلى بها الجمعة. فخطب الناس الخطبة الأولى جالسا، ثم قام فخطب الثانية قائما. فقال رجل لرجاء بن حَيْوَة: "أهكذا يصنعون؟" قال: "نعم، وهكذا صنع معٰوية، وهلم جرا." فقيل له: "ألا تكلمه؟" فقال: "أخبرني قبيصة بن ذؤيب أنه كلم عبد الملك في القعود، فلم يتركه، وقال: "هكذا خطب عثمان." قال: "فقلت: والله، ما خطب إلا قائما." قال رجاء: "روى ٥ لهم شيء، فأخذوا به."[٢٦]

١ أموالا : تصحيح في الأصل بخط المقريزي. ‖ الأولى : "الاولي" في الأصل. ٢ لرجاء : "لرجآ" في الأصل. ‖ بن حَيْوَة : تصحيح في الأصل بخط المقريزي. ٤ قائما : "قايما" في الأصل. ‖ رجاء : "رجآ" في الأصل. ٥ شيء : "شي" في الأصل.

[٢٦] راجع هذا الخبر على نفس الشكل تقريبا في ابن الأثير، الكامل، ج. ٤، ص. ٢٦٤؛ وأيضا في الطبري، تاريخ الرسل والملوك، ج. ٢/٢، ص. ١٢٣٤.

§ 49 He distributed a lot of riches in Medina, and performed the Friday prayer there. He delivered the first public Friday sermon before the people while he was sitting down. Then he stood up and delivered the second Friday sermon while he was standing up. A man said to Raǧāʾ b. Ḥaywah:[97] "Is this 5 the way [the caliphs] perform [the sermon]?" He said: "yes, for this is how it was done by Muʿāwiyah and so on." But it was said to him: "Aren't you going to speak to him [about it]?" He said: "Qabīṣah b. Ḏuʾayb[98] reported to me that he spoke to ʿAbd al-Malik on the matter of sitting down, but he did not [want to] refrain from it, saying: 'This is how ʿUṯmān performed the Friday 10 sermon.' [Qabīṣah] said: 'I said: By God, ʿUṯmān only delivered the Friday sermon while standing up.'" Raǧāʾ said: "They just follow anything that is transmitted to them."[99]

---

97 Raǧāʾ b. Ḥaywah b. Ḫanzal al-Kindī was an influential religious and political adviser at the Umayyad court from the reign of ʿAbd al-Malik up to ʿUmar's; it is said that he had a hand in ʿUmar's succession of his nephew Sulaymān in 99/717. Raǧāʾ is also known as a man of piety and religious learning. He died in 112/730 (C.E. Bosworth, "Radja' b. Ḥaywa", in *EI*² http://referenceworks.brillonline.com/entries/encyclopaedia-of-islam-2/radja-b-haywa-SIM_8865).

98 Qabīṣah b. Ḏuʾayb (d. 86/705) was a jurist and traditionist, who worked as a leading figure in the administration of ʿAbd al-Malik (see al-Ṭabarī, *History* XXXIX, 317, fn. 1469).

99 For the translation of the parallel text of this story, transmitted by Muḥammad b. ʿUmar, in al-Ṭabarī's *History*, see al-Ṭabarī, *History* XXIII, 180–181 (according to this account, the man who spoke to Raǧāʾ was known as Isḥāq b. Yaḥyá).

سليمان بن عبد الملك بن مروان

بويع بعد موت أخيه الوليد في نصف جمادى الآخرة وهو بالرملة. فاقام في الخلافة سنتين وثمانية أشهر وخمسة أيام—وقيل: إلا خمسة أيام.

وحج بالناس سنة سبع وتسعين، وكتب إلى خالد بن عبد الله القَسْرِي—وهو على مكة—أن "أجر لي عينا يخرج من مائها العذب الزلال حتى تخرج بين زمزم والمقام." فعمل خالد بركة بأصل ثَبِيْر ٥

٥ من: ناقصة في الأصل، مضافة بخط المقريزي في الهامش الأيمن، من الأعلى إلى الأسفل + صح؛ يشير إليها الرمز ⸢ بعد كلمة "يخرج". ‖ ثَبِيْر: كذا في الأصل (أشكال الحركات مضافة بخط المقريزي).

100 Sulaymān b. ʿAbd al-Malik b. Marwān succeeded his brother al-Walīd in the Umayyad caliphate in 96/715 without opposition; his reign ended abruptly in 99/717 when he died in Northern Syria, leading a campaign against the Byzantine empire that included an unsuccessful siege of Constantinople (R. Eisener, "Sulaymān b. ʿAbd al-Malik", in *EI*[2] http://referenceworks.brillonline.com/entries/encyclopaedia-of-islam-2/sulayman-b-abd-al-malik-SIM_7156).

8. Sulaymān b. ʿAbd al-Malik b. Marwān[100]

§ 50 The oath of allegiance was sworn to him after the death of his brother al-Walīd on 15 Ǧumādá II of the year 96 [25 February 715], while he was at al-Ramlah.[101] He remained in the post of caliph for 2 years, 8 months, and 5 days—it was said: less 5 days.

§ 51 He led the people on the pilgrimage in the year 97 [716]. He wrote to Ḫālid b. ʿAbd Allāh al-Qasrī[102]—he was [governor] over Mecca: "Make me a spring producing sweet and cold water [and make it thus] that [its water] wells up between Zamzam[103] and the *Maqām*."[104] So Ḫālid created a rock

101 The coastal town of al-Ramlah was founded and developed as the new capital of the *ǧund Filasṭīn*, the Umayyad province of Palestine, when Sulaymān was governor there during the caliphate of al-Walīd; Sulaymān alledgedly also continued to live in al-Ramlah when he became Umayyad caliph (E. Honigmann, "al-Ramla", in *EI*^{2} http://referenceworks.brillonline.com/entries/encyclopaedia-of-islam-2/al-ramla-SIM_6215).

102 Ḫālid b. ʿAbd Allāh al-Qasrī was an Umayyad governor, first of Mecca and later of the province of Iraq; he finally fell from office and favour in 120/738 and died under torture in 126/743–744; there is an unresolved discussion in historiography about whether Ḫālid remained governor of Mecca under Sulaymān, and hence whether this fountain, intended to supplant Zamzam, was constructed on the orders of Sulaymān or rather of al-Walīd before (as al-Ṭabarī suggests) (G.R. Hawting, "Khālid b. ʿAbd Allāh al-Ḳasrī", in *EI*^{2} http://referenceworks.brillonline.com/entries/encyclopaedia-of-islam-2/khalid-b-abd-allah-al-kasri-SIM_4145).

103 Zamzam is the name of the well inside the Ḥaram mosque of Mecca, east of the Kaʿbah, from which water is believed to have welled up for the first time in the days of the prophet Ibrāhīm and which is then believed to have been rediscovered by the grandfather of the prophet Muḥammad in the sixth century; as a result of these mythic origins, water from Zamzam is traditionally considered to possess particular qualities (J. Chabbi, "Zamzam", in *EI*^{2} http://referenceworks.brillonline.com/entries/encyclopaedia-of-islam-2/zamzam-SIM_8112).

104 The *maqām Ibrāhīm* refers to a little building close to Zamzam and to the northeast façade of the Kaʿbah; inside there is preserved a stone with the prints of two human feet, which are believed to have remained when the prophet Ibrāhīm stood on it for building the Kaʿbah (M.J. Kister, "Maḳām Ibrāhīm", in *EI*^{2} http://referenceworks.brillonline.com/entries/encyclopaedia-of-islam-2/makam-ibrahim-SIM_4815).

من حجارة، وأحكمها وأنبط ماءها وشق لها فلجا يسكب فيها من شعب في الجبل، ثم شق من البركة عينا تخرج إلى المسجد الحرام تجري في قصب من رصاص حتى أظهره من فوارة تسكب في فسقينة من رخام بين زمزم والمقام. فلما جرت وظهر ماءها، أمر القسْري بجُزُرٍ، فنُحِرت بمكة وقسمت بين الناس وعمل طعاما دعا إليه الناس. ثم أمر صائحا، فصاح: "الصلاة جامعة."

٥ وأمر بالمنبر فوضع في وجه الكعبة، ثم صعد فحمد الله وأثنى عليه، وقال: "أيها الناس، إحمدوا الله وادعوا لأمير المؤمنين الذي سقاكم الماء العذب الزلال النُقَاخَ العَذْب." فكانت تفرغ تلك الفسقينة في سَرْب من رصاص يخرج إلى موضع {وضوء} كان عند باب الصفا وفي بركة كانت في السوق. وكان الناس لا يقفون على تلك الفسقينة ولا يكاد أحد يقربها، وكانوا على شرب ماء زمزم أحرص وفيه أرغب. فصعد خالد المنبر وأنّبَ الناس وأقْذَع في كلامه.

١٠ فلم تزل البركة حتى هدمها داود بن علي بن عبد الله بن عباس في خلافة أبي | العباس السفاح، [120b] وصرف العين إلى بركة بباب المسجد. وبقي السرْب من الرصاص حتى قدم يُسْر الخادم من بغداد

١ ماءها: "ماها" في الأصل. ٣ بجُزُرٍ: تصحيح في الأصل بخط المقريزي. || فنُحِرت: تصحيح في الأصل بخط المقريزي. ٤ صائحا: "صايحا" في الأصل. ٦ الماء: "المآ" في الأصل. ٧ الفسقينة: تصحيح في الأصل بخط المقريزي (من "الفسقية"). || وضوء: "وضو" في الأصل. ٨ الفسقينة: تصحيح في الأصل بخط المقريزي (من "الفسقية"). || شرب: تصحيح في الأصل بخط المقريزي. || ماء: "مآ" في الأصل. ١٠ أبي: تصحيح في الأصل بخط المقريزي. ١١ وبقي: تصحيح في الأصل بخط المقريزي. || السرْب: تصحيح في الأصل بخط المقريزي؛ مضافة في السطر في مكانها الصحيح في الجملة ولكن مكتوبة من الأسفل إلى الأعلى.

105 Ṯubayr is the name of a mountain near Mecca.

106 Bāb al-Ṣafā is the name for one of the many gates that traditionally regulated access to the Meccan sanctuary of the sacred mosque, *al-masǧid al-ḥarām*.

basin at the foot of Ṯubayr,[105] he made it solid and he made its water rise, by cutting a fissure in it through which [water] could pour in it from a canyon in the mountain. Then he cut through [the other side] of the basin, [creating] a spring from which [water] poured down to the sacred mosque. It ran through a pipe of lead until it appeared again through a jet of water that poured into a marble drinking fountain between Zamzam and the *Maqām*. When it was all set up and its water appeared, al-Qasrī ordered camels to slaughter. They were slaughtered in Mecca and distributed among the people, and he organised a banquet to which he invited the people. Then he ordered with a loud voice, shouting: "all to prayer." He ordered for the *minbar* [to be brought]. It was put in front of the Kaʿbah, whereupon he mounted [it]. He praised and lauded Allah, and said: "O people, praise God and pray for the Commander of the Faithful, who has given you sweet, cold, and fresh water to drink." This drinking fountain poured out in a conduit of lead that ran to a place for ritual ablution which used to be at the Bāb al-Ṣafāʾ,[106] as well as in a basin that was at the market. The people did not take up the habit of stopping at this fountain, and in fact hardly anyone came near to it, for they were more intent on and longing for drinking the water of Zamzam. So Ḫālid mounted the *minbar* and blamed the people, speaking in a slanderous way.

§ 52 The basin [at the market] remained until Dāwūd b. ʿAlī b. ʿAbd Allāh b. ʿAbbās[107] destroyed it, during the caliphate of Abū l-ʿAbbās al-Saffāḥ.[108] The spring was transformed into a basin at the mosque's gate. The conduit of lead remained until Yusr al-Ḫādim[109] came from Baghdad to Mecca in the year

---

107 Dāwūd b. ʿAlī b. ʿAbd Allāh b. ʿAbbās was one of the most respected uncles of the first two ʿAbbāsid caliphs; he died in 133/750–751 (al-Ṭabarī, *History* XXXIX, 277, fn. 1258).

108 Abū l-ʿAbbās ʿAbd Allāh b. Muḥammad b. ʿAlī b. ʿAbd Allāh b. al-ʿAbbās was the first caliph of the ʿAbbāsid dynasty; he was proclaimed as caliph with the title al-Saffāḥ in 132/749 and died in 136/754 (S. Moscati, "Abū ʾl-ʿAbbās al-Saffāḥ", in *EI*² http://referenceworks.brillonline.com/entries/encyclopaedia-of-islam-2/abu-l-abbas-al-saffah-SIM_0150).

109 Yusr al-Ḫādim (also sometimes referred to as Bišr al-Ḫādim, Yusr al-Afšim, or Bišr al-Afšīnī) was a member of the ʿAbbāsid court in the second half of the ninth century who supervised the restoration of the mosques of Mecca and Medina in 256/870, at which occasion he was also involved in the restoration of the *maqām Ibrāhīm* (see Kister [1971]: 485) and—as explained here—of Zamzam. See also al-Ṭabarī, *History* XXXVIII, 164; Id., *History* XXXIV, 219–220; Id., *History* XXXVI, 31.

إلى مكة في سنة ست وخمسين ومائتين، فعمل القبة بجانب بيت الشراب، وأخرج قصب خالد فجعلها في سَرْب الفوارة التي يخرج منها الماء إلى حياض زمزم، فتصب في هذه البركة.[٢٧]

١ ومائتين : "مايتين" في الأصل. ٢ الماء : "المآ" في الأصل. || فتصب : تصحيح في الأصل بخط المقريزي. || في : تصحيح في الأصل بخط المقريزي.

٢٧ خبر البركة والفسقينة موجود على شكل مساو ولكن بتفاصيله في الأزرقي، أخبار مكة، ص. ٣٣٩-٣٤٠.

256 [870]. He had the dome constructed next to the drinking place and he removed the pipe of Ḫālid and used it for the conduit of the jet of water that poured into the cisterns of Zamzam, [enabling it] to overflow into this basin [at the mosque's gate].

هشام بن عبد الملك بن مروان

استخلف بعد موت أخيه يزيد بن عبد الملك لليال بقين من شعبان سنة خمس ومائة. فقام في الخلافة تسع عشرة سنة وتسعة أشهر وأحد وعشرين يوما، وقيل: وثمانية أشهر ونصف.

حج فيها مرة واحدة سنة ست ومائة. وكتب له أبو الزناد سُنَن الحج. قال أبو {الزناد}: "لقيت هشاما.
٥ فإني لفي الموكب إذ لقيه سعيد بن عبد الله بن الوليد بن عثمان بن عفان، فسار إلى جنبه فسمعته يقول له: "يا أمير المؤمنين، إن الله لم يزل ينعم على أهل بيت أمير المؤمنين وينصر خليفته المظلوم، ولم يزالوا يلعنون في هذه المواطن أبا تراب. فإنها مواطن صالحة وأمير المؤمنين ينبغي له أن يلعنه فيها." فشق على هشام قوله وقال: "ما قدمنا لشتم أحد ولا للعنه. قدمنا حجاجا." ثم قطع كلامه وأقبل

٢ ومائة: "ماية" في الأصل. ٤ ومائة: "وماية" في الأصل. ‖ الزناد: "الزياد" في الأصل، وهو خطأ.

110 Hišām b. ʿAbd al-Malik b. Marwān succeeded his older brother Yazīd in the Umayyad caliphate in 105/724 without opposition; he reigned in relative peace, stability and prosperity for 19 years, until his death in 125/743, which made him the longest reigning of the Syrian Umayyad caliphs (F. Gabrieli, "Hisẖām", in *EI*² http://referenceworks.brillonline.com/entries/encyclopaedia-of-islam-2/hisham-SIM_2901).

9. Hišām b. ʿAbd al-Malik b. Marwān[110]

§ 53 He was appointed as caliph after the death of his brother Yazīd b. ʿAbd al-Malik[111] in the course of the last ten days of Šaʿbān of the year 105 [late January 724]. He performed the office of caliph for 19 years, 9 months, and 21 days—it was said 8 months and a half.

§ 54 During [his term], he went on pilgrimage once, in the year 106 [725]. [On the caliph's request] Abū l-Zinād[112] wrote up for him the traditions of the pilgrimage. Abū l-Zinād said: "I have met Hišām [as follows]: I was in the procession [behind the caliph], when Saʿīd b. ʿAbd Allāh b. al-Walīd b. ʿUṯmān b. ʿAffān[113] encountered him. He came riding beside him, and I heard him saying to [Hišām]: 'O Commander of the Faithful, God has not ceased his benevolence toward the house of the Commander of the Faithful, and He [has not ceased] to stand by his ill-treated caliph;[114] [likewise] have they not ceased to curse Abū Turāb[115] in these lands; as they are virtuous lands, the Commander of the Faithful ought to curse him [too while he is] in them.' His talk troubled Hišām, so he said: 'We have not come to vilify nor to curse anyone; we have come as pilgrims.' Then he stopped talking and turned

111 Yazīd b. ʿAbd al-Malik succeeded his nephew ʿUmar in the Umayyad caliphate in 101/720 without opposition; he reigned until his death in 105/724 (H. Lammens, Kh.Y. Blankinship, "Yazīd (II) b. ʿAbd al-Malik", in *EI*² http://referenceworks.brillonline.com/entries/encyclopaedia-of-islam-2/yazid-ii-b-abd-al-malik-SIM_8001).

112 Abū l-Zinād (sometimes also referred to as Abū l-Zanād) is the nickname of ʿAbd Allāh b. Ḏakwān, an Umayyad administrator in Iraq who died in 130/747–748; together with his three sons, Abū l-Zinād is considered an important transmitter of *ḥadīṯ*, and one of these sons, known as Ibn Abī l-Zinād (d. 174/790–791), also gained fame as an early specialist of Medinan jurisprudence (*fiqh*) (Ed., "Ibn Abī ʾl-Zinād", in *EI*² http://referenceworks.brillonline.com/entries/encyclopaedia-of-islam-2/ibn-abi-l-zinad-SIM_8635).

113 Saʿīd b. ʿAbd Allāh b. al-Walīd was a great-grandson of the third caliph ʿUṯmān, and also a great-great-grandson of the first caliph Abū Bakr (al-Ṭabarī, *History* XXV, 19, fn. 19).

114 That is, Saʿīd's great-grandfather, the caliph ʿUṯmān, who was murdered in 35/656.

115 Abū Turāb is a pejorative nickname for the fourth caliph ʿAlī b. Abī Ṭālib ("Abū Turāb", in *EI*² http://referenceworks.brillonline.com/entries/encyclopaedia-of-islam-2/abu-turab-DUM_0104).

علي فسألني عن الحج، فأخبرته بما كتبت له، قال: "وشق على سعيد أني سمعتُه تكلم بذلك، فكان منكسرا كلما رآني."[٢٨]

وكلم إبراهيم بن محمد بن طلحة هشاما وهو في الحِجْر بمكة، فقال له: "أسألك بالله وبحرمة هذا البيت الذي خرجت معظما له ألا رددت علي ظلامتي." قال: "أي ظلامة؟" قال: "داري." قال: "فأين ٥ كنت عن أمير المؤمنين عبد الملك؟" قال: "ظلمني." قال: "فالوليد وسليمان؟" قال: "ظلماني." قال: "فعمر؟" قال: "{يرحمه} الله، ردها علي." قال: "فيزيد بن عبد الملك؟" قال: "ظلمني وقبضها مني بعد قبضي لها وهي في يدك." فقال هشام: "لو كان فيك ضرب لضربتك." فقال: "في والله ضرب بالسيف والسوط." فانصرف هشام وقال لمن معه: "كيف سمعت هذا اللسان؟" قال: "ما أجوده!" قال: "هي قريش وألسنتها، ولا يزال في الناس بقايا ما رأيت مثل هذا."[٢٩]

١٠ ولم يحج بعد هشام أحد من بني أمية وهو خليفة.

٦ فعمر: تصحيح في الأصل بخط المقريزي. || يرحمه: "يرحمة" في الأصل.

[٢٨] راجع هذا الخبر على نفس الشكل تماما في ابن الأثير، الكامل، ج. ٤، ص. ٣٧٤؛ وراجع أيضا على نفس الشكل تقريبا في الطبري، تاريخ الرسل والملوك، ج. ٢/٢، ص. ١٤٨٢-١٤٨٣. [٢٩] راجع هذا الخبر على نفس الشكل تماما في ابن الأثير، الكامل، ج. ٤، ص. ٣٧٦؛ وراجعه أيضا على نفس الشكل تقريبا في الطبري، تاريخ الرسل والملوك، ج. ٢/٢، ص. ١٤٨٣-١٤٨٤.

towards me. He asked me about the pilgrimage, and I informed him about what I had written for him." [Abū l-Zinād] said: "It troubled Saʿīd that I had heard him saying that, so he was broken-hearted every time he saw me."[116]

§ 55 Ibrāhīm b. Muḥammad b. Ṭalḥah[117] spoke to Hišām when he was in the *ḥiğr* in Mecca. He said to him: "By God and by the sacredness of this house for which you have gone out expanding its greatness, I supplicate you not to bring over me once again my injustice." [Hišām] said: "What injustice?" He said: "my house." [Hišām] said: "Where were you with respect to the Commander of the Faithful ʿAbd al-Malik?" He said: "He treated me unjustly." [Hišām] said: "What about al-Walīd and Sulaymān?" He said: "They both treated me unjustly." [Hišām] said: "What about ʿUmar?" He said: "May God have mercy upon him, he returned it to me." [Hišām] said: "What about Yazīd b. ʿAbd al-Malik?" He said: "He treated me unjustly, taking it from me just after I had taken it, so that it is [now] in your possession." Hišām said: "If you could bear a beating, I would beat you." He said: "By God, I can stand a beating with the sword and with the whip!" Hišām went away, saying to whoever was with him: "What did you make of hearing this tongue?" [The other person] said: "How skilful it is!". [Hišām] said: "It is the tongues of Quraysh, and among the people there continue to be remnants similar to this which I just noticed."[118]

§ 56 After Hišām, no one from the Banū Umayyah went on pilgrimage while he was caliph.

116 For the translation of the parallel text of this story, transmitted by al-Wāqidī on authority of Ibn Abī al-Zinād, in al-Ṭabarī's *History*, see al-Ṭabarī, *History* XXV, 19.

117 Ibrāhīm b. Muḥammad b. Ṭalḥah (also known as al-Aʿrağ) was a grandson of Ṭalḥah b. ʿUbayd Allāh, an early convert and prominent Companion of Muḥammad who was killed in 36/656 in the Battle of the Camel near Basra, when he rose with other companions against the succession to the caliphate of ʿAlī b. Abī Ṭālib (W. Madelung, "Ṭalḥa", in EI[2] http://referenceworks.brillonline.com/entries/encyclopaedia-of-islam-2/talha-SIM_7362; al-Ṭabarī, *History* XXV, 19–20, fn. 99).

118 For the translation of the parallel text of this story in al-Ṭabarī's *History*, see al-Ṭabarī, *History* XXV, 20.

ثم كانت دولة بني العباس. فأول من حج منهم وهو خليفة:

أبو جعفر المنصور

واسمه عبد الله بن محمد بن علي بن عبد الله بن عباس بن عبد المطلب، أمير المؤمنين، العباسي الهاشمي.

٥ بُويع بعد موت أخيه أبي العباس | السفاح عبد الله بن محمد—وهو بطريق مكة—سنة ست وثلٰثين ومائة. 121a

فقدم الكوفة، ثم حج في سنة أربعين ومائة، فأحرم من الحيرة، ولما قضى حجه، توجه إلى بيت

٦ ومائة : "وماية" في الأصل. ٧ ومائة : "وماية" في الأصل.

Then there was the reign of the ʿAbbāsids. The first of them to go on pilgrimage while he was caliph was:

10. Abū Ǧaʿfar al-Manṣūr[119]

His name is ʿAbd Allāh b. Muḥammad b. ʿAlī b. ʿAbd Allāh b. ʿAbbās b. ʿAbd
5 al-Muṭṭalib, Commander of the Faithful, al-ʿAbbāsī l-Hāšimī.

§ 57 The oath of allegiance was sworn [to him] after the death of his brother Abū l-ʿAbbās al-Saffāḥ ʿAbd Allāh b. Muḥammad, while he was on the road to Mecca, in the year 136 [754].

§ 58 He came to [live in] Kufa.[120] In the year 140 [758] he went on pilgrimage.
10 He entered into *iḥrām* from al-Ḥīrah[121] onwards. Once he had concluded

119 Abū Ǧaʿfar al-Manṣūr was the second caliph of the ʿAbbāsid dynasty, succeeding his brother al-Saffāḥ in 136/754 and reigning until his death in 158/775; the successful longevity of his rule consolidated the ʿAbbāsid take-over of the caliphate and meant the starting point of many decades of ʿAbbāsid imperial prosperity emanating from Iraq and integrating elites and regions from North Africa to Transoxania (H. Kennedy, "al-Manṣūr", in *EI*² http://referenceworks.brillonline.com/entries/encyclopaedia-of-islam-2/al-mansur-SIM_4935).

120 Kufa (al-Kūfah) was established in Iraq—together with Basra to the south—as a military encampment (*miṣr*) and control center in the course of the Arab conquest of the region in the 630s; it soon transformed into a regional capital for, as well as a hotbed of regional (especially pro-ʿAlid) dissent with, caliphal authority as emanating from the Hijaz and then from Syria; in the mid-eighth century, it briefly became the centre of the new ʿAbbāsid caliphate, before its transfer to Baghdad in the course of the reign of al-Manṣūr; throughout the caliphal era, Kufa (and Basra) operated as key centers of Arabo-Islamic cultural formation and efflorescence (H. Djaït, "al-Kūfa", in *EI*² http://referenceworks.brillonline.com/entries/encyclopaedia-of-islam-2/al-kufa-COM_0536).

121 Al-Ḥīrah was a settlement in Iraq that was the most important Arab city in the region before the rise of Islam, due its being the political and cultural capital of the pre-Islamic Lakhmid dynasty, a bulwark in the Sasanid protection system against nomads and Byzantines, and a crucial caravan stop in the transit trade between Persia and Arabia; with the advent of Islam, the Christian city of al-Ḥīrah was gradually eclipsed by new settlements in the region, especially by Kufa (A.F.L. Beeston, I. Shahîd, "al-Ḥīra", in *EI*² http://referenceworks.brillonline.com/entries/encyclopaedia-of-islam-2/al-hira-SIM_2891).

المقدس وسار منها إلى الرقة ومضى إلى الكوفة.

وحج ثانيا سنة أربع وأربعين. فلما حج بالناس ورجع، لم يدخل المدينة ومضى إلى الربَذة وأحضر بني حسن بن علي إليه في القيود والأغلال. فسار بهم إلى الكوفة، وعتا عتوا كبيرا في ظلمهم.

ثم حج بالناس في سنة سبع أربعين ومائة.

---

٢ الربَذة: تصحيح في الأصل بخط المقريزي. ٤ ومائة: "ومابة" في الأصل.

his pilgrimage, he headed for Jerusalem,[122] and from there he traveled to Raqqa[123] and [then] he proceeded to Kufa.

§ 59 He went on pilgrimage a second time in the year [1]44 [762]. When he had led the people on the pilgrimage and returned, he did not enter 5 Medina but went to al-Rabaḏah.[124] He had the descendants of Ḥasan b. ʿAlī[125] brought to him in chains and shackles, and he took them to Kufa, mistreating them in an extremely violent way.

§ 60 Then he led the people on the pilgrimage in the year 147 [765].

---

122 Jerusalem, the third sacred city of Islam after Mecca and Medina, was identified here by the name of "al-Bayt al-Muqaddas", often encountered in Arabic sources as a corruption of the early Islamic name "Bayt al-Maqdis" ("[The City of] the Temple"—a shorthand for "Īlyāʾ Madīnat Bayt al-Maqdis", "Aelia, the City of the Temple") and as an equivalent for the common Arabic name of Jerusalem until today, "al-Quds" (S.D. Goitein, "al-Ḳuds", in *EI*² http://referenceworks.brillonline.com/entries/encyclopaedia-of-islam-2/al-kuds-COM_0535).

123 Raqqa (al-Raqqah) on the left bank of the Euphrates is an ancient town on the route connecting Syria with northern Mesopotamia (the Jazira) and Iraq; after the Arab conquest, it was gradually transformed into an important regional metropolis, especially in the early ʿAbbāsid period, under the caliph al-Manṣūr and his successors; it lingered on thereafter as a regional urban centre until its destruction in the mid-thirteenth century (M. Meinecke, "al-Raḳḳa", in *EI*² http://referenceworks.brillonline.com/entries/encyclopaedia-of-islam-2/al-rakka-COM_0907).

124 Al-Rabaḏah was the name of a settlement in early Islamic Arabia, at the eastern foot of the Hijaz mountain chain some 200 kilometers east of Medina; it lay on the main pilgrimage route from Kufa to Mecca, providing all kinds of facilities to pilgrims (S.ʿA.ʿA. Rashid, "al-Rabad͟ha", in *EI*² http://referenceworks.brillonline.com/entries/encyclopaedia-of-islam-2/al-rabadha-SIM_6152).

125 In 145/762–763 al-Manṣūr was confronted with a last ʿAlid rebellion against his rule, led by the brothers Muḥammad—also know as al-Nafs al-Zakiyyah ("the Pure Soul")—and Ibrāhīm, who claimed on the basis of their direct descent from the Prophet's grandson Ḥasan b. ʿAlī that they had better rights to the caliphate than al-Manṣūr had; an important phase in the build-up of tension concerned this arrest and maltreatment in 144/762 of several members of their family (here referred to as "descendants of al-Ḥasan b. ʿAlī", the Prophet's grandson) by al-Manṣūr (F. Buhl, "Muḥammad b. ʿAbd Allāh b. al-Ḥasan al-Mut͟hannā b. al-Ḥasan b. ʿAlī b. Abī Ṭālib, called al-Nafs al-Zakiyya", in *EI*² http://referenceworks.brillonline.com/entries/encyclopaedia-of-islam-2/muhammad-b-abd-allah-b-al-hasan-al-muthanna-b-al-hasan-b-ali-b-abi-talib-called-al-nafs-al-zakiyya-SIM_5331).

وحج رابعا في سنة ثمان وأربعين.

وحج خامسا في سنة اثنتين وخمسين.

وسار في سنة أربع وخمسين إلى الشام وبيت المقدس. ثم سار في سنة ثمان وخمسين ومائة من بغداد إلى مكة ليحج. واستخلف ابنه محمد المهدي ووصاه وصية بليغة جدا—لولا طولها لذكرتها، ٥ وودعه، وبكى وأعلمه أنه ميت في سفره هذا. ثم سار إلى الكوفة، وجمع بين الحج والعمرة، وساق الهدي وأشعره وقلده لأيام [خلت] من ذي القعدة. فعرض له—وهو سائر—وجع اشتد به حتى مات في بئر ميمون خارج مكة لست خلون من ذي الحجة. فكتم الربيع الحاجب موته حتى بايع للمهدي.[٣٠]

٣ ومائة: "ومابة" في الأصل. ٦ خلت: ناقصة في الأصل مضافة من السياق. || سائر: "ساير" في الأصل. ٧ بئر: "بير" في الأصل. || خلون: تصحيح في الأصل بخط المقريزي. || الحاجب: ناقصة في الأصل، مضافة بخط المقريزي في الهامش الأيمن، من الأعلى إلى الأسفل + صح؛ يشير إليها الرمز ⌝ بعد كلمة "الربيع".

[٣٠] راجع خبر موت المنصور بكماله—الذي اختصره المقريزي هنا—في ابن الأثير، الكامل، ج.٥، ص. ٢١٦-٨. راجع أيضا الطبري، تاريخ الرسل والملوك، ج. ٣/ ١، ص. ٣٨٧-٣٩٠.

§ 61 He went on pilgrimage a fourth time in the year [1]48 [766].

§ 62 He went on pilgrimage a fifth time in the year [1]52 [769].

§ 63 In the year [1]54 [771] he travelled to Syria and Jerusalem. Thereafter, in the year 158 [775] he travelled from Baghdad[126] to Mecca for the performance of the pilgrimage. He appointed his son Muḥammad al-Mahdī[127] as caliph, commissioning him by a most eloquently produced will of his—if it were not for its length, I would mention it [here]. He bid him farewell, wept, and informed him that he would die on this trip of his. Then he left for Kufa. He combined the pilgrimage and the lesser pilgrimage, and he drove the oblational animals [towards Mecca], marking them for sacrifice by stabbing them in the hump and by hanging something upon their necks.[128] [This happened] in the course of early Ḏū l-Qaʿdah [September]. But when he was travelling, a pain befell him that became unbearable, until he died at Biʾr Maymūn,[129] outside Mecca, on the 6th of Ḏū l-Ḥiǧǧah [7 October]. Al-Rabīʿ the Ḥāǧib[130] concealed his death until allegiance was sworn to al-Mahdī.

---

126 Baghdad was constructed on the Tigris in Iraq as the new capital of the new ʿAbbāsid dynasty in the reign of al-Manṣūr, and it retained its status as one of the most important centres of the Islamic world until the 7th/13th century (A.A. Duri, "Baghdād", in *EI*² http://referenceworks.brillonline.com/entries/encyclopaedia-of-islam-2/baghdad-COM_0084).

127 Muḥammad al-Mahdī succeeded his father al-Manṣūr without opposition as the third ʿAbbāsid caliph in 158/775; his reign, which lasted until his death in 169/785, was very much a continuation of the long and prosperous reign of his father's (H. Kennedy, "al-Mahdi", in *EI*² http://referenceworks.brillonline.com/entries/encyclopaedia-of-islam-2/al-mahdi-SIM_4779).

128 For the translation of a parallel but more detailed text of this fragment on the 158/775 pilgrimage, including reference to the combination with the lesser pilgrimage and to the slaughter animals, in al-Ṭabarī's *History*, see al-Ṭabarī, *History* XXIX, 88–89.

129 Biʾr Maymūn is the name of an oasis just outside Mecca, mostly known for being the place where al-Manṣūr died (see al-Ṭabarī, *History* XXIX, 88).

130 Al-Rabīʿ b. Yūnus b. ʿAbd Allāh b. Abī Farwah (d. c. 169–170/785–786) was a manumitted slave who served in various capacities under the first four ʿAbbāsid caliphs; al-Manṣūr first made him his chamberlain (hence the title 'the Ḥāǧib', the Chamberlain) and then his vizir, reflecting al-Rabīʿs powerful position at his court; as a result, he is often also very present in stories about al-Manṣūr as the caliph's righthand (A.S. Atiya, "al-Rabīʿ b. Yūnus", in *EI*² http://referenceworks.brillonline.com/entries/encyclopaedia-of-islam-2/al-mahdi-SIM_4779).

فكانت خلافة أبي جعفر اثنين وعشرين سنة تنقص أياما قد اختلف في عدتها.[٣١]

واتفق أنه لما نزل آخر منزل بطريق مكة نظر في صدر البيت فإذا فيه بعد البسملة: [الطويل]

أبا جعفر، حانت وفاتك وانقضت سنوك وأمر الله لا بد واقع

أبا جعفر، هل كاهن أو منجم لك اليوم من حد المنية مانع؟

٥ فأحضر متولي المنازل وقال له: "ألم آمرك: لا يدخل المنازل أحد من الناس؟" وكانت الخلفاء يبنَى لهم في كل منزلة ينزلونها بطريق مكة دار، ويعد لهم فيها سائر ما يحتاج إليه من الستور والفرش والأواني وغير ذلك. فقال: "والله، ما دخله أحد منذ فرغ." فقال: "إقرأ ما في صدر البيت." فقال: "ما أرى شيئا." فأحضر غيره فلم ير شيئا. فقال: "يا رَبيع، قف بيني وبين الحائط." فقام الربيع بينه وبين الجدار، فرأى البيتين كما كان يراهما قبل وقوف الربيع، فعلم أنه قد نعيت إليه نفسه. فقال:
١٠ "يا ربيع، إقرأ آية من كتاب الله." فقرأ: ﴿وَسَيَعْلَمُ ٱلَّذِينَ ظَلَمُوٓاْ أَيَّ مُنْقَلَبٍ يَنْقَلِبُونَ﴾.[٣٢] فرحل من المنزل، وقد تطَير، فسقط عن دابته فاندق عنقه—وقيل: بل مات | من مرضه. ودفن ببئر ميمون.[٣٣] 121b

٣ حانت : تصحيح في الأصل بخط المقريزي. ‖ وفاتك : ناقصة في الأصل، مضافة بخط المقريزي في الهامش الأيمن، من الأعلى إلى الأسفل + صح، يشير إليها الرمز ⌐ بعد كلمة "حانت". ٥ الخلفاء : "الحلفآ" في الأصل. ٦ سائر: "ساير" في الأصل. ٧ منذ: تصحيح في الأصل بخط المقريزي. ٨ شيئا١ : "شيا" في الأصل. ‖ شيئا٢ : "شيا" في الأصل. ‖ الحائط : "الحايط" في الأصل. ٩ فرأى : "فراي" في الأصل. ١١ مات : تصحيح في الأصل بخط المقريزي. ‖ ببئر: "ببير" في الأصل.

[٣١] راجع تفاصيل الاختلاف في ابن الأثير، الكامل، ج. ٥، ص. ٢١٨، وفي الطبري، تاريخ الرسل والملوك، ج. ٣/ ١، ص. ٣٩٠-٣٩١. [٣٢] القرآن، سورة الشعراء، الآية ٢٢٧. [٣٣] راجع هذا الخبر على نفس الشكل تقريبا في ابن الأثير، الكامل، ج. ٥، ص. ٢١٨-٢١٩؛ وراجع هذا الخبر على شكل مساو أيضا في الطبري، تاريخ الرسل والملوك، ج. ٣/ ١، ص. ٤٤٩.

§ 64 The caliphate of Abū Ǧaʿfar lasted for 22 years less some days—their number is disputed.

§ 65 It so happened that when he halted at the last stop on the road to Mecca, he looked inside the lodge,[131] and behold [he saw verses written on 5 its main wall], which—after the *basmalah*—went as follows: [*Ṭawīl* meter]

§ 66 Abū Ǧaʿfar: your demise is drawing near
and your years are coming to an end—God's command: there is no escape from its reality.

Abū Ǧaʿfar: is there a sorcerer or astrologer
10 with you today who can push back the limits of mortality?

§ 67 [Al-Manṣūr] had the caretaker of the halting places brought and said to him: "Did I not order you not to let anyone of the people enter [the caliphal lodges at] the halting places?" The caliphs had constructed for themselves at every halting place along the road to Mecca a house in which everything 15 necessary was prepared for them, including curtains, carpets, dishes, and the like. [The caretaker] said: "By God, no one has entered it since it was finished." [Al-Manṣūr] said: "Read what is [written on the wall] inside the lodge." He said: "I don't see anything." Then he summoned another one, but he did not see anything either. So he said: "O, al-Rabīʿ, stand between me 20 and the wall." So al-Rabīʿ stood between him and the wall, but he still saw the two verses as he had seen them before al-Rabīʿ came to stand there. So he knew that his soul was announcing his own death to himself. He said: "O, al-Rabīʿ, recite a verse from the Book of God." So he recited: "Those who do wrong shall surely know by what overturning they will be overturned."[132] He 25 left from the halting place after he had seen the evil omen, and he fell from his riding animal and broke his neck. There was said that he rather died from a disease he had. He was buried at Biʾr Maymūn.[133]

---

131 The author is playing here with the double meaning of the Arabic phrase *fī ṣadr al-bayt*, which can mean both 'inside the lodge' and 'at the first hemistich of the verse'.

132 Qurʾān, s. 26: 227. Translation from Arberry (1955).

133 For the translation of a parallel, only slightly diverging story, transmitted by Mūsá b. Hārūn on authority of ʿĪsá b. Muḥammad, in al-Ṭabarī's *History*, see al-Ṭabarī, *History XXIX*, 155–156.

126a ومن بديع ما يحكى عنه أنه لما حج وأشرف على المدينة النبوية | ترجل الناس له لما استقبلوه إلا محمد ابن عمران—قاضي المدينة. فقال المنصور: "يا ربيع، ما له لا يترجل لي؟ يتجالد علي ويمتنع مما فعله بنو عبد المطلب وبنو علي، فلم ينزل إلى الأرض لما بصر بي؟" فقال الربيع: "يأمير المؤمنين، لو رأيته على الأرض، لرحمته ورثيت له من ثقله وعظمه." فأمره بالدنو، فدنا منه راكبا عند تمهيد الربيع

٥ له العذر، فسأله عن حاله. ثم قال: "يابن عمران، أيُما رجل أنت؟ لولا خصال فيك ثلاث كنت أنت الرجل." قال: "وما هن، يأمير المؤمنين؟" قال: "قعودك عن الصلاة في مسجد رسول الله ﷺ في جماعة، فتصلي وحدك. وثانية أنك لا تكلم إنسانا في الطريق تيها وعظمة. وثالثة أنك رجل

١ ومن ... النبوية : تصحيح في الأصل، مضافة في السطر في مكانها في النص بخط المقريزي. || النبوية : بقية نص المنصور ناقصة في الأصل ومكتوبة بخط المقريزي على جزازة منفردة مضافة في هذه المخطوطة في المكان الغلطان (صفحة ١٢٦أ-ب)، يشير إليها الرمز ⌐ بعد الكلمة "النبوية".

134 Muḥammad b. ʿImrān b. Ibrāhīm b. Muḥammad al-Taymī was the last Umayyad *qāḍī* of Medina (Judd [2014], Appendix 2: Qāḍīs *of Medina*, 159); Judd explains that little is known about his life, tenure in office, and scholarship, referring to Wakīʿs entry on him, which mainly consisted of reports of several incidents in which Muḥammad met al-Manṣūr (see Wakīʿ, *Aḫbār al-quḍāt*, 1:181–199).

§ 68 Among the unusual things that were told about him, [there was the following]. When he had performed the pilgrimage and was about to reach the Prophet's Medina, [all] the people dismounted for him when they went out to meet him, [all] except for Muḥammad b. ʿImrān,[134] the judge of Medina. Al-Manṣūr said: "O, al-Rabīʿ, what is it about him that he does not dismount for me? Does he want to engage in a fight with me, and abstain from what [even] the descendants of ʿAbd al-Muṭṭalib[135] and the descendants of ʿAlī[136] have done, by not dismounting to the ground when he saw me?" Al-Rabīʿ said: "O, Commander of the Faithful, if you had seen him [standing] on the ground, you would have had compassion with him and you would have felt sorry for him, due to his greatness and importance." [Al-Manṣūr] commanded him to come closer, so he approached him, but he remained mounted as a result of al-Rabīʿ's providing him with an excuse. [Al-Manṣūr] asked him how he was. Then he said: "O, Ibn ʿImrān, what kind of a man are you? If it were not for three of your characteristics, you would have been a great man." [Ibn ʿImrān] said: "What are they, O Commander of the Faithful?" He said: "Your abstinence from the communal prayer in the mosque of God's Messenger—may God bless him and grant him salvation—for you pray on your own; secondly, that you do not talk to anyone on the road, which is a token of haughtiness and pride; thirdly, that you are a greedy man who lives

135 ʿAbd al-Muṭṭalib b. Hāšim was the grandfather of the prophet Muḥammad; the ʿAbbāsids claimed the legitimacy of their rule on the basis of the fact that they descendend from the same ancestor—ʿAbd al-Muṭṭalib, via his son al-ʿAbbās—as the prophet Muḥammad did—via another son, ʿAbd Allāh; this passage then alludes to this particular claim to legitimacy as residing in and accepted by the broad group of descendants of ʿAbd al-Muṭṭalib (see U. Rubin, "ʿAbd al-Muṭṭalib b. Hāshim", in *EI*³ http://referenceworks.brillonline.com/entries/encyclopaedia-of-islam-3/abd-al-muttalib-b-hashim-SIM_0156).

136 As referred to above (fn. 125), in 145/762–763, al-Manṣūr overcame a last rebellion against his rule from partisans for and supporters of a more narrow definition of legitimate claims to rule, as residing only in the direct descendants of the prophet Muḥammad, via his daughther and his nephew ʿAlī, rather than in the broader clan that also included the ʿAbbāsids; as referred to in this passage, throughout the remainder of al-Manṣūr's reign and for some time thereafter, these ʿAlids seem to have accepted—or at least they posed no further threat to—ʿAbbāsid political authority.

بخيل فيك ضيق شديد." فقال: "يأمير المؤمنين، أما الأولى فإني أكره أن أصلي بصلاة الإمام، فما يدخل علي من فسادها أعظم عندي من تركي إياها لشغلي. وإني لا أدرك معهم ركوعا ولا سجودا، فأرى أن أصلي وحدي أفضل. وأما الثانية فإني قاض ولا يجوز أن أعطي من نفسي التسليم عليهم والابتذال لنفسي، فيكون في ذلك مفسدة للخصوم. وأما الثالثة فإني لا أَجْمُد في حق ولا أذوب
٥ في باطل." قال: "خرجت منهن، يابن عمران؟ يا ربيع، إدفع إليه ثلاثة آلاف درهم."[٣٤]

قال: "يأمير المؤمنين، بالباب مسْتَعْدون عليك يذكرون أن في يدك حقا من دار كذا." قال: "فأنصفهم مني." قال: "وكِل وكيلا يقوم مقامك أو احضر معهم مجلس القضاء." قال: "قد وكلت الربيع." قال: "أشهد على وكالتك إياه عيسى بن علي والعباس بن محمد." ففعل. ثم أخرج حدود الدار التي ينازعونه فيها. ودعا بالربيع وخصمائه، وأحضر شهادته على الوكالة وأنفذها. ثم سأل القوم عن
١٠ دعواهم وعن شهودهم. ثم قضى لهم عليه.

126b واستعدى | أيضا الجمالون على المنصور بالمدينة. فقال القاضي محمد بن عمران للشبلي: "أكتب إليه في ذلك." فأبى عليه وقال: "تعفيني." فقال: "لتكتبن." فكتب. فلما استتم الكتاب وختمه، قال له:

---

٧ القضاء: "القضآ" في الأصل. ٩ وخصمائه: "خصمايه" في الأصل.

---

[٣٤] راجع هذا الخبر، على شكل مختلف تماما، في وكيع، أخبار القضاة، ج. ١، ص. ١٩٣-١٩٤.

---

137 ʿĪsá b. ʿAlī (d. 163/780) was one of al-Manṣūr's paternal uncles; he was a powerful, well-known, and influential character at the early ʿAbbāsid court (see al-Ṭabarī, *History* XXIX, 7, fn. 14).

138 Al-ʿAbbās b. Muḥammad was another well-known protagonist of the early ʿAbbāsid ruling circle, a brother of the caliphs al-Saffāḥ and al-Manṣūr who was last recorded at the ʿAbbāsid court in 170/786–787 (see al-Ṭabarī, *History* XXIX, 21, fn. 58).

in grave poverty." He said: "O, Commander of the Faithful, as far as the first [characteristic] is concerned, I abhor to pray the prayer of the prayer leader, because the imperfection which this would cause with me would be more distressing for me than my abstaining [from prayer] for some preoccupation. I therefore do not pursue any bow nor any prostration with them, but I rather consider it better to pray on my own. As for the second [characteristic], I am a judge and it is not permitted that I myself would greet them and hence debase myself, because therein would be a cause of [accusations of] corruption for opponents. As for the third [characteristic], I do not freeze for the truth and I do not melt for deception." [Al-Manṣūr] said: "You have freed yourself from them, O, Ibn ʿImrān. O, al-Rabīʿ, pay him 3,000 *dirhams*."

§ 69 [Ibn ʿImrān] said: "O, Commander of the Faithful, there are people at the gate appealing for assistance against you, claiming that you have a [disputed] right of property for such and such a house." He said: "See that justice is done to them on my behalf." [But Ibn ʿImrān] said: "Appoint a representative to stand in your place or appear with them in the court of justice." He said: "I have appointed al-Rabīʿ." [Ibn ʿImrān] said: "Call upon ʿĪsá b. ʿAlī[137] and al-ʿAbbās b. Muḥammad[138] as witnesses for your appointment of him." [This] he did. Then [Ibn ʿImrān] established the borders of the house which they were challenging his rights to, and he summoned al-Rabīʿ and his adversaries. [Al-Rabīʿ] produced [al-Manṣūr's] document for the appoinment of a representative and he acted accordingly. Then [Ibn ʿImrān] asked the people about their claim and about their witnesses. Eventually, he passed judgement in favour of them against him.

§ 70 In Medina, the cameleers also appealed for assistance against al-Manṣūr. The judge Muḥammad b. ʿImrān said to al-Šiblī:[139] "Write to him on that." But he refused that, saying: "Excuse me [from this task]." But [Ibn ʿImrān] said: "You have to write!" So he wrote. When the letter was completed

139 This al-Šiblī remains to date unidentified; in Wakīʿ's version of this report, however, the scribe (and transmitter of this story) is identified differently, as one Numayr al-Šaybānī, who explains the wider context of this event: "I was a scribe for Muḥammad b. ʿImrān while he was occupying the post of *qāḍī* in Medina. [One day] Abū Ǧaʿfar performed the pilgrimage, and he wanted to take away the carriers [*al-ḥammālīn*, as opposed to *al-ǧammālīn* in Maqrīzī's text] to Syria. They appealed to Muḥammad b. ʿImrān for assistance against him…" (Wakīʿ, *Aḫbār al-quḍāt*, 1:193). There is thus a likely possibility that the *nisbah* al-Šaybānī was corrupted to al-Šiblī in the transmission process of this story.

"لا يمضي به سواك." فمضى ووافى إلى باب المنصور وسلم الكتاب إلى الربيع فأوصله إلى المنصور، فقرأه. وعاد الشبلي إلى محمد بن عمران، فعرفه أنه سلم ما كتب إلى الربيع، فأوصله، فقرأه المنصور، وأجاب إلى الحضور. ثم خرج المنصور مؤتزرا ببردة، مرتديا بأخرى، ومشى إلى أن قارب مجلس محمد بن عمران، ووقعت عينه عليه—والربيع بين يديه—فقال له: "يا ربيع، نُفِيت عن العباس.
٥ لئن تحرك محمد بن عمران من مجلسه هيبة لي، لأولى ولاية أبدا." ثم صار إلى محمد بن عمران. فلما رأى المنصور—وكان متكئًا—أطلق رداءه على عاتقه، ثم اجْتَبَى ودعا بالخصوم، فحكم لهم عليه وأمره بإنصافهم، وانصرف أبو جعفر. وأمر الربيع بإحضار محمد بن عمران. فلما دخل عليه، قال له: "يابن عمران، جزاك الله عن دينك وعن نبيك وعن حسبك وعن خليفتك أحسن الجزاء." وأمر له بعشرة آلاف درهم.[٣٥]

---

٣ ومشى: "ومشي" في الأصل. ٥ لئن: "لين" في الأصل. ٦ رأى: "رأي" في الأصل. || متكئًا: "متكيا" في الأصل. || رداءه: "رداه" في الأصل. ٨ الجزاء: "الجزآ" في الأصل.

---

[٣٥] راجع هذا الخبر، على شكل مختلف تماما، في وكيع، أخبار القضاة، ج. ١، ص. ١٩٣.

and he had sealed it, [Ibn ʿImrān] said to him: "There is no one but you who should deliver it." So he went, arrived at the gate of al-Manṣūr and handed the letter to al-Rabīʿ. He brought it to al-Manṣūr, who read it. Al-Šiblī returned to Muḥammad b. ʿImrān, and he informed him that he had delivered what had been written to al-Rabīʿ, who had brought it, and that al-Manṣūr had read it and had agreed to appear. Thereafter, al-Manṣūr left [for Ibn ʿImrān], wrapping a shawl against the cold over the other one he was already wearing. He walked until he approached the court of Muḥammad b. ʿImrān and he caught sight of it, while al-Rabīʿ was in front of him. He said to him: "O, al-Rabīʿ, I have been excluded from [the lineage of] al-ʿAbbās, because if Muḥammad b. ʿImrān had left from his court out of respect for me, I would have been entrusted with sovereignty for ever." Then he came to Muḥammad b. ʿImrān. When [Muḥammad] noticed al-Manṣūr taking a seat, he took off his cloak. Then he selected [the witnesses], he called for the opponents, and he passed judgement in favour of them against him. [Ibn ʿImrān] ordered him to see that justice is done to them, and Abū Ǧaʿfar [al-Manṣūr] left. He ordered al-Rabīʿ to summon Muḥammad b. ʿImrān. When he came to him, he said to him: "O, Ibn ʿImrān, may God award you the best possible reward for your religion, your prophet, your noble descent, and your caliph." He ordered [to pay] him 10,000 *dirhams*.

121b

المهدي

أبو عبد الله محمد بن أبي جعفر عبد الله بن محمد المنصور، أمير المؤمنين.

ولي بعد وفاة أبيه بعهده إليه، فقام في الخلافة عشر سنين {وتسعة} وأربعين يوما.

وحج في سنة ستين ومائة، واستخلف ببغداد ابنه موسى، ومعه خاله يزيد بن منصور. وحج معه ابنه
٥ هرون بن محمد في جماعة من أهله.

فلما قدم مكة، نزع الكسوة عن الكعبة عندما رفع إليه سدنة البيت أنهم يخافون على الكعبة أن تنهدم لكثرة ما عليها من الكسوة. فوجد كسوة هشام بن عبد الملك من الديباج الثخين، وكانت

٢ الله١ : تصحيح في الأصل بخط المقريزي. ٣ وتسعة : "وتسعا" في الأصل. ٤ ومائة : "ومايه" في الأصل. || وحج : تصحيح في الأصل بخط المقريزي.

11. Al-Mahdī

Abū ʿAbd Allāh Muḥammad b. Abī Ǧaʿfar ʿAbd Allāh b. Muḥammad al-Manṣūr, Commander of the Faithful.

§ 71 He was appointed after the demise of his father, by his designation of
5 him. He performed the office of caliph for ten years and forty-nine days.

§ 72 He went on pilgrimage in the year 160 [777]. He appointed his son Mūsá[140] as his representative in Baghdad, while his uncle Yazīd b. Manṣūr[141] remained with him. His son Hārūn b. Muḥammad[142] went on pilgrimage with him, in a group of his folk.[143]

10 § 73 When he arrived in Mecca, he removed the *kiswah*[144] from the Kaʿbah. This was because the custodians of the [sacred] house raised the issue before him that they feared that the Kaʿbah would be damaged due to the great number of *kiswah* covers that were on it. The *kiswah* of Hišām b. ʿAbd al-Malik, made from thick brocade, was found: the *kiswah* was not annually

---

140 Mūsá b. al-Mahdī succeeded his father in 169/785 as the fourth ʿAbbāsid caliph al-Hādī; this succession was however contested, especially by his brother Hārūn, a conflict which was resolved by the sudden death of Mūsá l-Hādī in 170/786, an event in which according to some Hārūn's mother had a hand (D. Sourdel, "al-Hādī Ilā ʾl-Ḥaḳḳ", in *EI*² http://referenceworks.brillonline.com/entries/encyclopaedia-of-islam-2/al-hadi-ila-l-hakk-SIM_2587).

141 Yazīd b. Manṣūr (d. 163/779–780) was the brother of Arwá, wife of the caliph al-Manṣūr and mother of the caliph al-Mahdī; he came from Yemen, acted at one point as ʿAbbāsid governor of Yemen, and also became a respected member of al-Mahdī's court (see al-Ṭabarī, *History XXIX*, p. 62, fn. 163).

142 Hārūn b. al-Mahdī succeeded his brother al-Hādī in 170/786 as the fifth ʿAbbāsid caliph al-Rašīd; his long, successful, and eventful reign until 193/809 marked an important stage in early ʿAbbāsid history (F. Omar, "Hārūn al-Ras̲h̲īd", in *EI*² http://referenceworks.brillonline.com/entries/encyclopaedia-of-islam-2/harun-al-rashid-SIM_2747).

143 For the translation of a parallel, slightly more detailed, version of this fragment in al-Ṭabarī's *History*, see al-Ṭabarī, *History XXIX*, 193–194; there remains some ambiguity on Yazīd's role, rendered by Kennedy's translation of al-Ṭabarī's report as follows: "with him [= al-Mahdī] left Yazīd b. Manṣūr, the maternal uncle of al-Mahdī, as his vizier and administrator of his affairs" (194).

144 The *kiswah* is the richly decorated veil that covers the four walls of the Kaʿbah in Mecca; until today, the privilege of providing the *kiswah* is considered a powerful political symbol of islamic sovereignty (see Wensinck & Jomier, "Kaʿbah"; Mortel [1988]).

الكسوة لا تنزع عن الكعبة في كل سنة كما هو العمل الآن، بل تلبس كل سنة كسوة فوق تلك الكسوة. فلما تكاثر العهد وكثر ذلك خافت السدنة على الأركان أن تنهدم لثقل ما صار عليها من الكسوة—وكانت كسوة الكعبة تعمل من الديباج المذهب.[٣٦]

وأنفق المهدي في هذه الحجة مالا عظيما قدم به معه من العراق مبلغ ثلثين ألف ألف درهم سوى ٥ ما وصل إليه من مصر—وهو مبلغ ثلثمائة ألف دينار عينا—ومن اليمن مبلغ مائتي ألف دينار عينا. فرق ذلك كله، ومعه مائة ألف وخمسون ألف ثوب.[٣٧]

ووسع مسجد رسول الله ﷺ. وأخذ خمسمائة من الأنصار جعلهم حرسا له، وأقطعهم بالعراق الإقطاعات وأجرى عليهم الأرزاق.[٣٨]

وحمل إليه محمد بن سليمن الثلج إلى مكة—وهو أول خليفة حمل إليه الثلج إلى مكة.[٣٩]

١٠ وأمر ببناء القصور بطريق مكة أوسع من القصور التي بناها السفاح، وأمر باتخاذ المصانع في كل منهل منها وتجديد الأميال وحفر الركايا.

٥ مائتي: "مايتي" في الأصل. ٦ مائة: "ماية" في الأصل. ٧ خمسمائة: "خمس ماية" في الأصل.
١٠ ببناء: "ببنآ" في الأصل.

[٣٦] راجع مثل هذا الخبر تقريبا في ابن الأثير، الكامل، ج. ٥، ص. ٢٣٦، وفي الطبري، تاريخ الرسل والملوك، ج. ٣/ ١، ص. ٤٨٣. [٣٧] راجع هذا الخبر على شكل مساو في ابن الأثير، الكامل، ج. ٥، ص. ٢٣٦؛ وراجع أيضا خبرا مساويا في الطبري، تاريخ الرسل والملوك، ج. ٣/ ١، ص. ٤٨٣. [٣٨] راجع نفس الخبر تماما في ابن الأثير، الكامل، ج. ٥، ص. ٢٣٦؛ وراجع هذا الخبر بتفاصيله في الطبري، تاريخ الرسل والملوك، ج. ٣/ ١، ص. ٤٨٣. [٣٩] راجع نفس الخبر تماما في ابن الأثير، الكامل، ج. ٥، ص. ٢٣٦-٢٣٧؛ وراجع أيضا هذا الخبر على شكل مساو في الطبري، تاريخ الرسل والملوك، ج. ٣/ ١، ص. ٤٨٤.

removed from the Kaʿbah, as it is the practice now, but every year a *kiswah* rather was draped over this *kiswah*. When the decades grew in number and that [number of *kiswah*s] increased, the guardians feared that the pillars would collapse from the heaviness of the *kiswah*s that were coming to rest on them. The *kiswah* of the Kaʿbah was made from [very heavy] gilded silk brocade.[145]

§ 74 For this pilgrimage al-Mahdī spent an enormous sum of money, which he brought with him from Iraq, amounting to 30,000,000 *dirham*s, not taking into account what arrived with him from Egypt—an amount of 300,000 *dīnār*s in cash—and from Yemen—an amount of 200,000 *dīnār*s in cash. He distributed all of that. There also came with him 150,000 garments.[146]

§ 75 He extended the mosque of the Messenger of God—may God bless him and grant him salvation. He took 500 from the *Anṣār*[147] and made them guardians for him. He granted them allotments in Iraq and he assigned salaries to them.[148]

§ 76 Muḥammad b. Sulaymān[149] brought ice to him in Mecca; he is the first caliph to have ice brought to him in Mecca.[150]

§ 77 He ordered the construction of palaces along the road to Mecca, more extensive than the palaces which al-Saffāḥ had constructed. He ordered the construction of reservoirs at every watering place along it, the renewal of the milestones, and the digging of watering troughs.[151]

145 For the translation of a variant version of this story, see al-Ṭabarī, *History* XXIX, 194.

146 For the translation of a variant version of this report, see ibid.

147 The *Anṣār* refers here to a particular social group in Medina; the descendants of the original inhabitants of the oasis of Yaṯrib (Medina), known as the *Anṣār* or Helpers because they welcomed the Prophet and his Meccan supporters in 622 in their midst, accepted his leadership, and supported him until his death in 10/632 (W.M. Watt, "al-Anṣār", in *EI*² http://referenceworks.brillonline.com/entries/encyclopaedia-of-islam-2/al-ansar-SIM_0678).

148 For the translation of a more expanded version of this report, see al-Ṭabarī, *History* XXIX, 194.

149 Muḥammad b. Sulaymān b. ʿAlī (d. 173/789–790) was a wealthy and important member of the ʿAbbāsid family who served several terms as governor of Basra and Kufa (see al-Ṭabarī, *History* XXIX, 12, fn. 29).

150 For the translation of this same report, see al-Ṭabarī, *History* XXIX, 195.

151 For the translation of a slightly more expanded version of this report, see al-Ṭabarī, *History* XXIX, 198.

وبعث ابنه موسى الهادي فحج بالناس سنة إحدى وستين.

وأمر في سنة ست وستين ومائة بإقامة البريد بين مكة والمدينة واليمن بغالا وإبلا، ولم يكن هناك بريد قبل ذلك.

وحكى محمد بن عبد الله بن محمد بن علي بن عبد الله بن جعفر بن أبي طالب، قال: "رأيت فيما يرى
٥ النائم—في آخر سلطان بني أمية— كأني دخلت مسجد رسول الله ﷺ، فرفعت رأسي، فرأيت الكتاب الذي بالفُسَيْفسَاء، فإذا فيه: "مما أمر به أمير المؤمنين الوليد بن عبد الملك،" وإذا قائل يقول: "يمحى الكتاب ويُكتب مكانه اسم رجل من بني هاشم يقال له محمد." قلت: "فأنا محمد، فابن من؟"
124a قال: "ابن عبد الله." قلت: | "فأنا ابن عبد الله، فابن من؟" قال: "ابن محمد." قلت: فأنا {ابن} محمد، فابن من؟" قال: "ابن علي." قلت: "فأنا ابن علي، فابن من؟" قال: "ابن عبد الله." قلت: "فأنا ابن
١٠ عبد الله، فابن من؟" قال: "{ابن} عباس." فلو لم يبلغ العباس ما شككت أني صاحب الأمر. فتحدث بها ذلك الزمان ونحن لا نعرف المهدي حتى ولي المهدي، فدخل مسجد رسول الله

١ الهادي: تصحيح في الأصل بخط المقريزي. ٢ ومائة: "وماية" في الأصل. ٤ قال رأيت: ناقصتان في الأصل ومضافتان بخط المقريزي إلى آخر السطر في مكانهما الصحيح في الجملة، مكتوبتان من الأسفل إلى الأعلى. || فيما يرى: تصحيح في الأصل بخط المقريزي. ٥ سلطان: تصحيح في الأصل بخط المقريزي. ٦ بالفُسَيْفسَاء: تصحيح في الأصل بخط المقريزي. || قائل: "قايل" في الأصل. ٨ قلت٢: أضيفت هنا في الأصل جزازتان منفردتان مكتوبتان بخط المقريزي [١٢٢أ-١٢٣ب] ولكنهما في المكان الغلطان في النص حتى يتم نص المهدي (و تتم المخطوطة الأصلية، كما أشارت إليه كلمة الإشارة "فأنا" المضافة تحت نص صفحة ١٢١ب بخط الناسخ) في صفحة ١٢٤أ. || ابن٣: "بن" في الأصل. ٩ ابن٢: الألف من إضافة المقريزي. || ابن٣: الألف من إضافة المقريزي. || ابن١: الألف من إضافة المقريزي. ١٠ ابن٢: "بن" في الأصل. ١١ مسجد: تصحيح في الأصل، مضافة بخط المقريزي في الهامش الأيمن، من الأعلى إلى الأسفل + صح، يشير إليها الرمز ⌐ بعد كلمة "فدخل".

§ 78 He sent his son Mūsá l-Hādī to lead the people on the pilgrimage in the year [1]61 [778].

§ 79 In the year 166 [782–783] he ordered the set up of the *barīd*[152] between Mecca and Medina and Yemen, by mule and by camel. There was no *barīd* there before.

§ 80 Muḥammad b. ʿAbd Allāh b. Muḥammad b. ʿAlī b. ʿAbd Allāh b. Ǧaʿfar b. Abī Ṭālib[153] narrated, saying: "By the end of the rule of the Banū Umayyah, I saw as a sleeper sees [the following vision]: it was as if I was entering the mosque of the Messenger of God—may God bless him and grant him salvation—, and when I raised my head, I saw the writing which is done in mosaic; and behold, there stood in it: '[This] is part of what the Commander of the Faithful al-Walīd b. ʿAbd al-Malik has ordered'. Then there was someone saying: 'The writing should be erased and there should be written instead of it the name of a man from the Banū Hāšim, known as Muḥammad'. I said: 'But I am Muḥammad, but the son of whom?' He said: 'The son of Ibn ʿAbd Allāh'. I said: 'But I am the son of Ibn ʿAbd Allāh, but the son of whom?' He said: 'The son of Muḥammad'. I said: 'But I am the son of Muḥammad, but the son of whom?' He said: 'The son of ʿAlī'. I said: 'But I am the son of ʿAlī, but the son of whom?' He said: 'The son of ʿAbd Allāh'. I said: 'But I am the son of ʿAbd Allāh, but the son of whom?' He said: 'The son of ʿAbbās'. If al-ʿAbbās had not been reached, I would not have doubted that I should be the lord of the command. I spoke about it at that time, while we did not know al-Mahdī until al-Mahdī was appointed. [When that had happened] he entered the mosque of the Messenger of God—may God bless him and

152 The *barīd* is the term used for the postal communication system of routes, relays, riding-mounts, and couriers, that was especially well organised in the early ʿAbbāsid period, connecting the different regions and elites of the realm. See A. Silverstein, "Barīd", in *EI*[3] http://referenceworks.brillonline.com/entries/encyclopaedia-of-islam-3/barid-COM_23475.

153 Muḥammad b. ʿAbd Allāh b. Muḥammad b. ʿAlī b. ʿAbd Allāh b. Ǧaʿfar b. Abī Ṭālib was a descendant of ʿAlī's brother Ǧaʿfar who, indeed, shared identical names for five generations with al-Mahdī (al-Ṭabarī, *History* XXIX, 254, fn. 831).

ﷺ، فرأى اسم الوليد، فقال: "أرى اسم الوليد إلى اليوم." فدعا بكرسي، فألقى في صحن المسجد، وقال: "ما أنا ببارح حتى يمحى ويكتب اسمي مكانه." ففعل ذلك وهو جالس."[٤٠]

وطاف بالبيت مرة ليلا، فسمع أعرابية تقول: "قومي مُقْتِرون، نَبَتْ عنهم العيون، وَفَدَحَتْهم الديون، وعَضَّتْهم السُنون، بادَتْ رجالهم وذهبت أموالهم، وكثرت عيالهم أبناء سبيل وأنضاء ٥ طريق وصية الله ووصية الرسول. فهل من آمر لي بجبّر كلأه الله في نفسه، وخَلَفه في أهله؟" فأمر لها بخمسمائة درهم.[٤١]

١ فرأى: تصحيح في الأصل بخط المقريزي. ٤ أبناء: "أبنآ" في الأصل. ‖ وأنضاء: "وانضآ" في الأصل. ٥ آمر: تصحيح في الأصل بخط المقريزي. ‖ بجبّر: تصحيح في الأصل بخط المقريزي. ‖ كلأه: تصحيح في الأصل بخط المقريزي. ‖ في نفسه: ناقصة في الأصل مضافة بخط المقريزي في آخر السطر بعد كلمة "الله". ‖ وخَلَفه: تصحيح في الأصل بخط المقريزي. ٦ بخمسمائة: "بخمس مایة" في الأصل.

[٤٠] راجع هذا الخبر على نفس الشكل تماما في ابن الأثير، الكامل، ج. ٥، ص. ٢٦٢؛ وراجع أيضا هذا الخبر على شكل مساو في الطبري، تاريخ، ج. ٣/ ١، ص. ٥٣٥. [٤١] راجع هذا الخبر على نفس الشكل تماما في ابن الأثير، الكامل، ج. ٥، ص. ٢٦٢؛ وراجع أيضا هذا الخبر على نفس الشكل في الطبري، تاريخ الرسل والملوك، ج. ٣/ ١، ص. ٥٣٥-٥٣٦.

grant him salvation—, he saw the name of al-Walīd, and said: 'Until today, I see the name of al-Walīd.' He called for a chair, had [it] put in the court of the mosque, and said: 'I will not leave until it is erased and my name is written in its place.' That was done while he was sitting down."[154]

5 § 81 One time, he circumambulated the [sacred] house at night, and he heard a Bedouin woman saying: "My people are living in poor circumstances: eyes look at them with repugnance, debts burden them, the years make them suffer, their men pass away, their wealth dissolves, and their dependents multiply, [becoming] vagabonds and wanderers, as a result of the instruction 10 of God and of the Messenger: is there anyone who can give me advice on a decree of fate [such as this]—may God watch over him and his soul and may He appoint him as his successor over His people?" [Al-Mahdī] ordered to [give her] 500 *dirhams*.[155]

154 For the translation of a slightly more expanded version of this report, narrated on the authority of ʿAlī b. Muḥammad b. Sulaymān al-Nawfalī via his father, see al-Ṭabarī, *History* XXIX, 254–255.

155 For the slightly diverging translation of a similar report, narrated on the authority of Aḥmad b. al-Hayṯam al-Qurašī via ʿAbd Allāh b. Muḥammad b. ʿAṭāʾ, see al-Ṭabarī, *History* XXIX, 255.

هٰرون الرشيد

ابن محمد المهدي بن أبي جعفر المنصور عبد الله بن محمد بن علي بن عبد الله بن عباس رضي الله عنهم.

بويع بالخلافة بعد موت أخيه موسى الهادي في ليلة الجمعة للنصف من ربيع الأول—وقيل لأربع
٥ عشرة خلت منه—سنة سبعين ومائة. فأقام في الخلافة ثلٰثا وعشرين سنة وشهرين وثمانية عشر يوما، يغزو سنة ويحج سنة. فحج تسع حجج، ولم يحج بعده خليفة من بغداد.

فأول ما حج—وهو خليفة—سنة سبعين، وقسم في أهل الحرمين عطاء كثيرا، وقيل إنه غزا أيضا فيها بنفسه.

وحج ثانيا في سنة ثلٰث وسبعين، وأحرم من بغداد.

١٠ وحج بالناس سنة أربع وسبعين، وقسم في الناس مالا كثيرا.

ثم حج في سنة سبع وسبعين، وخرج عليه الوليد بن طَرِيف الشاري—أحد الخوارج من بني تَغْلِب—بنَصيبين، وأخذ أرمينية، وحصر خلاط، وعاث في بلاد الجزيرة. فسير إليه الرشيد يزيد

---

٣ عنهم: تصحيح في الأصل بخط المقريزي. ٥ ومائة: "ومایة" في الأصل. ٧ عطاء: "عطآ" في الأصل.

12. Hārūn al-Rašīd

b. Muḥammad al-Mahdī b. Abī Ǧaʿfar al-Manṣūr ʿAbd Allāh b. Muḥammad b. ʿAlī b. ʿAbd Allāh b. ʿAbbās—may God be pleased with them.

§ 82 The oath of allegiance for the caliphate was sworn [to him] after the death of his brother Mūsá l-Hādī, during the night of Friday, 15 Rabīʿ I—it was said the 16th of it—of the year 170 [14–15 September 786]. He remained in the office of caliph for 23 years, two months and 18 days, carrying out military expeditions in one year and performing the pilgrimage in the other. He went on pilgrimage nine times, and after him there was no other caliph who performed the pilgrimage from Baghdad.

§ 83 The first time he went on pilgrimage when he was a caliph was in the year [1]70 [787]. He distributed a lot of gifts among the people of the two sacred places. It was said that he then also personally led a military expedition.

§ 84 He went on pilgrimage a second time in the year [1]73 [790], entering into *iḥrām* from Baghdad onwards.

§ 85 He led the people on the pilgrimage in the year [1]74 [791], and he distributed a lot of money among the people.

§ 86 Then he went on pilgrimage in the year [1]77 [794]. Al-Walīd b. Ṭarīf al-Šārī, one of the *Ḫāriǧī*s from the Banū Taġlib,[156] rebelled against him in Naṣībīn,[157] taking Armenia, besieging Ḫilāṭ[158] and causing havoc in the

---

156 Al-Walīd b. Ṭarīf al-Taġlibī l-Šaybānī l-Šārī was a famous *Ḫāriǧī* rebel, who successfully confronted Hārūn's agents and armies in 178–179/794–795, until he was defeated and killed; his own verses and elegies for him by his sister Laylá (see also below) have been preserved in collections of Arabic poetry (H. Eisenstein, "Al-Walīd b. Ṭarīf", in *EI*² http://referenceworks.brillonline.com/entries/encyclopaedia-of-islam-2/al-walid-b-tarif-SIM_7849).

157 Naṣībīn was an ancient town in upper Mesopotamia, now known as Nusaybin, in modern Turkey close to the Syrian border (E. Honigmann, C.E. Bosworth, "Naṣībīn", in *EI*² http://referenceworks.brillonline.com/entries/encyclopaedia-of-islam-2/nasibin-SIM_5818).

158 Ḫilāṭ, or Aḫlāṭ, is an Armenian town near Lake Van, on the road between upper Mesopotamia and eastern Armenia (V. Minorsky, "Akhlāṭ", in *EI*² http://referenceworks.brillonline.com/entries/encyclopaedia-of-islam-2/akhlat-COM_0036).

ابن مزيد بن زائدة الشيباني—وهو ابن أخي معْن بن زائدة—على العساكر، فلم يزل يحاربه حتى قتله. وفيه تقول أخته ليلى بنت طريف ترثيه بالأبيات المشهورة التي فيها قولها: [الطويل]

فيا شجر الخابور، ما لك مورقا   كأنك لم تجزع على ابن طريف

الأبيات.[٤٢]

٥ فاعتمر الرشيد في شهر رمضان سنة تسع وسبعين ومائة شكرا لله تعالى على قتل الوليد، وعاد إلى المدينة، فأقام بها إلى وقت الحج. فحج بالناس، ومشى من مكة إلى منى إلى عرفات، وشهد المشاعر كلها ماشيا، ورجع على طريق البصرة.[٤٣] ولا يعرف | من ملوك الدنيا ملك حج ماشيا 124b سوى ملكين: هرقل بن هرقل بن أنتونيش—من أهل صلوقيا—حج من حمص إلى إيليا—التي

١ ابن: الألف من إضافة المقريزي. ٣ ابن: الألف من إضافة المقريزي. ٥ ومائة: "ومابة" في الأصل.

[٤٢] راجع هذا الخبر بتفاصيله في ابن الأثير، الكامل، ج. ٥، ص. ٣٠٢-٣٠٣. [٤٣] راجع هذا الخبر على نفس الشكل تقريبا في ابن الأثير، الكامل، ج. ٥، ص. ٣٠٦، وكذلك في الطبري، تاريخ الرسل والملوك، ج. ٣/ ١، ص. ٦٣٨-٦٣٩.

Jazira region.[159] Al-Rašīd sent Yazīd b. Mazyad b. Zāʾidah al-Šaybānī, the nephew of Maʿn b. Zāʾidah,[160] at the head of the army against him. He continued fighting him until he killed him. His sister, Laylá bt. Ṭarīf, lamented him in famous verses, including the following: [*Ṭawīl* meter]

5 § 87 O elder tree, how green are your leaves!
It is as though you do not mourn for Ibn Ṭarīf.

[and many similar] verses.

§ 88 Al-Rašīd performed the lesser pilgrimage in the month Ramaḍān of the year 179 (November–December 795), thanking God the exalted for the killing 10 of al-Walīd. He returned to Medina and stayed there until the time of the pilgrimage. He led the people on the pilgrimage, he walked from Mecca to Miná to ʿArafah, and he attended on foot all the pilgrimage sites and rites. He returned via the road of Basra.[161] Among the rulers of the world, there is no ruler known to have performed the pilgrimage while walking, except for two: 15 Hercules, son of Hercules, son of Antonius, from the people of Seleucia,[162] who went on pilgrimage from Ḥimṣ[163] to Aelia—which is the [the City of]

159 The Jazira is the name used in Arabic sources to denote the rich and fertile northern part of the area between and beyond the rivers Tigris and Euphrates (M. Canard, "al-Djazīra", in *EI*² http://referenceworks.brillonline.com/entries/encyclopaedia-of-islam-2/al-djazira-SIM_2054).

160 Yazīd b. Mazyad b. Zāʾidah al-Šaybānī and his uncle Maʿn b. Zāʾidah al-Šaybānī (d. 152/769–770) were famous Arab Bedouin chiefs and military commanders who led the tribe of Shaybān and acquired important court positions in the late Umayyad and early ʿAbbāsid periods (H. Kennedy, "Maʿn b. Zāʾida", in *EI*² http://referenceworks.brillonline.com/entries/encyclopaedia-of-islam-2/man-b-zaida-SIM_4899; Kennedy (2001): 103).

161 For the translation of the same report of the 179/795 pilgrimage, in al-Ṭabarī's *History*, see al-Ṭabarī, *History* XXX, 154.

162 This is the standard way for Arabo-Muslim tradition to refer to the Byzantine emperor Heraclius (r. 610–641); on the functionality and meaning of reports of a correspondence between Heraclius and Muḥammad, see Conrad (2002).

163 The ancient town of Ḥimṣ (Homs, Latin: Emesa) in Syria, on the east bank of the Orontes river, has a longstanding history at or near the crossroads of empires, as an important site for early and late antique Christianity, and, since its integration in the early Arabo-Islamic polity in 16/637, as a well-known regional or local center of Muslim government (N. Elisséeff, "Ḥimṣ", in *EI*², http://referenceworks.brillonline.com/entries/encyclopaedia-of-islam-2/Hims-COM_0289).

هي بيت المقدس—ماشيا، ووافاه كتاب رسول الله ﷺ في سفرته هذه يدعوه إلى الإسلام، كما وقع في **الصحيحين** وغيرهما، والملك الثاني هٰرون الرشيد.

وذكر أبو محمد بن حزم في كتاب **جمهرة الأنساب** أن موسى الهادي بن محمد المهدي كان له أم ولد تسمى أمة العزيز تزوجها أخوه هٰرون من بعده، وهي التي كان حَلَف الرشيد لأخيه بالمشي إلى الكعبة أن لا يتزوجها. فلما مات الهادي تزوجها. ومشى راجلا من بغداد إلى مكة—وهو خليفة. فولدت له عليا، وكان أقبح الناس صورة.[٤٤] ٥

ولما دخل الرشيد مكة، كان يطرح له الرمل حول البيت—ومقدار عرضه {ذراعان}—، ويرش بالماء، ويقوم الحرس بينه وبين الناس، وكان يطوف بين المغرب والعشاء ثلٰثة عشر أسبوعا، ولا يطيق ذلك أحد ممن كان معه. وكان إذا سعى شمر إزاره وجعل له ذنبين، فكان يفتن من يراه.

١٠ وكذلك حجت زبيدة—أم جعفر—بنت جعفر بن أبي جعفر، زوج هٰرون الرشيد، ماشية أيضا، وكانت حجة عظيمة غير أن ذكرها ليس من شرط هذا الجزء، فلذلك تركت ذكرها.

٧ له : كشط المقريزي نهاية الكلمة وأثبتها كما هي الآن. ‖ حول : تصحيح في الأصل بخط المؤلف. ‖ ذراعان : "ذراعين" في الأصل، وهو خطأ. ٨ بالماء : "بالمآء" في الأصل. ‖ والعشاء : "والعشآ" في الأصل. ٩ ممن كان : تصحيح في الأصل بخط المقريزي. ‖ فكان : تصحيح في الأصل بخط المؤلف. ١١ الجزء : "الجزو" في الأصل.

[٤٤] راجع هذا الخبر على نفس الشكل تماما في ابن حزم، جمهرة أنساب العرب، ص. ٢٣.

164 The phrase "the two *Ṣaḥīḥ*s" refers to the two most authoritative—compiled by the scholars Muslim and al-Bukhārī—of the six canonic collections of Sunni *Ḥadīṯ*.

the Temple [Jerusalem]—while he was walking. The letter of the Messenger of God—may God bless him and grant him salvation—came to him during this journey of his, calling him to Islam, as that is reported in the two *Ṣaḥīḥ*s and elsewhere;[164] the second ruler is Hārūn al-Rašīd.

5 § 89 Abū Muḥammad Ibn Ḥazm reported in the book *Ǧamharat al-ansāb* [The Collection of Genealogies][165] that Mūsá l-Hādī b. Muḥammad al-Mahdī had a slave concubine known as Amat al-ʿAzīz, whom his brother Hārūn married after him. This is the one for whom al-Rašīd had sworn to his brother to walk to the Kaʿbah or else he could not marry her. So when al-Hādī died, 10 he married her and walked on foot from Baghdad to Mecca, while he was caliph. She gave birth for him to ʿAlī, and by appearance he was the ugliest of [all] people.

§ 90 When al-Rašīd entered Mecca, the dust was removed for him [in a zone of] two cubits wide around the House, water was sprinkled, and a guard was 15 stationed between him and the people. For thirteen weeks in a row he [daily] performed the circumambulation between the evening prayer and the night prayer. No one of those who were with him was able to do that. When he performed the ritual of running, he rolled up his shawl, making two tails from it. He used to charm everyone who saw him.

20 § 91 Zubaydah,[166] the mother of Ǧaʿfar, the daughter of Ǧaʿfar b. Abī Ǧaʿfar, the wife of Hārūn al-Rašīd, equally performed the pilgrimage [in this year], while she too was walking. It was an impressive pilgrimage, although its report does not fit within the parameters of this volume, and therefore, I left out this report.

165 See Ibn Ḥazm, *Ǧamharat ansāb al-ʿArab*, 23. Abū Muḥammad ʿAlī b. Aḥmad b. Saʿīd b. Ḥazm (384–456/994–1064) was an Andalusian poet, historian, jurist, philosopher, and theologian of great renown; his *Ǧamharat al-Ansāb* is a work of Arabic genealogy (R. Arnaldez, "Ibn Ḥazm", in *EI*² http://referenceworks.brillonline.com/entries/encyclopaedia-of-islam-2/ibn-hazm-COM_0325; see also Adang et al. [2012]).

166 Zubaydah bt. Ǧaʿfar (145–210/763–831) was a granddaughter of al-Manṣūr, a niece of Hārūn al-Rašīd, his wife, and the mother of his son and successor Muḥammad al-Amīn; she was remembered for her beauty, intelligence, and generosity, for her patronising of scholars, poets, and musicians, and for her public works, in Mecca in particular; she also became a famous literary figure in Arabic prose and in popular stories (R. Jacobi, "Zubayda bt. Djaʿfar", in *EI*² http://referenceworks.brillonline.com/entries/encyclopaedia-of-islam-2/zubayda-bt-djafar-SIM_8187).

وحج الرشيد أيضا بالناس في سنة إحدى وثمانين ومائة.

وحج في سنة ست وثمانين ومائة من الأنبار ومعه ابناه عبد الله المأمون ومحمد الأمين. فبدأ بالمدينة، فأعطى فيها ثلث أعطية: أعطى هو عطاء وكل من ولديه عطاء، وسار إلى مكة فأعطى أهلها ألف ألف دينار وخمسين ألف دينار، وكان قد ولى الأمين العراق والشام إلى آخر الغرب وجعله ولي ٥ عهده، وضم إلى المأمون من همَذان إلى آخر المشرق وعهد إليه بعد الأمين. ثم بايع لابنه القاسم بولاية العهد بعد المأمون ولقبه المؤتمن وضم إليه الجزيرة والثغور والعواصم. فجمع بمكة القضاة والفقهاء، وكتب كتابا أشهدهم فيه على الأمين بالوفاء للمأمون، وكتب كتابا أشهدهم فيه على المأمون بالوفاء للأمين، وعلق الكتابين بالكعبة.[٤٥] وقد ذكرت خبر ذلك مبسوطا في ترجمة المأمون من **تاريخ مصر الكبير المقفى**. فإنه قدم مصر في سنة سبع عشرة ومائتين.[٤٦]

١ ومائة: "ومايه" في الأصل. ٢ وثمانين ومائة: "وثمانن ومايه" في الأصل. ٣ عطاء: "عطآ" في الأصل. ‖ عطاء: "عطآ" في الأصل. ٧ والفقهاء: "والفقهآ" في الأصل. ‖ بالوفاء[١]: "بالوفآ" في الأصل. ٨ بالوفاء[٢]: "بالوفآ" في الأصل. ٩ المقفى: "المقفا" في الأصل. ‖ ومائتين: "ومايتين" في الأصل.

[٤٥] راجع هذا الخبر على شكل مساو في ابن الأثير، الكامل، ج. ٥، ص. ٣٢٥-٣٢٦؛ راجع هذا الخبر بتفاصيله في الطبري، تاريخ الرسل والملوك، ج. ٣/ ٢، ص. ٦٥١-٦٦٧. [٤٦] ترجمة المأمون مفقودة في المخطوطات المعروف وجودها لكتاب المقفى للمقريزي. راجع المقفى، ج. ٨.

167 Al-Anbār was an ancient strategic town on the left bank of the Euphrates, some 60 kilometers west from Baghdad; it had strong connections with the early ʿAbbāsid caliphs, who regularly resided there (M. Streck, A.A. Duri, "al-Anbār", in *EI*[2] http://referenceworks.brillonline.com/entries/encyclopaedia-of-islam-2/al-anbar-SIM_0659).

§ 92 Al-Rašīd led the people on the pilgrimage in the year 181 [798].

§ 93 He went on pilgrimage in the year 186 [802] from al-Anbār,[167] and his two sons ʿAbd Allāh al-Maʾmūn[168] and Muḥammad al-Amīn[169] were with him. He began in Medina, presenting there three gifts, one given by himself and one by each of his two sons. He went to Mecca and presented to its people 1,050,000 *dīnār*s. He had already appointed al-Amīn over Iraq and Syria, until the far end of the West, and he had made him his heir apparent; he had brought together [the region] from Hamadān until the far end of the East for al-Maʾmūn [to rule], and he had made him his heir after al-Amīn; then he had pledged allegiance to his son al-Qāsim[170] as heir apparent after al-Maʾmūn, giving him the title of al-Muʾtaman, and he had brought together for him [to rule] the Jazira and the Anatolian frontier zone. In Mecca, he gathered the judges and the jurisprudents, and he wrote a letter in which he confirmed their witnessing for al-Amīn the pledge to al-Maʾmūn, and he wrote a letter in which he confirmed their witnessing for al-Maʾmūn the pledge to al-Amīn, and he had the two letters hung up in the Kaʿbah. I have extensively reported the story of that in the biography of al-Maʾmūn in the *Tārīḫ Miṣr al-kabīr al-muqaffá* [The Great History of Egypt in Continuation], because he came to Egypt in the year 217 [832].[171]

168 ʿAbd Allāh al-Maʾmūn succeeded his brother Muḥammad al-Amīn, after several years of internecine warfare, as seventh ʿAbbāsid caliph in the period 196–198/812–813; begun in difficult circumstances, al-Maʾmūn's caliphate was eventually succesful in regaining control over most of, and then pacifying, his father's empire; he reigned until his death in 218/833 (M. Rekaya, "al-Maʾmūn", in *EI*² http://referenceworks.brillonline.com/entries/encyclopaedia-of-islam-2/al-mamun-SIM_4889).

169 Muḥammad al-Amīn succeeded his father Hārūn al-Rašīd as ʿAbbāsid caliph in 193/809, but he was ousted from the caliphate by his brother ʿAbd Allāh; he was executed by his brother's agents in 198/813 (M. Cooperson, "al-Amīn, Muḥammad", in *EI*³ http://referenceworks.brillonline.com/entries/encyclopaedia-of-islam-3/al-amin-muhammad-COM_22995).

170 Al-Qāsim al-Muʾtaman (d. 208/823) was another son and third designated heir of Hārūn al-Rašīd, but he never succeeded to the caliphate (see Rekaya, "al-Maʾmūn"; al-Ṭabarī, *History XXX*, xx, 181, 327).

171 The meaning of this passage is that it was a result of this Egyptian connection that al-Maʾmūn's biography was recorded in this "Egyptian" biographical dictionary (al-Maqrīzī, *al-Muqaffá* [but the entry for al-Maʾmūn does not seem to have survived]).

وفي عود الرشيد من هذه الحجة نكب البرامكة النكبة المشهورة بالأنبار سلخ المحرم سنة سبع | وثمانين 125a
ومائة.

ثم حج الرشيد في سنة ثمان وثمانين راجلا، وقسم أموالا كثيرة، وهي آخر حجة حجها.[٤٧]

وكان إذا حج حج معه مائة من الفقهاء وأبنائهم. فإذا لم يحج أحج ثلثمائة رجل بالنفقة السابغة
٥ والكسوة الظاهرة. ولم ير خليفة قبله أكثر عطاء منه، ويقال: "لو قيل للدنيا: متى أيام شبابك،
لقالت: أيام هرون الرشيد." | 123b

ومن فضائل الرشيد ما أخرجه الحافظ أبو نعيم في **كتاب الحلية**:[٤٨] ثنا سليمن بن أحمد—يعني

١–٢ وثمانين ومائة: "وثمانين وماية" في الأصل. ٤ مائة: "ماية" في الأصل. ‖ الفقهاء: "الفقهآ" في الأصل. ٥ عطاء: "عطا" في الأصل. ٦ الرشيد: بقية نص هارون الرشيد ناقصة في الأصل ومضافة على جزازتين منفردتين مكتوبتين بخط المقريزي ومضافتين في هذه المخطوطة في المكان الغلطان في النص (ص. ١٢٢ و١٢٣)، وفي الترتيب الغلطان (الترتيب الصحيح هو ١٢٣ب-١٢٣أ-١٢٢ب-١٢٢أ)؛ يشير إليها الرمز ⌝ بعد كلمة "الرشيد". ٧ فضائل: "فضايل" في الأصل.

[٤٧] راجع هذا الخبر على نفس الشكل تقريبا في ابن الأثير، الكامل، ج. ٥، ص. ٣٣٧؛ وراجع أيضا خبرا مساويا في الطبري، تاريخ الرسل والملوك، ج. ٣/ ٢، ص. ٧٠١. [٤٨] راجع الحاشيتين ٥٠ و٥١.

§ 94 On the return of al-Rašīd from this pilgrimage, the Barmakids[172] were afflicted by their famous calamity at al-Anbār, towards the end of Muḥarram of the year 187 [January 803].

§ 95 Thereafter al-Rašīd performed the pilgrimage in the year [1]88 [804], on foot and distributing great wealth. It is the last pilgrimage that he performed.

§ 96 It used to be so that if he performed the pilgrimage, 100 from the jurisprudents and their sons would perform the pilgrimage with him; and if he did not perform the pilgrimage, he would make 300 men perform the pilgrimage, [bringing along as always] the full charitable gift and the external *kiswah*. There was no caliph before him who was known to have given more than he did. It is said: "if it were said to the material world: 'When were the days of your youth?', it would reply: '[In] the days of Hārūn al-Rašīd.'"

§ 97 Among the qualities of al-Rašīd, there was what the great transmitter Abū Nuʿaym selected in the book *al-Ḥilyah* [The Ornament].[173] There was transmitted to us by Sulaymān b. Aḥmad—that is, al-Ṭabarānī[174]—, via

172 The Barmakids were a powerful and influential family of non-Arab origins, supplying viziers, administrators, and advisors to the courts of the first ʿAbbāsid caliphs, until their leading members were suddenly removed from power in 187/803; this sudden fall of the Barmakids has become a powerful trope for the fickleness and transient nature of power and authority (K. van Bladel, "Barmakids", in *EI*³ http://referenceworks.brillonline.com/entries/encyclopaedia-of-islam-3/barmakids-COM_24302).

173 See Abū Nuʿaym, *Ḥilyat al-awliyāʾ*, 8:105–108. Abū Nuʿaym Aḥmad al-Iṣfahānī (336–430/948–1038) was a religious scholar and traditionist from Isfahan, who is best known as the author of this *Ḥilyat al-awliyāʾ*, a biographical encyclopaedia of individuals from the earliest days of Islam onwards, who, at least according to the author, were to be regarded as ascetics and mystics (J. Chabbi, "Abū Nuʿaym al-Iṣfahānī", in *EI*³ http://referenceworks.brillonline.com/entries/encyclopaedia-of-islam-3/abu-nuaym-al-isfahani-COM_23648).

174 Abū l-Qāsim Sulaymān b. Ayyūb b. Muṭayyir al-Laḫmī l-Ṭabarānī (260–360/873–971) was one of the most important traditionists of his age; after many years of travelling in search for knowledge, he spent most of his life in Isfahan, where Abū Nuʿaym was one of his many students (M. Fierro, "al-Ṭabarānī", in *EI*² http://referenceworks.brillonline.com/entries/encyclopaedia-of-islam-2/al-tabarani-SIM_7246).

الطبراني، نا محمد بن زكرياء الغلابي، نا الغلابي، نا أبو عمر الجرمي النحوي، نا الفَضْل بن الربيع، قال:

"حج أمير المؤمنين—يعني هٰرون الرشيد—فأتاني، فخرجت مُسْرعا، فقلت: "يٰأمير المؤمنين، لو أرسلت إليّ أتيتك." فقال: "ويحك! قد حاك في نفسي شيء، فانظر لي رجلا أسأله." فقلت: "هاهنا سفيٰن بن عيينة." فقال: "إمض بنا إليه." فأتيناه، فقرعت الباب، فقال: "من ذا؟" قلت: "أجب أمير المؤمنين!" فخرج مسرعا، فقال: "يٰأمير المؤمنين، لو أرسلت إلي أتيتك." فقال له: "خذ لما جئناك له رحمك الله." فحدثه ساعة، ثم قال له: "عليك دين؟" قال: "نعم." قال: "أبا عباس، إقض دينه."

فلما خرجنا قال: "ما أغنى عني صاحبك شيئا. أنظر لي رجلا أسأله." قلت: "هاهنا عبد الرزاق بن همام." قال: "إمض بنا إليه." فأتيناه، فقرعت الباب، فقال: "من هذا؟" قلت: "أجب أمير المؤمنين!"

---

٤ شيء: "شي" في الأصل. ٦ جئناك: "جيناك" في الأصل. ٨ شيئا: "شيا" في الأصل.

Muḥammad b. Zakariyyāʾ al-Ġallābī,[175] via al-Ġallābī, via Abū ʿUmar al-Ǧarmī the Grammarian,[176] from al-Faḍl b. al-Rabīʿ,[177] who said:

§ 98 "The Commander of the Faithful—that is, Hārūn al-Rašīd—performed the pilgrimage, and he came to me. I quickly went out and said: 'O Commander of the Faithful, if you had sent me [word], I would have come to you.' He said: 'Woe onto you. Something has come up in my mind. Look for me for a man whom I may question.' So I said: 'Sufyān b. ʿUyaynah[178] [lives] over there.' So he said: 'Let us go to him.' So we came to him, and I knocked at the door. He said: 'Who is it?' I said: 'Accede to the request of the Commander of the Faithful.' So he quickly came out and said: 'O Commander of the Faithful, if you had sent me [word], I would have come to you.' He said to him: 'Behold what we have come to you for, may God's mercy be upon you.' He spoke with him for an hour. Then he said to him: 'Do you have a debt?' He said: 'Yes.' He said: 'Abū ʿAbbās, settle his debt.'

§ 99 When we left, he said: 'Your friend has not been of any benefit to me; look for me for a man whom I may question.' I said: "Abd al-Razzāq b. Hammām[179] [lives] over there.' He said: 'Let us go to him.' So we came to him, and I knocked at the door. He said: 'Who is this?' I said: 'Accede to the request of the Commander of the Faithful.' So he quickly came out and said: 'O

175 Muḥammad b. Zakariyyāʾ b. Dīnār al-Ġallābī (d. 298/910) was a traditionist and historian from Basra (al-Ziriklī [2002], 6:130).

176 Abū ʿUmar al-Ǧarmī was a scholar from Basra, especially known as a key figure in the early grammatical tradition (see Bernards [1990]).

177 Al-Faḍl b. al-Rabīʿ (138–208/757–824) was the son of al-Manṣūr's chamberlain al-Rabīʿ b. Yūnus (see above, fn. 130); just as his father, he was a person of status and influence at the early ʿAbbāsid court, and he served as vizier to the caliphs Hārūn al-Rašīd and al-Amīn (D. Sourdel, "al-Faḍl b. al-Rabīʿ", in *EI*[2] http://referenceworks.brillonline.com/entries/encyclopaedia-of-islam-2/al-Fadl-b-al-rabi-SIM_2227).

178 Sufyān b. ʿUyaynah b. Maymūn al-Hilālī (107–196/725–811) was a famous traditionist who lived and studied for most of his life in Mecca (S.A. Spectorsky, "Sufyān b. ʿUyayna", in *EI*[2] http://referenceworks.brillonline.com/entries/encyclopaedia-of-islam-2/sufyan-b-uyayna-SIM_7131).

179 ʿAbd al-Razzāq b. Hammām b. Nāfiʿ al-Ṣanʿānī l-Ḥimyarī (126–211/744–827) was a leading Yemeni scholar and specialist of *ḥadīṯ* and history (H. Motzki, "al-Ṣanʿānī", in *EI*[2] http://referenceworks.brillonline.com/entries/encyclopaedia-of-islam-2/al-sanani-SIM_6597).

فخرج مسرعا، فقال: "يأمير المؤمنين، لو أرسلت إلي أتيتك." فقال: "خذ لما جئناك له." فحادثه ساعة ثم قال له: "عليك دين؟" قال: "نعم." قال: "أبا عباس، إقض دينه."

فلما خرجنا قال: "ما أغنى عني صاحبك شيئا. أنظر لي رجلا أسأله." قلت: "هاهنا الفضيل بن عياض." قال: "إمض بنا إليه." فأتيناه، فإذا هو قائم يصلى، يتلو آية من القرآن يرددها. فقال:
٥ "إقرع الباب!" فقرعت الباب، فقال: "من هذا؟" قلت: "أجب أمير المؤمنين!" فقال: "ما لي ولأمير المؤمنين؟" فقلت: سبحٰن الله، أما عليك طاعة؟ أليس قد روي عن النبي ﷺ أنه قال: "ليس للمؤمن أن يذل نفسه؟" فنزل ففتح الباب. ثم ارتقى الغرفة فأطفأ السراج. ثم التجأ إلى زاوية من زوايا البيت. فدخلنا، فجعلنا نجول عليه بأيدينا. فسبقت كف هٰرون قبلي إليه، فقال: "يا لها من كف! ما ألينها إن نجت غدا من | عذاب الله عز وجل." فقلت في نفسي: ليكلمنه الليلة بكلام من قلب تقي. 123a
١٠ فقال له: "خذ لما جئناك له رحمك الله." فقال: "إن عمر بن عبد العزيز لما ولي الخلافة دعا سالم بن عبد الله ومحمد بن كعب القرظي ورجاء بن حَيْوَة، فقال لهم: "إني قد ابتليت بهذا البلاء. فأشيروا

١ جئناك : "جيناك" في الأصل. ٣ شيئا : "شيا" في الأصل. ١٠ جئناك : "جيناك" في الأصل.
١١ ورجاء : "رجا" في الأصل. ‖ البلاء : "البلا" في الأصل.

180 Al-Fuḍayl b. ʿIyāḍ al-Tamīmī l-Yarbūʿī (d. 187/803) was a leading religious scholar and transmitter of *ḥadīṯ*; he lived and worked in Kufa and then in Mecca, where he acquired a reputation as an exemplary ascetic; he appears in various bigraphical anecdotes—such as those preserved in the *Ḥilyah*—demonstrating his superiority and authority

Commander of the Faithful, if you had sent me [word], I would have come to you.' He said: 'Behold what we have come to you for.' So he talked with him for an hour. Then he said to him: 'Do you have a debt?' He said: 'Yes.' He said: 'Abū 'Abbās, settle his debt.'

5 §100 When we left, he said: 'Your friend has not been of any benefit to me; look for me for a man whom I may question.' I said: 'Al-Fuḍayl b. 'Iyāḍ[180] [lives] over there.' He said: 'Let us go to him.' So we came to him. But he was just beginning his prayer, reciting a verse from the Qur'ān which he repeated all the time. [Al-Rašīd] said: 'Knock at the door.' So I knocked at the 10 door. He said: 'Who is this?' I said: 'Accede to the request of the Commander of the Faithful.' He said: 'What is my business with the Commander of the Faithful?' I said: 'Praise God! Do you not owe allegiance? Is it not transmitted about the Prophet—may God bless him—that he said: It is not up to the believer to submit himself [to a trial]?' So he came down and opened the 15 door. Then he ascended to the room [which he had been praying in], put out the lamp, and then he resorted to one of the corners of the house. We entered and we tried to [follow him by] laying our hands on him, Harūn's hand palm preceding mine [in our movement] towards him. He said: 'What kind of a hand palm is this? How can I soften it so that it may be rescued 20 tomorrow from the punishment of God, may He be great and exalted.' I said to myself: '[I hope] that he may speak with him overnight with words from a devout heart.' [Harūn] said to him: 'Behold what we have come to you for, may God's mercy be upon you.' He said: 'When 'Umar b. 'Abd al-'Azīz[181] performed the office of caliph, he called for Sālim b. 'Abd Allāh,[182] 25 Muḥammad b. Ka'b al-Quraẓī,[183] and Raǧā' b. Ḥaywah.[184] He said to them: I have been afflicted by this tribulation, so give me advice—he considered

over Hārūn al-Rašīd (D. Tor, "al-Fuḍayl b. 'Iyāḍ", in *EI*³ http://referenceworks.brillonline.com/entries/encyclopaedia-of-islam-3/al-fudayl-b-iyad-COM_27202).

181 'Umar b. 'Abd al-'Azīz was Umayyad caliph between 99/717 and 101/720 [see fn. 91].

182 This may well refer to a grandson of the second caliph 'Umar, Sālim b. 'Abd Allāh b. 'Umar b. al-Ḫaṭṭāb (d. 107/725–726) (Ḫalīfah b. Ḫayyāṭ, *al-Ṭabaqāt*, 427 [n° 2113]; al-Maqrīzī, *al-Ḏahab al-masbūk*⁴, 119, fn. 7).

183 This may well refer to Muḥammad b. Ka'b al-Quraẓī (d. 117/735) (Ḫalīfah b. Ḫayyāṭ, *al-Ṭabaqāt*, 459 (n° 2344); al-Maqrīzī, *al-Ḏahab al-masbūk*⁴, 119, fn. 8).

184 Raǧā' b. Ḥaywah b. Ḫanzal al-Kindī (d. 112/730) was an influential advisor at the courts of the Umayyad caliphs 'Abd al-Malik, al-Walīd, Sulaymān, and 'Umar [see footnote 97].

علي، فعد الخلافة بلاء، وعدد‌تها أنت وأصحابك نعمة." فقال له سالم بن عبد الله: "إن أردت النجاة من عذاب الله فصم الدنيا وليكن إفطارك منها الموت." وقال له محمد بن كعب: "إن أردت النجاة من عذاب الله فليكن كبير المسلمين عندك أبا وأوسطهم عندك أخا وأصغرهم عندك ولدا. فوقر أباك وأكرم أخاك وتحنن على ولدك." وقال له رجاء بن حيوة: "إن أردت النجاة من عذاب الله فأحب للمسلمين ما تحب لنفسك وأكره لهم ما تكره لنفسك. ثم مت إذا شئت." وإني أقول لك: فإني أخاف عليك أشد الخوف يوم تزل فيه الأقدام. فهل معك رحمك الله مثل هذا أو من يشير عليك بمثل هذا؟"

فبكى هٰرون بكاء شديدا حتى غشي عليه. فقلت له: "إرفق بأمير المؤمنين!" قال: "يٰابن أم الربيع، تقتله أنت وأصحابك وأرفق به أنا؟" ثم أفاق فقال له: "زدني رحمك الله." فقال: "يٰأمير المؤمنين، بلغني أن عاملا لعمر بن عبد العزيز شكا إليه، فكتب إليه عمر: يٰابن أخي، أذكرك طول سهَرِ أهل النار في النار مع خلود الأبد، وإياك أن ينصرف بك من عند الله إلى عذاب الله، فيكون آخر العهد وانقطاع الرجاء." فلما قرأ الكتاب طوى البلاد حتى قدم على عمر بن عبد العزيز، فقال له: "ما أقدمك؟" فقال: "خلعت قلبي بكتابك. لا أعود إلى ولاية حتى ألقى الله"."

فبكى هٰرون بكاء شديدا، ثم قال له: "زدني رحمك الله." فقال: "يٰأمير المؤمنين، إن العباس— عم المصطفى ﷺ—قال: "يٰرسول الله، أمِرْني على إمارة." فقال له النبي ﷺ: "إن الإمارة حسرة وندامة يوم القيامة. فإن استطعت أن لا تكون أميرا فافعل"."

---

١ بلاء: "بلاً" في الأصل. ٣ عندك²: تصحيح بخط المقريزي في الأصل. ٤ رجاء: "رجا" في الأصل.
٥ شئت: "شيت" في الأصل. ٨ فبكى: "فبكي" في الأصل. ‖ بكاء: "بكا" في الأصل. ١٠ شكا: "شكى" في الأصل. ١٢ الرجاء: "الرجا" في الأصل. ‖ له: تصحيح بخط المقريزي في الأصل. ١٣ ألقى: "القا" في الأصل. ١٤ بكاء: "بكا" في الأصل. ١٥ أمِرْني: "امرْني" في الأصل.

the caliphate a tribulation and you and your companions consider it a gift. Sālim b. ʿAbd Allāh said to him: If you want to be rescued from the punishment of God, abstain from this world so that death may be as your fast-breaking. Muḥammad b. Kaʿb said to him: If you want to be rescued from the punishment of God, make the elder of the Muslims like a father with you, the intermediate of them like a brother with you, and the junior of them like a son with you; respect your father, honour your brother, and feel compassion for your son. Raǧāʾ b. Ḥaywah said to him: If you want to be rescued from the punishment of God, love for the Muslims what you love for yourself and dislike for them what you dislike for yourself, and then die if you want. Now I [= al-Fuḍayl] say to you [= Hārūn] that I greatly dread for you the day on which the feet will slip; is there with you—may God's mercy be upon you—anyone like this or who advises you anything like this?'

§ 101 Hārūn wept heavily until he lost consciousness. I said to him: 'Be kind to the Commander of the Faithful'. He said: 'O son of the mother of al-Rabīʿ, you and your companions will kill him and I should be kind to him?' Then [Hārūn] regained consciousness. He said to him: 'Give me more, may God's mercy be upon you.' He said: 'O Commander of the Faithful, I was informed that an agent of ʿUmar b. ʿAbd al-ʿAzīz complained to him, so ʿUmar wrote to him: O my nephew, let me remind you of the people of the fire [= the unbelievers] who have to stay awake in the fire for as long as the infinity of time; be careful that you are not made to move away from [being] with God to [undergoing] God's punishment, for that is the end of time and the cutting off of hope. When he read the letter, he traversed the lands to come to ʿUmar b. ʿAbd al-ʿAzīz. He said to him: What has made you come? He said: My heart is wrenched by your letter; I will not return to a governorship until I have met with God.'

§ 102 Hārūn wept heavily. Then he said to him: 'Give me more, may God's mercy be upon you.' He said: 'O Commander of the Faithful, al-ʿAbbās, the uncle of the chosen one—may God bless him and grant him salvation—said to the Messenger of God: Appoint me to a command. But the Prophet—may God bless him and grant him salvation—said to him: The command is the grief and regret of the Day of Resurrection; if you can manage not to be a commander, then do so.'

فبكى هرون بكاء شديدا، وقال: "زدني رحمك الله." | قال: "يا حسن الوجه، أنت الذي يسألك الله 122b
عز وجل عن هذا الخلق يوم القيامة. فإن استطعت أن تقي هذا الوجه من النار فإياك أن تصبح
وتمسي وفي قلبك غش لأحد من رعيتك. فإن النبي ﷺ قال: "من أصبح لهم غاشا لم يرح رائحة
الجنة"."

٥ فبكى هرون وقال له: "عليك دين؟" قال: "نعم، دين لربي لم يحاسبني عليه. فالويل لي إن ساءلني،
والويل لي إن ناقشني، والويل لي إن لم ألهم حجتي." قال: "إنما أعني من دين العباد." قال: "إن ربي
عز وجل لم يأمرني بهذا. إنما أمرني أن أصدق وأطيع أمره." فقال: ﴿وَمَا خَلَقْتُ ٱلْجِنَّ وَٱلْإِنْسَ
إِلَّا لِيَعْبُدُونِ. مَآ أُرِيدُ مِنْهُم مِّن رِّزْقٍ وَمَآ أُرِيدُ أَن يُطْعِمُونِ. إِنَّ ٱللَّهَ هُوَ ٱلرَّزَّاقُ ذُو ٱلْقُوَّةِ ٱلْمَتِينُ﴾ ."[49]
فقال له: "هذه ألف دينار. خذها فأنفقها على عيالك، وتقو بها على عبادتك." فقال: "سبحٰن الله، أنا
١٠ أدلك على طريق النجاة وأنت تكافيني بمثل هذا؟ سلمك الله ووفقك!" ثم صمت فلم يكلمنا. فخرجنا
من عنده. فلما صرنا على الباب، قال هرون: "أبا عباس، إذا دللتني على رجل، فدلني على مثل
هذا. هذا سيد المسلمين!"

فدخلت عليه امرأة من نسائه، فقالت: "يا هذا، قد ترى ما نحن فيه من ضيق. فلو قبلت هذا المال
فتفرجنا به." فقال لها: "مثلي ومثلكم كمثل قوم كان لهم بعير يأكلون من كسبه. فلما كبر نحروه
١٥ فأكلوا لحمه." فلما سمع هرون هذا الكلام، قال: "ندخل. فعسى أن يقبل المال." فلما علم الفضيل،
خرج فجلس في السطح على باب | الغرفة، فجاء هرون وجلس إلى جنبه، فجعل يكلمه، فلا يجيبه. 122a
فبينا نحن كذلك إذ خرجت جارية سوداء، فقالت: "يا هذا، قد آذيت الشيخ منذ الليلة. فانصرف
رحمك الله." فانصرفنا."[50]

١ بكاء: "بكا" في الأصل. ١٣ نسائه: "نسايه" في الأصل. ١٦ فجاء: "فجآ" في الأصل. ١٧ سوداء:
"سودآ" في الأصل.

[49] القرآن، سورة الذريات، الآيات ٥٦-٥٨. [50] راجع خبر الفضل بن الربيع وهارون الرشيد هذا كله (من
"حدثنا سليمان بن أحمد" إلى هنا) وعلى نفس الشكل تماما في أبو نعيم، الحلية، ج. ٨، ص. ١٠٥-١٠٨.

§ 103 Hārūn wept heavily, and said to him: 'Give me more, may God's mercy be upon you.' He said: 'O beautiful one, you are the one whom God—may He be great and exalted—will ask about this creation on the Day of Resurrection; if you want to protect this [handsome] face against the fire, take care not to have in your heart from morning to evening deception towards anyone from your flock; the Prophet—may God bless him and grant him salvation—said: He who tends to treat them with deception will not smell the fragrance of paradise.'

§ 104 Hārūn wept and said to him: 'Do you have a debt?' He said: 'Yes, a debt to my Lord which He has not yet settled with me. Woe onto me if He asks me, and woe onto me if He discusses with me, and woe onto me if He does not direct my argument with inspiration.' But he said: 'But I mean a debt of the human beings.' He said: 'My Lord—may He be great and exalted—did not command me to such a thing; rather He commanded me to believe and to obey His command, saying: I have not created *ǧinn* and mankind except to serve Me. I desire of them no provision, neither do I desire that they should feed Me. Surely, God is the All-Provider, the Possessor of Strength, the Ever-Sure.'[185] He said to him: 'These are 1,000 *dīnār*s; take them, spend them on your family, and strengthen your worship with it.' He said: 'Praise God! I guide you along the road of deliverance, while you recompense me in this way? May God grant you salvation and may he give you success.' Then he became silent and he did not speak to us. So we left from him. When we reached the door, Hārūn said: 'Abū 'Abbās, when you bring me to a man, bring me to someone like this; this one is the best of the Muslims.'

§ 105 A woman from his wives went to him [= al-Fuḍayl] and said: 'You there, you know the need we are in. If you took this money, we would be relieved by it.' But he said to her: 'Me and you, we are just like people who have a camel [that produces] a surplus which they eat from; but when it grows old, they slaughter it so as to eat its meat.' When Hārūn heard this talk, he said: 'Let us enter; maybe he will accept the money.' When al-Fuḍayl was informed, he came out and sat on the floor at the door of the room. Hārūn came and sat next to him. He began to speak to him, but he did not reply. While we were in the midst of this, a black slave girl suddenly came out and said: 'You there, you have troubled the old man all night, so leave now—may God's mercy be upon you.' So we left."

185 Qur'ān, s. 51: 56–58. Translation from Arberry (1955), 2:239–240.

نا إبرٰهيم بن عبد الله، نا محمد بن إسحٰق، حدثني إسمٰعيل بن عبد الله أبو النضر، نا يحيى بن يوسف الزَمّي عن فضيل بن عياض، قال:

"لما دخل علي هٰرون—أمير المؤمنين—قال: "أيكم هو؟" فأشاروا إلى أمير المؤمنين. فقال: "أنت هو، يا حسن الوجه. لقد كلفت أمرا عظيما. إني ما رأيت أحدا أحسن وجها منك. فإن قدرت أن لا تسود هذا الوجه بلفحة من النار فافعل." فقال لي: "عظني." فقلت: "ماذا أعظك؟ هذا كتاب الله تعالى بين الدفتين. أنظر ماذا عمل بمن أطاعه وماذا عمل بمن عصاه." وقال: "إني رأيت الناس يعرضون على النار عرضا شديدا ويطلبونها طلبا حثيثا. أما والله! لو طلبوا الجنة بمثلها أو أيسر لنالوها!" فقال: "عُد إلي." فقال: "لو لم تبعث إلي لم آتك. وإن انتفعت بما سمعت مني عدت إليك"."[٥١]

---

٣ إلى: "الي" في الأصل.

---

[٥١] راجع خبر فضيل بن عياض وهارون الرشيد على نفس الشكل تماما في أبو نعيم، الحلية، ج. ٨، ص. ١٠٥.

§ 106 There was transmitted to us by Ibrahīm b. ʿAbd Allāh,[186] via Muḥammad b. Isḥāq,[187] via Ismaʿīl b. ʿAbd Allāh Abū l-Naḍr,[188] via Yaḥyá b. Yūsuf al-Zammī,[189] from Fuḍayl b. ʿIyāḍ, who said:

§ 107 "When Hārūn, the Commander of the Faithful, entered to me, he said: 'Which one of you is it? Advise the Commander of the Faithful.' [Fuḍayl] said: 'It is you, O handsome one. You have been entrusted an important command; never have I seen anyone with a face more beautiful than yours. If you are able not to blacken this face with heat from the fire, then do so.' He said to me: 'Caution me.' So I said: 'What should I caution you for? This is the book of God, the Elevated One, between the two covers: look at what happened to who obeyed Him and at what happened to who opposed Him.' He said: 'I saw the people submitting themselves eagerly to the fire and aspiring to it hastily; truly, by God, if they aspired to paradise in a similar or lesser way, they would attain it.' He said: 'Come back to me.' [Fuḍayl] said: 'If you had not sent [word] to me, I would not have come to you, and if you take advantage of what you heard from me, I will come back to you.'"

186 Abū Isḥāq Ibrāhīm b. ʿAbd Allāh b. Muḥammad b. Ḫurrašīḏ Qūlah al-Iṣbahānī was a *ḥadīṯ* transmitter and merchant from Isfahan, who lived and worked in Baghdad, where he died in 400/1009 (al-Ḏahabī, *Siyar*, 17:69–71).

187 Abū l-ʿAbbās al-Sarrāǧ Muḥammad b. Isḥāq b. Ibrāhīm b. Mihrān al-Taqafī was a *ḥadīṯ* scholar and transmitter of towering importance who lived and worked in Nishapur and Baghdad, and who died in 313/925 (al-Ḏahabī, *Siyar*, 14:388–398).

188 Abū l-Naḍr Ismaʿīl b. ʿAbd Allāh: I have so far not been able to establish any information on the identity of this transmitter.

189 Abū Zakariyyāʾ Yaḥyá b. Yūsuf b. Abī Karīmah al-Zammī was an important *ḥadīṯ* scholar and transmitter from Baghdad, who died in 229/844 (al-Ḏahabī, *Siyar*, 11:38–39).

125[a]

الحاكم بأمر الله أبو العباس أحمد

ابن محمد بن الحسن بن أبي بكر بن أبي علي القُبِّي بن الحسن الخليفة الراشد بالله، على خلاف في نسبه، ثاني خلفاء بني العباس بديار مصر.

خرج من بغداد في واقعة هولاكو، وجمع طائفة من الناس ولقي الإمام المستنصر بالله أبا العباس
٥ أحمد بن الخليفة الظاهر بأمر الله أبي نصْر محمد بن الخليفة الناصر لدين الله العباسي المجهز من ديار

٣ خلفاء: "خلفاً" في الأصل. ٤ أبا: تصحيح في الأصل بخط المقريزي.

190 The refugee ʿAbbāsid scion al-Ḥākim (d. 701/1302) was installed as ʿAbbāsid caliph in Cairo by the sultan Baybars, after the violent termination of the ʿAbbāsid caliphate of Baghdad by the Mongols in 656/1258—when in the sultanate the wish to re-establish the caliphate arose for reasons of legal and, especially, political exigency—, after al-Ḥākim's earlier proclamation as caliph in Aleppo by an opponent of sultan Baybars, and after the violent death of his shortlived predecessor and ʿAbbāsid rival in Cairo al-Mustanṣir (see below). See B. Lewis, "ʿAbbāsids", in *EI*[2] http://referenceworks.brillonline.com/entries/encyclopaedia-of-islam-2/abbasids-COM_0002; for a detailed discussion of this transition of the caliphate from Baghdad to Cairo, see Heidemann (1994).

191 Al-Rāšid bi-llāh briefly performed the caliphate in Baghdad between 529/1135 and 530/1136; after him, the caliphate moved back to the line of his father's brother, al-Muqtafī (r. 530–555/1136–1160); some accounts claim al-Ḥākim's descent from al-Rāšid, others from al-Rāšid's father, the caliph al-Mustaršid (r. 512–529/1118–1135), via a brother of al-Rāšid (mostly identified as al-Ḥusayn, but here by al-Maqrīzī as al-Ḥasan) (Lewis, "ʿAbbāsids", in *EI*[2]; Heidemann [1994]: 71–75 [for a detailed discussion of the debate on al-Ḥākim's contested lineage]).

13. Al-Ḥākim bi-Amr Allāh Abū l-ʿAbbās Aḥmad[190]

b. Muḥammad b. al-Ḥasan b. Abī Bakr b. Abī ʿAlī l-Qubbī b. al-Ḥasan, [who was] the caliph al-Rāšid bi-llāh;[191] there is, however, disagreement on his pedigree. [He was] the second caliph of the descendants of al-ʿAbbās in 5 Egypt.

§ 108 He left Baghdad during the event involving Hülegü.[192] He gathered a group of people, and encountered the *Imām* al-Mustanṣir bi-llāh Abū l-ʿAbbās Aḥmad,[193] son of the caliph al-Ẓāhir bi-Amr Allāh Abū Naṣr Muḥammad,[194] son of the caliph al-Nāṣir li-Dīn Allāh al-ʿAbbāsī,[195] who was sent

---

192 Hülegü (1217–1265) was a grandson of the Mongol conqueror Jinghiz Ḫān (d. 1227), who successfully extended Mongol control over Iran, Iraq, Azerbaijan, and Anatolia, in a long military campaign that lasted from 1253 to 1260; his successors ruled over this wide area until 1335, as the Mongol dynasty of the Īl-Ḫāns; in Muslim sources, Hülegü's name remained infamously connected with one event in particular: the conquest and sack of the ancient Islamic capital of Baghad in 656/1258, and with the subsequent execution of the last ʿAbbāsid caliph of Baghdad, al-Mustaʿṣim (W. Barthold, J.A. Boyle, "Hūlāgū", in *EI*² http://referenceworks.brillonline.com/entries/encyclopaedia-of-islam-2/abbasids-SIM_2940; A.A. Duri, "Bag̱hdād", in *EI*2 http://referenceworks.brillonline.com/entries/encyclopaedia-of-islam-2/baghdad-COM_0084).

193 Abū l-Qāsim Aḥmad b. al-Ẓāhir Muḥammad, known by his caliphal title al-Mustanṣir bi-llāh (r. 659–660/1261), was an ʿAbbāsid scion from Baghdad who managed to escape to Egypt, where he was proclaimed the new ʿAbbāsid caliph in 659/1261; he was sent on an expedition to reclaim his ancestral dominions from the Mongols in Iraq, but he was defeated and killed in battle (P.M. Holt, "al-Mustanṣir", in *EI*² http://referenceworks.brillonline.com/entries/encyclopaedia-of-islam-2/al-mustansir-SIM_5628; Heidemann [1994]: 91–107, 145–157).

194 Abū Naṣr Muḥammad, known by his caliphal title al-Ẓāhir bi-Amr Allāh (r. 622–623/1225–1226), succeeded his father al-Nāṣir, but only reigned for nine months due to his untimely death (A.M. Eddé, "al-Ẓāhir bi-Amr Allāh", in *EI*² http://referenceworks.brillonline.com/entries/encyclopaedia-of-islam-2/al-zahir-bi-amr-allah-SIM_8079).

195 Abū l-ʿAbbās Aḥmad, reigning with the caliphal title al-Nāṣir li-Dīn Allāh from 575/1180 to 622/1225, is best known for (re-)establishing ʿAbbāsid local and regional authority and power in Baghdad and Iraq, and for restoring the primacy of ʿAbbāsid sovereignty over the entire Sunni Muslim world (A. Hartmann, "al-Nāṣir Li-Dīn Allāh", in *EI*² http://referenceworks.brillonline.com/entries/encyclopaedia-of-islam-2/al-nasir-li-din-allah-COM_0854).

مصر لقتال الططر، وصار في جملته. فلما قتل المستنصر في وقائع الططر قدم إلى القاهرة في سابع عشرين ربيع الأول سنة ستين وستمائة، فبايعه الملك الظاهر ركن الدين بيبرس البندقداري في يوم الخميس ثامن المحرم سنة إحدى وستين وستمائة.

فلم يزل خليفةً لا أمر له ولا نهي ولا نفوذ كلمة حتى مات بمناظر الكبش خارج القاهرة ليلة الجمعة ثامن عشر جمادى الأولى سنة إحدى وسبع مائة. فكانت خلافته أربعين سنة، وهو أول ٥ خليفة عباسي مات بمصر. واستمرت الخلافة في عقبه إلى اليوم.

٤ يزل: تصحيح في الأصل بخط المقريزي. ٥ الأولى: "الاولي" في الأصل.

from Egypt to fight the Mongols. He joined his group, but when al-Mustanṣir was killed during the confrontations with the Mongols, he came to Cairo, [arriving] on 27 Rabīʿ I of the year 660 [19 February 1262]. Al-Malik al-Ẓāhir Rukn al-Dīn Baybars al-Bunduqdārī[196] swore the oath of allegiance to him on Thursday 8 Muḥarram of the year 661 [23 November 1262].

§ 109 He remained a caliph, without any [power to] command and forbid and without any effective authority, until he died at Manāẓir al-Kabš,[197] outside Cairo, in the night of Friday, 18 Ǧumādá I of the year 701 [19 January 1302]. His caliphate lasted for 40 years, and he was the first ʿAbbāsid caliph to die in Egypt. The caliphate has remained with his offspring to this day.[198]

196 Al-Ẓāhir Baybars (r. 658–676/1260–1277) was the first succesful *mamlūk* sultan of Egypt and Syria; he was especially remembered for successfully staging the consolidation and (re-)organisation of the realm (P. Thorau, "Baybars I, al-Malik al-Ẓāhir Rukn al-Dīn", in *EI*³ http://referenceworks.brillonline.com/entries/encyclopaedia-of-islam-3/baybars-i-al-malik-al-zahir-rukn-al-din-COM_23709; Thorau [1987]).

197 Manāẓir al-Kabš, the "Pavillions of Kabsh Hill", refers to the residences that had mostly been constructed by Ayyūbid princes on a hilly platform some two kilometers south of historic Cairo, behind the Ibn Ṭūlūn mosque; in the course of the thirteenth century this pleasant area overlooking the Elephant Lake to the North became a residential district for royals and also, in alternation with the Cairo Citadel, for the ʿAbbāsid caliphs of Cairo (Raymond [2001]: 98, 133–135).

198 That is, up to the time of al-Maqrīzī's writing of the text of *al-Ḏahab al-masbūk*.

وحج في سنة تسع وتسعين وستمائة[52] والسلطان يومئذ الملك المنصور لاجين، وأعطاه مبلغ سبع مائة ألف درهم فضة. ولما قدم مكة أراد من الشريف أبي نُمَي —أمير مكة— أن يدعو له على منبر مكة، فامتنع من ذلك وجرت {بينهما} مفاوضة ترفع فيها عليه أبو نمي تفاخُرًا بنسبه الشريف. واستمر الأمر على ذلك إلى اليوم لم يخطب قط بمكة لأحد من خلفاء مصر العباسيين سوى الخليفة المستعين بالله أبي الفضل العباس بن محمد أياما يسيرة في سنة خمس عشرة وثماني مائة. ٥

١ يومئذ : "يوميذ" في الأصل. ٢ مائة : "مايه" في الأصل. || نُمَي أمير : تصحيح في الأصل بخط المقريزي. || يدعو : "يدعوا" في الأصل. ٣ بينهما : "بينها" في الأصل. ٤ خلفاء : "خلفآ" في الأصل. ٥ وثماني مائة : ناقصة في الأصل مضافة بخط المقريزي ("وثمانى مايه") في السطر على آخر نص الحاكم بعد كلمة "عشرة".

[52] كذا في الأصل، وهو خطأ لأن سلطنة المنصور لاجين انتهت في ربيع الآخر سنة ٦٩٨، والأصح أن حجة الحاكم كانت في سنة ٦٩٧ ولا في سنة ٦٩٩ (راجع نفس الملاحظة في المقريزي، الذهب المسبوك، تحقيق الشيال، ص. ٦١، وتحقيق فرحات أحمد، ص. ١٢٥).

§ 110 He went on pilgrimage in the year 699 (1300),[199] the sultan at that time being al-Manṣūr Lāǧīn.[200] He gave him an amount of 700 silver *dirhams* [for distribution in Mecca]. When he wanted from the Sharif Abū Numayy,[201] the amir of Mecca, that the Friday sermon would be delivered in his name from 5 the *minbar* of Mecca, [Abū Numayy] refused that. So there was a discussion between them, in which Abū Numayy declared himself of higher birth than [al-Ḥākim], boasting about his noble descent. Until today, the situation has remained like that, the Friday sermon in Mecca never being delivered in the name of any of the ʿAbbāsid caliphs of Egypt, except for the caliph al- 10 Mustaʿīn bi-llāh Abū l-Faḍl al-ʿAbbās b. Muḥammad,[202] [in whose name the Friday sermon was delivered] for a few days in the year 815 [1412].

---

199 This is an obvious mistake in the text, because sultan Lāǧīn's sultanate ended in early 698/1299; al-Ḥākim rather participated in the *ḥaǧǧ* season of the year 697/1298: on this caliphal *ḥaǧǧ* and the conflict with Abū Numayy, see especially Heidemann (1994): 190–191.

200 Al-Manṣūr Lāǧīn was sultan over Egypt and Syria between 696/1296 and 698/1299 (see Holt [1973]).

201 Muḥammad Abū Numayy was a member of a local dynasty of rulers or Sharifs of Mecca, which came to power in the course of the tenth century, and which only lost its power with the rise of the Kingdom of Saudi Arabia in the mid-1920s; they supported their successful claims to rule by their descent from the Prophet via his grandson al-Ḥasan; the Sharif Abū Numayy (r. 652–700/1254–1301) was one of the more energetic and successful rulers of this longlasting dynasty (A.J. Wensinck, C.E. Bosworth, "Makka, 2. From the ʿAbbāsid to the Modern Period", in *EI*[2] http://referenceworks.brillonline .com/entries/encyclopaedia-of-islam-2/makka-COM_0638; Meloy [2010a]: 15–16, 47–48; Mortel [1987]: 461–462).

202 Al-Mustaʿīn bi-llāh, regnal title of Abū l-Faḍl al-ʿAbbās, was the tenth ʿAbbāsid so-called "shadow" caliph in Egypt, reigning from 808/1406 to 816/1414; he died from the plague in 833/1430; al-Mustaʿīn's name is especially remembered for the fact that for six months in 815/1412, he was also endowed with the sultanate in Cairo, an unusual arrangement that did not arise from any renewed ʿAbbāsid empowerment, but rather from the contingent need to organise and legitimate the transition from the murder of the preceding sultan to the enthronement of one of his murderers as the next sultan (P.M. Holt, "al-Mustaʿīn", in *EI*[2] http://referenceworks.brillonline.com/entries/ encyclopaedia-of-islam-2/al-mustain-SIM_5620).

[فصل في] ذكر من حج من الملوك وهو ملك

الصُلَيْحي

واسمه علي بن محمد بن علي—أحد ثوار العالم—، كنيته أبو الحسن بن أبي محمد.

كان أبوه على قضاء اليمن ومن أهل السُنة، وكان في عشيرة من قومه. فصحب عليٌ داعيَ اليمن
٥ عامرَ بن عبد الله الزواحي—أحد دُعاة الدولة الفاطمية—، ومال إلى مذهب التشيع، وتضلع من
علوم الشيعة حتى صار إماما فيه.

---

٣ كنيته: تصحيح في الأصل بخط المقريزي. ٤ قضاء: "قضا" في الأصل.

[Chapter with] the Report of the Kings Who Went on Pilgrimage When They were King

1. Al-Ṣulayḥī[203]

§ 111 His name is ʿAlī b. Muḥammad b. ʿAlī, [and he is] one of this world's
5 revolutionaries; his *kunyah* is Abū l-Ḥasan b. Abī Muḥammad.

§ 112 His father held the judgeship of Yemen. He belonged to the adherents of the Sunna and lived amidst a clan of his people. ʿAlī became a companion of the missionary of Yemen, ʿĀmir b. ʿAbd Allāh al-Zawāḥī,[204] one of the missionary agents of the Fāṭimid dynasty.[205] [As a result] [ʿAlī] started
10 sympathising with the path of Shiism and he became proficient in the sciences of Shiism, until eventually he [himself] became a leading figure in it.

---

203 ʿAlī b. Muḥammad al-Ṣulayḥī (d. 473/1081) was the first ruler of the Ṣulayḥid dynasty of Yemen, a Shii Ismāʿīlī dynasty that ruled over the southern highlands and the Tihāmah region of the Yemen between approximately 439/1047 and 532/1138 (G.R. Smith, "Ṣulayḥids", in *EI*² http://referenceworks.brillonline.com/entries/encyclopaedia-of-islam-2/sulayhids-COM_1112).

204 ʿĀmir b. ʿAbd Allāh al-Zawāḥī was a missionary agent from Fāṭimid Egypt, sent to his native region of Yemen to spread the Fāṭimid Ismāʿīlī cause; his first name is mostly rendered as Sulaymān, however, and that of his son—a powerful Ṣulayḥid—as Sulṭān ʿĀmir (Smith, "Ṣulayḥids"; I. Poonawala, "Shahriyār b. al-Ḥasan", in *EI*² http://referenceworks.brillonline.com/entries/encyclopaedia-of-islam-2/shahriyar-b-al-hasan-SIM_6777).

205 The Fāṭimids were an Ismāʿīlī dynasty that emerged in North Africa in 297/909, from where they successfully established their rule over Sicily, Egypt, the Hijaz, and southern Syria; from 358/969 they reigned over their empire from Egypt, where they founded a new capital, al-Qāhirah (Cairo); with Ṣulayḥid support, their sovereignty was eventually also acknowledged in Yemen. The Fāṭimid rulers asserted direct descent from the Prophet's daughter Fāṭimah and her husband, ʿAlī, generating divine inspiration and special status, to support their claims to Muslim leadership; as a result of these claims, they assumed the title of caliph and developed an amibitous anti-ʿAbbāsid policy of eastward military expansion and Ismāʿīlī missionary activities; this was only succesful until the early decades of the eleventh century; the dynasty was brought to an end in 567/1171 by the Sunni military leader Saladin (M. Canard, "Fāṭimids", in *EI*² http://referenceworks.brillonline.com/entries/encyclopaedia-of-islam-2/fatimids-COM_0218; Halm [1996]).

125b ثم ثار سنة تسع وعشرين | وأربع مائة بستين رجلا—أصحاب عشائر—، فصار في عشرين ألف ضارب سيف من يومه. ودعا للإمام المستنصر بالله أبي تميم معد بن الظاهر بن الحاكم—أحد الخلفاء الفاطمية بالقاهرة—، وملك اليمن كله—سهله وجبله ووعره وبره وبحره—وخطب بنفسه، وكانت قاعدة ملكه صنعاء.

٥ وحج سنة خمس وخمسين وأربع مائة، وملك مكة في سادس ذي الحجة منها ونشر بها العدل وأكثر فيها من الإحسان، ومنع المفسدين وأمن الناس أمنا لم يعهدوه قبله. ورخصت بها الأسعار لكثرة ما جلب اليها بأمره، فأحبه الناس حبا زائدا. وكسا الكعبة الديباج الأبيض—وهو كان شعار الدولة الفاطمية—وأقام بها دعوتهم.[٥٣]

ثم حج في سنة ثلٰث وسبعين وأربعمائة. فلما نزل ظاهر المهجم، قتِل في ثاني عشر ذي الحجة بيد سعيد ١٠ الأحول بن نجاح، وملك بعده.

١ مائة: "ماية" في الأصل. || عشائر: "عشاير" في الأصل. ٣ الخلفاء: "الخلفآ" في الأصل. ٤ صنعاء: "صنعآ" في الأصل. ٥ وأربع: الكلمة غير واضحة في الأصل بسبب ثقب في المخطوطة. ٦ المفسدين: تصحيح في الأصل بخط المقريزي. ٧ زائدا: "زايدا" في الأصل. ٩ وأربعمائة: "واربعمايه" في الأصل.

[٥٣] راجع هذا الخبر على شكل مساو ولكن بعدة تفاصيل زائدة في الفاسي، شفاء الغرام، ج. ٢، ص. ٢٧٢-٢٧٣.

§ 113 Then he revolted in the year 429 [1037–1038], with 60 men, all clan chiefs. Soon thereafter, he got 20,000 swordsmen, and he publicly proclaimed allegiance to the *imām* al-Mustanṣir bi-llāh Abū Tamīm Maʿadd b. al-Ẓāhir b. al-Ḥākim, one of the Fāṭimid caliphs in Cairo.[206] He took control over all of Yemen, its coasts, mountains, and wildness, and its land and its sea. He delivered the Friday sermon in his own name. The seat of his reign was Sanaa.

§ 114 He went on pilgrimage in the year 455 [1063]. He took control of Mecca on the sixth of Ḏū l-Ḥiǧǧah of this year [30 November 1063], and he spread justice in it. He increased the performance of good deeds in [Mecca], hindered the evil doers, and provided safety for the people such as they had not experienced before him. Prices in it got cheap because of the multitude of what was imported to it by his order. People loved him enormously. He covered the Kaʿbah with a *kiswah* of white brocade, which is one of the symbols of the Fāṭimid dynasty, and he established their religious cause there.

§ 115 Then he went on pilgrimage in the year 473 [1081]. When he settled down outside al-Mahǧam,[207] he was killed, on the twelfth of Ḏū l-Ḥiǧǧah [24 May], by the hand of Saʿīd al-Aḥwal b. Naǧāḥ,[208] [who] took power after him.

206 Al-Mustanṣir bi-llāh, regnal title of Abū Tamīm Maʿadd b. ʿAlī al-Ẓāhir b. al-Ḥākim, was the eighth Fāṭimid caliph (b. 420/1029, r. 427–487/1036–1094); his reign of some 60 years is the longest recorded of any Muslim ruler, and it witnessed substantial changes in the nature and extent of Fāṭimid authority (H.A.R. Gibb, P. Kraus, "al-Mustanṣir", in *EI*² http://referenceworks.brillonline.com/entries/encyclopaedia-of-islam-2/al-mustansir-COM_0817).

207 Today Mahjamm, in the Yemeni Hajja governorate.

208 Saʿīd al-Aḥwal b. Naǧāḥ (d. 481/1088) was a member of a dynasty of former Abyssinian slaves, the Naǧāḥids, that ruled over the Yemenite city of Zabīd and over the northern Tihāmah for most of the period between 412/1022 and 553/1158; the murder of the dynasty's founder Naǧāḥ by ʿAlī b. Muḥammad in 452/1060, the subsequent Ṣulayḥid occupation of Zabīd, and the murder of ʿAlī by Naǧāḥ's sons, Saʿīd and Ǧayyāš, near the Tihāmah town of al-Mahǧam in 473/1081, marked a first and defining phase in the long competition of the Naǧāḥids with the Ṣulayḥids for control over the Tihāmah (R. Strothmann, G.R. Smith, "Nadjāḥīds", in *EI*² http://referenceworks.brillonline.com/entries/encyclopaedia-of-islam-2/nadjahids-SIM_5717).

ثم حج

الملك العادل نور الدين محمود

ابن عماد الدين أتابك بن زنكي بن أبي سعيد قسيم الدولة بن آقسنقر—المعروف بالحاجب—بن عبد الله.

٥ كان جده آقسنقر مملوكا تركيا للسلطان ملك شاه بن ألب أرسلان السلجوقي، وترقى إلى أن استنابه تاج الدولة تتش بن أرسلان في حلَب لما ملكها في سنة ثمان وسبعين وأربع مائة. فعصى عليه وحاربه. فقتل في جمادى الأول سنة سبْع وثمانين وأربع مائة. وصار ابنه عماد الدين زنكي من

١ ثم حج : ناقصة في الأصل، مضافة بخط المقريزي في الهامش الأيسر، من الأسفل إلى الأعلى + صح، يشير إليها الرمز ٦ بعد كلمة "بعده". ٦ مائة : "مايه" في الأصل. || فعصى : "فعصا" في الأصل. ٧ مائة : "مايه" في الأصل.

Then there went on pilgrimage

2. Al-Malik al-ʿĀdil Nūr al-Dīn Maḥmūd[209]

b. ʿImād al-Dīn [the] Atābak, [i.e.] b. Zankī b. Abī Saʿīd Qasīm al-Dawlah, [i.e.] b. Āqsunqur, known as al-Ḥāǧib, b. ʿAbd Allāh.

5 § 116 His grandfather Āqsunqur[210] was a Turkish military slave of the sultan Malik Šāh b. Alp Arslān al-Salǧūqī.[211] He rose in the ranks until Tāǧ al-Dawlah Tutuš b. Arslān[212] appointed him as his representative in Aleppo, when he took hold of it in the year 478 [1085–1086]. [But then] he rebelled against [Tutuš] and engaged into battle against him. [Āqsunqur] was killed 10 in Ǧumādá I of the year 487 [May–June 1094]. His son ʿImād al-Dīn Zankī

---

209 Al-Malik al-ʿĀdil Nūr al-Dīn Maḥmūd (d. 569/1174) ruled from 541/1146 until his death over most of Northern Mesopotamia and Syria; the main components of these domains first had been brought together by his father Zankī's military campaigning and they had then been divided among Maḥmūd and his Zankid brothers; from his appanage in Aleppo Maḥmūd succeeded to gradually extend his authority over family, friends, and foes in the region and thus to transform into the uncontested Muslim leader West of the Tigris; under the banner of *ǧihād* he was regularly engaged in warfare against Crusaders of the Levantine coast, and eventually he even obtained control over Egypt (N. Elisséeff, "Nūr al-Dīn Maḥmūd b. Zankī", in *EI*² http://referenceworks.brillonline.com/entries/encyclopaedia-of-islam-2/nur-al-din-mahmud-b-zanki-SIM_5988).

210 Qasīm al-Dawlah Āqsunqur al-Ḥāǧib (d. 487/1094) was a *mamlūk* or military slave in Salǧūq service who eventually served as Salǧūq governor in Aleppo; he was executed in the course of a Salǧūq succession conflict; his son Zankī (d. 541/1146) followed in his footsteps (H.A.R. Gibb, "Āḳ Sunḳur", in *EI*² http://referenceworks.brillonline.com/entries/encyclopaedia-of-islam-2/ak-sunkur-SIM_0451).

211 Ǧalāl al-Dawlah Muʿizz al-Dīn Abū l-Fatḥ Malik Šāh b. Alp Arslān (b. 447/1055, r. 465–485/1072–1092) was the greatest of all Salǧūq rulers (*sulṭāns*), a Turkish dynasty different branches of which dominated the eastern Islamic world for most of the eleventh and a great part of the twelfth centuries (C.E. Bosworth, "Malik-S͟hāh", in *EI*² http://referenceworks.brillonline.com/entries/encyclopaedia-of-islam-2/malik-shah-COM_0651); Peacock (2015).

212 Tāǧ al-Dawlah Tutuš b. Arslān (458–488/1066–1095) was the brother of sultan Malik Šāh, who was given Syria as his Salǧūq appanage; he was killed in a prolonged conflict for the succession of his brother (C.E. Bosworth, "Tutus͟h (I) b. Alp Arslan." in *EI*² http://referenceworks.brillonline.com/entries/encyclopaedia-of-islam-2/tutush-i-b-alp-arslan-COM_1267).

الأمراء ببغداد، ثم ولي الموصل سنة {اثنتين} وعشرين وخمسمائة، وأخذ الرها. وقتل على جعبر في ربيع الآخر سنة إحدى وأربعين وخمس مائة—وهو على فراشه.

ووُلِد نور الدين محمود في سابع عشر شوال سنة إحدى عشرة وخمسمائة. فقام بعد قتل أبيه، وأخذ قلعة حلب وجد في قتال الفرنج—وبيدهم حينئذ من الرها إلى السوادة من حدود أرض مصر—وافتتح عدة حصون. وأظهر بحلب مذهب أهل السنة—وكان أهلها ٥

١ الأمراء : "الامرآ" في الأصل. ‖ اثنتين : "اثنين" في الأصل. ‖ وخمسمائة : "وخمسمايه" في الأصل.
٢ مائة : "مايه" في الأصل. ٣ وخمسمائة : "وخمسمايه" في الأصل. ٤ حينئذ : "حينيد" في الأصل.

became [one] of the amirs in Baghdad. Then he was appointed over Mosul[213] in the year 522 [1128]. He took Edessa [from the Crusaders].[214] He was killed near Ǧaʿbar[215] in Rabīʿ II of the year 541 [September–October 1146], while he was in his bed.

5 § 117 Nūr al-Dīn Maḥmūd was born on 17 Šawwāl of the year 511 [11 February 1118]. He rose [to power] after the murder of his father, taking the citadel of Aleppo [as his seat]. He made every effort in fighting the Franks,[216] who controlled at that time [an area stretching] from Edessa to al-Sawwādah,[217] near the frontier of the territory of Egypt. He conquered several fortresses. 10 He made the path of the people of the Sunna dominant in Aleppo, [where most of] its people had belonged to the *Rāfiḍah*.[218] He abolished the [Shiite]

---

213 Mosul, or al-Mawṣil, is an old city in Northern Mesopotamia, or the Jazira, on the west bank of the Tigris, in present-day Iraq (P. Sluglett, "al-Mawṣil", in *EI*² http://referenceworks.brillonline.com/entries/encyclopaedia-of-islam-2/al-mawsil-COM_0717).

214 Al-Ruhā, traditionally known as Edessa in European sources and today as Urfa (also Şanlıurfa) in the southeast of modern Turkey, is the Arabic name of a city with ancient roots in Eastern Anatolia; between 1098 and 1144, following the first crusade, it was the capital of the Latin "County of Edessa", until its conquest and sack by Zankī; this event gave Zankī and his offspring the empowering aura of champions of Islam and holy war, but it also triggered the second crusade (E. Honigmann, C.E. Bosworth, "al-Ruhā", in *EI*² http://referenceworks.brillonline.com/entries/encyclopaedia-of-islam-2/al-ruha-COM_0936).

215 Ǧaʿbar, better known as Qalʿat Ǧaʿbar, is situated on the east bank of the upper Euphrates, to the west of the regional center of Raqqa; it is a fortified site on a hill, overlooking the river valley and controling its passage since pre-Islamic times (see Tonghini [1998]).

216 "Franks" (*firanǧ, ifranǧ*) is the generic name used in medieval Muslim sources to refer to Latin Christians, including those coming or originating from Europe in the context of crusading and the set-up of Levantine crusader principalities (A. Mallett, "Franks", in *EI*³ http://referenceworks.brillonline.com/entries/encyclopaedia-of-islam-2/franks-COM_27178).

217 Al-Sawwādah was the name of one of the stops on the postal route connecting Cairo with Gaza; it was the fourteenth station from Cairo, the second from Qaṭyā, and the third before al-Arish (see al-Qalqašandī, *Ṣubḥ al-aʿšá*, 14:378).

218 Rāfiḍah ('those who reject' [the first three caliphs]) is a term used in medieval Sunni Muslim sources to refer to Twelver-Šīʿah, mostly with an antagonistic and pejorative undertone (E. Kohlberg, "al-Rāfiḍa", in *EI*² http://referenceworks.brillonline.com/entries/encyclopaedia-of-islam-2/al-rafida-SIM_6185).

من الرافضة—، وأبطل الأذان بحي على خير العمل، وأنشأ بها المدارس على مذاهب الأئمة الأربعة.

ثم ملك دمشق بعدما أشرف الفرنج على أخذها، وضبط أمورها وأنشأ بها المدارس والمساجد والمارستان، وعمرها، وأبطل المكوس كلها ومنع المنكرات بأسرها وعاقب عليها.

٥ واستنقذ من الفرنج عدة معاقل، وبنى في أكثر ممالكه دار العدل وأحضرها القضاة والفقهاء وجلس فيها بنفسه | لإزالة المظالم. 127a

وبالغ في الإحسان لأهل مكة والمدينة، وبعث العساكر لحفظ المدينة النبوية، وأقطع أمير مكة إقطاعا، وأقطع أمراء العربان إقطاعات لحفظ الحاج فيما بين دمشق والحجاز، وأكمل سور المدينة النبوية، واستخرج لها العين، فدُعي له بالحرمين على منبريهما.

١ الأئمة: "الايمة" في الأصل. ٥ وبنى: "وبنا" في الأصل. ‖ القضاة: تصحيح في الأصل بخط المقريزي. ‖ والفقهاء: "الفقهآ" في الأصل. ٦ بنفسه: أضيفت هنا في الأصل جزازة منفردة مكتوبة بخط المقريزي [١٢٦] ولكنها في المكان الغلطان في النص حتى يتم نص نور الدين (وتتم المخطوطة الأصلية، كما أشارت إليه كلمة الإشارة "لازاله" المضافة بخط الناسخ تحت نص ص. ١٢٥ب) في ص. ١٢٧أ. ٨ أمراء: "امرآ" في الأصل. ‖ فيما ... والحجاز: ناقصة في الأصل، مضافة بخط المقريزي في الهامش الأيمن، من الأعلى إلى الأسفل + صح؛ يشير إليها الرمز ⌐ بعد كلمة "الحاج". ٩ بالحرمين: تصحيح في الأصل. ‖ منبريهما: تصحيح في الأصل.

219 The call to prayer of Sunni Muslims consists of seven formulas; that of the Shiites differs in that it has an eighth formula: "Come to the best of works" (*ḥayya ʿalā ḥayr al-ʿamal*) (Th.W. Juynboll, "Adhān", in *EI*² http://referenceworks.brillonline.com/entries/encyclopaedia-of-islam-2/adhan-SIM_0302).

call to prayer [that includes the phrase:] 'Come to the best of works',[219] and he erected there *madrasas* for the four schools of [Sunni] law of the four eponyms [Abū Ḥanīfah, Mālik b. Anas, al-Šāfiʿī and Aḥmad b. Ḥanbal].

§ 118 Then he gained possession of Damascus, after the Franks had been
5 about to take it.[220] He inspected its affairs, he erected *madrasas*, mosques and a hospital in it, and he developed [the city]. He abolished all the non-*sharʿī* taxes,[221] he prevented all reprehensible things, and he had [people] punished for [committing] them.

§ 119 He recovered several strongholds from the Franks. He built houses of
10 justice in most ruling centres of his realm, and he had judges and jurisprudents brought to them. He himself presided over sessions in them to remove injustices.

§ 120 He went to the greatest lengths to perform good deeds for the people of Mecca and Medina, sending the armies to protect the Prophet's Medina,
15 assigning an *iqṭāʿ*[222] to the ruler of Mecca, and assigning *iqṭāʿ*s to the amirs of the Bedouin Arab tribes for guarding the pilgrimage [route] between Damascus and the Hijaz. He completed the wall of the Prophet's Medina and he had a well dug for it. His name was proclaimed in the two august places, from their *minbars*.

---

220 Between 541/1147 and 549/1154, Damascus was a bone of contention in the competition for regional hegemony in southern Syria between the Latin Kingdom of Jerusalem, Nūr al-Dīn, and local military and urban leaders; in the end, Nūr al-Dīn emerged victoriously as a result of succesful military operations and shrewd diplomacy (Elisséeff, "Nūr al-Dīn Maḥmūd b. Zankī", in *EI*[2]).

221 Non-*šarʿī* taxes (*mukūs*) are levies on rural and urban goods and services that are not prescribed or condoned by Muslim scripture, and that therefore—despite their ubiquitousness and importance for the region's political economies—tend to be negatively perceived.

222 An *iqṭāʿ* ('apportionment') refers to a distinctive form of tributary remuneration in return for—mostly—military service; it was dominant in the Islamic world between the tenth and the eighteenth centuries and consisted basically of the assignment to its holder of the usufruct of designated rural estates; the actual nature and conditions of the assignment varied greatly according to time and place (Cl. Cahen, "Iḳṭāʿ", in *EI*[2] http://referenceworks.brillonline.com/entries/encyclopaedia-of-islam-2/ikta-SIM_3522).

وبعث الأمير أسد الدين شيركوه بالغُزّ إلى مصر، واستنقذ القاهرة من الفرنج بعد ما حصرها مُري لعنه الله بعساكر الفرنج أياما. ولم يبق إلا أن يملكها. فلما استولى شيركوه على القاهرة، دعي لنور الدين على منابر القاهرة ومصر.

ومات في حادي عشر شوال سنة تسع وستين وخمسمائة بدمشق، بعدما حج في سنة ست وخمسين {وخمسمائة}. وأكثر من فعل الخير بالحرمين وبالغ في الإحسان. ٥

١ واستنقذ: تصحيح في الأصل بخط المقريزي. ٣ على٢: "علي" في الأصل. ٤ وخمسمائة: "وخمسمايه" في الأصل. ٥ وخمسمائة: "وستمايه" في الأصل وهو خطأ واضح من السياق.

§ 121 He sent the amir Asad al-Dīn Šīrkūh[223] with the Ġuzz [Turks][224] to Egypt and he recovered Cairo from the Franks, after [King] Amaury[225]—may God curse him—and the armies of the Franks had besieged it for some days and [after he] had almost taken control of it. When Šīrkūh took control over 5 Cairo, the name of Nūr al-Dīn was proclaimed from the *minbar*s of Cairo and of Miṣr [al-Fusṭāṭ].[226]

§ 122 He died on 11 Šawwāl of the year 569 [15 May 1174] in Damascus, after he had performed the pilgrimage in the year 556 [1161]. He did a lot of good in the two august places and he went to the greatest lengths to perform 10 benevolent deeds.

---

223 Asad al-Dīn Šīrkūh (d. 564/1169), belonging to a Kurdish family from Armenia, was a military leader and agent of Nūr al-Dīn Maḥmūd, active in Syria and then in Egypt; he secured Egypt for Nūr al-Dīn in 564/1169, by rescuing Fāṭimid Egypt from an attack from the Kingdom of Jerusalem and by becoming the vizier of the last Fāṭimid caliph; he died shortly afterwards, leaving his role in Egypt as Fāṭimid vizier and agent of Nūr al-Dīn to his nephew Saladin (D.S. Richards, "Shīrkūh", in *EI*² http://referenceworks.brillonline.com/entries/encyclopaedia-of-islam-2/shirkuh-SIM_6966).

224 *Ġuzz* is the form that is generally used by medieval Arabic authors to refer to the Turkish Oghuz people, a grouping of western Turkish tribes in Central Asia that entered the Muslim world through migration and conquest in the 5th/11th century, led by the Saljuq family; in later times, the term is also used to refer to Turkman mercenary troops (Cl. Cahen, "Ghuzz: I.-Muslim East", in *EI*² http://referenceworks.brillonline.com/entries/encyclopaedia-of-islam-2/ghuzz-COM_0240).

225 Murī is the Arabic name used to refer to one of Nūr al-Dīn Maḥmūd's most formidable opponents for hegemony in Syria and in Egypt, the king of the Kingdom of Jerusalem, Amaury (or Amalric) I of Jerusalem (r. 1163–1174) (Elisséeff, "Nūr al-Dīn Maḥmūd b. Zankī", in *EI*²).

226 Miṣr al-Fusṭāṭ is the name of the city that predated Cairo as the Muslim capital of Egypt, lying some kilometers to the south, along the Nile's eastern shore; it first emerged at the time of the Arab conquest of Egypt, soon transformed into a thriving Mediterranean metropolis, and remained an important urban centre when Cairo took over its role as regional political and commercial center from the twelfth century onwards (J. Jomier, "al-Fusṭāṭ", in *EI*² http://referenceworks.brillonline.com/entries/encyclopaedia-of-islam-2/al-fustat-SIM_2409; Raymond [2001], 7–30, 98–102, 162–164).

الملك المعظم شمس الدولة تُورَان شاه

ابن والد الملوك نجم الدين أيوب بن شادي بن مروان الكردي.

نشأ بدمشق وقدم إلى القاهرة مع أهله في سنة أربع وستين وخمسمائة، وقد تقلد أخوه الملك الناصر صلاح الدين يوسف بن أيوب وزارة مصر للخليفة العاضد لدين الله أبي محمد عبد الله بن ٥ الأمير يوسف بن الحافظ لدين الله. فكان من أعظم الأسباب في نصرة أخيه صلاح الدين يوم

١ تُورَان: تصحيح في الأصل بخط الناسخ. ٣ وخمسمائة: "وخمسمايه" في الأصل. ٥ من: ناقصة في الأصل، مضافة بخط المقريزي في الهامش الأيمن، من الأعلى إلى الأسفل + صح؛ يشير إليها الرمز ⌐ بعد كلمة "فكان".

3. Al-Malik al-Muʿaẓẓam Šams al-Dawlah Tūrān Šāh[227]

Son of the father of kings, Naǧm al-Dīn Ayyūb b. Šādī b. Marwān al-Kurdī.[228]

§ 123 He was raised in Damascus and in the year 564 [1169] he came to Cairo with his family, when his brother al-Malik al-Nāṣir Ṣalāḥ al-Dīn Yūsuf b. 5 Ayyūb[229] had been invested with the post of vizier of Egypt for the caliph al-ʿĀḍid li-Dīn Allāh Abū Muḥammad ʿAbd Allāh b. al-Amīr Yūsuf b. al-Ḥāfiẓ li-Dīn Allāh.[230] [Tūrān Šāh] was one of the foremost reasons for the victory

227 Al-Malik al-Muʿaẓẓam Šams al-Dawlah Faḫr al-Dīn Tūrān Šāh b. Ayyūb (d. 576/1178) was the older brother of Ṣalāḥ al-Dīn (Saladin), who is mainly remembered for his conquest of the Yemen in 569/1173 and its addition to his Ayyūbid family's territorial control over Syria and Egypt (G.R. Smith, "Tūrānshāh b. Ayyūb", in *EI*² http://referenceworks.brillonline.com/entries/encyclopaedia-of-islam-2/turanshah-b-ayyub-COM_1258).

228 Naǧm al-Dīn Ayyūb b. Šādī b. Marwān al-Kurdī was the eponym of the Ayyūbid dynasty, which was established after Ṣalāḥ al-Dīn's taking control over Egypt in 564/1169, and which remained in power in Egypt and Syria into the later thirteenth century; Ayyūb (and his brother Šīrkūh) was of Kurdish origins, born in Armenia in the early twelfth century, and he served as a local agent and governor to various Saljuq and post-Salǧūq rulers, including Nūr al-Dīn Maḥmūd (A.-M. Eddé, "Ayyūbids", in *EI*³ http://referenceworks.brillonline.com/entries/encyclopaedia-of-islam-3/ayyubids-COM_0164).

229 Al-Malik al-Nāṣir Abū l-Muẓaffar Ṣalāḥ al-Dīn Yūsuf b. Ayyūb (b. 532/1138, r. 564–589/1169–1193), better known as Saladin, was the first ruler of the Ayyūbid dynasty; he began his career as an agent in Egypt of Nūr al-Dīn Maḥmūd and as a vizier to the Fāṭimid caliph; shortly afterwards, he ended the Shiite Fāṭimid caliphate in Egypt, established Sunni Islam as its main creed, and transformed Egypt into a powerbase and stronghold for his own family and followers; from Egypt he engaged in a successful project of the expansion of his authority over Syria, Yemen, and northern Mesopotamia, culminating in the 583/1187 conquest of the capital of the Crusader Kingdom of Jerusalem, which catapulted him to the eternal status of a Muslim hero; in the last years of his life, his territorial successes were somewhat mitigated by the impact of the Third Crusade (1189–1192) (D.S. Richards, "Ṣalāḥ al-Dīn", in *EI*² http://referenceworks.brillonline.com/entries/encyclopaedia-of-islam-2/salah-al-din-SIM_6517; Eddé, "Ayyūbids", in *EI3*; Lyons & Jackson [1982]; Mouton [2001]; Eddé [2008]).

230 Al-ʿĀḍid li-Dīn Allāh, regnal title of Abū Muḥammad ʿAbd Allāh b. Yūsuf b. al-Ḥāfiẓ li-Dīn Allāh (b. 546/1151, r. 555–567/1160–1171), was the fourteenth and last Fāṭimid caliph of Egypt; upon his death (at the age of twenty), Saladin formally restored the authority of the ʿAbbāsid caliph in Cairo (M.J. Salih, "al-ʿĀḍid li-Dīn Allāh", in *EI*³ http://referenceworks.brillonline.com/entries/encyclopaedia-of-islam-3/al-adid-li-din-allah-COM_22734).

وقعة السودان حتى هزمهم وأفناهم بالسيف. فأقطعه قوص وأسوان وعيذاب، وعِبْرتها يومئذ مائتا ألف دينار وستة وستون ألف دينار مصرية في كل سنة.

ثم {غزا} النوبة في سنة ثمان وستين، وأخذ قلعة إبريم، وعاد غانما.

١ وقعة: تصحيح في الأصل بخط المقريزي. ‖ وعِبْرتها: تصحيح في الأصل بخط المقريزي. ‖ يومئذ: "يوميذ" في الأصل. ‖ مائتا: "مايتا" في الأصل. ٣ غزا: "غز" في الأصل.

of his brother Ṣalāḥ al-Dīn on the day of the confrontation with the blacks,[231] in which he managed to defeat them and to wipe them out with the sword. [Ṣalāḥ al-Dīn] assigned Qus,[232] Aswan[233], and Aydhab[234] as an *iqṭāʿ* to him, its estimated income at that time being 266,000 Egyptian *dīnār*s annu-
5 ally.

§ 124 Then he invaded Nubia[235] in the year [5]68 [1172–1173]. He took Qalʿat Ibrīm[236] and returned plundering.

---

231 This refers to a critical episode in the beginning of Saladin's take-over of power from the Fāṭimids, in 564/1169, when the Sudanese regiments of the Fāṭimid caliphate revolted and Tūrān Šāh was reported to have taken charge in subduing the revolt and destroying the regiments after two days of fighting (Eddé, "Ayyūbids", in *EI*³; Lyons & Jackson [1982]: 34–36).

232 The ancient town of Qus (Qūṣ) in Upper Egypt, on the Nile's east bank, became a strategic local site in late antiquity, and developed into an important regional centre of trade, agriculture, and government especially from the fourth/tenth century onwards, reaching its zenith in the eighth/fourteenth century (Garcin [2005]; Id., "Kūṣ," in *EI*², http://brillonline.com/entries/encyclopaedia-of-islam-2/Hims-SIM_4555).

233 The town of Aswan (Uswān) in the south of Egypt, on the Nile's east bank, grew into an important regional center of Muslim government and trade from the first/seventh century onwards, controling Egypt's connections with Nubia and operating as a stop on the pilgrim routes; it fell in decay in the later eighth/fourteenth century (J.-C. Garcin & M. Tuscherer, "Uswān," in *EI*², http://brillonline.com/entries/encyclopaedia-of-islam-2/uswan-COM_1314).

234 Aydhab (ʿAyḏāb) was a port town on the African coast of the Red Sea, which was used by pilgrims to Mecca and as a central hub in the commercial networks that linked Yemen to Egypt; the port and its town flourished in particular between the eleventh and fourteenth centuries, but they were both destroyed in the early fifteenth century (H.A.R. Gibb, "ʿAyd͟hāb", in *EI*² http://referenceworks.brillonline.com/entries/encyclopaedia-of-islam-2/aydhab-SIM_0900).

235 Nubia, or al-Nūbah in medieval Arabic sources, refers to the land and its people south of Egypt, beyond Aswan and the first cataract of the Nile and into the Land of the Blacks (al-Sūdān) ("Nūba", in *EI*² http://referenceworks.brillonline.com/entries/encyclopaedia-of-islam-2/nuba-COM_0870).

236 Qalʿat Ibrīm, better known as Qaṣr Ibrīm, is an ancient fortified site on the Nile's east bank between the first and second Cataract, in the frontier region between Muslim Egypt and the Nubian Christian kingdoms in the south (S. Munro-Hay, "al-Marīs," in *EI*², http://brillonline.com/entries/encyclopaedia-of-islam-2/almaris-SIM_4967).

ثم سار إلى بلاد اليمن في سنة تسع وستين، وعلى مُلك زبيد أبو الحسن علي بن مهدي الملقب عبد النبي. وقدم مكة معتمرا، وتوجه إلى زبيد واستولى على ممالك اليمن، وتلقب بالملك المعظم وخطب لنفسه بعد الخليفة العباسي.

ثم توجه في سنة إحدى وسبعين إلى الشام، فملكه أخوه صلاح الدين دمشق في ربيع الأول سنة
٥ اثنتين وسبعين.

ثم جهزه إلى القاهرة في ذي القعدة سنة أربع وسبعين، وأنعم عليه بالإسكندرية، فأقام بها إلى أن مات هناك أول صفر سنة ست وسبعين وخمسمائة. فوجد عليه مبلغ مائتي ألف دينار مصرية دينا قضاها عنه السلطان صلاح الدين، وسبب هذا الدين كثرة جوده وسعة عطائه.

ومن غريب ما يحكى عنه أن الأديب الفاضل مهذب الدين أبا طالب محمد بن علي —ابن الخيمي—
١٠ قال: "رأيت في النوم المعظم شمس الدولة | توران شاه، وقد مدحته وهو في القبر ميت، فلف كفنه 127b
ورماه وأنشدني: [البسيط]

٤ ثم: ناقصة في الأصل، مضافة بخط المقريزي في الهامش الأيمن، من الأعلى إلى الأسفل + صح، يشير إليها الرمز ⌐ بعد كلمة "العباسي". ‖ إحدى: "احدي" في الأصل. ٧ وخمسمائة: "وخمسمايه" في الأصل. ‖ مائتي: "مايتي" في الأصل. ٨ قضاها: تصحيح في الأصل بخط المقريزي. ‖ عطائه: "عطايه" في الأصل. ٩ ابن: تصحيح في الأصل بخط المقريزي.

§125 Then he went to the land of Yemen, in the year [5]69 [1173–1174], when Zabīd[237] was controlled by Abū l-Ḥasan ʿAlī b. Mahdī,[238] whose honorific was ʿAbd al-Nabī. He came to Mecca and performed the lesser pilgrimage, and he moved on to Zabīd and took control of the territories of Yemen. He assumed the honorific al-Malik al-Muʿaẓẓam and had the Friday sermon delivered in his own name, after [that of] the ʿAbbāsid caliph.

§126 Then, in the year [5]71 [1175–1176], he travelled to Syria. His brother Ṣalāḥ al-Dīn put him in charge of Damascus in Rabīʿ I of the year [5]72 [September 1176].

§127 Then [Ṣalāḥ al-Dīn] sent him to Cairo, in Ḏū l-Qaʿdah of the year [5]74 [April 1179], and he granted him Alexandria [as an *iqṭāʿ*?]. He lived in [Alexandria] until he died there, on the first of Ṣafar of the year 576 [27 June 1180]. He was found to be in debt for an amount of 200,000 Egyptian *dīnār*s and the sultan Ṣalāḥ al-Dīn settled it in his stead. The reason for this debt was the wealth of his generosity and the wide extent of his benevolence.

§128 A curious thing that is told about him is that the excellent man of letters Muhaḏḏab al-Dīn Abū Ṭālib Muḥammad b. ʿAlī Ibn al-Ḫaymī[239] said: "I saw al-Muʿaẓẓam Šams al-Dawlah Tūrān Šāh in a dream. I had written a eulogy to him, while he was [lying] dead in his grave; he took off his burial shroud and threw it [at me], reciting [the following] verses to me: [*Basīṭ* meter]

237 The town of Zabīd, in the Tihāmah plain on Yemen's Red Sea coast, was founded in 204/820 by the ʿAbbāsid representative in the region, upon which it remained a regional seat of government, a prosperous centre of commerce, and an important station for pilgrims travelling to Mecca until the late ninth/fifteenth century (N. Sadek, "Zabīd," in *EI*², http://referenceworks.brillonline.com/entries/encyclopaedia-of-islam-2/zabid-COM_1372).

238 Abū l-Ḥasan ʿAlī b. Mahdī, known as ʿAbd al-Nabī, was a ruler of *Ḫāriǧī* reputation from the Mahdid dynasty of Zabīd, who pursued a violent policy of expansion in the Yemen, against other local rulers, that may actually have triggered the Ayyūbid invasion by Tūrān Šāh; he was arrested and executed by the Ayyūbids in 571/1176 (G.R. Smith, "Mahdids", in *EI*² http://referenceworks.brillonline.com/entries/encyclopaedia-of-islam-2/mahdids-COM_0620).

239 Muhaḏḏab al-Dīn Abū Ṭālib Muḥammad b. ʿAlī Ibn al-Ḫaymī (549–642/1155–1245) was a well-known *littérateur* and linguist from Cairo (Ibn Ḫallikān, *Wafayāt al-aʿyān*, 2:342).

لا تستقلن معروفا سمحت به ميتا وأمسيت منه عاريا بدني

ولا تظنن جودي شأنه بخل من بعد بذلي ملك الشام واليمن

إني خرجت من الدنيا وليس معي من كل ما ملكت كفي سوى كفني

وإليه ينسب درب شمس الدولة بالقاهرة.

٥ وقد ذكرت ترجمته مبسوطة في **كتاب المواعظ والاعتبارات بذكر الخطط والآثار** وفي **كتاب التاريخ الكبير المقفى لمصر**.[٥٤]

١ تستقلن : تصحيح في الأصل بخط المقريزي. ‖ وأمسيت : تصحيح في الأصل بخط المقريزي. ‖ منه : ناقصة في الأصل، مضافة بخط المقريزي في الهامش الأيسر، على نفس السطر + صح؛ يشير إليها الرمز ⌐ بعد كلمة "أمسيت". ٥ ترجمته : تصحيح في الأصل بخط المقريزي. ‖ والاعتبارات : كذا في الأصل.

[٥٤] راجع المقريزي، الخطط، ج. ٣، ص. ١٠٩-١١١؛ وترجمة شمس الدولة توران شاه مفقودة في المخطوطات المعروف وجودها للتاريخ الكبير المقفى للمقريزي. راجع المقفى، ج. ٨.

§ 129 You should really not underestimate a recompense which I grant
while being dead and of which I have deprived my body.

You should really not consider my generosity as a case of greed,
after my renunciation of the rule of Šām and of Yemen.

5 Because I left from the world only taking with me
from all that I possessed in abundance my burial shroud!"

§ 130 The Darb Šams al-Dawlah[240] in Cairo was named after him.

§ 131 I [= al-Maqrīzī] reported his biography in detail in the book *al-Mawāʿiẓ wa-l-iʿtibārāt bi-ḏikr al-ḫiṭaṭ wa-l-āṯār* [Admonitions and Reflections on the
10 Quarters and Monuments (in Fusṭāṭ and Cairo)] and in the book *al-Tārīḫ al-kabīr al-muqaffá li-Miṣr* [The Great History of Egypt in Continuation].[241]

240 For the neighbourhood of Darb Šams al-Dawlah in late medieval Cairo, see al-Maqrīzī, *al-Ḫiṭaṭ*, 3:108–111.

241 See al-Maqrīzī, *al-Ḫiṭaṭ*, 3:109–111; Id., *al-Muqaffá* (but the entry for Tūrān Šāh does not seem to have survived).

الملك المعظم شرف الدين أبو الفتح عيسى

ابن الملك العادل سيف الدين أبي بكر محمد بن نجم الدين أيوب بن شادي بن مروان الكردي الأيوْبي، الفقيه الحنفي النحوي الأديب الشاعر.

ولد بدمشق في خامس رجب سنة ست وخمسين وخمس مائة. وتفقه على مذهب الإمام أبي
٥ حنيفة بالشيخ {جمال الدين} أبي المحامد محمود بن أحمد الحَصِيْري البخاري الحنفي، وأخذ العربية عن التاج أبي اليُمن زيد بن الحسن الكندي، وكان يسعى إلى منزليهما على قدميه لأخذه العلم عنهما، وأفرط في العصبية لمذهب الحنفية.

---

٤ وخمس مائة: تصحيح في الأصل بخط المقريزي ("وخمس مايه"). ٥ جمال الدين: "جمالدين" في الأصل.
٦ منزليهما: تصحيح في الأصل بخط المقريزي.

4. Al-Malik al-Muʿaẓẓam Šaraf al-Dīn Abū l-Fatḥ ʿĪsá[242]

§ 132 [He is] the son of al-Malik al-ʿĀdil Sayf al-Dīn Abū Bakr Muḥammad b. Naǧm al-Dīn Ayyūb b. Šādī b. Marwān al-Kurdī l-Ayyūbī;[243] [he was] a Ḥanafī jurisprudent, a grammarian, a man of letters, and a poet.

5 § 133 He was born in Damascus on 5 Rajab of the year 556 [30 June 1161]. He was trained in the jurisprudence of the rite of the *imām* Abū Ḥanīfah by the *šayḫ* Ǧamāl al-Dīn Abū l-Maḥāmid Maḥmūd b. Aḥmad al-Ḥaṣīrī l-Buḫārī l-Ḥanafī.[244] He read Arabic with al-Tāǧ Abū l-Yumn Zayd b. al-Ḥasan al-Kindī.[245] He used to hurry walking to the places where they live, so as to 10 obtain knowledge from them. He was quite excessive in his partisanship of the Ḥanafī rite.

---

242 Al-Malik al-Muʿaẓẓam ʿĪsá (b. 576/1180, r. 594–624/1198–1227) was an Ayyūbid ruler of Damascus, with a substantial role in and impact on the organisation of the Ayyūbid dynastic political formation dominating Egypt, Syria, Armenia, and northern Mesopotamia in the first half of the 7th/13th century; he is also remembered as an active jurisprudent and staunch supporter of the Ḥanafī school of law (R.S. Humphreys, "al-Muʿaẓẓam", in *EI*² http://referenceworks.brillonline.com/entries/encyclopaedia-of-islam-2/al-muazzam-SIM_5288).

243 Al-Malik al-ʿĀdil Sayf al-Dīn Abū Bakr (b. 540/1145, r. 596–615/1200–1218), known in Western sources as Saphadin, was a younger brother of Saladin, who emerged victoriously from the long power struggle within the Ayyūbid family that followed Saladin's death; with his sons performing his power and authority as royal princes in Egypt, Syria, northern Mesopotamia, and Armenia, and he himself moving from place to place as circumstances required, he firmly controlled the Ayyūbid territories, thus managing to consolidate his brother's Ayyūbid legacy; al-ʿĀdil died while preparing for the defense of Egypt against the forces of the Fifth Crusade (H.A.R. Gibb, "al-ʿĀdil", in *EI*² http://referenceworks.brillonline.com/entries/encyclopaedia-of-islam-2/al-adil-SIM_0312).

244 Ǧamāl al-Dīn Maḥmūd b. Aḥmad al-Ḥaṣīrī (546–636/1151–1239) was an eminent Ḥanafī scholar from Bukhara, who spent a large part of his life teaching in Damascus (Ibn Ḫallikān, *Wafayāt al-aʿyān*, 4:259).

245 Al-Tāǧ (or Tāǧ al-Dīn) Abū l-Yumn Zayd b. al-Ḥasan al-Kindī (520–613/1126–1217) was a *littérateur* and scholar from Baghdad, who came to Syria in 563/1168, entered the service of the Ayyūbid family, and eventually settled down in Damascus as a scholar of widespread reputation (Ibn Ḫallikān, *Wafayāt al-aʿyān*, 2:339–342).

وشرح **الجامع الكبير** في الفقه وصنف **السهم المصيْب في الرد على الحافظ أبي بكر الخطيب**. وَرُئِي بخطه على **كتاب سيبويه**: إنني قطعته حفظا من خاطري، وعلى **كتاب النكت في الفقه على مذهب أبي حنيفة** أنه: قطعته حفظا—وهو في مجلدين.

واعتنى بالعلم وأهله عناية تامة، وسمع الحديث من حنبل وعمر بن طبرزد وغيره وحدث.

٣ قطعته : تصحيح في الأصل بخط المقريزي.

§ 134 He wrote a comment on *al-Ǧāmiʿ al-kabīr fī l-fiqh* [The Great Compilation in Jurisprudence][246] and he composed *al-Sahm al-muṣīb fī l-radd ʿalá l-ḥāfiẓ Abī Bakr al-Ḫaṭīb* [The Arrow that Hits Its Target Responding to the *ḥāfiẓ* Abū Bakr al-Ḫaṭīb].[247] [The following] was seen [to have been written] in his handwriting on [a copy of] the *Kitāb Sībawayhi* [The Book of Sībawayhi]:[248] "I have entirely absorbed it, learning it by heart with my mind", and on [a copy of] the *Kitāb al-Nukat fī l-fiqh ʿalá maḏhab Abī Ḥanīfah* [The Book of Anecdotes Concerning the Juridsprudence Following the Rite of Abū Ḥanīfah]:[249] "I have entirely absorbed it, learning it by heart"—this one consists of two volumes.

§ 135 He was deeply concerned for knowledge and for its people. He studied *ḥadīṯ* with Ḥanbal,[250] ʿUmar b. Ṭabarzad,[251] and others, and he transmitted *ḥadīṯ*.

246 *Al-Ǧāmiʿ al-kabīr* is a work of jurisprudence attributed to a student of Abū Ḥanīfah, al-Šaybānī (d. 189/805); it is considered a cornerstone for the thought and practice of the Ḥanafī school (E. Chaumont, "al-S̲h̲aybānī", in *EI*² http://referenceworks.brillonline.com/entries/encyclopaedia-of-islam-2/al-shaybani-COM_1051).

247 *Al-Sahm al-muṣīb fī l-radd ʿalá l-Ḫaṭīb* is a polemical work written by al-Muʿaẓẓam ʿĪsá to counter the partial biography of Abū Ḥanīfah by the Šāfiʿī scholar al-Ḫaṭīb al-Baġdādī (d. 463/1071), in his voluminous *Tārīḫ Baġdād* (*GAL* S. 1:563).

248 *Kitāb Sībawayhi* is one of the most important, founding texts of the Arabic grammatical tradition, composed by the grammarian Sībawayhi (d. c. 180/796) (M.G. Carter, "Sībawayhi", in *EI*² http://referenceworks.brillonline.com/entries/encyclopaedia-of-islam-2/sibawayhi-COM_1068).

249 *Kitāb al-Nukat fī l-fiqh ʿalá maḏhab Abī Ḥanīfah* probably refers to al-Šaybānī's *Nukat al-Ǧāmiʿ al-kabīr* (also known as *Išārāt al-Ǧāmiʿ al-kabīr*) (*GAL* S. 1:289) (see fn. 246).

250 Abū ʿAlī Ḥanbal b. ʿAbd Allāh b. Farağ b. Saʿādah was a *ḥadīṯ* transmitter, of the *Musnad* of Aḥmad b. Ḥanbal in particular, who lived and worked in Iraq and Syria and who died in 604/1207 (al-Ḏahabī, *Siyar*, 21:431–433).

251 Abū Ḥafṣ ʿUmar b. Abī Bakr Muḥammad b. Ṭabarzad (actually: Ṭabarzaḏ) al-Baġdādī l-Dāraquzī (516–607/1123–1210) was a renowned *ḥadīṯ* scholar from Baghdad, who visited Syria to transmit *ḥadīṯ* there towards the end of his life (Ibn Ḫallikān, *Wafayāt al-aʿyān*, 3:452–453).

وأعطاه أبوه الملك العادل دمشق وجعل في ولايته غزة والكرك والشوبك، وذلك سنة ست وتسعين وخمسمائة، فلم يزل حتى مات بدمشق آخر ذي القعدة سنة أربع وعشرين وستمائة.

وحج، فخرج من دمشق في حادي عشر ذي القعدة سنة إحدى عشرة وستمائة على الهجن، وسار على طريق تبوك، وبنى البركة وعدة مصانع، وتصدق على أهل الحرمين بصدقات جزيلة.

٥ وقدم منها إلى القاهرة وافدى على أبيه ومعه الشريف سالم بن قاسم—أمير المدينة—شافعا فيه، فأكرمه الملك العادل وبعث معه عسكرا إلى المدينة، وعاد المعظم إلى دمشق.

٢ وخمسمائة: "وخمسمايه" في الأصل. || وستمائة: "وستمايه" في الأصل. ٣ وستمائة: "وستمايه" في الأصل. ٥ وافدى: "وأفدا" في الأصل ويبدو أن المقريزي كشط ياء وحولها إلى ألف. ٦ الملك: تصحيح في الأصل بخط المقريزي. || عسكرا: الألف من إضافة المقريزي. || المعظم: تصحيح في الأصل بخط المقريزي.

252 The placement of the ancient Mediterranean town of Gaza in southern Palestine, on the junction of overland roads and routes that connect Egypt, Syria, and the Arabian peninsula, and amidst rich agricultural lands, has defined its destiny as a major commercial centre, as a bone of political contention, and as a meeting place for learning and scholarship, since immemorial times; integrated in the Crusader Kingdom of Jerusalem throughout the sixth/twelfth century, it remained an object of competition between Ayyubid and 'Frankish' leaders from the 560s/1170s until 642/1244 (J. Büssow, "Gaza", in *EI*[3]).

§ 136 His father al-Malik al-ʿĀdil gave him Damascus [to rule] and he put Gaza,[252] Karak[253], and Shawbak[254] under his authority. That happened in the year 596 [1200]. [This] did not change until he died in Damascus by the end of Ḏū l-Qaʿdah of the year 624 [November 1227].

5 § 137 He went on pilgrimage, leaving from Damascus on camels on 11 Ḏū l-Qaʿdah of the year 611 [14 March 1215]. He followed the Tabūk[255] road. He constructed the pond and several installations. He gave abundant alms to the people of the two august places.

§ 138 From there, he came to Cairo, coming to see his father, and with
10 him there was the Sharif Sālim b. Qāsim, the amir of Medina,[256] whom he interceded for. Al-Malik al-ʿĀdil honoured him and sent an army with him to Medina. Al-Muʿaẓẓam returned to Damascus.

253 Karak (al-Karak) is the name of another stronghold with adjacent settlement in Transjordan, east of the Dead Sea, with ancient origins but appearing in Muslim sources only from the mid-twelfth century onwards, in a Crusader context; its strategic location derived from its commanding the route to Egypt as well as the pilgrimage route from Damascus; it was taken by Saladin's brother, al-Malik al-ʿĀdil, in 584/1188, after which it also became an important site and occasional bone of contention for the Ayyūbid dynasty (D. Sourdel, "al-Karak", in *EI*² http://referenceworks.brillonline.com/entries/encyclopaedia-of-islam-2/al-karak-SIM_3906; Milwright [2008]).

254 Shawbak (al-Šawbak) is the name of a fortified place with adjacent settlement, originally constructed by the Crusaders (as Montréal), in Transjordan, on a strategic position commanding the route to Egypt; it was conquered by Saladin in 585/1189, after which it became an important site and an occasional bone of contention for the Ayyūbid dynasty (M.A. Bakhit, "al-Shawbak", in *EI*² http://referenceworks.brillonline.com/entries/encyclopaedia-of-islam-2/al-shawba-SIM_6872).

255 Tabūk is an ancient town in northwestern Arabia that was an important station of the Syrian *ḥağğ* route (M.A. al-Bakhit, "Tabūk", in *EI*², http://brillonline.com/entries/encyclopaedia-of-islam-2/tabuk-SIM_7267).

256 The Sharif Sālim b. Qāsim (d. 612/1215) was *amīr* of Medina after his father Qāsim b. Muhannā b. al-Ḥusayn; they were members of the Ḥusaynid dynasty that had founded the amirate of Medina early in the last third of the tenth century, legitimating their rule by successfully claiming direct descent from the Prophet's grandson al-Ḥusayn b. ʿAlī; Sālim is especially remembered for his successful resistance, with Ayyūbid assistance (referred to in this passage), of the attempts by the Sharif of Mecca to incorporate Medina into his domains (Mortel [1991]: 69–71).

وقد ذكرت[1] ترجمته مستوفاة في التاريخ الكبير المقفى لمصر.[٥٥]

١ ذكرت: تصحيح في الأصل بخط المقريزي.

٥٥ ترجمة المعظم عيسى مفقودة في المخطوطات المعروف وجودها للتاريخ الكبير المقفى للمقريزي. راجع المقفى، ج. ٨.

§ 139 I [al-Maqrīzī] reported his biography in detail in *al-Tārīḫ al-kabīr al-muqaffá li-Miṣr* [The Great History of Egypt in Continuation].[257]

257 Al-Maqrīzī, *al-Muqaffá* (but the entry for al-Muʿaẓẓam ʿĪsá does not seem to have survived).

128a

الملك المسعود صلاح الدين أبو المظفر يوسف—ويقال له أطسز |

ويقال أقسيس—بن السلطان الملك الكامل ناصر الدين أبي المظفر محمد بن السلطان الملك العادل سيف الدين أبي بكر محمد بن والد الملوك نجم الدين أبي الشكر أيوب بن شادي بن مروان الكردي الأيُوبي.

٥ ولد في ربيع الآخر سنة سبع وتسعين وخمسمائة، وولاه أبوه مملكة اليَمن في أيام جده سنة إحدى عشرة وستمائة. فسار إليها في ألف فارس، ومن الجاندارية والرماة خمسمائة وقدم مكة وتوجه منها إلى زَبيد، وملكها واستولى على تهامة وتعِزّ وصَنْعاء وسائر ممالك اليمن.

وحج في سنة تسع عشرة وستمائة، وقاتل أمير مكة الشريف حسن بن قتادة الحسني، وهزمه ونهب مكة. فلما كان يوم عرفة منع أعلام الخليفة من التقَدُم على أعلام أبيه. وأظهر من الجرأة على

٣ أبي: تصحيح في الأصل بخط الناسخ. ٥ وخمسمائة: "وخمسماية" في الأصل. ٦ وستمائة: "وستمايه" في الأصل. ‖ خمسمائة: "خمسماية" في الأصل. ٧ وصَنْعاء: "صَنْعا" في الأصل. ‖ وسائر: "وسآير" في الأصل. ٨ وستمائة: "وستمايه" في الأصل. ٩ مكة: تصحيح في الأصل بخط المقريزي.

5. Al-Malik al-Masʿūd Ṣalāḥ al-Dīn Abū l-Muẓaffar Yūsuf,[258] known as Aṭsiz

§ 140 [He was also] known as Aqsīs; [he was] the son of the sultan al-Malik al-Kāmil Nāṣir al-Dīn Abū l-Muẓaffar Muḥammad,[259] [who was] the son of the sultan al-Malik al-ʿĀdil Sayf al-Dīn Abū Bakr Muḥammad, [who was] the son of the father of kings, Naǧm al-Dīn Abū l-Šukr Ayyūb b. Šādī b. Marwān al-Kurdī l-Ayyūbī.

§ 141 He was born in Rabīʿ II of the year 597 [January 1201]. In the year 611 [1214–1215], in the days of his grandfather [al-Malik al-ʿĀdil], his father appointed him over the territory of Yemen. He went there amidst 1,000 horsemen and 500 [men] from the armour bearers and the bowmen. He came to Mecca and from there he proceeded to Zabīd. He occupied it, and he acquired control over Tihama, Taʿizz, Sanaa and all the territories of Yemen.

§ 142 He performed the pilgrimage in the year 619 [1223]. He fought the amir of Mecca, the Sharif Ḥasan b. Qatādah al-Ḥasanī.[260] He overcame him and plundered Mecca. When it was the Day of [the standing at] ʿArafah, he prevented the standards of the caliph from preceding his father's standards. He publicly committed gravely sinful deeds of insolence towards God, among

258 Al-Malik al-Masʿūd Yūsuf (d. 626/1229) was the son of al-Malik al-Kāmil Muḥammad, the Ayyūbid ruler of Egypt, and the grandson of the Ayyūbid ruler al-Malik al-ʿĀdil; he is mostly remembered for his rule over Yemen in his father's name, between 612/1215 and 626/1229 (Eddé, "Ayyūbids", in *EI*³).

259 Al-Malik al-Kāmil Muḥammad (b. 573/1177, r. 604–635/1207–1238) was the eldest son of Saladin's brother al-Malik al-ʿĀdil, who was given Egypt to rule by his father, and who managed after his father's death in 615/1218 and after a prolonged struggle with his brothers to have his authority acknowledged over the entire Ayyūbid polity of Egypt, Syria, Armenia, Mesopotamia, and Yemen (H.L. Gottschalk, "al-Kāmil", in *EI*² http://referenceworks.brillonline.com/entries/encyclopaedia-of-islam-2/sibawayhi-COM_1068).

260 Ḥasan b. Qatādah al-Ḥasanī was ruler or amir of Mecca after his father Qatādah b. Idrīs (r. 597–619/1201–1221), who according to some reports was one of the greatest of the long line of Ḥasanid Sharifs of Mecca (see also fn. 201); Ḥasan took power by killing his father in 618/1221, ushering in a period of internecine warfare that culminated in the Ayyūbid occupation of Mecca in 620/1223 (referred to here) and the loss of Ḥasanid effective control until 652/1254 (A.S. Wensinck, S. Zakkar, "Ḳatāda b. Idrīs", in *EI*² http://referenceworks.brillonline.com/entries/encyclopaedia-of-islam-2/katada-b-idris-SIM_4015; Mortel [1987]: 461).

الله قبائح منها أنه كان يصعد أعلى زمزم فيرمي حمام الحرم بالبُنْدق، ويستخفُ بحُرْمة الكعبة، وأكثر من سفك الدماء. وكان إذا نام في داره بالمسعى ضربت الجاندارية الطائفين بالمسعى بأطراف السيوف لئلا يشوشوا عليه وهو في نوم من شدة سكره بالخمر.

ثم عاد إلى اليمن، وخرج منها بعدما استخلف عليها نور الدين عمر بن علي بن رسول الكردي في سنة
٥ اثنتين وعشرين، وقدم القاهرة بهدايا جليلة، ونزل بالقصر وأقام لأبيه حرمة وافرة. نخافه الأمراء والأجناد، وخشوا سطوته.

ثم توجه إلى اليمن بعدما أتاه التشريف الخليفتي من بغداد، فأقام بها إلى أن بلغه ان أباه أخذ دمشق. فتاق إلى أخذها عوضا عن اليمن، وخرج بأمواله وأثقاله. فمات بمكة في ثالث عشر جمادى الأولى سنة ست وعشرين وستمائة. فدفن بالمعلا. وقام بأمر اليمن بعده نائبه عمر بن علي بن رسول.

---

١ قبائح : "قبآيح" في الأصل. ‖ أعلى : "أعلا" في الأصل. ٢ الدماء : "الدما" في الأصل. ‖ كان : ناقصة في الأصل، مضافة بخط المقريزي في الهامش الأيمن، من الأعلى إلى الأسفل + صح؛ يشير إليها الرمز ⌝ بعد كلمة "الدماء و". ٥ الأمراء : "الامرآ" في الأصل. ٩ وستمائة : "وستمايه" في الأصل. ‖ نائبه : "نايبه" في الأصل.

which [the following]: he took the habit of hunting from atop Zamzam, shooting bullets at the pigeons of the sacred mosque, and thus not taking the sacrosanctity of the Kaʿbah seriously and causing a lot of bloodshed; it used to be so that when he was asleep in his house at the time of the ritual of running [between al-Ṣafā and al-Marwah], the armour bearers would hit the two groups at the running course with the tips of their swords to make them not disturb him while he was asleep [and recovering from] his heavy drunkenness from wine.

§ 143 Then he returned to Yemen. In the year [6]22 [1225] he left from it, leaving Nūr al-Dīn ʿUmar b. ʿAlī b. Rasūl al-Kurdī[261] as his agent to govern it. He came to Cairo with fine presents and he settled down in the palace. Due to his father he obtained lofty status, the amirs and soldiers fearing him and dreading his influence.

§ 144 When there came to him from Baghdad the caliphal robe of honour, he moved back to Yemen. He remained there until he was informed that his father had taken Damascus and he wished to take it instead of Yemen. He left with his possessions and goods, but he died [on his way North,] in Mecca, on 13 Ǧumādá I of the year 626 [9 April 1229]. He was buried at al-Maʿlāh.[262] After him, Yemen was ruled by his representative ʿUmar b. ʿAlī b. Rasūl.

261 Al-Malik al-Manṣūr ʿUmar b. ʿAlī (r. 626–647/1229–1249) started as an Ayyūbid deputy in Yemen, but soon transformed into an independent ruler and became the eponymous founder of the Sunni Rasūlid dynasty of Yemen (632–858/1235–1454) (G.R. Smith, "Rasūlids", in *EI*² http://referenceworks.brillonline.com/entries/encyclopaedia-of-islam-2/rasulids-COM_0912). See Vallet (2010).

262 Al-Maʿlāh is the name of the place that houses the main historical graveyard of Mecca, the Maʿlāh cemetery, also known as the cemetery of al-Ḥaǧūn, north of the *Ḥaram*; several members of the Prophet's family as well as prominent Companions and early Muslims are buried here (S. Ory, "Maḳbara: 1. In the central Arab lands", in *EI*² http://referenceworks.brillonline.com/entries/encyclopaedia-of-islam-2/makbara-COM_0636; R.B. Winder, "Makka: 3. The Modern City", in *EI*2 http://referenceworks.brillonline.com/entries/encyclopaedia-of-islam-2/makka-COM_0638).

وقد استوفيت أخباره في **تاريخ مصر المقفى**.[٥٦]

وإليه تُنسب الدراهم المسعودية بمكة.

[٥٦] ترجمة الملك المسعود يوسف مفقودة في المخطوطات المعروف وجودها لكتاب المقفى للمقريزي. راجع المقفى، ج. ٨.

§ 145 I have recorded his stories in much more detail in the *Tārīḫ Miṣr al-muqaffá* [The History of Egypt in Continuation].[263]

§ 146 The Masʿūdī *dirhams*[264] in Mecca are named after him.

263 Al-Maqrīzī, *al-Muqaffá* (but the entry for al-Masʿūd Yūsuf does not seem to have survived).

264 These Masʿūdī *dirhams*, struck by order of al-Malik al-Masʿūd, marked an important stage in the monetary history of the Hijaz, to the extent that they continued to provide the standard for the striking of new *dirhams* in the area into the sixteenth century (Meloy [2010b]).

الملك المنصور نور الدين عمر

ابن علي بن رسول الكُردي

ملك اليمن بعد موت الملك المسعود، وبعث الملك الكامل هدية جليلة وقال: "أنا نائب السلطان على البلاد." فأقره عليها.

٥ وعُمر هذا أول من ملك اليمن من بني رسول.

وبويع له بها سنة تسع وعشرين، وخطب له بمكة فيها أيضا، ودامت مملكته إلى أن قتل في سنة سبع وأربعين وستمائة. وملك بعده ابنه الملك المظفر شمس | الدين يوسف. 128b

وحج نور الدين هذا في سنة إحدى وثلثين وستمائة على النجب.

وبعث في سنة {اثنتين} وثلثين إلى الكعبة قناديل من ذهب وفضة.

١٠ وحج أيضا في سنة تسع وثلثين، وأبطل المكوس والجنايات من مكة، وكتب ذلك تجاه الحجر الأسود. فاستمر ذلك حتى إزالة ابن المسيب لما ولي مكة سنة ست وأربعين وستمائة، وأعاد المكوس والجنايات، وصام شهر رمضان بمكة.[٥٧]

٣ نائب : "نايب" في الأصل. ٧ وستمائة : "وستمايه" في الأصل. ٨ وستمائة : "وستمايه" في الأصل.
٩ اثنتين : "ثنى" في الأصل. ١١ ابن : الألف من إضافة المقريزي. || وستمائة : "وستمايه" في الأصل.

[٥٧] راجع هذا الخبر على شكل مساو تماما في الفاسي، شفاء الغرام، ج. ٢، ص. ٢٨٦.

6. Al-Malik al-Manṣūr Nūr al-Dīn ʿUmar

[He was] the son of ʿAlī b. Rasūl al-Kurdī.

§ 147 After the death of al-Malik al-Masʿūd he acquired control over Yemen. He sent a precious gift to al-Malik al-Kāmil [in Egypt] and he said: "I am the representative of the sultan over the lands." [Al-Malik al-Kāmil] confirmed his [authority] over it.

§ 148 This ʿUmar is the first of those who were in control of Yemen from the Rasūlids.

§ 149 The oath of allegiance was sworn to him there in the year [6]29 [1232]. In [this year], the sermon in Mecca was also said in his name. His reign continued until he was killed in the year 647 [1249]. His son al-Malik al-Muẓaffar Šams al-Dīn Yūsuf[265] ruled after him.

§ 150 This Nūr al-Dīn performed the pilgrimage in the year 631 [1234], [travelling there] on especially bred she-camels.

§ 151 In the year [6]32 [1235] he sent lamps made from gold and silver to the Kaʿbah.

§ 152 He also performed the pilgrimage in the year [6]39 [1242]. He abolished the non-*sharʿī* taxes and [removed other] illegal customs from Mecca. He had that written down [on a slab] opposite the [Kaʿbah's] black stone; that [writing] remained until Ibn al-Musayyab[266] had it removed when he took control over Mecca in the year 646 [1248] and [when] he reinstated the non-*sharʿī* taxes and [other] illegal customs. [Nūr al-Dīn] performed the ritual of fasting during the month of Ramaḍān in Mecca.

---

265 Al-Malik al-Muẓaffar Yūsuf (r. 647–694/1249–1295) was the second Rasūlid ruler of Yemen, who reaped the fruits of his father's territorial and political achievements and whose longstanding and stable rule represents a high point in Rasūlid history (Smith, "Rasūlids", in *EI*²).

266 Aḥmad b. al-Musayyab al-Yamanī was appointed as local representative in Mecca by Nūr al-Dīn ʿUmar in 646/1249, but he was taken prisoner later in the same year by the Ḥasanid Ḥasan b. ʿAlī b. Qatādah, who thus resumed full control over Mecca for the Banū Ḥasan (al-Fāsī, *Šifāʾ al-ġarām*, 2:240; Mortel [1985]: 50).

واتفق في سنة ثلث وأربعين وستمائة—وقيل أربع وأربعين—أن هاجت ريح شديدة مزقت كسوة الكعبة وألقتها، وبقيت الكعبة عارية. فأراد عمر بن رسول أن يكسوها، فامتنع من ذلك شيخ الحرم عفيف الدين منصور بن مَنعة البغدادي، وقال: "لا يكون ذلك إلا من الديوان"—يعني الخليفة—، وكساها ثيابا من قطن مصبوغة بالسواد، وركب عليها الطرز القديمة.[٥٨]

---

١ وستمائة: "وسماه" في الأصل.

---

[٥٨] راجع هذا الخبر على شكل مساو تقريبا في الفاسي، شفاء الغرام، ج. ١، ص. ١٦٨.

§ 153 It so happened in the year 643 [1246]—it was said [6]44 [1247]—that a strong wind was stirred up and tore apart the *kiswah* of the Kaʿbah, throwing it off, the Kaʿbah remaining uncovered. ʿUmar b. Rasūl wanted to cover it [with a new *kiswah*]. But the *šayḫ al-ḥaram* ʿAfīf al-Dīn Manṣūr b. Manʿah al-Baġdādī[267] prevented him from doing that, saying: "That can only come from the *dīwān*", that is, [from] the caliph. So [Ibn Manʿah] had it covered with a cloth made from cotton dyed in black, on which he mounted the old embroidered inscription bands.

267 ʿAfīf al-Dīn Manṣūr b. Manʿah al-Baġdādī was supervisor of the Mecca sanctuary (*šayḫ al-ḥaram*) in the mid-thirteenth/mid-seventh century; not much is known about him, apart from the fact that after his death (at an unknown date) he was succeeded in this position of *šayḫ al-ḥaram* by his nephew, the Baġdādī *ḥadīṯ* scholar Ẓahīr al-Dīn Abū ʿAbd Allāh Muḥammad b. ʿAbd Allāh b. Abī l-Faḍl b. Manʿah al-Baġdādī (d. 708/1308–1309) (Ibn Kaṯīr, *al-Bidāyah*, 14:49).

الملك الناصر

أبو شادي داود بن الملك المعظم أبي الفتح عيسى بن الملك العادل سيف الدين أبي بكر محمد بن نجم الدين أبي الشكر أيوب بن شادي بن مروان الكردي الأيوبي.

ولد في تاسع عشر جمادى الآخرة سنة ثلث وستمائة، وحفظ القرآن وعمره تسع سنين، وقال الشعر وهو ابن عشر سنين، وبرع في كل فن من علوم الأدب والحكمة وغير ذلك. ٥

وولي سلطنة دمشق بعد موت أبيه—وهو في السنة {الحادية والعشرين} من عمره—أول ذي الحجة سنة أربع وعشرين وستمائة، وأقبل على اللهو.

فطلب منه عمه السلطان الملك الكامل قلعة الشوبك، فامتنع. فتنكر عليه وعزم على المسير إليه ونزعه من سلطنة {دمشق}. وأخذ الناصر في ظلم الرعية وأخذ أموالهم والانهماك في اللعب، واستدعى عمه الملك الأشرف شاه أرمن موسى، فقدم عليه من الشرق وحكمه في المملكة. فآل ١٠ الأمر أن حاصر الملك الكامل دمشق حتى أخذ الناصر، وعوضه عن دمشق بالكرك والشوبك

---

٤ وستمائة: "وستمايه" في الأصل. ‖ القرآن: تصحيح في الأصل بخط المقريزي. ٥ ابن: الألف ناقصة في الأصل ومضافة فوق السطر. ‖ وبرع: تصحيح في الأصل بخط المقريزي. ٦ سلطنة: تصحيح في الأصل بخط المقريزي. ‖ الحادية والعشرين: "الحادي عشر" في الأصل، والتصحيح من السياق. ٧ وستمائة: "وستمايه" في الأصل. ٩ دمشق: في الأصل "من سلطنة مصر"، وهو خطأ لأن الناصر ما ولي سلطنة مصر أبدا، والتصحيح من السياق. ١١ أخذ: تصحيح في الأصل بخط المقريزي.

7. Al-Malik al-Nāṣir

Abū Šādī Dāwūd b. al-Malik al-Muʿaẓẓam Abū l-Fatḥ ʿĪsá b. al-Malik al-ʿĀdil Sayf al-Dīn Abū Bakr Muḥammad b. Naǧm al-Dīn Abū l-Šukr Ayyūb b. Šādī b. Marwān al-Kurdī l-Ayyūbī.[268]

5 §154 He was born on 19 Ǧumādá II of the year 603 [21 January 1207]. He memorised the Qurʾān at the age of nine. He said poetry at the age of ten. He excelled in every branch of the sciences of literature and wisdom and their like.

§155 Upon the death of his father, on the first of Ḏū l-Ḥiǧǧah of the year 624 10 [12 November 1227], he was appointed sultan of Damascus. [At that time] he was twenty-one years old, and he devoted himself to amusement [instead of government].

§156 His uncle, the sultan al-Malik al-Kāmil, demanded the citadel of Shawbak from him. But he refused. So [al-Malik al-Kāmil] turned against him, 15 making plans to march against him and to take the sultanate of Damascus from him. Al-Nāṣir began to oppress the populace, seizing their properties and abandoning himself to amusements. His uncle [al-Kāmil] summoned al-Malik al-Ašraf Šāh Arman Mūsá,[269] who came to him from the East and who confirmed him [= al-Kāmil] as ruler over the realm. Eventually, the matter 20 came to al-Malik al-Kāmil besieging Damascus until he took [the city from] al-Nāṣir and he compensated him for [the loss of] Damascus with Karak,

268 Al-Malik al-Nāṣir Dāwūd (603–656/1207–1258) succeeded his father al-Muʿaẓẓam ʿĪsá as Ayyūbid ruler of Damascus in 624/1227, but he soon lost the city to his uncles al-Kāmil Muḥammad and al-Ašraf Mūsá, in Raǧab 626/June 1229, and after that he was mainly left with the region of Transjordan to rule, eventually ending up deeply embroiled in squabbles and conflicts for control over land with other members of his family until he lost all (K.V. Zettersteen, "al-Nāṣir: i. al-Malik al-Nāṣir Ṣalāḥ al-Dīn Dāwūd b. al-Malik al-Muʿaẓẓam", in *EI*² http://referenceworks.brillonline.com/entries/encyclopaedia-of-islam-2/al-nasir-COM_0851).

269 Al-Malik al-Ašraf Mūsá (d. 635/1237) was another son of Saladin's brother al-Malik al-ʿĀdil, who controled parts of Armenia and northern Mesopotamia and eventually, from 626/1229 onwards, Damascus, under the suzerainty of his brother in Egypt (Gottschalk, "al-Kāmil", in *EI*²).

والصلت والبلقاء والأغوار جميعها ونابلس وأعمال القدس وبيت جبريل. وكانت هذه الأعمال يومئذ عامرة جليلة القدر. ثم نزل الناصر عن الشوبك لعمه الكامل، وتسلم الكامل دمشق أول شعبان سنة ست وعشرين.

فأقام بالكرك، وكانت له قصص وأنباء ذكرتها في **التاريخ الكبير المقفى** آلت به أن التشتت في

٥ البلاد. وموته في إحدى قرى دمشق يوم السادس عشرين من جمادى الأولى سنة | ست وخمسين 129a

وستمائة، فدفن بصالحية دمشق.[٥٩]

١ والبلقاء : "البلقا" في الأصل. ‖ هذه : تصحيح في الأصل بخط المقريزي. ٢ يومئذ : "يوميذ" في الأصل. ‖ عامرة : تصحيح في الأصل بخط المقريزي. ٤ وأنباء : تصحيح في الأصل بخط المقريزي ("وانبآ"). ٥ جمادى : "حمادي" في الأصل. ‖ سنة : في الأصل الكلمة مكتوبة مرتين، مرة في آخر ص. ١٢٨ب ومرة أخرى في أول ص. ١٢٩أ. ٦ وستمائة : "وستمايه" في الأصل. ‖ بصالحية : تصحيح في الأصل بخط المقريزي.

[٥٩] ترجمة الملك الناصر داود مفقودة في المخطوطات المعروف وجودها للتاريخ الكبير المقفى للمقريزي. راجع المقفى، ج. ٨.

Shawbak, al-Ṣalt,[270] al-Balqāʾ,[271] the entire Jordan valley, Nablus,[272] the districts of Jerusalem, and Bayt Ǧibrīl.[273] At that time, these districts consisted of cultivated lands of high value. Only then did al-Nāṣir renounce Shawbak in his uncle al-Kāmil's favour. Al-Kāmil took hold of Damascus on the first of 5 Šaʿbān of the year [6]26 [25 June 1229].

§ 157 He [= al-Nāṣir] remained in Karak; there are tales and tidings about him which I have reported in *al-Tārīḫ al-kabīr al-muqaffá* [The Great History in Continuation], and in which he ended up moving from one region to another. His death occurred in a village near Damascus, on 26 Ǧumādá I of 10 the year 656 [31 May 1258]. He was buried at the Ṣāliḥiyyah [cemetery] of Damascus.[274]

---

270 The ancient town of al-Ṣalt (or al-Salṭ), in the Balqāʾ region, west of Amman, is known for the rich agricultural production of its orchards; a bone of contention in Crusader times, in 588/1192 it came in the hands of Ayyūbid kinsmen, who had the town's citadel constructed; it remained, next to Ḥiṣbān and Amman, a local centre of trade and government into the Ottoman period (M.A. Bakhīt, "al-Salṭ", in *EI*², http://referenceworks.brillonline.com/entries/encyclopaedia-of-islam-2/al-salt-SIM_6562).

271 Al-Balqāʾ is the name given to the relatively fertile limestone plateau of the middle-Transjordanian region, which had, depending on the period, Ḥisbān, Amman, or al-Ṣalt as its main center; it often also appeared as an administrative unit in the southern Bilād al-Šām, dependent either on the leadership of Damascus, or on that of Karak (J. Sourdel-Thomine, "al-Balḳāʾ", in *EI*², http://referenceworks.brillonline.com/entries/encyclopaedia-of-islam-2/al-balka-SIM_1151).

272 Nablus (Nābulus) is a town of Roman origins in a very fertile valley in central Palestine, with a complex history related to Judaism, Samaritanism, late antique Christianity, and the Crusades; it remained disputed territory between the latter and the Muslim rulers of the region until the mid-seventh/mid-thirteenth century (F. Buhl & C.E. Bosworth, "Nābulus", in *EI*², http://referenceworks.brillonline.com/entries/encyclopaedia-of-islam-2/nabulus-SIM_5706).

273 Bayt Ǧibrīl, also known as Bayt Ǧibrīn (and as Beth Gebrim, or also as Gibelin, in Crusader times), is a town of ancient origins in central Palestine, southwest of Jerusalem; it was a local commercial center and, from the sixth/twelfth century onwards, a fortified seat of government that acted as a local satellite for the leaderships of Gaza and Damascus (J. Sourdel-Thomine, "Bayt Djibrīn", in *EI*², http://referenceworks.brillonline.com/entries/encyclopaedia-of-islam-2/bayt-djibrin-SIM_1336).

274 Al-Ṣāliḥiyyah refers to a settlement north of Damascus, on the slopes of Mount Qāsyūn, known for containing many saints' tombs and a majority population of Ḥanbalī scholars ("al-Ṣāliḥiyya", in *EI*² http://referenceworks.brillonline.com/entries/encyclopaedia-of-islam-2/al-salihiyya-COM_0986).

وحج في سنة ثلٰث وخمسين وستمائة، وسبب حجه أنه لما تنكر له الملك الصالح نجم الدين أيوب بن الكامل وبعث إليه الأمير فخر الدين يوسف بن شيخ الشيوخ صدر الدين بن حَمُّويَه على العساكر، فهزمه وأوقع الحوطة على بلاده ونازل الكرك حتى طلب منه الأمان. فرحل عنه وقد ضاقت الأمور بالناصر، فخرج إلى حلب ومعه جواهر جليلة قيمتها ما ينيف ٥ على مائة ألف دينار، فبعثها إلى الخليفة المستعصم بالله ببغداد لتكون عنده وديعة، فقبضت من رسوله، وكتب الخط الشريف بقبضها، فشق ذلك على أولاده وخرجوا عن طاعته ولحق بعضهم بالملك الصالح نجم الدين أيوب بمصر، وسلمه الكرك. فجرت أمور آلت بالناصر إلى مسيره إلى بغداد لطلب وديعته. فمنعه الخليفة من الدخول إليها ومظله بالجوهر. فلما

١ وستمائة: "وستمايه" في الأصل. ٥ مائة: "ماية" في الأصل. ٨ إليها: تصحيح في الأصل بخط المقريزي.

275 Al-Malik al-Ṣāliḥ Ayyūb (603–647/1206–1249) was the son and successor of al-Malik al-Kāmil in Ayyūbid Egypt, who was first given Ayyūbid territories in Northern Mesopotamia and Armenia to rule, but who managed to obtain control over southern Syria and eventually also of Egypt after the death of his father, in 635/1238;

§158 [Al-Nāṣir Dāwūd] performed the pilgrimage in the year 653 [1256]. The cause for his pilgrimage was [the following:] When al-Malik al-Ṣāliḥ Naǧm al-Dīn Ayyūb b. al-Kāmil[275] turned against him, he sent the amir Faḫr al-Dīn Yūsuf b. Šayḫ al-Šuyūḫ Ṣadr al-Dīn Ḥammūyah[276] at the head of the armies
5 against him. He routed him and occupied his lands, [eventually] getting into a fight over Karak, until [al-Nāṣir] demanded a safe-conduct [for his departure] from him. [Thus being forced] to leave from [Karak], things had gotten into dire straits for al-Nāṣir. He went away to Aleppo, and he took splendid jewels with him, their value exceeding 100,000 *dīnār*, which he sent
10 on to the caliph al-Mustaʿṣim bi-llāh[277] in Baghdad, entrusting them to his custody. But they were taken from his envoy, [after] an official letter [from the sultan of Egypt] was written [ordering] their confiscation. That troubled his sons, and they left his dispensation, one of them joining up with al-Malik al-Ṣāliḥ Naǧm al-Dīn Ayyūb in Egypt, who handed him [the rule over] Karak
15 [in return]. [Many] things then happened that ended with al-Nāṣir's going to Baghdad to request his deposit. But the caliph refused to let him enter [Baghdad] and the place where he preserved the jewel. When he despaired

---

this appears as a long, complex, and violent process of re-establishing Ayyūbid coherence under al-Ṣāliḥ's authority, as the sultan of Egypt, that was all but finished when he died (D.S. Richards, "al-Malik al-Ṣāliḥ Nadjm al-Dīn Ayyūb", in *EI*[2] http://referenceworks.brillonline.com/entries/encyclopaedia-of-islam-2/al-malik-al-salih-najm-al-din-ayyub-SIM_6543).

276 Faḫr al-Dīn Yūsuf b. Šayḫ al-Šuyūḫ (580–647/1184–1250) was a military commander in Ayyūbid service and one of the main political advisors of al-Malik al-Kāmil and al-Malik al-Ṣāliḥ; he stemmed from a Syrian branch of an Iranian family of mystics and Šāfiʿī jurisprudents, the *Awlād al-Šayḫ* or Banū Ḥammūyah/Ḥammawayh, that monopolised the position of head of the mystics of Damascus (*Šayḫ al-Šuyūḫ*) for more than a century; Faḫr al-Dīn served as al-Kāmil's ambassador to the Holy Roman emperor Frederick II Hohenstaufen, in the context of the conclusion of the sixth crusade; when al-Ṣāliḥ assumed power in Egypt, Faḫr al-Dīn was made commander-in-chief of the Egyptian armies, in which capacity he was killed when leading his armies to repell an attack by the armies of Louis IX of France at al-Manṣūra (A.-M. Eddé, H.L. Gottschalk, "Awlād al-Shaykh", in *EI*[3] http://referenceworks.brillonline.com/entries/encyclopaedia-of-islam-3/awlad-al-shaykh-COM_23034).

277 Al-Mustaʿṣim bi-llāh (r. 640–657/1247–1258) was the last ʿAbbāsid caliph of Baghdad; he was put to death after his surrender of the city of Baghdad to the Mongol ruler Hülegü (K.V. Zetterstéen, "al-Mustaʿṣim Bi'llāh", in *EI*[2] http://referenceworks.brillonline.com/entries/encyclopaedia-of-islam-2/al-mustasim-bi-llah-SIM_5632).

أيس من ذلك سار إلى مكة من طريق العراق، وحج. فلما قدم المدينة النبوية تعلق بأستار الحجرة بحضرة الناس، وقال: "إشهدوا أن هذا مقامي من رسول الله داخلا عليه مستشفعا به إلى ابن عمه المستعصم في أن يرد علي وديعتي." فأعظم الناس ذلك وجرت عبراتهم وارتفع ضجيجهم بالبكاء. وكتب بصورة ما جرى مكتوب في يوم السبت ثامن عشرين ذي الحجة تسلمه أمير حاج العراقي، ومضى الناصر معه إلى بغداد. فعوض الجوهر بشيء تافه، وعاد إلى الشام مقهورا. ٥

١ إلى: "الي" في الأصل. ٢ مستشفعا: تصحيح في الأصل بخط المقريزي. ٣ بالبكاء: "بالبكا" في الأصل. ٤ بصورة: تصحيح في الأصل بخط المقريزي. ٥ إلى[1]: "الي" في الأصل. || بشيء: "بشي" في الأصل.

of [retrieving] that, he left for Mecca via the Iraq route, and he performed the pilgrimage. When he arrived in the Prophet's Medina, he hung on to the curtains of the sacrosanct area in the presence of the people, saying: "Bear witness that this is where I am standing vis-à-vis the Messenger of God, entering his house and appealing for his mediation with his cousin al-Mustaʿṣim, so as to make him return my deposit to me." People found that distressing, their tears running [down their cheeks] and their cries rising in loud wailing. A report of what had happened was written on Saturday 28 of Ḏū l-Ḥiǧǧah [29 January], which was handed to the amir of the Iraqi pilgrimage caravan. Al-Nāṣir left with him to Baghdad, and in compensation for the jewel something was given that still made him mutter in complaint; humiliated, he returned to Syria.

الملك المظفر شمس الدين يوسف

ابن الملك المنصور نور الدين عمر بن علي بن رسول.

قام بعد أبيه بملك اليمن في سنة سبع وأربعين وستمائة، وحج سنة تسع وخمسين، وغسل الكعبة بنفسه وطيبها وكساها من داخلها وخارجها.

٥ وهو أول من كسا الكعبة بعد قتل الخليفة المستعصم ببغداد من الملوك، وذلك أن الحاج انقطع من العراق عن مكة من سنة خمس وخمسين وستمائة إلى سنة ست وستين، فلم يرد من هناك حاج في هذه المدة. وقام المظفر بمصالح الحرم وأهله، وأكثر من الصدقات، ونثر على الكعبة الذهب والفضة، وخطب له بمكة واستمر يخطب بعده لملوك اليمن على منبر مكة إلى يومنا هذا بعد الخطبة لسلطان مصر.[٦٠]

١٠ ولم تزل كسوة المظفر التي كساها للكعبة من داخلها باقية إلى | أن كساها الملك الناصر حسن 129b ابن محمد بن قلاوون هذه الكسوة—الموجودة اليوم—في سنة إحدى وستين وسبعمائة.

٣ وأربعين وستمائة: "واربعن وستمايه" في الأصل. ٥ كسا: "كسى" في الأصل. ٦ وستمائة: "وستمايه" في الأصل. ١٠ إلى: "الي" في الأصل. ١١ وستين وسبعمائة: "وسىن وسبعمايه" في الأصل.

[٦٠] راجع هذا الخبر على شكل مساو في الفاسي، شفاء الغرام، ج. ٢، ص. ٢٨٨.

8. Al-Malik al-Muẓaffar Šams al-Dīn Yūsuf

[He was] the son of al-Malik al-Manṣūr Nūr al-Dīn ʿUmar b. ʿAlī b. Rasūl.

§ 159 In the year 647 [1249], he took up rule over Yemen, succeeding his father. He performed the pilgrimage in the year [6]59 [1261]. [On that occasion], he washed the Kaʿbah by himself, perfumed it, and covered it with a *kiswah* on the inside and on the outside.

§ 160 He is the first of the rulers who covered the Kaʿbah with a *kiswah* after the killing of the caliph al-Mustaʿṣim in Baghdad.[278] The reason for that was that pilgriming between Iraq and Mecca was interrupted from the year 655 [1257] until the year [6]66 [1268]. During this period there did not come from there any pilgrim anymore. As a result, al-Muẓaffar took responsibility for the wellbeing of the Ḥaram and its people, increasing the alms that were given and sprinkling gold and silver over the Kaʿbah. The Friday sermon in Mecca was delivered in his name, and the sermon thus continued to be delivered from the *minbar* of Mecca in the name of the rulers of Yemen until our own days, [but then nowadays only] after the sermon [is delivered] in the name of the sultan of Egypt.

§ 161 The *kiswah* of al-Muẓaffar, which he had the inside of the Kaʿbah covered with, continued to be present until in the year 761 [1360] al-Malik al-Nāṣir Ḥasan b. Muḥammad b. Qalāwūn[279] covered it with this *kiswah* which is still present today.

278 For the events involving the execution of the last ʿAbbāsid caliph of Baghdad, al-Mustaʿṣim, in 656/1258 by the Mongol ruler Hülegü, see fn. 192, 277.

279 Al-Malik al-Nāṣir Ḥasan b. Muḥammad b. Qalāwūn (r. 748–752/1347–1351; 755–762/1354–1361) was sultan of Egypt and Syria and a member of the Qalāwūnid dynasty; he was made sultan twice, first as a minor and then again when he was about twenty; during his second term of office, he eventually managed to impose his authority more firmly than before, but he yet failed to hold onto power and was killed by members of his own entourage; he is remembered especially for his impressive public works, especially his huge religio-economic complex at the foot of the Cairo citadel (known as the sultan Ḥasan mosque or *madrasah*) (J. Wansbrough, "Ḥasan", in *EI*² http://referenceworks.brillonline.com/entries/encyclopaedia-of-islam-2/hasan-SIM_2752).

السلطان الملك الظاهر ركن الدين أبو الفتح بيبرس البندقداري الصالحي النجمي

اشتراه السلطان الملك الصالح نجم الدين أيوب بن الملك الكامل ناصر الدين محمد بن الملك العادل سيف الدين أبي بكر محمد بن نجم الدين أيوب، وعمله أحد المماليك البحرية بقلعة الروضة. فترقى في خدمته واستفاد من أخلاقه وتنقلت به الأحوال حتى ملك مصر بعد قتل الملك المظفر سيف

٥ الدين قطز، وتسلم قلعة الجبل ليلة الاثنين تاسع عشر ذي القعدة سنة ثمان وخمسين وستمائة. واستمر ملكه حتى مات بدمشق في سابع عشرين المحرم سنة ست وسبعين وستمائة. وقد ملك مدة سبع عشرة سنة وشهرين واثني {عشر} يوما.

وحج سنة سبع وستين وستمائة، ولذلك خبر طويل قد ذكرته في ترجمته من **كتاب التاريخ الكبير المقفى** و**كتاب أخبار ملوك مصر**.[٦١]

٥ وتسلم : تصحيح في الأصل. ‖ وستمائة : "وستمايه" في الأصل. ٦ سنة[١] : تصحيح في الأصل. ‖ وسبعين : تصحيح في الأصل بخط المقريزي. ‖ وستمائة : "وستمايه" في الأصل. ٧ عشرة : تصحيح في الأصل بخط المقريزي. ‖ عشر : "عشرة" في الأصل. ٨ وستمائة : "وستمايه" في الأصل.

[٦١] لـ"أخبار ملوك مصر"—يعني السلوك—راجع المقريزي، السلوك، ج. ١، ص. ٥٧٣–٥٨٣. وترجمة الملك الظاهر بيبرس مفقودة في المخطوطات المعروف وجودها لكتاب المقفى للمقريزي. راجع المقفى، ج. ٨.

9. The sultan al-Malik al-Ẓāhir Rukn al-Dīn Abū l-Fatḥ Baybars al-Bunduqdārī l-Ṣāliḥī l-Naǧmī[280]

§ 162 The sultan al-Malik al-Ṣāliḥ Naǧm al-Dīn Ayyūb b. al-Malik al-Kāmil Nāṣir al-Dīn Muḥammad b. al-Malik al-ʿĀdil Sayf al-Dīn Abū Bakr Muḥammad b. Naǧm al-Dīn Ayyūb bought him and he made him one of the Baḥriyyah *mamlūk*s[281] in the citadel of al-Rawḍah.[282] [Baybars] advanced in his service, benefitting from his noble character. All kinds of things happened to him, until he took power over Egypt after the murder of al-Malik al-Muẓaffar Sayf al-Dīn Quṭuz.[283] [Baybars] was handed over [Cairo's] citadel of the mountain in the night of Monday, 19 Ḏū l-Qaʿdah of the year 658 [25 October 1260]. His rule lasted until he died in Damascus on 27 Muḥarram of the year 676 [30 June 1277], [after] he had ruled for a period of 17 years, two months, and 12 days.

§ 163 He went on pilgrimage in the year 667 [1269]. There is a long story of that which I have reported in his biography in the book *al-Tārīḫ al-kabīr al-muqaffá* [The Great History in Continuation] and the book *Aḫbār Mulūk Miṣr* [The Stories of the Kings of Egypt].[284]

280 For sultan al-Malik al-Ẓāhir Baybars (r. 658–676/1260–1277), remembered as a pioneering ruler of the sultanate of Egypt and Syria, see fn. 196.

281 The Baḥriyyah *mamlūk*s were a corps of elite military slaves of the last Ayyūbid ruler of Egypt, stationed on the island of al-Rawḍah in the Nile (*al-Baḥr*) (D. Ayalon, "al-Baḥriyya", in EI² http://referenceworks.brillonline.com/entries/encyclopaedia-of-islam-2/al-bahriyya-SIM_1075).

282 The citadel of al-Rawḍah was constructed by the last Ayyūbid ruler of Egypt between 637/1240 and 641/1243 on the island of al-Rawḍah in the Nile, East of Fusṭāṭ; it consisted of palaces for the sultan and his family and retainers, and of barracks for his *mamlūk*s; after the sultan's death, this citadel was abandonned by Egypt's new rulers (Raymond [2001]: 101–102).

283 Sultan al-Muẓaffar Quṭuz (r. 657–658/1259–1260) was a *mamlūk* commander who ruled Egypt at the time of the Mongol invasion of Syria; he is remembered for the victory that his armies won near the town of ʿAyn Ǧālūt in 658/1260 against the hitherto invincible Mongols; shortly afterwards, Quṭuz was murdered by a band of peers that included his successor, sultan al-Ẓāhir Baybars (Thorau, "Baybars I, al-Malik al-Ẓāhir Rukn al-Dīn", in EI²).

284 See al-Maqrīzī, *al-Sulūk*, 1:573–583 (= *Kitāb Aḫbār Mulūk Miṣr*); al-Maqrīzī, *al-Muqaffá* (but the entry for al-Ẓāhir Baybars does not seem to have survived).

وملخص ذلك أنه أجلس ابنه الملك السعيد محمد بركة خان في مرتبة الملك وحضر الأمراء فقبلوا الأرض بين يديه، وجلس الأمير عز الدين أيدمر الحِلي—نائب السلطنة—وجلس الأتابك والصاحب بهاء الدين علي بن حنا وكتّاب الإنشاء والقضاة والشهود، وحلف له الأمراء وسائر العساكر في تاسع صفر منها، وركب في ثالث عشره الموكب كما يركب والده، وجلس في الإيوان
٥ وقرئت عليه القصص، وقرئ في العشرين منه تقليد بتفويض السلطنة له في الإيوان، واستمر جلوسه فيه لقضاء الأشغال، ووَقّع وأطلق وركب في المواكب.[٦٢]

وأقام السلطان الأمير بدر الدين بيليك الخازندار نائبا عنه عوضا عن الحلي. وسار الى الشام في ثاني عشر جمادى الآخرة بِحصة من العساكر، وترك أكثرها مع ولده الملك السعيد. ونزل بخربة اللصوص—خارج دمشق—، وسار منها متنكرا إلى القاهرة ليشاهد أحوال ولده: نخفي

١ الأمراء: "الامرآ" في الأصل. ٣ بهاء: "بهآ" في الأصل. ‖ الإنشاء: "الانشآ" في الأصل. ‖ الأمراء وسائر: "الامرآ وساير" في الأصل. ٥ منه: ناقصة في الأصل، مضافة بخط المقريزي في الهامش الأيسر، من الأسفل إلى الأعلى + صح؛ يشير إليها الرمز ⌐ بعد كلمة "العشرين". ٦ جلوسه: تصحيح في الأصل بخط المقريزي. ‖ فيه: ناقصة في الأصل، مضافة بخط المقريزي في الهامش الأيسر، من الأعلى إلى الأسفل + صح؛ يشير إليها الرمز ⌐ بعد كلمة "جلوسه". ‖ لقضاء: "لقضآ" في الأصل. ٧ الأمير: ناقصة في الأصل، مضافة بخط المقريزي في الهامش الأيسر، من الأعلى إلى الأسفل + صح؛ يشير إليها الرمز ⌐ بعد كلمة "السلطان". ‖ نائبا: "نايبا" في الأصل. ٩ متنكرا: تصحيح في الأصل.

[٦٢] راجع هذا الخبر على نفس الشكل تقريبا في ابن عبد الظاهر، الروض الزاهر، ص. ٣٣٨.

285 Sultan al-Saʿīd Barakah Ḫān (also Berke Ḫān) (658–678/1260–1280) was the son of al-Ẓāhir Baybars, who co-ruled with his father since 662/1264 and who succeeded him briefly upon his death in 676/1277, without however ever managing to impose his authority against that of his father's entourage; he was forced into exile in 678/1279 (Stewart [2007]: 49–51).

§ 164 The short version of that [story] is [the following]: He made his son al-Malik al-Saʿīd Muḥammad Barakah Ḫān[285] sit on the seat of the ruler, in the presence of the amirs. They kissed the ground before him, and the amir ʿIzz al-Dīn Aydamur al-Ḥillī, the viceroy,[286] sat down, as did the commander of the army,[287] the lord Bahāʾ al-Dīn ʿAlī Ibn Ḥinnā,[288] the scribes of the chancery, the *qāḍī*s, and the legal witnesses. The amirs and the entire army swore an oath to him [= al-Malik al-Saʿīd Barakah] on 9 Ṣafar of [667] [18 October 1268]. On 13 [Ṣafar] [22 October] he rode in the public procession—just as his father used to ride—, he held session in the audience hall, and the petitions were read to him. On 20 [Ṣafar] [29 October] an official diploma was read out in the audience hall for the delegation of the sultanate to him. [Thereafter] he continued to hold session there to deal with royal business, [including] putting his signature [on documents and decrees], expressing [his will] without restriction, and riding in the public processions.

§ 165 The sultan [Baybars] installed the amir Badr al-Dīn Bīlīk al-Ḫāzindār[289] as his representative [in Egypt] instead of al-Ḥillī. [Baybars] left for Syria on 12 Ǧumādá II [667] [16 February 1269] with a small part of the army, leaving most of it behind with his son al-Malik al-Saʿīd. He settled down at Ḫirbat al-Luṣūṣ[290] outside Damascus and he went from there to Cairo in disguise, so as to see with his own eyes how his son was doing. That remained

286 ʿIzz al-Dīn Aydamur al-Ḥillī (d. 667/1269) was a senior commander and peer of Baybars, who acted as *nāʾib al-salṭanah* or vice-gerent in Egypt for some time (Ibn Taġrī Birdī, *al-Manhal al-ṣāfī*, 3:170–171; Amitai [1997]: 293, no. 9).

287 The commander of the army, or *atābeg*, at that time was the senior commander Fāris al-Din Aqṭāy al-Ṣāliḥī (d. 672/1273–1274) (Amitai [1997]: 292, no. 1).

288 Bahāʾ al-Dīn ʿAlī b. Muḥammad b. Ḥinnā (603–677/1206–1278) was the highly respected right-hand and vizier of al-Ẓāhir Baybars, who arranged the sultan's affairs throughout his reign (Ibn Taġrī Birdī, *al-Manhal al-ṣāfī*, 8:150–151).

289 Badr al-Dīn Bīlīk al-Ḫāzindār (d. 676/1278) was a *mamlūk* of al-Ẓāhir Baybars from before the time he became sultan; he became Baybars' vice-gerent and the right-hand of his son Barakah Ḫān (Ibn Taġrī Birdī, *al-Manhal al-ṣāfī*, 3:512–514; Amitai [1997]: 292–293, no. 4).

290 Ḫirbat al-Luṣūṣ: I have so far not been able to retrieve any more specific information on this site, apart from that, obviously, it lay south of Damascus, on the road to Cairo, and that—given its name, Ḫirbah, 'The Ruins'—it may have been connected to the remains, along the Damascus-Cairo road, of some ancient construction.

ذلك على جميع من معه من العسكر حتى عاد إليهم، وفي حكاية ذلك هنا طول ليس من قصد هذا {الجزء}.[٦٣]

فاتفق الاختلاف بين الشريف نجم الدين أبي نمي وبين عمه الشريف {بهاء} الدين إدريس—أميري مكة—، فرتب السلطان لهما عشرين ألف درهم نقرة في كل سنة عوضا | عما يؤخذ بمكة 130a
٥ من المكوس وأن لا يُمنَع أحد من دخول الكعبة وأن يُخطَب له بمكة والمشاعر وتضرَب السكة باسمه. فأجاباه، وكتب لهما تقليد الإمارة، وسلمت أوقاف الحرم بمصر والشام لنوابهما.

وسُلم للشريف قاضي المدينة النبوية وخطيبها ووزيرها، عندما حضر برسالة الأمير عز الدين جماز، أمير المدينة، الجمال التي نهبها الأمير أحمد بن حجي لأشراف المدينة—وهي ثلٰثة آلاف

١ هنا: ناقصة في الأصل، مضافة بخط المقريزي في الهامش الأيسر، من الأعلى إلى الأسفل + صح؛ يشير إليها الرمز ⌐ بعد كلمة "ذلك". ١-٢ هذا الجزء: "هذا الجزو" في الأصل. ٣ الشريف¹: ناقصة في الأصل، مضافة بخط المقريزي في الهامش الأيمن، على نفس السطر + صح؛ يشير إليها الرمز ⌐ بعد كلمة "بين". || بهاء: "بهاي" في الأصل. ٤ عما: في الأصل الكلمة مكتوبة مرتين، مرة في آخر ص.١٢٩ب ومرة ثانية في بداية ص.١٣٠أ.

[٦٣] راجع هذا الخبر بتفاصيله كله في ابن عبد الظاهر، الروض الزاهر، ص. ٣٤٢-٣٤٦.

hidden for all who were with him from the army, until he returned to them. The narrative of that [story] is so long that it does not suit the purpose of this volume to tell it here.

§ 166 There occurred discord between the Sharif Naǧm al-Dīn Abū Numayy[291] and his uncle, the Sharif Bahāʾ al-Dīn Idrīs, the two amirs of Mecca. The sultan assigned to both of them 20,000 high quality *dirhams*[292] annually, instead of the non-*šarʿī* taxes that used to be collected in Mecca, and [on the condition] that no one would be prevented from entering the Kaʿbah, that the sermon in Mecca and at the ceremony shrines would be said in his name, and [that] the coin would be struck in his name. They both accepted and the official diploma for the amirate was written for both of them. The [responsibility for the] pious foundations for the *Ḥaram* in Egypt and Syria was handed over to their representatives.

§ 167 Upon the arrival [in Ḫirbat] of the Sharif [Šams al-Dīn]—[who was] the *qāḍī*, the *ḫaṭīb* and the vizier of the Prophet's Medina—with a letter from the amir ʿIzz al-Dīn Ǧammāz,[293] the amir of Medina, there were handed over to him the camels which the amir Aḥmad b. Ḥiǧǧī[294] had looted from the

291 On the Sharif Abū Numayy (r. 652–700/1254–1301) and his family of Ḥasanid rulers of Mecca, see fn. 201.

292 The actual meaning of the Arabic numismatic terminology used here, *dirham nuqrah*, remains an issue of debate; it either refers to a particular type of *dirhams* of higher than standard silver purity, or to a fixed-weight money of account used to determine the actual, weighed value of silver coins of irregular weight (Schultz [2004]: 231–234).

293 ʿIzz al-Dīn Ǧammāz b. Šīḥah (d. 704/1304) was a member of the Ḥusaynid ruling family of Medina (see also fn. 256); Ǧammāz seems to have shared the amirate of Medina with his brother Munīf from 649/1251 until the latter's death in 657/1259; thereafter Ǧammāz continued as the independent and ambitious ruler of Medina until 700/1301 or 702/1303; in the period 665–667/1266–1268, however, his authority was successfully albeit only briefly challenged by his brother's son, Mālik b. Munīf, who received the support for this from the sultan Baybars (Mortel [1994]: 99–103).

294 Aḥmad b. Ḥiǧǧī b. Yazīd (d. 682/1283) was a leader of the Āl Murrah tribal group, a powerful tribe of nomadic pastoralists still present in contemporary Saudi Arabia, which in the later medieval period controled much of the region in the triangle between Syria, lower Mesopotamia, and the central Arabian Najd (E. Landau-Tasseron, "Murra", in *EI*[2] http://referenceworks.brillonline.com/entries/encyclopaedia-of-islam-2/murra-SIM_5546; al-Kutubī, *Fawāt al-wafayāt*, 1:425).

بعير—ليوصلها لأربابها. وأنعم على الطواشي جمال الدين محسن الصالحي—شيخ الخدام بالحجرة الشريفة—بمائتي ألف درهم، وأعاده مع القاضي صحبة الركب الشامي.[٦٤]

وجهز الكسوة لمكة والمدينة.[٦٥]

وقَدم الأمير شرف الدين عيسى بن مهنا إلى الدهليز بالخربة، فأوهم السلطان أنه يريد الحركة إلى العراق، وأمره بالتأهب ليركب إذا دعي، ورده إلى بلاده، وكان السلطان في الباطن إنما يريد ٥ الحركة للحجاز، لكنه وَرَّى بالعراق.[٦٦]

فلما دخل شوال أنفق في العساكر جميعها وجرد طائفة مع الأمير آقوش الرومي السلاح دار ليكونوا صحبة الرِكاب السلطاني، وجرد طائفة مع الأمير شمس الدين آق سُنقر الفارقاني أُسْتادار إلى دمشق

١ جمال الدين: تصحيح في الأصل بخط المقريزي. ٢ بمائتي: "بمايتى" في الأصل. ٧ طائفة: "طايفه" في الأصل. ٨ السلطاني: ناقصة في الأصل، مضافة بخط المقريزي في الهامش الأيمن، من الأعلى إلى الأسفل + صح، يشير إليها الرمز ⌐ بعد كلمة "الركاب". ‖ طائفة: "طايفه" في الأصل. ‖ شمس: ناقصة في الأصل مضافة بخط المقريزي فوق كلمة "الامير" على آخر السطر. ‖ الدين: تصحيح في الأصل بخط المقريزي. ‖ أُسْتادار: تصحيح في الأصل بخط المقريزي.

[٦٤] راجع هذا الخبر بتفاصيله في ابن عبد الظاهر، الروض الزاهر، ص. ٣٥١-٣٥٣. [٦٥] راجع هذا الخبر بتفاصيل لتاريخ الكسوة في ابن عبد الظاهر، الروض الزاهر، ص. ٣٥٣. [٦٦] راجع هذا الخبر على شكل مساو في ابن عبد الظاهر، الروض الزاهر، ص. ٣٥٨.

nobles of Medina—they were 3,000 camels—, so that he could lead them back to their owners. To the eunuch Ǧamāl al-Dīn Muḥsin al-Ṣāliḥī, the *šayḫ* of the eunuch servants in the noble enclosure,[295] [who had also come to Ḫirbat,] there were granted 200,000 *dirhams*. [Al-Ẓāhir Baybars] sent him as well as the *qāḍī* [Šams al-Dīn and his camels] back [to Medina] with the Syrian pilgrimage caravan.

§ 168 [Baybars] sent the *kiswah* to Mecca and Medina.

§ 169 The amir Šaraf al-Dīn ʿĪsá b. Muhannā[296] came to the royal tent at Ḫirbat [al-Luṣūṣ]. The sultan made believe that he wanted to proceed to [Mongol] Iraq and he ordered him to be prepared to ride out if he is summoned. [Thereupon] he sent him back to his lands. Secretly, the sultan only wanted to move to the Hijaz, but he pretended [to march] for Iraq.

§ 170 When Šawwāl [667] [June 1269] began, he disbursed a sum of money over the entire army. He sent a party ahead with the amir Āqqūš al-Rūmī l-Silāḥdār[297] to accompany the sultan's caravan. He sent a party ahead to Damascus with the amir Šams al-Dīn Āq Sunqur al-Fāriqānī l-Ustā-

295 Since the twelfth century, a corps of eunuchs guarded the access to the Prophet's tomb and to the noble enclosure (*al-ḥuǧrah al-šarīfah*, the structure that enclosed the tombs of the Prophet and of the first two caliphs) in Medina; the leader of this eunuch community, the *šayḫ al-ḫuddām*, always combined this position with that of *šayḫ* of the Prophet's sanctuary (*šayḫ al-ḥaram*), which made him one of the most powerful figures in Medina; this situation lasted until the mid-nineteenth century; the eunuch Ǧamāl al-Dīn Muḥsin al-Ṣāliḥī (d. 668/1269–1270), who had been a powerful member of the Egyptian court since the days of the last Ayyubid ruler al-Ṣāliḥ Ayyūb, occupied this position of high status at the time of Baybars' pilgrimage (Marmon [1995]: 31–53, 93–112; al-Maqrīzī, *al-Sulūk*, 1:342, 356, 512, 580, 588).

296 Šaraf al-Dīn ʿĪsá b. Muhannā (d. 683/1284) was the leader of the Arab clan of the Āl Faḍl in Syria; his charismatic leadership over the Arab Bedouin clans and groupings in Syria was acknowledged by the sultan Baybars through his appointment as *amīr al-ʿArab* in 663/1264; as a widely respected and successful local leader, ʿĪsá always managed to negotiate a reasonable autonomy vis-à-vis the sultan's suzerainty, including via occasional rapprochements to the Mongol Īlḫānids (M.C. Şehabeddin Tekindağ, "ʿĪsā b. Muhannā", in *EI*² http://referenceworks.brillonline.com/entries/encyclopaedia-of-islam-2/isa-b-muhanna-SIM_3599; Hiyari [1975]: 516–517).

297 Ǧamāl al-Dīn Āqqūš al-Rūmī l-Silāḥdār was a peer of Baybars from the time of their membership in the corps of the last Ayyūbid ruler of Egypt; in the 650s/1250s they had continued their partnership in Syria; Āqqūš remained an important supporter for Baybars throughout his reign (Amitai [1997]: 299, no. 57).

ليقيموا ظاهرها. وتوجه السلطان إلى الحج ومعه الأمير بدر الدين الخازندار وقاضي القضاة صدر الدين سليمٰن الحنفي وفخر الدين إ براهيم بن لقمان— كاتب السر—وتاج الدين بن الأثير ونحو ثلٰثمائة مملوك وعدة من أجناد الحلقة. وسار من الفوار يوم الخميس خامس شهر شوال كأنه متوجه إلى الكرك كأنه يتصيد، ولم يجسر أحد يتحدث بأنه متوجه إلى الحجاز، وذلك أن الحاجب جمال ٥ الدين بن الداية كتب إلى السلطان يسأله: "إني أشتهي أن أتوجه صحبة السطان إلى الحجاز." فأمر بقطع لسانه، فلم يتفوه أحد بعدها بذلك.

فوصل إلى الكرك أول يوم من ذي القعدة، وكان قد دبر أموره في خفية من غير أن يطلع أحد على شيء مما فعله، بحيث أنه جهز البشماط والدقيق والروايا والقرب والأشربة، وعين العربان المتوجهين معه والمرتبين في المنازل من غير أن يشعر أحد من الخاصة فضلا عن العامة بذلك.

---

٣ من[٢]: تصحيح في الأصل بخط المقريزي. ‖ الفوار: تصحيح في الأصل بخط المقريزي. ٤ أن: ناقصة في الأصل، مضافة بخط المقريزي في الهامش الأيمن، من الأعلى إلى الأسفل + صح؛ يشير إليها الرمز ⌐ بعد كلمة "ذلك". ٤–٥ جمال ... بن: تصحيح في الأصل بخط المقريزي. ٨ شيء: "شي" في الأصل.

dār,[298] to set up camp outside it[s walls]. The sultan proceeded to perform the pilgrimage, together with the amir Badr al-Dīn al-Ḫāzindār, the chief judge Ṣadr al-Dīn Sulaymān al-Ḥanafī,[299] the chancery chief Faḫr al-Dīn Ibrāhīm b. Luqmān,[300] Tāǧ al-Dīn Ibn al-Aṯīr,[301] about 300 *mamlūk*s and a number of rank-and-file troops. He left without delay on Thursday the fifth of the month Šawwāl [6 June], pretending to proceed towards Karak to go hunting. No one dared to talk about his proceeding towards the Hijaz. [The reason for] that was the doorkeeper Ǧamāl al-Dīn Ibn al-Dāyah's[302] writing to the sultan, asking him: "I would like to go with the sultan to the Hijaz": it was ordered to cut his tongue [for this disclosure of the sultan's secret], and afterwards no one dared to speak about that again.

§ 171 He arrived in Karak on the first day of Ḏū l-Qaʿdah [2 July]. He had already secretly arranged his affairs [for the journey to Mecca], without informing anyone of what he was doing. In this way, he had sent ahead biscuits, flour, camels that carry water, waterskins, and drinks; he had appointed Bedouins to proceed with him as well as to be in charge of the halting places; [he had organised all this] without anyone from his entourage, let alone from the commoners, realising that.

---

298 Šams al-Dīn Āq Sunqur al-Fāriqānī l-Ustādār (d. 677/1278) became an important agent of al-Ẓāhir Baybars' royal authority, after a career of *mamlūk* service in Syria and then in Egypt, where Baybars eventually made him his main steward (*ustādār*) and one of the leading men in his entourage; after Baybars' death, he was caught by his opponents and remained in prison until he died (Ibn Taġrī Birdī, *al-Manhal al-ṣāfī*, 2:494–496).

299 Ṣadr al-Dīn Sulaymān b. Abī l-ʿIzz al-Ḥanafī (d. 677/1278) was a highly respected scholar of the Ḥanafī creed; he was a teacher and chief judge in Damascus, and also in Egypt (Ibn Taġrī Birdī, *al-Manhal al-ṣāfī*, 6:57–58).

300 Faḫr al-Dīn Ibrāhīm b. Luqmān al-Šaybānī l-Isʿardī (612–693/1215–1293) was a well-known and widely respected scribe in the royal chancery in Cairo, with a long-standing track record that had started in the reign of the Ayyūbid ruler al-Kāmil Muḥammad (Ibn Taġrī Birdī, *al-Manhal al-ṣāfī*, 1:136–138).

301 Tāǧ al-Dīn Aḥmad b. Saʿīd b. al-Aṯīr al-Ḥalabī (d. 691/1291) was a leading scribe in the chancery in Damascus, and then in the royal chancery in Egypt, during the reign of al-Ẓāhir Baybars and during those of his successors (Ibn Taġrī Birdī, *al-Manhal al-ṣāfī*, 1:300–302).

302 Nothing further is known about this Ǧamāl al-Dīn Ibn al-Dāyah, apart from the fact that he was one of the sultan's doorkeepers (*ḥāǧib*s) at this particular moment (thus, he is merely referred to as "some person from [the group of] doorkeepers known as Ǧamāl al-Dīn Ibn al-Dāyah" in the version of this story by the early-fourteenth-century historian Baybars al-Manṣūrī, *Zubdat al-fikrah*, 121).

ففرق في المجردين معه الشعير، وبعث الثقل في رابعه، وتبعه في سادسه، فنزل الشوبك، ورسم بإخفاء خبره، واستقل بالمسير في حادي عشره، وأنفذ | البريد إلى قلعة الجبل لمهمات له. فجهزت الكتب مع العربان وقدم المدينة النبوية في خامس عشرينه، فلم يقابله الشريف جماز ولا مالك — {أميرا} المدينة —، وفرا منه، فأعرض عنهما. 130b

٥ ورحل في سابع عشرينه، وأحرم، فدخل مكة في خامس ذي الحجة، وأعطى خواصه جملة أموال لتفرق في الناس سرا، وعم أهل الحرمين بالكسوة التي فرقها فيهم، وصار كآحاد الناس لا يحجبه أحد ولا يحرسه إلا الله تعالى، وبقي منفردا يصلي وحده ويطوف وحده ويسعى وحده، فلا يعرفه إلا من يعرفه. وغسل الكعبة بيده بماء الورد، وصار بين جميع الناس على اختلاف طبقاتهم وتباين أجناسهم، وما منهم إلا من يرمي إليه إحرامه، فيغسله بيده ويناوله صاحبه. وجلس على ١٠ باب الكعبة وأخذ بأيدي الناس ليطلعهم إليها، فتعلق بعض العامة بإحرامه ليطلع فقطعه، وكاد يرمي السلطان عن العتبة إلى الأرض وهو مستبشر بجميع ذلك، وعلق كسوة الكعبة بيده ومعه خواصه، وتردد إلى من بمكة والمدينة من أهل الخير يلتمس بركتهم ويسأل دعاءهم.

هذا وقاضي القضاة صدر الدين معه طول طريقه يستفتيه ويتفهم منه أمور دينه.

---

٢ بإخفاء: "باخفآ" في الأصل. ٣ الشريف: ناقصة في الأصل، مضافة بخط المقريزي في الهامش الأيسر، من الأسفل إلى الأعلى + صح، يشير إليها الرمز ¬ بعد كلمة "يقابله". ٤ أميرا: "امرى" في الأصل، والتصحيح من السياق. ٨ بماء: "بمآ" في الأصل. ‖ الورد: تصحيح في الأصل بخط المقريزي. ‖ جميع: ناقصة في الأصل، مضافة بخط المقريزي في الهامش الأيسر، من الأسفل إلى الأعلى + صح، يشير إليها الرمز ¬ بعد كلمة "بين". ٩ من: ناقصة في الأصل، مضافة بخط المقريزي في الهامش الأيسر، من الأعلى إلى الأسفل + صح، يشير إليها الرمز ¬ بعد كلمة "الا". ١٢ دعاءهم: "دعآهم" في الأصل.

§ 172 He distributed the barley among those that were proceeding with him, and he sent the supplies ahead on 4 [Ḏū l-Qaʿdah] [5 July], and he followed them on 6 [Ḏū l-Qaʿdah] [7 July]. He set up camp at Shawbak, and he gave the command to conceal any news about him. On 11 [Ḏū l-Qaʿdah] [12 July] he set out alone. [In the course of this] he set the postal service to the citadel of the mountain in operation for some business of his, sending the letters with Bedouins. He arrived in the Prophet's Medina on the 25 [Ḏū l-Qaʿdah] [26 July]. Neither the Sharif Ǧammāz nor Mālik—the two amirs of Medina—received him. They fled away from him, and he left them alone.[303]

§ 173 He departed on 27 [Ḏū l-Qaʿdah] [28 July] and entered into *iḥrām*. He entered Mecca on 5 Ḏū l-Ḥiǧǧah [5 August], providing his retainers riches to secretly distribute among the people, and many of the inhabitants of the two august places were dotted with the garments that he had distributed among them. He became like one of the people, not sheltered nor guarded by anyone unless by God the Exalted. He remained alone, praying on his own, making the circumambulation on his own, and running on his own, without anyone recognising him, except for those who knew him. With his own hands he washed the Kaʿbah with rose water, and he got among all the people, with all the differences of their classes and the variety of their ethnic backgrounds. One of them even threw his ritual garb to him, which he washed with his own hands and which he then handed back to its owner. He sat down at the gate of the Kaʿbah and took the people's hands to help them climb it; one of the commoners clung to his ritual garb to climb up, tearing it and almost throwing the sultan from the step to the ground; but [Baybars] only rejoiced in all that. He hung up the *kiswah* of the Kaʿbah with his own hands, together with his retainers. He frequented those in Mecca and Medina that belonged to the people of goodness to request their blessing and to ask for their supplication.

§ 174 So far [this story of the pilgrimage of sultan Baybars]. The chief judge Ṣadr al-Dīn [Sulaymān] was with him all along his route, so that [Baybars] could ask his counsel and could try to understand from him the issues of his religion.

303 It is very likely that this refusal of the two Ḥusaynid amirs of Medina at that time, Ǧammāz b. Šīḥah and his nephew Mālik b. Munīf b. Šīḥah, to welcome the sultan was due to a dispute in the previous year on revenue generated from the collection of taxes in Medina (Mortel [1994]: 101).

ولم يغفل مع ذلك عن تدبير الممالك، وكتّاب الإنشاء تكتب عنه في المهمات، وكتب إلى صاحب اليمن ينكر عليه أمورا ويقول: "سطرتها من مكة المشرفة وقد أخذت طريقها في سبع عشرة خطوة"—يعني بالخطوة المنزلة—ويقول: "الملك هو الذي يجاهد في الله حق جهاده ويبذل نفسه في الذب عن حوزة الدين. فإن كنت ملكا، فاخرج والق الططر!"

٥ وأحسن إلى إميرَيْ مكة وإلى أمير ينبع وأمير خُلَيص وأكابر الحجاز، وكتب منشورين لأميري مكة، ورتب معهما الأمير شمس الدين مروان—نائب أمير جاندار—يقيم معهما بمكة حسب سؤالهما ليكون مرجع الأمور إليه والحل والعقد على يديه. وزاد أميري مكة مالا وغلالا في كل سنة لأجل تسبيل الكعبة للناس.

وسار من مكة بعد قضاء النسك في ثالث عشره، وقدم المدينة النبوية ثانيا في عشرينه، فبات بها
١٠ وسار من غده، فجد في السير ومعه عدة يسيرة. فقدم الكرك بكرة يوم الخميس سلخه من غير أن يعلم

١ عن: ناقصة في الأصل، مضافة بخط المقريزي في الهامش الأيسر، من الأسفل إلى الأعلى + صح؛ يشير إليها الرمز ⌐ بعد كلمة "ذلك". ‖ الإنشاء: "الانشآ" في الأصل. ٢ عشرة: تصحيح في الأصل بخط المقريزي. ٣ في الله: تصحيح في الأصل بخط المقريزي. ٥ وأحسن: تصحيح في الأصل بخط المقريزي. ‖ مكة: ناقصة في الأصل ومضافة بخط المقريزي في مكانها الصحيح في الجملة، في آخر السطر بعد كلمة "أميرَيْ". ٦ نائب: "نايب" في الأصل. ٩ قضاء: "قضآ" في الأصل. ‖ عشره: ناقصة في الأصل ومضافة بخط المقريزي في مكانها الصحيح في الجملة، في آخر السطر فوق كلمة "ثالث". ‖ وقدم: تصحيح في الأصل بخط المقريزي.

304 Yanbuʿ is the name of a port town on the Red Sea coast of the Hijaz; it was the ancestral home of the branch of the Ḥasanid family that controlled Mecca from the early thirteenth century onwards, but it was ruled more or less independently from Mecca by its own amir in this period and beyond (E. van Donzel, "Yanbuʿ", in *EI*² http://referenceworks.brillonline.com/entries/encyclopaedia-of-islam-2/yanbu-SIM_7979).

§175 Despite that [pre-occupation with the pilgrimage rituals], [Baybars] did not neglect the government of his realms, [since] the scribes of the chancery wrote down on his behalf [documents] concerning weighty affairs. [An example of this is that] he wrote to the ruler of Yemen reproaching him for certain things. He said: "I have composed [this letter] from glorious Mecca, which I have travelled to in seventeen steps"—by step he meant halting place—and he said: "the ruler is he who performs for God the duty of his *ǧihād*, and who exerts himself in defending the territory of Islam. If I were a ruler, I would go out and confront the Mongols!"

§176 He was benevolent towards the two amirs of Mecca, towards the amir of Yanbuʿ,[304] the amir of Ḫulayṣ,[305] and the chiefs of the Hijaz. He had two diplomas of investiture written for the two amirs of Mecca, and he assigned next to them the amir Šams al-Dīn Marwān, Nāʾib Amīr Ǧāndār,[306] to stay with them in Mecca, following the request of both of them, so as to be consulted in the affairs and so that the authority to rule would be in his hands. He increased the annual amount of money and crops to the two amirs of Mecca, for the facilitation of the people's access to the Kaʿbah.

§177 He left Mecca after the completion of the ceremonies on 13 [Ḏū l-Ḥiǧǧah] [13 August], and he arrived again in the Prophet's Medina on 20 [Ḏū l-Ḥiǧǧah] [20 August]. He spent the night there and left the next morning. He made every effort in going on, together with a small band, and he arrived in Karak in the morning of Thursday, the last day of [the month], without

305 Ḫulayṣ is the name of a settlement in the Hijaz on the coastal road between Mecca and Medina, set back some distance from the coast; in the later medieval period period this cultivated area was also ruled by its own amir (G. Rentz, "al-Ḥidjāz", in *EI*² http://referenceworks.brillonline.com/entries/encyclopaedia-of-islam-2/al-hidjaz-SIM_2857).

306 Šams al-Dīn Marwān, an assistant (*nāʾib*) of the amir ʿIzz al-Dīn Amīr Ǧāndār, was appointed by Baybars as his local representative in Mecca, to rule in his name and to confirm the sultan's local sovereignty; by lack of military resources Marwān's local authority remained very limited and the arrangement was more symbolic than real; within a year after Marwān's appointment the two amirs of Mecca removed him from Mecca, took matters again in their own hands, and were acknowledged as Mecca's sole rulers by the sultan in Cairo (Ibn Fahd, *Itḥāf al-wará*, 3:98–99; Mortel [1985]: 56).

أحد بوصوله حتى نزل مشهد جعفر بقرية مُؤتَة. فتلقاه الناس بها، ودخل المدينة وعليه عباءته التي سار بها—وهو راكب راحله—فبات بها.[٦٧]

131a ورحل من الغد، بعدما | صلى الجمعة مستهل المحرم سنة ثمان وستين وستمائة، ومعه مائة فارس بيد كل فارس منهم فرس، وساق إلى دمشق وسائر من في بلاد مصر وبلاد الشام مِن الأمراء ومَن
٥ دونهم لا يعرفون شيئا من خبر السلطان، هل هو في الشام أو الحجاز أو غير ذلك من بلاد الله. ولا يجسر أحد، لشدة مهابة السلطان والخوف منه، أن يتكلم بشيء من خبره ولا يسأل عنه. فلما قارب دمشق بعث أحد خاصته على البريد بكتب البشارة إلى دمشق بالسلامة بعد قضاء الحج. فلما دخل على الأمير جمال الدين النجيبي—نائب دمشق—جمع الأمراء لقراءة الكتب السلطانية، فبينا هم في القراءة إذ قيل لهم: "قد نزل السلطان بالميدان!" فتبادروا إلى لقائه، فإذا به وحده وقد
١٠ أعطى فرسه لبعض دلالي سوق الخيل لينادى عليه وهو لا يعرفه أنه السلطان. فعندما شاهدوه

١ عباءته: "عبآته" في الأصل. ٣ ما: في الأصل الكلمة مكتوبة مرتين، مرة في آخر ص ١٣٠ب ومرة ثانية في بداية ص. ١٣١أ. || وستمائة: "وستمايه" في الأصل. || مائة: "مايه" في الأصل. ٤ وسائر: "وساير" في الأصل. || في: ناقصة في الأصل ومضافة بخط المقريزي في الهامش الأيمن، من الأعلى إلى الأسفل + صح، يشير إليها الرمز ⌐ بعد كلمة "من". || الأمراء: "الامرآ" في الأصل. ٥ شيئا: "شيا" في الأصل. || هو: ناقصة في الأصل ومضافة بخط المقريزي في الهامش الأيسر، على نفس السطر + صح، يشير إليها الرمز ¬ بعد كلمة "هل". ٦ لشدة: تصحيح في الأصل بخط المقريزي. || بشيء: "بشى" في الأصل. ٧ خاصته: تصحيح في الأصل بخط المقريزي. || قضاء: "قضآ" في الأصل. || الحج: تصحيح في الأصل بخط المقريزي. ٨ جمال الدين: تصحيح في الأصل بخط المقريزي. || نائب: "نايب" في الأصل. || الأمراء لقراءة: "الامرآ لقراة" في الأصل. || السلطانية: تصحيح في الأصل. ٩ القراءة: "القراه" في الأصل. || إلى: "الي" في الأصل. || لقائه: "لقايه" في الأصل. ١٠ أعطى: تصحيح في الأصل. || فرسه: ناقصة في الأصل، مضافة بخط المقريزي في الهامش الأيمن، من الأعلى إلى الأسفل + صح، يشير إليها الرمز ⌐ بعد كلمة "أعطى".

[٦٧] راجع خبر حج السلطان بيبرس من "فلما دخل شوال" (356، ٧) إلى هنا على شكل مساو في ابن عبد الظاهر، الروض الزاهر، ص. ٣٥٤-٣٥٧.

anyone knowing about his arrival, until he set up camp at Mašhad Ǧaʿfar, at the village of Muʾtah.[307] The people came to see him there. He entered the town, while he was wearing the cloak which he had left with, and while he was mounted on his riding camel. He spent the night there.

5 §178 He left the next morning, after he had prayed the Friday prayer of 1 Muḥarram of the year 668 [30 August 1269]. With him were 100 horsemen, every horseman among them having a horse in his hand. He moved on to Damascus, while all those who were in Egypt and Syria, from the amirs and from those lower in status than them, were unaware of any news about the 10 sultan: was he in Syria, or in the Hijaz, or at any other place of God's lands? Because of the strong reverence and fear for the sultan no one dared to say anything about his whereabouts nor ask after him. When he approached Damascus, he sent one of his retainers via the postal system with letters of good news to Damascus, [announcing] the safe return after the completion 15 of the pilgrimage. When he entered with the amir Ǧamāl al-Dīn al-Naǧībī, the governor of Damascus,[308] the amirs had gathered to read the sultan's letters. While they were reading, there suddenly was said to them: "The sultan has set up camp on the hippodrome [outside the city wall]". They hurried to meet with him. There he was all by himself, having given his horse 20 to one of the stewards of the horse market, who had been called for [by Baybars] without knowing that he was the sultan. When they sighted him,

307 Muʾtah is the name of a village south of Karak, on the Syrian *ḥaǧǧ* route, in the centre of a fertile plain in the lower Transjordan region; Mašhad Ǧaʿfar refers to the mausoleum that was built over the tombs of the Arab leaders, including the Prophet's nephew, Ǧaʿfar b. Abī Ṭālib, who, in 8/629, fell at Muʾtah, defeated by Byzantine forces (F. Buhl, "Muʾta", in *EI*², http://brillonline.com/entries/encyclopaedia-of-islam-2/muta-SIM_5637).

308 Ǧamāl al-Dīn Āqqūš al-Naǧībī (d. 677/1278) was a peer of Baybars since the time of the last Ayyūbid ruler of Egypt, al-Ṣāliḥ Ayyūb; after having been steward (*ustādār*) in Egypt, he was governor in Syria from around 660/1262 until 670/1271 (Amitai [1997]: 294, no. 13). His name and tenure of office in Syria are also mentioned in the Maqām Nabī Mūsá inscription that includes an explicit reference to Baybars' *ḥaǧǧ*: "[the construction of this shrine in the course of 668/late 1269 happened during] the governorship of his slave and agent, the great amir, the frontier warrior, Ǧamāl al-Dīn ʾĀqqūsh al-Naǧībī, governor of the Syrian provinces" (Amitai [2006]: 46–49).

قبل النائب الارض وتلاه الأمراء، وحضر الأمير آق سنقر الفارقاني ومن معه من عسكر مصر، فأكل السلطان شيئا، وقام ليستريح، وانصرف الناس.

فركب في نفريسير وتوجه في خفية يريد حلب. فلما حضر الأمراء خدمة العصر لم يجدوا السلطان ولا عُرِف له خبر. فبينما نائب حلب والأمراء في الموكب تحت قلعة حلب وإذا بالسلطان قد ساق ٥ ووقف ساعة، فلم يعرفه أحد حتى فطن به بعضهم. فنزل عن فرسه وقبل له الأرض، فبادر الجميع ونزلوا وقبلوا الأرض، وساروا في ركابه حتى دخل دار نائب حلب. ثم كشف القلعة وخرج من حلب ولم يعرف أحد به.

فدخل دمشق في ثالث عشره على حين غفلة، ولعب بالكرة، وسار ليلا إلى القدس، وسار إلى الخليل، وتصدق بعدة صدقات.

١٠ وكان الأمير آق سنقر قد سار بمن معه من عسكر مصر، ونزل تل العجول، فوافاه السلطان هناك وعليه عباءته لم يغيرها، وسار من تل العجول بالعسكر في حادي عشرينه، وقدم القاهرة أول صفر وعليه عباءته التي حج بها لم يغيرها نحو خمسة وسبعين يوما. فخرج الملك السعيد إلى لقائه، وصعد قلعة الجبل.[٦٨]

١ النائب: "النايب" في الأصل. ‖ الأمراء: "الامرآ" في الأصل. ٢ شيئا: "شيا" في الأصل. ٣ الأمراء: "الامرا" في الأصل. ٤ نائب: "نايب" في الأصل. ‖ والأمراء: "والامرآ" في الأصل. ٦ نائب: "نايب" في الأصل. ٨ حين: تصحيح في الأصل بخط المقريزي. ‖ إلى: ناقصة في الأصل ومضافة بخط المقريزي ("الي") في الهامش الأيمن، من الأعلى إلى الأسفل + صح؛ يشير إليها الرمز ⁊ بعد كلمة "سار". ١١ عباءته: "عباته" في الأصل. ١٢ عباءته: "عباته" في الأصل. ‖ لقائه: "لقايه" في الأصل.

[٦٨] راجع خبر زيارات السلطان السرية في دمشق وحلب والقدس والخليل من "ورحل من الغد" (354، ٣) إلى هنا على شكل مساو في ابن عبد الظاهر، الروض الزاهر، ص. ٣٥٩-٣٦٠.

the governor kissed the ground and the amirs followed him. The amir Āq Sunqur al-Fāriqānī and those who were with him from the army of Egypt were present. The sultan ate something and stood up to take a rest and the people left.

5 § 179 He mounted with a handful of people and headed secretly for Aleppo. When the amirs [in Damascus] attended the evening public audience, they did not find the sultan, and no news was known about him. While the governor of Aleppo and the amirs were in the midst of the ceremonial procession below the citadel of Aleppo, there suddenly appeared the sultan, who had 10 come riding and who stood for an hour without anyone recognising him, until one of them became aware of him. [This one then] dismounted from his horse and kissed the ground to honour [the sultan], and all [thereupon] hastened to dismount and to kiss the ground. They proceeded in his escort until he entered the residence of the governor of Aleppo. Then he inspected 15 the citadel and left from Aleppo.

§ 180 No one knew about him, and then he entered Damascus unnoticed on 13 [Muḥarram] [11 September], he played [a game of] polo and left at night for Jerusalem. He went to Hebron and he made several charitable donations.

§ 181 The amir Āq Sunqur had left with who was with him from the army 20 of Egypt and he had set up camp at Tall al-ʿAǧūl.[309] The sultan joined him there, wearing his cloak which he had not changed. From Tall al-ʿAǧūl he left with the army on 21 [Muḥarram] [19 September], and he arrived in Cairo on 1 Ṣafar [29 September], wearing the cloak which he had performed the pilgrimage in, without changing it for about 75 days. Al-Malik al-Saʿīd came 25 out to meet him and he ascended the citadel of the mountain.

309 Tall al-ʿAǧūl is a place in Palestine, near Gaza; it is best known for the fact that a Fāṭimid army gained a victory there against the Crusader Kingdom of Jerusalem, in 553/1158 (See M. Canard, "Ḍirghām", in *EI*² http://referenceworks.brillonline.com/entries/encyclopaedia-of-islam-2/dirgham-SIM_1874).

السلطان الملك الناصر ناصر الدين أبو المعالي محمد بن الملك المنصور سيف الدين قلاوون الألفي الصالحي النجمي

ولد يوم السبت نصف المحرم سنة أربع وثمانين وستمائة، وأقيم في السلطنة بعد | قتل أخيه الملك 131b
الأشرف صلاح الدين خليل بن قلاوون في رابع عشر المحرم سنة ثلث وتسعين، وعمره تسع سنين
٥ تنقص يوما واحدا. فأقام سنة إلا ثلثة أيام، وخلع بمملوك أبيه زين الدين كتبغا—الملك العادل—

١ قلاوون: "قلاون" في الأصل. ٣ ولد: كلمة غير واضحة بسبب ثقب في المخطوطة ومضافة هنا من أ (ص. ٦٤أ). || وستمائة: "وستمايه" في الأصل. ٥ بمملوك: تصحيح في الأصل بخط المقريزي.

10. The sultan al-Malik al-Nāṣir Nāṣir al-Dīn Abū l-Maʿālī Muḥammad b. al-Malik al-Manṣūr Sayf al-Dīn Qalāwūn al-Alfī l-Ṣāliḥī l-Naǧmī[310]

§182 He was born on Saturday 15 Muḥarram of the year 684 [23 March 1285], and he was installed in the position of sultan after the murder of his
5 brother al-Malik al-Ašraf Ṣalāḥ al-Dīn Ḫalīl b. Qalāwūn[311] on 14 Muḥarram of the year [6]93 [15 December 1293], at the age of nine years minus one day. He remained in office for one year less three days, and he was deposed [and replaced] by the *mamlūk* of his father, Zayn al-Dīn Kitbuġā, al-Malik

310 Al-Nāṣir Muḥammad b. Qalāwūn (684–741/1285–1341; r. 693–694/1293–1294, 698–708/1299–1309, 709–741/1310–1341) was the third Qalāwūnid sultan of Egypt and Syria; he was made sultan twice at a young age by prominent amirs from his father's entourage, but in the first case he was soon deposed as a result of this entourage's fragmentation, and in the second instance he resigned from office to escape the impotence of his nominal rule; he eventually returned to power a third time by his own doing, embarking upon three decades of increasingly stable, powerful, and successful rule, marking a high point in the sultanate's history, a remarkable era of economic and cultural efflorescence for Egypt and Syria, and the formation of a Qalāwūnid dynastic state that survived him by many decades (P.M. Holt, "al-Nāṣir. 1. al-Nāṣir Muḥammad b. Ḳalāwūn", in *EI*² http://referenceworks.brillonline.com/entries/encyclopaedia-of-islam-2/al-nasir-COM_0852; Levanoni [1995]; Flinterman & Van Steenbergen [2015]).

311 Al-Ašraf Ḫalīl b. Qalāwūn (r. 689–693/1290–1293) was the second Qalāwūnid sultan of Egypt and Syria; he succeeded his father upon the latter's untimely death, bringing to a victorious end the campaign which his father had begun against the Latin Crusaders, the city of Acre and a handful of other remaining crusader strongholds on the Syrian littoral falling into his hands in 690/1291; his reign and fame are therefore especially remembered in this context of the final expulsion of the Crusaders; but Ḫalīl never really managed to fully impose his authority on his father's former entourage of senior amirs, and he was killed by some of them eventually (U. Haarmann, "Khalīl", in *EI*² http://referenceworks.brillonline.com/entries/encyclopaedia-of-islam-2/khalil-SIM_4163).

في حادي عشر المحرم سنة أربع وتسعين، وأخرج مع أمه أشلون بنت شكناي إلى الكرك.

فثار الأمير حسام الدين لاجين المنصوري—نائب السلطنة—على العادل كتبغا، وتسلطن عوضه. فثار عليه {طغجي} وكرجي، فقتلاه، وقتلا أيضا، واستدعى الناصر من الكرك. فقدم إلى قلعة الجبل، وأعيد إلى السلطنة مرة ثانية في سادس جمادى الأولى سنة ثمان وتسعين.

---

٢ نائب: "نايب" في الأصل. ٣ طغجي: "طغى" في الأصل وهو خطأ، والتصحيح من السياق.

al-ʿĀdil,[312] on 11 Muḥarram of the year [6]94 [1 December 1294]. He was removed to Karak with his mother Ašlūn bt. Šaknāy.[313]

§ 183 The amir Ḥusām al-Dīn Lāǧīn al-Manṣūrī,[314] who was viceroy, revolted against al-ʿĀdil Kitbuġā, and he became sultan instead of him. [The amirs] Ṭuġǧī and Kurǧī[315] revolted against him, and they killed him, but they were also killed. [Thereupon] al-Nāṣir was summoned from Karak. He came to [Cairo's] citadel of the mountain and he was reinstated in the position of sultan a second time, on 6 Jumāda I of the year [6]98 [9 February 1299].

---

312 Al-ʿĀdil Kitbuġā l-Manṣūrī (r. 694–696/1294–1296) was a former *mamlūk* of Oirat Mongol origins in the service of sultan al-Manṣur Qalāwūn; as a senior member from Qalāwūn's entourage, he managed to become vicegerent and the strong man behind the throne of the child-ruler al-Nāṣir Muḥammad, until he deposed him and took the throne and position of sultan for himself; his short reign was marked by dearth and famine in Egypt, and by the settlement in Palestine of Mongol refugee warriors with their families; eventually, he was deposed by a party headed by his own vicegerent, Lāǧīn al-Manṣūrī, who succeeded him as sultan (P.M. Holt, "Lād̲j̲īn", in EI^2 http://referenceworks.brillonline.com/entries/encyclopaedia-of-islam-2/ladjin-SIM_4611; Elham [1977]).

313 Ašlūn was the daughter of a Mongol notable, Šaknāy (more commonly known as Šaktāy), who moved with his family from Anatolia to Egypt in 675/1276; Ašlūn's marriage to sultan Qalāwūn was concluded in 680/1281–1282 (Holt [1995]: 314).

314 Ḥusām al-Dīn Lāǧīn l-Manṣūrī (r. 696–698/1296–1299) was a former *mamlūk* in the service of sultan al-Manṣūr Qalāwūn, in whose name he successfully performed the position of governor of Syria for many years; as one of the strong men from Qalāwūn's entourage, he continued to dominate the political theatre of Cairo after Qalāwūn's death throughout the 690s/1290s; he became vicegerent of sultan al-ʿĀdil Kitbuġā, and upon his deposition Lāǧīn was himself installed as sultan al-Manṣūr; he however equalled failed to fully impose his authority on his fellow amirs, and when he tried to reform and re-organise the allocation of fiscal resources to the realm's elites in an attempt to strengthen his position as sultan, he was murdered (Holt, "Lād̲j̲īn", in EI^2; Id. [1973]; Elham [1977]).

315 The amirs Kurǧī and Ṭuġǧī l-Ašrafī were two former *mamlūk*s of al-Ašraf Ḫalīl, who promoted them to high status and office; they retained their positions after Ḫalīl's murder, but in the reign of al-Manṣūr Lāǧīn they got into conflict with the sultan's vicegerent and organised a successful conspiracy as a result; in the days following their murder of the sultan and his vicegerent their plan to usurp their victims' power and positions failed and they were both killed (Ibn Taġrī Birdī, *al-Manhal al-ṣāfī*, 6:414–415; 9:125–126; Holt [1973]: 529–531).

فأقام عشر سنين وخمسة أشهر وستة عشر يومًا محجورا عليه لا يملك التصرف في أكلة طعام يشتهيه، والقائم بتدبير الدولة الأميران بيبرس الجاشنكير—أستادار السلطان—وسلار—نائب السلطنة—، فدبر لنفسه في سنة ثمان وسبعمائة، وأظهر أنه يريد الحج بعياله. فوافقه الأميران على ذلك، وشرعوا في تجهيزه، وكتب إلى دمشق والكرك برمي الإقامات، وألزم عرب الشرقية ٥ بحمل الشعير. فلما تهيأ ذلك أحضر الأمراء تقادمهم من الخيل والجمال في العشرين من شهر رمضان. فقبلها، وركب في خامس عشرينه من القلعة، ومعه الأمراء، إلى بركة الحاج وتعين

١ فأقام: تصحيح في الأصل بخط المقريزي. ٢ والقائم: "القايم" في الأصل. ‖ بيبرس: تصحيح في الأصل بخط المقريزي. ‖ نائب: "نايب" في الأصل. ٣ وسبعمائة: "وسبعمايه" في الأصل. ٥ الأمراء: "الامرآ" في الأصل. ٦ الأمراء: "الامرآ" في الأصل.

§184 He remained in office for ten years, five months, and 16 days, while he was placed under guardianship, without even possessing the authority to eat the food that he desired, the state being run by the two amirs Baybars al-Ǧāšnikīr,[316] who was the steward of the sultan, and Sallār,[317] who was the vicegerent. Therefore, he hatched up a plan for himself in the year 708 [1309]. He made it look as though he wanted to perform the pilgrimage with his family. The two amirs agreed with him on that, and they began to prepare for it. There was written to Damascus and Karak to sent forth supplies, and the Bedouin of al-Šarqiyyah[318] were obliged to provide barley. When that was prepared, the amirs presented their ceremonial gifts, consisting of horses and camels, on the 20th of the month Ramaḍān [3 March]. He received them and rode from the citadel on 25 [Ramaḍān] [8 March], together with the amirs, until the Birkat al-Ḥāǧǧ.[319] To accompany him on

316 Baybars al-Manṣūrī l-Ǧāšnikīr (r. 708–709/1309–1310) was a former *mamlūk* in the service of sultan al-Manṣūr Qalāwūn, who acted as taster (*ǧāšnikīr*) in Qalāwūn's household, and who rose to prominence after Qalāwūn's death, eventually obtaining the position of royal steward (*ustādār*); after the killing of al-Manṣūr Lāǧīn, and together with his peer Sallār, Baybars emerged as one of the new leading amirs behind al-Nāṣir Muḥammad's throne, establishing a *duumvirate* that lasted until al-Nāṣir Muḥammad's abdication; the widely respected Baybars was then proclaimed sultan al-Muẓaffar, but support for his unexpected rule soon proved fickle and eventually he was deposed by al-Nāṣir Muḥammad and strangled (L. Fernandes, "Baybars II, al-Malik al-Muẓaffar Jāšnikīr", in *EI*³ http://referenceworks.brillonline.com/entries/encyclopaedia-of-islam-3/baybars-ii-al-malik-al-muzaffar-jashnikir-COM_24315).

317 The amir Sayf al-Dīn Sallār (d. 710/1310) (also known as Sālār) was a former *mamlūk* of Oirat Mongol origins in the service of al-Manṣūr Qalāwūn, who had been captured by Qalāwūn during a military expedition in Anatolia; just as his peer Baybars, he rose to prominence after Qalāwūn's death, and he eventually obtained the position of vicegerent (*nā'ib al-salṭanah*) when he took power with Baybars behind al-Nāṣir Muḥammad's throne; he retained the viceregency when Baybars was enthroned, but when al-Nāṣir Muḥammad marched on Cairo, Sallār delivered the city to him; eventually, he was arrested and starved to death (Holt [1986]: 110–112).

318 Al-Šarqiyyah was (and still is) the name of one of the largest provinces of the eastern part of lower Egypt, with the town of Bilbays as its administrative centre (al-Qalqašandī, *Ṣubḥ al-aʿšá*, 3:400–401).

319 Birkat al-Ḥāǧǧ, the Pond of the Pilgrim (also known as Birkat al-Ḥaǧǧ, the Pond of the Pilgrimage, or Birkat al-Ḥuǧǧāǧ, The Pond of the Pilgrims), refers to a small lake northeast of Cairo, formed by the waters of the ancient Canal (*Ḫalīǧ*) that had been blocked there; it was the first station on the Muslim pilgrimage to Mecca from Egypt (Raymond [2001]: 16).

معه للسفر أيدمر الخطيري والحاج ألْ مَلِك الجوكندار وقرا لاجين—أمير مجلس—وبلبان—أمير جاندار—وأيبك الرومي—أمير سلاح—وبيبرس الأحمدي وسنجر الجمقدار وتقطاي الساقي

١ ألْ: تصحيح في الأصل بخط المقريزي. ‖ لاجين: تصحيح في الأصل بخط المقريزي.

320 Aydamur al-Ḫaṭīrī (d. 737/1337) was a former *mamlūk* of al-Manṣūr Qalāwūn, who rose to prominence during the successive reigns of al-Nāṣir Muḥammad (Ibn Taġrī Birdī, *al-Manhal al-ṣāfī*, 3:180–182; Amitai [1990]: 161, no. 1).

the voyage, there were appointed Aydamur al-Ḫaṭīrī,[320] the *ḥāǧǧ* Āl Malik al-Ǧūkandār,[321] Qarā Lāǧīn,[322] who was master of the audience, Balabān,[323] who was master of the reception, Aybak al-Rūmī,[324] who was master of arms, Baybars al-Aḥmadī,[325] Sanǧar al-Ǧamaqdār,[326] Tuqṭāy al-Sāqī,[327] Sunqur al-

---

321 Āl Malik al-Ǧūkandār (d. 747/1346) was a former *mamlūk* of al-Manṣūr Qalāwūn, acquired from the spoils of war of a campaign in Anatolia by sultan Baybars; he rose to prominence during the successive reigns of al-Nāṣir Muḥammad, becoming a highly venerated and widely respected veteran amir in the 730s/1330s and 740s/1340s; he was known as *al-ḥāǧǧ* as a token of his piety and interest in the pilgrimage (Ibn Taġrī Birdī, *al-Manhal al-ṣāfī*, 3:85–88; Amitai [1990]: 162, no. 12; Van Steenbergen [2005]: 197).

322 Qarā Lāǧīn al-Manṣūrī (d. 715/1315) was a former *mamlūk* of al-Manṣūr Qalāwūn who rose to prominence after the latter's death, eventually obtaining the position of steward (*ustādār*) under al-Nāṣir Muḥammad, apparently after also having served as his master of the audience (*amīr maǧlis*) (Ibn Taġrī Birdī, *al-Manhal al-ṣāfī*, 9:53; Amitai [1990]: 162, no. 9).

323 Balabān (d. 734/1333), also known as Balabān Ṭurnā,—whose origins remain unclear—was an amir and master of the reception (*amīr ǧāndār*) in Egypt until al-Nāṣir Muḥammad made him governor of Karak in Syria; shortly afterwards, in 714/1315, he was arrested and forced to spend a decade in the prison of the governor of Syria; he ended his days as a senior amir in the retinue of the same governor (Ibn Taġrī Birdī, *al-Manhal al-ṣāfī*, 3:421–422; al-Ṣafadī, *Aʿyān al-ʿaṣr*, 2:44–45).

324 Aybak al-Rūmī l-Manṣūrī (d. ?) was a former *mamlūk* of al-Manṣūr Qalāwūn who rose to prominence after the latter's death, apparently eventually obtaining the position of master of arms (*amīr silāḥ*) at al-Nāṣir Muḥammad's court; he fell from favour in 713/1314, after which all traces of him are lost in extant sources (Amitai [1990]: 162, no. 14; al-Maqrīzī, *al-Sulūk*, 2:128).

325 Baybars al-Aḥmadī (d. 746/1345) was a senior amir who soon after al-Nāṣir's third accession became master of the reception (*amīr ǧāndār*), which he remained throughout the rest of the sultan's reign; as one of the Qalāwūnid state's most longstanding agents, he became a highly respected and powerful veteran amir in the 730s/1330s and 740s/1340s (Ibn Taġrī Birdī, *al-Manhal al-ṣāfī*, 3:479–481; Amitai [1990]: 163, no. 19; Van Steenbergen [2005]: 197–198).

326 Sanǧar al-Manṣūrī l-Ǧamaqdār (d. 745/1345) was a former *mamlūk* of al-Manṣūr Qalāwūn who rose to prominence after the latter's death; he remained a senior amir in Egypt until al-Nāṣir Muḥammad transferred him to a position of senior amir in Damascus in 730/1330 (al-Ṣafadī, *Aʿyān al-ʿaṣr*, 2: 465; Amitai [1990]: 161, no. 5).

327 No information has been retrieved for this amir; he obviously had been a member of one of the preceding sultans' household corps of cupbearers (*sāqī*), and he had risen to rank and prominence in the first decade of the eighth/fourteenth century, but nothing further is known about him.

وسنقر السعدي—النقيب—وخمسة وسبعين مملوكا. وعاد بيبرس وسلار من غير أن يترجلا له عند نزوله بالبركة.

فرحل من ليلته وعرج إلى الصالحية وعيد بها، وتوجه إلى الكرك. فقدمها في عاشر شوال، وبها الأمير جمال الدين آقوش الأشرفي نائبا. فنزل بقلعتها وصرح بأنه قد انثنى عزمه عن الحج واختار ٥ الإقامة بالكرك وترك السلطنة ليستريح. وكتب إلى الأمراء بذلك وسأل أن ينعم عليه بالكرك والشوبك. وأعاد من كان معه من الأمراء وسلمهم الهجن—وعدتهم خمسمائة هجين—والمال والجمال وجميع ما قدمه له الأمراء، وأخذ ما كان من المال بالكرك—وهو ستمائة ألف درهم فضة وعشرون ألف دينار—، وأمر نائب الكرك أيضا بالمسير عنه، فسار إلى مصر.

١ النقيب: تصحيح في الأصل بخط المقريزي. ٤ جمال: تصحيح في الأصل بخط المقريزي. || نائبا: "نايبا" في الأصل. || بأنه: ناقصة في الأصل ومضافة بخط المقريزي في الهامش الأيسر، من الأسفل إلى الأعلى + صح، يشير إليها الرمز ⌐ بعد كلمة "صرح". ٥ الأمراء: "الامرآ" في الأصل. ٦ الأمراء: "الامرآ" في الأصل. || خمسمائة: "خمسمايه" في الأصل. ٧ الأمراء: "الامرآ" في الأصل. || ستمائة: "ستمايه" في الأصل. ٨ نائب: "نايب" في الأصل.

Sa'dī,[328] who was parade officer, and 75 *mamlūk*s. When he had set up camp at the pond, Baybars and Sallār returned, without having dismounted for him [as protocol demands].

§ 185 He left the same night, and halted at al-Ṣāliḥiyyah,[329] where he cele-
5 brated the Feast [of Fast-breaking]. [Then] he headed for Karak. He arrived there on 10 Šawwāl [23 March], and the amir Ǧamāl al-Dīn Āqqūš al-Ašrafī[330] was there as a governor. [The sultan] settled down in its citadel, and declared that he no longer wished to perform the pilgrimage, and [that] he prefered to stay at Karak, renouncing the post of sultan so as to find some rest. He
10 wrote about that to the amirs and asked that Karak and al-Shawbak would be granted to him. He sent back those from the amirs who were with him, handing over to them the dromedaries—their number was 500 dromedaries—, the money, the camels, and everything that the amirs had presented to him. He took the money that was in Karak—600,000 high quality silver *dirham*s
15 and 20,000 *dīnār*s. [Finally] he ordered the governor of Karak to also leave him alone, so [Āqqūš al-Ašrafī] left for Egypt.

---

328 Sunqur al-Sa'dī (d. 728/1328) was an amir in the entourage of al-Nāṣir Muḥammad, and a parade officer (*naqīb*) of the royal *mamlūk*s, until his removal to Tripoli in 723/1323, where he remained until his death; he is remembered especially for the peculiar *madrasah* for women with attached domed mausoleum which he had constructed south of Cairo, between 715/1315 and 721/1321 (and which is still standing there) (al-Maqrīzī, *al-Sulūk*, 2:246; Id., *al-Ḫiṭaṭ*, 4:598–602; Behrens-Abouseif [1989]: 107–108; Warner [2005]: 137, no. 263).

329 Al-Ṣāliḥiyyah refers to the name of a settlement on the north-eastern fringe of al-Šarqiyyah province of Egypt, on the route connecting Cairo with Syria, via Bilbays and Gaza; it was founded by the last Ayyūbid ruler of Egypt, al-Ṣāliḥ Ayyūb (hence its name), as a strategic stopping place for caravans and troops travelling from and to Egypt (al-Qalqašandī, *Ṣubḥ al-a'šá*, 3:400; 14:377).

330 Ǧamāl al-Dīn Āqqūš al-Ašrafī (d. 736/1336) was a former *mamlūk* of al-Ašraf Ḫalīl, who rose to prominence during the successive reigns of al-Ašraf Ḫalīl and of al-Nāṣir Muḥammad, securing throughout his long career various high positions in Egypt and Syria, including the governorships of Karak (which he retained for 18 years, until 708/1309, hence his nickname 'the Governor of Karak' [Nā'ib al-Karak]), and—briefly—of Damascus and of Tripoli; he died in the prison of Alexandria, after having been arrested in 734/1333 (Ibn Taġrī Birdī, *al-Manhal al-ṣāfī*, 3:27–30).

وتسلطن بيبرس الجاشنكير | وتلقب بالملك المظفر، وكتب للناصر تقليدا بنيابة الكرك وجهزه مع 132[a]
الحاج أل ملك. فأظهر الملك الناصر البشر وخطب باسم المظفر على منبر الكرك، وأنعم على الحاج
أَلْ ملِك وأعاده. فلم يتركه المظفر، وأخذ يناكره ويطلب منه من معه من المماليك الذين اختارهم
للإقامة عنده والخيول التي أخذها من قلعة الجبل والمال الذي أخذه من الكرك، وهدده بتجهيز
٥ العساكر إليه وأَخْذِهِ. فحنق لذلك وكتب لنواب الشام يشكو ما هو فيه. فحثوه على القيام لأخذ
ملكه ووعدوه بالنصر. فتحرك لذلك وسار إلى دمشق، وأتته النواب، وقدم إلى مصر، ففر بيبرس
وطلع الناصر القلعة يوم عيد الفطر سنة تسع وسبعمائة.

فأقام في الملك اثنتين وثلٰثين سنة وشهرين وعشرين يوما. ومات في ليلة الخميس حادي عشرين
ذي الحجة سنة إحدى وأربعين وسبعمائة، وعمره سبع وخمسون سنة وأحد عشر شهرا وخمسة أيام.

١٠ ومدة سلطنته في المدد الثلاث ثلاث وأربعون سنة وثمانية أشهر وتسعة أيام. حج فيها ثلٰث مرات:

الأولى في سنة اثنتي عشرة وسبعمائة، وسببها أن خربندا تحرك لأخذ الشام ونزل على الفرات.
فخرج السلطان بعساكر مصر في ثالث شوال، وسار إلى الصالحية، فقدم البريد من حلب ودمشق

---

١ الجاشنكير: تصحيح في الأصل بخط المقريزي. ‖ تقليدا: "تقليد" في الأصل، والألف لتنوين الفتح مضافة بخط المقريزي في مكانها فوق السطر. ٢ الملك الناصر: ناقصة في الأصل ومضافة بخط المقريزي في الهامش الأيمن، من الأعلى إلى الأسفل + صح، يشير إليها الرمز ⌝ بعد كلمة "فأظهر". ٣ الذين: تصحيح في الأصل بخط المقريزي. ٤ التي: تصحيح في الأصل بخط المقريزي. ٥ وأَخْذِهِ: تصحيح في الأصل بخط المقريزي. ‖ يشكو: "يشكوا" في الأصل. ٧ وسبعمائة: "وسبعمايه" في الأصل. ٨ اثنتين: تصحيح في الأصل بخط المقريزي. ٩ وأربعين وسبعمائة: "واربعن وسبعمايه" في الأصل. ‖ وأحد: تصحيح في الأصل. ١٠ ثلاث: تصحيح في الأصل بخط المقريزي. ١١ الأولى: تصحيح في الأصل. ‖ اثنتي: "ننتى" في الأصل. ‖ وسبعمائة: "وسبعمايه" في الأصل.

§ 186 Baybars al-Ǧāšnikīr assumed the position of sultan, with the royal style of al-Malik al-Muẓaffar. He had a diploma of investiture written for al-Nāṣir for the position of governor of Karak, and he had it sent over with the *ḥāǧǧ* Āl Malik. Al-Malik al-Nāṣir made the glad tidings public [in Karak], and he had the Friday sermon delivered in the name of al-Muẓaffar from the *minbar* of Karak. He showed his benevolence towards the *ḥājj* Āl Malik and then he sent him back. But al-Muẓaffar did not leave him alone. He began to distrust him and to demand from him the *mamlūk*s who were with him and whom he had chosen to stay with him, the horses which he had taken from the citadel of the mountain, and the money that he had taken from Karak. [Al-Muẓaffar] threatened him with sending the armies against him and with his arrest. [Al-Nāṣir] became angry because of that, and wrote to the governors of Syria to complain about his situation. They prompted him to rise and take his realm, and they promised him victory. Therefore, he started to organise his campaign and he proceeded towards Damascus, [where] the governors came to him. [When he marched on and] arrived in Egypt, Baybars fled, and al-Nāṣir ascended to the citadel on the day of the Feast of Fast-breaking of the year 709 [4 March 1310].

§ 187 He continued to rule for 32 years, two months, and 20 days. He died in the night of Thursday 21 Ḏū l-Ḥiǧǧah of the year 741 [7 June 1341], at the age of 57 years, 11 months, and five days.

§ 188 The period of his sultanate over the three terms is 43 years, eight months, and nine days, during which he went on pilgrimage three times.

§ 189 The first one was in the year 712 [1313]. The reason for it was that Ḫarbandā[331] was organising a campaign to take Syria, and [that] he was setting up camp near the Euphrates. The sultan left with the armies of Egypt on 3 Šawwāl [1 February 1313], proceeding up to al-Ṣāliḥiyyah. The postal system then brought message from Aleppo and Damascus that Ḫarbandā had left

331 Ḫarbandā refers to the penultimate Mongol ruler of the Īlḫānid realm in Iraq and Persia, Ġiyāṯ al-Dīn Muḥammad Ḫarbandā (later changed to Ḫudābandā) Öljeytü (r. 704–716/1304–1316); he is remembered in particular in Arabic sources for mounting the last but unsuccessful Īlḫānid campaign against the Syro-Egyptian sultanate, in 712/1312–1313 (D.O. Morgan, "Öl<u>dj</u>eytü", in *EI*² http://referenceworks.brillonline.com/entries/encyclopaedia-of-islam-2/oldjeytu-SIM_6018).

برحيل خربندا عن الرحبة يوم عيد الفطر يريد بلاده. فسر السلطان بذلك وعزم على الحج. ودخل دمشق في ثالث عشرينه، وفرق العساكر في الجهات، وركب في أربعين أميرا وستة آلاف مملوك على الهجن في أول ذي القعدة، وأخذ معه مائة فرس. فقضى نسكه وعاد إلى دمشق بعد مروره بالمدينة النبوية ودخوله الكرك. فدخل في حادي عشر المحرم سنة ثلث عشرة وهو راكب ناقة ٥ لطيفة القد بعمامة مدورة ولثام وعليه بشت من أبشات العرب وفي يده حربة، وتلقاه شيخ الإسلام تقي الدين أحمد بن تيمية وسائر الفقهاء وجميع الناس. فكان يوما مشهودا بلغ كراء دار للتفرج على السلطان ستمائة درهم فضة. ثم سار إلى مصر وصعد قلعة الجبل في ثاني عشر صفر.

ثم حج في سنة تسع عشرة وسبعمائة. فلما تحرك لذلك أنته تقادم الأمراء وسائر نواب الشام وأمراء دمشق وحلب، وأول من بعث تقدمته الأمير تنكز—نائب—وفيها الخيل والهجن بأكوار الذهب

٣ مائة: "ماية" في الأصل. ٥–٦ شيخ ... أحمد: ناقصة في الأصل ومضافة بخط المقريزي في الهامش الأيمن، من الأعلى إلى الأسفل + صح، يشير إليها الرمز ⌐ بعد كلمة "تلقاه". ٦ وسائر: تصحيح في الأصل بخط المقريزي ("وساير"). ‖ الفقهاء: "الفقهآ" في الأصل. ‖ كراء: "كرآ" في الأصل. ٧ ستمائة: "ستمايه" في الأصل. ٨ وسبعمائة: "وسبعمايه" في الأصل. ‖ الأمراء: "الامرآ" في الأصل. ‖ وسائر: تصحيح في الأصل بخط المقريزي ("وساير"). ‖ وأمراء: "وامرآ" في الأصل. ٩ نائب: "نايب" في الأصل. ‖ بأكوار: كلمة غير واضحة بسبب ثقب في المخطوطة ومضافة هنا من أ (ص. ٦٦ب).

332 Al-Raḥbah, or Raḥbat al-Šām is the name of a town with a citadel on the right bank of the middle Euphrates; in the later medieval period it functioned both as a strategic military stronghold and as an important caravan station, on the natural frontier between Syria and Mongol/post-Mongol Iraq (E. Honigmann, Th. Bianquis, "al-Raḥba", in *EI*[2] http://referenceworks.brillonline.com/entries/encyclopaedia-of-islam-2/al-rahba-SIM_6190).

333 Aḥmad b. Taymiyyah (661–728/1263–1328) was a Ḥanbalī theologian and jurist from Damascus, whose charismatic personality and controversial thinking had a substantial impact—during and after his own lifetime—upon the social and intellectual life of Damascus, of Syria, of the Syro-Egyptian sultanate, of the Ḥanbalī socio-intellectual

from al-Raḥbah[332] on the day of the Feast of Fast-breaking, heading back to his lands. The sultan was happy with that, and he set his mind on performing the pilgrimage. He entered Damascus on 23 [Šawwāl] [21 February], and he spread the armies over the different regions [in the Damascus province]. 5 He then rode off amidst 40 amirs and 6,000 *mamlūk*s, on dromedaries, on 1 Ḏū l-Qaʿdah [28 February], taking 100 horses with him. He fulfilled his pilgrimage rituals, and returned to Damascus, passing by the Prophet's Medina and entering Karak on the route. He made his entry [into Damascus] on 11 Muḥarram of the year [7]13 [8 May 1313], riding a she-camel of fine 10 stature, [wearing] a round turban with a veil and one of the Bedouin's cloaks, and [holding] a spear in his hand. The *šayḫ al-Islām* Taqī l-Dīn Aḥmad b. Taymiyyah,[333] all the jurisprudents, and the entire population came out to meet him. It was a memorable day, the rent for a house from which one could watch the sultan reaching [no less than] 600 silver *dirhams*. Then he 15 proceeded to Egypt, and he ascended the citadel of the mountain on 12 Ṣafar [8 June].

§190 Then he went on pilgrimage in the year 719 [1319–1320]. When he started organising that campaign, there came to him ceremonial gifts from the amirs, from all governors of Syria, and from the amirs of Dam- 20 ascus and Aleppo. The first who sent his ceremonial gift was the amir Tankiz,[334] the governor of Syria. It consisted of horses and dromedaries with

community, and beyond; the polemicist Ibn Taymiyyah clashed regularly with the authorities of his day, to the extent that he was persecuted and enjailed on various occasions; at first, sultan al-Nāṣir Muḥammad sympathised with Ibn Taymiyyah, but as a consequence of the latter's uncompromising attitude, their relationship soon changed for the worse, and eventually Ibn Taymiyyah died in the citadel of Damascus, after having been imprisonned for more than two years by order of the sultan (H. Laoust, "Ibn Taymiyya", in *EI*[2] http://referenceworks.brillonline.com/entries/encyclopaedia-of-islam-2/ibn-taymiyya-SIM_3388; Bori [2003]).

334 Tankiz al-Ḥusāmī (d. 740/1340) was a former *mamlūk* of Lāǧīn and of al-Nāṣir Muḥammad, who rose to prominence during al-Nāṣir Muḥammad's second reign, and who became the sultan's right hand in Syria in 712/1312; as governor of Damascus his authority stretched over the entire region of Syria, and as the prime regional agent of al-Nāṣir Muḥammad's state, also related to the sultan through various marriages, Tankiz remained in power until 740/1340, over time increasingly transforming into a semi-autonomous Syrian ruler; eventually, al-Nāṣir Muḥammad had his overpowerful agent Tankiz arrested and executed (S. Conermann, "Tankiz", in *EI*[2] http://referenceworks.brillonline.com/entries/encyclopaedia-of-islam-2/tankiz-COM_1168; Conermann [2008]).

والسلاسل من الذهب والفضة وجميع المقاود والمخاطم والآلات | من الحرير الملون المحكم الصنعة، 132b
ثم تقادم الملك المؤيد عماد الدين—صاحب حماة—، ثم تلاه الأمراء.

وشرع القاضي كريم الدين عبد الكريم—ناظر الخاص—في تجهيز ما يحتاج إليه، وخرج إلى ناحية سرياقوس، وصار يقف—وهو مشدود الوسط—أو يجلس على كرسي وسائر أرباب الوظائف

---

١ والآلات : تصحيح في الأصل بخط المقريزي. ٢ تقادم : تصحيح في الأصل بخط المقريزي. ‖ الأمراء : "الامرآ" في الأصل. ٣ القاضي كريم الدين عبد الكريم : مضافة بخط المقريزي في الأصل في مكانها الصحيح في السطر. ٤ هو : تصحيح في الأصل بخط المقريزي. ‖ مشدود : ناقصة في الأصل ومضافة بخط المقريزي في الهامش الأيسر، من الأسفل إلى الأعلى + صح؛ يشير إليها الرمز ٦ بعد كلمة "هو".

golden camel saddles and chains of gold and silver, and all the reins, halters, and equipments were of coloured silk, constructed in a solid fashion. Then [came] the ceremonial gift of al-Malik al-Mu'ayyad 'Imād al-Dīn, the lord of Ḥamāh;[335] thereafter followed [the gifts of] the amirs.

5 § 191 The judge Karīm al-Dīn 'Abd al-Karīm,[336] who was controller of the privy purse, began to prepare what was necessary. He left for Siryāqūs,[337] and he began to organise things, either standing up as the central point of intense [hustle and bustle], or sitting on a chair, while all the officials

335 Al-Malik al-Mu'ayyad 'Imād al-Dīn Abū l-Fidā' Ismā'īl b. 'Alī b. Maḥmūd (672–732/1273–1331) was a scion of the Ayyūbid family, who also obtained fame as a historian and a geographer; as the only remaining Ayyūbid in Syria, he was proclaimed lord of Ḥamāh and beyond upon his father's death; soon loosing his authority to the sultan, Abū l-Fidā' always maintained close and constructive relationships with rulers in Cairo and their representatives in Ḥamāh; as a result, in 710/1310 Ḥamāh was restored to him by al-Nāṣir Muḥammad, and in 720/1320 Abū l-Fidā' was even made sultan of Ḥamāh, an unusual title and position that were inherited by his son after him; this local restoration of the Ayyūbid sultanate came to an end upon the latter's death in 742/1341 (D.J. Talmon-Heller, "Abū l-Fidā', al-Malik al-Mu'ayyad 'Imād al-Dīn", in *EI*³ http://referenceworks.brillonline.com/entries/encyclopaedia-of-islam-3/abu-l-fida-al-malik-al-muayyad-imad-al-din-SIM_0286).

336 Karīm al-Dīn Ibn al-Sadīd (c. 654–724/c. 1256–1324), also known as Karīm al-Dīn al-Kabīr, was a member of the Egyptian Coptic scribal class, who converted to Islam during his career as a scribe, taking the name 'Abd al-Karīm; a scribe in the royal financial administration, Karīm al-Dīn rose to prominence and to remarkable influence during the first decade of al-Nāṣir Muḥammad's third reign; he was the first to occupy the position of controller of the privy purse (*nāẓir al-ḫāṣṣ*) in its new capacity as supreme financial administrator of al-Nāṣir Muḥammad's state; in 723/1323, he fell from royal favour and was tried for embezzlement, and he ended up strangled (W.M. Brinner, "Ibn al-Sadīd", in *EI*² http://referenceworks.brillonline.com/entries/encyclopaedia-of-islam-2/ibn-al-sadid-SIM_3345; Eychenne [2012]).

337 Siryāqūs was the name of a village to the North of Cairo, where there appeared between 723/1323 and 725/1325 by order of the Qalāwūnid sultan al-Nāṣir Muḥammad (d. 741/1341) an enormous hospice (*ḫānqāh*) for the housing of 100 mystics, a hippodrome for the polo game, and palaces for the sultan and his amirs, surrounded by lush gardens; Siryāqūs allegedly remained a royal resort and a place of elite entertainment until the end of the eighth/fourteenth century, after which the place was left to ruin (Levanoni [1995]: 160).

في خدمته وهو يرتب الأمور، فعمل عدة قدور من فضة ونحاس تحمل على البخاتي ليطبخ فيها، وأحضر الخولة لعمل مَباقِل وخضراوات ورياحين ومشمومات في أحْواض خشب لتحمل على الجمال وتسقى طول الطريق ويؤخذ منها كل يوم ما يحتاج إليه. ورتب الأفران وقلائي الجبن وصناع الكماج والسميد وغير ذلك مما يحتاج إليه. وأعطى العربان أجر الجمال التي تحمل الشعير والبشماط
٥ والدقيق، وجهز مركبين في البحر إلى ينبع ومركبين إلى جدة بعدما اعتبر كلفة العليق بأوراق كتب فيها أسماء اثنين وخمسين أميرا منهم من له في اليوم مائة عليقة ومنهم من له خمسون عليقة وأقلهم من له عشرون عليقة. فكانت جملة الشعير المحمول مائة ألف إردب وثلٰثين ألف إردب. وجهز من الشام خمسمائة جمل تحمل الحلوى والسكردانات والفواكه، وحضرت أيضا حوائج خاناه على مائة وثمانين جملا تحمل الحب رمان واللوز وما يحتاج إليه في المطبخ سوى ما حمل من
١٠ الحوائج خاناه من القاهرة، وجهز ألف طائر إوز وثلاثة آلاف طائر دجاج.

فلما تهيأ ذلك ركب السلطان مستهل ذي القعدة ومعه المؤيَد—صاحب حماة—وقاضي القضاة

٣ وتسقى: "وتسقا" في الأصل. ٤ وأعطى: "واعطا" في الأصل. ٦ أسماء: "اسمآ" في الأصل. ‖ مائة: "مايه" في الأصل. ٧ مائة: "مايه" في الأصل. ٨ خمسمائة: "خمسمايه" في الأصل. ‖ وحضرت: تصحيح في الأصل. ٩ مائة: "مايه" في الأصل. ‖ سوى: "سوي" في الأصل. ١٠ ألف طائر: تصحيح في الأصل بخط المقريزي ("الف طاير"). ‖ طائر: "طاير" في الأصل.

were in his service. He arranged for several silver and copper kettles to be carried on Bactrian camels for cooking purposes, and he had servants brought to arrange herbs, vegetables, aromatic plants, and sweet-smelling plants in wooden containers that were to be carried on camels, that were to be watered along the road, and from which there was to be taken daily what was needed. He organised the ovens, the cheese pans, and the hard bread and semolina makers, and similar things that were needed. He gave the Bedouin the rent for the camels that were to carry the barley, the biscuits, and the flour. He arranged for two boats to sail to Yanbuʿ and two boats to sail to Jeddah, after assessing the expenditure for the fodder [that was transported on the boats] on sheets of paper. The names of 52 amirs were written [on these sheets]: among them there were those who had 100 daily fodder rations, among them there were those who had 50 fodder rations, and the lowest among them were those who had 20 fodder rations. The total amount of the barley that was transported was 130,000 *irdabb*.[338] From Syria, there were sent 500 camels carrying sweets, sugar pots, and fruits. There were also brought containers for provisions on 180 camels, containing pomegranate seeds, almonds, and what is needed for cooking. On top of [all that], provision containers were also brought from Cairo, and there were sent along 1,000 geese and 3,000 chickens.

§192 When all that had been prepared, the sultan rode out on 1 Ḏū l-Qaʿdah [14 December 1319], together with al-Muʾayyad, the lord of Ḥamāh, and

338 *Irdabb* is an ancient measure of capacity for grain, used in Egypt in particular; its actual weight varied according to time and place, and is therefore difficult to reconstruct; in general, one *irdabb* is equaled to five bushels or about 200 litres ("irdabb", in *EI*², *Glossary and Index of Terms*. http://referenceworks.brillonline.com/entries/encyclopaedia-of-islam-2-Glossary-and-Index-of-Terms/irdabb-SIM_gi_01803).

بدر الدين محمد بن جماعة الشافعي، بعدما مهدت عقبة أيلة من الصخور ووسع مضيقها بعدما كان سلوكه مشقا، وفتح مغارة شعيب.

فلما قدم مكة أظهر من التواضع والذلة والمسكنة أمرا زائدا، وسجد عند معاينة البيت سجود عَبْدٍ ذليل. ثم التفت إلى الأمير بدر الدين جنكلي بن البابا وقال: "لا زلت أعظم نفسي حتى رأيت البيت. فذكرت تقبيل الناس الأرض لي، فدخل قلبي مهابة عظيمة لم تزل حتى سجدت لله تعالى شكرا." وتقدم إليه قاضي القضاة بدر الدين ابن جماعة وحسن له أن يطوف راكبا. فإن النبي ﷺ طاف راكبا. فقال: "يا قاضي، ومن أنا حتى اتشبه بالنبي ﷺ؟ والله لا طفت إلا كما يطوف الناس." فطاف من غير أن يكون معه أحد من الحجاب، فصار الناس يزاحمونه ويزاحمهم كواحد منهم حتى قضى | طوافه وسعيه. 133[a]

٣ زائدا: "زايدا" في الأصل. ٦ قاضي ... الدين: ناقصة في الأصل ومضافة بخط المقريزي في الهامش الأيسر، من الأسفل إلى الأعلى + صح (بدون رمز إشارة). || ابن: "بن" في الأصل، والألف مضافة بخط المقريزي قبل كلمة "بن" في مكانها الصحيح فوق السطر. || جماعة: كلمة غير واضحة بسبب ثقب في المخطوطة ومضافة هنا من أ (ص. ٦٨أ). || ﷺ: ناقصة في الأصل ومضافة بخط المقريزي في الهامش الأيسر، من الأعلى إلى الأسفل + صح؛ يشير إليها الرمز ˥ بعد كلمة "النبي". ٧ ﷺ: ناقصة في الأصل ومضافة بخط المقريزي في الهامش الأيمن، على نفس السطر والتالي + صح؛ يشير إليها الرمز ˥ بعد كلمة "النبي". ٩ طوافه: في الأصل الكلمة مكتوبة مرتين، مرة في آخر ص. ١٣٢ب ومرة أخرى في بداية ص. ١٣٣أ.

339 Badr al-Dīn Muḥammad b. Ǧamāʿah (639–733/1241–1333) was a member of a notable family of Šāfiʿī scholars in late medieval Syria and Egypt; he became chief judge of Egypt three times, and twice of Damascus, thus making the fortune of his family and establishing it among the leading families of scholars of the period, especially during the eighth-/fourteenth-century period of the Qalāwūnid sultanate (K.S. Salibi, "Ibn Djamāʿa", in *EI*[2] http://referenceworks.brillonline.com/entries/encyclopaedia-of-islam-2/ibn-djamaa-SIM_3133; Salibi [1958]).

340 The town of Aylah, also known as ʿAqabat Aylah, on the Gulf of ʿAqabah, was an ancient commercial port at the crossroads of various overland and maritime routes; it also served since early Islamic times as an important station on the Egyptian overland *ḥağğ* route; when over time the town developed further to the southeast, its name shifted along to that of ʿAqabat Aylah, 'the Pass of Aylah' (referring to the mountain pass that served as the town's overland access) and, ultimately, to the

with the Šāfiʿī chief judge Badr al-Dīn Muḥammad Ibn Ǧamāʿah.[339] [They proceeded over the land-route only] after the pass at Aylah[340] had been cleared from rocks, [after] its narrowness which used to hinder traffic had been widened, and [after the passage to] Maġārat Šuʿayb[341] had been opened 5 for traffic.

§ 193 When he arrived in Mecca, he displayed a great amount of modesty, submissiveness, and humbleness, and when he saw the House [of God] with his own eyes, he prostrated just as a humble servant would do. Then he turned to the amir Badr al-Dīn Ǧankalī b. al-Bābā[342] and he said: "I 10 have always considered myself important, until I saw the House. I remembered people kissing the ground for me, an enormous [feeling of] dignity entering my heart and continuing to do so, until I prostrated for God, the Exalted, out of gratitude." The chief judge Badr al-Dīn Ibn Ǧamāʿah came to him and presented as good to him that he would circumambulate rid- 15 ing his mount, "because the Prophet—may God bless him and grant him salvation—circumambulated riding his mount". But he said: "O, judge, who am I to imitate the Prophet—may God bless him and grant him salvation. By God, I will only circumambulate just as the people circumambulate." So he circumambulated without any of the guardians being with him, and the 20 people crowded around him and he joined their ranks as one of them, until he completed his circumambulation and his running.

---

shortened form of al-ʿAqabah (M. Lecker, "Ayla", in EI3; H.W. Glidden, "al-ʿAḳaba", in EI2, http://referenceworks.brillonline.com/entries/encyclopaedia-of-islam-2/al-akaba-SIM_0454).

341 Maġārat Šuʿayb (the 'Cave of Šuʿayb', better known locally as Maġāʾir Šuʿayb, the 'Caves of Šuʿayb') refers to a large necropolis with tombs carved into limestone (mainly Nabataean, just as the much better preserved Petra to the north), near the northwest Arabian town of Madyan Šuʿayb; this town and necropolis were lying in the Wādī l-Abyaḍ, a valley lying inland from the eastern shore of the Gulf of Aqaba which hosted the ancient pilgrimage route from Aqaba to Mecca that ran inland there to avoid the mountainous coast of the Gulf (F. Buhl, C.E. Bosworth, "Madyan Shuʿayb", in *EI*2 http://referenceworks.brillonline.com/entries/encyclopaedia-of-islam-2/ibn-djamaa-SIM_3133).

342 Badr al-Dīn Ǧankalī b. al-Bābā (675–746/1276–1346) had been a high-ranking officer in Ilḫānid Persia before fleeing to Egypt in 704/1304; he was welcomed with great respect and allowed to become a highly revered senior amir in Cairo, which he remained throughout the rest of his career (Ibn Taġrī Birdī, *al-Manhal al-ṣāfī*, 5:22–25; Amitai [1990]: 163, no. 22; Van Steenbergen [2005]: 198).

وكان قد حج جماعة من المغل، فأحضرهم وأنعم عليهم إنعاما زائدا. وأمر أن تكسى الكعبة بالحرير الأطلس، وأخرج الثياب للصناع فعملوها. وفرق في أهل مكة مالا عظيما، وأفاض التشاريف على أمراء مكة وأرباب وظائفها وأمير ينبع وأمير خليص. وأنعم عليه بخمسة آلاف درهم برسم عمارة عين خليص، وكان لها مدة سنين قد انقطعت، وجعل ذلك مقررا له في كل سنة برسم عمارتها. ٥

واجتمع عند السلطان من العربان [من] لم يجتمع لملك قبله وهم: سائر بني مهدي وأمرائها، وشطي وأخوه عساف وأولاده، وأمراء مكة وأشرافها، وأمراء المدينة، {وصاحبا} ينبع وخليص، {وبنو} لام، وعَرب حَوْران وكبارها، وأولاد مهنا. وصاروا يدِلون عليه إدلالا زائدا بحيث قام في بعض الأيام ابن لموسى بن مهنا وقال للسلطان: "يأبا علي، بحيات هذى"—ومد يده إلى لحية

١ زائدا : "زايدا" في الأصل. ‖ تكسى : "تكسا" في الأصل. ‖ بالحرير : ناقصة في الأصل ومضافة بخط المقريزي في الهامش الأيمن، من الأعلى إلى الأسفل + صح؛ يشير إليها الرمز ⌝ بعد كلمة "الكعبة". ٣ أمراء : "امرآ" في الأصل. ‖ وظائفها : "وظايفها" في الأصل. ‖ درهم : ناقصة في الأصل، مضافة بخط المقريزي في الهامش الأيمن، من الأعلى إلى الأسفل + صح؛ يشير إليها الرمز ⌝ بعد كلمة "آلاف". ٦ من[٢]: ناقصة في الأصل، مضافة من السياق. ‖ سائر : "ساير" في الأصل. ‖ وأمرائها : "وامرايها" في الأصل. ٧ وأمراء[١] : تصحيح في الأصل بخط المقريزي ("وامرا"). ‖ وأمراء[٢] : تصحيح في الأصل بخط المقريزي ("وامرا"). ‖ وصاحبا : "صاحبي" في الأصل وهو خطأ، والتصحيح من السياق. ٨ وبنو : "وبني" في الأصل وهو خطأ، والتصحيح من السياق. ‖ وعَرب : تصحيح في الأصل بخط المقريزي. ‖ مهنا : تصحيح في الأصل بخط المقريزي. ‖ وصاروا : تصحيح في الأصل بخط المقريزي. ‖ يدِلون : "يَدِلون" في الأصل ومن الظاهر أن الناسخ كتب "يَدلوا" وكشط المقريزى الألف فأضاف نونا ولكن لم يصحح الفتحة في بداية الفعل. ‖ زائدا : "زايدا" في الأصل. ٩ ابن : تصحيح في الأصل بخط المقريزي.

343 The Banū Mahdī was a tribal grouping that mainly dominated the Balqāʾ region, the eastern plateau of the Jordan valley; its leaders were integrated into the sultanate via the installation of the amirate of the Banū Mahdī, usually divided among four tribal leaders and an important vehicle for the negotiation of relationships between tribe and sultanate (al-Qalqašandī, *Ṣubḥ al-aʿšá*, 4:212–213, 12:135–140).

§ 194 A group of Mongols turned out to have made the pilgrimage, so he had them brought to him and he gave them a lot gifts. He commanded that the Kaʿbah be covered with satin silk and he had the textiles brought to the artisans, who prepared them. He distributed among the people of Mecca a lot of money and he overwhelmed the amirs and officials of Mecca, the amir of Yanbuʿ, and the amir of Ḫulayṣ with ceremonial gifts and robes. He granted to the latter 5,000 *dirhams* for the benefit of constructing the well of Ḫulayṣ, which for many years had been cut off. He made that into a regular annual stipulation for him, for the purpose of its upkeep.

§ 195 There gathered with the sultan from the Bedouin who had not gathered for any ruler before him: all the Banū Mahdī and its amirs;[343] Šaṭī, his brother ʿAssāf, and his sons,[344] the amirs and notables of Mecca, the amirs of Medina, the lords of Yanbuʿ and of Ḫulayṣ, the Banū Lām,[345] the Bedouin of Ḥawrān[346] with their chiefs, and the sons of Muhannā. They got on increasingly amiable terms with him, to the extent that one day a son of Mūsá b. Muhannā[347] rose and said to the sultan: "O, Abū ʿAlī, by the life of this

344 Šāṭī, his brother ʿAssāf, and his sons: I have so far not been able to retrieve further information on these Bedouin leaders from the Hijaz.

345 The Banū Lām is the name of a sizeable and varied Arab tribal grouping that long time dominated the area East of the lower Tigris region in Iraq and Iran; its exact origins and its whereabouts in the later medieval period remain obscure, however (V. Minorsky, R.M. Burell, "Lām", in *EI*[2] http://referenceworks.brillonline.com/entries/encyclopaedia-of-islam-2/lam-SIM_4629).

346 Ḥawrān refers to the region between the Damascus plain and the Yarmūk river, which separates Syria from Transjordan; in the fourteenth century, nomad groups belonging to the Banū Rabīʿah and led by the Āl Muhannā gradually settled in this region, which they came to share with the Āl Murrah (D. Sourdel, "Ḥawrān", in *EI*[2] http://referenceworks.brillonline.com/entries/encyclopaedia-of-islam-2/hawran-SIM_2817).

347 Mūsá b. Muhannā (d. 742/1341) was a son of the Syrian Āl Faḍl tribal leader Muhannā b. ʿĪsá b. Muhanná (d. 735/1334), the *amīr al-ʿArab* who experienced very mixed relations with al-Nāṣir Muḥammad and who on various occasions therefore moved from Syria to Īlḫānid Iraq; Mūsá performed the position of *amīr al-ʿArab* between c. 735/1334 and his sudden death at Tadmur (Palmyra) in 742/1341 (M.A. Bakhīt, "Muhannā", in *EI*[2] http://referenceworks.brillonline.com/entries/encyclopaedia-of-islam-2/muhanna-SIM_5423; Hiyari [1975]: 519–520; al-Ṣafadī, *Aʿyān al-ʿaṣr*, 5:490).

السلطان ومسكها—"إلا أعطيتني الضيعة الفلانية." فصرخ فيه الفخر—ناظر الجيش—فقال: "إرفع يدك قطع الله يدك! والك، يا ولد زناء، تمد يدك إلى السلطان!" فتبسم السلطان وقال: "يا قاضي، هذه عادة العرب. إذا قصدوا كبيرا في شيء يكون عظمته عندهم مسك ذقنه—يعني أنه قد استجار به—فهو عندهم سنة." فقام الفخر مغضبا وهو يقول: "والله، إن هاؤلاء مناحيس ٥ وسنتهم أنحس منهم، لا بارك الله فيهم!"

وصلى السلطان الجمعة بمكة، فدعي له وللشريف فقط ولم يدع لصاحب اليمن تأدبا مع السلطان. وقضى نسكه، وسار إلى المدينة النبوية وصلى بها الجمعة أيضا، وأقام يومين حتى قدم الركب، وبعث المبشرين إلى مصر والشام، وسار إلى ينبع، فلم يجد المراكب وصلت. فحصلت مشقة زائدة من قلة العليق، ومشى أكثر المماليك لوقوف الجمال حتى أتت الإقامات من مصر والشام.

١٠ ونزل السلطان بركة الحاج في ثاني عشر المحرم سنة عشرين وسبعمائة، فعمل له سماط عظيم جدا، وركب في موكب جليل إلى القلعة. فكان يوما مشهودا. وجلس يوم الخميس نصف المحرم بدار العدل وخلع على سائر الأمراء وأرباب الوظائف وأمراء العربان.

وحج ثالثا في سنة {اثنتين} وثلثين وسبعمائة، ورسم بسفر الخواتين وبعض السراري، وكتب لنائب الشام بتجهيز ما يحتاج إليه. فوصلت التقادم على العادة من النواب وأمراء الشام وأمراء العربان، ١٥ وطلب سائر صناع مصر لعمل الاحتياجات.

٢ زناء : "زنا" في الأصل. ٣ شيء : "شي" في الأصل. ٤ مغضبا : تصحيح في الأصل بخط المقريزي. ‖ هاؤلاء : "هاولا" في الأصل. ٨ زائدة : "زايده" في الأصل. ٩ ومشى : "ومشا" في الأصل. ١٠ عشرين وسبعمائة : "عشرن وسبعمايه" في الأصل. ١١ المحرم : أداة التعريف من إضافة المقريزي. ١٢ سائر الأمراء : "ساير الامرآ" في الأصل. ‖ الوظائف وأمراء : "الوظايف وامرآ" في الأصل. ١٣ اثنتين : "اسن" في الأصل. ‖ وسبعمائة : "وسبعمايه" في الأصل. ‖ لنائب : "لنايب" في الأصل. ١٤ وأمراء[١] : كلمة غير واضحة بسبب ثقب في المخطوطة ومضافة هنا من أ (ص. ٦٩ب) ("وامرَآ"). ‖ وأمراء[٢] : "وامرآ" في الأصل. ١٥ سائر : "ساير" في الأصل.

one"—and he stretched out his hand to the beard of the sultan and grasped it—"[I will consider you in default] if you do not give me estate such-and-such." Al-Faḫr, the controller of the military bureau, called out to him, saying: "Remove your hand—may God cut off your hand—, woe onto you, o son of adultery, for stretching out your hand to the sultan." But the sultan smiled and said: "O judge, this is the custom of the Bedouin: when they go to see someone important on an issue, his high status with them is [indicated] by grasping his beard, meaning that his patronage is being sought; it is a tradition with them." Al-Faḫr stood up angrily, while he was saying: "By God, these are ill-fated ones and their tradition is even more ill-fated than they are; may God not give his blessing to them."

§196 The sultan prayed the Friday prayer at Mecca. It was delivered in his name and in the name of the Sharif only, and not in the name of the lord of Yemen, out of courtesy for the sultan. He fulfilled his pilgrimage rituals, and then he proceeded to the Prophet's Medina. He prayed the Friday prayer there as well, and remained for two days, until the caravan arrived. He sent the messengers to spread the good news [of his successful pilgrimage] in Egypt and Syria, and he proceeded to Yanbuʿ. [There] he did not find any ships arriving, so that great calamity occurred due to the shortage of fodder. Most of the *mamlūk*s had to walk [back] on foot, due to the camels' having to wait [near Yanbuʿ] until the supplies would come from Egypt and Syria.

§197 The sultan settled down at Birkat al-Ḥāǧǧ on 12 Muḥarram of the year 720 [25 February 1320]. A huge banquet was organised for him, and he rode in a splendid procession to the citadel. It was a memorable day. On Thursday 15 Muḥarram [28 February] he held session in the Palace of Justice, and he gave a robe of honour to all the amirs, to the officials, and to the amirs of the Bedouin.

§198 He went on pilgrimage a third time in the year 732 [1332]. He ordered the royal ladies and some concubines to travel along. He wrote to the governor of Syria to prepare what he needed. As usual, the ceremonial gifts from the governors, from the amirs of Syria, and from the amirs of the Bedouin arrived. He required from all the artisans of Egypt to make everything necessary.

وخرج | المحمل على العادة وأمر الركب الأمير عز الدين أيدمر الخطيري، فرحل في عشرين 133b
شوال. وركب السلطان في سبعين أميرا من قلعة الجبل يوم الخامس والعشرين منه، وسفر الحريم
مع الأمير سيف الدين طقزتمر. فلما قارب عقبة أيلة بلغه أن الأمير بكتمر الساقي على نية المخامرة،
فهم بالرجوع وبعث ابنه آنوك وأمه الى الكرك. ثم قوي عزمه على المسير، فسار وهو محترز، ورسم
٥ أن كلا من الأمراء يحضر على باب الدهليز بثلثين مملوكا، فصار الجميع ينامون وعددهم تحت
{رؤوسهم}، والأحمدي مستمر عليه زرديه وسيفه متقلد به وترسه على كتفه، وترك السلطان
النوم في مبيته.

---

٢ أميرا: تصحيح في الأصل بخط المقريزي. ٤ آنوك: تصحيح في الأصل بخط المقريزي. ٥ الأمراء: "الامرا" في الأصل. || وعددهم: تصحيح في الأصل بخط المقريزي. || تحت: ناقصة في الأصل ومضافة بخط المقريزي في الهامش الأيسر، من الأسفل إلى الأعلى + صح، يشير إليها الرمز ⌐ بعد كلمة "عددهم".
٦ رؤوسهم: "روسهم" في الأصل. ٧ في: تصحيح في الأصل بخط المقريزي.

§199 The *maḥmal*[348] left as usual, and the commander of the caravan was the amir ʿIzz al-Dīn Aydamur al-Ḫaṭīrī. He set out on 20 Šawwāl [15 July], and the sultan rode from the citadel of the mountain, amidst 70 amirs, on 25 [Šawwāl] [20 July]. The women travelled with the amir Sayf al-Dīn Ṭuquztamur.[349] When [al-Nāṣir Muḥammad] approached ʿAqabat Aylah,[350] he was informed that the amir Baktamur al-Sāqī[351] intended to revolt. He wanted to return, and he sent his son Ānūk and his mother to Karak. Then his determination to go along was strengthened, so he proceeded while he was on his guard. He ordered that each of the amirs should be present at the entrance of the royal tent, with 30 *mamlūk*s. All took the habit of going to sleep with their gears under their heads; [the amir Baybars] al-Aḥmadī continued to have his chain mail on, his sword girded, and his shield [hanging] from his shoulders; the sultan forsook to sleep in his sleeping quarters.

348 The *maḥmal* or empty palanquin in the pilgrimage caravan was a central component of rulers' pilgrimage paraphernalia from the mid-thirteenth to the early twentieth centuries (see fn. 29).

349 Sayf al-Dīn Ṭuquztamur al-Ḥamawī (d. 746/1345) was a former *mamlūk* of Abū l-Fidāʾ, the sultan of Ḥamāh (see fn. 319), who had offered him as a gift to al-Nāṣir Muḥammad; Ṭuquztamur rose to prominence in the latter's service, eventually becoming one of the leading figures at court; after al-Nāṣir Muḥammad's death, he remained an important and highly respected senior amir, and he secured various leading positions in Egypt and Syria (Ibn Taġrī Birdī, *al-Manhal al-ṣāfī*, 6:420–422; Van Steenbergen [2005]: 198).

350 For the town of ʿAqabat Aylah, also known as Aylah, on the Gulf of ʿAqabah, see fn. 340.

351 Baktamur al-Sāqī (d. 733/1333) was a former *mamlūk* of Baybars al-Ǧāšnikīr and then of al-Nāṣir Muḥammad; as a privileged member of the latter's private retinue, he soon earned the sultan's close friendship and great esteem, becoming a high-ranking amir as well as the recipient of all kinds of exceptional royal privileges that made him be remembered as one of the closest and most prestigious intimates of al-Nāṣir Muḥammad; eventually, however, for a combination of political and personal reasons, the sultan had Baktamur and his twenty-year old son Aḥmad—also a high-ranking amir—poisoned (Behrens-Abouseif [2000]: 55–60).

فلما وصل إلى ينبع تلقاه الشريف أسد الدين رميثة—أمير مكة—بينبع ومعه القواد والأشراف، فأكرمه ورحب به، وتوجه حتى نزل خُلَيص. ففر عند الرحيل ثلاثون مملوكا، فاهتم السلطان لذلك وسار حتى قدم مكة، وجرى على عادته في التواضع لله تعالى وكثر الصدقات على أهل مكة والإنعام على الأمراء والأجناد، وقضى نسكه. وبعث الأمير أيتمش المحمدي ومعه مائة {حجار} إلى العقبة، ٥ فوسعها ونظفها. ودخل السلطان المدينة النبوية، فهبت بها رياح عاصفة قلعت الخيم وأظلم الجو وصار كل أحد يهجم على غير خيمته ولا يعرف موضعه. فانزعج السلطان انزعاجا زائدا، وخاف من أن يفتك به أحد أو يغتاله، ووقع الصياح في الوطاقات، فكان أمرا موهولا طول الليل، حتى طلع الفجر. فانجلى ذلك، وحضر أمراء العربان بالمماليك الهاربين عن آخرهم، ورحل من المدينة.

فتوعك أحمد بن الأمير بكتمر الساقي، ومات بعد أيام، ولم يقم بعده بكتمر سوى ثلثة أيام، ومات ١٠ أيضا بالقرب من عيون القصب. فتحدث الناس أن السلطان سقاهما. فدفنا بعيون القصب، ثم نقلا إلى تربة بكتمر بالقرافة.

٢-٣ حتى ... وسار: ناقصة في الأصل، مضافة بخط المقريزي في الهامش الأيمن، على نفس السطر وعلى السطور الأربعة التالية + صح؛ يشير إليها الرمز ⌝ بعد كلمة "توجه". ٣ وكثر: تصحيح في الأصل بخط المقريزي. ٤ الأمراء: "الامرآ" في الأصل. ‖ مائة: "ماية" في الأصل. ‖ حجار: في الأصل "حجارا" وهو خطأ، والتصحيح من السياق. ٦ زائدا: "زايدا" في الأصل. ٧ الصياح: تصحيح في الأصل بخط المقريزي. ٨ أمراء: "امرآ" في الأصل. ٩ الساقي: ناقصة في الأصل ومضافة بخط المقريزي في الهامش الأيسر، من الأسفل إلى الأعلى + صح؛ يشير إليها الرمز ⌝ بعد كلمة "بكتمر". ‖ أيام: "امام" في الأصل.

---

352 Rumayṯah b. Abī Numayy (d. 746/1346) was a member of the Banū Ḥasan, and a son of the great Sharif Muḥammad Abū Numayy (see fn. 201); throughout the first and second decades of the eighth/fourteenth century Rumayṯah and his brothers continuously competed for the amirate over Mecca, trying to play out against each other the Īlḫān and the sultan in their various bids for power; eventually, al-Nāṣir Muḥammad managed to impose his authority, establishing Rumayṯah and a brother of his as joint amirs, but the relationship between Rumayṯah and al-Nāṣir Muḥammad remained vexed (Mortel [1987]: 462–466; Meloy [2010a]: 47–48, 245).

§ 200 When he arrived at Yanbuʿ, the Sharif Asad al-Dīn Rumayṯah,[352] the amir of Mecca, came to meet him at Yanbuʿ, with the commanders and notables, and he honoured him and welcomed him. He moved on until he settled down at Ḫulayṣ. En route, 30 *mamlūk*s fled, and the sultan was worried because of that and he proceeded until he arrived at Mecca. He acted as usual in humbling himself before God the Exalted, in the multitude of alms for the people of Mecca, and in giving gifts to the amirs and the soldiers. He fulfilled his pilgrimage rituals. He sent the amir Ayitmiš al-Muḥammadī[353] with 100 stonemasons to ʿAqabah to make it[s passage] wider and to clean it up. The sultan entered the Prophet's Medina. Stormy winds raged there, tearing down the tents and darkening the sky. Every one started to enter without permission into another tent than his own, not knowing his location. The sultan got extremely upset, and feared that someone would slay or murder him. There was clamour in the pavilions, and it was a frightening situation all night long, until dawn rose and that cleared up. The amirs of the Bedouin came [bringing] every single one of the *mamlūk*s who had fled. [Thereuon, al-Nāṣir Muḥammad] departed from Medina.

§ 201 Aḥmad, the son of the amir Baktamur al-Sāqī, was unwell and died after a couple of days. After him, Baktamur only remained for three days, and he also died, close to ʿUyūn al-Qaṣab.[354] The people were saying that the sultan had poisoned both of them. They were both burried at ʿUyūn al-Qaṣab; later they were transferred to the mausoleum of Baktamur at the Qarāfah.[355]

353 Ayitmiš al-Muḥammadī l-Nāṣirī (d. 755/1354) was a former *mamlūk* of al-Nāṣir Muḥammad, who became an amir during al-Nāṣir Muḥammad's third reign, and who obtained various leading positions in Egypt and Syria after the latter's death (Ibn Taġrī Birdī, *al-Manhal al-ṣāfī*, 3:137–138; al-Ṣafadī, *Aʿyān al-ʿaṣr*, 1:648–649).

354 ʿUyūn al-Qaṣab is the name of an oasis settlement near the North-Arabian Red-Sea coast, where the Egyptian *ḥaǧǧ* route coming from ʿAqabat Aylah turns southwest and starts following the coastal line.

355 This so-called mausoleum actually was a richly endowed and lavishly furnished Sufi hospice with attached mausoleum, built in 726/1326 at the foot of the Muqattam hill, a desert area southeast of Cairo also known (until today) as the small cemetery (al-Qarāfāh al-Ṣughrá) (Behrens-Abouseif [2000]: 56–57).

وسار السلطان وقد اطمأن بعدما كان خائفا فزعا، فقدم بركة الحاج يوم السبت ثاني عشر المحرم
سنة ثلث وثلثين وسبعمائة، وصعد القلعة في موكب عظيم لم ير مثله، ومشى على شقاق الحرير
بفرسه وهو ضارب اللثام، وفرح الناس به فرحا زائدا، ودقت البشائر وطبلخاناة الأمراء ثلثة
أيام، وعملت الأفراح، وجلس في يوم الاثنين وخلع على سائر الأمراء والمقدمين وأنعم إنعاما
٥ عظيما.

---

١ خائفا : "خايفا" في الأصل. ٢ وسبعمائة : "وسعمايه" في الأصل. ٣ زائدا : "زايدا" في الأصل. ‖ البشائر: "البشاير" في الأصل. ‖ الأمراء: "الامرآ" في الأصل. ٤ الأفراح : كلمة غير واضحة بسبب ثقب في المخطوطة ومضافة هنا من أ (ص. ١٧١أ). ‖ سائر الأمراء: "ساير الامرا" في الأصل.

§ 202 The sultan proceeded, having become at ease after having been terribly afraid. He arrived at Birkat al-Ḥājj on Saturday, 12 Muḥarram of the year 733 [3 October 1332]. He ascended the citadel in a magnificent procession, the likes of which have not been seen. He walked over strips of silk with his horse, while he was [showing his face to the people by] striking off the veil [that was covering the lower part of his face]. The people were extremely happy with [his safe return]. For three days, the royal drums and the orchestras of the amirs played, and feasts were organised. On Monday, he held a public session, awarding robes of honour to all the amirs and commanders, and giving lavish gifts.

{مَنسَا} مُوسَى ملك التكرور

أول من حج من ملوك التكرور سَرْبَندانه—ويقال برمَنْدانه—. ثم حج مَنْسَا وَلي بن ماري بن جَاطه في أيام الملك | الظاهر بيبرس. ثم حج ساكوره وكان قد تغلب على ملكهم وفتح بلاد كَوكَو. 134a

ثم حج مَنْسَا موسى لما قدم إلى مصر سنة أربع وعشرين وسبعمائة بهدايا جليلة وذهب كثير. فأرسل السلطان الملك الناصر محمد بن قلاوون المهمندار لتلقيه، وركب به إلى القلعة في يوم الخدمة. فامتنع ٥ أن يقبل الأرض، وقال للترجمان: "أنا رجل مالكي المذهب ولا أسجد لغير الله." فأعفاه السلطان

١ مَنسَا : "مَسَّا" في الأصل، والتصحيح من كتابة الاسم في الصفحة التالية (١٣٤أ، سطر ٢) ومن أ (ص. ٧١أ).   ٢ سَرْبَندانه : كلمة غير واضحة بسبب ثقب في المخطوطة، متممة هنا من أ (ص. ٧١أ).   ٣ الظاهر : في الأصل الكلمة مكتوبة مرتين، مرة في آخر ص. ١٣٣ب ومرة أخرى في بداية ص. ١٣٤أ.   ٤ وعشرين وسبعمائة : "وعشرن وسعمايه" في الأصل.

11. Mansā Mūsá,[356] the ruler of Takrūr[357]

§ 203 The first to undertake the pilgrimage from the rulers of Takrūr was Sarbandānah—it was said: Barmandānah. Then Mansā Walī b. Mārī b. Ǧāẓah performed the pilgrimage, in the days of al-Malik al-Ẓāhir Baybars. 5 Then Sākūrah performed the pilgrimage. He had subdued their ruler and he had conquered the lands of Kawkaw.[358]

§ 204 Then Mansā Mūsá performed the pilgrimage, arriving in Egypt in the year 724 [1324], with impressive gifts and lots of gold. The sultan al-Malik al-Nāṣir Muḥammad b. Qalāwūn sent the *mihmandār*[359] to meet him, and 10 he rode with him to the citadel on the day of the public audience. [When he entered the sultan's public audience, Mansā Mūsá] refused to kiss the ground, saying to the interpreter: "I am a man of Mālikī creed and I prostrate

356 Mansā Mūsá (r. 712–738/1312–1337 [alternative reign dates that are also encountered are 707–732/1307–1331]), also known as Kankan Mūsá, was a Muslim ruler (*mansa*) of the kingdom of Mali, reigning at the height of this polity's prosperity; his 724/1324 pilgrimage, which took him and the enormous entourage that accompanied him via Timbuktu to Cairo, made him into one of the most famous of all royal West African pilgrims, firmly establishing the fame of Mali as an immensily wealthy Muslim polity (D.C. Conrad, "Mansa Mūsā", in *EI*² http://referenceworks.brillonline.com/entries/encyclopaedia-of-islam-2/hasan-SIM_2752; Lewis, *Islam* ["7. The Pilgrimage of Kankan Mūsā (1324–1325)"]; Schultz [2006]: 430–431).

357 Takrūr is the Arabised form of an African ethnonym that by the later medieval period tended to be used as a name for Muslim West Africa, either in part or in whole, and for its inhabitants (J.O. Hunwick, "Takrūr", in *EI*² http://referenceworks.brillonline.com/entries/encyclopaedia-of-islam-2/takrur-SIM_7348).

358 Sarbandānah, Mansā Walī (= Mansā Ulī) (r. 1255–1270), and Sākūrah (r. 1285–1300) are the names of the first set of rulers who, in the course of the thirteenth century, created through expansion and trade (including in the region of Kawkaw, the commercial settlement of Gao on the left bank of the Niger), and through conversion to Islam, the kingdom of Mali in West Africa; as a token of their power and of their piety, they each participated in the tradition of royal pilgrimage from West Africa to Mecca, thus creating important connections with the central lands of the Muslim world (N. Levtzion, "Mali", in *EI*² http://referenceworks.brillonline.com/entries/encyclopaedia-of-islam-2/mali-SIM_4860; Möhring [1999]: 324–326).

359 The *mihmandār* is the name of a court position commissioned to receive and to provide hospitality for guests, including foreigners and envoys (C.E. Bosworth, "Mihmān", in *EI*² http://referenceworks.brillonline.com/entries/encyclopaedia-of-islam-2/mihman-SIM_8826).

من ذلك وقربه إليه وأكرمه وسأله عن سبب مجيئه، فقال: "أردت الحج." فرسم للوزير أن يجهزه بكل ما يحتاج إليه.

ويقال إنه قدم معه أربع عشرة ألف جارية برسم خدمته خاصة. فأقبل أصحابه على شراء الجواري من الترك والحبوش والمغنيات والثياب، فانحط سعر الدينار الذهب ستة دراهم.

٥ وقدم هديته، وخرج مع الركب بعدما أوصى به السلطان الأمير سيف الدين أيتمش—أمير الركب—، فسار ركبا وحده ساقة الحاج حتى قضى حجه.

وتأخر بمكة بعد الموسم أياما وعاد. فهلك كثير من أصحابه وجماله بالبرد حتى لم يصل معه إلا نحو الثلث منهم. فاحتاج إلى قرض مال كثير من التجار.

واشترى عدة كتب من فقه المالكية، وأنعم السلطان عليه بخيول وجمال.

١٠ وسافر إلى بلاده بعدما تصدق في الحرمين بمال كثير.

وكان إذا حدثه أصحابه في أمر، كشفوا {رؤوسهم} عند مخاطبته عادة لهم.

١ من : كتب الناسخ "عن" وكشط المقريزي العين وكتب في مكانها ميما. ‖ مجيئه : "محيه" في الأصل. ٣ عشرة : تصحيح في الأصل بخط المقريزي. ‖ شراء : "شرا" في الأصل. ٤ الدينار : تصحيح في الأصل بخط المقريزي ("الدنار"). ‖ الذهب ستة : ناقصة في الأصل ومضافة بخط المقريزي في الهامش الأيمن، من الأعلى إلى الأسفل + صح؛ يشير إليها الرمز ⌝ بعد كلمة "الدينار". ٧ بمكة : تصحيح في الأصل بخط المقريزي. ‖ لم : ناقصة في الأصل ومضافة بخط المقريزي في الهامش الأيسر، على نفس السطر + صح؛ يشير إليها الرمز ⌐ بعد كلمة "حتى". ٩ فقه : تصحيح في الأصل. ١١ رؤوسهم : "روسهم" في الأصل.

to none but God." The sultan forgave him for that. He made him come nearer to him, he honoured him, and he asked him about the cause for his coming. He said: "I want to perform the pilgrimage." [The sultan] ordered the vizier to send him everything that he needed.

§ 205 It is said that there came with him 14,000 slave girls for the benefit of his service alone. His companions began to purchase Turkish and Abyssinian slave girls, female singers, and textiles. The price of the gold dinar was lowered by six *dirham*s.

§ 206 [When] he had presented his gift [to the sultan], he left with the [regular pilgrimage] caravan after the sultan had entrusted him to the care of the amir Sayf al-Dīn Ayitmiš, the commander of the caravan. He proceeded along the pilgrim's itinerary, riding alone, until he had completed his pilgrimage.

§ 207 After the [pilgrimage] season, he remained behind in Mecca for a couple of days, and then he returned [to Egypt]. But [on the road back] many of his companions and of his camels perished from the cold, so that only a third of them arrived [in Cairo] with him. [As a result of his misfortune] he needed to borrow a lot of money from the merchants [for his home journey].

§ 208 [In Cairo] he bought a number of books of Mālikī jurisprudence. The sultan gave him horses and camels.

§ 209 He travelled back to his homeland after he had left a lot of money for almsgiving in the two august places [Mecca and Medina].

§ 210 It was customary for them [that] when his companions would talk to him about anything, they would uncover their heads while addressing him.

الملك المجاهد علي

ابن الملك المؤيد داود بن الملك المظفر يوسف بن الملك المنصور عمر بن علي بن رسول، صاحب اليمن.

حج في سنة اثنتين وأربعين وسبعمائة، وأطلع علمه جبل عرفة وقد وقف بنو حسن في خدمته حتى ٥ قضى حجه. وعزم على كسوة الكعبة، فلم يمكنه أمير مكة من ذلك، فسار وهو حنق.

ثم حج ثانيا في سنة اثنتين وخمسين وسبعمائة، وقد قدم عليه الشريف ثقبة بن رميثة، وأغراه بأخيه عجلان، وأطمعه في مكة وكسوة الكعبة. فسار في عسكر كبير. فبلغ ذلك الشريف عجلان. وكان الأمير طاز قد حج في جماعة من الأمراء. فبلغهم قدوم صاحب اليمن في جحفل عظيم وأنه يريد

٤ اثنتين: تصحيح في الأصل بخط المقريزي. || وسبعمائة: تصحيح في الأصل ("وسبع مايه"). || قد: ناقصة في الأصل ومضافة بخط المقريزي في الهامش الأيمن، من الأعلى إلى الأسفل + صح، يشير إليها الرمز ⌜ بعد حرف "و". ٦ اثنتين: تصحيح في الأصل بخط المقريزي. || وخمسين وسبعمائة: "وخمسن وسبعمايه" في الأصل. ٨ الأمراء: "الامرآ" في الأصل. || في جحفل: غير واضحة في الأصل بسبب ثقب في المخطوطة ومضافة هنا من أ (ص. ٧٢ب).

360 Al-Malik al-Muǧāhid ʿAlī (r. 721–764/1322–1363) was the fifth of the Rasūlid rulers of Yemen (Smith, "Rasūlids", in *EI*[2]).

12. Al-Malik al-Muǧāhid ʿAlī[360]

[He was] the son of al-Malik al-Muʾayyad Dāwūd b. al-Malik al-Muẓaffar Yūsuf b. al-Malik al-Manṣūr ʿUmar b. ʿAlī b. Rasūl;[361] [he was] lord of Yemen.

§ 211 He performed the pilgrimage in the year 742 [1342]. He raised his
5 banner on the mountain of ʿArafah, and the Banū Ḥasan[362] remained in his service until he completed his pilgrimage. [But when] he wished to cover the Kaʿbah with a *kiswah*, the amir of Mecca did not enable him to do that, so he left in anger.

§ 212 Thereafter he performed the pilgrimage a second time in the year 752
10 [1352].[363] The Sharif Ṯaqabah b. Rumayṯah had come to him [in Yemen] and had set him up against his brother ʿAǧlān [b. Rumayṯah],[364] making him covetous for Mecca and for covering the Kaʿbah with a *kiswah*. [Al-Malik al-Muǧāhid] left [for Mecca] with a great army, but that reached the ears of the Sharif ʿAǧlān [just when] the [Egyptian] amir Ṭāz[365] had been performing
15 the pilgrimage amidst a group of [Egyptian] amirs. He informed them of the coming of the lord of Yemen with an enormous host, and that he wanted to

---

361 Al-Malik al-Muʾayyad Dāwūd (r. 696–721/1296–1322) was the fourth Rasūlid ruler of Yemen, son and successor of the long-reigning al-Muẓaffar Yūsuf (Smith, "Rasūlids", in *EI*²).

362 Banū Ḥasan refers to the ruling elite of Mecca, the sharifian family that claimed to be descended from the Prophet's grandson al-Ḥasan b. ʿAlī b. Abī Ṭālib and that was therefore collectively known by this name (Meloy [2010a]: 47; Mortel [1987]: 455). See also fn. 201, 352.

363 Although the Arabic text has clearly been corrected by al-Maqrīzī to refer to the year 752, the story's continuation, as well al-Maqrīzī's own discussion of the same event in his chronicle *Kitāb al-Sulūk*, make amply clear that this second pilgrimage actually happened towards the end of 751 [early 1351] (see al-Maqrīzī, *al-Sulūk*, 2:831–832).

364 ʿAǧlān b. Rumayṯah (r. 747–776/1346–1375) was a member of the Banū Ḥasan (see fn. 362), a son of the Sharif Rumayṯah (see fn. 352), and a grandson of the great Sharif Muḥammad Abū Numayy (see fn. 201); his rule as Sharif over Mecca was highly contested, including by his brother Ṯaqabah (d. 762/1362) (A.J. Wensinck, C.E. Bosworth, "Makka. 2. From the ʿAbbāsid to the Modern Period"; Meloy [2010a]: 245, 246).

365 Ṭāz al-Nāṣirī (d. 763/1362) was a high-ranking military commander (*amīr*) in Cairo; in the early 750s/1350s, he was one of the most powerful political leaders at the court of Cairo (Wansbrough, "Ḥasan", in *EI*²; Van Steenbergen [2006]: 187).

يدخل مكة بلامة الحرب وحوله سلاح داريته وطبرداريته ليقيم فتنة. فبعثوا إليه أنه "من يريد الحج إنما يدخل مكة بذلة ومسكنة، وأنت تريد تبتدع بدعة فاحشة، ونحن لا نمكنك من الدخول على هذه الصفة. فإن اردت السلامة، فابعث إلينا الشريف ثقبة يكون عندنا حتى | تقضي الحج." 134b
فلم يجد بدا من الإذعان، وبعث ثقبة. فأكرمه الأمراء وبعث الأمير طاز إلى صاحب اليمن بالأمير
٥ طقطاي في جماعة من المماليك ليكونوا في خدمته حتى يقضي حجه. فساروا إليه وأبطلوا السلاح دارية وحَمْل الغاشية وسائر ما كان قد اهتم به، ومشوا في خدمته حتى دخل الحرم، وسلم على الأمراء واعتذر إليهم وأضمر أنه يصبر حتى يرحل الأمير طاز ويثور—هو وثقبة—على من بقي مع أمير الركب ويأخذا عجلان ويملكا مكة.

فلما كان يوم منى ركب الأمير بزلار—أمير الركب—من مكة، فرأى خادم صاحب اليمن،
١٠ فاستدعاه إليه. فامتنع من الحضور، وضرب مملوك بزلار بعض جنده بحربة. فوقع الصوت في الركب، وركب بزلار إلى طاز وثار أهل اليمن بالسلاح. فركب أمراء مصر وقت الظهر واقتتلوا مع اليمنيين وهزموا بزلار هزيمة قبيحة، وأقبل عجلان—أمير مكة—بجيش كبير. فأمره طاز أن

١ مكة: ناقصة في الأصل ومضافة بخط المقريزي في الهامش الأيمن، من الأعلى إلى الأسفل + صح؛ يشير إليها الرمز ⌝ بعد كلمة "يدخل". ‖ وحوله: كلمة غير واضحة في الأصل بسبب ثقب في المخطوطة ومضافة هنا من أ (ص. ٧٢ب). ٢ بذلة: كلمة غير واضحة في الأصل بسبب ثقب في المخطوطة ومضافة هنا من أ (ص. ٧٢ب). ٤ الأمراء: "الامرآ" في الأصل. ‖ إلى: "الي" في الأصل. ٥ إليه: تصحيح في الأصل بخط المقريزي. ٦ وسائر: "وساير" في الأصل. ‖ ومشوا: الألف من إضافة المقريزي. ٧ الأمراء: "الامرآ" في الأصل. ‖ هو: تصحيح في الأصل. ‖ بقي: تصحيح في الأصل بخط المقريزي. ٨ ويأخذا: "ياخذ" في الأصل، والألف مضافة بخط المقريزي إلى آخر الفعل فوق السطر. ١٠ فامتنع: تصحيح في الأصل بخط المقريزي. ١١ أمراء: "امرآ" في الأصل. ١٢ مع اليمنيين: ناقصة في الأصل ومضافة بخط المقريزي في الهامش الأيسر، من الأسفل إلى الأعلى + صح؛ يشير إليها الرمز ⌝ بعد كلمة "اقتتلوا".

enter Mecca in a wartime cuirass and surrounded by his corps of weapons-bearers and axe-bearers, so as to arouse chaos. So they sent [a message] to him, [stating] that: "whoever wants to perform the pilgrimage can only enter Mecca in submissiveness and humbleness. You, you want to contrive a despicable innovation, but we will not make it possible for you to enter in this fashion. If you want safety, then send to us the Sharif Ṯaqabah to stay with us until you have finished the pilgrimage." [Al-Malik al-Muǧāhid] saw no other option than to yield, so he sent Ṯaqabah. The amirs treated him honourably, and the amir Ṭāz sent the amir Ṭuqṭāy[366] with a group of mamluks to the lord of Yemen, to be in his service until he completed his pilgrimage. They went to him and they abolished the corps of arms-bearers, the carrying of the saddle blanket,[367] and everything that he had been attaching importance to. They walked in his service until he entered the *ḥaram*. He greeted the amirs and apologised to them. He kept a secret that he was really only waiting his time until the amir Ṭāz would leave and he and Ṯaqabah could rise up against whoever remained with the commander of the [Egyptian] caravan and [until] they both could take ʿAǧlān and take possession of Mecca.

§ 213 When it was the day of Miná, the amir Buzlār,[368] the commander of the caravan, rode from Mecca. He saw the servant of the lord of Yemen, and he called him to him. But he refused to appear and the *mamlūk* of Buzlār hit one from [al-Muǧāhid's] army with a spear, and there occurred noise in [Buzlār's] following. Buzlār rode to Ṭāz [to complain], and the people of Yemen revolted in arms. The amirs of Egypt rode out at the time of the midday prayer, and they clashed with the Yemenites. Buzlār was defeated in a disgraceful way, but then ʿAǧlān, the amir of Mecca, arrived with a large

366 Ṭuqṭāy al-Nāṣirī (719–760/1319–1358) was a *mamlūk* amir in the entourage of the amir Ṭāz; he was married to one of the latter's daughters (Van Steenbergen [2006]: 59, 83).

367 The *ġāšiyah* or covering for the saddle was one of the insignia of royal status in the medieval Nile-to-Oxus region; it used to be carried before the ruler during public processions ("Ghāshiya", in *EI*² http://referenceworks.brillonline.com/entries/encyclopaedia-of-islam-2/ghashiya-DUM_1422).

368 Buzlār al-Nāṣirī (d. 756/1355) was a high-ranking *mamlūk* amir who led the Egyptian pilgrimage caravan in this particular pilgrimage season (al-Ṣafadī, *Aʿyān al-ʿaṣr*, 1:689).

يحفظ الحاج، واستمرت الحرب إلى العصر فانكسر جيش اليمن وقتل منهم جماعة وقطع دهليز المجاهد وقبض عليه ونهبت أثقاله.

وقضى الناس حجهم وسار الأمير طاز بالمجاهد معه ورتب في خدمته جماعة من مماليكه، وبالغ في إكرامه ووصى الأمير عجلان بأمه وحرمه، وكتب إلى السلطان يعرفه بما وقع، وتوجه إلى مصر.
٥ فقدم به في العشرين من المحرم سنة اثنتين وخمسين وسبعمائة، وصعد به إلى القلعة مقيدا في يوم الخدمة. فأوقف تجاه النائب، والأمراء قعود، حتى خرج أمير جاندار ودخل الأمراء إلى الخدمة بالإيوان وهو معهم. فقبل الأرض بين يدي السلطان الملك الناصر حسن بن محمد بن قلاوون. ثم فك قيده وأنزل بالأشرفية من القلعة، وأطلق له راتب وأقيم له من يخدمه.

ثم رسم بسفره إلى بلاده، فخرج معه الأمير قشتمر—شاد الدواوين—، وكتب للشريف
١٠ عجلان—أمير مكة—أن يجهزه، وخلع عليه أطلسين وركب في الموكب واستأنس السلطان به وتردد إليه الناس، واقترض مالا كثيرا، واشترى المماليك والخيل والجمال، وأتته الإنعامات من السلطان والتقادم من الأمراء والتزم بحمل المال في كل سنة على العادة. وسار أول ربيع الأول.

---

٣ ورتب: تصحيح في الأصل بخط المقريزي. ٥ اثنتين: تصحيح في الأصل ومضافة بخط المقريزي في الهامش الأيسر، من الأسفل إلى الأعلى + صح؛ يشير إليها الرمز ˥ بعد كلمة "سنة". || وخمسين وسبعمائة: "وخمسن وسبعمايه" في الأصل. || مقيدا: "مقيد" في الأصل، والألف لتنوين الفتح مضافة بخط المقريزي في مكانها بعد كلمة "مقيد" في السطر. ٦ والأمراء: "والامرآ" في الأصل. || الأمراء: "الامرآ" في الأصل. ٨ وأطلق: تصحيح في الأصل بخط المقريزي. ٩ إلى: "الي" في الأصل. ١١ واشترى: "واشترا" في الأصل. || وأتته: كلمة غير واضحة في الأصل بسبب ثقب في المخطوطة ومضافة هنا من أ (ص. ٧٣ب). ١٢ والتقادم من: تصحيح في الأصل، مضافة بخط المقريزي في الهامش الأيسر، من الأسفل إلى الأعلى + صح؛ يشير إليها الرمز ˥ بعد كلمة "و". || الأمراء: "الامرا" في الأصل.

army, and Ṭāz commanded him to protect the pilgrims. The battle went on until the afternoon prayer, [when] the army of Yemen was defeated and a group of them were killed. The tent of al-Muǧāhid was torn, he was caught, and his baggage was looted.

5 § 214 The people completed their pilgrimage and the amir Ṭāz left, [taking] al-Muǧāhid with him. He assigned a group from his *mamlūks* to [al-Muǧāhid's] service and did his utmost to treat him honourably. He entrusted [al-Muǧāhid's] mother and his wives to the care of the amir ʿAǧlān. He wrote to the sultan to inform him of what had happened, and he headed for Egypt, 10 which he reached on 20 Muḥarram of the year 752 [19 March 1351]. On the day of the [sultan's] public session, [Ṭāz] entered the [Cairo] citadel with him, in chains. [Al-Malik al-Muǧāhid] was made to wait standing in front of the viceroy, while the amirs were sitting down, until the commander of the bodyguard came out [to summon them to enter]. The amirs entered the pub-15 lic session in the great hall together with him. He kissed the ground before the sultan al-Malik al-Nāṣir Ḥasan b. Muḥammad b. Qalāwūn[369] and then his chains were undone. He was made to stay in the Ašrafiyyah-palace of the citadel,[370] there was awarded a stipend to him, and there were installed for him those who were to serve him.

20 § 215 Then it was ordered that he should travel to his land. The amir Qaštamur, the controller of the financial departments,[371] left with him. There was written to the Sharif ʿAǧlān, the amir of Mecca, that he should equip him. Two robes of honour of black satin were granted to him, he rode in the [sultan's] public procession, the sultan got on friendly terms with him, and the 25 people frequented him. He borrowed a lot of money, and he bought *mamlūks*, horses, and camels. Grants from the sultan and ceremonial gifts from the amirs came to him, and he was obliged to annually transfer money [to the sultan], as was the habit. He left on 1 Rabīʿ I [28 April].

---

369 For al-Malik al-Nāṣir Ḥasan b. Muḥammad b. Qalāwūn (r. 748–752/1347–1351; 755–762/1354–1361), see fn. 279.

370 The Ašrafiyyah-palace was one of the main palaces in the southern enclosure of the citadel of Cairo, constructed by order of the Qalāwūnid sultan al-Ašraf Ḫalīl (r. 689–693/1290–1293) (Rabbat [1995]: 36–38, 156–180; Warner [2005]: 185).

371 The *mamlūk* amir Qaštamur al-Manṣūrī (710–770/1310–1369) was *šādd al-dawāwīn* or controller of the financial departments, involved in issues of tax collection, in the late 740s/1340s and early 750s/1350s (Ibn Ḥaǧar, *al-Durar al-kāminah*, 3:249).

فبعث قشتمر بالشكوى منه، فرسم له أن يقبض عليه ويسيره إلى الكرك. ففعل ذلك وقبض عليه بالينبع وبعث به إلى الكرك، وأقام بالكرك قليلا. | ثم أفرج عنه وأحضر إلى القاهرة، ووبخ وعنف تعنيفا كثيرا من الأمراء. ثم خلع عليه وجهز في النيل ليتوجه إلى بلاده من عيذاب في البحر، وأنعم عليه الأمراء والسلطان بأشياء كثيرة. 135[a]

٥ فوصل إلى بلاده وقد ضبطت له أمه المملكة، وأقام بها حتى مات في سنة تسع وستين وسبعمائة، وملك بعده ابنه الملك الأفضل عباس.

٢ قليلا: كلمة غير واضحة في الأصل بسبب ثقب في المخطوطة ومضافة هنا من أ (ص. ٧٤أ). ‖ ثم: في الأصل الكلمة مكتوبة مرتين، مرة في آخر ص. ١٣٤ب ومرة اخرى في بداية ص. ١٣٥أ. ٣ من: تصحيح في الأصل بخط المقريزي. ‖ الأمراء: "الامرآ" في الأصل. ٤ الأمراء: "الامرا" في الأصل. ‖ بأشياء كثيرة: "باشيا كبيرة" في الأصل. ٥ وسبعمائة: "وسبعمايه" في الأصل. ٦ بعده: تصحيح في الأصل.

§ 216 But [on the road] Qaštamur sent [an envoy to Cairo] to complain about him. There was ordered to him that he should arrest him and bring him to Karak. He did that, arresting him at Yanbuʿ and sending him to Karak. He remained in Karak for a little while. Then he was set free and brought to Cairo. He was chided and seriously reprimanded by the amirs. Then a robe of honour was given to him and he was sent along the Nile, so as to head towards his land by sea, via Aydhab. The amirs and the sultan awarded a lot of things to him.

§ 217 He arrived in his land, [where] his mother had held the realm for him. He remained there until he died in the year 769 [1368].[372] After him, his son al-Malik al-Afḍal ʿAbbās[373] reigned.

372 The Arabic text here clearly refers to 769 as the year of al-Muǧāhid's death; there is however considerable confusion on this issue: in his chronicle *al-Sulūk* al-Maqrīzī himself mentions al-Muǧāhid among those that died in the year 767 (al-Maqrīzī, *al-Sulūk*, 3:125); other sources and studies, however, rather refer to the year 764 in this context (see Smith, "Rasūlids", in *EI*²).

373 Al-Malik al-Afḍal ʿAbbās (r. 764–778/1363–1377) was the sixth of the Rasūlid rulers of Yemen (Smith, "Rasūlids", in *EI2*).

الملك الأشرف شعبان بن حُسَين بن محمد بن قلاوون

جلس على تخت الملك—وعمره عشر سنين—في نصف شعبان سنة أربع وستين وسبعمائة، وقام بأمر المملكة الأمير يلبغا العُمري الخاصكي إلى أن قتل في ربيع الآخر سنة ثمان وستين وسبعمائة، فقوي أمره قليلا، ثم قتل أسندمر بعد يلبغا، واشتد أمره، وأوقع باليلبغاوية الأجلاب.

٥ وشرع في الاهتمام بالحج في سنة ثمان وسبعين، وخرج أطلاب الأمراء للسفر في يوم السبت ثاني عشر شوال، وخرج طلب السلطان يوم الأحد ثالث عشره. فجر عشرين قطار هجن بقماش ذهب

١ قلاوون: "قلاون" في الأصل. ٢ وسبعمائة: "وسبعمايه" في الأصل. ٣ وسبعمائة: "وسبعمايه" في الأصل. ٥ في[1]: تصحيح في الأصل بخط المقريزي. || الأمراء: "الامرآ" في الأصل.

13. Al-Malik al-Ašraf Šaʿbān b. Ḥusayn b. Muḥammad b. Qalāwūn[374]

§ 218 He sat on the royal throne at the age of ten, on 15 Šaʿbān of the year 764 [30 May 1363]. The command over the realm was performed by the amir Yalbuġā l-ʿUmarī l-Ḫāṣṣakī,[375] until he was killed in Rabīʿ II of the 5 year 768 [December 1366]. [Thereupon] his [= Šaʿbān's] authority slightly increased. Then, after Yalbuġā, [the new powerholder] Asandamur[376] was killed. His [= Šaʿbān's] authority became strong, and he brought down the young Yalbuġāwiyyah *mamlūk*s.[377]

§ 219 [Sultan Šaʿbān] began to take an interest in the pilgrimage in the year 10 [7]78 [1377]. The regiments of the amirs went out [of the city in preparation] for the voyage on Saturday 12 Šawwāl [21 February], and the regiment of the sultan left on Sunday 13 [Šawwāl] [22 February]. He took along twenty

374 Al-Malik al-Ašraf Šaʿbān b. Ḥusayn b. Muḥammad b. Qalāwūn (r. 764–778/1363–1377) was sultan of Egypt and Syria and a member of the Qalāwūnid dynasty, made sultan at a young age by prominent amirs from his father's entourage; after a number of years of mere nominal rule, from 1366 onwards he increasingly managed to impose his effective authority, eventually sitting firmly on the throne for about a decade, until he was deposed and killed in a rebellion against his rule (P.M. Holt, "Shaʿbān. 2. al-Malik al-Ashraf", in *EI*² http://referenceworks.brillonline.com/entries/encyclopaedia-of-islam-2/shaban-SIM_6718).

375 Yalbuġā l-ʿUmarī l-Ḫāṣṣakī (d. 768/1366) was a *mamlūk* amir and one of the leading figures at the Qalāwūnid court of Cairo in the 1360s; he was one of the main instigators of the fall of the Qalāwūnid sultan al-Nāṣir Ḥasan in 762/1361, and his empowerment thereafter was only thwarted in 768/1366 by a rebellion, which began in his own entourage and which ended in 769/1367 with the rather unexpected victory of sultan al-Ašraf Shaʿban b. Ḥasan (Van Steenbergen [2011b]).

376 Asandamur al-Nāṣirī (d. 769/1368) was a *mamlūk* amir who emerged from the entourage of Yalbuġā l-Ḫāṣṣakī after the latter's murder in 768/1366: he became one of the new leaders in Cairo in the subsequent year, but he was eventually arrested and equally murdered (Van Steenbergen [2006]: 179–180).

377 The young Yalbuġāwiyyah *mamlūk*s (*al-Yalbuġāwiyyah al-Aǧlāb*) is a term used to refer to the mass of young and unemancipated *mamlūk*s in the military corps of the amir Yalbuġā l-Ḫāṣṣakī, many of whom played a role in the murder of their master in 768/1366: they caused havoc and chaos in Cairo for some months thereafter, until in 769/1368 they were subdued and punished for this by sultan al-Ašraf Šaʿbān; many of those that survived this purge (including the later sultan al-Ẓāhir Barqūq) re-emerged from the second half of the 770s/1370s onwards, to dominate Syro-Egyptian politics into the 790s/1390s (Van Steenbergen [2011a]).

وخمسة عشر قِطارا بعُبْي حرير وقطارا ملبس خليفتي وقطارا بقماش أبيض برسم الإحرام ومائة رأس خيل مشهرة وكحاوتين وتسع محفات—وهو محفات كلها بأغشية حرير مزركش—وستة وأربعين زوج محاير وخزانة عشرين جملا وقطارين جمال تحمل خُضَر مُزدَرعة ومن الجمال المحملة شيئا كثيرا.

٥ وركب يوم الاثنين رابع عشره، فأقام بسرياقوس إلى يوم الثلثاء ثاني عشرينه، واستقل بالمسير—ومعه من الأمراء المقدمين تسعة ومن الطبلخاناه خمسة وعشرون ومن العشراوات خمسة عشر.

فركب طاش تمر المحمدي اللفاف—أحد العشرات—وقرطاي—رأس نوبة—وجماعة في يوم السبت ثالث ذي القعدة خارج القاهرة، وسلطنوا أمير علي بن السلطان. فقدم الخبر يوم الأحد

١–٢ ومائة رأس: "ومائة راس" في الأصل. ٢ محفات: تصحيح في الأصل بخط المقريزي. ‖ كلها: تصحيح في الأصل بخط المقريزي. ٣ جمال: تصحيح في الأصل بخط المقريزي. ٤ شيئا: "شيا" في الأصل. ٥ يوم الاثنين: تصحيح في الأصل بخط المقريزي. ‖ بسرياقوس ... الثلثاء: جزء غير واضح في الأصل بسبب ثقب في المخطوطة ومضاف هنا من أ (ص. ٧٥أ) ("بسرياقوس الى يوم الثلثا"). ‖ بالمسير: تصحيح في الأصل. ٦ الأمراء: "الامرآ" في الأصل. ٧ فركب: تصحيح في الأصل بخط المقريزي.

convoys of dromedaries with gold cloth, fifteen convoys with packs of silk, a convoy with caliphal clothing and a convoy of white cloth for *iḥrām*; [he also took along] 100 head of thoroughbred horses, two camel litters,[378] and nine stretchers, all of them with covers of silk embellished with brocade embroi-
5 dery; [he took with him] 46 pairs of water tanks, a treasury [carried by] 20 camels, and two convoys of camels that carried freshly sown vegetables; [and finally,] there also was a great lot of pack camels.

§ 220 [The sultan] rode out on Monday 14 [Šawwāl] [23 February]. He stayed in Siryāqūs until Tuesday 22 [Šawwāl] [3 March]. He went ahead alone,
10 together with nine from the [group of] amirs commanders, with 25 from the amirs of 40, and with 15 from the amirs of ten.

§ 221 On Saturday 3 Ḏū l-Qaʿdah [14 March] Ṭāštamur al-Muḥammadī l-Laffāf[379]—one of [the amirs of] ten—, Qaraṭāy[380]—the head of the royal guard—, and a group rode out [in rebellion] and left Cairo, and they pro-
15 claimed sultan the amir ʿAlī, the son of the sultan.[381] The news arrived [in

378 According to Ǧamāl al-Dīn al-Šayyāl the unfamiliar word *al-kaǧāwah* that is used here in the text comes from Persian and is used to refer to a camel litter for women (al-Maqrīzī, *al-Ḏahab al-masbūk*², 119, fn. 6).

379 Ṭāštamur al-Muḥammadī l-Laffāf (d. 779/1377) was one of the small-time amirs who rose to prominence after a successful rebellion against sultan al-Ašraf Šaʿbān in 778/1377; Ṭāštamur however succumbed to the plague before he could reap the fruits of his sudden empowerment (Ibn Taġrī Birdī, *al-Manhal al-ṣāfī*, 6:394).

380 Qaraṭāy al-Ṭāzī (d. 779/1378), a mamlūk and a member of the personal household of sultan al-Ašraf Šaʿbān's son ʿAlī, appears to have been one of the instigators of the successful rebellion against the sultan in 778/1377, whereupon he immediately rose to prominence, to high income and status, and to the effective leadership in Cairo; within less than two months, however, he was defeated by one of his rivals for power and sent off to Syria, where, eventually, he was put to death (Van Steenbergen [2006]: 165, 184, 195).

381 Al-Malik al-Manṣūr ʿAlī b. Šaʿbān b. Ḥusayn b. Muḥammad b. Qalāwūn (r. 778–783/1377–1381) was one of the last Qalāwūnid sultans of Egypt and Syria; in 778/1377, he was made to succeed his deposed father at a very young age and subsequently throughout his short reign he never managed to have more than nominal authority, the amir and later sultan Barqūq rising to power behind his throne and soon ruling in his name (Van Steenbergen [2006]: 164–168).

ثانيه بأن السلطان وصل إلى عقبة أيلة يوم الثلاثاء وأقام إلى ليلة الخميس، فركب عليه المماليك ليلة الخميس بسبب تأخير النفقة، فانهزم السلطان في نفر يسير، فخرجوا إلى قبة النصر. فقبضوا على الأمير صرغتمش وغيره من الأمراء وقتلوهم، وقبض على الأشرف من بيت إمرأة في ليلة الاثنين خامس ذي القعدة. فكان آخر العهد به. قتل خنقا. والله أعلم.

٥ حرره جهد القدرة فصح مؤلفه أحمد بن علي المقريزي في ذي القعدة سنة ٨٤١.

---

١ إلى : "الي" في الأصل. ‖ الثلاثاء : "الثلاثا" في الأصل. ‖ فركب : تصحيح في الأصل بخط المقريزي. ٣ على[1] : ناقصة في الأصل ومضافة بخط المقريزي في الهامش الأيمن، من الأعلى إلى الأسفل + صح؛ يشير إليها الرمز ⌐ بعد كلمة "فقبضوا". ‖ الأمراء : "الامرآ" في الأصل. ‖ وقتلوهم : تصحيح في الأصل بخط المقريزي. ٤ والله أعلم : ناقصة في الأصل ومضافة بخط المقريزي في مكانها الصحيح في النص في آخر السطر بعد كلمة "خنقا". ٥ حرره : كلمة غير واضحة في الأصل بسبب ثقب في المخطوطة مصححة هنا من السياق ووفقا للشكل المستقل الواضح لحرف الهاء الأخير؛ ولكن هذه الكلمة كتبت "حَرَّرْته" في آخر أ (ص. ٧٥ب). ‖ حرره ... ٨٤١ : هذه الجملة كلها مضافة بخط المقريزي تحت النصّ في السطر الأخير للصفحة.

Cairo] on the next [day,] Sunday, that the sultan had arrived at ʿAqabat Aylah on Tuesday, [where] he had stayed until Thursday night. But in the night of Thursday [—this news said—] the *mamlūk*s had ridden against him, because of the delay of the travel allowance; the sultan had been routed, 5 [remaining only] with a few people, and they had left for Qubbat al-Naṣr [near Cairo].[382] [The new rulers in Cairo then] caught the amir Ṣarġitmiš[383] and others from the amirs [while they were at Qubbat al-Naṣr], and they killed them. Al-Ašraf [escaped, but then he] was taken from [his hiding place in] the house of a woman, in the night of Monday 5 Ḏū l-Qaʿdah [15 March]. 10 The last that is known about him is that he was killed by strangulation.

God knows best.

[This Book of Moulded Gold] was corrected to the best of [his] abilities by its author Aḥmad b. ʿAlī al-Maqrīzī, so that it is correct, in Ḏū l-Qaʿdah of the year 841 [May 1438].

382 Qubbat al-Naṣr refers to a domed commemorative monument outside Cairo, of unknown origins (Mouton & Dayoub [2013]: 520).

383 Ṣarġitmiš al-Ašrafī (d. 778/1377) was a leading *mamlūk* amir in the entourage of al-Ašraf Šaʿbān, until he, his peers, and the sultan were brutally murdered outside Cairo (Ibn Taġrī Birdī, *al-Manhal al-ṣāfī*, 6:341–342).

Bibliography

Primary Sources (incl. Translations)

Abū Dāwūd, *al-Sunan*

Abū Dāwūd al-Siǧistānī (d. 275/889), *Sunan Abī Dāwūd*, ed. M.ʿA. al-Ḫālidī (Beirut: Dār al-Kutub al-ʿIlmiyyah, 2005).

Abū l-Fidāʾ, *al-Tibr al-masbūk*

Al-Malik al-Muʾayyad Ismāʿīl b. ʿAlī Abū l-Fidāʾ (672–732/1273–1331), *Kitāb al-Tibr al-masbūk fī tawārīḫ al-mulūk*, ed. M.Z.M. ʿAzab (Cairo: Maktabat al-Ṯaqāfah al-Dīniyyah, 1995).

Abū Nuʿaym, *Ḥilyat al-awliyāʾ*

Abū Nuʿaym b. ʿAbd Allāh al-Iṣfahānī (336–430/948–1038), *Kitāb Ḥilyat al-awliyāʾ wa-ṭabaqāt al-aṣfiyāʾ*, ed. M.ʿA. ʿAṭā (Beirut: Dār al-Kutub al-ʿIlmiyyah, 2010), 12 vols.

Arberry, A.J., *The Koran Interpreted* (London and New York: Allen & Unwin and Macmillan, 1955).

Al-ʿAynī, *ʿIqd al-ǧumān*

Badr al-Dīn Maḥmūd b. Aḥmad al-ʿAynī (762–855/1361–1451), *ʿIqd al-ǧumān fī tārīḫ ahl al-zamān: ḥawādiṯ wa-tarāǧim 824h–850h*, ed. ʿA. al-Ṭanṭāwī l-Qarmūṭ (Cairo: al-Zahrāʾ li-l-Iʿlām al-ʿArabī, 1989).

Al-Azraqī, *Aḫbār Makkah*

Abū l-Walīd Muḥammad b. ʿAbd Allāh al-Azraqī (d. c. 251/865), *Aḫbār Makkah šarrafahā llāh wa-mā fīhā min al-āṯār*, ed. F. Wüstenfeld, *Die Chroniken der Stadt Mekka, Teil 1: el-Azrakis Geschichte und Beschreibung der Stadt Mekka* (Leipzig: Brockaus, 1858; repr. Hildesheim-New York: Georg Olms Verlag, 1981).

Baybars al-Manṣūrī, *Zubdat al-fikrah*

Baybars al-Manṣūrī (d. 725/1325), *Zubdat al-fikrah fī tārīḫ al-hiǧrah*, ed. D.S. Richards (Beirut-Berlin: Orient-Institut der DMG, Das Arabische Buch, 1998).

Al-Buḫārī, *al-Ǧāmiʿ al-ṣaḥīḥ*

Abū ʿAbd Allāh Muḥammad b. Ismāʿīl al-Buḫārī (194–256/810–870), *al-Ǧāmiʿ al-ṣaḥīḥ wa-huwa al-Ǧāmiʿ al-musnad al-ṣaḥīḥ al-muḫtaṣar min umūr rasūl Allāh ṣallá llāh ʿalayhi wa-sallama wa-sunanihi wa-ayyāmihi li-l-imām Abī ʿAbd Allāh Muḥammad al-Buḫārī*, ed. M. Zuhayr b. Nāṣir al-Nāṣir (Būlāq, 1312 AH).

———, *al-Taʾrīḫ al-kabīr*

al-Taʾrīḫ al-kabīr (Hyderabad: Dāʾirat al-Maʿārif al-ʿUṯmāniyyah, 1941; repr. Beirut: Dār al-Kutub al-ʿIlmiyyah, 1986), 8 vols.

Al-Ḏahabī, *Siyar*

Abū ʿAbd Allāh Muḥammad b. Aḥmad b. ʿUṯmān al-Ḏahabī (673–748/1274–1348), *Siyar aʿlām al-nubalāʾ*, ed. Sh. Arnāʾūṭ & Ḥusayn Asad (Beirut: Muʾassassat al-Risālah, 1981–1996), 28 vols.

Al-Fāsī, *Šifāʾ al-ġarām*

Abū l-Ṭayyib Muḥammad b. Aḥmad al-Fāsī l-Makkī (775–832/1373–1429), *Šifāʾ al-ġarām bi-aḫbār al-Balad al-Ḥarām* (Beirut: Dār al-Kutub al-ʿIlmiyyah, 2000), 2 vols.

Al-Ǧazīrī, *Durar al-farāʾid*

ʿAbd al-Qādir b. Muḥammad b. ʿAbd al-Qādir b. Muḥammad al-Anṣārī l-Ǧazīrī l-Ḥanbalī (d. c. 977/1570), *Durar al-farāʾid al-munaẓẓamah fī aḫbār al-ḥāǧǧ wa-ṭarīq Makkah al-muʿaẓẓamah*, ed. M.Ḥ.M.Ḥ. Ismāʿīl (Beirut: Dār al-Kutub al-ʿIlmiyyah, 2002), 2 vols.

Al-Ḫālidiyyān, *al-Tuḥaf wa-l-hadāyā*

Abū Bakr Muḥammad b. Hāšim al-Ḫālidī (d. 380/990) & Abū ʿUṯmān Saʿīd b. Hāšim al-Ḫālidī (d. 371/982), *al-Tuḥaf wa-l-hadāyā. Le livre des dons et des cadeaux*, ed. and transl. S. Dahhan (Cairo: Institut français d'archéologie orientale, 1956).

Ḫalīfah b. Ḫayyāṭ, *al-Ṭabaqāt*

Abū ʿUmar Ḫalīfah b. Ḫayyāṭ al-Šaybānī (d. 240/854), *Ṭabaqāt Ḫalīfah b. Ḫayyāṭ*, ed. S. Zakkār (Beirut: Dār al-Fikr, 1993).

Ibn ʿAbd al-Barr, *al-Istīʿāb*

Abū ʿUmar Yūsuf b. ʿAbd Allāh Ibn ʿAbd al-Barr al-Namarī l-Qurṭubī (368–463/978–1070), *al-Istīʿāb fī maʿrifat al-aṣḥāb*, ed. ʿA.M. Muʿawwaḍ, ʿĀ.A. ʿAbd al-Mawǧūd et al. (Beirut: Dār al-Kutub al-ʿIlmiyyah, 1995), 4 vols.

Ibn ʿAbd al-Ḥakam, *Futūḥ Miṣr*

Abū l-Qāsim ʿAbd al-Raḥmān b. ʿAbd Allāh Ibn ʿAbd al-Ḥakam (d. 257/871), *Kitāb Futūḥ Miṣr wa-aḫbārihā*, ed. C.C. Torrey, *The History of the Conquest of Egypt, North Africa and Spain known as the* Futūḥ Miṣr *of Ibn ʿAbd al-Ḥakam, edited from the manuscripts in London, Paris and Leyden* (New Haven: Yale University Press, 1922).

Ibn ʿAbd al-Ẓāhir, *al-Rawḍ al-zāhir*

Muḥyī l-Dīn Abū l-Faḍl ʿAbd Allāh Ibn ʿAbd al-Ẓāhir (620–692/1223–1292), *al-Rawḍ al-zāhir fī sīrat al-Malik al-Ẓāhir*, ed. ʿA. al-Ḫuwayṭir (Riyadh: Muʾassasat Fuʾād, 1976).

Ibn al-Aṯīr, *al-Kāmil*

ʿIzz al-Dīn Abū l-Ḥasan ʿAlī b. Muḥammad Ibn al-Aṯīr (d. 630/1233), *al-Kāmil fī l-tārīḫ*, ed. A.ʿA. al-Qāḍī (Beirut: Dār al-Kutub al-ʿIlmiyyah, 2006 [4th ed.]), 11 vols.

———, *Chronicle*

The Chronicle of Ibn al-Athir for the Crusading Period from al-Kamil fi'l-Ta'rikh. *Parts 1–3*, translated by D.S. Richards (*Crusade Texts in Translation* 13, 15, 17) (Farnham: Ashgate, 2006–2010), 3 vols.

Ibn Fahd, *Itḥāf al-wará*

ʿUmar b. Muḥammad Ibn Fahd al-Makkī (812–885/1409–1480), *Itḥāf al-wará bi-aḫbār Umm al-Qurá*, ed. F.M. Šaltūt (Mecca: Ǧāmiʿat Umm al-Qurá, Markaz al-Baḥṯ al-ʿIlmī wa-Iḥyāʾ al-Turāṯ al-Islāmī, 1983–1990), 5 vols.

Ibn al-Ǧawzī, *Ḫulāṣat al-Ḏahab al-masbūk*

Ǧamāl al-Dīn Abū l-Farağ ʿAbd al-Raḥmān b. ʿAlī Ibn al-Ǧawzī (510–597/1117–1201) /

ʿAbd al-Raḥmān Sunbuṭ Qanītū l-Irbīlī, *Ḫulāṣat al-Ḏahab al-masbūk, Muḫtaṣar min Siyar al-mulūk*, ed. M. Ǧāsim (Baghdad: Maktabat al-Muṯannā, 1964).

Ibn Ḥağar, *al-Durar al-kāminah*

Šihāb al-Dīn Aḥmad b. ʿAlī Ibn Ḥağar al-ʿAsqalānī (773–852/1372–1449), *al-Durar al-kāminah fī aʿyān al-miʾah al-ṯāminah*, s.e. (Beirut: Dār al-Ǧīl, 1993), 4 vols.

———, *Inbāʾ al-ġumr*

Inbāʾ al-ġumr bi-abnāʾ al-ʿumr, ed. ʿA. Ḫān et al. (Beirut: Dār al-Kutub al-ʿIlmiyyah, 1986, 2nd ed.), 9 vols.

Ibn Ḫaldūn, *al-Muqaddimah*

Walī l-Dīn Abū Zayd ʿAbd al-Raḥmān b. Muḥammad Ibn Ḫaldūn (732–808/1332–1406), *The Muqaddimah: an introduction to history*, translated from the Arabic by Franz Rosenthal (New York: Pantheon Books, 1958), 3 vols.

Ibn Ḫallikān, *Wafayāt al-aʿyān*

Šams al-Dīn Abū l-ʿAbbās Aḥmad b. Muḥammad Ibn Ḫallikān (608–671/1211–1282), *Wafayāt al-aʿyān wa-anbāʾ abnāʾ al-zamān*, ed. I. ʿAbbās (Beirut: Dār Ṣādir, 1968–1978), 8 vols.

Ibn Ḥanbal, *al-Musnad*

Aḥmad Ibn Ḥanbal (164–241/780–855), *Musnad al-imām Aḥmad b. Ḥanbal*, ed. Š. al-Arnaʾūṭ and ʿĀ. Murshid (Beirut: Muʾassasat al-Risalah, 1993–2001), 50 vols.

Ibn Ḥazm, *Ǧamharat ansāb al-ʿArab*

Abū Muḥammad ʿAlī b. Aḥmad Ibn Ḥazm al-Andalusī (384–456/994–1064), *Ǧamharat ansāb al-ʿArab* (Beirut: Dār al-Kutub al-ʿIlmiyyah, 2003).

———, *Ḥiǧǧat al-wadāʿ*

Ḥiǧǧat al-wadāʿ, ed. ʿA. b. Malik Ḥaqqī al-Turkumānī (Beirut, 2008).

Ibn Hišām, *al-Sīrah*

Abū Muḥammad ʿAbd al-Malik Ibn Hišām (d. 218/833), *al-Sīrah al-nabawiyyah*, ed. M. al-Saqā, I. al-Abyārī, and ʿA. Šiblī (Damascus, Beirut: Dār Ibn Kaṯīr, 2005 [3rd ed.]).

Ibn Kaṯīr, *al-Bidāyah*

Abū l-Fidāʾ Ismāʿīl b. ʿUmar Ibn Kaṯīr (701–774/1301–1372), *al-Bidāyah wa-l-nihāyah fī l-tārīḫ* (Beirut: Maktabat al-Maʿārif, 1990, 2nd ed.), 15 vols.

———, *al-Fuṣūl*

Al-Fuṣūl fī ḫtiṣār sīrat al-rasūl, ed. ʿA.M. al-Darwīš (Damascus, Beirut, Hawally: Dār al-Nawādir, 2010).

Ibn Māǧah, *al-Sunan*

Abū ʿAbd Allāh Muḥammad b. Yazīd Ibn Māǧah al-Qazwīnī (d. 273/887), *Ṣaḥīḥ Sunan Ibn Māǧah*, ed. M.N. al-Albānī (Riyadh: Maktabat al-Maʿārif li-l-Našr wa-l-Tawzīʿ, 1997).

Ibn Saʿd, *al-Ṭabaqāt*

Muḥammad Ibn Saʿd b. Manīʿ (167–230/784–845), *Kitāb al-Ṭabaqāt al-kabīr*, ed.

E. Sachau et al., *Biographien Muhammeds, seiner Gefährten und der späteren Träger des Islams bis zum Jahre 230 der Flucht* (Leiden: Brill, 1905–1917 [facsimile]), 9 vols.

Ibn Taġrī Birdī, *al-Manhal al-ṣāfī*

Ǧamāl al-Dīn Abū l-Maḥāsin Yūsuf Ibn Taġrī Birdī (813–874/1411–1470), *al-Manhal al-ṣāfī wa-l-mustawfī baʿda l-Wāfī*, ed. Muḥammad Muḥammad Amīn (Cairo: al-Hay'ah al-Miṣriyyah al-ʿĀmmah li-l-Kitāb & al-Hay'ah al-ʿĀmmah li-Dār al-Kutub wa-l-Waṯā'iq al-Qawmiyyah, 1984–2006), 12 vols.

———, *al-Nuǧūm al-zāhirah*

Al-Nuǧūm al-zāhirah fī mulūk Miṣr wa-l-Qāhirah (Cairo: al-Mu'assassah al-Miṣriyyah al-ʿĀmmah, 1963–1972), 16 vols.

———, *History of Egypt*

History of Egypt, 1382–1469 A.D., translated from the Arabic Annals of Abu l-Maḥâsin ibn Taghrî Birdî. Transl. W. Popper (Berkeley and Los Angeles: University of California Press, 1954–1963), 8 vols.

Kātib Çelebī, *Kašf al-ẓunūn*

Muṣṭafá b. ʿAbd Allāh Kātib Çelebī Ḥāǧǧī Ḫalīfah (1017–1067/1609–1657), *Kašf al-ẓunūn fī asāmī l-kutub wa-l-funūn*, ed. M.Sh. Yāltqāyā & R.B. al-Kilīsī (Beirut: Dār Iḥyā' al-Turāṯ al-ʿArabī, s.d. [reprint]), 2 vols.

Al-Kutubī, *Fawāt al-wafayāt*

Muḥammad b. Šākir al-Kutubī (d. 764/1363), *Fawāt al-wafayāt wa-l-ḏayl ʿalayhā*, ed. I. ʿAbbās (Beirut: Dār al-Ṯaqāfah, 1973–1974), 4 vols.

Lewis, *Islam*

Islam from the Prophet Muhammad to the Capture of Constantinople. Volume II: Religion and Society, ed. and trans. B. Lewis (New York & Oxford: Oxford University Press, 1987).

Al-Maqrīzī, *al-Bayān*

Taqī l-Dīn Aḥmad b. ʿAlī l-Maqrīzī (766–845/1364–1442), *Kitāb al-Bayān wa-l-iʿrāb ʿammā bi-arḍ Miṣr min al-Aʿrāb = El-Macrizi's Abhandlung über die in Aegypten eingewanderten arabische Stämme. Aus den Handschriften zu Leyden, Paris und Wien herausgegeben und übersetst von F. Wüstenfeld* (Göttingen: Vandenhoeck und Ruprecht, 1847).

———, *Bināʾ al-Kaʿbah*

Bināʾ al-Kaʿbah al-bayt al-ḥarām: risālah fī tārīḫ al-Kaʿbah al-mušarrafah min bidāyat bināʾihā ḥattá bināyat al-Ḥaǧǧāǧ, ed. ʿA.ʿA. Ibn Duhayš (Beirut: Dār al-Bašā'ir al-Islāmiyyah, 2005).

———, *al-Ḏahab al-masbūk*[1]

Al-Ḏahab al-masbūk fī ḏikr man ḥaǧǧa min al-ḫulafāʾ wa-l-mulūk, ed. Ḥ. al-Ǧāsir, in *Maǧallat al-Ḥaǧǧ* 6/1 (Raǧab 1371/April 1952): 1–52.

———, *al-Ḏahab al-masbūk*[2]

Al-Ḏahab al-masbūk fī ḏikr man ḥaǧǧa min al-ḫulafāʾ wa-l-mulūk, ed. Ǧ. al-D. al-

Šayyāl (*Maktabat al-Maqrīzī al-Ṣaġīrah* 3) (Cairo and Baghdad: Maktabat al-Ḫanjī and Maktabat al-Muṯannā, 1955).

———, *al-Ḏahab al-masbūk*[3]

Al-Ḏahab al-masbūk fī ḏikr man ḥaǧǧa min al-ḫulafāʾ wa-l-mulūk, ed. Ǧ. al-D. al-Šayyāl (al-Ẓāhir, Cairo: Maktabat al-Ṯaqāfah al-Dīniyyah, 2000).

———, *al-Ḏahab al-masbūk*[4]

Al-Ḏahab al-masbūk fī ḏikr man ḥaǧǧa min al-ḫulafāʾ wa-l-mulūk, ed. K. Faraḥāt (Cairo: ʿEin for Human and Social Studies, 2009).

———, *Ḍawʾ al-sārī*

Ḍawʾ al-sārī li-maʿrifat ḫabar Tamīm al-Dārī = On Tamīm al-Dārī and his Waqf in Hebron. Critical edition, annotated translation and introduction by Y. Frenkel (*Bibliotheca Maqriziana, Opera Minora*, vol. 2) (Leiden: Brill, 2014).

———, *Durar al-ʿuqūd al-farīdah*

Durar al-ʿuqūd al-farīdah fī tarāǧim al-aʿyān al-mufīdah, ed. M. al-Ǧalīlī (Beirut: Dār al-Ġarb al-Islāmī, 2002), 4 vols.

———, *al-Ḫiṭaṭ*

Al-Mawāʿiẓ wa-al-iʿtibār fī ḏikr al-ḫiṭaṭ wa-l-aṯār, ed. A.F. Sayyid (London: Muʿassassat al-Furqān li-l-Turāth al-Islāmī, 2002–2003), 6 vols.

———, *Imtāʿ al-asmāʿ*

Imtāʿ al-asmāʿ bi-mā li-l-nabī min al-aḥwāl wa-l-amwāl wa-ḥafaḍah wa-l-matāʿ, ed. M.ʿA. al-Numaysī (Beirut: Dār al-Kutub al-ʿIlmiyyah, 1999), 15 vols.

———, *al-Maqāṣid al-saniyyah*

Kitāb al-Maqāṣid al-saniyyah li-maʿrifat al-aǧsām al-maʿdiniyyah = Al-Maqrīzīs Traktat über die Mineralien. Herausgegeben, übersetzt und kommentiert von Fabian Käs (*Bibliotheca Maqriziana, Opera Minora*, vol. 3) (Leiden: Brill, 2015).

———, *al-Muqaffá*

Kitāb al-Muqaffá al-kabīr, ed. M. al-Yaʿlāwī (Beirut: Dār al-Ġarb al-Islāmī, 2006), 8 vols.

———, *al-Sulūk*

Kitāb al-Sulūk li-maʿrifat duwal al-mulūk, ed. M.M. Ziyādah and S.ʿA ʿĀšūr (Cairo: Maṭbaʿat Lajnat al-Taʾlīf wa-l-Tarǧama wa-l-Našr, 1934–1958; Cairo: Maṭbaʿat Dār al-Kutub, 1970–1973), 4 vols.

Al-Nasāʾī, *al-Sunan*

Aḥmad b. Šuʿayb al-Nasāʾī (d. 303/915), Ǧalāl al-Dīn al-Suyūṭī (849–911/1445–1505), and al-Imām al-Sindī, *Sunan al-Nasāʾī bi-šarḥ al-ḥāfiẓ Ǧalāl al-Dīn al-Suyūṭī wa-ḥāšiyat al-imām al-Sindī*, ed. Ḥ.M. al-Masʿūdī (Cairo: al-Maṭbaʿah al-Miṣriyyah, 1930), 8 vols.

Al-Qalqašandī, *Ṣubḥ al-aʿšá*

Šihāb al-Dīn Aḥmad b. ʿAbd Allāh l-Qalqašandī (756–821/1355–1418), *Ṣubḥ al-aʿšá fī ṣināʿat al-inšāʾ* (Cairo: al-Maṭbaʿah al-Amīriyyah, 1913–1919), 14 vols.

Al-Ṣafadī, *Aʿyān al-ʿaṣr*

Ṣalāḥ al-Dīn Ḫalīl b. Aybak al-Ṣafadī (d. 764/1363), *Aʿyān al-ʿaṣr wa-aʿwān al-naṣr*, ed. ʿA. Abū Zayd et al. (Damascus, Beirut: Dār al-Fikr al-Muʿāṣir, 1998), 6 vols.

Al-Saḫāwī, *al-Ḍawʾ al-lāmiʿ*

Šams al-Dīn Muḥammad b. ʿAbd al-Raḥmān al-Saḫāwī (831–902/1424–1497), *al-Ḍawʾ al-lāmiʿ li-ahl al-qarn al-tāsiʿ*, s.e. (Beirut: Dār al-Ǧīl, 1992), 12 vols.

———, *al-Tibr al-masbūk*

Kitāb al-Tibr al-masbūk fī ḏayl al-Sulūk, ed. S.ʿA. ʿĀšūr, N.M. Kāmil & L.I. Muṣṭafā (Cairo: Dār al-Kutub wa-l-Waṯāʾiq al-Qawmiyyah, 2002–2007), 4 vols.

Al-Ṣayrafī, *Nuzhat al-nufūs*

ʿAlī b. Dāwūd al-Ṣayrafī (d. 900/1495), *Nuzhat al-nufūs wa-l-abdān fī tawārīḫ al-zamān*, ed. Ḥ. Ḥabašī (Cairo: Wizārat al-Ṯaqāfah, Markaz Taḥqīq al-Turāṯ; al-Hayʾah al-Miṣriyyah al-ʿĀmmah li-l-Kitāb, 1970–1994), 4 vols.

Al-Ṭabarī, *Tārīḫ*

Abū Ǧaʿfar Muḥammad b. Ǧarīr al-Ṭabarī (d. 310/923), *Tārīḫ al-rusul wa-l-mulūk*, ed. M.J. De Goeje et al., *Annales quos scripsit Abu Djafar Mohammed ibn Djarir al-Tabari* (Leiden: Brill, 1964 [facsimile]), 16 vols.

———, *History* XIII

The History of al-Ṭabarī. Volume XIII. The Conquest of Iraq, Southwestern Persia and Egypt, transl. G.H.A. Juynboll (Albany: SUNY Press, 1989).

———, *History* XIV

The History of al-Ṭabarī. Volume XIV. The Conquest of Iran, transl. G. Rex Smith (Albany: SUNY Press, 1994).

———, *History* XV

The History of al-Ṭabarī. Volume XV. The Crisis of the Early Caliphate, transl. R. Stephen Humphreys (Albany: SUNY Press, 1990).

———, *History* XXIII

The History of al-Ṭabarī. Volume XXIII. The Zenith of the Marwānid House, transl. Martin Hinds (Albany: SUNY Press, 1990).

———, *History* XXV

The History of al-Ṭabarī. Volume XXV. The End of Expansion, transl. Kh.Y. Blankinship (Albany: SUNY Press, 1989).

———, *History* XXIX

The History of al-Ṭabarī. Volume XXIX. Al-Manṣūr and al-Mahdī, transl. H. Kennedy (Albany: SUNY Press, 1990).

———, *History* XXX

The History of al-Ṭabarī. Volume XXX. The ʿAbbāsid Caliphate in Equilibrium, transl. C.E. Bosworth (Albany: SUNY Press, 1989).

———, *History* XXXIV

The History of al-Ṭabarī, Volume XXXIV. Incipient Decline: the Caliphates of al-Wāt-

hiq, al-Mutawakkil and al-Muntaṣir, transl. J.L. Kraemer (Albany: SUNY Press, 1989).

———, *History XXXVI*

The History of al-Ṭabarī, Volume XXXVI, The Revolt of the Zanj, transl. D. Waines (Albany: SUNY Press, 1992).

———, *History XXXVIII*

The History of al-Ṭabarī, Volume XXXVIII, The Return of the Caliphate to Baghdad: The Caliphates of al-Muʿtaḍid, al-Muktafī and al-Muqtadir, transl. F. Rosenthal (Albany, SUNY Press, 1985).

———, *History XXXIX*

The History of al-Ṭabarī. Volume XXXIX. Biographies of the Prophet's Companions and Their Successors, transl. E. Landau-Tasseron (Albany: SUNY Press, 1998).

Wakīʿ, *Aḫbār al-quḍāt*

Muḥammad b. Ḫalaf Wakīʿ al-Ǧarrāḥ (d. 306/918), *Aḫbār al-quḍāt*, ed. ʿA.ʿA.M. al-Marāġī (Cairo: al-Maktabah al-Tiǧāriyyah al-Kubrá, 1947–1950), 3 vols.

Al-Wāqidī, *al-Maġāzī*

Muḥammad b. ʿUmar al-Wāqidī (130–207/748–822), *Kitāb al-Maġāzī*, ed. M. Jones, *The Kitāb al-Maghāzī of al-Wāqidī* (London: Oxford University Press, 1966), 3 vols.

Studies

Abdel Haleem (2012)

Abdel Haleem, M.A.S., "The Importance of ḥajj: Spirit and Rituals", in *Hajj. Journey to the Heart of Islam*, ed. V. Porter (London: British Museum Press, 2012), 26–63.

——— (2013)

"The Religious and Social Importance of Hajj", in *The Hajj: Collected Essays*, ed. V. Porter and L. Saif (London: The British Museum, 2013), 1–5.

ʿAbd al-Rāziq (1977)

ʿAbd al-Rāziq, A., "La *ḥisba* et le *muḥtasib* en Égypte au temps des Mamluks", *AI* 13 (1977): 115–178.

Abū Ġāzī (2000)

Abū Ġāzī, ʿI., *Taṭawwur al-ḥiyāzah al-zirāʿiyyah fī Miṣr zaman al-Mamālīk al-Ǧarākisah (Dirāsah fī bayʿ amlāk bayt al-māl)* (al-Haram: ʿAyn li-l-Dirāsāt wa-l-Buḥūṯ al-Insāniyyah wa-l-Iǧtimāʿiyyah, 2000).

Adang (2005)

Adang, C., "The Prophet's farewell pilgrimage (*Ḥijjat al-wadāʿ*): the true story, according to Ibn Ḥazm", *JSAI* 30 (2005): 112–153.

——— et al. (2012)

Adang, C., M. Fierro, and S. Schmidtke (eds.), *Ibn Ḥazm of Cordoba. The Life and Works of a Controversial Thinker* (Leiden: Brill, 2012).

Adriaenssens & Van Steenbergen (2016)

Adriaenssens, V., and J. Van Steenbergen, "Mamluk authorities and Anatolian realities: Jānibak al-Ṣūfī, sultan al-Ashraf Barsbāy, and the story of a social network in the Mamluk/Anatolian frontier zone, 1435–1438", *JRAS* (2016): 1–40.

Allouche (1994)

Allouche, A., *Mamluk Economics: A Study and Translation of al-Maqrīzī's* Ighāthah (Salt Lake City: University of Utah Press, 1994).

Amitai (1990)

Amitai, R., "The Remaking of the Military Elite of Mamlūk Egypt by al-Nāṣir Muḥammad b. Qalāwūn", *SI* 72 (1990): 145–163.

——— (1997)

"The Mamluk Officer Class during the Reign of Sultan Baybars", in *War and Society in the Eastern Mediterranean, 7th–15th Centuries*, ed. Yaacov Lev (Leiden: Brill, 1997), 267–300.

——— (2006)

"Some remarks on the inscription of Baybars at Maqam Nabi Musa", in *Mamluks and Ottomans. Studies in honour of Michael Winter*, ed. David J. Wasserstein & Ami Ayalon (London: Routledge, 2006), 45–53.

ʿAnkawi (1974)

ʿAnkawi, A., "The Pilgrimage to Mecca in Mamlūk Times", *Arabian Studies* 1 (1974): 146–170.

Apellániz (2009)

Apellániz Ruiz de Galarreta, F.J., *Pouvoir et finance en Méditerranée pré-moderne: le deuxième État mamelouk et le commerce des épices (1382–1517)* (Madrid: Consejo Superior de Investigaciones Cientificas, 2009).

Armstrong (2012)

Armstrong, K., "Pilgrimage: Why do they do it?", in *Hajj. Journey to the Heart of Islam*, ed. V. Porter (London: British Museum Press, 2012), 18–23.

Ayalon (1960)

Ayalon, D., "The Historian al-Jabartī and his Background", *BSOAS* 23/2 (1960): 217–249.

——— (1990)

"Baḥrī Mamlūks, Burjī Mamlūks—Inadequate Names for the Two Reigns of the Mamlūk Sultanate", *Tārīkh* 1 (1990): 3–52.

Bacharach (1973)

Bacharach, J.L., "The Dinar versus the Ducat", *IJMES* 4 (1973): 77–96.

Bauden (2008)

Bauden, F., "Maqriziana II: Discovery of an Autograph Manuscript of al-Maqrīzī:

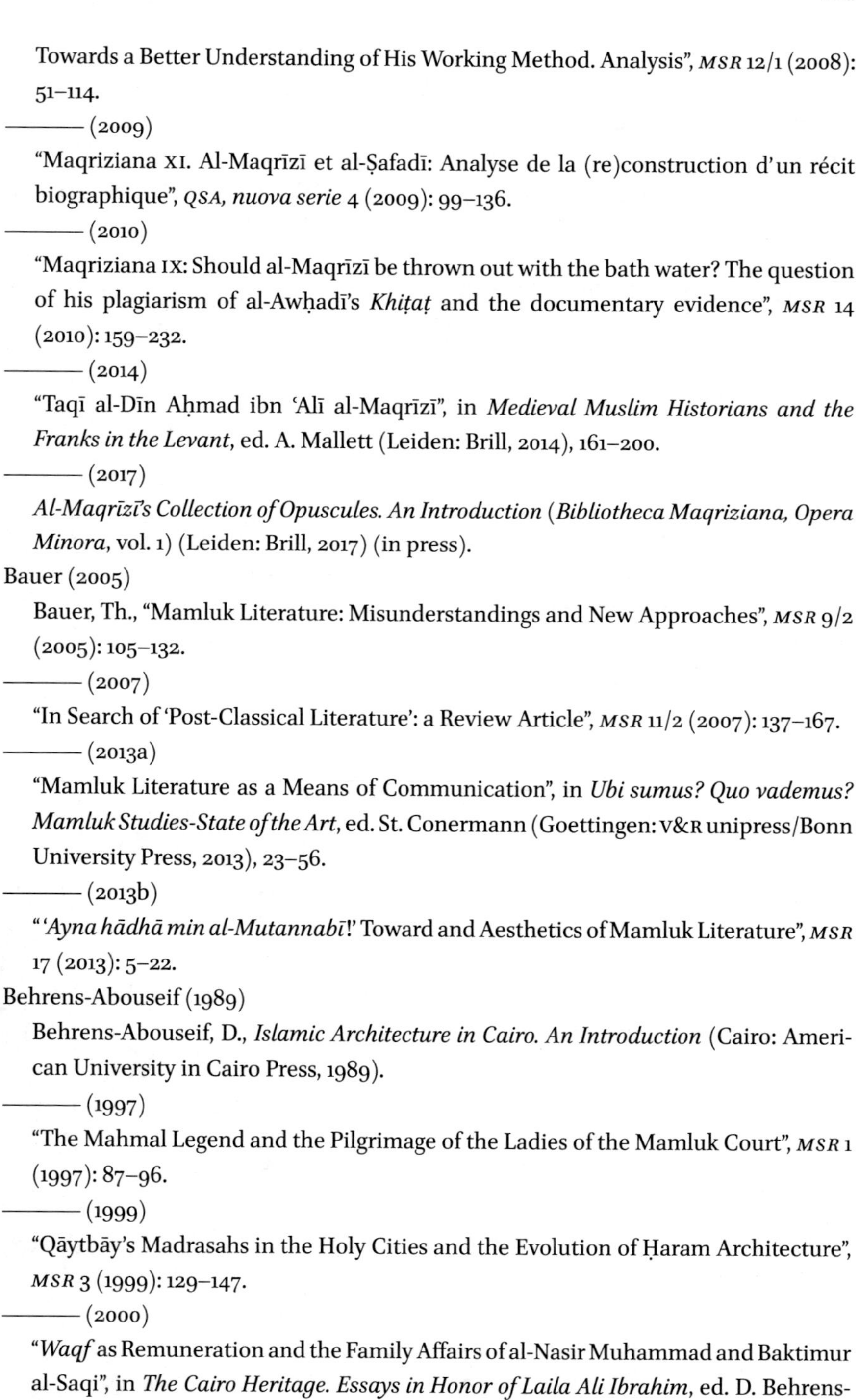

Towards a Better Understanding of His Working Method. Analysis", *MSR* 12/1 (2008): 51–114.

——— (2009)

"Maqriziana XI. Al-Maqrīzī et al-Ṣafadī: Analyse de la (re)construction d'un récit biographique", *QSA, nuova serie* 4 (2009): 99–136.

——— (2010)

"Maqriziana IX: Should al-Maqrīzī be thrown out with the bath water? The question of his plagiarism of al-Awḥadī's *Khiṭaṭ* and the documentary evidence", *MSR* 14 (2010): 159–232.

——— (2014)

"Taqī al-Dīn Aḥmad ibn 'Alī al-Maqrīzī", in *Medieval Muslim Historians and the Franks in the Levant*, ed. A. Mallett (Leiden: Brill, 2014), 161–200.

——— (2017)

Al-Maqrīzī's Collection of Opuscules. An Introduction (*Bibliotheca Maqriziana, Opera Minora*, vol. 1) (Leiden: Brill, 2017) (in press).

Bauer (2005)

Bauer, Th., "Mamluk Literature: Misunderstandings and New Approaches", *MSR* 9/2 (2005): 105–132.

——— (2007)

"In Search of 'Post-Classical Literature': a Review Article", *MSR* 11/2 (2007): 137–167.

——— (2013a)

"Mamluk Literature as a Means of Communication", in *Ubi sumus? Quo vademus? Mamluk Studies-State of the Art*, ed. St. Conermann (Goettingen: V&R unipress/Bonn University Press, 2013), 23–56.

——— (2013b)

"'*Ayna hādhā min al-Mutannabī*!' Toward and Aesthetics of Mamluk Literature", *MSR* 17 (2013): 5–22.

Behrens-Abouseif (1989)

Behrens-Abouseif, D., *Islamic Architecture in Cairo. An Introduction* (Cairo: American University in Cairo Press, 1989).

——— (1997)

"The Mahmal Legend and the Pilgrimage of the Ladies of the Mamluk Court", *MSR* 1 (1997): 87–96.

——— (1999)

"Qāytbāy's Madrasahs in the Holy Cities and the Evolution of Ḥaram Architecture", *MSR* 3 (1999): 129–147.

——— (2000)

"*Waqf* as Remuneration and the Family Affairs of al-Nasir Muhammad and Baktimur al-Saqi", in *The Cairo Heritage. Essays in Honor of Laila Ali Ibrahim*, ed. D. Behrens-Abouseif (Cairo, New York: The American University in Cairo Press, 2000), 55–67.

——— (2007)
Cairo of the Mamluks. A History of the Architecture and Its Culture (Cairo: The American University in Cairo Press, 2007).

Berkey (1992)
Berkey, J.P., *The Transmission of Knowledge in Medieval Cairo: A Social History of Islamic Higher Education* (Princeton: Princeton University Press, 1992).

——— (1998)
"Culture and Society during the Late Middle Ages", in *The Cambridge History of Egypt*. Vol. 1: *Islamic Egypt, 640–1517*, ed. C.F. Petry (Cambridge: Cambridge University Press, 1998), 375–411.

——— (2003)
The Formation of Islam. Religion and Society in the Near East, 600–1800 (Cambridge: Cambridge University Press, 2003).

Bernards (1990)
Bernards, M., "The Basran Grammarian Abu 'Umar al-Jarmi: His Position between Sibawayhi and Mubarrad", in *Studies in the History of Arabic Grammar II*, ed. K. Versteegh and M.G. Carter (Amsterdam, 1990), 35–47.

Bianchi (2004)
Bianchi, R.R., *Guests of God: Pilgrimage and Politics in the Islamic World* (Oxford: Oxford University Press, 2004).

Bori (2003)
Bori, C., *Ibn Taymiyya, una vita esemplare: analisi delle fonti classiche della sua biografia* (Pisa and Rome: Istituti editoriali e poligrafici internazionali, 2003).

Borsch (2005)
Borsch, St.J., *The Black Death in Egypt and England. A Comparative Study* (Austin: University of Texas Press, 2005).

Broadbridge (1999)
Broadbridge, A.F., "Academic Rivalry and the Patronage System in Fifteenth-Century Egypt: al-ʿAynī, al-Maqrīzī, and Ibn Ḥajar al-ʿAsqalānī", *MSR* 3 (1999): 85–107.

——— (2003)
"Royal Authority, Justice, and Order in Society: The Influence of Ibn Khaldūn on the Writings of al-Maqrīzī and Ibn Taghrībirdī", *MSR* 7/2 (2003): 231–245.

——— (2008)
Kingship and Ideology in the Islamic and Mongol Worlds (Cambridge: Cambridge University Press, 2008).

Brown (1900)
Brown, E.G., *A Handlist of Muhammadan Manuscripts including All Those Written in the Arabic Character Preserved in the Library of the University of Cambridge* (Cambridge: Cambridge University Press, 1900).

Chamberlain (1994)
Chamberlain, M., *Knowledge and Social Practice in Medieval Damascus, 1190–1350* (Cambridge: Cambridge University Press, 1994).
Conermann (2008)
Conermann, St., "Tankiz ibn ʿAbd Allāh al-Ḥusāmī al-Nāṣirī (d. 740/1340) as Seen by His Contemporary al-Ṣafadī (d. 764/1363)", *MSR* 12/2 (2008): 1–24.
Conrad (2002)
Conrad, L., "Heraclius in early Islamic Kerygma", in *The Reign of Heraclius (610–641): Crisis and Confrontation*, ed. G.J. Reinink and B.H. Stolte (Peeters: Leuven, 2002).
Cook (1983)
Cook, M., *Muhammad* (Oxford: OUP, 1983).
Crone (1987)
Crone, P., "Did al-Ghazālī write a mirror for princes? On the authorship of *Naṣīḥat al-mulūk*", *JSAI* 10 (1987): 167–191.
——— (2004)
Medieval Islamic Political Thought (Edinburgh: Edinburgh University Press, 2004).
Darrag (1961)
Darrag, A., *L'Égypte sous le règne de Barsbay, 825–841/1422–1438* (Damas: Institut Français de Damas, 1961).
Dekkiche (2014–2015)
Dekkiche, M., "New Source, New Debate: Reevaluation of the Mamluk-Timurid Struggle for Religious Supremacy in the Hijaz (Paris, BnF MS ar. 4440)", *MSR* 18 (2014–2015): 247–271.
Dekkiche & Van Steenbergen (forthcoming)
Dekkiche, M., & J. Van Steenbergen, "The Politics of the Hajj: Networks and Meanings from Shaykh to Khushqadam (815–872 AH/1412–1467 CE)", (forthcoming).
Dozy (1847–1851)
Dozy, R.P.A., *Notices sur quelques manuscrits arabes* (Leiden: Brill, 1847–1851).
Eddé (2008)
Eddé, Anne-Marie, *Saladin* (Paris: Flammarion, 2008).
——— (2012)
"Baybars et son double. De l'ambiguïté du souverain idéal", in *Le Bilād al-Šām face aux mondes extérieurs. La perception de l'Autre et la représentation du Souverain*, ed. Denise Aigle (Damascus and Beirut: Presses de l'IFPO, 2012), 73–86.
Elbendary (2012)
Elbendary, A., *Between Riots and Negotiations: Urban Protests in Late Medieval Egypt and Syria* (Schenefeld, 2012).
——— (2015)
Crowds and Sultans. Urban Protest in Late Medieval Egypt and Syria (Cairo: AUC Press, 2015).

Elham (1977)
Elham, Sh.M., *Kitbuġā und Lāǧīn: Studien zur Mamluken-Geschichte nach Baibars al-Manṣūrī und al-Nuwairī* (*Islamkundliche Untersuchungen* 46) (Freiburg: Klaus Schwartz, 1977).
Eskoubi (2006)
Eskoubi, K., "Brief report on the archaeological survey of Wadi al-Aqiq, Madinah al-Munawwarah 1422 H/2001G", *Atlal: the Journal of Saudi Arabian Archaeology* 19 (2006): 35–37.
Eychenne (2012)
Eychenne, M., "Réseau, pratiques et pouvoir(s) au début du XIVe siècle. L'exemple de Karīm al-Dīn al-Kabīr, un administrateur civil dans le système mamelouk", *AI* 46 (2012): 45–66.
Faraḥāt (2009)
Faraḥāt, K.Ḥ. "al-Qism al-awwal: Dirāsat al-mu'allif wa-kitābihi 'al-Ḏahab al-masbūk'", in Taqī l-Dīn Aḥmad b. 'Alī l-Maqrīzī, *al-Ḏahab al-masbūk fī ḏikr man ḥaǧǧa min al-ḫulafā' wa-l-mulūk*, ed. Faraḥāt (Cairo: 'Ein for Human and Social Studies, 2009), 5–68.
Faroqhi (2014)
Faroqhi, S., *Pilgrims and Sultans: the Hajj under the Ottomans 1517–1683* (London: I.B. Tauris, 2014 [New Paperback Edition]).
Flinterman & Van Steenbergen (2015)
Flinterman, W., & J. Van Steenbergen, "Al-Nasir Muhammad and the Formation of the Qalawunid State", in *Pearls on a String: Art in the Age of Great Islamic Empires*, ed. A. Landau (Baltimore and Seattle: The Walters Art Museum and University of Washington Press, 2015), 86–113.
Al-Ġabbān (2011)
Al-Ġabbān, A.I., *Les Deux Routes syrienne et égyptienne de pèlerinage au nord-ouest de l'Arabie Saoudite* (Cairo: Institut français d'archéologie orientale, 2011).
Gacek (2009)
Gacek, A., *Arabic Manuscripts. A Vademecum for Readers* (Leiden & Boston: Brill, 2009).
Garcin (1973–1974)
Garcin, J.-C., "La 'Méditerranéisation' de l'empire mamlouk sous les sultans bahrides", *RSO* 48 (1973–1974): 109–116.
——— (2005)
Qūṣ. Un centre musulman de la Haute-Egypte Médiévale (Le Caire: Institut Français d'archéologie orientale, 2005 [2nd ed.]).
Al-Ǧāsir (1952)
Al-Ǧāsir, Ḥ, "al-Ta'rīf bi-l-kitāb", in Taqī l-Dīn Aḥmad b. 'Alī l-Maqrīzī, *al-Ḏahab al-masbūk fī ḏikr man ḥaǧǧa min al-ḫulafā' wa-l-mulūk*, ed. al-Ǧāsir, in *Maǧallat al-Ḥaǧǧ* 6/1 (Raǧab 1371/April 1952)—*mulḥaq*: 1–10.

Gaudefroy-Demombynes (1923)
Gaudefroy-Demombynes, M., *Le Pèlerinage à la Mekke. Étude d'histoire religieuse* (Paris: Librairie orientaliste Paul Geuthner, 1923).
——— (1954)
"Le Voile de la Kaʿbah", *SI* 2 (1954): 5–21.
Gellens (1990)
Gellens, S.I., "The search for knowledge in medieval Muslim societies: a comparative approach", in *Muslim Travellers: Pilgrimage, Migration and the Religious Imagination*, ed. D.F. Eickelman & J. Piscatori (Abingdon: Routledge, 1990), 50–65.
Gosden & Marshall (1999)
Gosden, Chris and Yvonne Marshall, "The cultural biography of objects", *World Archaeology* 31/2 (1999): 169–178.
Grabar (1985)
Grabar, O., "Upon reading al-Azraqi", *Muqarnas: An Annual on Islamic Art and Architecture* 3 (1985): 1–7.
Guo (1997)
Guo, L., "Mamluk Historiographic Studies: The State of the Art", *MSR* 1 (1997): 15–43.
——— (1998)
Early Mamluk Syrian Historiography: al-Yūnīnī's Dhayl Mirʾāt al-Zamān (Leiden: Brill, 1998), 2 vols.
——— (2010)
"History Writing", in *The New Cambridge History of Islam*. Vol. 4: *Islamic Cultures and Societies to the End of the Eighteenth Century*, ed. R. Irwin (Cambridge: Cambridge University Press, 2010), 444–457.
Haarmann (1969)
Haarmann, U., *Quellenstudien zur frühen Mamlukenzeit* (Freiburg: Robischon, 1969).
Halm (1996)
Halm, H., *The empire of the Mahdi: the rise of the Fatimids*, transl. M. Bonner (Leiden: Brill, 1996).
Al-Harigi (1994)
Al-Harigi, F.N., "The early development of the relationship between the Prophet's mosque and its surrounding physical environment", *Arabic Journal for the Humanities/al-Maǧallah al-ʿArabiyyah li-l-ʿUlūm al-Insāniyyah* 12/46 (1994): 298–313.
Hawting (1993)
Hawting, G.R., "The Hajj in the Second Civil War", in *Golden Roads: Migration, Pilgrimage and Travel in Mediaeval and Modern Islam*, ed. I.R. Netton (Wiltshire, 1993), 31–42.
——— (2001)
"Pilgrimage", *EQ*, 4:91–100.

Heidemann (1994)
Heidemann, St., *Das Aleppiner Kalifat (A.D. 1261): vom Ende des Kalifates in Bagdad über Aleppo zu den Restaurationen in Kairo* (Leiden: Brill, 1994).

Hiyari (1975)
Hiyari, M.A., "The Origins and Development of the Amīrate of the Arabs during the Seventh/Thirteenth and Eighth/Fourteenth Centuries", *BSOAS* 38 (1975): 509–524.

Hillenbrand (1988)
Hillenbrand, C., "Islamic orthodoxy or realpolitik? Al-Ghazālī's views on government", *Iran* 26 (1988): 81–94.

Hinds (1972)
Hinds, M., "The Siffin arbitration agreement", *JSS* 17 (1972): 93–129.

Hirschler (2006)
Hirschler, K., *Medieval Arabic Historiography. Authors as Actors* (London: Routledge, 2006).

——— (2012)
The Written Word in the Medieval Arabic Lands: A Social and Cultural History of Reading Practices (Edinburgh: Edinburgh University Press, 2012).

——— (2013)
"Studying Mamluk Historiography: from source-criticism to the cultural turn", in *Ubi sumus? Quo vademus? Mamluk Studies-State of the Art*, ed. St. Conermann (Goettingen: V&R unipress/Bonn University Press, 2013), 159–186.

Holt (1973)
Holt, P.M., "The Sultanate of al-Manṣūr Lāchīn (696–8/1296–9)", *BSOAS* 36/3 (1973): 521–532.

——— (1982)
"Three biographies of al-Ẓāhir Baybars", in *Medieval historical writing in the Christian and Islamic Worlds*, ed. D.O. Morgan (London: School of Oriental and African Studies, 1982), 19–29.

——— (1985)
"The Sultan as Ideal Ruler: Ayyubid and Mamluk Prototypes", in *Süleyman the Magnificent and His Age: The Ottoman Empire in the Early Modern World*, ed. M.I. Kunt & Chr. Woodhead (London and New York: Longman, 1985), 122–137.

——— (1986)
The Age of the Crusades. The Near East from the eleventh century to 1517 (London, New York: Longman, 1986).

——— (1995)
"An-Nāṣir Muḥammad b. Qalāwūn (684–741/1285–1341): his Ancestry, Kindred and Affinity", in *Egypt and Syria in the Fāṭimid, Ayyūbid and Mamlūk Eras. Proceedings of the 1st, 2nd and 3rd International Colloquium Organized at the Katholieke Universiteit*

Leuven in May 1992, 1993 and 1994, ed. U. Vermeulen and D. De Smet (Leuven: Peeters, 1995), 313–324.

Humphreys (2006)

Humphreys, R.S., *Mu'awiya b. Abi Sufyan: from Arabia to Empire* (Oxford: Oneworld, 2006).

Irwin (2012)

Irwin, R., "Journey to Mecca: A History (Part 2)", in *Hajj. Journey to the Heart of Islam*, ed. V. Porter (London: British Museum Press, 2012), 137–219.

Johnson (2000)

Johnson, K.V., "Royal Pilgrims: Mamluk Accounts of the Pilgrimages to Mecca of the Khawand al-Kubra (Senior Wife of the Sultan)", *SI* 91 (2000): 107–131.

Jomier (1953)

Jomier, J., *Le* Maḥmal *et la caravane égyptienne des pèlerins à La Mecque (XIIIe-XXe siècles)* (Cairo: Institut Français d'Archéologie Orientale, 1953).

Judd (2014)

Judd, S.C., *Religious Scholars and the Umayyads. Piety-Minded Supporters of the Marwānid caliphate* (Abingdon: Routledge, 2014).

Kecia (2011)

Kecia, Ali, *Imam Shafi'i: scholar and saint* (Oxford: Oneworld, 2011).

Kennedy (2001)

Kennedy, H., *The Armies of the Caliphs. Military and Society in the Early Islamic State* (London and New York: Routledge, 2001).

——— (2012)

"Journey to Mecca: A History", in *Hajj. Journey to the Heart of Islam*, ed. V. Porter (London: British Museum Press, 2012), 68–135.

Khalidi (1994)

Khalidi, T., *Arabic Thought in the Classical Period* (Cambridge: Cambridge University Press, 1994).

Kister (1971)

Kister, M.J., "Maqām Ibrāhīm. A Stone with an Inscription", *Le Muséon* 84 (1971): 477–491.

Kopytoff (1986)

Kopytoff, I., "The cultural biography of things: commoditization as process", in *The social life of things. Commodities in cultural perspective*, ed. Arjun Appadurai (Cambridge: Cambridge University Press, 1986), 64–91.

Lapidus (1967)

Lapidus, I.M., *Muslim Cities in the Later Middle Ages* (Cambridge: Harvard University Press, 1967).

Lebling (2010)

Lebling, R., *Legends of the fire spirits: jinn and genies from Arabia to Zanzibar* (London: Tauris, 2010).

Levanoni (1995)

Levanoni, A., *A Turning Point in Mamluk History. The Third Reign of al-Nāṣir Muḥammad Ibn Qalāwūn. 1310–1341* (Leiden: Brill, 1995).

——— (2001)

"Al-Maqrīzī's Account of the Transition from Turkish to Circassian Mamluk Sultanate: History in the Service of Faith", in *The Historiography of Islamic Egypt* (*c. 950–1800*), ed. H. Kennedy (Leiden: Brill, 2001), 93–105.

——— (2004)

"The Sultan's Laqab—A Sign of a New Order in Mamluk Factionalism?", in *The Mamluks in Egyptian and Syrian Politics and Society*, ed. A. Levanoni & M. Winter (Leiden: Brill, 2004), 79–115.

Little (1970)

Little, D.P., *An Introduction to Mamlūk Historiography: an Analysis of Arabic Annalistic and Biographical Sources for the Reign of al-Malik al-Nāṣir Muḥammad ibn Qalā'ūn* (Wiesbaden: Franz Steinter Verlag, 1970).

——— (1998)

"Historiography of the Ayyūbid and Mamlūk epochs", in *Cambridge History of Egypt. Vol. 1: Islamic Egypt, 640–1517*, ed. C.F. Petry (Cambridge: Cambridge University Press, 1998), 412–444.

Loiseau (2010)

Loiseau, J., *Reconstruire la maison du sultan, 1350–1450: ruine et recomposition de l'ordre urbain au Caire* (Le Caire: Institut Français d'archéologie orientale, 2010), 2 vols.

——— (2014)

Les Mamelouks, xiiie–xvie siècle. Une expérience de pouvoir dans l'Islam médiéval (Paris: éditions du Seuil, 2014).

Lucas (2004)

Lucas, S.C., *Constructive Critics, Ḥadīth Literature and the articulation of Sunnī Islam: the legacy of the generation of Ibn Sa'd, Ibn Ma'īn and Ibn Ḥanbal* (Leiden: Brill, 2004).

Lyons & Jackson (1982)

Lyons, M.C., & D.E.P. Jackson, *Saladin: the politics of the Holy War* (Cambridge, 1982).

Madelung (1997)

Madelung, W., *The Succession to Muḥammad: a study of the early Caliphate* (Cambridge: Cambridge University Press, 1997).

Manz (1999)

Manz, B.F., *The Rise and Rule of Tamerlane* (Cambridge: Cambridge University Press, 1999, Canto Edition).

Marlowe

Marlowe, L., "Advice and Advice Literature", in *EI*³ (http://referenceworks.brillonline.com/entries/encyclopaedia-of-islam-3/advice-and-advice-literature-COM_0026).

Marmon (1995)
Marmon, Sh., *Eunuchs and Sacred Boundaries in Islamic Society* (New York: Oxford University Press, 1995).
Marsham (2009)
Marsham, A., *Rituals of Islamic Monarchy: Accession and Succession in the First Muslim Empire* (Edinburgh: Edinburgh University Press, 2009).
Martel-Thoumian (2001)
Martel-Thoumian, B., "Les élites urbaines sous les Mamlouks circassiens: quelques éléments de réflexion", in *Egypt and Syria in the Fatimid, Ayyubid and Mamluk Eras III*, ed. U. Vermeulen & J. Van Steenbergen (Leuven: Peeters, 2001), 271–308.
Massoud (2003)
Massoud, S., "Al-Maqrīzī as a Historian of the Reign of Barqūq", *MSR* 7/2 (2003): 119–136.
——— (2007)
The Chronicles and Annalistic Sources of the Early Mamluk Circassian Period (Leiden & Boston: Brill, 2007).
Mayer (1933)
Mayer, L.A., "Two inscriptions of Baybars", *Quarterly of the Department of Antiquities in Palestine* 2 (1933): 28–29.
McMillan (2011)
McMillan, M.E., *The Meaning of Mecca. The Politics of Pilgrimage in Early Islam* (London: Saqi Books, 2011).
Melchert (1997)
Melchert, Chr., *The Formation of the Sunni Schools of Law, 9th and 10th Centuries C.E.* (Leiden: Brill, 1997).
——— (2006)
Ahmad b. Hanbal (Oxford: Oneworld, 2006).
——— (2008)
"Life and works of Abū Dāwūd al-Sijistānī", *al-Qanṭara: Revista de Estudios Árabes* 29/1 (2008): 9–44.
Meloy (2003a)
Meloy, J.L., "Imperial Strategy and Political Exigency: The Red Sea Spice Trade and the Mamluk Sultanate in the Fifteenth Century", *JAOS* 123/1 (2003): 1–19.
——— (2003b)
"The Merits of Economic History: Re-Reading al-Maqrīzī's *Ighāthah* and *Shudhūr*", *MSR* 7/2 (2003): 183–203.
——— (2004)
"The Privatization of Protection: Extortion and the State in the Circassian Mamluk Period", *JESHO* 47/2 (2004): 195–212.

——— (2005)
"Economic Intervention and the Political Economy of the Mamluk State under al-Ashraf Barsbāy", *MSR* 9/2 (2005): 85–103.
——— (2006)
"Celebrating the *Maḥmal*: The Rajab Festival in Fifteenth Century Cairo", in *History and Historiography of Post-Mongol Central-Asia and the Middle East. Studies in Honor of John E. Woods*, ed. J. Pfeiffer & Sh.A. Quinn (Wiesbaden: Harrasowitz Verlag, 2006), 404–427.
——— (2010a)
Imperial Power and Maritime Trade: Mecca and Cairo in the Later Middle Ages (Chicago, 2010).
——— (2010b)
"Money and Sovereignty in Mecca: Issues of the Sharifs in the Fifteenth and Sixteenth Centuries", *JESHO* 53/5 (2010): 712–738.
Milwright (2008)
Milwright, M., *The Fortress of the Raven. Karak in the Middle Islamic Period (1100–1650)* (Leiden: Brill, 2008).
Miura (1997)
Miura, T., "Administrative Networks in the Mamlūk Period: Taxation, Legal Execution, and Bribery", in *Islamic Urbanism in Human History: Political Power and Social Networks*, ed. T. Sato (London and New York: Kegan Paul Internation, 1997), 39–76.
Möhring (1999)
Möhring, H., "Mekkawallfahrten orientalischer und afrikanischer Herrscher im Mittelalter", *Oriens* 34 (1999): 314–329.
Morisot (1998)
Morisot, C., "Conséquences économiques de la tutelle mamelouke sur le Ḥiǧāz", *AI* 32 (1998): 159–176.
Mortel (1985)
Mortel, R.T., *Al-Aḥwāl al-siyāsiyyah wa-l-iqtiṣādiyyah bi-Makkah fī l-ʿaṣr al-mamlūkī* (Riyadh: Ǧāmiʿat al-Malik Saʿūd, 1985).
——— (1987)
"Zaydi Shiism and the Hasanid Sharifs of Mecca", *IJMES* 19/4 (1987): 455–472.
——— (1988)
"The Kiswa: Its Origins and development from pre-Islamic times until the end of the Mamluk period", *al-Uṣūr/Ages* 3/2 (1988): 30–46.
——— (1991)
"The Origins and Early History of the Ḥusaynid Amirate of Medina to the End of the Ayyūbid Period", *SI* 74 (1991): 63–78.
——— (1994)
"The Ḥusaynid Amirate of Madīna during the Mamlūk Period", *SI* 80 (1994): 97–123.

——— (1997)
"Madrasas in Mecca during the Medieval Period: a Descriptive Study based on Literary Sources", *BSOAS* 30 (1997): 236–252.

Mouton (2001)
Mouton, J.-M., *Saladin, le sultan chevalier* (Paris: Découvertes Gallimard/Institut du Monde Arabe-Histoire, 2001).

Mouton & Dayoub (2013)
Mouton, J.-M., B. Dayoub, "Les Qubbat al-Naṣr de Damas et ses environs à l'époque mamlouke", in *Egypt and Syria in the Fatimid, Ayyubid and Mamluk Eras VII*, ed. U. Vermeulen, K. D'hulster, J. Van Steenbergen (Leuven: Peeters Publishers, 2013), 507–524.

Munt (2013)
Munt, H., "The Official Announcement of an Umayyad Caliph's Successful Pilgrimage to Mecca", in *The Hajj: Collected Essays*, ed. V. Porter and L. Saif (London: The British Museum, 2013), 15–20.

Musawi (2015)
Al-Musawi, M., *The Medieval Islamic Republic of Letters. Arabic Knowledge Construction* (Notre Dame: University of Notre Dame Press, 2015).

Nassar (2013)
Nassar, N., "Dar al-Kiswa al-Sharifa: Administation and Production", in *The Hajj: Collected Essays*, ed. V. Porter and L. Saif (London: The British Museum, 2013), 175–183.

Netton (2008)
Netton, I.R., *The Travels of Ibn Jubayr* (London: Routledge, 2008).

Onimus (2013)
Onimus, C., "Les Émirs dans le sultanat mamelouk sous les sultans Barqūq et Farağ (784–815/1382–1412). Restauration sultanienne et conflits émiraux", PhD thesis, École Pratique des Hautes Études & Universiteit Gent, 2013.

Ota (2002)
Ota, K., "The Meccan Sharifate and its Diplomatic Relations in the Bahri Mamluk Period", *AJAMES* 17/1 (2002): 1–20.

Peacock (2015)
Peacock, A.C.S., *The Great Seljuk Empire* (Edinburgh: Edinburgh University Press, 2015).

Pearson (1994)
Pearson, M.N., *Pious Passengers: the Hajj in earlier times* (London: Hurst, 1994).

Peters (1994)
Peters, F.E., *The Muslim Pilgrimage to Mecca and the Holy Places* (Princeton: Princeton University Press, 1994).

Petry (1981)
Petry, C.F., *The Civilian Elite in the Later Middle Ages* (Princeton: Princeton University Press, 1981).

——— (1993)
"Scholastic Stasis in Medieval Islam Reconsidered: Mamluk Patronage in Cairo", *Poetics Today* 14/2 (1993): 323–348.
Porter (2013)
Porter, V., "The *Mahmal* revisited", in *The Hajj: Collected Essays*, ed. V. Porter and L. Saif (London: The British Museum, 2013), 195–205.
Al-Qāḍī (1998)
Al-Qāḍī, W., "Biography, medieval", in *Routledge Encyclopaedia of Arabic Literature*, ed. J. Scott Meisami & P. Starkey (New York: Routledge, 1998, 2010): 150–152.
Rabbat (1995)
Rabbat, N., *The Citadel of Cairo: a new interpretation of royal Mamluk architecture* (Leiden: Brill, 1995).
——— (2000)
"Al-Maqrīzī's *Khitat*, an Egyptian *Lieu de Mémoire*", in *The Cairo Heritage: Essays in Honor of Laila Ali Ibrahim*, ed. D. Behrens-Abouseif (Cairo & New York: The American University in Cairo Press, 2000), 17–30.
——— (2003)
"Who Was al-Maqrīzī? A Biographical Sketch", *MSR* 7/2 (2003): 1–19.
——— (2012)
"Was al-Maqrīzī's *Khiṭaṭ* a Khaldūnian History?", *Der Islam* 89/1–2 (2012): 118–140.
Rapoport (2005)
Rapoport, Y., *Marriage, Money and Divorce in Medieval Islamic Society* (Cambridge: Cambridge University Press, 2005).
——— (2007)
"Women and Gender in Mamluk Society: An Overview", *MSR* 11/2 (2007): 1–47.
Raymond (2001)
Raymond, A., transl. W. Wood, *Cairo. City of History* (Cairo: American University in Cairo Press, 2001).
Richards (1982)
Richards, D.S., "Ibn al-Athīr and the later parts of the *Kāmil*: a study of aims and method", *Medieval Historical Writing in the Christian and Islamic Worlds*, ed. D.O. Morgan (London, 1982), 76–108.
Robinson (2003)
Robinson, C.F., *Islamic Historiography* (Cambridge: Cambridge University Press, 2003).
——— (2007)
Abd al-Malik (*Makers of the Muslim World*) (Oxford: Oneworld, 2007).
Sabra (2004)
Sabra, A.A., "The Rise of a New Class? Land Tenure in Fifteenth-Century Egypt: a Review Article", *MSR* 8/2 (2004): 203–210.

Salibi (1958)
Salibi, K.S., "The Banu Jamāʿa: A Dynasty of Shāfiʿite Jurists in the Mamluk Period", *SI* 9 (1958): 97–109.
Sardi (2013)
Sardi, M., "Weaving for the Hajj under the Mamluks", in *The Hajj: Collected Essays*, ed. V. Porter and L. Saif (London: The British Museum, 2013), 169–174.
Al-Šayyāl (1955)
Al-Šayyāl, Ǧ., "Muqaddimat al-nāšir", in Taqī l-Dīn Aḥmad b. ʿAlī l-Maqrīzī, *al-Ḏahab al-masbūk fī ḏikr man ḥaǧǧa min al-ḫulafāʾ wa-l-mulūk*, ed. al-Šayyāl (Cairo and Baghdad: Maktabat al-Ḫanǧī and Maktabat al-Muṯanná, 1955), 3–26.
——— (1971)
"Muʾallafāt al-Maqrīzī l-ṣaġīrah", in *Dirāsāt ʿan al-Maqrīzī*, ed. M.M. Ziyādah, Ǧ. al-Šayyāl, et al. (Cairo: al-Hayʾah al-Miṣriyyah al-ʿĀmmah li-l-Taʾlīf wa-l-Našr, 1971), 23–37.
——— (2000)
"Muqaddimat al-nāšir", in Taqī l-Dīn Aḥmad b. ʿAlī l-Maqrīzī, *al-Ḏahab al-masbūk fī ḏikr man ḥaǧǧa min al-ḫulafāʾ wa-l-mulūk*, ed. Ǧ. al-Šayyāl (al-Ẓāhir, Cairo: Maktabat al-Ṯaqāfah al-Dīniyyah, 2000), 3–27.
Sayyid (1979)
Sayyid, A.F., "Remarques sur la composition des *Ḫiṭaṭ* de Maqrīzī d'après un manuscrit autographe", in *Hommages à la mémoire de Serge Sauneron, 1927–1976*, II: *Égype post-pharaonique* (Cairo: Institut français d'archéologie orientale, 1979), 231–258.
Schultz (2004)
Schultz, W.C., "The Circulation of *Dirhams* in the Bahri Period", in *The Mamluks in Egyptian and Syrian Politics and Society*, ed. Michael Winter and Amalia Levanoni (Leiden, Boston: Brill, 2004), 221–244.
——— (2006)
"Mansa Mūsā's Gold in Mamluk Cairo: A Reappraisal of a World Civilizations Anecdote", in *History and Historiography of Post-Mongol Central-Asia and the Middle East. Studies in Honor of John E. Woods*, ed. J. Pfeiffer & Sh.A. Quinn (Wiesbaden: Harrasowitz Verlag, 2006), 428–447.
Sijpesteijn (2014)
Sijpesteijn, P.M., "An Early Umayyad Papyrus Invitation for the Ḥajj", *JNES* 73/2 (2014): 179–190.
Stewart (2007)
Stewart, A.D., "Under-age Rulers and Succession in the Early Mamlūk Sultanate", *al-Masāq* 19/1 (2007): 47–54.
Stilt (2011)
Stilt, K., *Islamic Law in Action. Authority, Discretion, and Everyday Experiences in Mamluk Egypt* (Oxford: Oxford University Press, 2011), 62–71.

Suhaib (2009)
Suhaib, A.Q., "Sukuk: an Islamic financial instrument", *Pakistan Journal of Islamic Research* 4 (2009): 47–65.
Thorau (1987)
Thorau, P., transl. P.M. Holt, *The Lion of Egypt. Sultan Baybars I and the Near East in the Thirteenth Century* (London & New York: Longman, 1987).
Tonghini (1999)
Tonghini, C., *Qal'at Ja'bar Pottery. A Study of a Syrian fortified site of the late 11th–14th centuries* (London: The British Academy, 1999).
Vallet (2010)
Vallet, E., *L'Arabie marchande. État et commerce sous les sultans rasūlides du Yémen (626–858/1229–1454)* (Paris: Publications de la Sorbonne, 2010).
Van Binsbergen (2005)
Van Binsbergen, W., "Commodification: Things, agency and identities: Introduction", in *Commodification: Things, Agency, and Identities*, ed. W.M.J. van Binsbergen & P.L. Geschiere (Münster: LIT Verlag, 2005), 9–51.
Van Gelder (1998)
van Gelder, G.H.J., "Hijaz", *Routledge Encyclopedia of Arabic Literature*, ed. J. Scott Meisami & P. Starkey (New York: Routledge, 1998, 2010), 285–286.
Van Nieuwenhuyse & Van Steenbergen (forthcoming)
Van Nieuwenhuyse, St., & J. Van Steenbergen, "Justice, Violence, and Truth in the late medieval Sultanate of Cairo. Qurqumās al-Shaʿbānī (d. 1438) and the Formation of Sultan Barsbāy's State (1422–1438)" (forthcoming).
Van Steenbergen (2005)
Van Steenbergen, J., "Mamluk Elite on the Eve of an-Nasir Muhammad's death (1341): A Look behind the Scenes of Mamluk Politics", *MSR* 9/2 (2005): 173–199.
——— (2006)
Order Out of Chaos. Patronage, Conflict and Mamluk Socio-Political Culture, 1341–1382 (Leiden: Brill, 2006).
——— (2011a)
"On the Brink of a New Era? Yalbughā al-Khāṣṣakī (d. 1366) and the Yalbughāwiyyah", *MSR* 15/1 (2011): 117–152.
——— (2011b)
"The amir Yalbughā al-Khāṣṣakī (d. 1366), the Qalāwūnid sultanate, and the cultural matrix of Mamluk society. A re-assessment of Mamluk Politics in the 1360s", *JAOS* 131/3 (2011): 423–443.
——— (2012)
"Qalāwūnid discourse, elite communication and the Mamluk cultural matrix: interpreting a 14th-century panegyric", *JAL* 43/1 (2012): 1–28.
——— (forthcoming)
"'Nomen Est Omen': David Ayalon, the Mamluk Sultanate, and the Rule of the Turks."

In *Egypt and Syria Under Mamluk Rule: Political, Social and Cultural Aspects*, ed. Amalia Levanoni (forthcoming).

Van Steenbergen, Wing & D'hulster (2016)
Van Steenbergen, J., P. Wing & K. D'hulster, "The Mamlukisation of the Mamluk Sultanate? State Formation and the History of Fifteenth Century Egypt and Syria: Part I—Old problems and new trends / Part II—Comparative solutions and a new research agenda", *History Compass* (2016).

Waines (2010)
Waines, D., *The odyssey of Ibn Battuta: uncommon tales of a medieval adventurer* (Chicago: University of Chicago Press, 2010).

Walker (2011)
Walker, B., *Jordan in the Late Middle Ages: Transformation of the Mamluk Frontier* (Chicago: Middle East Documentation Center, 2011).

Walker (2003)
Walker, P.E., "Al-Maqrizi and the Fatimids", *MSR* 7/2 (2003): 83–97.

Warner (2005)
Warner, N., *The Monuments of Historic Cairo. A Map and Descriptive Catalogue* (Cairo, New York: American University in Cairo Press, 2005).

Wasserstein (1998)
Wasserstein, D., "Ibn ʿAbd al-Barr al-Namarī", in *The Routledge Encyclopedia of Arabic Literature*, ed. Julie Scott Meisami and Paul Starkey (London & New York: Routledge, 1998, 2010), 302.

Wiederhold (1999)
Wiederhold, L., "Legal-Religious Elite, Temporal Authority, and the Caliphate in Mamluk Society: Conclusions Drawn from the Examination of a 'Zahiri Revolt' in Damascus in 1386", *IJMES* 31/2 (1999): 203–235.

Wing (2014)
Wing, P., "Indian Ocean Trade and Sultanic Authority: The *nāẓir* of Jedda and the Mamluk Political Economy", *JESHO* 57 (2014): 55–75.

——— (2015)
"Submission, Defiance, and the Rules of Politics on the Mamluk Sultanate's Anatolian Frontier", *JRAS* 25/3 (2015): 377–388.

Winter (1999)
Winter, S.H., "Shams al-Dīn Muḥammad ibn Makkī: 'al-Shahīd al-Awwal' (d. 1384) and the Shiʿah of Syria", *MSR* 3 (1999): 149–182.

Witkam (2014)
Witkam, J.J., "Reflections on al-Maqrīzī's Biographical Dictionary", in *History and Islamic Civilisation. Essays in honour of Ayman Fu'ad Sayyid*, ed. O. Kohela (Cairo: Al-Dār al Miṣriyya al-Lubnāniyya, 2014), 93–114.

Yosef (2012)
Yosef, K., "Dawlat al-atrāk or dawlat al-mamālīk? Ethnic origin or slave origin as the

defining characteristic of the ruling élite in the Mamlūk sultanate", *JSAI* 39 (2012): 387–410.

Al-Ziriklī (2002)

Al-Ziriklī, Ḫ., *al-A'lām. Qāmūs tarāǧim li-ašhar al-riǧāl wa-l-nisā' min al-'Arab wa-l-musta'ribīn wa-l-mustašriqīn* (Beirut: Dār al-'Ilm li-l-Malāyīn, 2002 [15th ed.]) 8 vols.

Ziyādah (1971a)

Ziyādah, M.M., "Aḥmad b. 'Alī l-Maqrīzī", in *Dirāsāt 'an al-Maqrīzī*, ed. M.M. Ziyādah, Ǧ. al-Šayyāl, et al. (Cairo: al-Hay'ah al-Miṣriyyah al-'Āmmah li-l-Ta'līf wa-l-Našr, 1971), 7–12.

——— (1971b)

"Tārīḫ ḥayāt al-Maqrīzī", in *Dirāsāt 'an al-Maqrīzī*, ed. M.M. Ziyādah, Ǧ. al-Šayyāl, et al. (Cairo: al-Hay'ah al-Miṣriyyah al-'Āmmah li-l-Ta'līf wa-l-Našr, 1971), 13–22.

List of Quoted Manuscripts

Cambridge, University Library, MS Add. 746, fols. 78^{a}–105^{b} (= Ca)
Cambridge, University Library, MS Qq. 141, fols. 1^{a}–37^{a} (= Cq)
El Escorial, Real Biblioteca del Monasterio, MS Árabe 1771, fols. 23^{a}–75^{b} (= E / أ)
Istanbul, Atıf Efendi Kütüphanesi, MS 2814, fols. 84^{a}–107^{a} (= Ia)
Istanbul, Nuruosmaniye Kütüphanesi, MS 4937, fols. 145^{a}–186^{a} (= In)
Istanbul, Beyazıt Devlet Kütüphanesi, MS Veliyüddin 3195, fols. 64^{a}–85^{a} (= Iv)
Leiden, Universiteitsbibliotheek, MS Or. 560, fols. 115^{b}–135^{a} (= L / أصل)
New Haven, Yale University, Beinecke Rare Book and Manuscript Library, MS Landberg 111, fols. 26^{a}–62^{b} (= Y)
Paris, Bibliothèque nationale de France, MS arabe 4657, fols. 101^{b}–131^{a} (= P)

Index of Qur'ānic Verses

Page and line numbers between parentheses refer to the translation.

Index of Prophetic Traditions

Page and line numbers between parentheses refer to the translation.

Index of Verses

Index of Names (People and Places)

Place names, tribes, dynasties, families, and ethnic groups are to be searched respectively under Places and Tribes, dynasties, families, and other groups

Index of Quoted Titles in *al-Ḏahab al-masbūk*

Index of Sources in *al-Ḏahab al-masbūk*

Facsimile of MS Or. 560
(Leiden, Universiteitsbibliotheek), fols. 115^{b}–135^{a}

∵

135

ثم اخرج عنه واحضر الى القاهرة ووبخ وعنف تعنيفا كثيرا من الامرا ثم خلع
عليه وجهز في النيل ليتوجه الى بلاده من عيذاب في البحر وانعم عليه الامرا
والسلطان باشيا كثيرة فوصل الى بلاده وتدضبطت له امر المملكة واقام بها
حتى مات في سنة تسع وستين وسبعمايه وملك بعده ابنه الافضل عباس
الملك الاشرف شعبان بن حسين بن محمد بن قلاون جلس على تخت الملك
وعمره عشر سنين في نصف شعبان سنة اربع وستين وسبعمايه وقام بامر
المملكه الامير يلبغا العمري الخاصكي الى ان قتل في ربيع الاخر سنة ثمان وستين
وسبعمايه فقوي امره قليلا ثم قتل اسندمر بعد يلبغا واشتد امره واوقع
باليلبغاويه الاجلاب وشرع في الاهتمام بالحج في سنة ثمان وسبعين وخرج
اطلاب الامرا للسفر في يوم السبت ثاني عشر شوال وخرج طلب السلطان
يوم الاحد ثالث عشره فجر عشرين قطار هجن بقماش ذهب وخمسة عشر
قطار البختي حرير وقطارا ملبس خليفتي وقطارا بقماش ابيض برسم الاحرام
ومايه راس خيل مشهرة وكجاوتين وتسع محفات وهي محفات كلها باغشية
حرير مزركش وستة واربعين زوج محاير وخزانه عشرين جملا وقطاري
جمال يحمل خضر مزدرعة ومن الجمال المحمله شيا كثيرا وركب يوم الاثنين
رابع عشره فاقام بسر[illegible] يوم الاربعا ثاني عشرينه واستقل بالمسير
ومعه من الامرا المقدمين تسعة ومن الطبلخاناه خمسة وعشرون ومن
العشراوات خمسة عشر فركب طاشتمر المحمدي اللفاف احد العشراوات وقرطاي
راس نوبة وجماعه في يوم السبت ثالث ذي القعدة خارج القاهرة وسلطنوا
امير علي بن السلطان فقدم الخبر يوم الاحد ثانيه بان السلطان وصل الى
عقبه ايله يوم الثلاثا واقام الى ليلة الخميس فركب عليه المماليك ليله الخميس
بسبب تاخير النفقه فانهزم السلطان في نفر يسير فخرجوا الى قبة النصر
فقبضوا الامير صرغتمش وعدة من الامرا وقتلوهم وقبض على الاشرف من بيت
امراة في ليلة الاثنين خامس ذي القعدة فكان اخر العهد به قتل خنقا والله اعلم

[illegible] جهد العدره فسح [illegible] احمد [illegible] المعز [illegible] في القعدة سنة ١٠٩٥

135a

نقضي الحج فلم يجد بدا من الاذعان وبعث ثقبة فاكرمه الامرا وبعث الامير
طاز الى صاحب اليمن بالامير طقطاي في جماعة من المماليك ليكونوا في خدمته
حتى يقضي حجه فساروا اليه واطلقوا السلاح داريه وحمل الغاشية وسائر
ما كان قد اهتم به ومشوا في خدمته حتى دخل الحرم وسلم على الامرا واعتذر
اليهم واضمر انه يصبر حتى يرحل الامير طاز ويثور هو وثقبه على من تخلف مع امير
الركب ويأخذ عجلان ويملكا مكه فلما كان يوم منى ركب الامير بزلار امير الركب
من مكه فراى خادم صاحب اليمن فاستدعاه اليه فامتنع من الحضور وضرب
مملوك بزلار بعض حزبه فوقع الصوت في الركب وركب بزلار الى طاز
وثار اهل اليمن بالسلاح وركب امرا مصر وقت الظهر واقتتلوا وهزموا بزلار
هزيمة قبيحة واقبل عجلان امير مكه بجيش كبير فامره طاز ان يحفظ الحاج
واستمرت الحرب الى العصر فانكسر جيش اليمن وقتل منهم جماعة وقطع
دهليز المجاهد وقبض عليه ونهبت اثقاله وقضى الناس حجهم وسار الامير
طاز بالمجاهد معه ورتب في خدمته جماعة من مماليكه وبالغ في اكرامه
ووصى الامير عجلان بامه وحرمه وكتب الى السلطان يعرفه بما وقع وتوجه
الى مصر فقدم به في العشرين من المحرم سنه اثنتين وخمسين وسبعمايه وصعد
به الى القلعه مقيدا الى يوم الخدمة فاوقف تجاه النايب والامرا قعود حتى خرج
امير جاندار ودخل الامرا الى الخدمة بالايوان وهو معهم فقبل الارض بين
يدي السلطان الملك الناصر حسن بن محمد بن قلاوون ثم فك قيده وانزل
بالاشرفية من القلعة واطلق له راتب واقيم له من يخدمه ثم رسم بسفره الى
بلاده فخرج معه الامير قشتمر شاد الدواوين وكتب للشريف عجلان امير مكه
ان يجهزه وخلع عليه اطلسين وركب في الموكب واستانس السلطان به وتردد
اليه الناس واقترض مالا كثيرا واشترى المماليك والخيل والجمال و[illegible] الانعاما
من السلطان والامرا والتزم بحمل المال في كل سنة على العاده وسار في ربيع
الاول فبعث قشتمر بالشكوى منه فرسم له ان يقبض عليه ويسير الى الكرك
ففعل ذلك وقبض عليه بالينبع وبعث به الى الكرك واقام بالكرك قليلا ثم

134b

134

الظاهر بيبرس ثم حج ساكوره وكان قد تغلب على ملكهم وفتح بلاد كوكو ثم حج
منسا موسى لما قدم الى مصر سنة اربع وعشرين وسبعمايه بهدايا جليلة وذهب
كثير فارسل السلطان الملك الناصر محمد بن قلاوون المهمندار ليلقيه وركب به
الى القلعه في يوم الخدمه فامتنع ان يقبل الارض وقال للترجمان انا رجل
مالكي المذهب ولا اسجد لغير الله فاعفاه السلطان من ذلك وقربه اليه واكرمه
وساله عن سبب مجيه فقال اردت الحج فرسم للوزير ان يجهزه بكل ما يحتاج
اليه وقال انه قدم معه اربع عشرة الف جاريه برسم خدمته خاصة فاقبل
اصحابه على شرا الجواري من الترك والحبوش والمغنيات والثياب فانحط سعر
الدينار ستة دراهم وقدم هديته وخرج مع الركب بعد ما وصى به السلطان الامير
سيف الدين ايتمش امير الركب فسار ركبا وحده ساقة الحاج حتى قضى حجه وتاخر
بمكه بعد الموسم اياما وعاد فهلك كثير من اصحابه وجماله بالبرد حتى لم يصل معه الا
نحو الثلث منهم فاحتاج الى قرض مال كثير من التجار واشترى عدة كتب من فقه
المالكيه وانعم السلطان عليه بخيول وجمال وسافر الى بلاده بعد ما تصدق في
الحرمين بمال كثير وكان اذا احدثه اصحابه في امر كشفوا روسهم عند مخاطبته
عادة لهم الملك المجاهد علي بن الملك المويد داود بن الملك المظفر
يوسف بن الملك المنصور عمر بن علي بن رسول صاحب اليمن حج في سنة اثنتين
واربعين وسبعمايه واطلع علمه جبل عرفه ووقف بنو حسن في خدمته حتى قضى
حجه وعزم على كسوة الكعبه فلم يمكنه امير مكه من ذلك فسار وهو حنق ثم حج ثانيا
في سنه اثنتين وخمسين وسبعمايه وقد قدم عليه الشريف ثقبة بن رميثة
واغراه باخيه عجلان واطمعه في مكه وكسوة الكعبه فسار في عسكر كبير
فبلغ ذلك الشريف عجلان وكان الامير طاز قد حج في جماعة من الامرا
فبلغهم قدوم صاحب اليمن في جحفل عظيم وانه يريد يدخل بلامة الحرب
وحمل السلاح دارية وطبر دارية ليقيم فتنه فبعثوا اليه انه من يريد الحج انما يدخل
مكه بذلة ومسكنة وانت تريد تبتدع بدعة فاحشة ونحن لا نمكنك من الدخول
على هذه الصفة فان اردت السلامه فابعث الينا الشريف ثقبة يكون عندنا حتى

134a

المحمل على العاده وامير الركب الامير عز الدين ايدمر الخطيري ورحل في عشرين
شوال وركب السلطان في سبعين اميرا من قلعه الجبل يوم الخامس والعشرين
منه وسفر الحريم مع الامير سيف الدين طقزتمر فلما قارب عقبة ايلة بلغه ان
الامير بكتمر الساقي على نية المخامرة فهم بالرجوع وبعث ابنه انوك وامه الى الكرك
ثم قوي عزمه على المسير فسار وهو محترز ورسم ان كلا من الامرا يحضر على باب
الدهليز بثلثين مملوكا فصار الجميع يبايتون بعدد [illegible] روسهم والاحمدي يستمر
عليه زرديه وسيفه متقلد به وترسه على كتفه وترك السلطان النوم في بيته
فلما وصل الى ينبع تلقاه الشريف اسد الدين رميثه امير مكه بينبع ومعه القواد
والاشراف فاكرمه ورحب به وتوجه مكه وجرى على عادته في التواضع لله
تعالى وكثر الصدقات على اهل مكه والانعام على الامرا والاجناد وقضى نسكه وبعث
الامير اينتمش المحمدي ومعه مايه حجارا الى العقبه فوسعها وقطعها ودخل
السلطان المدينه النبويه فهبت بها رياح عاصفه قلعت الخيم واظلم الجو وصار
كل احد يهجم على غير خيمته ولا يعرف موضعه فانزعج السلطان انزعاجا زايدا
وخاف من ان يفتك به احد او يغتاله ووقع الصياح في الوطاقات فكان امرا
مهولا طول الليل حتى طلع الفجر فانجلى ذلك وحضر امرا العربان بالمماليك الهاربين
عن احزهم ورحل من المدينه فتوعك احمد بن الامير بكتمر ومات بعد ايام
ولم تقم بعده بكتمر سوى ثلثه ايام ومات ايضا بالقرب من عيون القصب فتحدث
الناس ان السلطان سقاهما فدفنا بعيون القصب ثم نقلا الى تربة بكتمر بالقرافه
وسار السلطان وقد اطمان بعدما كان خايفا فزعا فتقدم بركه الحاج يوم
السبت ثاني عشر المحرم سنه ثلث وثلثين وسبعمايه وصعد القلعه في موكب
عظيم لم ير مثله ومشى على شقاق الحرير بفرسه وهو ضارب اللثام وعزم الناس
به فرحا زايدا ودقت البشاير وطبلخانات الامرا ثلثه ايام وعملت الافراح وجلس
في يوم الاثنين وخلع على ساير الامرا والمقدمين وانعم انعاما عظيما
منسا موسى ملك التكرور اول من حج من ملوك التكرور [illegible]دانه
ويقال برمندانه ثم حج منسا ولي بن ماري بن جاطه في ايام الملك الظاهر

133b

133

طوانه وسعيه وكان قد رح جماعة من المغل فاحضرهم وانعم عليهم انعاما زايدا
وامر ان تكسا الكعبة الاطلس واخرج الثياب للصناع فعملوها وفرق في اهل
مكه مالا عظيما وافاض التشاريف على امرا مكه وارباب وظايفها وامير ينبع
وامير خليص وانعم عليه بخمسة الاف برسم عمارة عين خليص وكان لها من
سنين قد انقطعت وجعل ذلك مقررا له في كل سنه برسم عمارتها واجتمع عند
السلطان من العربان لم يجتمع لملك قبله وهم ساير بني مهدي وامرايها وشطى
واخوه عساف واولاده وامرا مكة واشرافها وامرا المدينه وصاحبي ينبع وخليص
وبني لام وعرب حوران وكبارها واولاد مهنا وصار يدخلون عليه ادلالا زايدا
بحيث قام في بعض الايام ابو موسى بن مهنا وقال للسلطان يا باعلي بحيات هذه
ومد يده الى لحية السلطان ومسكها الا اعطيتني الضيعة الفلانيه فصرخ فيه الفخر
ناظر الجيش وقال ارفع يدك قطع الله يدك والك يا ولد زنا تمد يدك الى السلطان
فتبسم السلطان وقال يا قاضي هذه عادة العرب اذا قصد واكبيرا في شي يكون
عظمته عندهم مسك ذقنه يعني انه قد استجار به فهو عندهم سنه فقام الفخر
مغضبا وهو يقول والله ان هاولا مناحيس وسنتهم انحس منهم لا بارك الله
فيهم وصلى السلطان الجمعه بمكه فدعي له وللشريف فقط ولم يدع لصاحب اليمن
تادبا مع السلطان وقضى نسكه وسار الى المدينه النبوية وصلى بها الجمعه ايضا
واقام يومين حتى قدم الركب وبعث المبشرين الى مصر والشام وسار الى ينبع
فلم يجد المراكب وصلت فحصلت مشقة زايده من قلة العليق ومشا اكثر المماليك
لموت الجمال حتى اتت الاقامات من مصر والشام ونزل السلطان بركة الحاج
في ثاني عشر المحرم سنه عشرين وسبعماية فعمل له سماط عظيم جدا وركب في
موكب جليل الى القلعه فكان يوما مشهودا وجلس يوم الخميس نصف المحرم
بدار العدل وخلع على ساير الامرا وارباب الوظايف وامرا العربان وحج بالناس
في سنه اثنين وثلثين وسبعمايه ورسم ببعض الخواتين وبعض السراري وكتب
لنايب الشام بتجهيز ما يحتاج اليه فوصلت التقادم على العادة من النواب
واهل الشام وامرا العربان وطلب ساير صناع مصر لعمل الاحتياجات وخرج

من الحرير الملون المحكم الصنعة ثم تعاظم الملك المويد عماد الدين صاحب حماه
ثم تلاه الامرا وشرع القاضي كريم الدين عبد الكريم ناظر الخاص في تجهيز ما يحتاج
اليه وخرج الى ناحية سرياقوس وصار يقف وهو الاوسط او يجلس على
كرسي وساير ارباب الوظايف في خدمته وهو يرتب الامور فحمل عدة قدور من
فضه ونحاس تحمل على البخاتي ليطبخ فيها واحضر الخوله لعمل مباقل وخضراوات
ورياحين ومشمومات في احواض خشب لتحمل على الجمال وتسقا طول الطريق
ويوخذ منها كل يوم ما يحتاج اليه ورتب الافران وقلايي الجبن وصناع الكماج
والسميد وغير ذلك مما يحتاج اليه واعطا العربان اجر الجمال التي تحمل الشعير
والبشماط والدقيق وجهز مركبين في البحر الى ينبع ومركبين الى جدة بعد ما
اعتبر كلفة العليق باوراق كتب فيها اسما اثنين وخمسين اميرا منهم من له في
اليوم مايه عليقه ومنهم من له خمسون عليقه واقلهم من له عشرون عليقه فكانت
جملة الشعير المحمول مايه الف اردب وثلثين الف اردب وجهز من الشام
خمسمايه حمل تحمل الحلوى والسكر دانات والفواكه وحضرت ايضا حوايج
خاناه على مايه وثمانين جملا تحمل الحب رمان واللوز وما يحتاج اليه في
المطبخ سوى ما حمل من الحوايج خاناه من القاهره وجهز الوزير اوز وثلاثة
الاف طاير دجاج فلما انتهيا ذلك ركب السلطان مستهل ذي القعده ومعه
المويد صاحب حماه وقاضي القضاه بدر الدين محمد بن جماعه الشافعي بعد ما
مهدت عقبة ايله من الصخور ووسع مضيقها بعد ما كان سلوكه مشقا وفتح
مغارة شعيب فلما قدم مكة اظهر من التواضع والذله والمسكنه امرا زايدا وسجد
عند معاينه البيت سجود عبد ذليل ثم التفت الى الامير بدر الدين جنكل بن البابا
وقال لا زلت اعظم نفسي حتى رايت البيت ذكرت تقبيل الناس الارض لي فدخل
قلبي مهابة عظيمة لم تزل حتى سجدت لله تعالى شكرا وتقدم اليه ابن جماعه
وحسن له ان يطوف راكبا فان النبي طاف راكبا فقال يا قاضي ومن انا حتى
اتشبه بالنبي والله لا طفت الا كما يطوف الناس نطاف من غير ان يكون معه
احد من الحجاب فصار الناس يزاحمونه ويزاحمهم كواحد منهم حتى قضى طوافه

صلى الله عليه وسلم صح

132b

132.

وتلقب بالملك المظفر وكتب للناصر تقليد بنيابه الكرك وجهزه مع الحاج
الى ملكه فاظهر البشر وخطب باسم المظفر على منبر الكرك وانعم على الحاج الى
ملكه واعاده فلم يتركه المظفر واخذ يناكده ويطلب منه من معه من المماليك الذين
اختارهم للاقامه عنده والخيول التى اخذها من قلعة الجبل والمال الذى اخذه
من الكرك وهدده بتجهيز العساكر اليه واخذ يحنق لذلك وكتب لنواب الشام
يشكوا ما هو فيه فحثوه على القيام لاخذ ملكه ووعدوه بالنصر فتحرك لذلك وسار
الى دمشق واتته النواب وتقدم الى مصر ففر بيبرس وطلع الناصر القلعه يوم
عيد الفطر سنه تسع وسبعمايه فاقام فى الملك اثنتين وثلثين سنه وشهرين
وعشرين يوما ومات فى ليله الخميس حادى عشرين ذى الحجه سنه احدى
واربعين وسبعمايه وعمره سبع وخمسون سنه واحد عشر شهرا وخمسة ايام
ومدة سلطنته فى المده الثلاث [illegible] واربعون سنه وثمانيه اشهر وتسعة ايام
حج بها ثلث مرات الاولى فى سنه ثنتى عشره وسبعمايه وسببها ان خربندا
تحرك لاخذ الشام ونزل على الفرات فخرج السلطان بعساكر مصر فى ثالث
شوال وسار الى الصالحية فقدم البريد من حلب ودمشق برحيل خربندا عن
الرحبه يوم عيد الفطر يريد بلاده فسر السلطان بذلك وعزم على الحج ودخل
دمشق فى ثالث عشرينه وفرق العساكر فى الجهات وركب فى اربعين اميرا وستة
الاف مملوك على الهجن فى اول ذى القعده واخذ معه مايه فرس فقضى نسكه وعاد
الى دمشق بعد مروره بالمدينة النبويه ودخوله الكرك ودخل فى حادى عشر
المحرم سنه ثلث عشره وهو راكب ناقه لطيفه القد بعمامه مدوره ولثام وعليه
بشت من ابشات العرب وفى يده حربه وتلقاه ابن تيمية وساير الفقها وجميع
الناس وكان يوما مشهودا بلوكوا دار للتفرج على السلطان ستمايه درهم فضه
ثم سار الى مصر فصعد قلعة الجبل فى ثانى عشر صفر ثم حج فى سنه تسع عشر
وتعبا [illegible]ه فلما تحرك لذلك اتته تقادم الامرا وساير نواب الشام وامرا دمشق
وحلب واول من بعث تقدمته الامير تنكز نايب الشام وفيها الخيل والهجن
باكوار الذهب والسلاسل من الذهب والفضة وجميع المقاود والمخاطم والالات

قتل اخيه الملك الاشرف صلاح الدين خليل بن قلاوون في رابع عشر المحرم
سنة ثلث وتسعين وعمره تسع سنين تنقص يوما واحدا فاقام سنة الا ثلثه
ايام وخلع بمملوك ابيه زين الدين كتبغا الملك العادل في حادي عشر المحرم سنه
اربع وتسعين واخرج مع امه اشلون بنت شكتاي الى الكرك فثار الامير
حسام الدين لاجين المنصوري نايب السلطنه على العادل كتبغا وتسلطن عوضه
فثار عليه طغي وكرجي فقتلاه وقتلا ايضا واستدعي الناصر من الكرك فقدم
الى قلعه الجبل واعيد الى السلطنه مره ثانيه في سادس جمادى الاولى سنه
ثمان وتسعين ثم اقام عشر سنين وخمسة اشهر وستة عشر يوما محجورا عليه
لا يملك التصرف في اكلة طعام يشتهيه والقايم بتدبير الدوله الاميران بيبرس
الجاشنكير استادار السلطان وسلار نايب السلطنه فدبر لنفسه في سنة ثمان
وسبعمايه واظهر انه يريد الحج بعيا له فوافقه الاميران على ذلك وشرعوا في تجهيزه
وكتب الى دمشق والكرك برمي الاقامات والزم عرب الشرقيه بحمل الشعير
فلما تهيا ذلك احضر الامرا تقادمهم من الخيل والجمال في العشرين من شهر
رمضان فقبلها وركب في خامس عشرينه من القلعه ومعه الامرا الى بركة
الحاج وتعين معه للسفر ايدمر الخطيري والحاج ال ملك الجوكندار وقرا لاجين
امير مجلس وبلبان امير جاندار وايبك الرومي امير سلاح وبيبرس الاحمدي
وسنجر الجمقدار وتغطاي الساقي وسنقر السعدي النقيب وخمسه وسبعين
مملوكا وعاد بيبرس وسلار من غير ان يترجلا له عند نزوله بالبركه فرحل من
ليلته وعرج الى الصالحيه وعيد بها وتوجه الى الكرك فقدمها في عاشر شوال
وبها الامير جمال الدين اقوش الاشرفي نايبا فنزل بقلعتها وصرح بانثني عزمه
عن الحج واختار الاقامه بالكرك وترك السلطنه ليستريح وكتب الى الامرا بذلك
وسال ان ينعم عليه بالكرك والشوبك واعاد من كان معه من الامرا وسلم اليهم الهجن
وعدتهم خمسمايه هجين والماليك والجمال وجميع ما قدمه له الامرا واخذ ما كان
من المال بالكرك وهو ستمايه الف درهم فضه وعشرون الف دينار واعاد
نايب الكرك ايضا بالمسير عنه فسار الى مصر وتسلطن بيبرس الجاشنكير

وتلقب

131b

١٣١

ما صلى الجمعة مستهل المحرم سنة ثمان وستين وستماية ومعه ماية فارس
بيد كل فارس منهم فرس وساق الى دمشق وساير من في بلاد مصر وبلاد الشام
من الامرا ومن دونهم لا يعرفون شيا من خبر السلطان هل في الشام او الحجاز
او غير ذلك من بلاد الله ولا يجسر احد لشدة مهابة السلطان والخوف منه
ان يتكلم بشي من خبره ولا يسال عنه فلما قارب دمشق بعث احد خاصته
على البريد بكتب البشارة الى دمشق بالسلامة بعد قضا الحج فلما دخل على
الامير جمال الدين النجيبي نايب دمشق جمع الامرا لقراة الكتب السلطانية فبيناهم
في القراة اذ قيل لهم قد نزل السلطان بالميدان فتبادروا الى لقايه فاذا به
وحده وقد اعطى [illegible] لبعض دلالي سوق الخيل لينادي عليه وهو لا يعرفه انه
السلطان فعندما شاهدوه قبلوا له الارض وتلاه الامرا وحضر الامير اق
سنقر الفارقاني ومن معه من عسكر مصر فاكل السلطان شيا وقام ليستريح
وانصرف الناس فركب في نفر يسير وتوجه في خفية يريد حلب فلما حضر الامرا
خدمة العصر لم يجدوا السلطان ولا عرف له خبر فبينا نايب حلب والامرا في الموكب
تحت قلعة حلب واذا بالسلطان قد ساق ووقف ساعة فلم يعرفه احد حتى فطن
به بعضهم فنزل عن فرسه وقبل له الارض فبادر الجميع ونزلوا وقبلوا الارض
وساروا في ركابه حتى دخل دار نايب حلب ثم كشف القلعة وخرج من حلب
ولم يعرف احد به ودخل دمشق في ثالث عشره على حين غفلة ولعب بالكرة وسار
ليلا الى القدس وسار الى الخليل وتصدق بعدة صدقات وكان الامير اق سنقر
قد سار بمن معه من عسكر مصر ونزل تل العجول فوافاه السلطان هناك
وعليه عباته لم يغيرها وسار من تل العجول بالعسكر في حادي عشرينه
وقد [illegible] في اول صفر وعليه عباته التي حج بها لم يغيرها نحو خمسة وسبعين
يوما ثم خرج الملك السعيد الى لقايه وصعد قلعة الجبل

السلطان الملك الناصر ناصر الدين ابو المعالي محمد بن الملك المنصور سيف الدين قلاوون الالفي الصالحي النجمي

[illegible] يوم السبت نصف المحرم سنة اربع وثمانين وستماية واقيم في السلطنة بعد

131a

البريد الى قلعة الجبل بمهمات له فجهزت الكتب مع العربان وقدم المدينه
النبويه في خامس عشرينه فلم يقابله جماز ولا مالك اميرى المدينه وفرا منه
فاعرض عنهما ورحل في سابع عشرينه واحرم ودخل مكه في خامس ذى الحجه
واعطى خواصه جملة اموال لتفرق في الناس سرا وعم اهل الحرمين بالكسوه
التي بعث بها فيهم وصار كآحاد الناس لا يحجبه احد ولا يحرسه الا الله تعالى وبقي
منفردا يصلي وحده ويطوف وحده ويسعى وحده فلا يعرفه الا من يعرفه وغسل
الكعبه بيده بماء الورد وصار بين الناس على اختلاف طبقاتهم وتباين اجناسهم
وما منهم الا من يرمى اليه احرامه فيغسله بيده ويناوله صاحبه وجلس على باب
الكعبه واخذ بايدى الناس ليطلعهم اليها فتعلق بعض العامه باحرامه ليطلع
فقطعه وكاد يرمى السلطان عن العتبه الى الارض وهو مستبشر بجميع ذلك
وعلق كسوة الكعبه بيده ومعه خواصه وتردد الى من بمكه والمدينه من اهل
الخير يلتمس بركتهم ويسال دعاهم هذا وقاضى القضاة صدر الدين معه طول
طريقه يستفتيه ويتفهم منه امور دينه ولم يغفل مع ذلك تدبير الممالك وكتابه
الانشا تكتب عنه في المهمات وكتب الى صاحب اليمن ينكر عليه امورا ويقول
سطرتها من مكه المشرفه وقد اخذت طريقها في سبع عشر خطوه يعني بالخطوه
المنزله ويقول الملك هو الذى يجاهد في الله حق جهاده ويبذل نفسه
في الذب عن حوزة الدين فان كنت ملكا فاخرج والق التتر واحسن الى اميرى مكه
والى امير ينبع وامير خليص واكابر الحجاز وكتب منشورين لاميرى مكه ورتب
معهما الامير شمس الدين مروان نايب امير جاندار ليقيم معهما بمكه حسب سوالهما
ليكون مرجع الامور اليه والحل والعقد على يديه وزاد اميرى مكه مالا وغلالا
في كل سنه لاجل تسبيل الكعبه للناس وسار من مكه بعد قضا النسك في ثالث عشره
وقدم المدينه النبويه ثانى عشرينه فبات بها وسار من غد فجد في السير
ومعه عدة يسيرة فقدم الكرك بكرة يوم الخميس سلخه من غير ان يعلم احد به
بوصوله حتى نزل مشهد جعفر بقرية موته فتلقاه الناس بها ودخل المدينه
وعليه عباته التي سار بها وهو راكب راحله فبات بها ورحل من الغد بعد ما

130

عما يوخذ بمكه من المكوس وان لا يمنع احد من دخول الكعبة وان يخطب
له بمكه والمشاعر وتضرب السكه باسمه فاجاباه وكتب لهما تقليد الاسان
وسلمت اوقاف الحرم بمصر والشام لنوابهما وسلم للشريف قاضي المدينه النبويه
وخطيبها ووزيرها عندما حضر برسالة الامير عز الدين جماز امير المدينه
الجمال التي نهبها الامير احمد بن حجي لاشراف المدينه وهي ثلثه الاف بعير
ليوصلها لاربابها وانعم على الطواشي جمال الدين محسن الصالحي شيخ الخدام
بالحجرة الشريفه بمايتي الف درهم واعاده مع القاضي صحبه الركب الشامي وجهز
الكسوة لمكه والمدينه وقدم الامير شرف الدين عيسى بن مهنا الى الدهليز
بالخربة فاوهم السلطان انه يريد الحركه الى العراق وامره بالتاهب ليركب اذا
دعي ورده الى بلاده وكان السلطان في الباطن انما يريد الحركه للحجاز لكنه
ورى بالعراق فلما دخل شوال انفق في العساكر جميعها وجرد طايفه مع
الامير اقوش الرومي السلاح دار ليكونوا صحبة الركاب وجرد طايفه مع الامير
الدين اق سنقر الفارقاني استادار الى دمشق ليقيموا بظاهرها وتوجه
السلطان الى الحج ومعه الامير بدر الدين الخازندار وقاضي القضاه صدر الدين
سليمن الحنفي وفخر الدين ابراهيم بن لقمان كاتب السر وتاج الدين بن
الاثير ونحو ثلثمايه مملوك وعده من اجناد الحلقة وسار من الفوار يوم الخميس
خامس شهر شوال كانه متوجه الى الكرك كانه يتصيد ولم يجسر احد يتحدث
بانه متوجه الى الحجاز وذلك ان الحاجب جمال الدين بن الدايه كتب الى السلطان
يساله اي اشتهي ان اتوجه صحبه السلطان الى الحجاز فامر بقطع لسانه فلم
يتفوه احد بعدها بذلك فوصل الى الكرك اول يوم من ذي القعده وكان قد دبر
اموره في خفية من غير ان يطلع احد على شي مما فعله بحيث انه جهز البشماط
والدقيق والروايا والقرب والاشربه وعين العربان المتوجهين معه
وا[illegible]ين في المنازل من غير ان يشعر احد من الخاصه فضلا عن العامة بذلك
ففر[illegible] في المجردين معه الشعير وبعث الثقل في رابعه وتبعه في سادسه
ونزل الشوبك ورسم باخفا خبره واستقل بالمسير في حادي عشره وانفذ

130a

ان كسا ها الملك الناصر حسن بن محمد بن قلاوون هذه الكسوه الموجوده اليوم
في سنة احدى وستين وسبعمايه

السلطان الملك الظاهر ركن الدين ابو الفتح بيبرس البندقداري الصالحي النجمي

اشتراه السلطان الملك الصالح نجم الدين ايوب بن الملك الكامل ناصر الدين محمد
ابن الملك العادل سيف الدين ابي بكر محمد بن نجم الدين ايوب وعمله احد المماليك
البحريه بقلعه الروضه فترقى في خدمته واستفاد من اخلاقه وتنقلت به
الاحوال حتى ملك مصر بعد قتل الملك المظفر سيف الدين قطز وتسلم قلعه
الجبل ليله الاثنين تاسع عشر ذي القعده سنة ثمان وخمسين وستمايه
واستمر ملكه حتى مات بدمشق في سابع عشرين المحرم سنه ست وسبعين
وستمايه وقد ملك مده سبع عشره سنه وشهرين واثني عشره يوما وحج سنه
سبع وستين وستمايه وله ذلك خبر طويل قد ذكرته في ترجمته من كتاب التاريخ
الكبير المقفى وكتاب اخبار ملوك مصر وملخص ذلك انه اجلس ابنه الملك
السعيد محمد بركه خان في مرتبه الملك وحضر الامرا فقبلوا الارض بين يديه
وجلس الامير عز الدين ايدمر الحلي نايب السلطنه وجلس الاتابك والصاحب
بها الدين علي بن حنا وكتاب الانشا والقضاه والشهود وحلف له الامرا
وساير العساكر في تاسع صفر منها وركب في ثالث عشره الموكب كما ركب والده
وجلس في الايوان وقريت عليه القصص وقري في العشرين تقليده بتفويض
السلطنه له في الايوان واستمر جلوسه لقضا الاشغال ووقع واطلق
وركب في المواكب واقام السلطان بدر الدين بيليك الخازندار نايبا عنه عوضا
عن الحلي وسار الى الشام في ثاني عشر جمادى الاخره بخاصه من العساكر
وترك اكثرها مع ولده الملك السعيد ونزل بخربه اللصوص خارج دمشق
وسار منها متنكرا الى القاهره ليشاهد احواله ولده فخفي ذلك على جميع من معه
من العسكر حتى عاد اليهم وفي حكايه ذلك طول ليس من قصد هذا الجزو
واتفق الاختلاف بين نجم الدين ابي نمي وبين عمه الشريف بها الدين ادريس
اميري مكه فرتب السلطان لهما عشرين الف درهم نقره في كل سنه عوضا

الشريف

129.

سنه ست وخمسين وستمايه فدفن بصالحية دمشق وحج في سنه ثلث وخمسين
وستمايه وسبب حجه انه لما تنكر له الملك الصالح نجم الدين ايوب بن الكامل
وبعث اليه الامير فخر الدين يوسف بن شيخ الشيوخ صدر الدين بن حمويه
على العساكر فهزمه واوقع الحوطه على بلاده ونازل الكرك حتى طلب منه الامان
فرحل عنه وقد ضاقت الامور بالناصر فخرج الى حلب ومعه جواهر جليلة
قيمتها ما ينيف على مايه الف دينار فبعثها الى الخليفة المستعصم بالله ببغداد
لتكون عنده وديعه فقبضت من رسوله وكتب الخط الشريف بقبضها فشق
ذلك على اولاده وخرجوا عن طاعته ولحق بعضهم بالملك الصالح نجم الدين ايوب
بمصر وسلمه الكرك فجرت امور آلت بالناصر الى مسيره الى بغداد لطلب وديعته
فمنعه الخليفة من الدخول اليها ومطله بالجوهر فلما ايس من ذلك سار الى
مكه من طريق العراق وحج فلما قدم المدينه النبويه تعلق باستار الحجره بحضره
الناس وقال اشهدوا ان هذا مقامي من رسول الله داخلا عليه مستشفعا
به الى ابن عمه المستعصم في ان يرد علي وديعتي فاعظم الناس ذلك وجرت
عبراتهم وارتفع ضجيجهم بالبكا وكتب بصورة ما جرى مكتوب في يوم السبت
ثامن عشرين ذي الحجه تسلمه امير حاج العراقي ومضى الناصر معه الى
بغداد فعوض الجوهر بشي تافه وعاد الى الشام متهورا

الملك المظفر شمس الدين يوسف ابن الملك المنصور نور الدين عمر بن علي بن
رسول قام بعد ابيه بملك اليمن في سنة سبع واربعين وستمايه وحج سنة تسع
وخمسين وغسل الكعبه بنفسه وطيبها وكساها من داخلها وخارجها وهو
اول من كسى الكعبة بعد قتل الخليفه المستعصم ببغداد من الملوك وذلك ان
الحاج انقطع من العراق عن مكه من سنه خمس وخمسين وستمايه الى سنه
ست وستين فلم يرد من هناك حاج في هذه المده وقام المظفر بمصالح الحرم
واهله واكثر من الصدقات ونثر على الكعبة الذهب والفضه وخطب له بمكه
واستمر يخطب بعده لملوك اليمن على منبر مكه الى يومنا هذا بعد الخطبة
لسلطان مصر ولم تزل كسوة المظفر التي كساها للكعبه من داخلها باقيه الى

129a

الدين يوسف وحج نور الدين هذا في سنه احدى وثلثين وستمايه على النجب
وبعث في سنه ثنتين وثلثين الى الكعبه قناديل من ذهب وفضه وحج ايضا في سنة
تسع وثلثين وابطل المكوس والجبايات من مكه وكتب ذلك تجاه الحجر الاسود
فاستمر ذلك حتى ازاله ابن المسيب لما ولي مكه سنه ست واربعين وستمايه واعاد
المكوس والجبايات وصام شهر رمضان بمكه واتفق في سنه ثلث واربعين وستما
وقيل اربع واربعين ان هاجت ريح شديده مزقت كسوة الكعبه والقتها وبقيت
الكعبة عارية فاراد عمر بن رسول ان يكسوها فامتنع من ذلك شيخ الحرم عفيف
الدين منصور بن منعه البغدادي وقال لا يكون ذلك الا من الديوان يعني الخليفه
وكساها ثيابا من قطن مصبوغه بالسواد وركب عليها الطرز القديمه
الملك الناصر ابو شادي داود بن الملك المعظم ابي الفتح عيسى بن الملك
العادل سيف الدين ابي بكر محمد بن نجم الدين ابي الشكر ايوب بن شادي بن مروان
الكردي الايوبي ولد في تاسع عشر جمادى الاخره سنة ثلث وستمايه وحفظ
القران وعمره تسع سنين وقال الشعر وهو ابن عشر سنين وبرع في كل فن
من علوم الادب والحكمه وغير ذلك وولي سلطنه دمشق بعد موت ابيه وهو
في السنه الحادي عشر من عمره اول ذي الحجه سنه اربع وعشرين وستمايه
واقبل على اللهو فطلب منه عمه السلطان الملك الكامل قلعة الشوبك فامتنع
فتنكر عليه وعزم على المسير اليه ونزعه من سلطنة مصر واخذ الناصر في ظلم
الرعية واخذ اموالهم والانهماك في اللعب واستدعى عمه الملك الاشرف شاه
ارمن موسى فقدم عليه من الشرق وحكمه في المملكه فال الامر ان حاصر الملك
الكامل دمشق حتى اخذ الناصر وعوضه عن دمشق بالكرك والشوبك
والصلت والبلقا والاغوار جميعها ونابلس واعمال القدس وبيت جبريل
وكانت هذه الاعمال يوميذ عامره جليله القدر ثم نزل الناصر عن الشوبك لعمه
الكامل وتسلم الكامل دمشق اول شعبان سنه ست وعشرين فاقام بالكرك
وكانت له قصص وانباء ذكرتها في التاريخ الكبير المقفى اللايق به اثنا تشتته في
البلاد وموته في احدى قرى دمشق يوم السادس عشرين من جمادي الاولى سنة

128b

128

ويقال اقسيس بن السلطان الملك الكامل ناصر الدين ابي المظفر محمد بن السلطان
الملك العادل سيف الدين ابي بكر محمد بن والد الملوك نجم الدين ابي الشكر ايوب
ابن شادي بن مروان الكردي الايوبي ولد في ربيع الاخر سنه سبع وتسعين
وخمسمايه وولاه ابوه مملكة اليمن في ايام جده سنه احدى عشره وستمايه
فسار اليها في الف فارس ومن الجاندارية والرماه خمسماية وقدم مكه وتوجه
منها الى زبيد وملكها واستولى على تهامه وتعز وصنعا وساير ممالك اليمن
وحج في سنه تسع عشره وستمايه وقاتل امير مكه الشريف حسن بن قتاده
الحسني وهزمه ونهب مكه فلما كان يوم عرفه منع اعلام الخليفه من
التقدم على اعلام ابيه واظهر من الجراة على الله قبايح منها انه كان يصعد
اعلا زمزم فيرمي حمام الحرم بالبندق ويستخف بحرمه الكعبه واكثر من
سفك الدما واذا نام في دار بالمسعى ضربت الجاندارية الطايفين بالمسعى
باطراف السيوف ليلا يشوشوا عليه وهو في نوم من شده سكره بالخمر ثم
عاد الى اليمن وخرج منها بعدما استخلف عليها نور الدين عمر بن علي بن رسول
الكردي في سنه اثنتين وعشرين وقدم القاهره بهدايا جليله ونزل بالقصر
واقام لابيه حرمه وافره فخافه الامرا والاجناد وخشوا سطوته ثم توجه الى
اليمن بعدما اتاه التشريف الخليفتي من بغداد فاقام بها الى ان بلغه ان اباه اخذ
دمشق فتاق الى اخذها عوضا عن اليمن وخرج باموال واثقاله فمات بمكه في
ثالث عشر جمادى الاولى سنه ست وعشرين وستمايه ودفن بالمعلا وقام
بامر اليمن بعده نايبه عمر بن علي بن رسول وقد استوفيت اخباره في تاريخ مصر
المقفي واليه تنسب الدراهم المسعوديه بمكه

الملك المنصور نور الدين عمر بن علي بن رسول الكردي ملك اليمن
بعد موت الملك المسعود وبعث الى الملك الكامل هديه جليله وقال انا نايب
السلطان على البلاد فاقره عليها وعمر هذا اول من ملك اليمن من بني رسول
وبويع له بها سنه تسع وعشرين وخطب له بمكه فيها ايضا ودامت مملكته الى
ان قتل في سنه سبع واربعين وستمايه وملك بعده ابنه الملك المظفر شمس

128a

توران شاه وقد مدحته وهو في القبر ميت فلف كفنه ورماه وانشدني

لا تستعظن معروفا سمحت به ميتا واصبحت عاريا بدني — منه ح

ولا تظنن جودي شانه بخل من بعد بذلي ملك الشام واليمن

اني خرجت من الدنيا وليس معي من كل ما ملكت كفي سوى كفني

واليه ينسب درب شمس الدولة بالقاهرة وقد ذكرت ترجمته مبسوطة في كتاب
المواعظ والاعتبار بذكر الخطط والاثار وفي كتاب التاريخ الكبير المقفى لمصر

الملك المعظم شرف الدين ابو الفتح عيسى بن الملك العادل سيف الدين ابي بكر
محمد بن نجم الدين ايوب بن شادي بن مروان الكردي الايوبي الفقيه الحنفي النحوي
الاديب الشاعر ولد بدمشق في خامس رجب سنة ست وخمسين وخمسمائة
وتفقه على مذهب الامام ابي حنيفة بالشيخ جمال الدين ابي المحامد محمود بن احمد
الحصيري البخاري الحنفي واخذ العربية عن التاج ابي اليمن زيد بن الحسن الكندي
وكان يسعى الى منزليهما على قدميه لاخذ العلم عنهما وافرط في العصبية لمذهب
الحنفية وشرح الجامع الكبير في الفقه وصنف السهم المصيب في الرد على الحافظ
ابي بكر الخطيب وروي بخطه على كتاب سيبويه انني قطعته حفظا من خاطري
وعلى كتاب النكت في الفقه على مذهب ابي حنيفة انه قطعته حفظا وهو في
مجلدين واعتنى بالعلم واهله عناية تامة وسمع الحديث من حنبل وعمر بن
طبرزد وغيره وحدث واعطاه ابوه الملك العادل دمشق وجعل في ولايته غزة
والكرك والشوبك وذلك سنة ست وتسعين وخمسمائة فلم يزل حتى مات
بدمشق اخر ذي القعدة سنة اربع وعشرين وستمائة وحج فخرج من دمشق
في حادي عشر ذي القعدة سنة احدى عشرة وستمائة على الهجن وسار على
طريق تبوك وبنى البركة وعدة مصانع وتصدق على اهل الحرمين بصدقات
جزيلة وقدم منها الى القاهرة وافدا على ابيه ومعه الشريف سالم بن قاسم
امير المدينة شافعا فيه فاكرمه الملك العادل وبعث معه عسكرا الى المدينة
وعاد المعظم الى دمشق وقد ذكرت ترجمته مستوفاة في التاريخ الكبير المقفى لمصر — بلغ

الملك المسعود صلاح الدين ابو المظفر يوسف ويقال له اطسز

ويقال

127b

127

لازاله المظالم وبالغ في الاحسان لاهل مكه والمدينه وبعث العساكر لحفظ
المدينه النبويه واقطع امير مكه اقطاعا واقطع امرا العربان اقطاعات لحفظ
الحاج واكمل سور المدينه النبويه واستخرج لها العين فدعي له بالحرمين على منبرهما
وبعث الامير اسد الدين شيركوه بالعسكر الى مصر واستنقذ القاهره من
الفرنج بعد ما حصرها مرى لعنه الله بعساكر الفرنج اياما ولم يبق الا ان يملكها
فلما استولى شيركوه على القاهره دعي لنور الدين على منابر القاهره ومصر
ومات في حادي عشر شوال سنه تسع وستين وخمسمايه بدمشق بعد ما حج في
سنه ست وخمسين وخمسمايه واكثر من فعل الخير بالحرمين وبالغ في الاحسان

الملك المعظم شمس الدوله توران شاه بن والد الملوك نجم الدين ايوب بن
شادي بن مروان الكردي نشا بدمشق وقدم الى القاهره مع اهله في سنه اربع
وستين وخمسمايه وقد تقلد اخوه الملك الناصر صلاح الدين يوسف بن ايوب
وزارة مصر للخليفه العاضد لدين الله ابي محمد عبد الله بن الامير يوسف بن الحافظ
لدين الله فكان اعظم الاسباب في نصر اخيه صلاح الدين يوم وقعة السودان
حتى هزمهم وافناهم بالسيف فاقطعه قوص واسوان وعيذاب وعبرتها يوميذ
مايتا الف دينار وسته وستون الف دينار مصريه في كل سنه ثم غزا النوبه
في سنه ثمان وستين واخذ قلعه ابريم وعاد غانما ثم سار الى بلاد اليمن في
سنه تسع وستين وعلى ملك زبيد ابو الحسن علي بن مهدي الملقب عبد النبي
وقدم مكه معتمرا وتوجه الى زبيد واستولى على ممالك اليمن ولقب بالملك المعظم
وخطب لنفسه بعد الخليفه العباسي توجه في سنه احدي وسبعين الى الشام
فملكه اخوه صلاح الدين دمشق في ربيع الاول سنة اثنين وسبعين ثم
جهزه الى القاهره في ذي القعده سنه اربع وسبعين وانعم عليه بالاسكندريه
فاقام بها الى ان مات هناك اول صفر سنه ست وسبعين وخمسمايه فوجد
عليه مبلغ مايتي الف دينار مصريه دينا قضاها عنه السلطان صلاح الدين وسبب
هذا الدين كثرة جوده وسعة عطايه ومن غريب ما حكي عنه ان الاديب الفاضل
مهذب الدين اباطالب محمد بن علي ابن الخيمي قال رايته في النوم المعظم شمس الدوله

ايضا الجمالون على المنصور بالمدينة فقال الحاج محمد بن عمران للشبلي اكتب اليه في
ذلك فانا عليه وقال تعفيني فقال لتكتبن فكتب فلما استتم الكتاب وختمه
قال له لا يمضي به سواك فمضى ووافى الى باب المنصور وسلم الكتاب الى الربيع
فاوصله الى المنصور فقراه وعاد الشبلي الى محمد بن عمران فعرفه انه سلم ما
كتب الى الربيع فاوصله فقراه المنصور واجاب الى الحضور ثم خرج
المنصور موتزرا ببردة ومرتديا باخرى ومشى الى ان قارب مجلس محمد بن عمران
ووقعت عينه عليه والربيع بين يديه فقال له يا ربيع نفيت من العباس
لئن تحرك محمد بن عمران من مجلسه هيبة لي لا وليته ابدا ثم صار الى محمد بن عمران
فلما راى المنصور وكان متكيا اطلق رداه على عاتقه ثم احتبى ودعا
بالخصوم فحكم لهم عليه وامره بانصافهم وانصرف ابو جعفر وامر
الربيع باحضار محمد بن عمران فلما دخل عليه قال له يا ابن عمران جزاك الله
عن دينك وعن نبيك وعن حسبك وعن خليفتك احسن الجزا وامر له
بعشرة الاف درهم

126b

126.

ترجل الناس له لما استقبلوه الا محمد بن عمران قاضي المدينة فقال المنصور يا ربيع الا
يترجل لي ابن خالد علي وتشنيع بما فعله بنو عبد المطلب وبنو علي فلم ينزل الى الارض لما بصر
بي فقال الربيع يا امير المومنين لو رايته على الارض لرحمته ورثيت له من ثقله وعظمه
وامره بالدنو فدنا منه راكبا عند تمهيد الربيع له العذر فساله عن حاله ثم
قال يا ابن عمران ايما رجل انت لولا خصال فيك ثلاث كنت انت الرجل قال
وما هن يا امير المومنين قال قعودك عن الصلاة في مسجد رسول الله صلى الله عليه وسلم
في جماعة فتصلي وحدك والثانية انك لا تكلم انسانا في الطريق تيها وعظمة
والثالثة انك رجل بخيل فيك ضيق شديد فقال يا امير المومنين اما الاولى
فاني اكره ان اصلي بصلاة الامام مما يخطر علي من فسادها اعظم عندي من
تركي اياها في الشيء واني لا ادري معهم ركوعا ولا سجودا فاري ان اصلي وحدي
افضل واما الثانية فاني قاض ولا يجوز ان اعطي من نفسي التسليم عليهم
والابتذال لنفسي فيكون في ذلك مفسدة للخصوم واما الثالثة فاني لا
اجمد في حق ولا اذوب في باطل قال اخرج عنهم يا ابن عمران يا ربيع ادفع
اليه ثلاثة الاف درهم قال يا امير المومنين بالباب مستعدون عليك يذكرون
ان في يديك حمام دار كذا قال فانصفهم مني قال وكل وكيلا يقوم مقامك
او احضر معهم مجلس القضاء قال قد وكلت الربيع قال اشهد على وكالتك
اياه عيسى بن علي والعباس بن محمد ففعل ثم اخرج حدود الدار التي ينازعونه
فيها ودعا بالربيع وخصمائه واحضر شهادته على الوكالة وانفذها
ثم سال القوم عن دعواهم وعن شهودهم ثم قضى لهم عليه واستعدى

126a

واربع مايه بستين رجلا اصحاب عشاير فصار في عشرين الف ضارب سيف
من يومه ودعا للامام المستنصر بالله ابي تميم معد بن الظاهر بن الحاكم احد
الخلفا الفاطميه بالقاهره وملك اليمن كله سهله وجبله ووعره وبره وبحره
وخطب بنفسه وكانت قاعده ملكه صنعا وحج سنه خمس وخمسين واربعمايه
وملك مكه في سادس ذي الحجه منها ونشر بها العدل واكثر فيها من الاحسان
ومنع المفسدين وامن الناس امنا لم يعهدوه قبله ورخصت بها الاسعار لكثره
ما جلب اليها من ناحيه الناس جبارا يدا وكسا الكعبه الديباج الابيض وهو
كان شعار الدوله الفاطميه واقام بها دعوتهم ثم حج في سنه ثلث وسبعين
واربعمايه فلما نزل ظاهر المهجم قتل في ثاني عشر ذي الحجه بيد سعيد الاحول
ابن نجاح وملك بعده **الملك العادل نور الدين محمود** بن عماد الدين اتابك بن
زنكي بن ابي سعيد قسيم الدوله بن اقسنقر المعروف بالحاجب بن عبد الله كان جده
اقسنقر مملوكا تركيا للسلطان ملكشاه بن الب ارسلان السلجوقي وترقي
الى ان استنابه تاج الدوله تتش بن ارسلان في حلب لما ملكها في سنه ثمان
وسبعين واربعمايه فعصا عليه وحاربه فقتل في جمادي الاول سنه سبع و
وثمانين واربعمايه وصار ابنه عماد الدين زنكي من الامرا ببغداد ثم ولي الموصل
سنه اثنين وعشرين وخمسمايه واخذ الرها وقتل على جعبر في ربيع الاخر
سنه احدى واربعين وخمسمايه وهو على فراشه وولد نور الدين محمود في
سابع عشر شوال سنه احدى عشر وخمسمايه فقام بعد قتل ابيه واخذ
قلعه حلب وجد في قتال الفرنج وبيدهم حينيذ من الرها الى السواده من
حدود ارض مصر وافتتح عده حصون واظهر بحلب مذهب اهل السنه وكان
اهلها من الرافضه وابطل الاذان بحي على خير العمل وانشا بها المدارس على
مذاهب الايمه الاربعه ثم ملك دمشق بعد ما اشرف الفرنج على اخذها وضبط
امورها وانشا بها المدارس والمساجد والمارستان وعمرها وابطل المكوس
كلها ومنع المنكرات باسرها وعاقب عليها واستنقذ من الفرنج عده معاقل
وبنا في اكثر ممالكه دار العدل واحضرها القضاه والفقها وجلس فيها بنفسه

125b

-125-

وثمانين ومائة ثم حج الرشيد في سنة ثمان وثمانين راجلا وقسم اموالا كثيرة
وهي آخر حجة حجها وكان اذا حج حج معه مائة من الفقهاء وابنائهم فاذا لم يحج احج
ثلثمائة رجل بالنفقة السابغة والكسوة الظاهرة ولم ير خليفة قبله اكثر عطا
منه ويقال لو قيل للدنيا متى ايام شبابك لقالت ايام هرون الرشيد

الحاكم بامر الله ابو العباس احمد بن محمد بن الحسن بن ابي بكر بن ابي علي
القبي بن الحسن الخليفة الراشد بالله على خلاف في نسبه ثاني خلفاء بني العباس
بديار مصر خرج من بغداد في واقعة هولاكو وجمع طايفة من الناس ولقي الامام
المستنصر بالله ابا العباس احمد بن الخليفة الظاهر بامر الله ابي نصر محمد بن الخليفة
الناصر لدين الله العباسي المجهز من ديار مصر لقتال الططر وصار في جملته فلما
قتل المستنصر وتاخر الططر قدم الى القاهرة في سابع عشرين ربيع الاول سنة
ستين وستمائة فبايعه الملك الظاهر ركن الدين بيبرس البندقداري في يوم
الخميس ثامن المحرم سنة احدى وستين وستمائة فلم يزل خليفة لا امر له ولا نهي
ولا نفوذ كلمة حتى مات بمناظر الكبش خارج القاهرة ليلة الجمعة ثامن عشر جمادى
الاولى سنة احدى وسبعمائة فكانت خلافته اربعين سنة وهو اول خليفة عباسي
مات بمصر واستمرت الخلافة في عقبه الى اليوم وحج في سنة تسع وتسعين وستمائة
والسلطان يوميذ الملك المنصور لاجين واعطاه مبلغ سبعماية الف درهم فضة
ولما قدم مكة اراد منه الشريف ابي نمي امير مكه ان يدعو له على منبر مكة فامتنع من
ذلك وجرت بينهما معاوضة ترفع فيها عليه ابو نمي تفاخرا بنسبه الشريف
واستمر الامر على ذلك الى اليوم لم يخطب قط بمكة لاحد من خلفاء مصر العباسيين

٢٠

سوى الخليفة المستعين بالله ابي الفضل العباس بن محمد ايام سلطنته في سنة خمس
عشرة وثمانمائة

ذكر من حج من الملوك وهو ملك الصليحي

واسمه علي بن محمد بن علي احد ثوار العالم كنيته ابو الحسن بن ابي محمد كان ابوه
على قضاء اليمن ومن اهل السنة وكان في عشيرة من قومه فصحب علي داعي
اليمن عامر بن عبد الله الرواحي احد دعاة الدولة الفاطمية ومال الى مذهب
الشيعة وتضلع من علوم الشيعة حتى صار اماما فيه ثم ثار سنة تسع وعشرين

من ملوك الدنيا ملك حج ماشيا سوى ملكين هرقل بن هرقل بن انتونبش من
اهل صلوقيا حج من حمص الى ايليا التي هي بيت المقدس ماشيا ووافاه كتاب
رسول الله صلى الله عليه وسلم في سفرته هذه يدعوه الى الاسلام كما وقع في
الصحيحين وغيرهما والملك الثاني هرون الرشيد وذكر ابو محمد بن حزم في كتاب
جمهرة الانساب ان موسى الهادي بن محمد المهدي كان له ام ولد تسمى امة العزيز
تزوجها اخوه هرون من بعده وهي التي كان حلف الرشيد لاخيه بالمشي
الى الكعبة ان لا يتزوجها فلما مات الهادي تزوجها ومشى راجلا من بغداد
الى مكة وهو خليفة فولدت له عليا وكان اقبح الناس صورة ولما دخل الرشيد
مكة كان يطرح له الرمل حول البيت ومقدار عرضه ذراعين ويرش بالماء
ويقوم الحرس بينه وبين الناس وكان يطوف بين المغرب والعشا ثلثه عشر
اسبوعا ولا يطيق ذلك احد عمركا زمعه وكان اذا سعى شمر ازاره وجعل له
ذنبين وكان يعتق من براه وكذلك حجت زبيدة ام جعفر بنت جعفر بن ابي جعفر
زوج هرون الرشيد ماشية ايضا وكانت حجة عظيمة غير ان ذكرها ليس
من شرط هذا الجزو فلذلك تركت ذكرها وحج الرشيد ايضا بالناس في سنه
احدى وثمانين ومايه وحج في سنه ست وثمانين ومايه من الانبار ومعه
ابناه عبد الله المامون ومحمد الامين فبدا بالمدينه فاعطى فيها ثلث اعطيه اعطى
هو عطا وكل من ولديه عطا وسار الى مكه فاعطى اهلها الف الف دينار
وخمسين الف دينار وكان قد ولى الامين العراق والشام الى اخر المغرب
وجعله ولي عهده وضم الى المامون من همذان الى اخر المشرق وعهد اليه بعد
الامين ثم بايع لابنه القاسم بولايه العهد بعد المامون ولقبه المؤتمن وضم اليه
الجزيرة والثغور والعواصم وجمع بمكه القضاة والفقها وكتب كتابا اشهدهم فيه
على الامين بالوفا للمامون وكتب كتابا اشهدهم فيه على المامون بالوفا للامين
وعلق الكتابين بالكعبه وقد ذكرت خبر ذلك مبسوطا في ترجمه المامون من تاريخ
مصر الكبير المقفا فانه قدم مصر في سنه سبع عشره ومايتين وفي عود الرشيد
من هذه الحجه نكب البرامكه النكبة المشهوره بالانبار سلخ المحرم سنه سبع

وثمانين

124b

124

فانا ابن عبد الله فابن من قال ابن محمد قلت فانا ابن محمد فابن من قال ابن علي قلت
فانا ابن علي فابن من قال ابن عبد الله قلت فانا ابن عبد الله فابن من قال ابن
عباس قلو لو بلغ العباس ما شككت انك صاحب الامر فتحدث بها ذلك الزمان
ونحن لا نعرفه المهدي حتى ولي المهدي فدخل رسول الله صلى الله عليه وسلم
فذكر اسم الوليد فقال الهادي اسم الوليد الى اليوم فدعا بكرسي فالقي في صحن المسجد
وقال ما انا ببارح حتى يمحى ويكتب اسمي مكانه ففعل ذلك وهو جالس وطاف
بالبيت من ليلة فسمع اعرابية تقول قومي مقترون نبت عنهم العيون وفدحتهم
الديون وعضتهم السنون بادت رجالهم وذهبت اموالهم وكثرت عيالهم ابناء سبيل
وانضاء طريق وصية الله ووصية الرسول فهل من امر لي بخير كلاه الله في نفسه
وخلفه في اهله فامر لها بخمسماية درهم **هرون الرشيد** بن محمد المهدي
ابن ابي جعفر المنصور عبد الله بن محمد بن علي بن عبد الله بن عباس رضي الله عنهم
بويع بالخلافه بعد موت اخيه موسى الهادي في ليلة الجمعه للنصف من ربيع الاول
وقيل لاربع عشر خلت منه سنه سبعين ومايه فاقام في الخلافه ثلثا وعشرين
سنه وشهرين وثمانيه عشر يوما يغزو سنه ويحج سنه فحج تسع حجج ولم يحج بعده
خليفه من بغداد واول ما حج وهو خليفه سنه سبعين وقسم في اهل الحرمين عطا
كثيرا وقيل انه غزا الصايفه بنفسه ثم حج ثانيا في سنة ثلث وسبعين واحرم
من بغداد وحج بالناس سنه اربع وسبعين وقسم في الناس مالا كثيرا ثم حج في
سنه سبع وسبعين وخرج عليه الوليد بن طريف الشاري احد الخوارج من بني
تغلب بنصيبين واخذ ارمينيه وحصر خلاط وعاث في بلاد الجزيره فسير اليه
الرشيد يزيد بن مزيد بن زايدة الشيباني وهو ابن اخي معن بن زايده على العساكر
فلم يزل يحاربه حتى قتله وفيه تقول اخته ليلى بنت طريف ترثيه بالابيات
المشهوره التي فيها قولها فيا شجر الخابور ما لك مورقا كانك لم تجزع على ابن طريف
الابيات فاعتمر الرشيد في شهر رمضان سنه تسع وسبعين ومايه شكرا لله تعالى
على قتل الوليد وعاد الى المدينه فاقام بها الى وقت الحج فحج بالناس ومشى من مكه
الى منى الى عرفات وشهد المشاعر كلها ماشيا ورجع على طريق البصره ولا يعرف

124a

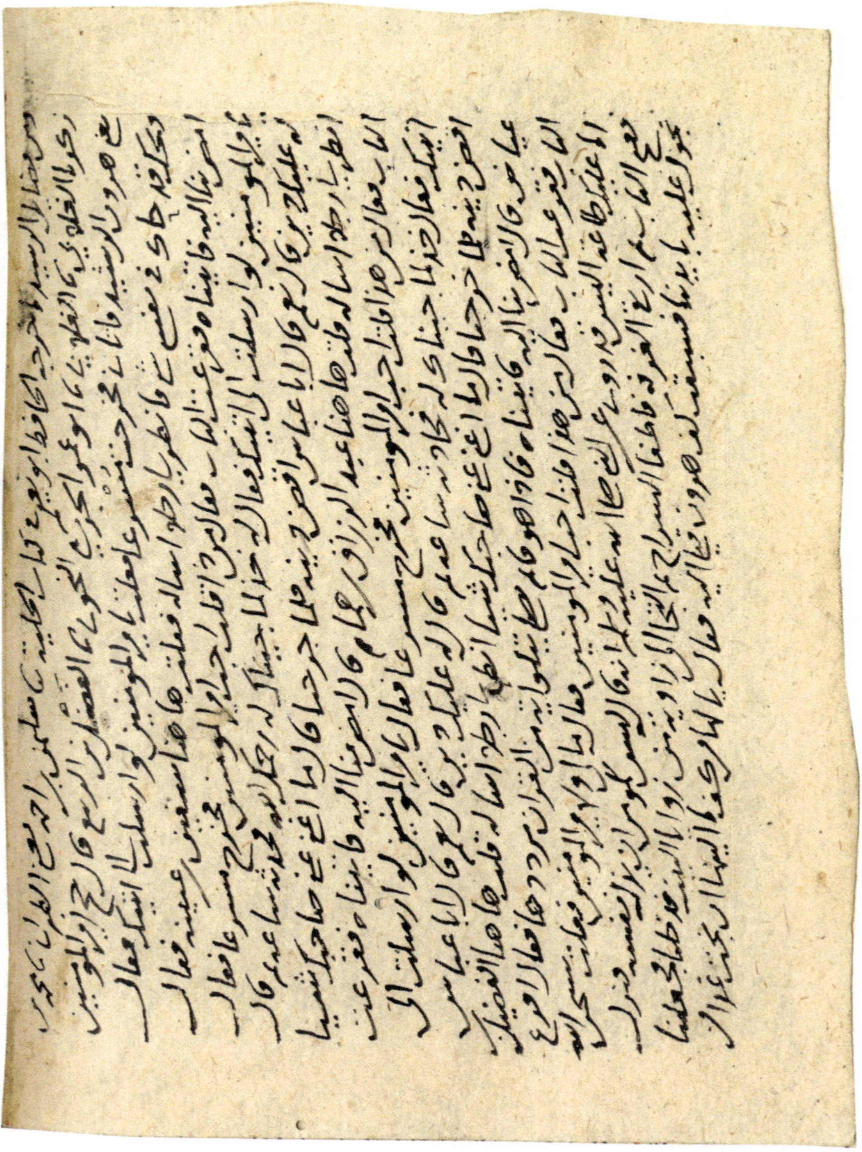

123b

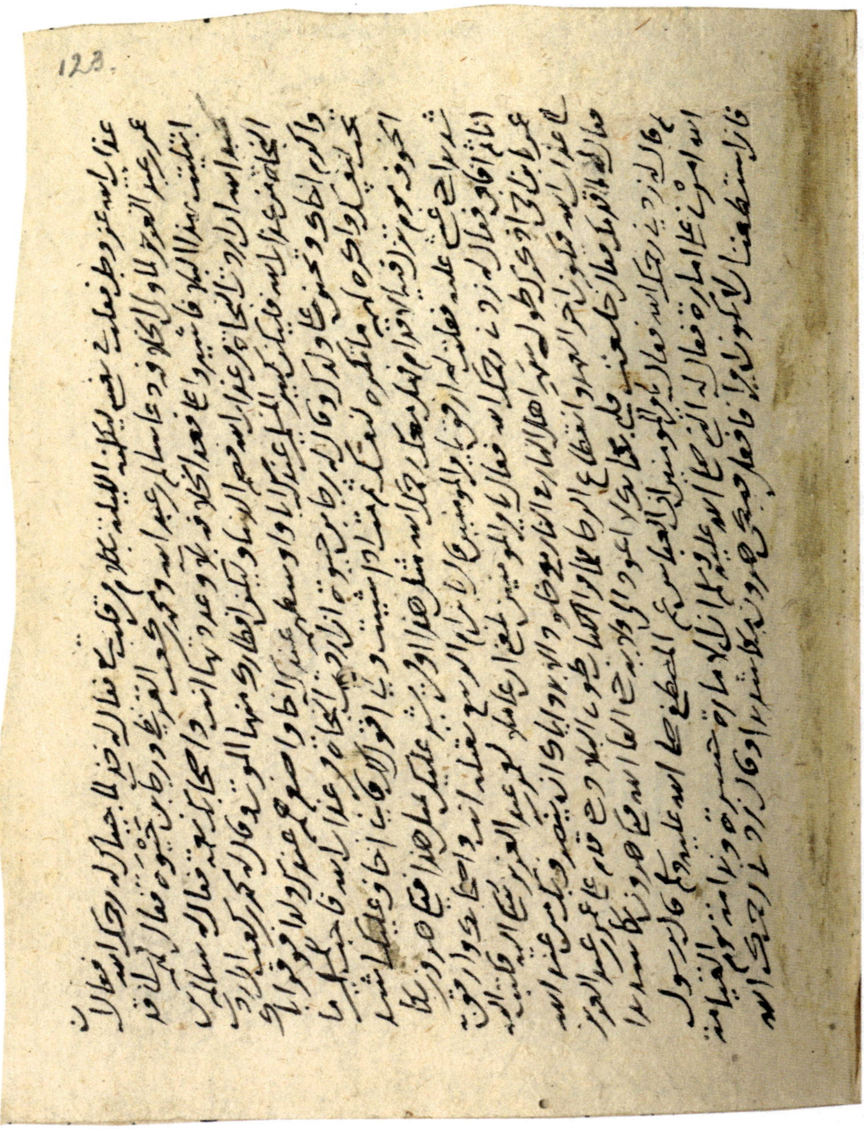

123.

123a

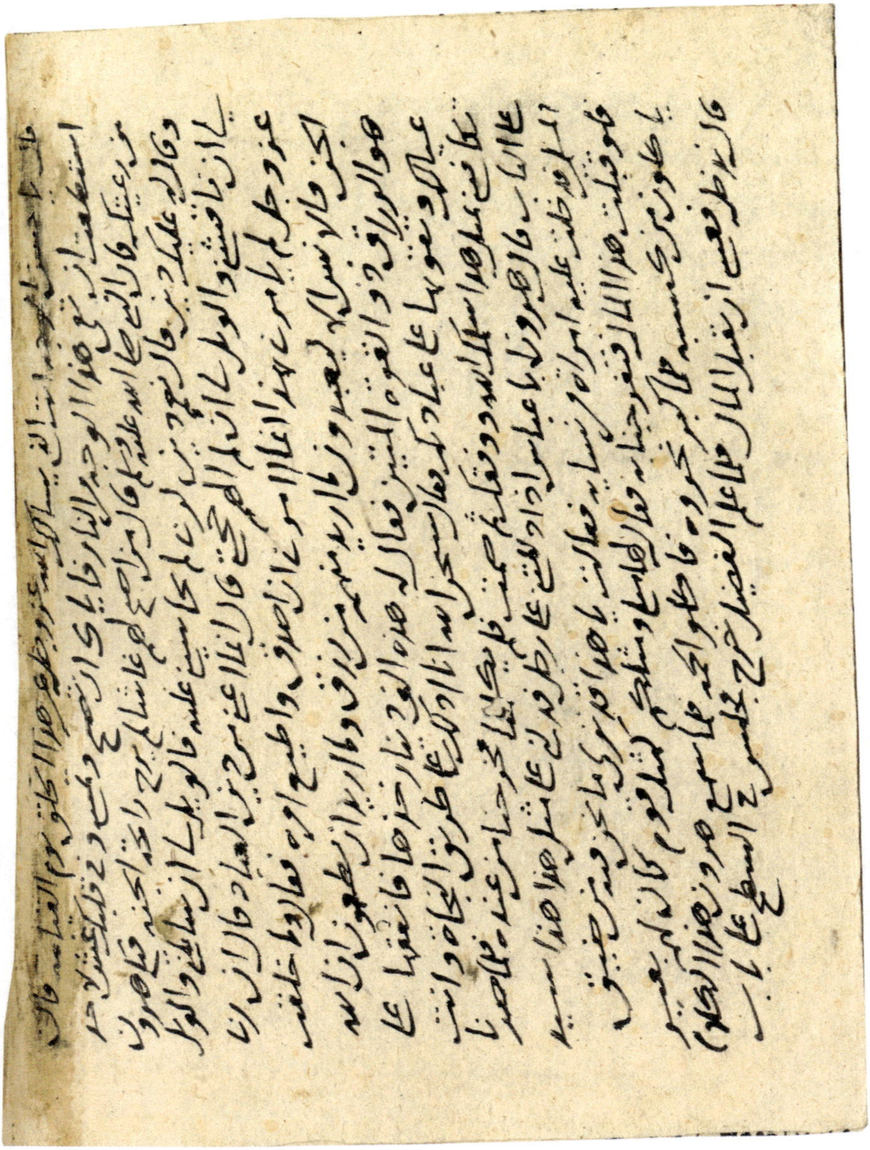

122b

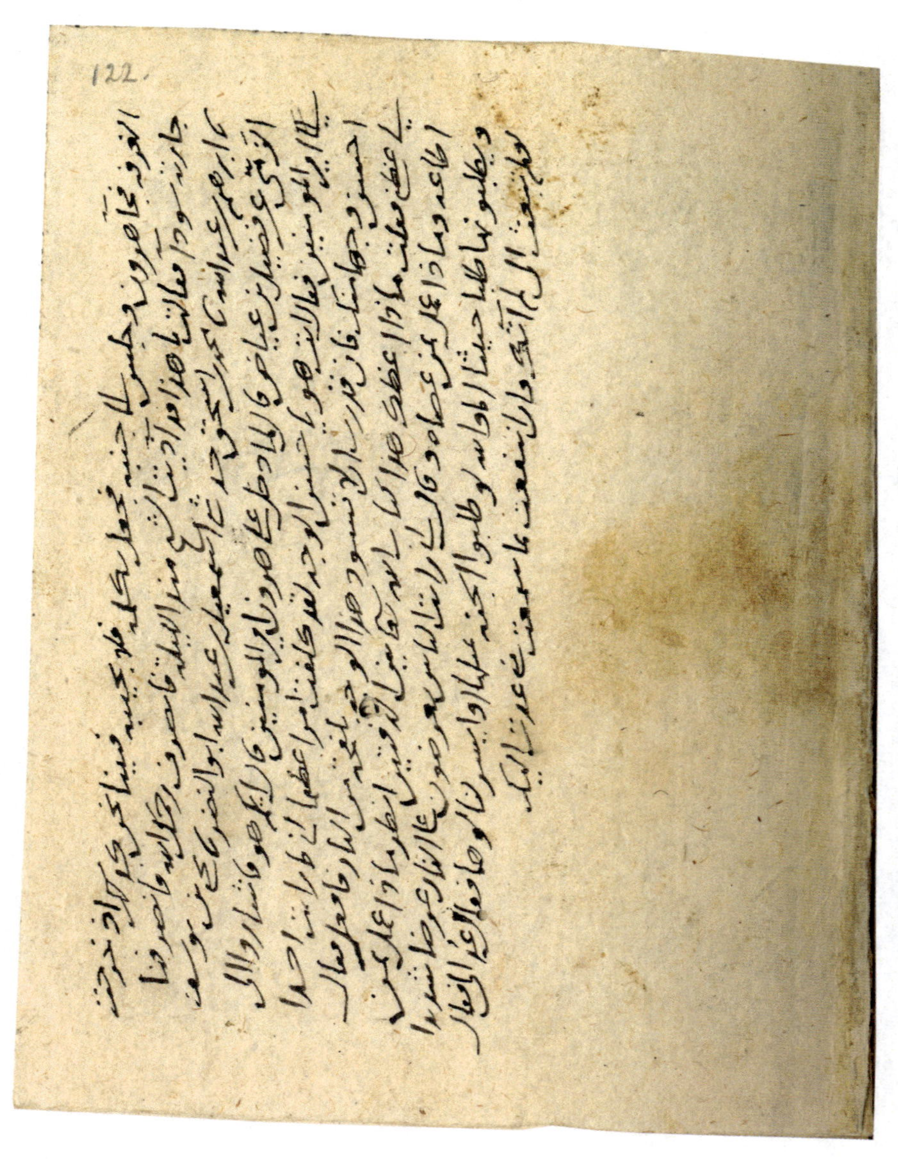

122a

من مرضه ودفن ببير ميمون ومما يحكى عنه انه لما حج واشرف على المدينه
النبويه **المهدي** ابو عبد الله محمد بن ابي جعفر عبد الله بن محمد المنصور
امير المومنين ولي بعد وفاة ابيه بعهده اليه فقام في الخلافه عشر سنين
وتسعا واربعين يوما وحج في سنه ستين ومايه واستخلف ببغداد ابنه موسى
ومعه خاله يزيد بن منصور وحج معه بابنه هرون بن محمد في جماعه من اهله
فلما قدم مكه نزع الكسوه عن الكعبه عندما رفع اليه سدنه البيت انهم يخافون
على الكعبه ان تنهدم لكثره ما عليها من الكسوه فوجد كسوة هشام بن عبد الملك
من الديباج الثخين وكانت الكسوه لا تنزع عن الكعبه في كل سنه كما هو العمل
الان بل تلبس كل سنه كسوه فوق تلك الكسوه فلما تكاثر العهد وكثر ذلك خافت
السدنه على الاركان ان تنهدم لثقل ما صار عليها من الكسوه وكانت كسوه الكعبه
تعمل من الديباج المذهب وانفق المهدي في هذه الحجه مالا عظيما قدم به معه
من العراق مبلغ ثلثين الف الف درهم سوى ما وصل اليه من مصر وهو مبلغ
ثلثمايه الف دينار عينا ومن اليمن مبلغ مايتي الف دينار عينا فرق ذلك كله
ومعه مايه الف وخمسون الف ثوب ووسع مسجد رسول الله صلى الله عليه وسلم
واخذ خمسمايه من الانصار جعلهم حرسا له واقطعهم بالعراق الاقطاعات واجرى
عليهم الارزاق وحمل اليه محمد بن سليمن الثلج الى مكه وهو اول خليفه حمل اليه
الثلج الى مكه وامر ببنا القصور بطريق مكه اوسع من القصور التي بناها السفاح
وامر باتخاذ المصانع في كل منهل منها وتجديد الاميال وحفر الركايا وبعث ابنه
موسى الهادي فحج بالناس سنه احدى وستين وامر في سنه ست وستين
ومايه باقامة البريد بين مكه والمدينه واليمن بغالا وابلا ولم يكن هناك بريد
قبل ذلك وحكى محمد بن عبد الله بن محمد بن علي بن عبد الله بن جعفر بن ابي طالب
فيما يرى النايم في اخر سلطان بني اميه كاني دخلت مسجد رسول الله صلى الله
عليه وسلم فرفعت راسي فرايت الكتاب الذي بالفسيفسا فاذا فيه مما امر
به امير المومنين الوليد بن عبد الملك واذا قايل يقول يمحى الكتاب ويكتب مكانه
اسم رجل من بني هاشم يقال له محمد قلت فانا محمد وابن من قال ابن عبد الله قلت

فانا

121

السفاح عبد الله بن محمد وهو بطريق مكه سنه ست وثلثين ومايه فقدم الكوفه
ثم حج في سنه اربعين ومايه فاحرم من الحيره ولما قضي حجه توجه الى بيت
المقدس وسار منها الى الرقه ومضى الى الكوفه وحج ثانيا سنه اربع واربعين
فحاج بالناس ورجع لم يدخل المدينه ومضى الى الربذه واحضر بني حسن بن علي
اليه في القيود والاغلال فسار بهم الى الكوفه وعتا عتوا كبيرا في ظلمهم ثم حج
بالناس في سنه سبع واربعين ومايه وحج رابعا في سنه ثمان واربعين وحج خامسا
في سنه اثني وخمسين وسار في سنه اربع وخمسين الى الشام وبيت المقدس
ثم سار في سنه ثمان وخمسين ومايه من بغداد الى مكه ليحج واستخلف ابنه
محمد المهدي ووصاه وصيه بليغه جدا لولا طولها لذكرتها وودعه وبكى واعلمه
انه ميت في سفره هذا ثم سار الى الكوفه وجمع بين الحج والعمره وساق الهدي
واشعره وقلده لايام من ذي القعده فعرض له وهو ساير وجع اشتد به حتى
مات في بير ميمون خارج مكه لست خلون من ذي الحجه فكتم الربيع موته حتى بايع
للمهدي فكانت خلافة ابي جعفر اثنين وعشرين سنه ينقص اياما قد اختلف في
عدتها واتفق انه لما نزل اخر منزل بطريق مكه نظر في صدر البيت واذا فيه
بعد البسمله

ابا جعفر حانت وفاتك وانقضت سنوك وامر الله لا بد واقع
ابا جعفر هل كاهن او منجم لك اليوم من حر المنيه مانع

فاحضر متولي المنازل وقال له الم امرك لا يدخل المنازل احد من الناس
وكانت الخلفا يبنى لهم في كل منزله ينزلونها بطريق مكه دار ويعد لهم فيها ساير
ما يحتاج اليه من الستور والفرش والاواني وغير ذلك فقال والله ما دخله
احد منذ فرغ فقال اقرا ما في صدر البيت فقال ما ارى شيا فاحضر غيره فلم
ير شيا فقال يا ربيع قف بيني وبين الحايط فقام الربيع بينه وبين الجدار فراي
البيتين كما كان يراهما قبل وتوقف الربيع فعلم انه قد نعيت اليه نفسه فقال
يا ربيع اقرا ايه من كتاب الله فقرا وسيعلم الذين ظلموا اي منقلب ينقلبون
ثم رحل من المنزل وقد تطير فسقط عن دابته فاندق عنقه وقيل بل مات

121a

العباس السفاح وصرف العين الى بركة بباب المسجد ونقع من الرصاص
حتى قدم بشر الخادم من بغداد الى مكة في سنة ست وخمسين ومائتين فعمل
القبة بجانب بيت الشراب واخرج قصب خالد فجعلها في سرب الفوارة التي
يخرج منها الماء الى حياض زمزم فتصب في هذه البركة **هشام بن عبد الملك
ابن مروان** استخلف بعد موت اخيه يزيد بن عبد الملك لليال بقين من شعبان
سنة خمس ومائة فعام في الخلافة تسع عشرة سنة وتسعة اشهر واحد وعشرين
يوما وقيل وثمانية اشهر ونصف حج فيها مرة واحدة سنة ست ومائة وكتب
له ابو الزناد سنن الحج قال ابو الزناد لقيت هشاما فاني لفي الموكب اذ لقيه
سعيد بن عبد الله بن الوليد بن عثمان بن عفان فسار الى جنبه فسمعته يقول
له يا امير المومنين ان الله لم يزل ينعم على اهل بيت امير المومنين وينصر خليفته
المظلوم ولم يزالوا يلعنون في هذه المواطن ابا تراب فانها مواطن صالحة وامير
المومنين ينبغي له ان يلعنه فيها فشق على هشام قوله وقال ما قدمنا لشتم
احد ولا للعنه قدمنا حجاجا ثم قطع كلامه واقبل علي فسالني عن الحج فاخبرته
ما كتبت له قال وشق على سعيد اني سمعته تكلم بذلك فكان منكسرا كلما رآني
وكلم ابراهيم بن محمد بن طلحة هشاما وهو في الحجر بمكة فقال له اسالك بالله
وبحرمة هذا البيت الذي خرجت معظما له الا رددت علي ظلامتي قال اي
ظلامة قال داري قال فاين كنت عن امير المومنين عبد الملك قال ظلمني قال
فالوليد وسليمان قال ظلماني قال فعمر قال يرحمه الله ردها علي قال فيزيد بن
عبد الملك قال ظلمني وقبضها مني بعد قبضي لها وهي في يدك فقال هشام لو كان
فيك ضرب لضربتك فقال في والله ضرب بالسيف والسوط فانصرف هشام
وقال لمن معه كيف سمعت هذا اللسان قال ما اجوده قال هي قريش والسنتها
ولا يزال في الناس بقايا ما رايت مثل هذا ولم يحج بعد هشام احد من بني امية
وهو خليفة ثم كانت دولة بني العباس فاول من حج منهم وهو خليفة **ابو
جعفر المنصور** واسمه عبد الله بن محمد بن علي بن عبد الله بن عباس بن عبد
المطلب امير المومنين العباسي الهاشمي بويع بعد موت اخيه ابي العباس

120

عمر نعم ومن حاله كذا وكذا ولو علم بمكانك لقام فسلم عليك وهو ضعيف البصر
قال الوليد قد [illegible] حاله ونحن نأتيه فدار في المسجد ثم اتاه فقال كيف انت ايها
الشيخ فوالله ما تحرك سعيد فقال بخير والحمد لله فكيف امير المومنين وكيف
حاله فانصرف الوليد وهو يقول لعمر هذا بقية الناس وقسم بالمدينة اموالا
كثيرة وصلى بها الجمعة فخطب الناس الخطبة الاولى جالسا ثم قام فخطب الثانية
قائما فقال رجل لرجاء بن حيوة اهكذا يصنعون قال نعم وهكذا صنع معوية وهلم
جرا فقيل له الا تكلمه فقال اخبرني قبيصة بن ذويب انه كلم عبد الملك بن
القعود فلم يتركه وقال هكذا خطب عثمان قال فقلت والله ما خطب الا قائما
قال رجاء روي لهم شي فاخذوا به سليمان بن عبد الملك بن مروان بويع بعد
موت اخيه الوليد في نصف جمادى الاخرة وهو بالرملة فاقام في الخلافة
سنتين وثمانية اشهر وخمسة ايام وقيل الا خمسة ايام وحج بالناس سنة
سبع وتسعين وكتب الى خالد بن عبد الله القسري وهو على مكة ان اجر
لي عينا تخرج ماها العذب الزلال حتى تخرج بين زمزم والمقام فعمل خالد بركة
باصل ثبير من حجارة واحكمها وانبط ماها وشق لها فلجا يسكب فيها من
شعب في الجبل ثم شق من البركة عينا تخرج الى المسجد الحرام تجري في
قصب من رصاص حتى اظهره من فوارة تسكب في فسقية من رخام بين
زمزم والمقام فلما جرت وظهر ماؤها امر القسري بجزر فنحرت بمكة
وقسمت بين الناس وعمل طعاما دعا اليه الناس ثم امر صايحا فصاح
الصلاة جامعة وامر بالمنبر فوضع في وجه الكعبة ثم صعد فحمد الله واثنى عليه
وقال ايها الناس احمدوا الله وادعوا لامير المومنين الذي سقاكم الماء العذب
الزلال النقاخ العذب وكانت تفرغ تلك الفسقية في سرب من رصاص يخرج
الى موضع وضو كان عند باب الصفا وفي بركة كانت في السوق وكان الناس
لا يقفون على تلك الفسقية ولا يكاد احد يقربها وكانوا على شرب ماء زمزم
احرص وفيه ارغب فصعد خالد المنبر وانب الناس واقذع في كلامه فلم
تزل البركة حتى هدمها داود بن علي بن عبد الله بن عباس في خلافة ابي

120a

والثنا عليه اما بعد فاني لست بالخليفه المستضعف يعني عثمن ولا بالخليفه
المداهن يعني معوية ولا بالخليفه المابون يعني يزيد بن معويه الا واني لا اداوي
هذه الامه الا بالسيف حتى تستقيم لي قناتكم وانكم تكلفونا اعمال المهاجرين
الاولين ولا تعملوا مثل اعمالهم وانكم تامروننا بتقوى الله وتنسون ذلك من
انفسكم والله لا يامرني احد بتقوى الله بعد مقامي هذا الا ضربت عنقه ثم نزل
الوليد بن عبد الملك بن مروان بويع بعد موت ابيه بعهده اليه للنصف
من شوال سنة ست وثمانين وكانت خلافته تسع سنين وسبعة اشهر وعمر
مسجد رسول الله صلى الله عليه وسلم في سنة ثمان وكان على يد عمر بن عبد
العزيز وهو على المدينه فكتب اليه في ربيع الاول يامره بادخال حجر ازواج
النبي في مسجد رسول الله صلى الله عليه وسلم وا[illegible] ما في نواحيه حتى
يكون ما يبنى ذراع في مثلها وان تقدم القبله فقوم عمر الاملاك قيمة عدل
واعطا الناس اثمانها وهدم بيوت ازواج النبي وبنا المسجد واتمه الفعلة
من الشام وبعث الوليد الى ملك الروم ما عزم عليه فبعث له مائة الف
مثقال ذهبا ومائه عامل واربعين حملا من الفسيفسا فحمل الوليد ذلك
الى عمر بن عبد العزيز فحضر عمر ومعه الناس فوضعوا اساس المسجد وابتدوا
بعمارته وكتب ايضا الى عمر ان يسهل الثنايا ويحفر الابار ويعمل الفوارة
بالمدينه فعملها واجرى ماها فلما حج الوليد وراها اعجبته فامر لها بقوام يقومون
عليها وامر اهل المسجد ان يسقوا منها وكتب الى جميع البلاد باصلاح
الطرق وعمل الابار بطريق الحجاز ومنع المجذمين من الخروج على الناس
واجرى لهم الارزاق وكان حجه في سنه احدى وتسعين فلما دخل المدينه
غدا الى المسجد ينظر الى بنايه واخرج الناس منه ولم يبق غير سعيد بن
المسيب فلم يجسر احد من الحرس يخرجه فقيل له لو قمت فقال لا اقوم حتى
ياتي الوقت الذي كنت اقوم فيه فقيل فلو سلمت على امير المومنين قال
والله لا اقوم اليه قال عمر بن عبد العزيز فجعلت اعدل بالوليد في ناحيه المسجد
لئلا يراه فالتفت الوليد الى القبله فقال من ذلك الشيخ اهو سعيد قال

نعم

119b

119

الله عنه بويع له بالخلافه سنه اربع وقيل خمس وستين بعد موت معاويه بن
يزيد بن معويه بن ابي سفين وكان قبل ذلك لا يدعي بالخلافه واجتمع علي طاعته
اهل الحجاز واليمن والعراق وخراسان وحج بالناس ثماني حجج وقتل رحمه الله على
يد الحجاج بن يوسف الثقفي في ايام عبد الملك بن مروان بن الحكم يوم الثلثا السبع
عشر خلت من جمادي الاولي وقيل جمادي الاخر سنه ثلث وسبعين وصلب
بعد قتله بمكه وبدا الحجاج بحصاره من اول ليله من ذي الحجه سنه اثنين وسبعين
وحج بالناس الحجاج في ذلك العام ووقف بعرفه وعليه درع ومغفر ولم يطوفوا
بالبيت في تلك الحجه فحاصر الحجاج سته اشهر وسبعه عشر يوما الى ان قتل
ولما غزاه اهل الشام في ايام يزيد بن معويه احترقت الكعبه في سنه اربع وستين
فتركها ابن الزبير ليشنع بذلك على اهل الشام فلما مات يزيد واستقر الامر
له هدمها الى الارض وبناها على قواعد ابرهيم وادخل فيها الحجر وجعل لها
بابين فلما قتل الحجاج عبد الله بن الزبير هدم بناء ابن الزبير من الكعبه في سنة
اربع وسبعين وجعلها على ما هي كما قد ذكرت ذلك في كتاب الاشان والاعلام
بنا الكعبه البيت الحرام ذكرا شافيا **عبد الملك بن مروان** بن الحكم بن
ابي العاص بن اميه بن عبد شمس بن عبد مناف بن قصي قام بدمشق بعد موت
ابيه في شهر رمضان سنه خمس وستين وبمكه عبد الله بن الزبير يدعا له
بالخلافه وعلى العراق المختار بن ابي عبيد الثقفي يدعوا لمحمد بن الحنفيه ٥٥
والارض تستعر حربا منذ قتل الحسين بن علي بن ابي طالب فساعدت الاقدار
عبد الملك بن مروان وقتل جميع من خالفه واقام في الخلافه بعد ابن الزبير
ثلث عشر سنه واربعة اشهر الا سبع ليال كما قد ذكرت ترجمته وترجمه
ابيه في التاريخ الكبير مفصلا بما دخلاها وحج عبد الملك في خلافته
سنتين احدهما سنه خمس وسبعين فهم شبيب بن يزيد احد الخوارج
ان يفتك به فبلغه ذلك فاحترس وكتب الى الحجاج بن يوسف بعد انصرافه
يامره بطلب صالح بن مسرح وغيره من الخوارج وكان من اخبارهم ما قد ذكر
في موضعه وخطب عبد الملك الناس بالمدينه المنوره بعد ان حمد الله ٥٥

119a

ركعتين وانت صليت ركعتين صدرا من خلافتك فما ادري ما يرجع اليه وقال
راي رايته وبلغ الخبر عبد الرحمن بن عوف وكان معه بمجاه وقال له الم تصل
في هذا المكان مع رسول الله صلى الله عليه وسلم وابي بكر وعمر ركعتين وصليتهما
انت ركعتين قال بلى ولكني اخبرت ان بعض من حج من اليمن وجفاة الناس
قالوا ان الصلاة للمقيم ركعتين واحتجوا بصلاتي وقد اتخذت بمكة اهلا ولي بالطايف
مال فقال عبد الرحمن بن عوف ما في هذا عذر اما قولك اتخذت بها اهلا فان
زوجتك بالمدينة تخرج بها اذا شيت وانما تسكن بسكناك واما مالك بالطايف
فبينك وبينه مسيرة ثلث ليال واما قولك عن حاج اليمن وغيرهم فقد كان رسول
الله صلى الله عليه وسلم ينزل عليه الوحي والاسلام قليل ثم ابو بكر وعمر فصلوا
ركعتين وقد ضرب الاسلام بجرانه فقال عثمن هذا راي رايته فخرج عبد الرحمن
فلقي عبد الله بن مسعود فقال ابا محمد قد غير ما تعلم قال فما اصنع قال اعمل
بما ترى وتعلم فقال ابن مسعود الخلاف شر وقد صليت باصحابي اربعا فقال
عبد الرحمن قد صليت باصحابي ركعتين واما الان فسوف اصلي اربعا وقيل
كان ذلك سنة ثلثين ولم يحج امير المومنين علي بن ابي طالب في خلافته لاشتغاله
بحرب الجمل وصفين معوية بن ابي سفين واسمه صخر بن حرب بن امية بن
عبد شمس بن عبد مناف القرشي الاموي ابو عبد الرحمن امير المومنين
كان اميرا بالشام نحو عشرين سنة وبايع له اهل الشام خاصة بالخلافة
سنة ثمان او تسع وثلثين واجتمع الناس عليه حين بايع له الحسن بن علي
وجماعة من معه في ربيع او جمادى سنة احدى واربعين وقيل سنة اربعين
واقام في الخلافة تسع عشرة سنة وتسعة اشهر وثمانية وعشرين يوما
وقيل غير ذلك وحج بالناس عدة سنين اولها سنة اربع واربعين ولم يحج سنة
خمس واربعين فحج بالناس مروان بن الحكم ثم حج معوية سنة خمسين وقيل
بل حج بالناس ابنه يزيد بن معوية وقيل حج معوية عدة سنين اكثر من هذا
عبد الله بن الزبير بن العوام بن خويلد بن اسد بن عبد العزى بن
قصي القرشي الاسدي ابو بكر وقيل ابو بكير وابو خبيب امير المومنين رضي

بلغ

اخبر الحافظ ابو عمر يوسف بن عبد الله بن عبد البر النمري وذكر محمد بن عمر الواقدي
في كتاب الفتوح هذه الابيات بزياده في عددها وقال ابو عثمان النهدي رايت
عمر يرمي الجمرة وعليه ازار مرقوع بقطعة جراب وقال علي بن ابي طالب رايت
عمر يطوف بالكعبة وعليه ازار فيه احدى وعشرون رقعة فيها من ادم وعن
سعيد بن المسيب قال حج عمر فلما كان بضجنان قال لا اله الا الله العلي العظيم
المعطي من شا ما شا كنت ارعى ابل الخطاب بهذا الوادي في مدرعة
صوف وكان فظا يتعبني اذا عملت ويضربني اذا قصرت وقد امسيت وليس
بيني وبين الله احد ثم تمثل

لا شي مما ترى تبقى بشاشته يبقى الاله ويودي المال والولد
لم تغن عن هرمز يوما خزائنه والخلد قد حاولت عاد فما خلدوا
ولا سليمان اذ تجري الرياح له والانس والجن فيما بينها برد
اين الملوك التي كانت نوافلها من كل اوب اليها راكب يفد
حوض هنالك مورود بلا كذب لا بد من ورده يوما كما وردوا

عثمان بن عفان بن ابي العاص بن امية بن عبد شمس بن عبد مناف بن قصي القرشي
الاموي ابو عبد الله وابو عمرو ذو النورين امير المومنين رضي الله عنه بويع
له بالخلافه يوم السبت غرة المحرم سنه اربع وعشرين بعد دفن عمر بن الخطاب
بثلاثه ايام باجتماع الناس عليه وقتل بالمدينه يوم الجمعه لثمان عشرة او
سبع عشرة خلت من ذي الحجة سنه خمس وثلثين وذلك على راس احدي
عشرة سنه واحد عشر شهرا واثنين وعشرين يوما من مقتل عمر رضي الله
عنه حج فيها كلها الا السنه الاولى والاخيرة وذكر ابن الاثير انه حج بالناس
في السنة الاولى وقيل بل حج بالناس عبد الرحمن بن عوف بامر عثمان ولما حج
في سنه تسع وعشرين ضرب فسطاطه بمنى فكان اول فسطاط ضربه عثمن
بمنى واتم الصلاه بها وبعرفه فكان اول ما تكلم به الناس في عثمان ظاهرا حين
اتم الصلوه بمنى فعاب ذلك غير واحد من الصحابة وقال له علي ما حدث
امر ولا قدم عهد ولقد عهدت النبي صلى الله عليه وسلم وابا بكر وعمر يصلون

118a

ابن نوفل بن اخرس واستاذنه اهل المياه في ان يبنوا منازل بين مكه والمدينه
فاذن لهم وشرط عليهم ان ابن السبيل احق بالظل والما ثم خرج من المدينه عام الرماده حاجا او معتمرا
فاتى الجار لينظر الى السفن التي قدمت من مصر في الخليج الذي احتفره عمرو بن العاص كما قد
ذكرنا خبره في كتاب المواعظ والاعتبار بذكر الخطط والاثار وقال للناس سيروا بنا ننظر الى
السفن التي سيرها الله الينا من ارض فرعون واكل في سفره هذا وهو محرم لحم ظبي اصابه
قوم حلال فلما نزل على البحر قال اغتسلوا من ما البحر فانه مبارك ثم صك للناس بذلك الطعام
صكوكا فتبايع التجار الصكوك بينهم قبل ان يقبضوها فلقي عمر العلا بن الاسود كم ربح حكيم بن حزام
فقال ابتاع من صكوك الجار مايه الف درهم وربح عليها مايه الف فلقيه عمر فقال يا حكيم كم ربحت
فاخبره بمثل خبر العلا قال فبعته قبل ان تقبضه قال نعم قال فان هذا
بيع لا يصلح فاردده قال ما علمت ان هذا لا يصلح وما اقدر على رده قال ما
بد قال والله ما اقدر على ذلك وقد تفرق وذهب ولكن راس مالي وربحي صدقه
واتفق في اخر حجة حجها انه لما رمى الجمرة اتاه حجر فوقع على صلعته فادماه وثم
رجل من بني لهب فقال اشعر امير المومنين لا يحج بعدها ثم جا الى الجمرة
الثانيه فصاح رجل يا خليفه رسول الله فقال لا يحج امير المومنين بعد عامه
هذا فقتل عمر رضي الله عنه بعد رجوعه من الحج لهب مكسور اللام قبيله من
قبايل الازد تعرف فيها العيافه والزجر وعن عايشه رضي الله عنها ان عمر
اذن لازواج النبي صلى الله عليه وسلم ان يحججن في اخر حجه حجها قالت فلما
ارتحل من الحصبة اقبل رجل متلثم فقال وانا اسمع اين كان منزل امير المومنين
فقال قايل وانا اسمع هذا كان منزله فاناخ في منزل عمر ثم رفع عقيرته
يتغنى عليك سلام من امير وباركت يد الله في ذاك الاديم الممزق
فمن يجر او يركب جناحي نعامة ليدرك ما قدمت بالامس يسبق
قضيت امورا ثم غادرت بعدها بوايج في اكمامها لم تفتق
قالت عايشه فقلت لبعض اهلي اعلموا لي من هذا الرجل فذهبوا فلم يجدوا
في مناخه احدا قالت عايشه فوالله اني لاحسبه من الجن فلما قتل عمر نحل
الناس هذه الابيات للشماخ بن ضرار او لاخيه مزرد هكذا اروي هذا

117b

117

له دينه لطيفة البدا ابالحج سنة للمسلمين وينادى بديار مصر فى رجب
وهو قياس ندايه عليه السلام اول ذى القعدة لان مسافة الحج من المدينة عشر
ايام فقدم النداء بثلاثة امثالها ومسافة الحج فى البر من مصر اربعون يوما
فقدم النداء بثلاثة امثالها فكانت الجملة من اول رجب الى انقضاء عشر ذى
الحجة خمسة اشهر وعشر ايام وكذلك بدمشق واول من ادار المحمل الملك
الظاهر بيبرس البندقدارى فصل فى ذكر من حج من الخلفاء فى مدة خلافته
ابو بكر الصديق رضى الله عنه اسمه عبد الله بن ابى قحافة عثمان بن عامر
ابن عمرو بن كعب بن سعد بن تيم بن مرة بن كعب بن لؤى بن غالب بن فهر
ابن مالك القرشى التيمى خليفة رسول الله صلى الله عليه وسلم بويع له بعد وفاة
رسول الله صلى الله عليه وسلم بيعة العامة يوم الثلثا ثالث عشر شهر ربيع
الاول سنة احدى عشر من الهجرة وحج بالناس فى هذه السنة عتاب بن اسيد
وقيل عبد الرحمن بن عوف رضى الله عنهما وحج ابو بكر رضى الله عنه بالناس
سنة اثنتى عشرة واستخلف على المدينة عثمان بن عفان رضى الله عنه وقيل حج
بالناس عمر بن الخطاب او عبد الرحمن بن عوف رضى الله عنهما والاول اصح
وتوفى ابو بكر رضى الله عنه على راس سنتين وثلثة اشهر واثنى عشر يوما
وقيل غير ذلك عمر بن الخطاب بن نفيل بن عبد العزى بن رباح بن عبد الله
ابن قرط بن رزاح بن عدى بن كعب القرشى العدوى ابو حفص امير المومنين
رضى الله عنه ولى الخلافة بعد ابى بكر الصديق رضى الله عنه بويع له بها باستخلا فه
له فى جمادى الاخرة سنة ثلث عشرة واختلف فى اليوم كما اختلف فى يوم وفاة
ابى بكر رضى الله عنه وقتل مطعونا بيد ابى لؤلؤة غلام المغيرة بن شعبة لثلاث
بقين من ذى الحجة سنة ثلث وعشرين فكانت خلافته عشر سنين ونصف حج
فى جميعها الا السنة الاولى فقط فانه حج بالناس فيها عتاب بن اسيد وقيل
بل حج عمر بالناس سنيه كلها وفى سنة سبع عشرة اعتمر رضى الله عنه
وبنى المسجد الحرام ووسع فيه واقام بمكة عشرين ليلة وهدم على قوم ابوا ان
يبيعوا دورهم وعوضهم اثمانها من بيت المال وجدد انصاب الحرم على يد مخرمة

117a

من ادجبه وممن قال بافضليته الامام ابو حنيفه النعمن بن ثابت رحمه الله
وهو رواية عن الامام ابي عبد الله احمد بن حنبل الشيباني رحمه الله وساق
صلى الله عليه وسلم الهدي من ذي الحليفه وامر من كان معه هدي ان يهل كما
اهل صلى الله عليه وسلم وسار صلى الله عليه وسلم والناس بين يديه وخلفه
وعن يمينه وشماله امما لا يحصون كثرة كلهم قدم ليأتم به صلى الله عليه وسلم فلما قدم
صلى الله عليه وسلم مكه لاربع ليال خلون من ذي الحجة طاف للقدوم ثم
سعى بين الصفا والمروه وامر الذين لم يسوقوا هديا ان يفسخوا حجهم الى عمره
ويحلوا حلا تاما ثم يهلوا بالحج وقت خروجهم الى منى وقال ثم لو استقبلت
من امري ما استدبرت ما سقت الهدي ولجعلتها عمره وهذا دليل ظاهر انه
صلى الله عليه وسلم لم يكن متمتعا كما ذهب اليه بعض اصحاب الامام احمد
وغيرهم وقدم علي بن ابي طالب رضي الله عنه من اليمن فقال له صلى الله عليه
وسلم بما اهللت قال باهلال كاهلال النبي صلى الله عليه وسلم فقال له النبي
صلى الله عليه وسلم اني سقت الهدي وقرنت روى هذا اللفظ ابو داود وغير
من الايمه باسناد صحيح وهو صريح في القران وقدم مع علي رضي الله عنه من اليمن
هدايا فاشركه صلى الله عليه وسلم في هديه ايضا فكان حاصلهما مايه بدنه
ثم خرج صلى الله عليه وسلم الى منى فبات بها وكانت ليلة الجمعه التاسع
من ذي الحجه ثم اصبح فسار الى عرفة وخطب بنمره خطبه عظيمه شهدها من
اصحابه نحو من اربعين الفا رضي الله عنهم اجمعين وجمع بين الظهر والعصر
ثم وقف بعرنه ثم على رحله وكانت زاملته ثم بات بالمزدلفه وجمع بين المغرب
والعشا ليلتئذ ثم اصبح فصلى الفجر اول وقتها ثم سار قبل طلوع الشمس الى
منى فرمى جمرة العقبه ونحر وحلق ثم افاض فطاف بالبيت طواف الفرض وهو طواف
الزيارة واختلف اين صلى الظهر يومئذ وقد اشكل ذلك على كثير من الحفاظ ثم حل
من كل شي حرم منه صلى الله عليه وسلم وخطب وانذر واشهدهم على انفسهم بانه بلغهم
الرسالة فنحن نشهد انه بلغ الرساله وادى الامانه ونصح الامه صلى الله عليه وسلم تسليما
كثيرا الى يوم الدين ثم اقبل صلى الله عليه وسلم منصرفا الى المدينه وقد اكمل الله

ه

116b

116

الشمس وروح الحيوة الى النفس غير ان في كريم اخلاقه الزكيه وزاكي
اعراقه المرضيه ما يقبل اليسير ويتجاوز عن الخطا والتقصير رعا الله الخدم
من حيث لا يرتقب وحرسه حيث لا يحتسب وكان له في سفره خفيرا او في حضره عونا
وظهيرا ابنه **فصل** في حجة رسول الله صلى الله عليه
وسلم افتتحت بها هذا الجزو اذ كان صلى الله عليه وسلم هو الذي بين للناس
معالم دينهم وقال خذوا عني مناسككم وقد امتلات كتب الحديث بذكر حجة رسول
الله صلى الله عليه وسلم وافردها الفقيه الحافظ ابو محمد علي بن احمد بن سعيد
ابن حزم الاندلسي مصنفا جليلا فيما اعترض عليه في مواضع منه اجبت عنها في
كتاب شارع النجاه وملخص حجة الوداع ان رسول الله صلى الله عليه وسلم لما دخل
ذو القعده تجهز للحج وامر الناس بالجهاز له واذن فيهم فاجتمعوا ثم صلى الظهر
يوم الخميس لست بقين من ذي القعدة سنه عشر من الهجرة بالمدينه اربعا
وخرج منها بمن معه من المسلمين من اهل المدينه ومن تجمع من الاعراب
وهم عشرة الاف بعدما استعمل على المدينه ابا دجانه الساعدي ويقال سباع بن
عرفطه الغفاري فصلى العصر بذي الحليفة ركعتين وبات بها واتاه آت من ربه
عز وجل في ذلك الموضع وهو وادي العقيق يامره عن ربه تعالى ان يقول في
حجته هذه حجة في عمرة ومعنى هذا ان الله سبحانه امره بان يقرن الحج مع العمرة
فاصبح صلى الله عليه وسلم فاخبر الناس بذلك وطاف على نسايه يوميذ بغسل
واحد وهن تسع وقيل احدى عشره ثم اغتسل وصلى عند المسجد ركعتين واهل
بحجة وعمرة معا هذا الذي رواه بلفظه ومعناه عنه صلى الله عليه وسلم سته
عشر صحابيا منهم خادمه انس بن مالك رضي الله عنه وقد رواه عنه صلى الله عليه
وسلم سته عشر تابعيا قد ذكرتهم في كتاب شارع النجاة وهذا صريح لا يحتمل
التاويل الا ان يكون بعيدا وما عدا ذلك جا من الاحاديث الموهمه التمتع
او ما يدل على الافراد فليس هذا محل ذكرها والقران في الحج هو مذهب
امامنا ابي عبد الله محمد بن ادريس الشافعي رحمة الله عليه وقد نص جماعة
من محققي اصحابه وهو الذي يحصل به الجمع بين الاحاديث كلها ومن العلما

116a

كتاب الذهب المسبوك في ذكر من حج من الخلفاء والملوك

تأليف المقريزي

بسم الله الرحمن الرحيم رب يسر يا كريم

الحمد لله وبه المستعان على ما عز وهان وصلى الله على نبينا محمد خاتم النبيين
وعلى آله وأصحابه والتابعين صلاة باقية إلى يوم الدين وبعد فأسأل الله مبتهلا
إليه بما أبدى له أن يتبع أيام المقر المخدوم بأخواتها الباقيات الصالحات والزيادات
الغامرات ليكون كل دهر يستقبله وأمل يستأنفه موفيا على المتقدم له قاصرا
عن المتأخر عنه ويؤتيه من العمر أطوله وأبعده ومن العيش أعذبه وأرغده عزيزا
منصورا محميا موفورا باسطا يده فلا يقبضها إلا على نواصي أعداء وحساد ساميا
طرفه فلا يغضه إلا على لذة غمض ورقاد مستريحة ركابه فلا يعملها إلا لاستنفاد
عز وملك حاجبه نداحه فلا يحيلها إلا لجيان مال يخفى بنيل أقصى ما تتوجه
إليه أمنيته جامحة وتسمو إليه طامحة وقد استفاض أن العزم الشريف قد
قوي على الحج والتحلي بالعج والثج وجرت العادة بألطاف العبيد السادة فتأملت
حال الأتباع الذين يجب عليهم الهدايا في مثل هذه الحركة فأردت التأسي بهم
ورأيتني إن أهديت نفسي فهي في ملك المقر المخدوم وإن أهديت مالي فهو منه
وإن أهديت مودتي وشكري فهما خالصين له غير مشتركين وكرهت أن أخلي
هذا العزم من سنته وأكون من المقصرين أو أدعي في ملكي ما هو حق المقر المخدوم
فأكون من الكاذبين

إن أهد نفسي فهو مالكها [illegible]
أو أهد مالاً فهو واهبه وأنا الحقيق عليه بالشكر
أو أهد شكري فهو مرتهن بجميل فعلك آخر الدهر
والشمس تستغني إذا طلعت أن تستضي بطلعة البدر

ولما كان العلم أنفس الذخائر وأعلاها قدرا وأعظم المآثر وأبقاها ذكرا جمعت
برسم الخزانة الشريفة المخدومية عمرها الله ببقاء مالكها جزءا يحتوي على ذكر من
حج من الخلفاء والملوك سميته الذهب المسبوك ليكون تذكرة للخاطر الشريف بما
هو مني أدرى وأحق بإفادته وأحرى وإني فيما فعلت وصنعت كمن أهدى القطر
إلى البحر أو بعث النور إلى القمر والأرج إلى الزهر بل كالذي أرسل الضياء إلى

الشمس

115b

Printed in the United States
By Bookmasters